P9-CAU-635

Third Edition

Algebra I

Expressions, Equations, and Applications

Paul A. Foerster

Addison-Wesley Publishing Company
Menlo Park, California • Reading, Massachusetts • New York
Don Mills, Ontario • Wokingham, England • Amsterdam • Bonn
Paris • Milan • Madrid • Sydney • Singapore • Tokyo
Seoul • Taipei • Mexico City • San Juan

To the women in my life:

My grandmother, Annie Higgins, whose foresight made teaching a feasible career.

My mother, Gladys Foerster, who inspired me by asking the right questions at the right time.

My wife, who makes it all worthwhile.

Paul A. Foerster has taught mathematics at Alamo Heights High School in San Antonio, Texas since 1961. In that same year he received his teaching certificate from Texas A&M University. His B.S. degree in Chemical Engineering and M.A. degree in Mathematics are from the University of Texas. Among many honors, he was awarded the Presidential Award for Excellence in Mathematics Teaching in 1983.

ISBN 0-13-165708
17

Foreword to the Student

You are about to embark on the course which lays the foundation for virtually all of higher mathematics. In previous courses you have occasionally used a letter to stand for a number you seek to find. Now you will be less concerned about what number the letter represents, and will concentrate on things that are true just because it is a *number*.

The letters used will be called variables, because they can stand for different numbers at different times. Expressions containing these variables can represent quantities in the real world, such as how high a ball is above the ground at various times after it was thrown. By learning how to operate with such expressions, you will be able to predict such things as how high the ball is at a given time, how long it takes to reach a given height, and when it will be back down.

Some of the things you will learn may not seem to have any immediate practical use. Learn them anyway, and learn them well! They are all part of a big picture which becomes clear only after you have unveiled its various parts.

The way to learn mathematics is by practice. Some things may seem clear when your teacher explains them. But they will not become a part of you until you can *do* them. Do your homework only after you have worked the text examples. Then do the problems without looking at the examples. Sometimes you will be asked to read the book and work new problems on your own prior to classroom discussion. Keep asking yourself how new problems relate to the ones you have done before. You have a chance to gain self-reliance that will help you the rest of your life.

Neatness is an asset in algebra. Clear writing will help you avoid mistakes. There will be times when you cannot tell what step to take next in a problem until you have done the step before. It is less time-consuming in the long run to write carefully and get things right the first time than it is to save a few minutes, then have to redo the work. Developing the habit of neatness and of saying exactly what you mean will help you in other subjects as well as mathematics.

In conclusion, let me wish you the best as you start the course. Remember that mathematics is not a spectator sport. May your hard work cause you to progress toward better understanding of mathematics.

Paul A. Foerster

Foreword to the Teacher

Algebra I: Expressions, Equations, and Applications presents the normal content of first-year high school algebra. It is designed to prepare students for a subsequent course in either geometry or second-year algebra. The materials were written for use in the author's own classes, and have been refined following successful pilot tests in public and private schools across the United States.

The unifying theme is the concept of an *expression*. For increasingly complex expressions, students do these three things:

1. Write an expression representing a variable quantity in some real-world situation,
2. Find the value of the expression when x is known,
3. Find x when the value of the expression is known.

The first part of the book is carefully sequenced to lead to the Quadratic Formula by mid-year. This departure from the more traditional sequence of topics is made possible by technology, specifically, the use of calculators to evaluate radicals. As a result, students are able to work more realistic word problems in which answers are decimals. Students must check their answers based on whether or not they are reasonable, not because they came out as small, whole numbers.

The second part of the book allows more flexibility in selection of sequence and topics to fit students' needs and available time. Expressions with two variables, harder factoring problems, algebraic fractions, radical equations, and inequalities appear here. Students can also learn that the computer is appropriate for repetitive evaluation of expressions, while the calculator or the brain is more appropriate for single calculations. The final chapter introduces topics to which the students will spiral back in geometry, algebra II, and trigonometry.

The Third Edition differs from the second by the addition of a new chapter on probability, scattered data, and linear functions. The chapter on two-variable expressions and equations is now Chapter 7. After learning about linear equations, students are prepared to see relationships in real-world data that are approximately linear. The chapter on BASIC programming has been deleted.

Chapter 8, the new chapter, introduces students to probability and data analysis. It begins with a discussion of linear functions and their application to real-world situations. Next, students are introduced to scatter plots, fitting a line to data, and using regression equations to make predictions. Probability concepts are then presented, including basic definitions and geometric probability.

The chapter concludes with a section on experimental probability. Students predict the probabilities of events, then see how well their predictions match the results of actual experiments. After completing this chapter, students should have a good understanding of the difference between probability (where they look at a real-world situation and predict what *should* happen in an experiment) and statistics (where they use the results of experiments to learn about a real-world situation).

The section on linear functions that opens Chapter 8 is taken from Chapter 14 in the Second Edition. Section 14-3 is new material on $f(x)$ notation. Introduction to this topic in Algebra I will help students feel more comfortable with its development and use in more advanced courses. Development of this notation comes late in the text so that students become familiar with the concept of a function before seeing unfamiliar terminology. The students seem to understand a function as something that "tells how y is related to x" this way, rather than just as "that $f(x)$ thing!"

Finally, the Problem Title Index and the General Index have been moved to the end of the book for easier access.

The main features of the First and Second Editions remain intact. Word problems involve variables that really *vary,* rather than standing for unknown constants. The "hand- holding" phase at the beginning of the text has problems with multiple parts. Students are asked to define variables and to write expressions representing the quantities in the problem. Then students either evaluate expressions if a value of the variable is given, or solve for the variable if a value of the expression is given. Thus, students quick enough to do easy problems in their heads are forced to learn proper algebraic techniques, while those who might have trouble are given successful experience by following the instructions.

Toward the middle of the book the word problems look rather like those in any good algebra I text. Students are expected to know that they should define a variable, and write and solve equations. By Chapter 10 students enter the "no-holds-barred" phase. Here, clever short-cuts and trial-and-error techniques are encouraged, as well as the traditional algebraic techniques. Students thus practice problem solving as advocated by the National Council of Teachers of Mathematics. The experience helps prepare them for contests and standardized tests, where the emphasis is on getting the right answer quickly.

Pedagogically, the first two chapters start slowly for the benefit of students who have never encountered negative numbers or variables, or who just need time to get started at the beginning of the course. Classes with a stronger background can move rapidly here, allowing time for the more difficult problems later on, or for the advanced topics at the end.

Some sections, particularly at the beginnings of chapters, are for students to read and work on their own. This feature provides a worthwhile assignment to be given following a test. Each section contains Oral Practice problems, where appropriate. These problems are *lettered* rather than numbered, so that students will not work orals by mistake when you assign "Problems 1 through 10" on a particular page.

The examples in each section specify that the student cover the answers at the dotted lines, then work the example himself or herself. The answers are to be uncovered only after the student has done the work. The technique is very effective, but students must be trained to do the work, and not just to look at the solutions.

Paul A. Foerster

Acknowledgements

Thanks go to my students starting in 1980 for putting up with "all those ditto sheets!" In particular, thanks to Maria Flores and Gilbert Rios whose good class notes provided input for much of the First Edition.

The following teachers pilot tested the materials for the First Edition or provided valuable input for the Second Edition.

Alamo Heights High School, San Antonio, Texas: Tammy Frietsch, Sharon Brassel, Bruce Fink, Kathy Schlosberg, Susan Thomas, Becky Wallace, Mercille Wisakowsky, Isabel Zsohar, Paul Foerster

Alamo Heights Junior School, San Antonio, Texas: Martha Jo Buckley

Eisenhower Middle School, San Antonio, Texas: Loren Caraway

John Evans Junior High, Greeley, Colorado: Gary Steward, Jack Pendar

Greenwich High School, Greenwich, Connecticut: Terry Lowe, William Bechem

Groton School, Groton, Massachusetts: Jonathan Choate

Lamar Middle School, Temple, Texas: Larry Scott, Mariella Morgan

Libertyville High School, Libertyville, Illinois: Barbara Schultz, Jack Zetterberg

Milwaukee Technical High School, Milwaukee, Wisconsin: Adele Hanson

Pan American University, Edinburg, Texas: Olga Ramirez, John Huber

Sandusky High School, Sandusky, Ohio: Paula Schmansky, Paul Dahnke

University of Massachusetts, Amherst, Massachusetts: Ron Narode, Jack Lochhead

Valley View Junior High, Omaha, Nebraska: David Thronson, Al Gloor

Westridge School for Girls, Pasadena, California: Jerry Pillsbury, Sandra Feeney

Thanks go to Jill Foerster for proofreading the original manuscript. Thanks also to Richard and Josephine Andree for letting their children Calvin Butterball and Phoebe Small join my own (the Dupp Family, etc.) in making the problems a bit more entertaining.

Photograph Acknowledgments

Cover: Alwyncooper/E+/Getty Images

Page 1: Dana Gluckstein*

Page 42: Jay Delaney/Getty Images

Page 89: Charlotte Pawel

Page 129: Don Mason/Blend Images/Getty Images

Page 104: Charlotte Pawel*

Page 213: Gchutka/E+//Getty Images

Page 271: Joao Inacio/Moment//Getty Images

Page 366: 123RF.com

Page 410: Feng Yu/Shutterstock

Page 455: Wayland Lee*/Addison-Wesley Publishing Company

Page 520: Temmuzcan/iStock/Getty Images

Page 568: Dana Gluckstein*

Page 615: Frantisekhojdysz/Shutterstock

*Photographs provided expressly for the publisher.

Contents

4 HARDER EQUATIONS 129

5 SOME OPERATIONS WITH POLYNOMIALS AND RADICALS 164

6 QUADRATIC EQUATIONS 213

7 EXPRESSIONS AND EQUATIONS CONTAINING TWO VARIABLES 271

1

Expressions and Equations

this course you will work with
ıantities that can vary. For in-
ance, if you mow lawns for $10
ch, you will earn varying
nounts depending on how many
wns you mow. One type of
oblem is: If you mow 3 lawns,
w much money will you make?
nother is: If you want to make
'0, how many lawns must you
ow? The answers, of course, are
'0 and 7 lawns, respectively. In
gebra you will learn to reduce
mplicated problems to easy
es like these. The name algebra
mes from the Arabic word al-
br. *It is part of the title of the*
nth century book hisab al-jabr
a'l muqabalah, *meaning "the*
ience of reduction *and com-*
ırison." Letters are used to
and for quantities whose value
ries, and expressions and equa-
ons are made using these vari-
les.

1-1 OPERATIONS WITH NUMBERS

An *operation* in mathematics is something you do to numbers, such as adding, subtracting, multiplying, or dividing. For instance, in

$$3 + 11,$$

the operation of addition is performed on the numbers 3 and 11.

Difficulties may arise if there are several different operations. For example, what number does

$$3 + 2 \times 7$$

represent? If you add 3 and 2 first and then multiply by 7, you get

$$5 \times 7 = \underline{\underline{35}}.$$

But if you multiply 2 by 7 first, then add the result to 3, you get a different number:

$$3 + 14 = \underline{\underline{17}}.$$

To avoid this difficulty, **symbols of inclusion**—parentheses, ( ), or brackets, [ ]—are used to tell which operation to do first.

$$(3 + 2) \times 7 \quad \text{means} \quad 5 \times 7, \quad \text{or} \quad 35.$$

$$3 + (2 \times 7) \quad \text{means} \quad 3 + 14, \quad \text{or} \quad 17.$$

$$12 \div [2 \times 3] \quad \text{means} \quad 12 \div 6, \quad \text{or} \quad 2.$$

Another symbol of inclusion is the bar used in fractions, called a **vinculum.** For example, in

$$\frac{6 + 7}{2 \times 7}$$

the operations 6 + 7 and 2 × 7 are done *first,* giving

$$\frac{13}{14}.$$

Then 13 is divided by 14, giving about 0.929.

A collection of numbers, operation signs, and symbols of inclusion (parentheses, brackets, vinculums) is called an **expression.** Finding the value of an expression is called **evaluating** the expression. An expression such as

$$36 \div 3 \times 4 + 2$$

can have different values, depending on how the operations are grouped.

EXAMPLE 1

Evaluate $[(36 \div 3) \times 4] + 2$.

$$\begin{aligned} & [(36 \div 3) \times 4] + 2 \\ = & [12 \times 4] + 2 \\ = & 48 + 2 \\ = & \underline{\underline{50}} \end{aligned}$$

Note that you do what is inside the *innermost* symbols of inclusion *first.*

EXAMPLE 2

Evaluate $[36 \div (3 \times 4)] + 2$.

$$\begin{aligned} & [36 \div (3 \times 4)] + 2 \\ = & [36 \div 12] + 2 \\ = & 3 + 2 \\ = & \underline{\underline{5}} \end{aligned}$$

Objective

Given an expression, be able to *evaluate* it.

As shown in the examples, you should do the following to evaluate an expression:

1. Write the given expression.
2. Do the innermost operation and write the result. Use an = sign to connect the new expression to the original one.
3. Keep doing operations until you reduce the expression to a *single* number. Use = signs to connect each expression to the one before, as shown in the examples.
4. Clearly indicate the answer by underlining or boxing it.

Now *you* work the examples on the next page. Put a piece of paper along the dotted lines. This will cover the answer, leaving only the original expression showing. (If the writing shows through, use more sheets of paper or an index card.) Then evaluate the expression. Last, uncover the answer in the book to make sure your *work* and your *answer* are right.

EXAMPLE 3

Evaluate $36 \div [3 \times (4 + 2)]$.

Think These Reasons

$36 \div [3 \times (4 + 2)]$	Write the given expression.
$= 36 \div [3 \times 6]$	Do the *innermost* operation first.
$= 36 \div 18$	Do operations in parentheses or brackets next.
$= \underline{\underline{2}}$	Do the arithmetic. Underline or box the answer.

Note: Be sure to write the given expression first and to use = signs to connect each simplified expression to the one on the line above.

EXAMPLE 4

Evaluate $(36 \div 3) \times (4 + 2)$.

$(36 \div 3) \times (4 + 2)$	Write the given expression.
$= 12 \times 6$	Do what is inside parentheses first.
$= \underline{\underline{72}}$	Underline or box the answer.

As you read the above material, you found the words *operation, expression,* and *evaluate*. It is important for you to know exactly what these words mean. This is why mathematicians make precise *definitions* of the words they use. You should learn the following definitions.

DEFINITIONS

ARITHMETIC OPERATION
Addition, subtraction, multiplication, and division are called **arithmetic operations.**

EXPRESSION
An **expression** is a collection of numbers, operation signs, and inclusion symbols that stands for a number.

EVALUATING
To **evaluate an expression** means to find the number for which the expression stands.

EXERCISE 1-1

Evaluate the following expressions.

1. $(5 + 7) \times 8$
2. $(4 + 9) \times 5$
3. $5 + (7 \times 8)$
4. $4 + (9 \times 5)$
5. $9 - (4 \times 2)$
6. $11 - (5 \times 2)$
7. $(9 - 4) \times 2$
8. $(11 - 5) \times 2$
9. $[8 \times 7] - 13$
10. $[7 \times 6] - 19$
11. $9 \times [4 + 2]$
12. $8 \times [2 + 5]$
13. $(36 \div 2) \times 6$
14. $(54 \div 3) \times 2$
15. $36 \div (2 \times 6)$
16. $54 \div (3 \times 2)$
17. $[16 - (3 \times 2)] - 4$
18. $[17 - (4 \times 3)] - 2$
19. $16 - [(3 \times 2) - 4]$
20. $17 - [(4 \times 3) - 2]$
21. $(10 + 6) \times (11 - 3)$
22. $(14 + 6) \times (9 - 2)$
23. $10 + [6 \times (11 - 3)]$
24. $14 + [6 \times (9 - 2)]$
25. $100 \div [(20 \div 5) - 3]$
26. $[800 \div (50 \div 2)] - 7$
27. $100 \div [20 \div (5 - 3)]$
28. $[(800 \div 50) \div 2] - 7$
29. $\frac{63 - 8}{3 + 8} - 2$
30. $19 - \frac{25 - 7}{5 + 4}$
31. $5 \times \frac{19 - 7}{5 + 1}$
32. $28 \div \frac{8 \times 6}{5 + 7}$

1-2 VARIABLES

In the last section you learned what it means to evaluate an expression such as

$$3 + (7 \times 9).$$

The answer is 66. Suppose that you are not told what one of the numbers in this expression is.

$$3 + (\_\_ \times 9)$$

The value of this expression *varies,* depending on what number you put in the blank space. Some examples are shown on the next page.

$$3 + (\underline{\ 2\ } \times 9)$$
$$= 3 + 18$$
$$= \underline{\underline{21}}$$

$$3 + (\underline{100} \times 9)$$
$$= 3 + 900$$
$$= \underline{\underline{903}}$$

$$3 + (\underline{5.7} \times 9)$$
$$= 3 + 51.3$$
$$= \underline{\underline{54.3}}$$

It is customary to use a letter such as x, y, or z to stand for a number that can take on different values at different times. Instead of using a blank space, the expression above would be written

$$3 + (x \times 9).$$

A letter such as x is called a *variable*.

DEFINITION

VARIABLE
A **variable** is a letter that represents a number. (It can represent different numbers at different times, but it represents the *same* number each place it appears in an expression.)

To evaluate an expression containing a variable, you must be told what value to use for the variable. Then you *substitute* that number for the variable and evaluate the expression as before. Symbols such as 14, 7.8, or $\frac{3}{4}$, which stand for the *same* number *all* the time, are called **constants.**

DEFINITION

SUBSTITUTING
To **substitute** means to replace a variable with a constant (such as 3, 158, or 1001).

For each of the examples on the next page, put a piece of paper along the dotted lines to cover the answer. Work the example. Then uncover the answer to be sure you are right.

EXAMPLE 1

Substitute 4 for x and evaluate: $(15 - x) \times 3$

Think These Reasons

$(15 - x) \times 3$	Write the given expression.
$= (15 - 4) \times 3$	Substitute 4 for x.
$= 11 \times 3$	Do what is inside the parentheses.
$= \underline{\underline{33}}$	Underline or box the answer.

Note: Be sure to use = signs to say that the first expression is *equal* to the next, and so forth.

EXAMPLE 2

Substitute 9 for x and evaluate: $(15 - x) \times 3$

$(15 - x) \times 3$	Write the given expression.
$= (15 - 9) \times 3$	Substitute 9 for x.
$= 6 \times 3$	Do what is inside the parentheses.
$= \underline{\underline{18}}$	Underline or box the answer.

Note: The *same* expression has *different* values when different numbers are substituted for the variable.

It is possible to write an expression that fits a given description. For instance, "the sum of x and 7" is written

$$x + 7.$$

You should recall from previous courses what the words *sum, difference, product,* and *quotient* mean.

$11 + 3$ is an indicated *sum.*

$11 - 3$ is an indicated *difference.*

11×3 is an indicated *product.*

$11 \div 3$ is an indicated *quotient.*

The numbers in a sum, difference, and product have special names, as shown at the top of the next page.

11 + 3 ← Terms → 11 − 3

Factors → 11 × 3

DEFINITION

TERMS AND FACTORS

Terms are numbers that are *added* to each other or *subtracted* from each other.

Factors are numbers that are multiplied together.

EXAMPLE 3

Cover the answers on the right. Write each expression described. Then uncover the answer to be sure that you are correct.

Question	*Possible Answer*
a. The sum of x, 5, and 2.	$x + 5 + 2$
b. The product of 2 and 11.	2×11
c. The difference 17 minus 4.	$17 - 4$
d. The quotient 13 divided by 7.	$13 \div 7 \left(\text{or } \frac{13}{7}\right)$
e. x decreased by 6.	$x - 6$
f. 10 more than y.	$y + 10$ or $10 + y$
g. 50 less than z.	$z - 50$

There are several ways to write the *product* of two numbers x and y:

$$x \times y \quad \text{or} \quad x \cdot y \quad \text{or} \quad (x)(y) \quad \text{or} \quad xy.$$

In the last two, there is no operation sign. So you must *understand* that multiplication is to be done. An expression such as

$$3x$$

means 3 *times* x.

Sometimes an expression may be described by a picture. For instance, the length marked by a question mark below is the *sum* of 3 and x.

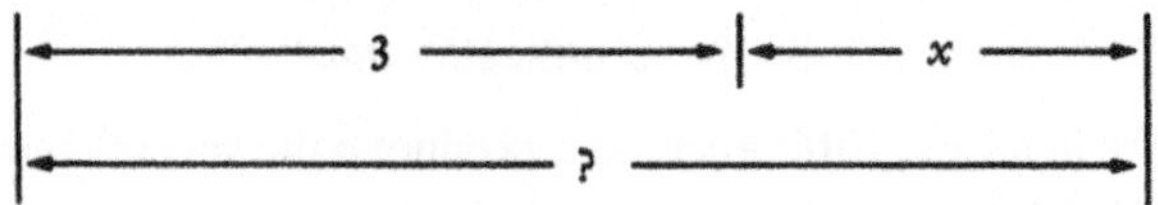

You would write $3 + x$ or $x + 3$ to represent this length.

Cover the answers below as you work the next examples.

EXAMPLE 4

Find the length marked "?".

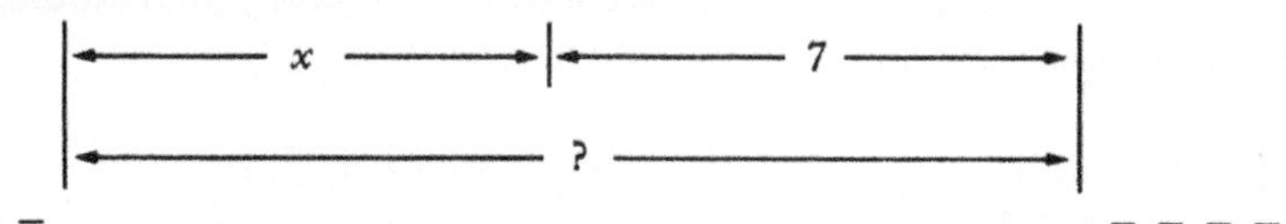

Think These Reasons

$\underline{\underline{x + 7}}$ or $\underline{\underline{7 + x}}$ $\quad$ x and 7 must be *added* to get the total length.

EXAMPLE 5

Find the length marked "?".

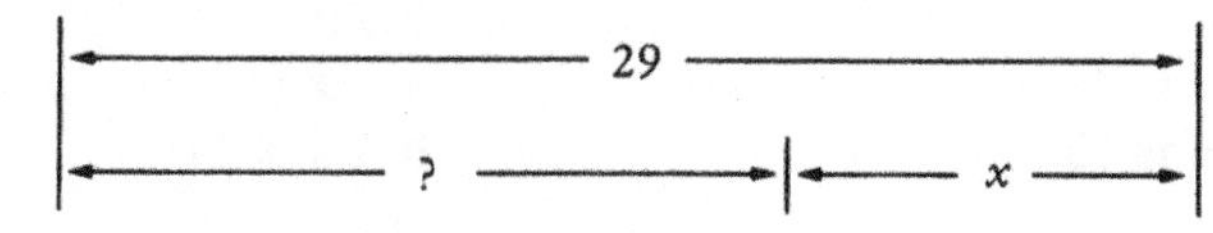

$\underline{\underline{29 - x}}$ $\quad$ 29 is the *whole* length. x is *part* of that length. So $29 - x$ is what is *left* when x is taken away. Note that $x - 29$ would not be correct.

Objective

Be able to write expressions from a verbal description and evaluate expressions by substituting a value for the variable.

EXERCISE 1-2

For Problems 1 and 2, write an expression representing the quantity described.

1. a. The product of 13 and 8.
   b. The product of x and 8.
   c. The product of 13 and y.
   d. The product of x and y.
   e. The sum of 3 and y.
   f. The sum of x and 7.
   g. The difference x minus y.
   h. The quotient x divided by y.
   i. 3 more than x.
   j. 3 times as much as x.
   k. 5 less than y.
   l. One-fifth of y.

2. a. The sum of 17 and 9.
   b. The sum of x and 9.
   c. The sum of 17 and y.
   d. The sum of x and y.
   e. The product of 9 and y.
   f. The product of x and 2.

g. The difference y minus z.
h. The quotient y divided by z.
i. 2 more than x.
j. 2 times as much as x.
k. 8 less than z.
l. One-eighth of z.

For Problems 3 through 14, evaluate the expressions by substituting the given values of the variable.

3. $5 + x$, if:
   a. x is 4;
   b. x is 17.
4. $x + 7$, if:
   a. x is 8;
   b. x is 93.
5. $(24 \div y) - 1$, if:
   a. y is 4;
   b. y is 12.
6. $(72 \div z) + 5$, if:
   a. z is 6;
   b. z is 9.
7. $(z - 19) \times 2$, if:
   a. z is 100;
   b. z is 37;
   c. z is 19.
8. $(y - 31) \times 4$, if:
   a. y is 80;
   b. y is 57;
   c. y is 31.
9. $9x$, if:
   a. x is 4;
   b. x is 13.
10. $7x$, if:
   a. x is 8;
   b. x is 11.
11. $\frac{30}{x}$, if:
   a. x is 6;
   b. x is 90;
   c. x is 45.
12. $\frac{40}{x}$, if:
   a. x is 5;
   b. x is 80;
   c. x is 60.
13. $\frac{p + 5}{2}$, if:
   a. p is 11;
   b. p is 95;
   c. p is 0.
14. $\frac{k + 7}{3}$, if:
   a. k is 5;
   b. k is 53;
   c. k is 0.

For Problems 15 through 34, write an expression for the length marked "?."

15. 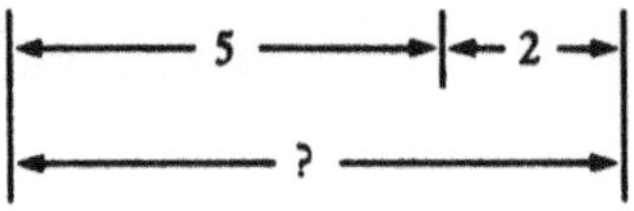 |← 5 →|← 2 →|
|← ? →|

16. 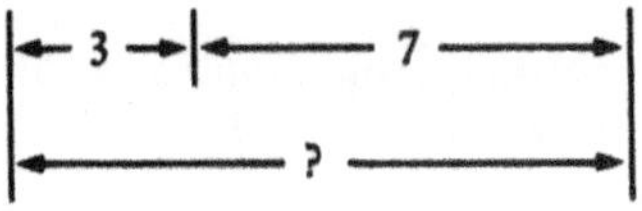 |← 3 →|← 7 →|
|← ? →|

17. 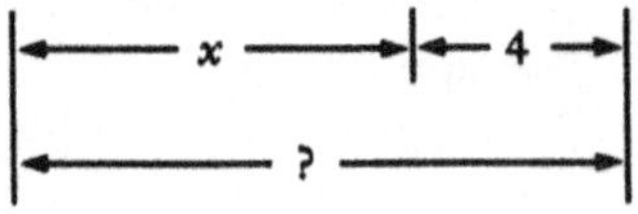 |← x →|← 4 →|
|← ? →|

18. 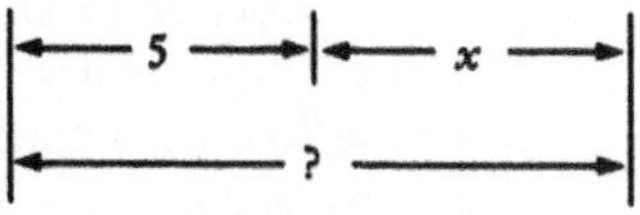 |← 5 →|← x →|
|← ? →|

19. 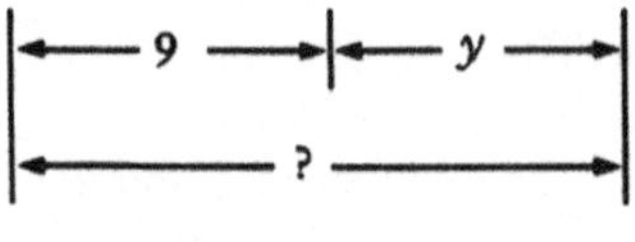 |← 9 →|← y →|
|← ? →|

20. 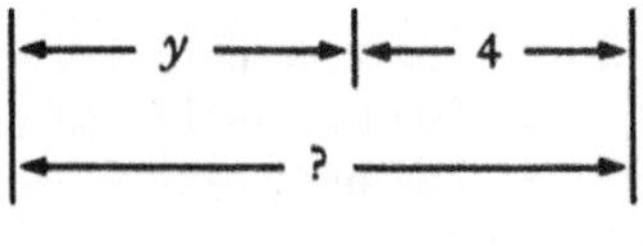 |← y →|← 4 →|
|← ? →|

21. 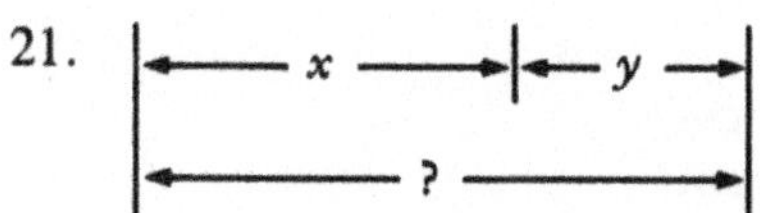

22. y x
?

23. 15
8 ?

24. 13
5 ?

25. 7
x ?

26. 12
x ?

27. y
? 5

28. z
? 5

29. y
? x

30. z
? y

31. ?
6 y x

32. ?
4 x z

33. 12
7 y ?

34. 25
9 x ?

Write expressions for the following quantities.

35. Les Moore is 57 years old.
   a. How old will he be in 4 years?
   b. How old will he be in y years?
   c. How old was he 8 years ago?
   d. How old was he z years ago?

   Manny Moore is x years old.
   e. How old will he be in 4 years?
   f. How old will he be in y years?
   g. How old was he 8 years ago?
   h. How old was he z years ago?

36. Stan Dupp is 127 cm tall.
    a. How tall will he be if he grows 7 cm?
    b. How tall will he be if he grows y cm?
    c. How tall was he when he was 13 cm shorter?
    d. How tall was he when he was z cm shorter?

    Phoebe Small is x cm tall.
    e. How tall will she be if she grows 3 cm?
    f. How tall will she be if she grows y cm?
    g. How tall was she when she was 9 cm shorter?
    h. How tall was she when she was z cm shorter?

1-3 POWERS AND EXPONENTS

You know that multiplication can be thought of as a shorthand way of writing repeated addition. For instance,

$$5 + 5 + 5 \quad \text{is written} \quad 3 \times 5.$$

There is also a short way of writing repeated multiplication.

$$5 \times 5 \times 5 \quad \text{is written} \quad 5^3.$$

The expression 5^3 is read "5 cubed," or "5 raised to the third power," or "the third power of 5." Parts of 5^3 are given names.

5 is called the *base*.
3 is called the *exponent*.
5^3 is called a *power*.

DEFINITION

POWER, BASE, AND EXPONENT
In the expression x^y,

x is called the **base,**

y is called the **exponent,** and

x^y is called a **power.**

Don't confuse the words *exponent* and *power*. The exponent 3 is just the number that tells how many 5s to multiply together. The power is the entire expression, 5^3. Power is similar in meaning to sum or product.

$5 + 3$	A *sum*.
$5 - 3$	A *difference*.
$5 \cdot 3$	A *product*.
$5 \div 3$	A *quotient*.
5^3	A *power*.

Objective

Be able to evaluate a given power and write a number as a power.

To evaluate a power, you simply do the multiplication. In each of the following examples, put a piece of paper along the dotted lines to cover the answer. Work the examples. Then uncover the answers to make sure you are right.

EXAMPLE 1

Evaluate 5^3 (read "five cubed").

- - - - - - - - - -

$$5^3$$
$$= 5 \cdot 5 \cdot 5$$
$$= \underline{\underline{125}}$$

Writing a number as a power might take some cleverness!

EXAMPLE 2

Write each of the following as a power.

Think These Reasons

a. 7 to the fourth power

- - - - - - - - - -

$\underline{\underline{7^4}}$ The base is 7, exponent is 4.

b. 13 squared.

- - - - - - - - - -

$\underline{\underline{13^2}}$ Squared means raised to the *second* power.

c. $x \cdot x \cdot x \cdot x \cdot x \cdot x$

- - - - - - - - - -

$\underline{\underline{x^6}}$ There are *six* x's multiplied together.

d. $3 \cdot 3 \cdot 3 \cdots 3$ (x of them)

- - - - - - - - - -

$\underline{\underline{3^x}}$ There are x 3s multiplied together.

e. 32 as a power of 2.

- - - - - - - - - -

$\underline{\underline{2^5}}$ "As a power of 2" means 2 is the *base*.

Note: To find out how *many* 2s are multiplied together to give 32, do some "upside down repeated short dividing," as shown at the right. Then count the number of 2s.

Five 2s: $2\overline{)32}$, $2\overline{)16}$, $2\overline{)8}$, $2\overline{)4}$, 2

Powers can represent geometrical ideas, such as area or volume.

EXAMPLE 3

How many dots are in this picture? Write the answer as a power.

$\underline{\underline{9^2}}$ 9 rows of 9 dots means 9×9 dots, and 9×9 is 9^2. You can check the answer by counting the dots. 9^2 is 81 and there are 81 dots.

ORAL PRACTICE

Evaluate.

A. 2^3 B. 3^2 C. 4^2 D. 3^3 E. 5^1 F. 1^{10}

Give these as powers.

G. $3 \cdot 3 \cdot 3 \cdot 3$ H. $4 \cdot 4 \cdot 4$ I. $x \cdot x \cdot x \cdot x \cdot x$ J. 7

Give the power represented.

K. ⠿ Number of dots. L. ⊞ Number of smallest squares.

Give the exponent needed.

M. $8 = 2^?$ N. $16 = 2^?$ O. $9 = 3^?$ P. $25 = 5^?$

EXERCISE 1-3

1. Evaluate.
   a. 2^7 b. 3^4 c. 4^3 d. 5^2
   e. 7^3 f. 10^5 g. 8^2 h. 0^4
   i. 13^1 j. 1^{1000}

2. Evaluate.
   a. 3^5 b. 2^6 c. 6^2 d. 5^4
   e. 11^3 f. 10^7 g. 9^2 h. 0^6
   i. 17^1 j. 1^{200}

3. For the expression x^3.
   a. What is the 3 called? b. What is the x called?
   c. Evaluate it if x is 6. d. Evaluate it if x is 10.
   e. Write two different ways x^3 could be read.

4. For the expression z^4.
   a. What is the 4 called? b. What is the z called?
   c. Evaluate it if z is 3. d. Evaluate it if z is 10.
   e. Write two different ways z^4 could be read.

For Problems 5 through 14, write a power representing the indicated quantity

5. Number of dots.

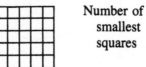

6.  Number of dots.

7. Number of smallest squares

8. 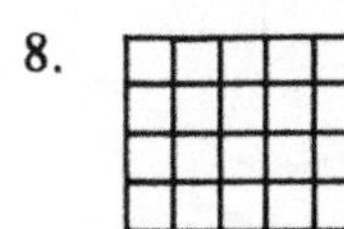 Number of smallest squares

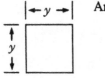

9. y, y Area.

10. 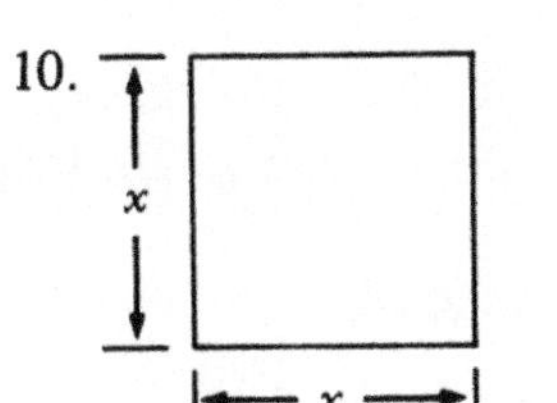

Area.

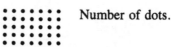

11. 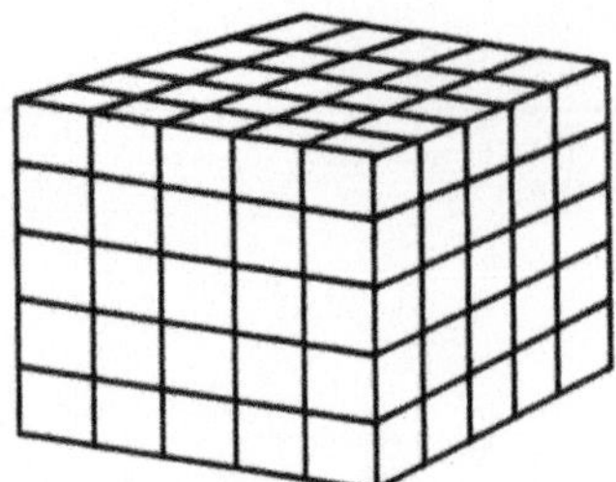

Number of small cubes.

12. 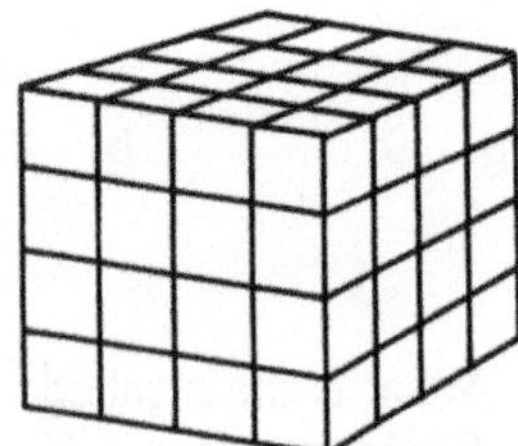

Number of small cubes.

13. 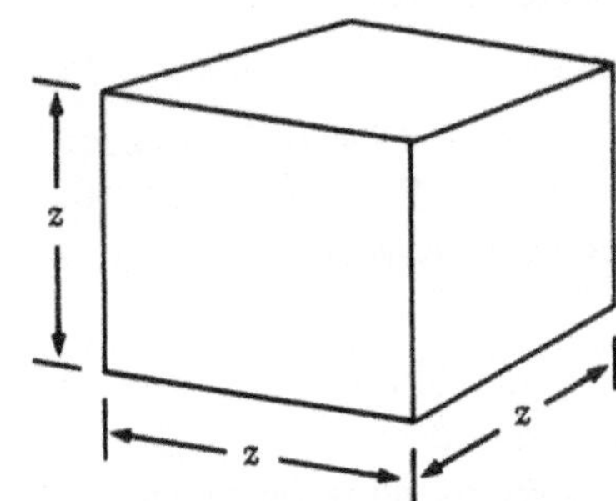

Volume.

14. 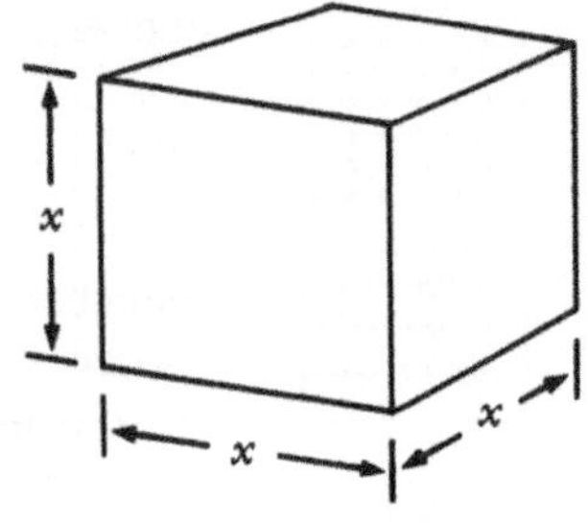

Volume.

For Problems 15 through 26, write the expression as a power.

15. $6 \cdot 6 \cdot 6 \cdot 6$

16. $9 \cdot 9 \cdot 9$

17. $4 \cdot 4 \cdot 4 \cdot 4 \cdot 4 \cdot 4$

18. $3 \cdot 3 \cdot 3 \cdot 3 \cdot 3 \cdot 3 \cdot 3 \cdot 3 \cdot 3$

19. $x \cdot x \cdot x \cdot x \cdot x$

20. $y \cdot y \cdot y \cdot y$

21. $2 \cdot 2 \cdot 2 \cdot \ldots \cdot 2$ (11 of them)

22. $5 \cdot 5 \cdot 5 \cdot \ldots \cdot 5$ (13 of them)

23. $2 \cdot 2 \cdot 2 \cdot \ldots \cdot 2$ (y of them)

24. $5 \cdot 5 \cdot 5 \cdot \ldots \cdot 5$ (x of them)

25. $y \cdot y \cdot y \cdot \ldots \cdot y$ (z of them)

26. $x \cdot x \cdot x \cdot \ldots \cdot x$ (y of them)

For Problems 27 through 34, write the power as a product. For instance, $3^4 = 3 \cdot 3 \cdot 3 \cdot 3$.

27. 7^6

28. 8^7

29. z^5

30. y^6

31. 5^x

32. 6^z

33. z^x

34. y^z

For Problems 35 through 44, write the given number as a power with the given base. For instance, 8 as a power of 2 is 2^3.

35. 81 as a power of 3.

36. 64 as a power of 4.

37. 343 as a power of 7.

38. 36 as a power of 6.

39. 64 as a power of 2.

40. 625 as a power of 5.

41. 100,000 as a power of 10.

42. 1,000,000 as a power of 10.

43. 12 as a power of 12.

44. 8 as a power of 8.

45. ***Calvin's Study-Time Problem*** Calvin Butterball studied algebra for 1 minute the first week of school. Then he studied 2 minutes the second week, 4 minutes the third week, 8 minutes the fourth week, and so on. Each week he doubled the number of minutes. If he keeps up this pattern, how many minutes will he study algebra the last week of an 18-week semester? Write the answer as a power.

46. ***Ancestors Problem*** Your ancestors in the first, second, and third generations back are your natural parents, grandparents, and great-grandparents, respectively. You have had 2 parents, 4 grandparents, and 8 great-grandparents. How many ancestors do you have in the 10th generation back? Write the answer as a power.

1-4 ORDER OF OPERATIONS

You have learned that symbols of inclusion can be used to tell which operation is to be performed first in an expression. If there are more than three operations, there would be so many parentheses and brackets that the expression would look untidy, like this:

$$(4 + [(9 \times 3) \div 6]) + [(5 \times 8) - 7].$$

To avoid all this clutter, users of mathematics have *agreed* on an order in which operations are to be performed. Parentheses are used only to *change* this order.

If an expression has no parentheses to tell you otherwise, then you raise to powers first. For example,

$$3 \cdot 2^4 \quad \text{means} \quad 3 \cdot 16, \quad \text{or} \quad \underline{\underline{48}}.$$

If you want the multiplication to be done first, you have to use parentheses.

$$\begin{aligned} &(3 \cdot 2)^4 \\ &= 6^4 \\ &= \underline{\underline{1296}} \end{aligned}$$

Multiplication and division are done before addition and subtraction. For example,

$$13 - 2 \cdot 4 \quad \text{means} \quad 13 - 8, \quad \text{or} \quad \underline{\underline{5}}.$$
$$15 + 35 \div 5 \quad \text{means} \quad 15 + 7, \quad \text{or} \quad \underline{\underline{22}}.$$

Parentheses must be used if you want to do the addition or subtraction first.

$$\begin{aligned} &(13 - 2) \cdot 4 \\ &= 11 \cdot 4 \\ &= \underline{\underline{44}} \end{aligned}$$

$$\begin{aligned} &(15 + 35) \div 5 \\ &= 50 \div 5 \\ &= \underline{\underline{10}} \end{aligned}$$

If an expression has only multiplication and division or only addition and subtraction, then these operations are done in order, from left to right. For example,

$$48 \div 6 \times 2 \quad \text{means} \quad 8 \times 2, \quad \text{or} \quad \underline{\underline{16}};$$
$$17 - 5 + 3 \quad \text{means} \quad 12 + 3, \quad \text{or} \quad \underline{\underline{15}}.$$

Again, parentheses must be used if you are supposed to do the operations in a different order:

$$48 \div (6 \times 2) = 48 \div 12 = \underline{\underline{4}};$$

$$17 - (5 + 3) = 17 - 8 = \underline{\underline{9}}.$$

AGREEMENT

ORDER OF OPERATIONS
If there are no parentheses to tell you otherwise, operations are performed in the following order:

1. Evaluate any *powers* first.
2. After powers, *multiply* and *divide,* in order, from left to right.
3. Last, *add* and *subtract,* in order, from left to right.

Objective

Be able to evaluate expressions using the agreed-upon order of operations.

For each of the following examples, put a piece of paper along the dotted lines to cover up the answer. Evaluate the expression. Then uncover the answer to be sure you are right.

EXAMPLE 1
Evaluate $60 - 7(5 + 6 \div 2) + 2^4$.

------ -----

	Think These Reasons
$60 - 7(5 + 6 \div 2) + 2^4$	Write the given expression.
$= 60 - 7(5 + 3) + 2^4$	Inside the parentheses, divide *before* adding.
$= 60 - 7(8) + 2^4$	Do what is inside parentheses *first.*
$= 60 - 7(8) + 16$	Evaluate *powers* next.
$= 60 - 56 + 16$	Multiply *before* adding and subtracting.
$= 4 + 16$	Add and subtract, in order, from left to right.
$= \underline{\underline{20}}$	Answer.

At first it is safer to evaluate expressions *one* step at a time. Later you will learn ways to combine steps. You do *not* need to write down the reason for each step, but you should *think* of what the reason is.

If you are evaluating an expression containing a variable, you must substitute a value for the variable first.

EXAMPLE 2

Evaluate $3x^2 - 5x$ if x is 4.

	Think These Reasons
$3x^2 - 5x$	Write the given expression.
$= 3 \cdot 4^2 - 5 \cdot 4$	Substitute 4 for x, *both* places.
$= 3 \cdot 16 - 5 \cdot 4$	Raise to powers *before* multiplying.
$= 48 - 20$	Multiply *before* adding or subtracting.
$= \underline{\underline{28}}$	Answer.

ORAL PRACTICE

Evaluate:

A. $10 - 4 + 3$
B. $10 - 4 - 3$
C. $12 \div 4 + 2$
D. $10 + 4 \div 2$
E. $4 + 3 \cdot 5$
F. $4 \cdot 3 + 5$
G. $12 \div 6 \cdot 2$
H. $12 \cdot 6 \div 2$
I. $3 \cdot 2^2$
J. $(3 \cdot 2)^2$
K. $(3 + 2)^2$
L. $3 + 2^2$
M. $23 - 3(2)$
N. $18 + 2(3)$
O. $12 - 2(3 + 1)$
P. $(12 - 2)(3 + 1)$

EXERCISE 1-4

For Problems 1 through 26, evaluate the given expression.

1. a. $24 - 6 + 2$
   b. $24 - 6 \cdot 2$
   c. $24 \cdot 6 - 2$
   d. $24 \div 6 \cdot 2$
   e. $24 \div 6 \div 2$

2. a. $36 - 9 + 2$
   b. $36 - 9 \cdot 2$
   c. $36 \cdot 9 - 2$
   d. $36 \div 9 \cdot 2$
   e. $36 \div 9 \div 2$

3. a. $5 + 2 \cdot 4 + 3$
   b. $(5 + 2) \cdot 4 + 3$
   c. $5 + 2 \cdot (4 + 3)$
   d. $(5 + 2) \cdot (4 + 3)$

4. a. $6 + 4 \cdot 5 - 2$
   b. $(6 + 4) \cdot (5 - 2)$
   c. $6 + 4 \cdot (5 - 2)$
   d. $(6 + 4) \cdot 5 - 2$

5. a. $5 + 2^3$
   b. $5 - 2^3$
   c. $5 \cdot 2^3$
   d. $(5 \cdot 2)^3$

6. a. $7 + 3^2$
   b. $7 - 3^2$
   c. $7 \cdot 3^2$
   d. $(7 \cdot 3)^2$

7. $10 - 3(8 - 6)$

8. $30 - 4(8 - 3)$

9. $4 + 6(5 - 2)$

10. $7 + 3(12 - 2)$

11. $8 + 5 \cdot 4^3$

12. $2 + 8 \cdot 3^2$

13. $33 - 3 \cdot 2^3$

14. $34 - 4 \cdot 2^3$

15. $16 + 4(7 - 4 + 1)$

16. $17 + 3(8 - 5 + 1)$

17. $14 + 8 \div 2 - 1$

18. $30 + 10 \div 5 - 3$

19. $4 \cdot 9 + 7 \cdot 8$

20. $9 \cdot 5 + 6 \cdot 7$

21. $37 + 3[16 \div (2 \cdot 4)]$

22. $48 + 2[12 \div (2 \cdot 3)]$

23. $102 - 2(3^4 - 51)$

24. $53 - 3(2^5 - 22)$

25. $33 - 3[4 \cdot (7 - 5)] + 3^2$

26. $74 - 4[3 \cdot (9 - 4)] + 5^2$

For Problems 27 through 40, evaluate the expression for the given values of x.

27. x^3, if:
   a. x is 3;
   b. x is 5;
   c. x is 1.

28. x^4, if:
   a. x is 2;
   b. x is 3;
   c. x is 0.

29. 3^x, if:
   a. x is 2;
   b. x is 4;
   c. x is 1.

30. 2^x, if:
   a. x is 3;
   b. x is 5;
   c. x is 1.

31. $4x^2$, if:
   a. x is 3;
   b. x is 5;
   c. x is 0.

32. $6x^2$, if:
   a. x is 3;
   b. x is 4;
   c. x is 1.

33. $x^2 + 2x + 1$, if:
   a. x is 6;
   b. x is 4;
   c. x is 1.

34. $x^2 + 4x + 4$, if:
   a. x is 3;
   b. x is 5;
   c. x is 0.

35. $(x + 1)^2$, if:
   a. x is 6;
   b. x is 4;
   c. x is 1.

36. $(x + 2)^2$, if:
   a. x is 3;
   b. x is 5;
   c. x is 0.

37. $(3x)^2$, if:
    a. x is 1;
    b. x is 2;
    c. x is 0.

38. $(5x)^2$, if:
    a. x is 1;
    b. x is 2;
    c. x is 0.

39. $56 - 6x$, if:
    a. x is 8;
    b. x is 1;
    c. x is 0.

40. $108 - 8x$, if:
    a. x is 12;
    b. x is 1;
    c. x is 0.

1-5 EXPRESSIONS FROM WORD STATEMENTS

In Section 1-2 you wrote expressions such as $x + 3$ to represent the sum of x and 3. In this section you will write expressions involving three or more numbers.

The expression

$$3 + 5x$$

means add 3 and the product of 5 and x. No parentheses are necessary since the multiplication, $5x$, is done before the addition. The expression

$$(3 + 5)x$$

is read "the *quantity* 3 plus 5, times x." The words "the quantity . . ." are used to say in English what the parentheses say in mathematics. The parentheses, of course, mean that the 3 and 5 are to be added *before* multiplying by x.

Objective

Given a description of an expression, write that expression using parentheses only when necessary.

For each of the following examples, put a piece of paper along the dotted lines to cover the answers. Work the example. Then uncover the answer to make sure you are right and did not leave any unneeded parentheses.

EXAMPLE 1
Subtract 6 from 21, then add 3.

- - - - -   - - - - -

Think These Reasons

$21 - 6 + 3$ — No parentheses are needed, because addition and subtraction are done in order from left to right.

EXAMPLE 2

Subtract 6 from 21, then divide by 3.

$(21 - 6) \div 3$, or $\dfrac{21 - 6}{3}$ — Parentheses or a vinculum *are* needed. Without them, the 6 would first be divided by the 3.

EXAMPLE 3

Add 3 to x, then square the result.

$(x + 3)^2$ — Parentheses *are* needed. Without them, only the 3 would be squared.

EXAMPLE 4

The sum of the squares of x and 3.

$x^2 + 3^2$, or $x^2 + 9$ — No parentheses are needed, because squaring is done *before* adding.

EXAMPLE 5

The quantity r minus s, cubed.

$(r - s)^3$ — Parentheses *are* needed since "the quantity . . ." means that the subtraction must be done *first*.

EXERCISE 1-5

Write the expression described. Use parentheses only where necessary.

1. Subtract 2 from x, then add y.
2. Add 5 to y, then multiply by x.
3. Subtract the sum of 2 and y from x.
4. Add the product of 5 and y to x.
5. Divide x by 3, then multiply by z.
6. Multiply x by the sum of 7 and y.
7. Divide x by the product of 3 and z.
8. Multiply x by 7, then add y.
9. Multiply x by 3, then add y.

10. Divide y by 7, then add z.
11. Add x and 3, then multiply by y.
12. Divide y by the sum of 7 and z.
13. Add x and y, then square the result.
14. Add 6 and x, then cube the result.
15. Add the squares of x and y.
16. Add the cubes of 6 and x.
17. Subtract the product of 5 and x from 7.
18. Subtract the product of 3 and y from 19.
19. Subtract the cube of z from 15.
20. Subtract the square of p from 18.
21. 5 more than the product of 3 and c.
22. 6 more than the quotient 7 divided by j.
23. 13 less than the quotient 5 divided by p.
24. 17 less than the product of 9 and k.
25. 4 times the sum of 10 and x.
26. 11 times the quantity y minus 3.
27. 5 divided by the quantity x minus 7.
28. 10 divided by the quantity r plus t.
29. The quantity $3x + 2$ divided by the quantity $1 - 3x$.
30. The quantity $4x - 7$ divided by the quantity $1 + 4x$.

1-6 INTRODUCTION TO EQUATIONS

This section is intended for you to read by yourself, without help from your teacher. Read the material below, work the examples to see what is being asked for, and then work the assigned problems.

You have learned how to find the value of an expression when you know what x equals. Here, you will find the value of x when you know what the *expression* equals. For example, if the expression is $x + 5$ and you know that it equals 17, you could write

$$x + 5 = 17.$$

This is called an **equation.** The expression on the left side is called the **left member** and the expression on the right is called the **right member.**

To find what x equals, you must have x alone on one side of the equation. To do this you must get rid of the unwanted 5 in the left member. You can *subtract* 5 from *each* member, getting

$$x + 5 - 5 = 17 - 5.$$

Simplifying leads to

$$\underline{\underline{x = 12.}}$$

As you can see, 12 + 5 really *does* equal 17!

Objective

Given the value of an expression, be able to find the value of the variable.

For each of the following examples, put a piece of paper along the dotted lines to cover the answer. After you do one step, uncover the work down to the next set of dotted lines to be sure you are right.

EXAMPLE 1

For the expression $x - 7$, find x when the expression equals 15.
First, you write an equation.

- - - - -   - - - - -

$$x - 7 = 15$$

Then you figure out how to get rid of the unwanted 7 in the left member so that x will be alone. *Adding* 7 to each member will do the job.

- - - - -   - - - - -

$$x - 7 + 7 = 15 + 7$$

Finally, you do the operations.

- - - - -   - - - - -

$$\underline{\underline{x = 22}}$$

EXAMPLE 2

For the expression $\frac{1}{3}x$, find x if the expression equals 13.

Your thought process should be, "I want to get x by itself. So I must get rid of the $\frac{1}{3}$ in front of the x. To do this I can *multiply* each member by 3."

Think These Reasons

$\frac{1}{3}x = 13$	Write an equation.
$3 \cdot \frac{1}{3}x = 3 \cdot 13$	Multiply each member by 3.
$\underline{x = 39}$	Do the operations to get x alone. Underline or box the answer.

EXAMPLE 3

For the expression $7x$, find x when the expression equals 42.

$7x = 42$	Write an equation.
$\frac{7x}{7} = \frac{42}{7}$	*Divide* each member by 7 to get rid of the 7 that is multiplied by x.
$\underline{x = 6}$	Do the operations to get x alone.

EXERCISE 1-6

1. For the expression $x - 3$, find x when the expression equals:
   a. 7 b. 10 c. 20
   d. 100 e. 1998
2. For the expression $x + 8$, find x when the expression equals:
   a. 10 b. 17 c. 35
   d. 107 e. 1776
3. For the expression $\frac{1}{2}x$, find x when the expression equals:
   a. 5 b. 13 c. 50
   d. 111 e. 65
4. For the expression $5x$, find x when the expression equals:
   a. 10 b. 75 c. 1000
   d. 15 e. 27

1-7 SOLVING EQUATIONS

In the last section you learned how to find the value of x if you are given the value of an expression containing x. For instance, by subtracting 5 from each member of the equation

$$x + 5 = 17,$$

you found that

$$x = 12.$$

If you substitute the number 12 for x in the original equation, you get the *true* statement

$$12 + 5 = 17.$$

The number 12 in this example is called a *solution* of the equation. The process of finding all values of the variable that make the equation true is called *solving the equation*. Taking a step such as subtracting 5 from each member is called *transforming* the equation. Thus to solve an equation, all you need to do is *transform* it until it says

x = some number.

The particular transformation you pick is the one that gets the variable by itself by getting *rid* of unwanted numbers surrounding the variable.

$x - 2 = 7$	*Add* 2 to each member to get rid of the 2.
$x + 3 = 8$	*Subtract* 3 from each member to get rid of the 3.
$\frac{1}{5}x = 9$	*Multiply* each member by 5 to get rid of the $\frac{1}{5}$.
$6x = 2$	*Divide* each member by 6 to get rid of the 6.

EXAMPLE

Solve $x + 3 = 8$. Show the transformation.

	Think These Reasons
$x + 3 = 8$	Write the given equation.
$x + 3 - 3 = 8 - 3$	Subtract 3 from each member.
$\underline{\underline{x = 5}}$	Do the operations.

See the examples of Section 1-6 if you need more practice.

Objective

Be able to solve equations by transforming them to the form x = some number.

You can probably tell that a simple equation like $x + 5 = 17$ has 12 as its solution *without* doing any transformations. However, soon you will have to solve equations like

$$3x^2 - 4x - 2 = 7.$$

It is almost impossible to figure out that 2.5225881 is a solution of this equation without doing some transformations. So it is a good idea to get used to doing the transformations while the problems are still relatively easy.

A transformation such as adding 3 to each member can be thought of as adding equal weights to both sides of a balance. If it was balanced before, it will still balance afterward. But if you add weight to only *one* side, it no longer balances!

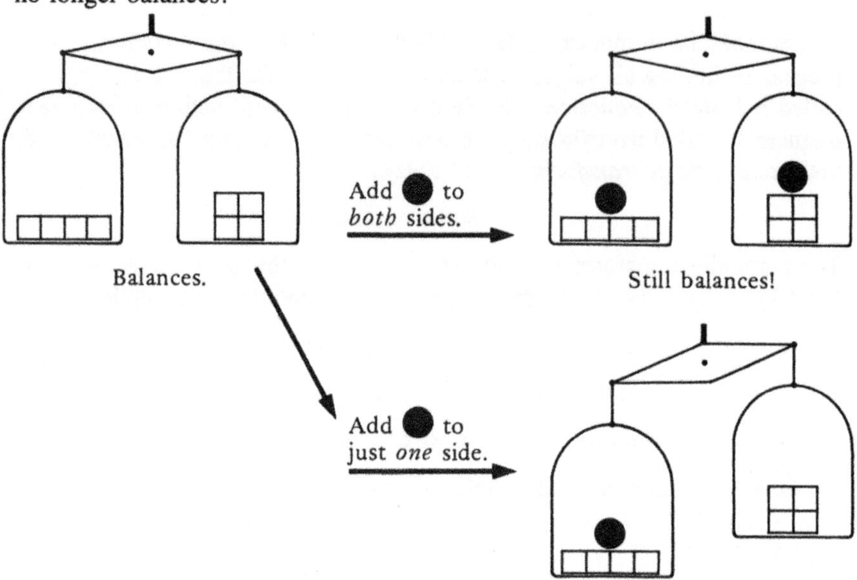
Add ● to
both sides.
Balances.
Still balances!
Add ● to
just *one* side.
Doesn't balance!!

You have read the words *equation, solution,* and *transform*. Here are formal definitions of these words.

DEFINITIONS

EQUATION
An **equation** is a sentence (such as $x + 3 = 5$) which says that one expression is equal to another expression.

SOLUTION
A **solution** of an equation is a number you can substitute for the variable that makes the sentence *true*. (For instance, 2 is a solution of $x + 3 = 5$ because $2 + 3$ equals 5.)

TRANSFORMING AN EQUATION
To **transform** an equation means to do the *same* operation to *each* member of the equation.

ORAL PRACTICE

Give the transformation needed to solve the equation.

A. $x + 4 = 13$	B. $x - 3 = 4$	C. $2x = 11$
D. $\frac{1}{6}x = 5$	E. $x - 5 = 6$	F. $\frac{1}{3}x = 9$
G. $7x = 5$	H. $x + 7 = 19$	I. $x - 7 = 4$
J. $x + 1 = 10$	K. $\frac{1}{4}x = 20$	L. $8x = 0$

Tell whether each is an equation or an expression.

M. $x + 6 - 8$	N. $x + 6 = 8$	O. $x = 4$
P. $x - 4$	Q. $3x \div 5$	R. $3x = 5$
S. $x^2 + 2x$	T. $x^2 = 2x$	U. $x^2 - 2x$
V. $2 = x + 3$	W. $2x = 3$	X. $2x + 3$

EXERCISE 1-7

Solve each equation. Show the transformation step.

1. $x - 10 = 17$	2. $x - 8 = 13$
3. $x + 4 = 13$	4. $x + 9 = 21$
5. $5x = 90$	6. $6x = 72$
7. $\frac{1}{3}x = 29$	8. $\frac{1}{5}x = 23$
9. $x - 16 = 7$	10. $x - 17 = 8$
11. $x - 32 = 95$	12. $x - 45 = 89$
13. $x + 58 = 74$	14. $x + 43 = 91$
15. $x + 91 = 247$	16. $x + 79 = 422$
17. $12x = 132$	18. $15x = 210$
19. $8x = 1000$	20. $4x = 100$
21. $\frac{1}{7}x = 68$	22. $\frac{1}{9}x = 58$
23. $\frac{1}{10}x = 100$	24. $\frac{1}{10}x = 1000$

25. $x + 5 = 4$

26. $x + 7 = 5$

27. $x - 94 = 362$

28. $x - 61 = 365$

29. $x + 1984 = 2001$

30. $x + 1066 = 1776$

31. $\frac{1}{3}x = 51$

32. $\frac{1}{3}x = 57$

33. $3x = 51$

34. $3x = 57$

35. $17x = 51$

36. $19x = 57$

37. $\frac{1}{17}x = 51$

38. $\frac{1}{19}x = 57$

39. $6x = 2$

40. $8x = 4$

Problems 41 through 50 involve fractions.

EXAMPLE

$\frac{2}{3}x = 12$ Given equation.

$\frac{3}{2} \cdot \frac{2}{3}x = \frac{3}{2} \cdot 12$ *Multiply* by the *reciprocal* of $\frac{2}{3}$.

$x = \underline{\underline{18}}$ Do the operations.

41. $\frac{2}{3}x = 6$

42. $\frac{3}{2}x = 6$

43. $\frac{3}{5}x = 30$

44. $\frac{4}{5}x = 20$

45. $\frac{7}{2}x = 28$

46. $\frac{5}{3}x = 30$

47. $x + \frac{2}{3} = \frac{5}{3}$

48. $x + \frac{3}{5} = \frac{13}{5}$

49. $x - \frac{3}{4} = 1\frac{3}{4}$

50. $x - \frac{2}{3} = 4\frac{2}{3}$

1-8 PROBLEMS THAT LEAD TO EQUATIONS

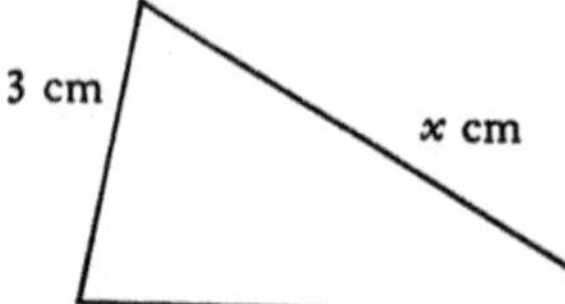

You have learned how to evaluate expressions and solve equations. Expressions can represent things in the real world. For instance, the *perimeter* of a figure is the *sum* of the lengths of its sides. In the triangle shown, the perimeter is the sum

$$x + 3 + 7, \quad \text{or} \quad x + 10.$$

If someone tells you that the perimeter is 18 centimeters (cm), you could write an equation stating this fact.

$$\underset{\text{The perimeter}}{\underset{\uparrow}{x + 10}} \quad \underset{\text{is}}{\underset{\uparrow}{=}} \quad \underset{18.}{\underset{\uparrow}{18}}$$

Then you could find the length of the variable side, x cm, by *solving* the equation. To isolate x you must get rid of the unwanted 10 on the left. So you subtract 10 from each member.

$$x + 10 = 18$$

$$x + 10 - 10 = 18 - 10$$

$$x = 8$$

Side is 8 cm.

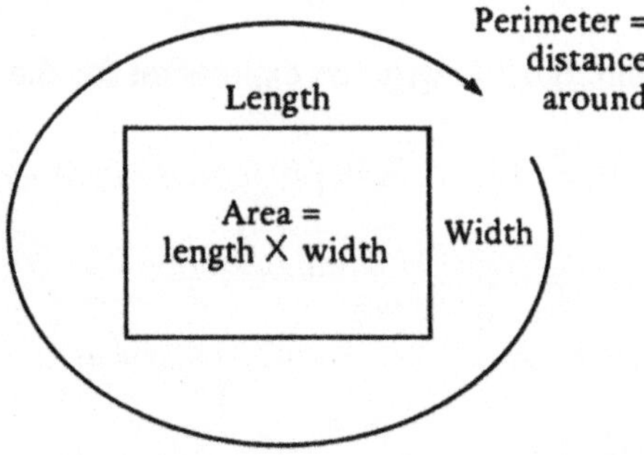

Objective

Be able to write and solve equations representing real-world situations.

For the problems in this section, you must keep in mind the difference between perimeter and area. **Perimeter** is the *distance* around a figure. **Area** is a measure of the "space" inside a figure. For a rectangle, area equals length times width.

ORAL PRACTICE

For items A through G on the next page, give an expression for the perimeter or area.

A. Perimeter

B. Area

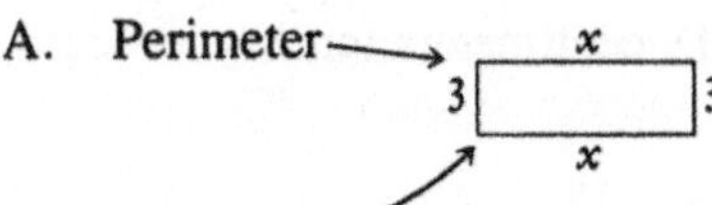

C. Perimeter

D. Area

E. Perimeter

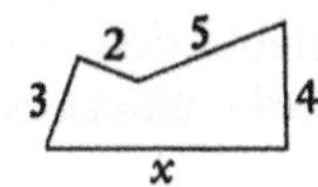

F. Area

G. Perimeter

EXERCISE 1-8

For Problems 1 through 10, write an expression for the perimeter of the figure.

1. 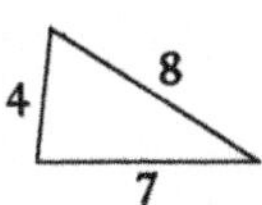

2. 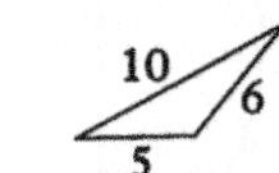

3. 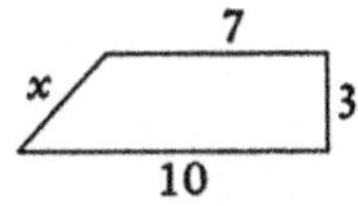

4. 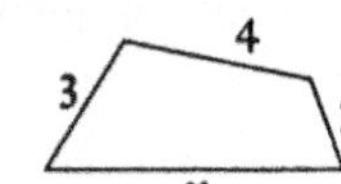

5. 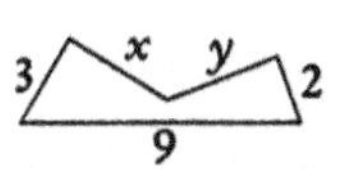

6. 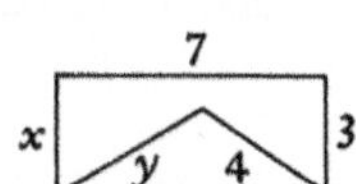

7. 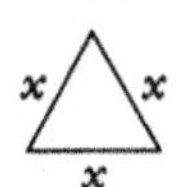

8. 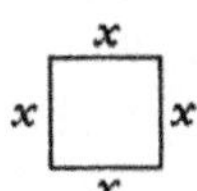

9. 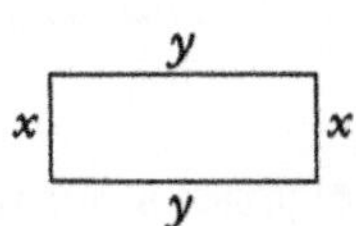

10. 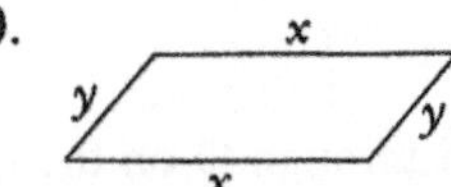

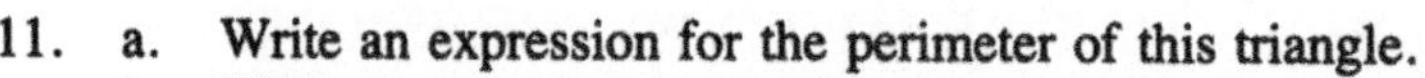

11. a. Write an expression for the perimeter of this triangle.
    b. Write an equation stating that the perimeter equals 47.
    c. Find x by solving the equation.

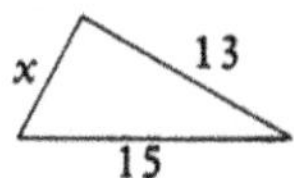

12. a. Write an expression for the perimeter of this triangle.
    b. Write an equation stating that the perimeter equals 62.
    c. Find x by solving the equation.

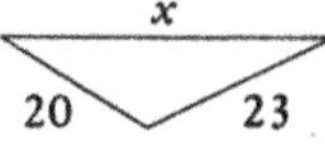

13. Find x if the perimeter of this triangle is 61.

14. Find x if the perimeter of this triangle is 56.

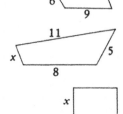

15. Find x if the perimeter of this figure is 30.

16. Find x if the perimeter of this figure is 28.

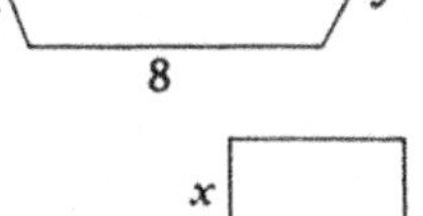

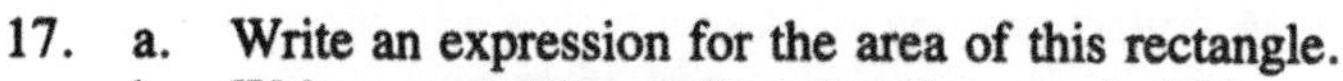

17. a. Write an expression for the area of this rectangle.
    b. Write an equation stating that the area is 584.
    c. Find x by solving the equation.

18. a. Write an expression for the area of this rectangle.
    b. Write an equation stating that the area is 105.
    c. Find x by solving the equation.

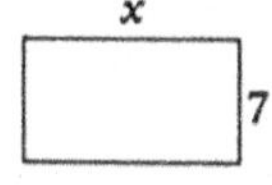

19. Find x if the area of this rectangle is 5.

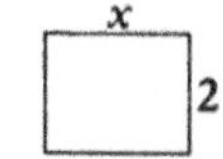

20. Find x if the area of this rectangle is 12.

21. Although circles do not have sides, they do have "perimeters."
    a. What special name is given to the perimeter of a circle?
    b. Measure the perimeter of this circle. Use centimeters. Find the answer correct to the nearest 0.1 cm. You must be very clever to figure out how to do this!

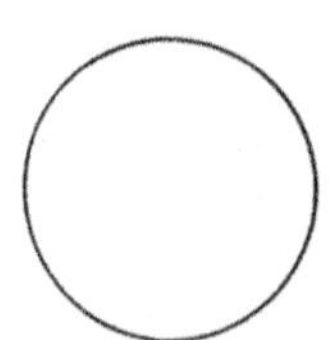

1-9 PROBLEMS THAT LEAD TO EXPRESSIONS AND EQUATIONS

In the last section you saw how expressions could be used to represent things such as perimeter and area of a rectangle. Now you are ready to use expressions to represent other quantities. By evaluating the expression or by solving an equation involving the expression, you can get answers to problems from the real world.

EXAMPLE 1

A cook makes \$16 per day more than a waiter makes. Let x be the number of dollars per day a waiter makes. Answer the following questions.

a. Write an expression for the dollars per day a cook makes.

b. If a waiter makes \$35 per day, how much does a cook make?

c. If waiters get a raise to \$40 per day, how much will a cook make?

d. If a cook makes \$65 per day, how much does a waiter make?

	Think These Reasons
a. Waiter: x dollars per day	Write the given variable.
Cook: $x + 16$ dollars per day	Cook makes \$16 *more*. So you add 16 to x.
b. $x + 16$	Write the expression from (a).
$= 35 + 16$	Substitute 35 for x.
$= 51$	Do the arithmetic.
Cook makes \$51 per day.	Answer the question.
c. $x + 16$	Write the expression from (a).
$= 40 + 16$	Substitute 40 for x.
$= 56$	Do the arithmetic.
Cook makes \$56 per day	Answer the question.
d. $x + 16 = 65$	Set cook's expression equal to 65.
$x + 16 - 16 = 65 - 16$	Subtract 16 from each member.
$x = 49$	Do the operations.
Waiter makes \$49 per day.	Answer the question.

Objectives

1. Be able to write expressions representing things in the real world.
2. Be able either to evaluate the expression or solve an equation containing the expression to answer a question about the real world.

For the following example, put a piece of paper along the dotted lines to cover the answer. Work each part. Then uncover the answer to be sure you are right before going on to the next part.

EXAMPLE 2

Genes Problem **If parents have a certain combination of genes, then about $\frac{1}{4}$ of their children will have attached earlobes. Let x be the number of children born to a group of couples with these genes.**

a. **Write an expression for the number of children with attached lobes.**

b. **If these couples have a total of 532 children, about how many of them will have attached lobes?**

c. **About how many children would the couples need to have in order for there to be 240 children with attached lobes?**

- - - - -

a. Total number: x — Write the given variable.

Attached lobes: $\underline{\underline{\frac{1}{4}x}}$ — "$\frac{1}{4}$ of" means "$\frac{1}{4}$ times."

- - - - -

b. $\frac{1}{4}x$ — Write the expression from (a).

$= \frac{1}{4}(532)$ — Substitute 532 for x.

$= 133$ — Do the arithmetic.

<u>133 children</u> — Answer the question.

- - - - -

c. $\frac{1}{4}x = 240$ — Write an equation.

$4\left(\frac{1}{4}x\right) = 4(240)$ — Multiply each member by 4.

$x = 960$ — Do the operations.

<u>960 children</u> — Answer the question.

ORAL PRACTICE

Give an expression representing each.

A. $\frac{1}{4}$ of x.

B. 7 less than x.

C. 5 more than x.

D. 3 fewer than x.

E. 6 years older than x.

F. 10 years younger than x.

G. 4 times x.

H. 30% of x (30% means $30 \div 100$, or 0.30).

I. 90% of x.

J. 2.3 times as much as x.

EXERCISE 1-9

1. *Freshmen Problem* Suppose that $\frac{1}{4}$ of the students in a school are freshmen. Let x stand for the total number of students.
   a. Write the definition of x. Then write an expression representing the number of freshmen.
   b. Write an equation stating that the number of freshmen is 312.
   c. Find the number of students in the school.
2. *Rain Problem* At Scorpion Gulch, it rains $\frac{1}{8}$ of the days. Let x stand for the total number of days that have passed.
   a. Write the definition of x. Then write an expression representing the number of days it rains.
   b. Write an equation stating that the number of days it rains is 31.
   c. Solve the equation to find the total number of days that have passed.
3. *Sid's and Tip's Age Problem* Sid Upp is 4 years younger than his brother, Tip. Let x stand for Tip's age.
   a. Write the definition of x. Then write an expression for Sid's age.
   b. Write an equation stating that Sid's age is 76.
   c. Find Tip's age by solving this equation.
4. *Tess and Clara's Allowance Problem* Tess T. Fye gets \$3 less allowance each week than her older sister Clara. Let x stand for the number of dollars Clara gets a week.
   a. Write the definition of x. Then write an expression for the number of dollars Tess gets a week.
   b. Write an equation stating that Tess gets \$11 per week.
   c. Find Clara's allowance by solving the equation.
5. *Rectangle Problem* The length of a rectangle is 7 cm more than its width. Let x be the number of cm in the width.
   a. Draw the rectangle. Then write an expression for its length.
   b. Find the length if the width is:
      i. 12 cm; ii. 37 cm; iii. 100 cm.

c. Write an equation stating that the length is 43 cm. Then solve the equation to find the width.
d. Repeat the procedure in part (c) to find the width if the length is:
i. 91 cm; ii. 34 cm.

6. *Age Problem* Inda Cates is 5 years younger than her sister Cindy. Let x be Cindy's age.
a. Write an expression for Inda's age.
b. How old will Inda be when Cindy is:
i. 17; ii. 23; iii. 100?
c. Write an equation stating that Inda is 24. Then solve the equation to find Cindy's age.
d. Repeat the procedure in part (c) to find Cindy's age when Inda is:
i. 13; ii. 72.

7. *Downstream Problem* When you travel downstream, your actual speed is your speed through the water *plus* the speed of the current. The San Antonio River flows at about 3 kilometers per hour (km/h). Let x be the number of kilometers per hour you go through the water.
a. Write an expression representing your actual speed downstream.
b. How fast would you go downstream in:
i. a pedalboat, which goes 5 km/h;
ii. a rowboat, which goes 11 km/h;
iii. a speedboat, which goes 42 km/h?
c. Write an equation stating that your actual speed is 21 km/h. Then solve the equation to find your speed through the water.
d. Repeat the procedure of part (c) to find your speed through the water if your actual speed is:
i. 9 km/h; ii. 65 km/h

8. *Upstream Problem* When you travel upstream, your actual speed is your speed through the water *minus* the speed of the current. The current in Snake River is 7 kilometers per hour (km/h). Let x be your speed through the water in kilometers per hour.
a. Write an expression for your actual speed upstream.
b. Find the actual speed of:
i. a canoe traveling 12 km/h through the water;
ii. a salmon swimming 9 km/h through the water;
iii. a sound wave traveling 2000 km/h through the water.
c. Write an equation stating that your actual speed is 15 km/h. Solve this equation to find your speed through the water.
d. Repeat the procedure of part (c) to find your speed through the water if your actual speed is:
i. 25 km/h; ii. 8 km/h.

9. *Left-Handers' Problem* About $\frac{1}{5}$ of all people are left-handed. Let x be the number of people in a particular group.
   a. Write an expression for the number of left-handed people in the group.
   b. Write an equation stating that the number of left-handers in a group is 47. Solve the equation to find the number of people in that group.
   c. Find the number of people in groups that have:
      i. 100 left-handers
      ii. 4000 left-handers.
   d. How many left-handers are there in a group of:
      i. 30 people; ii. 100 people;
      iii. 5000 people?

10. *Sale Problem* When an item is on sale for $\frac{1}{3}$ off, the number of dollars you save is $\frac{1}{3}$ of the normal price. Let x dollars be the normal price.
   a. Write an expression for the number of dollars you save.
   b. A tag says, "Save $43.00 on this pair of binoculars!" Write an equation expressing this fact. Then solve the equation to find the normal price of the binoculars.
   c. Find the normal selling price of:
      i. a tent, on which you save $37.00;
      ii. a scuba mask, on which you save $13.00.
   d. How much do you save on:
      i. a watch, normally priced at $12.00?
      ii. a video tape recorder, normally priced at $837.00?

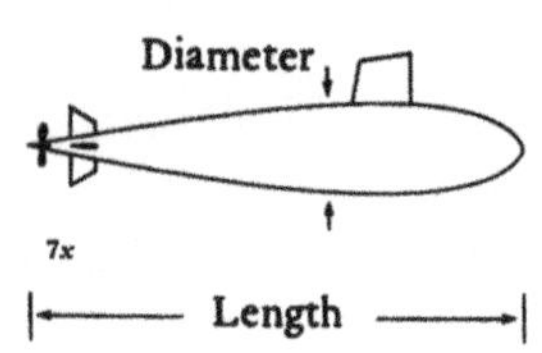

11. *Submarine Problem* To go through the water most efficiently, a submarine should be built so that its length is 7 times its diameter. Let x be the diameter in meters (m).
   a. Write an expression for the length.
   b. What should the length be if:
      i. the diameter is 8 meters (m);
      ii. the diameter is 10 m?
   c. Write and solve equations to find out what the diameter should be if:
      i. the length is 91 m;
      ii. the length is 50 m.

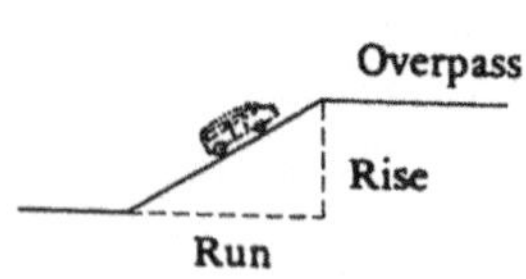

12. *Access Ramp Problem* When an overpass is built on an expressway, the run should be 15 times the rise (see the diagram). Let x be the number of meters in the rise.
   a. Write an expression representing the run.
   b. Find the run if the rise is:
      i. 7 m; ii. 20 m.
   c. Write and solve equations to find the rise if the run is:
      i. 195 m; ii. 243 m.

13. *Profit Problem* Mark Upp runs a retail store. On each item sold, he makes a profit of 20%, which means that he sells it for 1.2 times what he paid for it. Let x be the number of dollars he paid for an item.
    a. Write an expression for the number of dollars for which he sells an item.
    b. What is the selling price of:
        i. a flag for which he paid \$5.00;
        ii. a skillet for which he paid \$9.00;
        iii. a desk for which he paid \$140.00?
    c. Find out how much Mark paid for:
        i. a suitcase that he sells for \$84.00;
        ii. a clock that he sells for \$13.20.

14. *Laborer Problem* A construction company's rules say that a supervisor earns 1.5 times as much as a laborer. Let x be the number of dollars per hour a laborer earns.
    a. Write an expression for the number of dollars per hour a supervisor earns.
    b. Doug Upp is a laborer who earns \$6.00 per hour. How much does his supervisor earn?
    c. If Doug's pay is increased to \$8.00 per hour, how much will the supervisor earn?
    d. Suppose that a supervisor earns \$9.60 per hour. How much does a laborer earn under these conditions?

15. *Challenge Problem* Use the expression $2x + 5$.
    a. Evaluate the expression if:
        i. x is 7; ii. x is 13; iii. x is 58.
    b. Write an equation stating that the expression is 41.
    c. Solve the equation. Note that you will have to subtract *and* divide. See if you are clever enough to do these two transformations in the order that makes the problem the easiest!

1-10 CHAPTER REVIEW AND TEST

In this chapter, you have used the two basic processes of algebra. If you are given an expression such as

$$x + 3$$

you should be able to do the following:

1. Find out what the expression equals when you know the value of x.
2. Find out what x equals when you know the value of the expression.

The first is called *evaluating* an expression. The second is called *solving* an equation. Both processes are useful in solving problems from the real world.

One goal of your education should be to learn how to prepare for a test. Before you attempt the Chapter Test below, you should thumb through each section in this chapter and find the paragraph headed *Objective*. If you understand what the objective means, go right on to the next section and read its objective. If not, then look at the exercise for that section. If you still don't understand the objective, work examples in that section until you *do* get the idea.

CHAPTER TEST

T1. What is the difference in each case?
- a. Expression and an equation.
- b. Evaluating an expression and solving an equation.
- c. Order of operations in $(3 + 4) \times 5$ and in $3 + 4 \times 5$.
- d. Product and a power.
- e. Power and an exponent.
- f. Factors and terms.
- g. Perimeter of a rectangle and area of a rectangle.

T2. Evaluate each expression.
- a. $30 + 5 \cdot 6 - 3$
- b. $30 + 5 \cdot (6 - 3)$
- c. $30 \cdot 5 + 6 \div 3$
- d. $30 \cdot (5 + 6) \div 3$
- e. $30 \div 5 \cdot 6 - 3$
- f. $7 + 3^2$
- g. $7 \cdot 3^2$
- h. $7 \cdot (3^2)$
- i. $62 - 2[24 - 5 \cdot 3]$
- j. $5 + 5(11 \div 2^3)$
- k. $\frac{30}{10} + \frac{6}{2}$
- l. $\frac{30 + 6}{10 + 2}$

T3. Evaluate $2x^2 + 7x - 4$ if:
- a. x is 3;
- b. x is 6.

T4. Evaluate each expression (i) if x is 35, and (ii) if x is 400.
- a. $x + 7$
- b. $x - 16$
- c. $\frac{1}{7}x$
- d. $9x$

T5. Solve the equations.
- a. $x + 7 = 13$
- b. $x - 16 = 59$
- c. $\frac{1}{7}x = 19$
- d. $9x = 54$

T6. Write each as a power.
- a. $12 \cdot 12 \cdot 12 \cdot 12 \cdot 12 \cdot 12 \cdot 12$
- b. 243, with 3 as its base.
- c. 10,000, with 10 as its base.

T7. Write an expression for each of the following. Use parentheses only where necessary.

a. Eleven cubed.
b. The fifth power of y.
c. The sum of 17 and x.
d. The product of 17 and x.
e. Add 8 to z; then multiply the result by x.
f. Multiply 8 by z and add x to the result.
g. Divide the sum of r and s by the difference r minus s.

T8. Write an expression for the length marked "?."

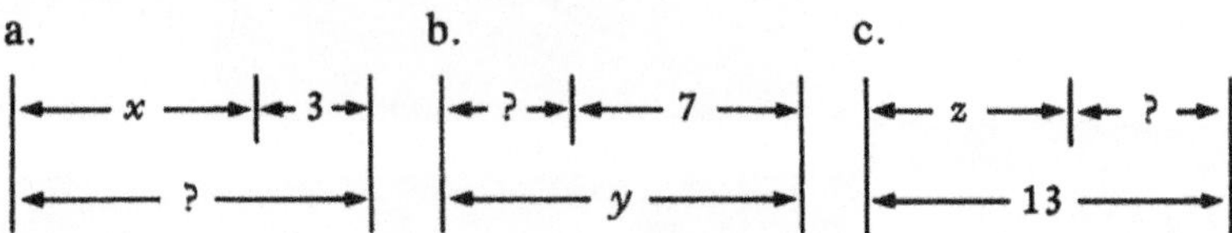

T9. *Savings Problem* When money is left in a savings account, it earns "simple interest." If the interest rate is 10% a year, you will have 1.1 times as much money at the end of 1 year as you had to start with. Each year the amount is multiplied by 1.1 again. If you start with $1, how much will you have at the end of 30 years? Write the answer as a power.

T10. *Thunder and Lightning Problem* The number of seconds it takes the thunder sound to reach you is 3 times the number of kilometers between you and the lightning. Let x be the number of kilometers.

a. Write an expression for the number of seconds the sound takes to reach you.
b. How long does it take the sound to reach you if the lightning is:
   i. 5 kilometers away;
   ii. 2.8 kilometers away?
c. Write an equation stating that the sound takes 12 seconds to reach you. Then solve it to find your distance from the lightning.

T11. *Bank Robbery Problem* Robin Banks robs a bank and takes off in the get-away car. Five minutes later, Willie Catchup starts after Robin. Let x be the number of minutes Robin has been driving.

a. Write an expression for the number of minutes Willie has been driving.
b. How long has Willie been driving when Robin has been going for:
   i. 13 minutes; ii. 21 minutes?
c. How long has Robin been driving when Willie has been going for:
   i. 17 minutes; ii. 24 minutes?

2

Operations with Negative Numbers

In the last chapter you learned how to write expressions representing such things as perimeter, area, dollars, and speed. In this chapter you will use the same techniques. But the answers will sometimes be negative *numbers. Negative numbers were invented to represent things like temperatures below freezing, overdrawn bank balances, and number of seconds ago. For instance, suppose you are riding a bike downhill and are gaining speed at* $\frac{2}{3}$ *mile per hour each second. If you are going 12 miles per hour now, positive values for time could be used to find your speed several seconds later. Negative values for time could be used to find your speed several seconds* ago. *In this chapter you will learn how to operate with negative numbers.*

Variable:

x	Represents number of seconds later.

Expression:

$12 + \frac{2}{3}x$	Represents speed x seconds later.
x is -3	Represents 3 seconds *ago*.

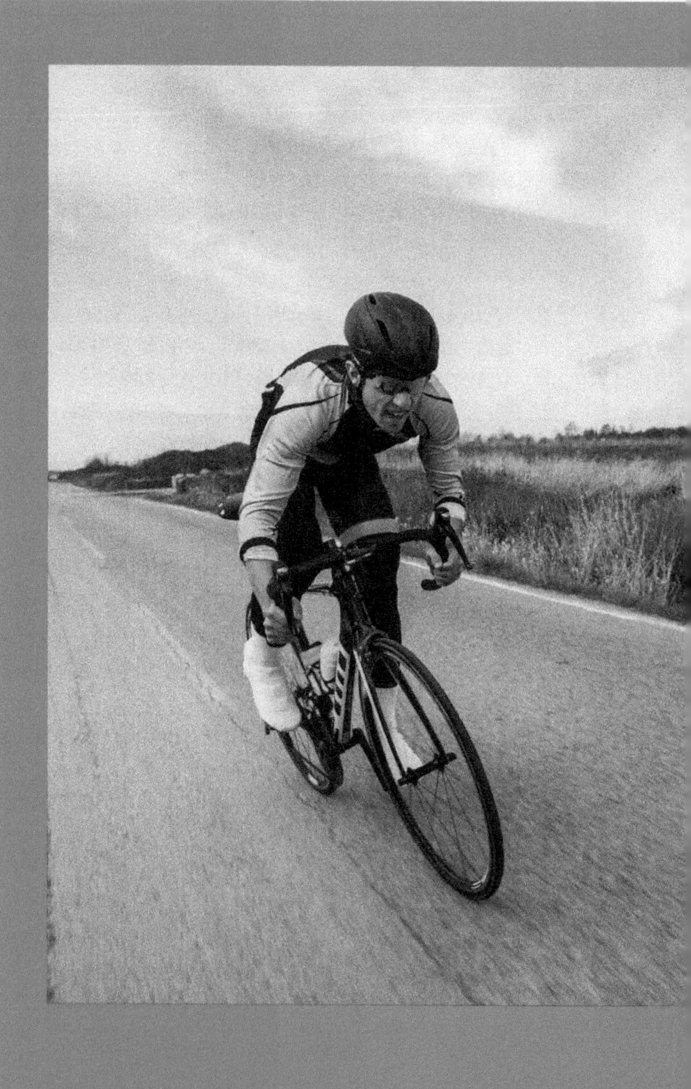

2-1 INTRODUCTION TO NEGATIVE NUMBERS

This section is meant for you to read and work on your own. If you have worked with negative numbers before, this will be review. If not, this will be a chance for you to try learning something new before hearing about it in class.

Numbers were invented by people. Different kinds of numbers are used for different purposes. The *positive integers* 1, 2, 3, 4, 5, . . . were invented for counting. The *fractions* and *decimals,* such as $3\frac{1}{2}$ or 98.6, were invented for measuring. In order to express things like temperatures colder than 0°, overdrawn bank accounts, and speeds when going backwards, people invented negative numbers. Negative numbers are numbers that are less than zero.

One of the best ways for you to visualize negative numbers is to look at a number line.

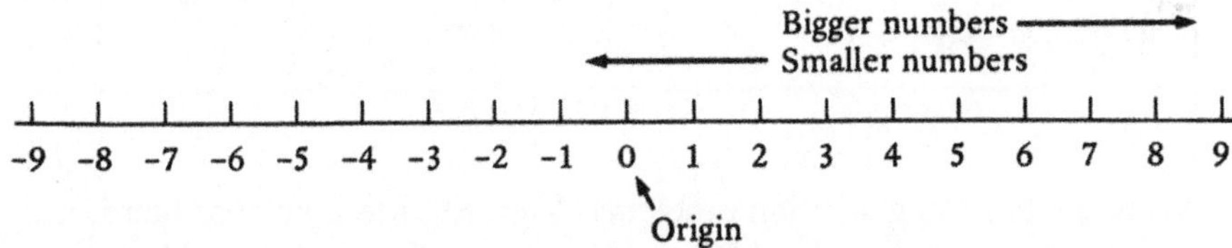

Each point on the line represents a number. The bigger the number, the farther it is to the *right*. Numbers to the left of 0 (the **origin**) are called *negative numbers*. The − sign is used to represent a negative number, as shown above. All numbers that have a place on the number line are called *real numbers*. These include decimals and fractions, both positive and negative.

To add two numbers such as 2 + 3, you start at 2 and move 3 spaces to the right, ending at 5.

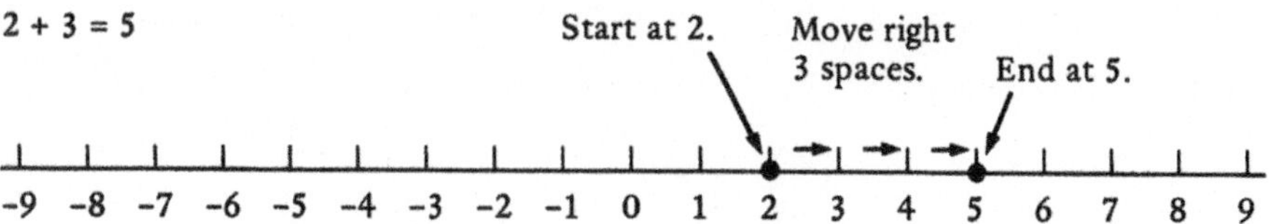

To add a *negative* number to a positive number, such as $4 + (-3)$, you start at 4 and then count 3 spaces to the *left*, ending at 1.

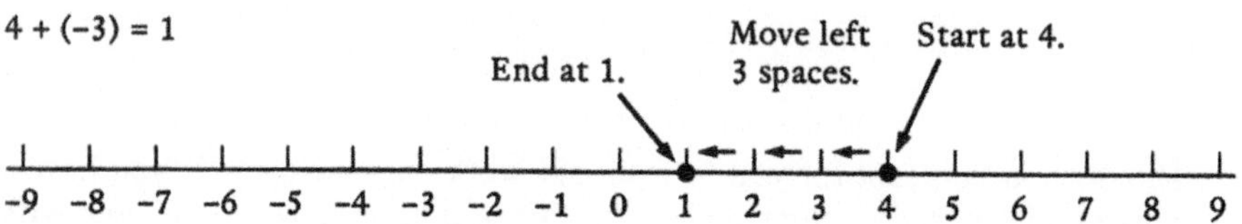

Objective

Be able to discover something about the answers to addition problems of the forms

$$\begin{gathered}\text{(positive)} + \text{(negative)},\\ \text{(negative)} + \text{(positive)},\\ \text{(negative)} + \text{(negative)}.\end{gathered}$$

Working the following exercise should allow you to reach some conclusions.

EXERCISE 2-1

Work the following addition problems. You may use a number line if necessary. You should work all 33 problems rather than just the odds or just the evens.

1. $5 + (-2)$
2. $7 + (-3)$
3. $6 + (-4)$
4. $8 + (-7)$
5. $2 + (-5)$
6. $9 + (-10)$
7. $13 + (-8)$
8. $1 + (-4)$
9. $3 + (-7)$
10. $2 + (-11)$
11. $-3 + (-2)$
12. $-5 + (-1)$
13. $-13 + (-4)$
14. $-1 + (-6)$

15. $-4 + (-5)$ 16. $-2 + (-9)$ 17. $-8 + (-9)$

18. $-1 + (-1)$ 19. $0 + (-3)$ 20. $-10 + (-10)$

21. $-3 + 5$ 22. $-2 + 7$ 23. $-4 + 1$

24. $-12 + 8$ 25. $-13 + 15$ 26. $-8 + 11$

27. $-27 + 1$ 28. $-4 + 15$ 29. $-11 + 35$

30. $-100 + 100$

31. True or false?
    a. The sum of two negative numbers is always negative.
    b. A negative number plus a positive number is always negative.
    c. A positive number plus a negative number is always positive.

32. Adding a *negative* number to another number is the same as what *other* operation?

33. What is meant by:
    a. a negative number; b. an integer; c. a real number?

2-2 ADDING SIGNED NUMBERS

In the previous section, you added signed numbers on a number line. In this section, you will learn a quicker way.

Objective

Be able to add positive and negative numbers *quickly*.

To accomplish this objective, you must first have two background concepts.

The first is that of *additive inverses (opposites):* Negative 5, written -5, is a number 5 units to the left of the origin on a number line. If you add 5 to it, the answer is 0.

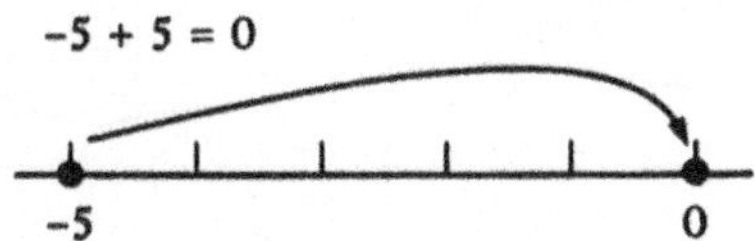

Any two numbers that have a sum of zero are called *additive inverses,* or *opposites,* of each other.

DEFINITION

ADDITIVE INVERSES, OR OPPOSITES
Two numbers are **additive inverses,** or **opposites,** of each other if their *sum* equals *zero.* (For instance, -5 and 5 are additive inverses because $-5 + 5 = 0$.)

Because $-5 + 5$ equals 0, you can say that -5 is the opposite of 5 and that 5 is the opposite of -5. The opposite of -5 can be written $-(-5)$. So you can write

$$-(-5) = 5.$$

In general, for any real number x,

$$-(-x) = x$$

The second concept is **absolute value.** The *absolute value* of a number, written

$$|\text{number}|,$$

is its distance from the origin on a number line. Because 5 and -5 are both 5 spaces from the origin,

$$|-5| = 5 \quad \text{and} \quad |5| = 5.$$

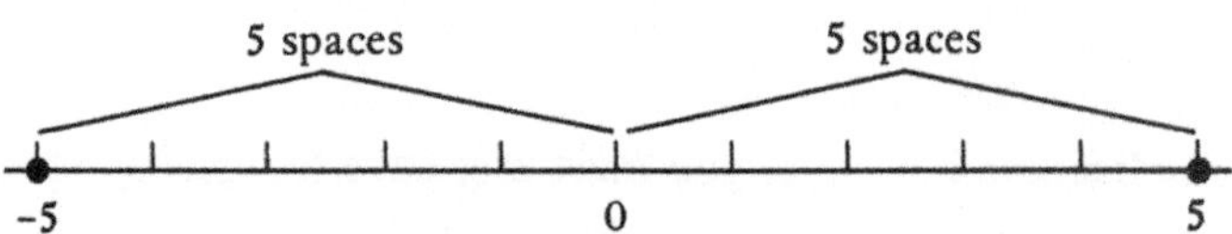

As you can see, the absolute value of a number tells you its "size." For instance, -7 has a larger absolute value than does 3, because -7 is farther from the origin than 3.

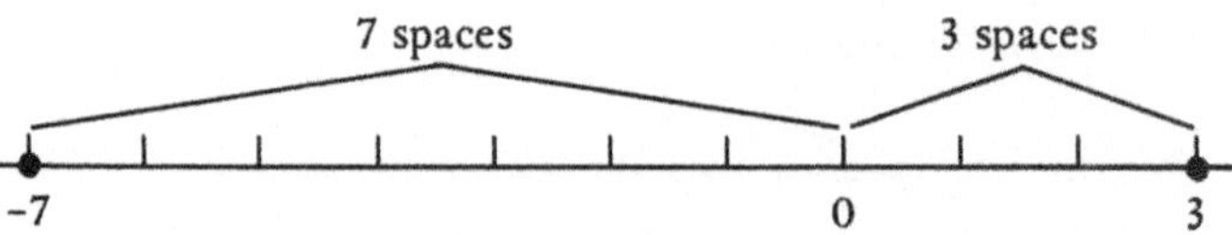

With these two concepts, you are ready to learn how to add negative numbers quickly. The following cases show how.

Case 1: Add $7 + (-4)$.

From the number line, the answer is 3.

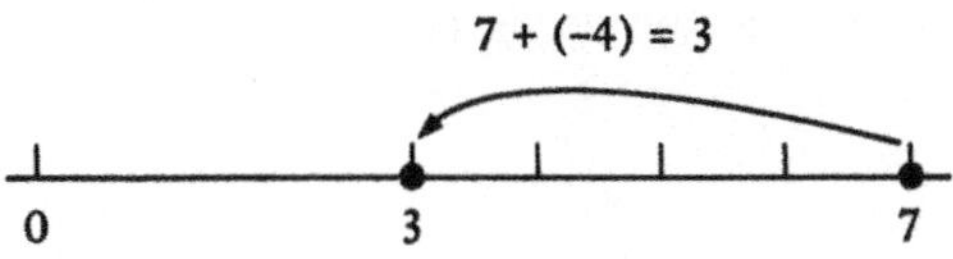

Quick way: $7 + (-4)$

$= 7 - 4 \leftarrow$ *Subtract* the numbers!

$= \underline{\underline{3}}$

Note that in expressions such as $7 + (-4)$, the parentheses are needed to separate the $+$ and $-$ signs. It is not correct notation to write two operation signs together without parentheses.

Case 2: Add $7 + (-9)$.

From the number line, the answer is -2.

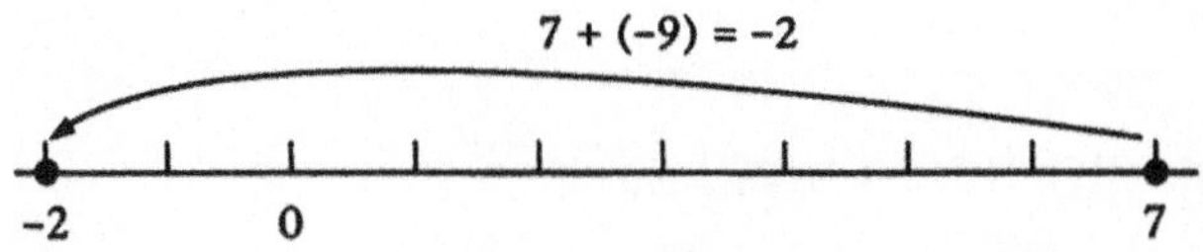

Quick way: $7 + (-9)$

$= 7 - 9$ Subtract the *absolute values,* 9 and 7.

$= \underline{\underline{-2}}$ The answer is *negative* since the absolute value of 9 is greater than the absolute value of 7.

Case 3: Add $-3 + (-4)$.

From the number line, the answer is -7.

-3 + (-4) = -7

-7 -3 0

Quick way: $-3 + (-4)$

$= \underline{\underline{-7}}$ ← *Add* the absolute values, 3 and 4. Then make the answer *negative*.

Case 4: Add $-3 + 4$.

From the number line, the answer is 1.

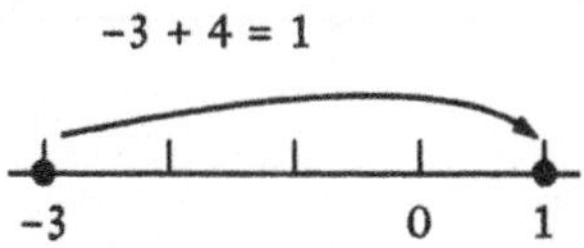

Quick way: $-3 + 4$

$= \underline{\underline{1}}$ ← *Subtract* the absolute values. The sign of the answer is the sign of the *greater* absolute value.

From these four cases, you can summarize the quick ways.

TECHNIQUE

TO ADD SIGNED NUMBERS:

1. If the two numbers have *opposite* signs:
   - *Subtract* the absolute values.
   - The answer has the sign of the term with the *greater* absolute value.

   Big minus small is *positive*.
   Small minus big is *negative*.

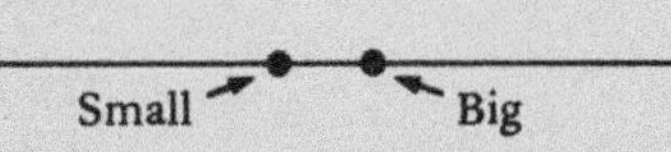

2. If the two numbers have the *same* sign:
   - *Add* the absolute values.
   - Use the sign of the two numbers for the answer.

   Positive plus positive is *positive*.
   Negative plus negative is *negative*.

You have read the words *positive number, negative number, integer,* and *real number*. Here are formal definitions of these sets of numbers.

DEFINITION

KINDS OF NUMBERS
Positive numbers are greater than zero.
Negative numbers are less than zero.
Integers are the numbers . . . −3, −2, −1, 0, 1, 2, 3, ... They do *not* include the fractions in between.
Real numbers are *all* numbers on the number line, positive, negative, and zero. They include fractions, decimals, etc., and fill the entire number line, leaving no gaps.

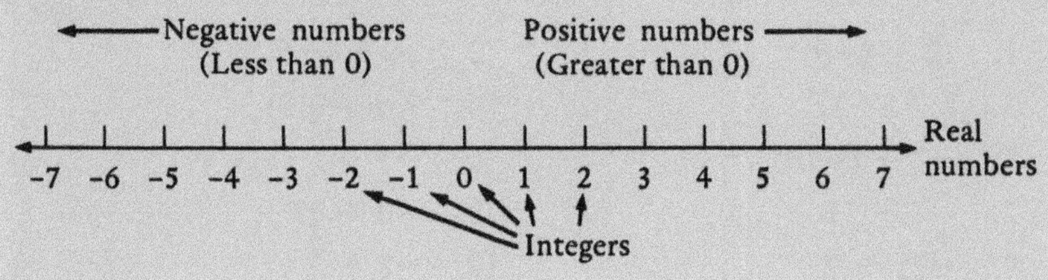

ORAL PRACTICE

Evaluate the following.

A. $|-3|$ B. $|4|$ C. $|7.2|$

D. $\left|\frac{-2}{3}\right|$ E. $|0|$ F. $3 + (-5)$

G. $8 + (-2)$ H. $-6 + 1$ I. $-3 + (-4)$

J. $-3 + 4$ K. $-2 + (-7)$ L. $-(-4)$

M. $-(-6.1)$ N. $\left|-5\frac{1}{3}\right|$ O. $-|-9|$

P. Tell why it would be bad form to write $3 + -7$.

Tell whether the parentheses are needed in each case.

Q. $6 + (-5)$ R. $-7 + (4)$ S. $-3 + (-1)$

T. $6.2 + (1.4)$ U. $-(-8)$

Give an example of each.

V. Negative number. W. Positive number.

X. **Real number that is *not* an integer.**

Y. **Negative integer.**

Z. **Negative real number that is not an integer.**

EXERCISE 2-2

For Problems 1 through 40, evaluate the expression. Write both the given expression and the answer.

1. $12 + (-9)$
2. $14 + (-6)$
3. $8 + (-13)$
4. $9 + (-19)$
5. $-2 + (-16)$
6. $-5 + (-11)$
7. $-4 + 11$
8. $-3 + 17$
9. $-21 + 7$
10. $-8 + 2$
11. $-5 + (-8)$
12. $-7 + (-9)$
13. $5 + (-8)$
14. $7 + (-9)$
15. $-5 + 8$
16. $-7 + 9$
17. $-8 + 5$
18. $-9 + 7$
19. $-23 + (-15)$
20. $-62 + (-38)$
21. $-6.3 + 2.1$
22. $-8.7 + 1.2$
23. $5.8 + (-4.1)$
24. $3.4 + (-2.1)$
25. $-1.8 + (-7.3)$
26. $-5.8 + (-7.4)$
27. $\frac{5}{13} + \left(-\frac{2}{13}\right)$
28. $\frac{7}{11} + \left(-\frac{4}{11}\right)$
29. $-1\frac{5}{7} + \frac{2}{7}$
30. $-6\frac{4}{5} + \frac{3}{5}$
31. $|-7|$
32. $|-6|$
33. $-(-7)$
34. $-(-6)$
35. $-7 + 7$
36. $-6 + 6$
37. $-7 + (-7)$
38. $-6 + (-6)$
39. $-(-(-7))$
40. $-(-(-(-6)))$

For Problems 41 through 54, evaluate the expression. Recall the agreed-upon order of operations.

41. $14 + (-3) + (-6)$
42. $21 + (-8) + (-7)$
43. $2 + (-7) + (-10)$
44. $5 + (-11) + (-2)$

45. $-19 + 8 + (-4)$
46. $-13 + 6 + (-1)$
47. $-30 + 6 + 29$
48. $-90 + 10 + 30$
49. $-5 + (-12) + (-13)$
50. $-4 + (-16) + (-27)$
51. $5 + (-32) + 16 + (-8)$
52. $12 + (-5) + 11 + (-29)$
53. $-29 + 4 + (-15) + 40$
54. $-17 + 6 + (-11) + 22$

For Problems 55 through 60, tell what kind(s) of number is (are) given: real, positive, negative, or integer.

EXAMPLE

-8 Real, negative, integer

55. 13
56. 7.2
57. -6.3
58. -11
59. $\frac{3}{4}$
60. $1\frac{4}{5}$

2-3 SUBTRACTING SIGNED NUMBERS

In the last section, you saw that addition of negative numbers can be turned into a subtraction problem. For example,

$$\begin{aligned} &7 + (-3) \\ &= 7 - 3 \\ &= 4. \end{aligned}$$

The reverse is also true. A subtraction problem can be turned into an addition problem. For instance,

$$7 - 3 = 7 + (-3).$$

This equation says

7 *minus* 3 equals 7 *plus* the *opposite* of 3.

This idea can be used as a definition of subtraction.

DEFINITION

SUBTRACTION
Subtracting a number means adding its opposite. That is,

$$x - y = x + (-y).$$

This definition is especially useful if you must subtract a *negative* number. The expression

$$9 - (-5)$$

can be written as

9 *plus* the *opposite* of −5.

Since the opposite of −5 is 5, you can write

$$\begin{aligned} &9 - (-5) \\ &= 9 + 5 \\ &= \underline{\underline{14}}. \end{aligned}$$

Objective

Be able to subtract positive and negative numbers.

The following rules can be used for quick subtraction of signed numbers.

TECHNIQUE

TO SUBTRACT SIGNED NUMBERS

1. Change subtracting to *adding* the *opposite*.
2. Follow the rules for *adding* signed numbers.

For each of the following examples, put a piece of paper along the dotted lines to cover the answer. Evaluate the expression. Then uncover the answer to be sure you are right.

EXAMPLE 1

Evaluate 13 − 29.

- - - - - - - - - -

	Think These Reasons
13 − 29	Write the given expression.
= 13 + (−29)	Change subtracting to adding the opposite.
= $\underline{\underline{-16}}$	*Subtract* the absolute values.

EXAMPLE 2

Evaluate −4 − 3.

- - - - - - - - - -

−4 − 3	Write the given expression.

$= -4 + (-3)$ Change subtracting to adding the opposite.

$= \underline{\underline{-7}}$ *Add* the absolute values. Make the answer *negative*.

EXAMPLE 3

Evaluate $11 - (-3) - 4$.

$11 - (-3) - 4$ Write the given expression.

$= 11 + 3 - 4$ Change subtracting to adding the opposite. (The "-4" does not need to be changed yet.)

$= 14 - 4$ Add and subtract from left to right.

$= \underline{\underline{10}}$ Do the arithmetic.

EXAMPLE 4

Evaluate $-3 - 7 - (-2)$.

$-3 - 7 - (-2)$ Write the given expression.

$= -3 + (-7) + 2$ Change subtracting to adding the opposite.

$= -10 + 2$ *Add* the absolute values. Make the answer negative.

$= \underline{\underline{-8}}$ *Subtract* the absolute values. Make the answer negative.

ORAL PRACTICE

Give the value of each expression.

A. $5 - 7$ B. $-6 - 2$ C. $8 - (-5)$

D. $7 - (-9)$ E. $-3 - (-1)$ F. $-4 - 6$

G. $5 - (-2)$ H. $7.3 - 9.8$ I. $6 + (-5)$

J. $-2 + (-5)$

K. Tell why it would be bad form to write $3 - -7$.

Tell whether or not the parentheses are needed in each case.

L. $6 - (-5)$ M. $-7 - (4)$ N. $-3 - (-1)$

O. $6.2 - (1.4)$ P. $0 - (2)$

Q. State the definition of subtraction.

EXERCISE 2-3

Evaluate.

1. $35 - 200$
2. $144 - 441$
3. $14 - (-17)$
4. $15 - (-21)$
5. $-11 - (-2)$
6. $-34 - (-7)$
7. $-99 - 59$
8. $-40 - 30$
9. $-241 - (-42)$
10. $-300 - (-88)$
11. $158 - (-115)$
12. $135 - (-165)$
13. $5.9 - 2.3$
14. $6.7 - 4.1$
15. $1.2 - 7.3$
16. $2.5 - 6.7$
17. $3.8 - (-2.7)$
18. $5.4 - (-6.9)$
19. $-\frac{5}{7} - \frac{2}{7}$
20. $-\frac{13}{11} - \frac{9}{11}$
21. $0 - (-15)$
22. $0 - (-21)$
23. $154 - (43 - 28)$
24. $200 - (68 - 50)$
25. $314 - (58 - 70)$
26. $190 - (40 - 85)$
27. $(33 - 45) - (64 - 78)$
28. $(36 - 46) - (22 - 30)$
29. $(13 - 5) - (-2 + 6)$
30. $(33 - 13) - (-8 + 10)$
31. $1066 - 1492 + 1984$
32. $1215 - 1776 + 2001$
33. $8 - (-3) - [4 - (-6)]$
34. $-10 - 4 - [-6 - (-11)]$
35. $1 - 2 + 4 - 8 + 16$
36. $17 - 13 + 12 + 3 - 19$
37. $45 - 7 - 58 + 11 - 21$
38. $35 - 15 + 8 - 20 - 48$
39. $19 - 2 + 23 - 54 + 34 - 29$
40. $200 - 195 + 71 - 66 + 18 - 29$

For Problems 41 through 50, the operations inside the absolute value sign must be done first.

41. $|3 - 7|$
42. $|2 - 9|$
43. $|8 - (-11)|$
44. $|6 - (-4)|$
45. $|13 - 5| + 4$
46. $|9 - 6| + 5$
47. $|-17 + 2| - 2$
48. $|-14 + 3| - 8$
49. $-|-2 + 5| + 1$
50. $-|-8 - (-5)| + 2$

2-4 MULTIPLYING SIGNED NUMBERS

You recall that multiplication can be thought of as repeated addition. For instance,

$$(4)(7) \quad \text{means} \quad 7 + 7 + 7 + 7, \quad \text{or} \quad 28.$$

Similarly,

$$(4)(-1) \quad \text{means} \quad (-1) + (-1) + (-1) + (-1), \quad \text{or} \quad -4.$$

Multiplying a number by -1 gives a special result. The answer is the *opposite* of the number multiplied. For example,

$$(13)(-1) = -13$$
$$(54)(-1) = -54$$
$$(1000)(-1) = -1000.$$

The two factors in a product can be written in either order. For example, (5)(7) and (7)(5) both equal 35. Therefore,

$$(-1)(13) = -13$$
$$(-1)(54) = -54$$
$$(-1)(1000) = -1000.$$

This fact is called the Multiplication Property of Negative One.

PROPERTY

MULTIPLICATION BY −1
-1 times a number equals the *opposite* of that number; that is, for any real number x,

$$-1 \cdot x = -x.$$

The property is true if x itself is negative. For instance, $(-1)(-7)$ is the *opposite* of -7, which is 7. Similarly,

$$(-1)(-12) = 12$$
$$(-1)(-88) = 88$$
$$(-1)(-100) = 100.$$

In these examples, a *negative* number times a *negative* number gives a *positive* answer. This always happens, even when neither number is -1.

For example,

$$(-5)(-3) = 15$$
$$(-9)(-8) = 72$$
$$(-7)(-6) = 42.$$

You can remember these simple statements to help you multiply negative numbers.

> Negative times negative is *positive*.
> Positive times negative is *negative*.

Objective

Be able to evaluate products that contain negative numbers.

Cover the answer as you work the example. Then uncover the answer to be sure you are right.

EXAMPLE 1

Evaluate $(-3)(-7)$.

- - - - - - - - - -

Think These Reasons

$(-3)(-7)$	Write the given expression.
$= \underline{\underline{21}}$	Negative times negative is *positive*.

EXAMPLE 2

Evaluate $(-5)(8)$.

- - - - - - - - - -

$(-5)(8)$	Write the given expression.
$= \underline{\underline{-40}}$	Negative times positive is *negative*.

EXAMPLE 3

Evaluate $(-5)(-3)(-2)$.

- - - - - - - - - -

$(-5)(-3)(-2)$	Write the given expression.
$= (15)(-2)$	Negative times negative is *positive*.
$= \underline{\underline{-30}}$	Positive times negative is *negative*.

EXAMPLE 4

Evaluate $(-3)(-8)(-2)(-1)$.

$(-3)(-8)(-2)(-1)$	Write the given expression.
$= (24)(-2)(-1)$	Negative times negative is *positive*.
$= (-48)(-1)$	Positive times negative is *negative*.
$= \underline{\underline{48}}$	Negative times negative is *positive*.

From these examples you should be able to see a shortcut for telling the *sign* of the answer. The product $(-5)(-3)(-2)$ has an *odd* number of negative factors and the answer is *negative*. The product $(-3)(-8)(-2)(-1)$ has an *even* number of negative factors and the answer is *positive*.

CONCLUSION

SIGN OF A PRODUCT
The sign of a product will be:
- *negative*, if it has an *odd* number of negative factors;
- *positive*, if it has an *even* number of negative factors.

The following examples involve *powers* of negative numbers.

EXAMPLE 5

Evaluate $(-2)^3$.

$(-2)^3$	Write the given expression.
$= (-2)(-2)(-2)$	Write the power as a product.
$= \underline{\underline{-8}}$	*Odd* number of negative factors.

EXAMPLE 6

Evaluate $(-2)^4$.

$(-2)^4$	Write the given expression.
$= (-2)(-2)(-2)(-2)$	Write the power as a product.
$= \underline{\underline{16}}$	*Even* number of negative factors.

EXAMPLE 7

Evaluate -2^4.

- - - - -

	Think These Reasons
-2^4	Write the given expression.
$= -(2)(2)(2)(2)$	Only *base* 2 is raised to the fourth power, not -2. You may think of -2^4 as meaning $(-1)(2^4)$.
$= \underline{\underline{-16}}$	Multiply *before* taking opposites.

The last three examples lead to a conclusion about the sign of a power.

CONCLUSION

> **SIGN OF A POWER OF A NEGATIVE NUMBER**
> (Negative number)$^{\textit{even exponent}}$ is *positive*.
> (Negative number)$^{\textit{odd exponent}}$ is *negative*.
>
> *Note:* An expression like -3^4 is *not* a power of a negative number, since taking the power is done *before* taking the opposite.
>
> -3^4 equals $-(3)(3)(3)(3)$, or -81.

ORAL PRACTICE

Evaluate.

A. $(-4)(6)$	B. $(3)(-8)$	C. $(-2)(-8)$
D. $(7)(-1)$	E. $(-9)(0)$	F. $(-8)(-7)$
G. $(-1)(-9)$	H. $(4)(-8)$	I. $(6)(7)$
J. $(1)(-27)$		

Give the sign of the answer.

EXAMPLES

	Answers
i. $(-2)(-3)$	i. Positive.
ii. $(-2)(3)$	ii. Negative.

K. $(-462)(-291)$ L. $(55)(-2)(-18)$
M. $(-73)(-54)(-66)$ N. $(-200)(35)(68)$
O. $(-2)(-3)(-4)(-5)(-6)$ P. $(-1)(2)(-3)(4)(-5)(-6)$
Q. $(-75)^2$ R. $(-51)^3$ S. $(-85)^{19}$
T. $(-21)^{100}$ U. -44^6 V. -26^{10}

Evaluate.

W. $(-1)^{70}$ X. $(-1)^{53}$ Y. -1^{28} Z. 0^{35}

EXERCISE 2-4

For Problems 1 through 40, evaluate the expression.

1. $(10)(-7)$
2. $(-8)(-6)$
3. $(-5)(-9)$
4. $(-3)(12)$
5. $(-6)(8)$
6. $(4)(-7)$
7. $(-1.2)(-5)$
8. $(10)(-3.4)$
9. $\left(-\frac{2}{3}\right)(6)$
10. $\left(\frac{3}{4}\right)(-12)$
11. $(-72)(1)$
12. $(-1)(54)$
13. $(-1)(-200)$
14. $(1)(-300)$
15. $(-53)(0)$
16. $(-82)(0)$
17. $(-3)(-5)(-7)$
18. $(-2)(-4)(-6)$
19. $(-2)(5)(-8)$
20. $(-3)(5)(-10)$
21. $(4)(-7)(2)$
22. $(7)(-4)(3)$
23. $(-1)(5)(-3)(-2)$
24. $(-6)(-1)(5)(-3)$
25. $(-4)^3$
26. $(-5)^3$
27. $(-4)^4$
28. $(-5)^4$
29. -4^4
30. -5^4
31. $(-1)^{15}$
32. $(-1)^{22}$
33. $(-1)^{18}$
34. $(-1)^{21}$
35. -1^{18}
36. -1^{20}
37. $(-1)(-3)^4$
38. $(-1)(-2)^4$
39. $(-3)^2(-2)^3$
40. $(-2)^4(-3)^3$

For Problems 41 through 50, evaluate the expression for the given values of the variable.

41. $(-5)^x$, if:
 a. x is 3;
 b. x is 2;
 c. x is 1.

42. $(-4)^x$, if:
 a. x is 3;
 b. x is 2;
 c. x is 1.

43. -5^x, if:
 a. x is 3;
 b. x is 2.

44. -4^x, if:
 a. x is 3;
 b. x is 2.

45. $(-x)^4$, if:
 a. x is 2;
 b. x is 1;
 c. x is 0.

46. $(-x)^2$, if:
 a. x is 3;
 b. x is 1;
 c. x is 0.

47. $-x$, if:
 a. x is 5;
 b. x is -3;
 c. x is -1.

48. $-x$, if:
 a. x is 8;
 b. x is -5;
 c. x is 0.

49. $-1 \cdot x$, if:
 a. x is 5;
 b. x is -3;
 c. x is -1.

50. $-1 \cdot x$, if:
 a. x is 8;
 b. x is -5;
 c. x is 0.

51. From the answers to Problems 47 through 50, you can see that $-x$ and $-1 \cdot x$ always stand for the *same* number. True or false: Does the expression $-x$ always stand for a *negative* number? Explain.

52. Explain the difference in meaning between $-x^2$ and $(-x)^2$.

2-5 DIVISION OF SIGNED NUMBERS

You have learned that two numbers with a sum of 0 are called *additive inverses*, or opposites, of each other. There is a similar relationship applying to multiplication. For example,

$$\frac{2}{3} \cdot \frac{3}{2} = 1.$$

Any two numbers whose product is 1 are called *multiplicative inverses*, or *reciprocals*, of each other. Some other examples are

$$4 \text{ and } \tfrac{1}{4};$$

$$-\tfrac{3}{5} \text{ and } -\tfrac{5}{3};$$
$$-1 \text{ and } -1.$$

The symbols

$$\frac{1}{x} \quad \text{or} \quad 1/x$$

are used for the reciprocal of x. Note that 0 has *no* reciprocal, since there is no number for which

$$0 \cdot \textit{number} = 1.$$

DEFINITION

MULTIPLICATIVE INVERSE, OR RECIPROCAL
Two nonzero numbers are **multiplicative inverses,** or **reciprocals,** of each other if their *product* equals 1. (For instance, $\frac{2}{3}$ and $\frac{3}{2}$ are reciprocals since $\frac{2}{3} \cdot \frac{3}{2} = 1$.)
Note: Zero has *no* reciprocal.

One-fourth *of* 20 means $\frac{1}{4}$ *times* 20, which equals 5. The 5 can be found by *dividing* 20 by 4. This fact provides a means of defining division in terms of multiplication.

$$20 \div 4 \quad \text{means} \quad 20 \cdot \frac{1}{4}.$$

DEFINITION

DIVISION
Dividing by a number means *multiplying* by its *reciprocal.* That is, for any real numbers x and y with $y \neq 0$,

$$x \div y = x \cdot \frac{1}{y}$$

or

$$\frac{x}{y} = x \cdot \frac{1}{y}$$

or

$$x/y = x \cdot \frac{1}{y}.$$

Because 0 has no reciprocal, division by 0 is *undefined*. The expression

$$\frac{3}{0} \quad \text{means} \quad 3 \cdot \frac{1}{0},$$

which does not equal a real number. However, division *of* 0 *by* another number *is* defined. For example,

$$\frac{0}{5} = 0 \cdot \frac{1}{5} = 0.$$

With this definition of division, the properties of multiplying by negative numbers carry over directly to division. For example, consider $(-15) \div (-5)$.

$\frac{-15}{-5}$

$= (-15)\left(-\frac{1}{5}\right)$ Definition of division.

$= \underline{\underline{3}}$ Negative times negative is positive.

To find this quotient, you must realize that the reciprocal of -5 is $-\frac{1}{5}$, because $(-5)(-\frac{1}{5}) = 1$.

You can remember the sign of a quotient as follows.

> Negative divided by negative is *positive*.
> Positive divided by negative is *negative*.
> Negative divided by positive is *negative*.

Later in your mathematical career you will be able to *prove* these properties. For the time being, you will be required only to *remember* them and use them.

Objective

Be able to evaluate quotients involving negative numbers.

Cover the answer as you work the example. Then uncover the answer to be sure you are right.

EXAMPLE

Evaluate $\frac{-54}{x}$ if:

a. x is 6; b. x is -3; c. x is 0.

- - - - - - - - - -

Think These Reasons

a. $\dfrac{-54}{x}$ Write the given expression.

$= \dfrac{-54}{6}$ Substitute 6 for x.

$= \underline{\underline{-9}}$ Negative divided by positive is *negative*.

- - - - - - - - - -

b. $\dfrac{-54}{x}$ Write the given expression.

$= \dfrac{-54}{-3}$ Substitute -3 for x.

$= \underline{\underline{18}}$ Negative divided by negative is *positive*.

- - - - - - - - - -

c. $\dfrac{-54}{x}$

$= \dfrac{-54}{0}$ (crossed out) Undefined.

Reason: Division by zero is undefined. Simply mark out the expression $-\frac{54}{0}$ and write the word *undefined*.

ORAL PRACTICE

Evaluate.

A. $\dfrac{24}{-6}$ B. $\dfrac{-30}{10}$ C. $\dfrac{-8}{-2}$

D. $\dfrac{15}{-3}$ E. $\dfrac{-20}{-2}$ F. $\dfrac{-42}{3}$

G. $\dfrac{5}{-4}$ H. $\dfrac{-7}{-1}$ I. $\dfrac{-12}{1}$

J. $\dfrac{10}{-1}$ K. $\dfrac{0}{-6}$ L. $\dfrac{-4}{0}$

Give the sign of the answer.

M. $\frac{-547}{261}$ N. $\frac{-82.8}{-0.03}$ O. $\frac{3840}{-125}$

P. $\frac{-6}{-100}$ Q. $\frac{41}{37}$

Tell the reciprocal of the given number.

R. 5 S. $\frac{2}{3}$ T. $-\frac{3}{5}$

U. -1 V. 1 W. 0

X. State the definition of division.

EXERCISE 2-5

For Problems 1 through 40, evaluate the expression.

1. $\frac{-21}{7}$
2. $\frac{35}{-5}$
3. $\frac{21}{-7}$
4. $\frac{-35}{5}$
5. $\frac{-21}{-7}$
6. $\frac{-35}{-5}$
7. $-\frac{-21}{-7}$
8. $-\frac{-35}{-5}$
9. $-\frac{21}{-7}$
10. $-\frac{-35}{5}$
11. $-\frac{-21}{7}$
12. $-\frac{35}{-5}$
13. $\frac{-26}{2}$
14. $\frac{-38}{2}$
15. $\frac{51}{-3}$
16. $\frac{57}{-3}$
17. $\frac{-55}{-11}$
18. $\frac{-39}{-13}$
19. $\frac{1000}{-10}$
20. $\frac{200}{-200}$
21. $\frac{7-19}{-3}$
22. $\frac{13-37}{-2}$
23. $\frac{45}{5-14}$
24. $\frac{200}{-50+10}$
25. $\frac{32-4}{8-15}$
26. $\frac{6-21}{6-1}$
27. $\frac{(8)(-3)}{-6}$
28. $\frac{(4)(-6)}{2}$
29. $\frac{(-3)(10)}{5}$
30. $\frac{(-14)(6)}{-3}$
31. $\frac{10}{-1}$
32. $\frac{20}{-1}$
33. $\frac{-10}{-1}$

34. $\frac{-20}{1}$ 35. $\frac{0}{10}$ 36. $\frac{20}{0}$

37. $\frac{0}{-10}$ 38. $\frac{0}{20}$ 39. $\frac{10}{0}$

40. $\frac{0}{-20}$

For Problems 41 through 50, evaluate the expression for the given values of x.

41. $\frac{15}{x}$, if:
 a. x is 5;
 b. x is -3;
 c. x is 0.

42. $\frac{-45}{x}$, if:
 a. x is -5;
 b. x is 3;
 c. x is 0.

43. $\frac{x}{-30}$, if:
 a. x is 5;
 b. x is -3;
 c. x is 0.

44. $-\frac{x}{15}$, if:
 a. x is -5;
 b. x is 3;
 c. x is 0.

45. $\frac{45}{x^2}$, if:
 a. x is -3;
 b. x is 5;
 c. x is -1.

46. $\frac{75}{x^2}$, if:
 a. x is -5;
 b. x is 3;
 c. x is -1.

47. $\frac{x+5}{x+3}$, if:
 a. x is -2;
 b. x is 5;
 c. x is -3.

48. $\frac{x-5}{x-3}$, if:
 a. x is 5;
 b. x is 3;
 c. x is 0.

49. $\frac{5-x}{3-x}$, if:
 a. x is 2;
 b. x is 5;
 c. x is -3.

50. $\frac{3-x}{5-x}$, if:
 a. x is 6;
 b. x is 5;
 c. x is 3.

51. **Explain why 0 has *no* reciprocal.**

52. **Explain why division by 0 is undefined, but division of 0 by a non-zero number is defined.**

For Problems 53 and 54, write the reciprocal of each given number in the simplest possible form.

53. a. 7 b. 5/9 c. $-\frac{2}{3}$
 d. -1 e. 0.25 f. 0

54. a. 13 b. 1/3 c. $-\frac{3}{5}$

d. 1 e. −0.5 f. 0

For Problems 55 and 56, change the division to multiplication by the reciprocal.

55. a. $x \div y$ b. $\frac{a}{3}$ c. $\frac{7}{p}$

d. $m \div \frac{2}{3}$

56. a. $k \div j$ b. $4/t$ c. $\frac{c}{8}$

d. $5 \div \frac{1}{x}$

2-6 COMMUTING AND ASSOCIATING

It is obvious that 5 + 3 and 3 + 5 are equal to each other because they each equal 8. The process of reversing the two terms in a sum is called *commuting* them.

DEFINITION

COMMUTE
To **commute** two numbers in an expression means to interchange their positions.

Since you can commute two terms in a sum without changing the answer, addition is said to be a *commutative* operation. So is multiplication. For example,

$$3 \cdot 7 \text{ and } 7 \cdot 3 \text{ each equal } 21.$$

CONCLUSION

COMMUTING TERMS AND FACTORS
You can commute the terms in a sum or the factors in a product. That is, if x and y are real numbers, then

$$x + y = y + x \qquad x \cdot y = y \cdot x$$

Not all operations are commutative. Commuting the numbers in a difference, a quotient, or a power *changes* the value of the expression.

Subtraction:

$$7 - 2 \qquad\qquad\qquad 2 - 7$$
$$= 5 \quad \longleftarrow \text{ Different! } \longrightarrow \quad = -5$$

Division:

$$6 \div 3 \qquad\qquad\qquad 3 \div 6$$
$$= 2 \quad \longleftarrow \text{ Different! } \longrightarrow \quad = 0.5$$

Power:

$$2^3 \qquad\qquad\qquad 3^2$$
$$= 8 \quad \longleftarrow \text{ Different! } \longrightarrow \quad = 9$$

Addition and multiplication are **binary** operations. This means that numbers are added or multiplied only *two* at a time. If a sum has three terms, such as

$$3 + 5 + 9,$$

it has been agreed to add in order from left to right. But the answer is the same no matter which order you add the terms.

$$(3 + 5) + 9 \qquad\qquad\qquad 3 + (5 + 9)$$
$$= 8 + 9 \qquad\qquad\qquad = 3 + 14$$
$$= 17 \quad \longleftarrow \text{ The same! } \longrightarrow \quad = 17$$

The process of grouping two numbers in an expression is called *associating* them.

DEFINITION

ASSOCIATE
To **associate** two of the numbers in an expression means to *group* them with parentheses (without changing their positions) so that the operation between them is done *first*.

Since you can associate any two terms in a sum without changing the answer, addition is said to be an *associative* operation. Multiplication is also an associative operation. For example,

$$(2 \cdot 3) \cdot 5 = 6 \cdot 5 = 30 \quad \longleftarrow \text{The same!} \longrightarrow \quad 2 \cdot (3 \cdot 5) = 2 \cdot 15 = 30$$

CONCLUSION

ASSOCIATING TERMS AND FACTORS
You can associate any two terms in a sum or any two factors in a product. That is, if x, y, and z are real numbers, then

$$(x + y) + z = x + (y + z)$$

$$(x \cdot y) \cdot z = x \cdot (y \cdot z).$$

Again, subtraction, division, and raising to a power are *not* associative operations.

Subtraction:

$$(12 - 7) - 2 = 5 - 2 = 3 \quad \longleftarrow \text{Different!} \longrightarrow \quad 12 - (7 - 2) = 12 - 5 = 7$$

Division:

$$(24 \div 6) \div 2 = 4 \div 2 = 2 \quad \longleftarrow \text{Different!} \longrightarrow \quad 24 \div (6 \div 2) = 24 \div 3 = 8$$

Power:

$$(2^3)^2 = 8^2 = 64 \quad \longleftarrow \text{Different!} \longrightarrow \quad 2^{(3^2)} = 2^9 = 512$$

Commuting and associating can be used to simplify expressions containing variables. Any subtraction or division must be changed to addition or multiplication before you commute or associate.

Objective

Be able to simplify expressions by commuting and associating.

Cover the answer as you work the example. Then uncover the answer to be sure you are right.

EXAMPLE 1

Simplify $3 + 2x + 7$.

	Think These Reasons
$3 + 2x + 7$	Write the given expression.
$= 2x + 3 + 7$	Commute the $2x$ and the 3.
$= \underline{\underline{2x + 10}}$	Associate the 3 and the 7 and add.

Note: In the given expression, $2x$ is the variable term and 3 and 7 are constant terms. The idea is to commute and associate the *constant* terms to simplify the expression. If you like, you can commute and associate at the same time. The minimum you should write is the given expression and the answer.

EXAMPLE 2

Simplify $7 - x - 12$.

$7 - x - 12$	Write the given expression.
$= 7 + (-x) + (-12)$	Change subtracting to adding the opposite.
$= -x + 7 + (-12)$	Commute $-x$ and 7.
$= -x + (-5)$	Associate 7 and -12 and simplify.
$= \underline{\underline{-x - 5}}$	Change adding the opposite back to subtracting.

Note: The form $-x - 5$ is considered to be simpler than $-x + (-5)$ because it has fewer symbols of inclusion.

EXAMPLE 3

Simplify $12x \cdot \frac{1}{4}$.

$12x \cdot \frac{1}{4}$	Write the given expression.
$= 12 \cdot \frac{1}{4} \cdot x$	Commute x and $\frac{1}{4}$.
$= \underline{\underline{3x}}$	Associate 12 and $\frac{1}{4}$ and simplify.

EXAMPLE 4

Simplify $\frac{-7x}{-7}$.

Think These Reasons

$\frac{-7x}{-7}$ Write the given expression.

$= -7x \cdot \left(-\frac{1}{7}\right)$ Change dividing to multiplying by the reciprocal.

$= -\frac{1}{7} \cdot (-7x)$ Commute $-7x$ and $-\frac{1}{7}$.

$= 1 \cdot x$ Associate $-\frac{1}{7}$ and -7 and simplify.

$= \underline{\underline{x}}$ Replace $1 \cdot x$ with x.

Note: x is considered to be simpler than $1 \cdot x$. The expression $1 \cdot x$ equals x because 1 times any number equals that number.

ORAL PRACTICE

Tell what was done to transform the expression on the left to the one on the right.

EXAMPLES

Answers

i. $5 + x + 3 = 5 + (x + 3)$ — i. Associate the x and the 3.

ii. $x - 7 = x + (-7)$ — ii. Change subtracting 7 to adding -7.

iii. $x + (-7) = -7 + x$ — iii. Commute the x and the -7.

A. $5 + x = x + 5$

B. $x \cdot 5 = 5x$

C. $3 + x + 4 = (3 + x) + 4$

D. $5 + x + 6 = 5 + (x + 6)$

E. $1 + (-x) = -x + 1$

F. $3 + (-x) = -x + 3$

G. $(x + 2) + 7 = x + (2 + 7)$

H. $4 + (5 + x) = (4 + 5) + x$

I. $x \cdot 3 = 3x$

J. $x + 7 = 7 + x$

K. $3(4x) = (3 \cdot 4)x$

L. $2(6x) = (2 \cdot 6)x$

M. $x - 2 = x + (-2)$

N. $5 - x = 5 + (-x)$

O. $x - 3 = -3 + x$

P. $x - 9 = -9 + x$

Q. $x \div 4 = x \cdot \frac{1}{4}$

R. $\frac{x}{7} = x \cdot \frac{1}{7}$

S. $\frac{1}{4}(4x) = \left(\frac{1}{4} \cdot 4\right)x$

T. $\frac{1}{7}(7x) = \left(\frac{1}{7} \cdot 7\right)x$

U. $5 + x + 7 = x + 5 + 7$

V. $3 + x + 4 = x + 3 + 4$

W. $x + 5 + 7 = x + (5 + 7)$

X. $x + 3 + 4 = x + (3 + 4)$

Y. $5 + x - 7 = 5 - 7 + x$

Z. $4 - x + 6 = 4 + 6 - x$

EXERCISE 2-6

For Problems 1 through 40, commute and associate the constants to simplify the expression as much as possible.

1. $4 + x + 3$
2. $5 + x + 4$
3. $6 + x + 7$
4. $8 + x + 13$
5. $5 + x - 3$
6. $7 + x - 9$
7. $-8 + x + 4$
8. $-3 + x + 11$
9. $15 - x + 9$
10. $16 - x + 5$
11. $6 - x - 37$
12. $12 - x - 15$
13. $-19 - x - 22$
14. $-2 - x - 71$
15. $9 - x - 9$
16. $-13 - x + 13$
17. $9 + 7x + 3$
18. $14 + 3x + 21$
19. $-18 - 3x + 7$
20. $8 - 5x - 13$
21. $5x \cdot 7$
22. $7x \cdot 9$
23. $(3x)(-8)$
24. $(5x)(-13)$
25. $20x \cdot \frac{1}{5}$
26. $30x \cdot \frac{1}{6}$
27. $-\frac{1}{8} \cdot 56x$
28. $-\frac{1}{3} \cdot 21x$
29. $9x \cdot \frac{1}{9}$
30. $\frac{1}{3}x \cdot 3$

31. $\dfrac{54x}{9}$

32. $\dfrac{86x}{2}$

33. $-88x \div 11$

34. $-18x \div 9$

35. $\dfrac{1000x}{-10}$

36. $\dfrac{100x}{-5}$

37. $-37x \div (-1)$

38. $-x \div (-1)$

39. $\dfrac{-19x}{-19}$

40. $\dfrac{-25x}{-25}$

41. Calvin Butterball simplifies the expression $2 + 3x$. He associates the 2 and 3, gets $5x$, and loses points on a test. Tell Calvin what he did wrong.

42. Phoebe Small simplifies the expression $-7 - x + 7$ by commuting and associating the -7 and the 7, getting x for the answer. Explain to Phoebe what mistake she made.

43. You can simplify $6 + x + 7$ either of two ways.

i.
$$\begin{aligned} &6 + x + 7 \\ &= (6 + x) + 7 \\ &= (x + 6) + 7 \\ &= x + (6 + 7) \\ &= \underline{\underline{x + 13}} \end{aligned}$$

ii.
$$\begin{aligned} &6 + x + 7 \\ &= 6 + (x + 7) \\ &= 6 + (7 + x) \\ &= (6 + 7) + x \\ &= \underline{\underline{13 + x}} \end{aligned}$$

a. For each way, write each step and write what was done at that step. For instance, in the second line of the first way, you would write

$= (6 + x) + 7$ Associate the 6 and the x.

b. Tell in words how $13 + x$ (from the second way) can be transformed into $x + 13$ (from the first way).

44. You can simplify $6x \cdot 7$ either of two ways.

i.
$$\begin{aligned} &6x \cdot 7 \\ &= x \cdot 6 \cdot 7 \\ &= x(6 \cdot 7) \\ &= \underline{\underline{x \cdot 42}} \end{aligned}$$

ii.
$$\begin{aligned} &6x \cdot 7 \\ &= 6 \cdot 7 \cdot x \\ &= (6 \cdot 7)x \\ &= \underline{\underline{42x}} \end{aligned}$$

a. For each way, write each step and write what was done at that step. For instance, in the second line of the first way, you would write

$= x \cdot 6 \cdot 7$ Commute the 6 and the x.

b. Tell in words how $x \cdot 42$ (from the first way) can be transformed into $42x$ (from the second way).

45. Give examples showing why addition *is* an associative operation but subtraction is *not*.

46. Give examples showing why multiplication *is* an associative operation but division is *not*.

47. Give examples showing why multiplication *is* a commutative operation but division is *not*.

48. Give examples showing why addition *is* a commutative operation but subtraction is *not*.

49. Give examples showing why raising to a power (*exponentiation*) is *not* a commutative operation.

50. Explain why raising to a power (*exponentiation*) is *not* an associative operation.

2-7 EQUATIONS THAT NEED TWO TRANSFORMATIONS

You have solved equations by adding (or subtracting) a number to (or from) each member. You have also solved equations by multiplying (or dividing) each member by a number. Some equations require *both* transformations. For example, to solve

$$\frac{1}{5}x + 4 = 13,$$

you would first subtract 4 from each member, getting

$$\frac{1}{5}x + 4 - 4 = 13 - 4$$

$$\frac{1}{5}x = 9.$$

From here on, the equation is just like those you have solved before. Multiplying each member by 5 gives

$$5 \cdot \frac{1}{5}x = 5 \cdot 9$$

$$\underline{\underline{x = 45}}.$$

To make sure you are correct, you can check the solution by substituting the value of x into the left member of the original equation and showing that you get the right member for the answer.

Check: $\frac{1}{5}x + 4$

$= \frac{1}{5}(45) + 4$

$= 9 + 4$

$= 13$ Correct.

The secret to solving these equations is to do whatever is needed to get the variable *by itself* on one side of the equation.

Objective

Be able to solve equations that require more than one transformation.

Cover up the answer at the dotted lines as you work these examples.

EXAMPLE 1

Solve and check: $2x + 3 = 19$.

\- - - - - - - - - -

$2x + 3 = 19$	Write the given equation.
$2x + 3 - 3 = 19 - 3$	Subtract 3 from each member.
$2x = 16$	Associate and do the operations.
$\frac{2x}{2} = \frac{16}{2}$	Divide each member by 2.
$\underline{\underline{x = 8}}$	Do the operations.
Check: $2x + 3$	
$= 2(8) + 3$	Substitute 8 for x.
$= 16 + 3$	Do the operations.
$= 19$ ✔	The "✔" shows that you have looked to see that the answer you get is the right member of the original equation.

EXAMPLE 2

Solve and check: $13 = 9 - \frac{1}{3}x$.

\- - - - - - - - - -

$13 = 9 - \frac{1}{3}x$	Write the given equation.
$13 - 9 = 9 - \frac{1}{3}x - 9$	Subtract 9 from each member.
$4 = -\frac{1}{3}x$	Do the operation on the left. Commute and associate 9 and −9 on the right.

$-3 \cdot 4 = -3\left(-\frac{1}{3}x\right)$	Multiply each member by -3.
$\underline{\underline{-12 = x}}$	Do the operation on the left. Associate -3 and $-\frac{1}{3}$ on the right.

Check: $9 - \frac{1}{3}x$

$= 9 - \frac{1}{3}(-12)$	Substitute -12 for x in the right member.
$= 9 + 4$	Do the operations.
$= 13$ ✓	Show that you got the correct left member.

EXAMPLE 3

Solve and check: $5 - 3c = 17$.

- - - - - - - - - -

$5 - 3c = 17$	Write the given equation. (The variable is c this time!)
$5 - 3c - 5 = 17 - 5$	Subtract 5 from each member.
$-3c = 12$	Do the operation on the right. Commute and associate 5 and -5 on the left. Remember $5 - 3c - 5$ is $5 - 3c + (-5)$.
$\frac{-3c}{-3} = \frac{12}{-3}$	Divide each member by -3.
$\underline{\underline{c = -4}}$	Do the arithmetic.

Check: $5 - 3c$

$= 5 - 3(-4)$	Substitute -4 for c in the left member.
$= 5 - (-12)$	Do the arithmetic.
$= 17$ ✓	Correct!

EXAMPLE 4

Solve and check: $\frac{3}{2}x + 4 = -9$.

- - - - - - - - - -

$\frac{3}{2}x + 4 = -9$	Write the given equation.
$\frac{3}{2}x + 4 - 4 = -9 - 4$	Subtract 4 from each member.

$\frac{3}{2}x = -13$	Associate; do the arithmetic.
$\frac{2}{3} \cdot \frac{3}{2}x = \frac{2}{3} \cdot (-13)$	Multiply each member by $\frac{2}{3}$, the *reciprocal* of $\frac{3}{2}$.
$1 \cdot x = -\frac{26}{3}$	Associate; multiply.
$x = -\frac{26}{3}$	$1 \cdot x = x$.

Check: $\frac{3}{2}x + 4$

$= \frac{3}{2}\left(-\frac{26}{3}\right) + 4$ Substitute $-\frac{26}{3}$ for x.

$= -13 + 4$ Multiply the fractions.

$= -9$ ✔ Correct!

ORAL PRACTICE

Tell what transformation is to be done *first* for each equation.

EXAMPLE

$\frac{1}{4}x + 6 = 19$ *Answer:* Subtract 6 from each member.

A. $\frac{1}{5}x + 3 = 7$	B. $\frac{1}{8}x - 7 = 45$	C. $2x - 5 = 9$
D. $6x + 4 = 7$	E. $4c - 2 = -1$	F. $5p + 1 = -13$
G. $\frac{1}{3}x = 5$	H. $4x = 7$	I. $5 + 2x = 3$
J. $6 + 7x = 4$	K. $-2 + 3x = 8$	L. $-6 + 5x = 2$
M. $3x = 10$	N. $5x = 8$	O. $3x + 0.7 = 4$
P. $4.6 + 5x = -9$	Q. $3x + \frac{4}{7} = 9$	R. $5x - \frac{2}{9} = 1$
S. $\frac{2}{3}x = 5$	T. $\frac{5}{4}x = 2$	U. $6 - x = 4$
V. $5 - x = -7$	W. $-3 + 5x = 0$	X. $-5x = 1$
Y. $-x = 8$	Z. $-x = -\frac{2}{3}$	

EXERCISE 2-7

Solve the following equations. Then check the solution by substituting it into one member and showing that you get the other member.

1. $\frac{1}{3}x + 5 = 7$
2. $\frac{1}{5}x + 3 = 9$
3. $\frac{1}{2}x - 8 = 3$
4. $\frac{1}{4}x - 7 = 2$
5. $5x + 4 = 39$
6. $6x + 5 = 53$
7. $3a - 7 = 26$
8. $2r - 13 = 95$
9. $-\frac{1}{6}x + 5 = 8$
10. $-\frac{1}{3}x + 6 = 10$
11. $-\frac{1}{4}x - 9 = 17$
12. $-\frac{1}{2}x - 7 = 23$
13. $13 - 4y = 25$
14. $5 - 3t = 56$
15. $8 - \frac{1}{7}v = -19$
16. $11 - \frac{1}{9}d = -45$
17. $53 = 5x + 11$
18. $22 = 4 + 5x$
19. $17 - x = 25$
20. $15 - x = 41$
21. $71 = 4 - x$
22. $13 = 17 - x$
23. $\frac{2}{3}x + 6 = 18$
24. $\frac{3}{4}x + 12 = 36$
25. $0.9 + 3x = 6$
26. $1.6 + 4x = 8$
27. $-21 + 4p = 10$
28. $-8 + 3f = 6$
29. $-\frac{4}{3} - x = -\frac{1}{3}$
30. $-\frac{2}{5} - x = \frac{1}{5}$
31. Jess Missed transforms $5 - x = 11$ by subtracting 5 from each member, getting $x = 6$. Explain to Jess what he did wrong.
32. K. Ann DeWitt solves $-3 - 4x = 8$ by ading 3 to each member, getting $4x = 11$. Explain to K. Ann what she did wrong.
33. Noah Lott transforms $3 + 4x = 21$ by associating the 3 and the 4, getting $7x = 21$. Tell Noah why he is wrong.
34. Will Geddit transforms $13 - 3x = 40$ by associating the 13 and the -3, getting $10x = 40$. Tell Will why what he did violates the order of operations.

2-8 PROBLEMS THAT LEAD TO TWO-TRANSFORMATION EQUATIONS

Now that you know how to solve slightly tougher equations, you can use these equations to solve more complicated problems.

Suppose that it takes 4 minutes to cook a batch of pancakes. Cooking 3 batches would take $4 \cdot 3$ minutes, or 12 minutes. Cooking x batches would take $4x$ minutes. In each case, you multiply the number of batches by 4. However, it usually takes some time beforehand to mix the batter and warm up the pan. If it takes 10 minutes to do these things, then the total time would be

$$4x + 10 \text{ min.}$$

In this expression, x is the number of batches. To find the time for 7 batches, you would substitute 7 for x.

$$\begin{aligned} &4x + 10 \\ &= 4 \cdot 7 + 10 \\ &= 28 + 10 \\ &= 38 \end{aligned}$$

$\underline{\underline{\text{38 minutes}}}$

To find out how many batches you could cook in 30 min, you set $4x + 10$ equals 30 and solve the equation for x.

$$\begin{aligned} 4x + 10 &= 30 \\ 4x + 10 - 10 &= 30 - 10 \\ 4x &= 20 \\ \frac{4x}{4} &= \frac{20}{4} \\ x &= 5 \end{aligned}$$

$\underline{\underline{\text{5 batches}}}$

The key to solving problems like this is to let a variable stand for one quantity, such as the number of batches. Then you write an expression for a related quantity, such as the number of minutes. The problem can then be answered either by evaluating the expression or by solving an equation.

Objective

Be able to write an expression representing a variable quantity and use this expression to answer questions.

For the following example, put a piece of paper along the dotted lines to cover the answer. Work each part. Then uncover the answer to be sure you are right.

EXAMPLE

Pedalboat Problem Flo Tilla is pedalboating on the lake. She starts back toward the dock, which is 800 yards away. She goes at a rate of 50 yd per minute toward the dock.

a. Draw a picture showing the place Flo starts, the dock 800 yards away, and Flo somewhere in between.

b. How far has Flo gone after:

i. 1 minute; ii. 2 minutes; iii. 5 minutes?

c. How far is Flo from the dock after:

i. 1 minute; ii. 2 minutes; iii. 5 minutes?

d. Let x be the number of minutes since Flo started for the dock. Write an expression in terms of x for:

i. the distance Flo has gone;

ii. the distance she is from the dock.

Write these expressions on the diagram.

e. Write an equation stating that Flo has reached a point 150 yards from the dock. Then solve the equation to find out *when* she is 150 yards from the dock.

- - - - - - - - - -

a.

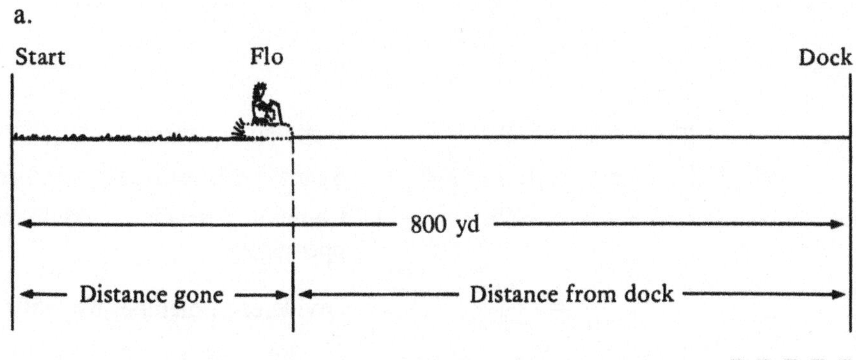

- - - - - - - - - -

		Think These Reasons
b.	i. 50 yards	She goes 50 yd *per minute*.
	ii. $50(2) = 100$ 100 yards	She goes 50(2) yd in 2 min. Write the answer.

iii. $50(5) = 250$	She goes 50(5) yd in 5 min.
250 yards	Write the answer.

- - - - -

c. i. $800 - 50 = 750$	There were 800 yards to go, and she has gone 50 yards. So there are still $800 - 50$ yards left to go.
750 yards	Write the answer.
ii. $800 - 100 = 700$	
700 yards	
iii. $800 - 250 = 550$	
550 yards	

- - - - -

d. i. x = number of minutes	Write the definition of x.
$50x$ = number of yards gone	She goes $50(x)$ yards in x minutes.
ii. $800 - 50x$ = number of yards from dock	She has already gone $50x$ of the 800 yards. So $800 - 50x$ is left.

- - - - -

e. $800 - 50x = 150$	Write an equation.
$800 - 50x - 800 = 150 - 800$	Subtract 800 from each member.
$-50x = -650$	Commute, associate, and do the operations.
$\dfrac{-50x}{-50} = \dfrac{-650}{-50}$	Divide each member by -50.
$x = 13$	Do the operations.
After 13 minutes.	Answer the question.

Note that the distance Flo travels, $50x$, is her *rate* multiplied by her *time*. This is an example of the *distance-rate-time formula*.

FORMULA

DISTANCE-RATE-TIME FORMULA

$$\text{Distance} = (\text{rate})(\text{time})$$

or

$$d = rt$$

ORAL PRACTICE

Give an expression representing each of the following.

EXAMPLE
Spend $50 per day for x days, plus $230. How much do you spend?
Answer: $50x + 230$

A. Make 5 dollars per hour for x hours, plus $7.50. How many dollars do you make?

B. Spend 65 cents per carton of milk for x cartons of milk, plus 80 cents. How many cents do you spend?

C. Go 40 miles per hour for x hours, then go 70 miles further. How many miles have you gone?

D. Fly 600 miles per hour for x hours, then fly 1000 miles further. How many miles have you flown?

E. Earn $6 per hour for x hours, then pay back $10. How much do you have?

F. Go 80 feet per minute for x minutes, then go back 30 feet. How many feet are you from where you started?

G. Start with 50 grapes and eat 3 grapes per minute for x minutes. How many grapes are left?

H. Start with 100 quarters and spend 2 quarters per minute for x minutes. How many quarters are left?

I. Start 20 miles from home. Walk 4 miles per hour toward home for x hours. How far are you from home?

J. Start 20 miles from home. Ride your bike 9 miles per hour away from home for x hours. How far are you from home?

EXERCISE 2-8

1. *Donuts Problem* Drenchin Donuts sells donuts for 20 cents each, plus 15 cents for the box in which they come. So the total number of cents you pay is 20 times the number of donuts, plus 15. Let x be the number of donuts.
   a. Write the definition of x on your paper. Then write an expression for the number of cents you pay for x donuts.
   b. How much will you pay for:
      i. 12 donuts;
      ii. 100 donuts?
      iii. What assumption must you make about the box in order for the answer to (ii) to be reasonable?
   c. Write an equation stating that the number of cents you pay is 355. Then solve the equation to find out how many donuts you get for \$3.55.

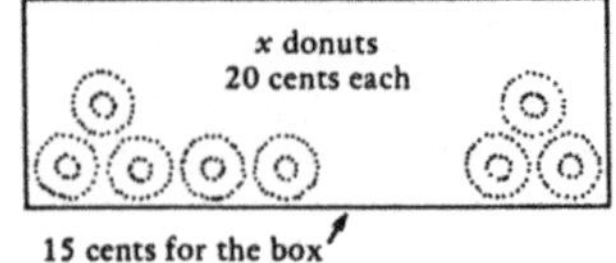

15 cents for the box

x cubic feet
\$ .50 each

Plus \$6.00 to deliver.

2. *Delivery Problem* Bill Dupp's Lumber Yard charges \$.50 for each cubic foot (ft^3) of sand you buy, plus \$6.00 to deliver the sand. So the total number of dollars you pay is 0.50 times the number of cubic feet, plus 6. Let x be the number of cubic feet.
   a. Write the definition of x on your paper. Then write an expression for the number of dollars you pay for x ft^3 of sand, delivered.
   b. How much would you pay to get 258 ft^3 delivered?
   c. Write an equation stating that you pay \$17.50 to get x ft^3 of sand delivered. Then solve the equation for x.
   d. How much sand could you get, delivered, for \$100?

3. *Plumbers' Wages Problem* Drane & Route Plumbing Co. charges \$42 per hour, plus \$35 for the service call. Let x be the number of hours they work.
   a. Write the definition of x. Then write an expression for the number of dollars you must pay if they work for x hours.
   b. How much would you pay for:
      i. 3 hours; ii. $4\frac{1}{2}$ hours?
   c. Write an equation stating that the amount you pay is \$140. Then solve the equation to find out how long they worked.
   d. How long did they work if the bill is \$56?

BILL

x hr. @ \$42/hr. . . . ____

Service . . . . . . ____

Total . . . . ____

4. *Taxi Fare Problem* When the meter in a taxi is first turned on, it reads $1.20. As the taxi travels, $1.60 is added for each mile driven. Let x be the number of miles driven.
   a. Write the definition of x. Then write an expression for the number of dollars the meter reads after x mi.
   b. How much would you pay to ride:
      i. 5 mi; ii. 13 mi?
   c. Write an equation stating that you paid $12.40. Then solve the equation to find out how far you rode.
   d. How far could you ride for $33.20?

5. *Dump Truck Problem* Doug Upp must shovel a pile containing 50 ft^3 of sand into a dump truck. With each scoop, he decreases the size of the pile by $\frac{1}{6}$ ft^3. Let x be the number of scoops he has shoveled.
   a. Write the definition of x. Then write an expression for the number of cubic feet of sand left in the pile after x scoops.
   b. How much sand is left after:
      i. 12 scoops; ii. 100 scoops?
   c. Doug takes a rest when 20 ft^3 of sand remain. Write an equation stating that 20 ft^3 remain. Then solve the equation to find out how many scoops Doug has shoveled before he rests.

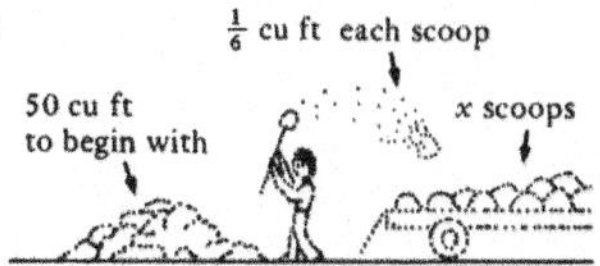

6. *Gasoline Consumption Problem* Suppose that the gas tank of a car holds 12 gallons, and that the car uses $\frac{1}{20}$ of a gallon per mile. Let x be the number of miles the car has gone since the tank was filled.
   a. Write the definition of x. Then write an expression for the number of gallons left after x miles.
   b. How many gallons are left after:
      i. 100 mi; ii. 170 mi?
   c. Write an equation stating that 5 gallons are left. Then solve it to find out how far the car has gone when 5 gallons remain.
   d. How far has the car gone when it runs out of gas?

7. *Hot Chocolate Consumption Problem* Suppose that the people living in Coe, CO, drink 3600 cups of hot chocolate per day when the temperature is 0° Celsius. For each rise of 1°C, their consumption decreases by 30 cups/day.
   a. How many cups would they drink at:
      i. 1°C;
      ii. 5°C;
      iii. T°C, where T is a variable?

b. Evaluate the expression you wrote in (iii) of part (a) if:
   i. T is 21; ii. T is -10.
c. Write an equation stating that the consumption is 2400 cups. Then solve it to find the temperature.
d. At what temperature would the town drink 4200 cups?

8. *Expansion Gap Problem* When bridges are built in expressways, a small gap is left between the bridge sections so that the bridge will have room to expand. That is why a car goes "bump-bump, bump-bump" as it goes across a bridge. As the temperature goes up, the bridge sections expand and the width of the gap goes down. Suppose that the gap is 21 millimeters (mm) at a temperature of 0°C and decreases by 0.4 mm for every 1°C increase in temperature.

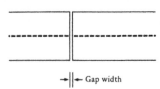

   Gap width

   a. How wide will the gap be if the temperature is:
      i. 1°C; ii. 5°C;
      iii. T°C?
   b. Evaluate the expression you wrote in (iii) of part (a) if:
      i. T is 30; ii. T is 17;
      iii. T is -10.
   c. Write an equation which says that the gap is 7 mm. Then find the temperature at which the gap is 7 mm.
   d. At what temperature will the gap be:
      i. 23 mm; ii. completely closed?

9. *Frosty Problem* The townspeople of Ledditston, OH, construct a 250-pound snow sculpture. It starts to melt at a rate of 3 pounds per day.
   a. Write an expression representing its weight after x days.
   b. Find its weight after
      i. 7 days; ii. 1 month (of 31 days).
   c. How long will it be before the sculpture weighs:
      i. 160 pounds; ii. 150 pounds?
   d. What assumption do you have to make in order for the answers to parts (b) and (c) to be meaningful?

10. *Weight Increase Problem* Grace, a Labrador Retriever, weighs 97 pounds. She goes on an eating spree, gaining $\frac{1}{4}$ pound per day.
    a. Write an expression representing her weight after x days.
    b. How much will she weigh after:
       i. 12 days; ii. 4 weeks?
    c. How long will it take her to reach:
       i. 150 pounds; ii. 160 pounds?

11. *Cycling Problem Number 1* Jewel Case is at a point 3 miles from her home. She rides her bike at $\frac{1}{4}$ mile per minute *away* from home.
    a. Draw a picture showing home, Jewel's starting point 3 miles from home, and Jewel some distance *beyond* the starting point.

b. Jewel rides for x minutes. Write expressions for:
   i. the number of miles Jewel has ridden (recall that distance = (rate)(time));
   ii. the number of miles Jewel is away from home.
   Write these expressions on your diagram.
c. How far is Jewel from home after:
   i. 20 minutes; ii. 1 hour?
d. When will she be 10 miles from home?

12. *Cycling Problem Number 2* Justin Case (Jewel's brother) is at a point 3 miles from home. He starts riding his bike at $\frac{1}{4}$ mile per minute *toward* home.
   a. Draw a picture showing home, Justin's starting point 3 miles from home, and Justin somewhere *between* start and home.
   b. Justin rides for x minutes. Write expressions for:
      i. the number of miles he has ridden (recall that distance = (rate)(time));
      ii. the number of miles he is away from home.
      Write these expressions on your diagram.
   c. How far is he from home after 8 minutes?
   d. When will he be:
      i. $\frac{1}{2}$ mile from home; ii. at home?

13. *Downhill Speed Problem* As you coast downhill on your bike, you find that the speed increases by $\frac{2}{3}$ mi/h each second. When you are going 12 mi/h you start a stopwatch.
   a. Define a variable for the number of seconds that have passed since you started the stopwatch. Then write an expression for the speed you are going.
   b. How fast will you be going after 15 sec?
   c. What will the stopwatch read when you are going 18 mi/h?
   d. How long *before* you started the stopwatch did you start coasting down the hill?

14. *Celsius and Fahrenheit Temperature Problem* To convert Celsius temperature to Fahrenheit temperature, you multiply the Celsius temperature by $\frac{9}{5}$, then add 32. Let C be the number of Celsius degrees.
   a. Write an expression representing the number of Fahrenheit degrees.
   b. Find the Fahrenheit temperature for:
      i. 35° Celsius; ii. −20° Celsius.
   c. Write and solve equations to find C if the Fahrenheit temperature is:
      i. 59°; ii. 14°.

15. *Temperature Inside the Earth Problem* The temperature inside the earth is assumed to increase by about 10° Celsius for every kilometer

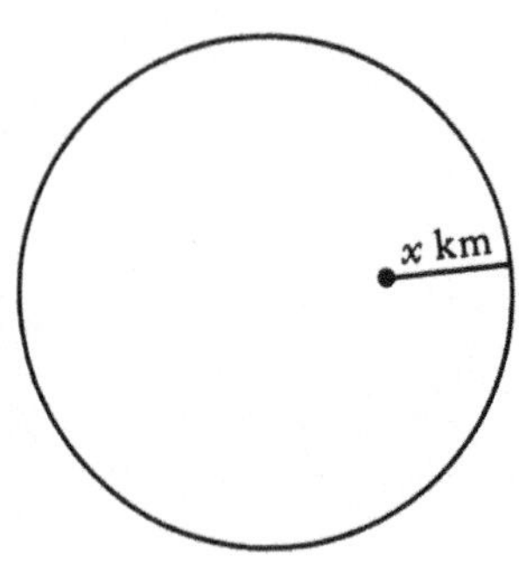

beneath the surface. Suppose that the temperature at the surface is 24°C. Let x be the number of kilometers beneath the surface.

a. Write an expression for the number of degrees at a depth of x kilometers.
b. Find the temperature inside a coal mine 1.3 kilometers deep.
c. Find the temperature at the bottom of an oil well 5 km deep.
d. Write an equation stating that the temperature at the bottom of a diamond mine is 61°C. Then solve the equation to find the depth of the mine.
e. At what depth would water boil (100°C)?

2-9 CHAPTER REVIEW AND TEST

In this chapter you have studied negative numbers. You added, subtracted, multiplied, and divided them, solved equations with them, and used them for such things as time *before* the present and temperatures *colder* than zero.

You also extended your equation-solving ability to equations like

$$7 + 5x = 3,$$

where *two* transformations are needed. You subtracted 7 from each member:

$$7 + 5x - 7 = 3 - 7.$$

Then you used the definition of subtraction to write

$$7 + 5x + (-7) = 3 - 7.$$

Then you *commuted* and *associated* the 7 and -7, and added them (getting 0); this left

$$5x = -4.$$

From here on it was an old problem. Dividing each member by 5 gave

$$x = -0.8.$$

You should now be able to appreciate the meaning of the word *algebra*, the "science of reduction and comparison." To solve a new problem, you *reduce* it to an old problem!

One thing you should teach yourself is how to review for a test. Something to try is making a list of key words. Before you attempt to work the following test, skim through the chapter and write down any word that sounds important. After you have made the list, write a phrase telling what each word means. For instance, if you have written

commute,

you might say:

to switch the numbers in a sum or a product.

If you cannot think of what to say, go back and look up the word. The index at the back of the book may help you locate the word.

The following test should take you about 45 minutes. For the most realistic practice, try putting yourself under "test conditions" and working the whole test without stopping. See if you really *can* do it in 45 minutes!

CHAPTER TEST

T1. What is the difference in meaning in each case?
- a. Negative number and positive number.
- b. -2^4 and $(-2)^4$.
- c. $\frac{5}{0}$ and $\frac{0}{5}$.
- d. Commute and associate.
- e. $0 \cdot x$ and $1 \cdot x$.

T2. Write each of the following.
- a. The definition of integer.
- b. The definition of real number.
- c. The definition of subtraction.
- d. The definition of division.
- e. The multiplication property of -1.

T3. Answer the following questions.
- a. Is a negative number a real number? Explain.
- b. Why does 0 have no reciprocal?
- c. How many members does the equation $5 + 8x + 7 = 12$ have?
- d. Write an equation relating rate, distance, and time.
- e. Why is subtraction *not* associative?
- f. Why is division *not* commutative?
- g. Why must there be parentheses in $5 + (-3)$?

T4. Evaluate each expression.
- a. $\frac{-52}{-4}$
- b. -2^4

c. $(-2)^4$
d. $(-2)^3$
e. $(-2)(-3)(-4)$
f. $(-1)(-5)(6)$
g. $(-3)^2(-4)^3$
h. $20 - (-3)$
i. $20 - 60$
j. $-6 - 8$
k. $-9 - (-3 + 5)$
l. $|-4|$
m. $|4 - 7|$

T5. Evaluate each expression if $x = -3$.
a. $-x$
b. x^2
c. x^3
d. $-x^2$
e. $7x^2$
f. $4x^2 - 5x$

T6. Simplify by commuting and associating the constants.
a. $-13 - 7x - 8$
b. $(4x)(-9)$
c. $50x \cdot \frac{1}{5}$

T7. Solve and check.
a. $9 - 7x = 51$
b. $13 = 25 - \frac{1}{4}x$
c. $5t + 34 = -9$

T8. *Fried Chicken Problem* A fried-chicken dealer makes boxes of chicken with various numbers of pieces. He charges 40 cents for each piece of chicken, plus a fixed charge of 55 cents for the box, the rolls, the service, and so on.
a. Write an expression for the number of cents charged for a box containing x pieces of chicken.
b. Write an equation stating that a box containing x pieces costs \$3.35. Then solve the equation to find the number of pieces in the box.
c. How much would you pay for:
i. a 5-piece box;
ii. a dozen-piece box?

T9. *Speed on a Hill Problem* On level ground (0 degrees slope), a car can go a top speed of 132 kilometers per hour (km/h). For each degree of uphill slope, the top speed is *decreased* by 11 km/h.
a. Write an expression for the top speed on an uphill slope of x degrees.
b. How fast can the car go on an uphill slope of 7 degrees?
c. A 3 degree *down*hill slope can be thought of as a -3 degree *up*hill slope. How fast could the car go on a 3 degree downhill slope?
d. Write an equation stating that the top speed is 187 km/h. Then solve it to find out how steep the hill is. Is it an *up*hill or a *down*hill slope? Explain.
e. If the top speed is 0 km/h, the hill is so steep that the car cannot go up it. How steep would that be?

3

Distributing: Axioms and Other Properties

u have learned what it means commute and associate num- rs in a sum or product. In this apter you will learn other prop- ies for transforming expres- ns. Some of the properties, lled axioms, *are assumed to be e without proof. Other proper- s can be proved by starting h the axioms. In the next chap- these properties will be used reduce complicated expressions d equations to simpler ones you eady know how to evaluate and lve.*

pression:
$x - 7)$
pression transformed distributing:
$- 21$

3-1 DISTRIBUTING

This section is meant for you to read and work on your own before the topic is discussed in class.

According to the agreed-upon order of operations, expressions such as

$$5(4 + 7)$$

should be evaluated by doing the operation inside parentheses *first:*

$$\begin{aligned} &5(4 + 7) \\ &= 5 \cdot 11 \\ &= 55. \end{aligned}$$

However, if the operation inside is addition and the operation outside is multiplication, there is another way to get the right answer. You can multiply *each* number inside the parentheses by 5 and then add the answers.

$$\begin{aligned} &5(4 + 7) \\ &= 5 \cdot 4 + 5 \cdot 7 \\ &= 20 + 35 \\ &= 55 \end{aligned}$$

To see why this result is reasonable, think of (4 + 7) as the length of a rectangle and 5 as its width (see the figure). The area of the rectangle is its width times its length, or

$$5(4 + 7).$$

But the area of the largest rectangle is also the *sum* of the areas of the smaller rectangles,

$$5 \cdot 4 + 5 \cdot 7.$$

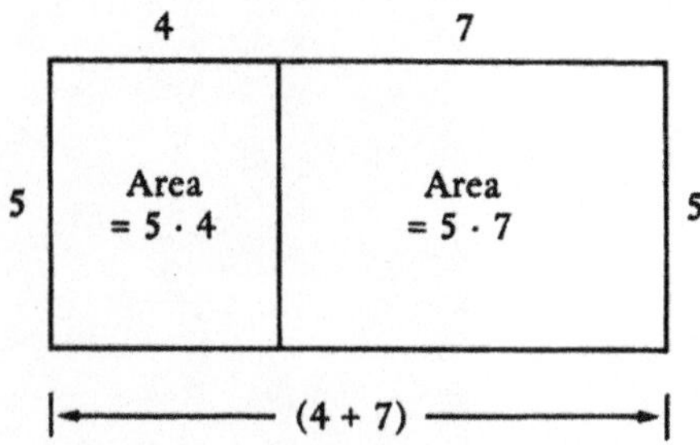

A 5 seems to be "passed out" to each number inside the parentheses. The 5 "goes over" the addition sign to get to the second term.

Goes over

$$5(4 + 7) = 5 \cdot 4 + 5 \cdot 7$$

Because of this property, multiplication is said to *distribute over addition.*

In algebra this property is most useful for simplifying expressions that contain variables, such as

$$3(x + 5) + 7.$$

The parentheses in $(x + 5)$ mean to do the addition *first*. But this is impossible until you know what number to substitute for x. However, you can *distribute* the 3 to the x and 5, getting

Distribute

$3(x + 5) + 7$	
$= 3x + 3 \cdot 5 + 7$	Distribute 3 to x and 5.
$= 3x + 15 + 7$	Multiply before adding.
$= 3x + 22$	Associate 15 and 7.

The expression $3x + 22$ is *simpler* than the original expression.

Objective

Be able to simplify expressions by distributing multiplication over addition.

Cover the answers as you work these examples.

EXAMPLE 1

Simplify $5(x + 2) + 9$.

- - - - - - - - - -

Think These Reasons

$5(x + 2) + 9$	Write the given expression.
$= 5x + 5 \cdot 2 + 9$	Distribute 5 to x and 2.
$= 5x + 10 + 9$	Multiply before adding.
$= \underline{\underline{5x + 19}}$	Associate 10 and 9.

Think These Reasons

EXAMPLE 2

Simplify $4(3x + 7) - 50$.

$4(3x + 7) - 50$	Write the given expression.
$= 4 \cdot 3x + 4 \cdot 7 - 50$	Distribute 4 to $3x$ and 7.
$= 12x + 28 - 50$	Multiply before adding or subtracting.
$= \underline{\underline{12x - 22}}$	Associate the 28 and -50.

EXAMPLE 3

Simplify $7 + 3(2x + 8)$.

$7 + 3(2x + 8)$	Write the given expression.
$= 7 + 3 \cdot 2x + 3 \cdot 8$	Distribute 3 to $2x$ and 8.
$= 7 + 6x + 24$	Multiply before adding. (*Don't* add 7 and 3 before you multiply!)
$= \underline{\underline{6x + 31}}$	Commute and associate 7 and 24.

EXERCISE 3-1

Simplify by distributing, commuting, and associating.

1. $3(x + 5) + 11$
2. $4(x + 3) + 20$
3. $7(6 + x) + 8$
4. $5(3 + x) - 9$
5. $2(3x + 8) + 40$
6. $8(5x + 7) - 60$
7. $9(4 + 8x) - 6$
8. $30 + 2(x + 8)$
9. $100 + 6(4x + 9)$
10. $-15 + 9(5 + 8x)$

3-2 DISTRIBUTING MULTIPLICATION OVER SUBTRACTION

In the last section you learned that multiplication distributes over addition. For instance,

Distribute

$$5(x + 3)$$

$$= 5x + 5 \cdot 3$$
$$= 5x + 15$$

Multiplication also distributes over *subtraction*. For instance, the parentheses in $5(7 - 3)$ mean, "Subtract 3 from 7 and then multiply by 5." However, you get the same answer by distributing.

Operation in parentheses first	Distribute first.
$5(7 - 3)$	$5(7 - 3)$
$= 5(4)$	$= 5 \cdot 7 - 5 \cdot 3$
	$= 35 - 15$
$= 20$ ⟵ The same! ⟶	$= 20$

The fact that multiplication distributes over addition and subtraction are called *properties*. Some properties are called *axioms*. An axiom is a property that is used as a starting point in the mathematics of real numbers. No attempt is made to *prove* an axiom. It is just assumed to be true.

DEFINITIONS

PROPERTY AND AXIOM

A **property** of a mathematical system is a fact that is true concerning that system.

An **axiom** is a property that forms the basis of a mathematical system. It is assumed to be true without proof.

The facts that multiplication distributes over addition and that multiplication distributes over subtraction are both *properties*. The first one is an *axiom* that is assumed to be true. The second one is not an axiom. It can be proved using the first one.

For future reference, here are formal statements of these two distributive properties.

THE DISTRIBUTIVE AXIOM

Multiplication distributes over addition.

That is, for real numbers x, y, and z,

$$x(y + z) = xy + xz.$$

PROPERTY

MULTIPLICATION DISTRIBUTES OVER SUBTRACTION
For real numbers x, y, and z,

$$x(y - z) = xy - xz.$$

Objective

Be able to simplify expressions by distributing multiplication over addition and subtraction.

Cover the answers as you work these examples.

EXAMPLE 1

Distribute $3(4x - 2)$.

	Think These Reasons
$3(4x - 2)$	Write the given expression.
$= \underline{\underline{12x - 6}}$	Distribute 3 to $4x$ and 2. (Do the computation in your head!) Write the subtraction sign.

EXAMPLE 2

Simplify $5 + 4(7x - 6)$.

$5 + 4(7x - 6)$	Write the given expression.
$= 5 + 28x - 24$	Distribute 4 to $7x$ and 6. Write the subtraction sign.
$= \underline{\underline{28x - 19}}$	Commute; then associate 5 and -24.

EXAMPLE 3

Simplify $9 - 2(x - 4)$.

$9 - 2(x - 4)$	Write the given expression.
$= 9 - 2x + 8$	Think of $9 - 2(x - 4)$ as $9 + (-2)(x - 4)$. Distribute -2 to x and 4. Then rewrite $9 + (-2x) - (-8)$ as $9 - 2x + 8$.
$= \underline{\underline{17 - 2x}}$	Commute; then associate 9 and 8.

ORAL PRACTICE

Distribute the multiplication over the addition or subtraction.

EXAMPLES

	Answers
i. $2(7 - 4)$	i. $14 - 8$
ii. $-3(6 - 4)$	ii. $-18 + 12$

A. $3(4 + 7)$ B. $6(3 + 8)$

C. $7(-9 + 3)$ D. $9(-8 + 1)$

E. $-4(2 + 10)$ F. $-3(9 + 11)$

G. $5(9 - 2)$ H. $4(7 - 2)$

I. $-4(3 - 10)$ J. $-5(3 - 13)$

K. $-2(-7 + 5)$ L. $-1(-6 - 8)$

EXERCISE 3-2

For Problems 1 through 20, distribute the multiplication over the addition or subtraction. Simplify, leaving no parentheses.

1. $3(x + 7)$
2. $8(x + 4)$
3. $7(3x - 8)$
4. $6(2x - 7)$
5. $x(3 + y)$
6. $x(5 + z)$
7. $-5(6 - x)$
8. $-2(11 - y)$
9. $-1(x - y)$
10. $-1(a - b)$
11. $x(x + 9)$
12. $x(10 + x)$
13. $6(9 + 7x)$
14. $5(7x + 2)$
15. $\frac{1}{3}(12x - 15y)$
16. $\frac{1}{6}(30x - 42y)$
17. $28\left(\frac{1}{4}z + \frac{1}{7}\right)$
18. $24\left(\frac{1}{12} + \frac{1}{3}y\right)$
19. $\frac{2}{3}\left(4x + \frac{3}{4}\right)$
20. $\frac{3}{5}\left(2x - \frac{2}{3}\right)$

For Problems 21 through 40, simplify the expression by distributing, commuting, and associating. Leave no parentheses.

21. $3(4x + 7) - 2$
22. $5(3x + 2) - 7$
23. $7(3x - 5) + 20$
24. $4(2x - 7) + 40$
25. $8(1 - 2x) + 5$
26. $9(4 - 5x) + 3$
27. $-5(2 + 3x) + 7$
28. $-6(3 + 4x) + 8$
29. $-1(x - 9) - 10$
30. $-1(x - 2) - 7$
31. $4 + 3(2x - 9)$
32. $7 + 3(5x - 1)$
33. $6 + 7(3x + 2) + 8$
34. $10 + 2(6x + 3) + 4$
35. $8 - 5(4 - 6x)$
36. $5 - 3(9 - 7x)$
37. $11 - 1(5x + 3)$
38. $21 - 1(3x + 8)$
39. $7 + \frac{3}{5}(10 + 35x)$
40. $11 + \frac{3}{2}(8 + 12x)$

Tell in words what was done.

41. $5(2x + 3) = 10x + 15$
42. $7(5 + 4x) = 35 + 28x$
43. $9(4x - 5y) = 36x - 45y$
44. $8(3z - 7a) = 24z - 56a$
45. $-4(5 - 7p) = -20 + 28p$
46. $-3(18m - 10) = -54m + 30$
47. $5 + 3x + (-4) = 5 + (-4) + 3x$
48. $6p + 2 + 11 = 6p + (2 + 11)$
49. $6 + 5 + k = (6 + 5) + k$
50. $-3c + 4 + 5c = 4 + (-3c) + 5c$

Solve the equation.

51. $3x + 71 = 44$
52. $5x - 19 = 44$
53. $0.4x - 9 = 13$
54. $0.3x + 13 = 46$
55. Write the equation in the distributive axiom.
56. Write the equation in the distributive property of multiplication over subtraction.

3-3 MORE DISTRIBUTIVE PROPERTIES

In Sections 3-1 and 3-2 you learned that multiplication distributes over addition and subtraction. For example,

$$5(x + 3) \qquad \text{and} \qquad 7(2x - 4)$$
$$= 5x + 15 \qquad\qquad = 14x - 28$$

In this section you will learn some more distributive properties.

If a sum or difference is divided by a number, you can distribute the division over the addition or subtraction.

Distributing division over addition:

$\frac{10 + 16}{2}$	Add first.	$= \frac{10 + 16}{2}$	Distribute first.
$= \frac{26}{2}$		$= \frac{10}{2} + \frac{16}{2}$	
		$= 5 + 8$	
$= 13$	⟵ The same! ⟶	$= 13$	

Distributing division over subtraction:

$\frac{12 - 27}{3}$	Subtract first.	$\frac{12 - 27}{3}$	Distribute first.
$= \frac{-15}{3}$		$= \frac{12}{3} - \frac{27}{3}$	
		$= 4 - 9$	
$= -5$	⟵ The same! ⟶	$= -5$	

These properties are true because division by a number can be changed into multiplication by the reciprocal of that number. For instance,

$\frac{10 + 16}{2}$

$= (10 + 16) \cdot \frac{1}{2}$ Change division by 2 to multiplication by $\frac{1}{2}$.

$= 10 \cdot \frac{1}{2} + 16 \cdot \frac{1}{2}$ Distribute multiplication over addition.

$= 5 + 8$ Do the multiplication.

$= 13$ Do the addition.

This is the answer as above.

From the second to the third line, the factor $\frac{1}{2}$ was distributed from the *right* side of the expression. If you have doubts that this is legal, just commute the two factors first.

$$(10 + 16) \cdot \frac{1}{2}$$

$= \frac{1}{2} \cdot (10 + 16)$ Commute $(10 + 16)$ and $\frac{1}{2}$.

$= 5 + 8$ Distribute $\frac{1}{2}$ from the *left*.

$= 13$ Do the addition.

If a sum or difference of *three* or more terms is multiplied or divided by a number, you can still distribute.

Distributing multiplication over three terms:

$2(4 + 5 - 6)$	Operations in parentheses first	$= 2(4 + 5 - 6)$	Distribute first.
$= 2(9 - 6)$		$= 2 \cdot 4 + 2 \cdot 5 - 2 \cdot 6$	
$= 2(3)$		$= 8 + 10 - 12$	
$= 6$ ←	Same	→ $= 6$	

Distributing division over three terms:

$\frac{15 - 35 + 60}{5}$	Add and subtract first.	$\frac{15 - 35 + 60}{5}$	Distribute first.
$= \frac{-20 + 60}{5}$		$= \frac{15}{5} - \frac{35}{5} + \frac{60}{5}$	
$= \frac{40}{5}$		$= 3 - 7 + 12$	
		$= -4 + 12$	
$= 8$ ←	Same	→ $= 8$	

The above work leads to the following conclusions.

CONCLUSIONS

DISTRIBUTING
Multiplication or division distribute over addition or subtraction of two or more terms from the left or from the right.

In this section you will use these properties to simplify expressions that contain variables.

Objective

Be able to use the distributive properties to transform expressions containing variables.

Cover the answer as you work the example.

EXAMPLE 1

Distribute $x(3x - 5)$.

	Think These Reasons
$x(3x - 5)$	Write the given expression.
$= x \cdot 3x - x \cdot 5$	Distribute the x.
$= \underline{\underline{3x^2 - 5x}}$	Commute and associate. Remember $x \cdot x$ equals x^2.

EXAMPLE 2

Simplify $\dfrac{45 + 12x - 3y}{3}$.

$\dfrac{45 + 12x - 3y}{3}$	Write the given expression.
$= \dfrac{45}{3} + \dfrac{12x}{3} - \dfrac{3y}{3}$	Distribute the division over the addition and subtraction.
$= \underline{\underline{15 + 4x - y}}$	Divide.

EXAMPLE 3

Simplify $-(x - 5)$.

$-(x - 5)$	Write the given expression.
$= -1 \cdot (x - 5)$	Multiplication property of -1.
$= -1 \cdot x - (-1)(5)$	Distribute -1 over the subtraction.
$= \underline{\underline{-x + 5}}$	$-1 \cdot x = -x$ and $-(-5) = +5$

ORAL PRACTICE

Distribute.

EXAMPLES

	Answers:
i. $(4 - 5)(6)$	i. $24 - 30$
ii. $\dfrac{20 + 30 - 40}{-10}$	ii. $-2 - 3 + 4$

A. $(3 - 7)(5)$

B. $-2(4 - 7)$

C. $3(4 + 5 + 6)$

D. $\dfrac{8 + 12}{4}$

E. $\dfrac{30 - 10}{5}$

F. $\dfrac{10 + 12 + 14}{2}$

G. $(2 - 4 + 5)(3)$

H. $-4(5 - 3 + 1)$

I. $-1(7 - 9)$

J. $-(5 - 2)$

K. $\dfrac{12 + 15 - 6}{-3}$

L. $\dfrac{3 - 5 + 7}{-1}$

M. State the definition of axiom.

N. State the distributive axiom.

EXERCISE 3-3

For Problems 1 through 50, transform the expression by distributing the multiplication or division over addition or subtraction. Simplify the answers.

1. $9(x - 8)$
2. $7(x - 9)$
3. $5(3x - 2)$
4. $6(8x - 7)$
5. $x(4 + z)$
6. $x(5 + y)$
7. $c(x + y)$
8. $r(x - y)$
9. $(-5 + y)(10)$
10. $(-10 + z)(13)$
11. $-7(x - 8)$
12. $-4(x - 7)$
13. $-(r - s)$
14. $-(a - b)$
15. $-(x + y)$
16. $-(p + z)$
17. $(x - 4)(x)$
18. $(x + 5)(x)$

19. $\frac{1}{4}(20x + 12)$

20. $\frac{1}{3}(18x + 27)$

21. $(100x + 35)\left(\frac{1}{5}\right)$

22. $(200x + 150)\left(\frac{1}{10}\right)$

23. $-\frac{1}{9}(-54x - 63)$

24. $-\frac{1}{7}(-63x - 42)$

25. $21\left(\frac{1}{3} - \frac{1}{7}x\right)$

26. $45\left(\frac{1}{9} - \frac{1}{5}x\right)$

27. $\frac{32 + 4x}{4}$

28. $\frac{56 + 8x}{8}$

29. $\frac{15 - 21x}{3}$

30. $\frac{20 - 4x}{2}$

31. $\frac{24x - 18}{-2}$

32. $\frac{33x - 66}{-11}$

33. $9(2x + 3y + 4)$

34. $8(5x + 4y + 3)$

35. $-2(5c - 2 + 7d)$

36. $-3(6r - 5 + 9s)$

37. $-(6 + 3x - 4y)$

38. $-(x - 7 + 2y)$

39. $(x + 2y - z)(-4)$

40. $(3x + y - z)(-5)$

41. $x(2x - 4y + 7)$

42. $x(3x + 4y - 13)$

43. $\frac{8x + 72 + 64c}{8}$

44. $\frac{7x + 63 - 14d}{7}$

45. $\frac{-30 - 65r + 100s}{-5}$

46. $\frac{-9 - 12x + 30z}{-3}$

47. $0.6(1.2 + 5x - 4y)$

48. $0.8(1.3 - 3x + 5y)$

49. $(12x - 18y + 6)\left(\frac{2}{3}\right)$

50. $(15 + 30x - 45y)\left(\frac{3}{5}\right)$

For Problems 51 through 60, tell in words what was done.

51. $3(x + y - z) = 3x + 3y - 3z$

52. $(a - b + c)(4) = 4a - 4b + 4c$

53. $\frac{1}{10}(20 + 15x) = 2 + 1.5x$

54. $\frac{1}{c}(x - y) = \frac{x}{c} - \frac{y}{c}$

55. $(3x + 5)(7) = 7(3x + 5)$

56. $5y(7 + 2x) = 5y(2x + 7)$

57. $3x - (-2x) = 3x + 2x$

58. $12x \div \frac{2}{3} = 12x \cdot \frac{3}{2}$

59. $(5 - 9)x = 5x - 9x$

60. $(7 + 3)x = 7x + 3x$

61. Show that

$$(2 \cdot 3)^5 \quad \text{equals} \quad 2^5 \cdot 3^5$$

by evaluating each expression using the agreed-upon order of operations. What property seems to relate the operations of multiplication and exponentiation (raising to a power)?

62. Using variables for the numbers, write an equation expressing each property:
    a. Multiplication distributes over subtraction.
    b. Division distributes over addition.
    c. Multiplication distributes over a sum of three terms.
    d. Multiplication distributes over addition from the right.
    e. The distributive axiom
    f. Multiplication is associative.
    g. Addition is commutative.

63. Tell the difference between an axiom and any other property.

3-4 LIKE TERMS AND COMMON FACTORS

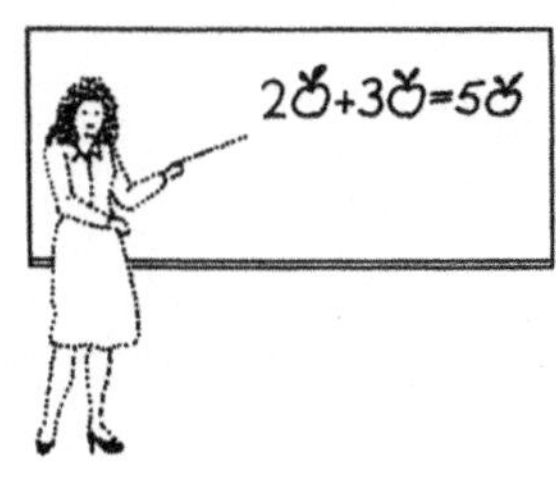

Grade school children learn that two apples plus three apples is five apples. It sounds reasonable that two x's plus three x's equals five x's, or more precisely,

$$2x + 3x = 5x.$$

Now that you know the distributive properties you can see *why* this is true. The expression

$$2x + 3x$$

looks like the *answer* to the problem

$$(2 + 3)x = 2x + 3x.$$

Since the $=$ sign can be read either way, the expression $2x + 3x$ can be transformed as follows:

$2x + 3x$	Write the given expression.
$= (2 + 3)x$	Use the distributive properties "backwards" to factor out x.
$= 5x$	Do the addition.

Therefore,

$2x + 3x = 5x$	The first expression equals the last one.

The two terms $2x$ and $3x$ are alike except for the constant. If the variables in two terms are exactly alike, the terms are said to be *like* terms, or *similar* terms. So $2x$ and $3x$ are like terms. Other examples of like terms are

$$\begin{array}{rcl} 5y & \text{and} & -13y \\ 2x^5 & \text{and} & 7x^5 \\ x & \text{and} & 8x \\ 6z & \text{and} & 6z \\ 4xy & \text{and} & -7xy. \end{array}$$

DEFINITION

LIKE TERMS
Two terms in an expression are called **like terms** (or **similar terms**) if they have the *same* variable(s) raised to the *same* powers.

The constant multiplied by the variable is called the *numerical coefficient,* or simply the *coefficient*. For instance, in $3x^2$, 3 is the coefficient of x^2.

DEFINITION

NUMERICAL COEFFICIENT
The **numerical coefficient** of a term is the constant that is multiplied by the variables. (For example, in $5xy$, 5 is the numerical coefficient of xy.)

The transformation

$$3x + 2x = 5x$$

is called *combining like terms*. So to combine like terms, you simply add their numerical coefficients.

In the expression $3x + 2x$, each term has x as a factor. So x is said to be a *common factor*. Similarly, in

$4x + 4y$, 4 is the common factor,

$3x - 6y$, 3 is the common factor,

$5x^2 - 7x$, x is the common factor,

$3x + 2y$, there are *no* common factors.

DEFINITION

COMMON FACTOR
In an expression, c is a **common factor** if c is a factor of *each term* in that expression.

The process of using the distributive property backwards, as in

$$4x + 4y = 4(x + y)$$

is called *factoring out a common factor*.

Objective

Be able to transform expressions by combining like terms or by factoring out common factors.

Cover the answers as you work the examples.

EXAMPLE 1

Simplify $7z - 5z$.

	Think These Reasons
$7z - 5z$	Write the given expression.
$= \underline{\underline{2z}}$	Combine like terms by subtracting the coefficients.

EXAMPLE 2

Factor out the common factor(s): $3x + 12y$.

$3x + 12y$	Write the given expression.
$= \underline{\underline{3(x + 4y)}}$	3 is a factor of each term.

EXAMPLE 3

Factor out the common factor(s): $5x^2 - 15x$.

$5x^2 - 15x$	Write the given expression.
$= \underline{\underline{5x(x - 3)}}$	5 and x are each common factors of $5x^2$ and $15x$.

EXAMPLE 4

Simplify $7x + x(4x + 3)$.

$7x + x(4x + 3)$	Write the given expression.
$= 7x + 4x^2 + 3x$	Distribute x.
$= 4x^2 + 7x + 3x$	Commute so that like terms are together.
$= \underline{\underline{4x^2 + 10x}}$	Associate and combine like terms.

Note: $4x^2$ and $10x$ are *not* like terms, because the powers of the variables are not alike.

EXAMPLE 5

Simplify $3(5x - 7) - 2(x + 8)$.

$3(5x - 7) - 2(x + 8)$	Write the given expression.
$= 3(5x - 7) + (-2)(x + 8)$	Change subtracting to adding the opposite.
$= 15x - 21 - 2x - 16$	Distribute 3 and -2.
$= 15x - 2x - 21 - 16$	Commute $-2x$ and -21 so that like terms are together.
$= \underline{\underline{13x - 37}}$	Associate and combine like terms.

EXAMPLE 6

Simplify $7(x + 3) - (x - 9)$.

$7(x + 3) - (x - 9)$	Write the given expression.
$= 7(x + 3) + (-1)(x - 9)$	Rewrite subtracting $(x - 9)$ as adding $(-1)(x - 9)$.
$= 7x + 21 - x + 9$	Distribute 7 and -1.
$= 7x - x + 21 + 9$	Commute $-x$ and 21.
$= \underline{\underline{6x + 30}}$	Combine like terms.

ORAL PRACTICE

Combine like terms.

A. $7x + 2x$

B. $3a + 4a$

C. $8x - 3x$

D. $6b - 11b$

E. $8r - r$

F. $5x^2 + 8x^2$

G. $10bc - 4bc$

H. $3x + 5y$

Factor out the common factor(s):

I. $4x + 4y$

J. $9x - 9y$

K. $5b + 20$

L. $8c - 4d$

M. $8c - 4$

N. $x^2 + 5x$

O. $6x^2 - 6x$

P. $3x + 5y$

EXERCISE 3-4

For Problems 1 through 20, combine like terms.

1. $5x + 9x$
2. $6x + 5x$
3. $8p - 3p$
4. $7k - 5k$
5. $9xy - 8xy$
6. $10yz - 9yz$
7. $6x - x$
8. $4y - y$
9. $3x + 7x + 8$
10. $5x + 8x + 3$
11. $5y + 9 + 7y$
12. $4y + 10 + 6y$
13. $3z - 2 - 8z$
14. $5z - 7 - 9z$
15. $-4 - 5x + 11x$
16. $-6 - 2x + 9x$
17. $-6c + 13 - 7c$
18. $-7d + 4 - 9d$
19. $4.5x - 7.1x + 11.6$
20. $3.1x - 8.5x + 2.4$

For Problems 21 through 40, factor out the common factor(s).

21. $3x + 3y$
22. $5x + 5y$
23. $5a - 5b$
24. $7p - 7f$
25. $7c - 14$
26. $3a - 6$
27. $16d - 8$
28. $20r - 10$
29. $6x + 8y$
30. $12x + 8y$
31. $3ab - 3ac$
32. $5bx - 5bz$
33. $4ax + 12bx$
34. $3cx + 15dx$
35. $x^2 - 9x$
36. $x^2 - 4x$
37. $7x^2 + 7x$
38. $3x^2 + 3x$
39. $3x + 3y - 6z$
40. $2x - 2y + 10z$

In Problems 41–70, simplify the expression by distributing, commuting, associating, and combining like terms.

41. $5x + 3(x - 2)$
42. $3x + 7(x - 9)$
43. $7 - 4(2x + 5)$
44. $13 - 2(3x + 4)$
45. $6x - (x - 1)$
46. $7x - (x - 2)$
47. $2(3x + 4) - 5x$
48. $5(3x + 4) - 15x - 20$
49. $-8(9x - 7) + 72x - 57$
50. $-7(6x - 4) + 41x$
51. $4(3x + 2) + 6(5x + 8)$
52. $5(2x + 6) + 3(6x + 7)$
53. $2(x - 5) + 5(4 - 2x)$
54. $4(x - 3) + 2(6 - 5x)$
55. $8(2x + 3) - 4(3x + 6)$
56. $8(3x + 2) - 4(7x + 4)$
57. $3(6 + 5x) - 7(2x - 1)$
58. $3(6 + 7x) - 5(4x + 9)$
59. $-6(x - 5) - 2(7 - 3x)$
60. $-3(4x - 5) - 6(7 - 2x)$
61. $8(x + 4) - (x - 5)$
62. $7(x + 2) - (x - 3)$
63. $5(2x - 3y + 7) - 4(3y + 5x - 1)$
64. $4(7x - 2y + 3) - 5(6x + 5y - 1)$
65. $3x + x(5 - 2x)$
66. $6x - x(4x + 1)$
67. $\frac{1}{4}(12x + 20) - \frac{1}{5}(30 - 15x)$
68. $\frac{1}{3}(15x - 21) - \frac{1}{4}(18 + 30x)$
69. $0.3(5x - 7) - 0.2(3x + 4)$
70. $0.4(2x - 9) - 0.6(4x + 5)$

For Problems 71 through 74, solve the equation.

71. $5x - 23 = 76$

72. $84 = 6x + 12$

73. $14 = 3 - 4x$

74. $11 - x = 44$

For Problems 75 through 80, write an expression for the quantity indicated.

75. Five times the quantity x plus 3
76. The quotient of the quantity f minus 5, and 4
77. The sum of the squares of d and e
78. The product of 15 and the quantity $3x$ minus 7
79. Three less than the product of 15 and y
80. The quotient of u and 3, diminished by 14

3-5 AXIOMS FOR ADDING AND MULTIPLYING

You have learned the words "commute," "associate," and "distribute" as *verbs*. They pertain to things you can do to change the form of an expression. For instance, commuting the terms in $2 + 5$ gives $5 + 2$. The fact that both expressions stand for the same number, 7, is an example of a *property* called the "commutative property for addition." The word "commutative" is the adjective that comes from "commute."

This commutative property is an *axiom*. It is a fact that is used as a basis for the system of real numbers. You can write an equation to express this fact in general, using variables for the numbers.

$$x + y = y + x$$

There are two commutative axioms, one for addition and one for multiplication.

There are also two *associative* axioms. They express the fact that you can associate the terms in a sum or the factors in a product any way you like, and still get the same answer. An equation for the associative axiom for addition is

$$(x + y) + z = x + (y + z).$$

A fifth axiom is the *distributive* axiom. An equation is

$$x(y + z) = xy + xz.$$

These five axioms are summarized in the following table.

AXIOMS

SOME AXIOMS FOR ADDITION AND MULTIPLICATION

In all the axioms, x, y, and z stand for real numbers.

Commutative axiom for addition

$$x + y = y + x$$

Commutative axiom for multiplication

$$xy = yx$$

Associative axiom for addition

$$(x + y) + z = x + (y + z)$$

Associative axiom for multiplication

$$(xy)z = x(yz)$$

Distributive axiom for multiplication over addition

$$x(y + z) = xy + xz$$

There are four other axioms for adding and multiplying. You have been using these axioms, perhaps without realizing it. They concern the numbers 0 and 1.

If you add 0 to a number or multiply a number by 1, the answer is *identical* to the original number. For instance,

$$3 + 0 = 3$$
$$7 \cdot 1 = 7$$

The axioms that express these facts are called the *identity* axioms.

If you add 5 and -5, you get 0. If you multiply $\frac{2}{3}$ by $\frac{3}{2}$, you get 1. The axioms that express these facts are called the *inverse* axioms. Formal statements of these axioms are in the box below.

AXIOMS

SOME MORE AXIOMS FOR ADDITION AND MULTIPLICATION

In all the axioms, x stands for a real number.

Additive Identity Axiom

Zero added to any number gives that number. That is,

$$x + 0 = x.$$

Multiplicative Identity Axiom

One times any number gives that number. That is,

$$x \cdot 1 = x.$$

Additive Inverses Axiom

Any number x has an opposite, $-x$, for which

$$x + (-x) = 0.$$

Multiplicative Inverses Axiom

Any number x (except for 0) has a reciprocal, $\frac{1}{x}$ for which

$$x \cdot \frac{1}{x} = 1.$$

There are two other important properties of multiplication. They tell what happens when you multiply a number by -1 or by 0. In Chapter 2 you learned that if a number is multiplied by -1, the result is the *opposite* of that number. For instance,

$$-1 \cdot 5 = -5, \quad \text{and} \quad -1 \cdot (-7) = 7.$$

This fact is named the *multiplication property of -1*. The fact that multiplying a number by 0 gives 0 for the answer is called the *multiplication property of 0*. For instance,

$$0 \cdot \left(-\frac{2}{3}\right) = 0.$$

Both properties can be proved using the other axioms, as you will learn in later courses. So these two are not called axioms.

PROPERTIES

x stands for a real number.

MULTIPLICATION PROPERTY OF −1
−1 times a number equals the *opposite* of that number.
That is,

$$-1 \cdot x = -x.$$

MULTIPLICATION PROPERTY OF 0
0 times a number equals 0. That is,

$$0 \cdot x = 0.$$

It will be your goal in this section to learn what these axioms and properties say by using them in various ways.

Objective

Given a step in a computation, tell which axiom or other property justifies that step.

Cover the answers as you work these examples.

EXAMPLE 1

Tell which axiom or property justifies the fact that the expression on the right is equal to the expression on the left.

Think These Reasons

a. $\frac{3x}{2} \cdot \frac{2}{3x} = 1$

- - - - -

Multiplicative inverses axiom

A number multiplied by its multiplicative inverse (reciprocal) is 1.

b. $(x + 3y) = 1 \cdot (x + 3y)$

- - - - -

Multiplicative identity axiom

Multiplying by 1 gives an identical number for the answer.

c. $5 \cdot (3x) = (5 \cdot 3)x$

Associative axiom for multiplication — The 5 and 3 were associated.

d. $7(2 + 4x) = 14 + 28x$

Distributive axiom — The 7 was distributed.

e. $7 + (x + 5) = (x + 5) + 7$

Commutative axiom for addition — The 7 and $(x + 5)$ were commuted.

f. $-(x + 5) = -1 \cdot (x + 5)$

Multiplication Property of -1 — The opposite of a number equals -1 times that number.

EXAMPLE 2

Write the axiom, definition, etc., justifying each step:

$7(3 + x) - 5$	
$= 21 + 7x - 5$	a.
$= 21 + 7x + (-5)$	b.
$= 21 + (-5) + 7x$	c.
$= [21 + (-5)] + 7x$	d.
$= 16 + 7x$	e.

$7(3 + x) - 5$	
$= 21 + 7x - 5$	a. *Distributive axiom*
$= 21 + 7x + (-5)$	b. *Definition of subtraction*
$= 21 + (-5) + 7x$	c. *Commutative axiom for addition*
$= [21 + (-5)] + 7x$	d. *Associative axiom for addition*
$= 16 + 7x$	e. *Arithmetic*

ORAL PRACTICE

Name the axiom or definition illustrated:

A. $4 + x = x + 4$

B. $3(y + 7) = 3y + 21$

C. $1x = x$

D. $x \div \left(\frac{2}{3}\right) = x \cdot \left(\frac{3}{2}\right)$

E. $3c + 0 = 3c$

F. $ab = ba$

G. $\left(\frac{5}{8}\right) \cdot \left(\frac{8}{5}\right) = 1$

H. $-\frac{2}{7} + \frac{2}{7} = 0$

I. $5x - (-3x) = 5x + 3x$

J. $5(3x) = (5 \cdot 3)x$

K. $5x + 3x = (5 + 3)x$

L. $5x + 3x = 3x + 5x$

M. $\frac{x}{y} = x \cdot \frac{1}{y}$

N. $3x \cdot 0 = 0$

O. $-1 \cdot xy = -xy$

EXERCISE 3-5

For Problems 1 through 30, name the axiom, other property, or definition which justifies that the expression on the left is equal to the expression on the right. Do not abbreviate! You must show that you know how to spell the words!!

1. $x + y = y + x$
2. $rs = sr$
3. $x - y = x + (-y)$
4. $c \div d = c \cdot \frac{1}{d}$
5. $a + (b + c) = a + (c + b)$
6. $p(mt) = p(tm)$
7. $a + (b + c) = (a + b) + c$
8. $p(mt) = (pm)t$
9. $3x + 4x = (3 + 4)x$
10. $7k + 7j = 7(k + j)$
11. $5m + 5n = 5(m + n)$
12. $6r + 9r = (6 + 9)r$
13. $k \cdot 5 = 5k$
14. $a + 5 = 5 + a$
15. $1 \cdot (4p - 2) = 4p - 2$
16. $0 + 3t = 3t$
17. $2n - 5 \cdot 3 = 2n + (-5 \cdot 3)$
18. $8f \div \left(\frac{2}{3}\right) = 8f \cdot \left(\frac{3}{2}\right)$

19. $\frac{11}{b} \cdot \frac{b}{11} = 1$

20. $0.3 + (-0.3) = 0$

21. $\frac{11}{b} = 11 \cdot \frac{1}{b}$

22. $0.3 + (-0.3) = 0.3 - 0.3$

23. $\frac{11}{b} \cdot 1 = \frac{11}{b}$

24. $0.3\left(\frac{1}{0.3}\right) = 1$

25. $4(pt) = 4(tp)$

26. $3 + (k + 2n) = (3 + k) + 2n$

27. $4(pt) = (pt) \cdot 4$

28. $(3 + k) + 2n = 2n + (3 + k)$

29. $2001x \cdot 0 = 0$

30. $-1 \cdot ahs = -ahs$

For Problems 31 through 50, copy the steps shown. Then name the axiom, definition, etc., which justifies each step. You may abbreviate the names.

31. $3y + 4y$
$= (3 + 4)y$ a.
$= 7y$ b.

32. $\frac{2}{3}x + \frac{10}{3}x$
$= \left(\frac{2}{3} + \frac{10}{3}\right)x$ a.
$= 4x$ b.

33. $9 - 7x$
$= 9 + (-7x)$ a.
$= -7x + 9$ b.

34. $-5 + 2y$
$= 2y + (-5)$ a.
$= 2y - 5$ b.

35. $4(3 + x) + 7$
$= 12 + 4x + 7$ a.
$= 12 + (4x + 7)$ b.
$= 12 + (7 + 4x)$ c.
$= (12 + 7) + 4x$ d.
$= 19 + 4x$ e.

36. $8 + 6(x + 4)$
$= 8 + 6x + 24$ a.
$= (8 + 6x) + 24$ b.
$= (6x + 8) + 24$ c.
$= 6x + (8 + 24)$ d.
$= 6x + 32$ e.

37. $7[x - 8]$
$= 7[x + (-8)]$ a.
$= 7x + 7(-8)$ b.
$= 7x + (-56)$ c.
$= 7x - 56$ d.

38. $[p - 5](3)$
$= [p + (-5)](3)$ a.
$= 3p + (-5)(3)$ b.
$= 3p + (-15)$ c.
$= 3p - 15$ d.

39. $5x + 13 - 2x$
$= 5x + 13 + (-2x)$ a.
$= (5x + 13) + (-2x)$ b.
$= (13 + 5x) + (-2x)$ c.
$= 13 + [5x + (-2x)]$ d.
$= 13 + [5 + (-2)]x$ e.
$= 13 + 3x$ f.

40. $11e - 7 - 3e$
$= 11e + (-7) + (-3e)$ a.
$= 11e + [(-7) + (-3e)]$ b.
$= 11e + [(-3e) + (-7)]$ c.
$= [11e + (-3e)] + (-7)$ d.
$= [11 + (-3)]e + (-7)$ e.
$= 8e + (-7)$ f.
$= 8e - 7$ g.

41.
$8n \div 4$
$= 8n \cdot \frac{1}{4}$ a.
$= 8\left(n \cdot \frac{1}{4}\right)$ b.
$= 8\left(\frac{1}{4} \cdot n\right)$ c.
$= \left(8 \cdot \frac{1}{4}\right)n$ d.
$= 2n$ e.

42.
$51t \div 17$
$= 51t \cdot \frac{1}{17}$ a.
$= 51\left(t \cdot \frac{1}{17}\right)$ b.
$= 51\left(\frac{1}{17} \cdot t\right)$ c.
$= \left(51 \cdot \frac{1}{17}\right)t$ d.
$= 3t$ e.

43.
$11x + 5 - 11x$
$= 11x + 5 + (-11x)$ a.
$= 11x + [5 + (-11x)]$ b.
$= 11x + [(-11x) + 5]$ c.
$= [11x + (-11x)] + 5$ d.
$= 0 + 5$ e.
$= 5$ f.

44.
$3 - 7.1a - 3$
$= 3 + (-7.1a) + (-3)$ a.
$= 3 + [(-7.1a) + (-3)]$ b.
$= 3 + [(-3) + (-7.1a)]$ c.
$= [3 + (-3)] + (-7.1a)$ d.
$= 0 + (-7.1a)$ e.
$= -7.1a$ f.

45.
$\frac{12x}{x}$
$= 12x \cdot \frac{1}{x}$ a.
$= 12\left(x \cdot \frac{1}{x}\right)$ b.
$= 12 \cdot 1$ c.
$= 12$ d.

46.
$\frac{4f}{f}$
$= 4f \cdot \frac{1}{f}$ a.
$= 4\left(f \cdot \frac{1}{f}\right)$ b.
$= 4 \cdot 1$ c.
$= 4$ d.

47.
$6u - u$
$= 6u - (1u)$ a.
$= 6u + (-1u)$ b.
$= [6 + (-1)]u$ c.
$= 5u$ d.

48.
$n - 7n$
$= 1n - 7n$ a.
$= 1n + (-7n)$ b.
$= [1 + (-7)]n$ c.
$= -6n$ d.

49.
$5 - [x + 2]$
$= 5 - 1[x + 2]$ a.
$= 5 + (-1)[x + 2]$ b.
$= 5 + [(-x) + (-2)]$ c.
$= 5 + [(-2) + (-x)]$ d.
$= [5 + (-2)] + (-x)$ e.
$= 3 + (-x)$ f.
$= 3 - x$ g.

50.
$7 - [k + 3]$
$= 7 - 1[k + 3]$ a.
$= 7 + (-1)[k + 3]$ b.
$= 7 + [(-k) + (-3)]$ c.
$= 7 + [(-3) + (-k)]$ d.
$= [7 + (-3)] + (-k)$ e.
$= 4 + (-k)$ f.
$= 4 - k$ g.

For Problems 51 through 60, if it is an expression, simplify it; if it is an equation, solve it.

51. $3x - 7 + 4$

52. $5x - 8 = 3$

53. $7x + 9 = 2$

54. $9x + 7 - 13$

55. $3x - 10 = 2x$ 56. $4x - 8 - 3x$

57. $3.1 - 2x - 41.9$ 58. $1.7 - 2x = 33.6$

59. $5(3x + 8) = -x$ 60. $7(8x + 3/7) - x$

61. The order of operations says multiplication such as $3 \cdot 2 \cdot 7$ should be done from left to right. What axiom says that you get the same answer if you multiply from right to left?

62. A problem on an algebra test says,

"Justify this statement: $-1 \cdot 0 = 0$."

Wanda Ngo says, "Multiplication Property of -1." Her sister Juana says, "Multiplication property of 0." Explain why *both* answers are right.

3-6 PROPERTIES OF EQUALITY

In the last section you learned names for some properties of multiplication and addition. In this section you will learn names for some of the properties that apply to the "=" sign.

When you evaluate an expression, you write something like this:

$$\begin{aligned} &3(5 - 1) + 7 \\ &= 3(4) + 7 \\ &= 12 + 7 \\ &= 19. \end{aligned}$$

What you really want to say is that the original expression equals the final one,

$$3(5 - 1) + 7 = 19.$$

The property that allows you to connect the first expression to the last is called the *transitive axiom of equality*. The word "transit" comes from the Latin *transire,* meaning "to go across." The equality goes across from the first number to the last one.

A second axiom of equality expresses the fact that, for example, $x = 5$ and $5 = x$ both say the same thing. It is called the *symmetric axiom of equality*. The name can be remembered because the "=" sign looks the same from either side. It is "symmetric." So it doesn't matter which direction you read an equation, left to right, or right to left.

The third axiom expresses the fact that a variable stands for the same number, no matter where it appears in an expression or equation. When you check an equation such as

$$3x + 20 = x,$$

you must substitute the *same* number for x in both places. The property is called the *reflexive axiom of equality*. The equation expressing this axiom is

$$x = x.$$

You can remember the name by thinking that x sees its own "reflection" when it looks into an "=" sign.

These three axioms are stated formally below.

AXIOMS OF EQUALITY

x, y, and z stand for real numbers.

TRANSITIVE AXIOM OF EQUALITY
If the first number equals a second number, and the second number equals a third number, then the first number equals the third number. That is,

$$\text{If } x = y \quad \text{and} \quad y = z, \quad \text{then} \quad x = z.$$

SYMMETRIC AXIOM OF EQUALITY
The two members of an equation can be reversed without affecting their equality. That is,

$$\text{If } x = y, \quad \text{then} \quad y = x.$$

REFLEXIVE AXIOM OF EQUALITY
A number equals itself. That is,

$$x = x.$$

Besides these three axioms, there are other properties which express the fact that you can add the same number to each member of an equation, or multiply each member by the same number. For instance,

$$\text{if} \quad 5x - 3 = 17 \quad \text{is true, then so is } 5x - 3 + 3 = 17 + 3.$$

This fact is called the *addition property of equality*. The same fact for multiplying is called the *multiplication property of equality*. For instance,

$$\text{if } 5x = 20 \text{ is true, then so is } 5x \cdot \left(\frac{1}{5}\right) = 20 \cdot \left(\frac{1}{5}\right).$$

These properties are stated formally below.

PROPERTIES FOR TRANSFORMING EQUATIONS

x, y, and z stand for real numbers.

ADDITION PROPERTY OF EQUALITY

If $x = y$, then $x + z = y + z$.

MULTIPLICATION PROPERTY OF EQUALITY

If $x = y$, then $xz = yz$.

Objective

Learn the axioms and properties of equality well enough so that you can tell which property you are using at each step in solving an equation.

Cover the answers as you work these examples.

EXAMPLE 1

Name the axiom, other property, or definition that justifies the following:

Think These Reasons

a. $3x + 5 = 14$
$\therefore 3x + 5 + (-5) = 14 + (-5)$

(The 3-dot symbol "∴" stands for "therefore.")

- - - - -

Addition property of equality — You added the same number to each member of the equation.

b. $13 = 13$

- - - - -

Reflexive axiom of equality — 13 sees its reflection in the "=" sign.

c. $8 + 12 = 20$, and $20 = 23 - 3$
$\therefore 8 + 12 = 23 - 3$

- - - - -

Transitive axiom of equality — The first number, $8 + 12$, is equal to the last one, $23 - 3$.

d. $7x = 28$
$\therefore 7x \cdot \left(\frac{1}{7}\right) = 28 \cdot \left(\frac{1}{7}\right)$

- - - - - - - - - -

Multiplication property of equality Each member of the equation was multiplied by the same number.

e. $6x + 17 = 89$
$\therefore 6x = 72$

- - - - - - - - - -

Addition property of equality -17 was added to each member of the equation. (Some associating and arithmetic were also done.)

f. $19 + 5x + 11$
$= 5x + 19 + 11$

- - - - - - - - - -

Commutative axiom of addition The $5x$ and 19 were commuted. (Note that this is a property of *addition,* not equality!)

EXAMPLE 2

Name the axiom, other property, or definition that justifies each step.

$15 = 8 + 2x$	
$8 + 2x = 15$	a.
$8 + 2x + (-8) = 15 + (-8)$	b.
$2x + 8 + (-8) = 15 + (-8)$	c.
$2x + [8 + (-8)] = 15 + (-8)$	d.
$2x + 0 = 15 + (-8)$	e.
$2x = 15 + (-8)$	f.
$2x = 15 - 8$	g.
$2x = 7$	h.
$\underline{\underline{x = 3.5}}$	i.

- - - - - - - - - -

$15 = 8 + 2x$	
$8 + 2x = 15$	a. Symmetric axiom of equality
$8 + 2x + (-8) = 15 + (-8)$	b. Addition property of equality
$2x + 8 + (-8) = 15 + (-8)$	c. Commutative axiom for addition
$2x + [8 + (-8)] = 15 + (-8)$	d. Associative axiom for addition
$2x + 0 = 15 + (-8)$	e. Additive inverse axiom
$2x = 15 + (-8)$	f. Additive identity axiom
$2x = 15 - 8$	g. Definition of subtraction
$2x = 7$	h. Arithmetic.
$\underline{\underline{x = 3.5}}$	i. Multiplication property of equality (Each member was multiplied by $\frac{1}{2}$).

EXAMPLE 3

State the addition property of equality.

- - - - - - - - - -

If $a = b$, *then* $a + c = b + c$.

"Stating" a property means telling what it *says*. You may use any variables you like, but you should not use constants.

ORAL PRACTICE

Tell which axiom, other property, or definition was used.

A. $2 + 3 = 5$ and $5 = 4 + 1$
$\therefore 2 + 3 = 4 + 1$

B. $2 + 3 = 5$
$\therefore 5 = 2 + 3$

C. $2 + 3 = 5$
$\therefore 2 + 3 + (-3) = 5 + (-3)$

D. $2 + 3 = 2 + 3$

E. $2 + 3 = 3 + 2$

F. $2 + (-3) = 2 - 3$

G. $2 + 3 + 4 = 2 + (3 + 4)$

H. $2 \div 3 = 2 \cdot (1/3)$

I. $2 \cdot 3 = 6$
$\therefore 2 \cdot 3 \cdot \left(\frac{1}{3}\right) = 6 \cdot \left(\frac{1}{3}\right)$

J. $2(3 + 4) = 6 + 8$

K. $2(3 + 4) = 2(4 + 3)$

L. $2(3 + 4) = (3 + 4)(2)$

M. $2(3 + 4) = 2(3 + 4)$

EXERCISE 3-6

For Problems 1 through 40, name the axiom, other property, or definition that justifies the statement.

1. If $19 = 5x + 3$, then $5x + 3 = 19$.
2. $5x + 3 = 5x + 3$
3. $5(x + 3) = 5x + 15$
4. $5(x + 3) = (x + 3)(5)$
5. $5(x + 3) = 5(3 + x)$
6. $5 + (x + 3) = (5 + x) + 3$
7. $x + 3 = x + 3$
8. If $p = a$ and $a = f$, then $p = f$.
9. $w + (-w) = 0$
10. $w + 0 = w$
11. $w \cdot \frac{1}{w} = 1$

12. $w \cdot 0 = 0$

13. $-1 \cdot 3t = -3t$

14. $1x = x$

15. $0x = 0$

16. $1066x + 2001x = (1066 + 2001)x$

17. $1492w + 1492v = 1492(w + v)$

18. $3c \div 3 = 3c\left(\frac{1}{3}\right)$

19. $3(50 \cdot 90) = (3 \cdot 50) \cdot 90$

20. $3(50 + 90) = 3 \cdot 50 + 3 \cdot 90$

21. $3(50 + 90) = (50 + 90)3$

22. $3(50 + 90) = 3(90 + 50)$

23. $3 + (50 + 90) = (3 + 50) + 90$

24. $3 - 50 = 3 + (-50)$

25. $3 - 50 = -47$, and $-47 = -40 - 7$, so $3 - 50 = -40 - 7$.

26. $-1 \cdot 3 = -1 \cdot 3$

27. $0 \cdot x = x \cdot 0$

28. Since $3x + 5x = 8x$, $8x = 3x + 5x$.

29. $3x + 5x = (3 + 5)x$

30. If $3x = 5x + 7$, then $3x + (-5x) = 5x + 7 + (-5x)$.

31. If $\left(\frac{2}{3}\right)x = 12$, then $\left(\frac{2}{3}\right)x \cdot \left(\frac{3}{2}\right) = 12 \cdot \left(\frac{3}{2}\right)$.

32. If $x = 7$ and $7 = z$, then $x = z$.

33. If $14x = 28$, then $x = 2$.

34. If $13 + t = 43$, then $t = 30$.

35. If $14x + 28 = n$, then $28 + 14x = n$.

36. If $13 \cdot t = 43$, then $t \cdot 13 = 43$.

37. $-d + d = 0$

38. $1p = p$

39. $d - d = d + (-d)$

40. $d\left(\frac{1}{d}\right) = 1$

For Problems 41 through 50, copy the steps in the solution of the equation. For each step, name the axiom, other property, or definition which justifies that step.

41. $x + 3 = 8$

$(x + 3) + (-3) = 8 + (-3)$	a.
$x + [3 + (-3)] = 8 + (-3)$	b.
$x + 0 = 8 + (-3)$	c.
$x = 8 + (-3)$	d.
$x = 5$	e.

42. $k + 8 = 3$

$(k + 8) + (-8) = 3 + (-8)$	a.
$k + [8 + (-8)] = 3 + (-8)$	b.
$k + 0 = 3 + (-8)$	c.
$k = 3 + (-8)$	d.
$k = -5$	e.

43. $3m = 21$

$3m \div 3 = 21 \div 3$	a.
$3m \div 3 = 7$	b.
$3m \cdot \frac{1}{3} = 7$	c.
$3\left(m \cdot \frac{1}{3}\right) = 7$	d.
$3\left(\frac{1}{3} \cdot m\right) = 7$	e.
$\left(3 \cdot \frac{1}{3}\right)m = 7$	f.
$1m = 7$	g.
$m = 7$	h.

44. $8m = 72$

$8m \div 8 = 72 \div 8$	a.
$8m \div 8 = 9$	b.
$8m \cdot \frac{1}{8} = 9$	c.
$8\left(m \cdot \frac{1}{8}\right) = 9$	d.
$8\left(\frac{1}{8} \cdot m\right) = 9$	e.
$\left(8 \cdot \frac{1}{8}\right)m = 9$	f.
$1m = 9$	g.
$m = 9$	h.

45. $4v + 21 = 3$

$(4v + 21) + (-21) = 3 + (-21)$	a.
$(4v + 21) + (-21) = -18$	b.
$4v + [21 + (-21)] = -18$	c.
$4v + 0 = -18$	d.
$4v = -18$	e.
$\left(\frac{1}{4}\right)(4v) = \left(\frac{1}{4}\right)(-18)$	f.
$\left(\frac{1}{4}\right)(4v) = -4.5$	g.
$\left(\frac{1}{4} \cdot 4\right)v = -4.5$	h.
$1v = -4.5$	i.
$v = -4.5$	j.

46. $5y + 37 = 11$

$(5y + 37) + (-37) = 11 + (-37)$	a.
$(5y + 37) + (-37) = -26$	b.
$5y + [37 + (-37)] = -26$	c.
$5y + 0 = -26$	d.
$5y = -26$	e.
$\left(\frac{1}{5}\right)(5y) = \left(\frac{1}{5}\right)(-26)$	f.
$\left(\frac{1}{5}\right)(5y) = -5.2$	g.

$\left(\frac{1}{5} \cdot 5\right)y = -5.2$	h.
$1y = -5.2$	i.
$y = -5.2$	j.

47. $10x - 31 = 45$
$10x = 76$ a.
$x = 7.6$ b.

48. $7x + 12 = 1$
$7x = -11$ a.
$x = -1.5714\ldots$ b.

49. $3x + 15 = 5x - 7$
$-2x + 15 = -7$ a.
$-2x = -22$ b.
$x = 11$ c.

50. $9x - 14 = 5x + 26$
$4x - 14 = 26$ a.
$4x = 40$ b.
$x = 10$ c.

Problems 51 through 56 show steps in proofs of some properties. Write the reasons that justify the steps.

51. *Multiplication Distributes over Subtraction*
Prove that $x(y - z) = xy - xz$.

PROOF:

$x(y - z)$
$= x[y + (-z)]$ a.
$= xy + x(-z)$ b.
$= xy + (-xz)$ c.
$= xy - xz$ d.
$\therefore x(y - z) = xy - xz$ e.

52. *Division Distributes over Addition*

Prove: If x, y, and z are any real numbers, $z \neq 0$, then

$$\frac{x+y}{z} = \frac{x}{z} + \frac{y}{z}.$$

PROOF:

$\frac{x+y}{z}$

$= (x + y) \cdot \frac{1}{z}$ a.

$= x \cdot \frac{1}{z} + y \cdot \frac{1}{z}$ b.

$= \frac{x}{z} + \frac{y}{z}$ c.

$\therefore \frac{x+y}{z} = \frac{x}{z} + \frac{y}{z}$ d.

53. *Multiplication Distributes over a Sum of Three Terms*

Prove: For any four real numbers w, x, y, and z,

$$w(x + y + z) = wx + wy + wz.$$

PROOF:

$w(x + y + z)$

$= w[x + (y + z)]$ a.

$= wx + w(y + z)$ b.

$= wx + wy + wz$ c.

$\therefore w(x + y + z) = wx + wy + wz$ d.

Hint: In (a), there are just *two* terms inside the parentheses, x and $(y + z)$. Thus you can use the distributive axiom in the next step.

54. *Combining Like Terms*

Copy the steps in the following proof that you can combine like terms by adding their coefficients. Then supply a reason for each step.

Prove: For any real numbers a, b, and x, $ax + bx = (a + b)x$.

PROOF:

$(a + b)x$

$= x(a + b)$ a.

$= xa + xb$ b.

$= ax + bx$ c.

$\therefore (a + b)x = ax + bx$ d.

$\therefore ax + bx = (a + b)x$ e.

55. *Property of the Opposite of a Sum:* The following is a proof that a "−" sign can distribute over addition. Name the axiom, other property, or definition which justifies each step.

PROOF:

$-(x + y)$

$= -1 \cdot (x + y)$ a.

$= -1x + (-1y)$ b.

$= -x + (-y)$ c.

$= -x - y$ d.

$\therefore -(x + y) = -x - y$ e.

56. *Multiplication Property of −1*

Prove that $-1x = -x$.

PROOF:

$-1x + x$	
$= -1x + 1x$	a.
$= (-1 + 1)x$	b.
$= 0x$	c.
$= 0$	d.
$= x + (-x)$	e.
$\therefore -1x + x = x + (-x)$	f.
$\therefore -1x + x = -x + x$	g.
$\therefore -1x = -x$	h.

57. What is wrong with this reasoning?

$5 \cdot 0 = 0$	Multiplication property of 0
$0 = 3 \cdot 0$	Multiplication property of 0
$\therefore 5 \cdot 0 = 3 \cdot 0$	Transitive axiom of equality
$\therefore 5 = 3$	Multiplication property of equality

58. One of these is an example of a commutative axiom. The other is an example of the symmetric axiom. Which is which?

If $3d + 5 = 14$, then $14 = 3d + 5$.
If $3d + 5 = 14$, then $5 + 3d = 14$.

59. State the axiom:
   a. Symmetric axiom of equality
   b. Reflexive axiom of equality
   c. Transitive axiom of equality
   d. Commutative axiom of multiplication
   e. Additive inverse axiom
   f. Multiplicative identity axiom

60. State the property or definition:
   a. Addition property of equality
   b. Multiplication property of equality
   c. Multiplication property of −1
   d. Multiplication property of 0
   e. Definition of division
   f. Definition of subtraction

For Problems 61 through 70, if it is an equation, solve it. If it is an expression, simplify it.

61. $5x - 7 = -34$
62. $3x - 5 + 7x$
63. $13 - x + 4x$
64. $8 - x = 51$

65. $4x - (2 - 11x)$

66. $5x = 4(x - 8)$

67. $21 = 5(2x + 4) - 3$

68. $2x + 3(4 - 7x)$

69. $(5)(3 \cdot 2x)$

70. $x(x + 5) + 17x$

3-7 CHAPTER REVIEW AND TEST

In this chapter you have learned an important new technique—distributing. Distributing multiplication over addition, such as in

$$3(x + y) = 3x + 3y,$$

is an *axiom*. Other distributive properties, such as

$$3(x - y) = 3x - 3y$$

or

$$3(x + y + z) = 3x + 3y + 3z,$$

can be *proved* from the axioms. The distributive properties were used for two other types of transformation, collecting like terms and factoring out common factors.

Like terms:	*Common factors:*
$4x + 3x - 5$	$4x - 12y$
$= 7x - 5$	$= 4(x - 3y)$

The chapter test below is one that you should be able to complete in 45 minutes. You will get the most benefit from it if you put yourself under test conditions (quiet room, no TV, etc.!). Don't just look at the problems and say, "Oh, I could do that." Actually write the problems and answers neatly and accurately as though it were a real test! Time yourself. When you finish, check the answers at the end of the book to see how well you did. If you do these things, you should be in good shape for the test your teacher will give you in class.

CHAPTER TEST

For Problems 1 through 20, simplify the expression by distributing, commuting, associating, and collecting like terms.

1. $7(9x - 8)$

2. $(3x + 5)(8)$

3. $\dfrac{72a - 36b}{-12}$

4. $x(x + 9)$

5. $-42\left(\frac{1}{3}x - \frac{1}{7}y\right)$

6. $-(x - 2)$

7. $5x + 7x + 11$

8. $10 + 5r - 2r$

9. $6 - 4x + 5x$

10. $7x - 5 - 4x$

11. $3x - x$

12. $4(x - 3) + 10x$

13. $3(x + 5) + 2(4x - 7)$

14. $-4(3x - 9) + 6(2x + 7)$

15. $5(x + 3) - (x - 7)$

16. $6 + 4(x + 5) - x$

17. $7x + x(2 - 5x)$

18. $\frac{1}{5}(35x - 50y) - \frac{1}{4}(24x - 20y)$

19. $0.4x + 0.7(x - 3)$

20. $\frac{3}{4}(20x - 1) - 14x$

For Problems 21 through 26, factor out the common factor(s).

21. $5x + 10y$

22. $6p - 9j$

23. $rx + rz$

24. $12x + 18$

25. $5x^2 - 3x$

26. $4x + 4y - 8z$

27. The expressions $3(4 + x)$ and $3(4 \cdot x)$ are the same except for the operation between 4 and x. Simplify each expression. Then tell in words the difference between what you did for the two expressions.

28. Explain the difference between an axiom and any other property.

29. Write a statement of each of the following.
    a. The commutative axiom for addition
    b. The associative axiom for multiplication
    c. The transitive axiom of equality
    d. The definition of subtraction
    e. The reflexive axiom of equality

30. Copy the steps in the following solution. Then supply a reason justifying each step.

$29 = 5 - 3x$	
$5 - 3x = 29$	a.
$5 + (-3x) = 29$	b.
$-3x + 5 = 29$	c.
$(-3x + 5) + (-5) = 29 + (-5)$	d.
$(-3x + 5) + (-5) = 24$	e.
$-3x + [5 + (-5)] = 24$	f.
$-3x + 0 = 24$	g.
$-3x = 24$	h.

$\left(-\frac{1}{3}\right)(-3x) = \left(-\frac{1}{3}\right)(24)$ i.

$\left(-\frac{1}{3}\right)(-3x) = -8$ j.

$\left[\left(-\frac{1}{3}\right)(-3)\right]x = -8$ k.

$1x = -8$ l.

$x = -8$ m.

31. Copy the steps in the following proof. Then supply a reason justifying each step.

Prove: For all real numbers w, x, y, and z, $\frac{w + x + y}{z} = \frac{w}{z} + \frac{x}{z} + \frac{y}{z}$.

PROOF:

$\frac{w + x + y}{z}$ a.

$= (w + x + y) \cdot \frac{1}{z}$ b.

$= \frac{1}{z}(w + x + y)$ c.

$= \frac{1}{z}[(w + x) + y]$ d.

$= \frac{1}{z}[w + x] + \frac{1}{z} \cdot y$ e.

$= \frac{1}{z} \cdot w + \frac{1}{z} \cdot x + \frac{1}{z} \cdot y$ f.

$= w \cdot \frac{1}{z} + x \cdot \frac{1}{z} + y \cdot \frac{1}{z}$ g.

$= \frac{w}{z} + \frac{x}{z} + \frac{y}{z}$ h.

$\therefore \frac{w + x + y}{z} = \frac{w}{z} + \frac{x}{z} + \frac{y}{z}$ i.

4

Harder Equations

e last chapter you learned the ibutive properties. These erties are useful in sim- ng expressions such as + 5) − 7. They also allow o simplify expressions like · 7x + 8 by combining like s. In this chapter you will equations that have expres- like these in one or both bers. These expressions could esent things in the real world as the amount of work done onstruction crews that start at rent times.

able:

Number of days first crew has worked.

ression:

2 Number of days second crew has worked.

ressions:

Amounts of work

− 2) each crew has done.

ation:

$= 12(x - 2)$ Says that each crew has done the same amount of work.

4-1 EQUATIONS WITH LIKE TERMS

This section is meant for you to read and work on your own. If you have understood what you have learned so far, you should be able to do this without prior classroom discussion.

You have learned how to solve equations like

$$3x + 5 = 17.$$

You also know how to simplify expressions such as

$$3x - 7 + 5x,$$

which have like terms. Now you are ready to put together these two techniques and solve equations that look like this:

$$3x - 7 + 5x = 25.$$

In such equations, the variable appears more than once.

Objective

Be able to solve equations that have like terms in one member.

The secret in working a new problem such as this is changing it to an old problem. The equation

$$3x - 7 + 5x = 25$$

can be transformed by combining like terms on the left. You get

$$8x - 7 = 25.$$

From here on, this is an old problem.

$$8x - 7 + 7 = 25 + 7 \quad \text{Add 7 to each member.}$$

$$8x = 32 \quad \text{Do the operations.}$$

$$\frac{8x}{8} = \frac{32}{8}$$ Divide each member by 8.

$\underline{\underline{x = 4}}$ Do the division.

Note: You can do some of the steps for solving this kind of equation in your head. For instance, you could write

$8x - 7 = 25$

$8x = 32$ Add 7 to each member.

$\underline{\underline{x = 4}}$ Divide each member by 8.

Cover the answers as you work these examples.

EXAMPLE

Solve and check: $2x - 8 + 7x = 19$.

	Think These Reasons
$2x - 8 + 7x = 19$	Write the given equation.
$9x - 8 = 19$	Combine like terms.
$9x - 8 + 8 = 19 + 8$	Add 8 to each member.
$9x = 27$	Do the operations.
$\frac{9x}{9} = \frac{27}{9}$	Divide each member by 9.
$\underline{\underline{x = 3}}$	Do the operations.
Check: $2x - 8 + 7x$	Write the left member.
$= 6 - 8 + 21$	Substitute 3 for x.
$= 19$ ✓	Do the arithmetic. The answer checks.

EXERCISE 4-1

For Problems 1 through 20, solve the equation and check your answer.

1. $2x + 6x = 56$
2. $5x + 4x = 45$
3. $7x - 4x = 15$
4. $8x - 3x = 35$
5. $3x + 4x + 8 = 22$
6. $6x + 2x + 7 = 31$

7. $10x - 7x + 18 = 6$
8. $7x - 4x + 21 = 15$
9. $5x - 7x + 21 = 27$
10. $6x - 10x + 2 = 22$
11. $7x + 3 + 3x = 63$
12. $2x + 3 + 5x = 31$
13. $9x - 14 - 5x = -10$
14. $8x - 4 - 2x = -10$
15. $10x - x = 90$
16. $6x - x = 30$
17. $7x - 4 - 6x = 5$
18. $9x - 3 - 8x = 7$
19. $2x + 3x + 4 + 5x = 34$
20. $3x + 4 + 5x + 6x = 32$

Problems 21 through 30 review other techniques.

21. Simplify: $3x - 4 + 5x$
22. Evaluate: $0.3 + 4.7(2)$
23. Evaluate $3x + 4.9$ if x is 5.
24. Simplify: $4 - (2x - 11)$
25. Evaluate: $|4 - 13|$
26. Evaluate $\left(\frac{2}{3}\right)x - 10$ if x is 24.
27. Write an expression for twelve less than x.
28. Write an expression for the product of 6 and x, increased by 5.
29. Name the axiom: $(ab)c = a(bc)$
30. Name the axiom: If $a = b$, then $b = a$.

4-2 EQUATIONS WITH LIKE TERMS AND DISTRIBUTING

In the last section you solved equations in which the left member has like terms. Equations such as

$$3x - 7 + 5x = 25$$

can be transformed into more familiar equations, like

$$8x - 7 = 25,$$

by combining like terms. In this section you solve more equations like this. You also solve equations such as

$$6(x - 2) + 5x = 43,$$

in which you must *distribute* before you can combine like terms.

Objective

Be able to solve equations with like terms in one member, some of which require distributing before like terms can be combined.

Cover the answers as you work these examples.

EXAMPLE 1

Solve and check: $6(x - 2) + 5x = 43$.

	Think These Reasons
$6(x - 2) + 5x = 43$	Write the given equation.
$6x - 12 + 5x = 43$	Distribute 6 to x and to -2.
$11x - 12 = 43$	Commute and combine like terms.
$11x = 55$	Add 12 to each member.
$\underline{\underline{x = 5}}$	Divide each member by 11.
Check: $6(x - 2) + 5x$	Write the left member.
$= 6(5 - 2) + 25$	Substitute 5 for x.
$= 6(3) + 25$	Do the arithmetic.
$= 18 + 25$	Do more arithmetic.
$= 43$ ✓	The answer checks.

Some equations may require distributing more than once or may have the variable in the right member instead of in the left.

EXAMPLE 2

Solve and check: $-1 = 5(x - 6) + 4(2 - 3x)$.

$-1 = 5(x - 6) + 4(2 - 3x)$	Write the given equation.
$-1 = 5x - 30 + 8 - 12x$	Distribute 5 and 4.
$-1 = -7x - 22$	Combine like terms.
$21 = -7x$	Add 22 to both members.
$\underline{\underline{-3 = x}}$	Divide both members by -7.
Check: $5(x - 6) + 4(2 - 3x)$	Write the right member of the equation.
$= 5(-3 - 6) + 4(2 + 9)$	Substitute -3 for x.
$= 5(-9) + 4(11)$	Do the arithmetic.

$= -45 + 44$ Do more arithmetic.

$= -1$ ✓ The answer checks.

ORAL PRACTICE

Tell what equation you get after the distributive step.

EXAMPLES

	Answers
i. $3(7 - 2x) + 4x = 19$	i. $21 - 6x + 4x = 19$
ii. $5x - 2(3x - 7) = -13$	ii. $5x - 6x + 14 = -13$

A. $6(4x + 7) + 2x = 9$

B. $5(2x - 3) + 4x = 11$

C. $4(3y + 5) - 2y = 6$

D. $6(3z - 2) - 5z = 1$

E. $-2(4x + 3) + 5x = 7$

F. $-8(3 - 2x) + 4x = 10$

G. $5x + 3(6 + x) = -4$

H. $4x - 2(3x + 7) = 8$

I. $6x - 1(4 - 2x) = 7$

J. $6x - (5x - 8) = 7$

EXERCISE 4-2

Solve and check.

1. $7x + 3x = 40$
2. $9x + 4x = 65$
3. $4x - 11x = 105$
4. $7x - 11x = 60$
5. $16x + 3 + 4x = 103$
6. $18x + 7 + 7x = 107$
7. $7r - 8 - 4r = 25$
8. $10s - 7 - 3s = 84$
9. $-5c + 17 - 8c = 56$
10. $-3t + 19 - 5t = 91$
11. $58 = 6 - 14x + 12x$
12. $65 = 5 - 8x + 2x$
13. $8t + 5 - 7t = 22$
14. $9r + 7 - 8r = 24$
15. $20x + 84 - 8x = 0$
16. $13x + 105 - 8x = 0$
17. $x + 21 + 4x = -33$
18. $9x + 33 + x = -93$
19. $2x - 5x + 13 + 9x = 67$
20. $3x - 7x + 15 + 6x = 41$
21. $5(x + 3) - 2x = -21$
22. $6(x + 2) - 4x = 48$

23. $2(3x - 7) + 4x = 26$

24. $3(2x - 5) + 2x = -7$

25. $5x + 3(x + 4) = 28$

26. $6x + 3(x + 7) = -15$

27. $7x - 4(2 - 3x) = -27$

28. $5x - 2(6 - 5x) = 18$

29. $7x - (5 + 6x) = 4$

30. $4x - (3x + 11) = -11$

31. $12 - 7(x - 4) + x = -2$

32. $17 - 7(x - 3) + x = 86$

33. $2(x + 3) - 5(x - 1) = 32$

34. $3(x + 4) - 5(x - 1) = 5$

35. $55 = 3(2x - 1) + 2(x + 5)$

36. $66 = 4(2x - 3) + 2(x + 4)$

37. $0 = 4(6 - x) + 7x$

38. $0 = 5(7 - x) + 12x$

39. $3(a + 2) - (a - 1) = 17$

40. $4(c + 3) - (c - 1) = 64$

Problems 41 through 44 require clever transformations or have surprising answers!

41. $9x + 35 = 4x$

42. $8x + 21 = 5x$

43. $3(4x + 5) - 2(6x - 1) = 17$

44. $3(4x + 5) - 2(6x - 1) = 18$

Problems 45 through 50 review other techniques.

45. What property is this? $-1 \cdot s = -s$

46. Evaluate $5x^2$ if x is 3.

47. Simplify: $19 - 9(2x - 4)$

48. Evaluate: $\frac{2}{3} + \frac{5}{6}$

49. Simplify: $-(-14x + 3) - 7$

50. What property is this? $(x)\left(\frac{1}{x}\right) = 1$

4-3 EQUATIONS WITH VARIABLES IN BOTH MEMBERS

The equations of Sections 4.1 and 4.2 had all the variable terms in either the left member or the right member. Equations such as

$$7x = 5x + 18$$

have variable terms in *both* members. These equations can readily be transformed so that all variable terms are in *one* member.

$7x = 5x + 18$	Write the given equation.
$7x - 5x = 5x + 18 - 5x$	Subtract $5x$ from each member.
$2x = 18$	Combine like terms on the left. Commute and associate $5x$ and $-5x$ on the right.
$\underline{\underline{x = 9}}$	Divide each member by 2.

By getting rid of the variable term in the right member, you have changed this new problem into an old problem. From there on, you use familiar techniques to solve the equation.

The check for such an equation is most easily done by substituting the solution into *both* members of the equation.

$7(9) \stackrel{?}{=} 5(9) + 18$	Substitute 9 for x.
$63 \stackrel{?}{=} 45 + 18$	Do the arithmetic.
$63 = 63$ ✓	The answer checks.

The $\stackrel{?}{=}$ sign asks: *Are* these equal?

Objective

Be able to solve equations with variables in both members.

Cover the answers as you work these examples.

EXAMPLE 1

Solve and check: $3x + 55 = 8x$.

- - - - - - - - - -

Think These Reasons

$3x + 55 = 8x$	Write the given equation.
$3x + 55 - 8x = 8x - 8x$	Subtract $8x$ from each member.
$-5x + 55 = 0$	Combine like terms.
$-5x = -55$	Subtract 55 from each member.
$\underline{\underline{x = 11}}$	Divide each member by -5.

Check:

$3(11) + 55 \stackrel{?}{=} 8(11)$	Substitute 11 for x.
$33 + 55 \stackrel{?}{=} 88$	Do the arithmetic.
$88 = 88$ ✓	Checks!

Sometimes there are surprises when you try to solve this kind of equation. For example, the equation

$$x = x + 5$$

has *no* solutions. It says that a number is 5 more than *itself*. If you try to solve such an equation, you get the following result.

$x = x + 5$	Write the given equation.
$x - x = x + 5 - x$	Subtract x from each member.
$0 = 5$	Combine like terms.
No solutions.	Write a conclusion.

The impossible statement $0 = 5$ indicates that there are *no* solutions. So you write a conclusion stating this fact.

Another surprise results from solving an equation like this:

$$2x + 3x + 7 = 5x + 1 + 6.$$

Upon combining like terms, you get

$$5x + 7 = 5x + 7.$$

The two expressions are identical. The equation is therefore true for *all* values of x. For instance, $5(3) + 7 = 5(3) + 7$, since both equal 22, and $5(-2) + 7 = 5(-2) + 7$, since both equal -3.

Such an equation is called an *identity*. The equations you have solved so far are called *conditional equations*, because they are true only under the condition that the variable has the "right" value.

DEFINITION

IDENTITIES AND CONDITIONAL EQUATIONS

An **identity** is an equation that is true for *all* values of the variable.

A **conditional equation** is one that is true for some value(s) of the variable and not true for other values of the variable.

If you try to solve the identity above, you get the following result.

$5x + 7 = 5x + 7$	
$5x + 7 - 5x = 5x + 7 - 5x$	Subtract $5x$ from each member.
$7 = 7$	Combine like terms.
Any number (identity).	Write a conclusion. The statement $7 = 7$ is *always* true, so the equation is an identity.

CONCLUSION

The following examples show what is true if the variable *disappears* from an equation.

$0 = 5$	*Never* true. *No* solutions
$7 = 7$	*Always* true. Any number is a solution. (Equation is an *identity*.)

The next two examples illustrate these ideas.

EXAMPLE 2

Solve $5 - 9x = -9x$.

$5 - 9x = -9x$	Write the given equation.
$5 - 9x + 9x = -9x + 9x$	Add $9x$ to each member.
$5 = 0$	Combine like terms.
No solutions.	Write a conclusion.

EXAMPLE 3

Solve $4(x + 3) = 3x + 12 + x$.

$4(x + 3) = 3x + 12 + x$	Write the given equation.
$4x + 12 = 4x + 12$	Distribute on the left. Combine like terms on the right.
Any number (identity).	Write a conclusion.

Note: It is not necessary for you to do any more steps once you have shown that the two members of the equation are exactly the same.

ORAL PRACTICE

Tell what you would do to get rid of the variable in the right member.

EXAMPLES

	Answers
i. $3x + 8 = 5x$	i. Subtract $5x$ from each member.
ii. $2x = 3 - 7x$	ii. Add $7x$ to each member.
iii. $x = 4x - 8$	iii. Subtract $4x$ from each member.

A. $9x - 2 = 4x$

B. $6x + 5 = -3x$

C. $4 - 2x = 7x$

D. $5x = 2 + 8x$

E. $7x = 5 - 9x$

F. $-10x = -4x + 3$

G. $-2x = 5 - x$

H. $5x - 4 = 3x + 7$

I. $2 + 8x = 5 - 7x$

J. $3 - 2x = -11x + 4$

K. Tell what $\stackrel{?}{=}$ means.

L. Give the definition of identity.

M. Give the definition of conditional equation.

The last step in solving an equation is given below. Tell whether the equation is *conditional*, is an *identity*, or has *no* solution.

EXAMPLES

	Answers
i. $4 = 0$	i. No solution
ii. $5 = 5$	ii. Identity
iii. $x = 7$	iii. Conditional

N. $x = 3$

O. $7 = 7$

P. $8 = x$

Q. $8 = 7$

R. $8 = 8$

S. $x = x$

T. $x = 0$

U. $0 = 0$

EXERCISE 4-3

For Problems 1 through 20, solve and check.

1. $5x + 27 = 2x$
2. $7x + 66 = 4x$
3. $6x - 28 = 8x$
4. $5x - 39 = 8x$
5. $9x = 4x - 65$
6. $8x = 2x - 60$
7. $55 - 3x = 8x$
8. $54 - 5x = 4x$
9. $5x = 48 - x$
10. $3x = 40 - x$
11. $10c - 51 = 7c$
12. $9j - 75 = 6j$
13. $29y + 56 = 27y$
14. $14b + 30 = 16b$
15. $-6a = a - 70$
16. $-a = 7a - 48$
17. $9x = 34 + 8x$
18. $7x = 45 - 2x$
19. $7z = -16 - 9z$
20. $11y = -400 - 9y$

For Problems 21–44, solve and check. If the equation is an identity or has no solution, write an appropriate conclusion.

21. $4u = 37 + 4u$
22. $5x + 7 = 4x + 7$
23. $5x + 8 = 7x + 8$
24. $5x + 7 = 5x + 8$
25. $2x - 5 = 3x + 4$
26. $4a - 3 = 5a + 6$
27. $5 - 2x = 3 - 2x + 2$
28. $4 - 3x = 5 - 6x - 7$
29. $6x + 7 - 2x = 3 + 5x - 9$
30. $5 + 2x - 9 = 7x - 4 - 5x$
31. $4(x + 3) = 6x$
32. $7x = 5(x - 12)$
33. $5(9 - x) = 4(x + 18)$
34. $7(2 - r) = 3(r + 8)$
35. $3s + 3(1 - s) = s - 17$
36. $2(5 - t) + 6t = t + 22$
37. $4x - 2(1 - x) = 2(3x - 2)$
38. $3(x - 4) - x = 2(x - 6)$
39. $4(r + 1) = 6 - 2(1 - 2r)$
40. $x + 2(x + 4) = 1 + 3(x + 2)$
41. $2[1 - 3(x + 2)] = -x$
42. $3(1 + x) = 2[3(x + 2) - (x + 1)]$
43. $6(x + 4) - (x + 3) = x - 1$
44. $3(3x + 1) - (x - 1) = 6(x + 10)$

Problems 45 through 50 review other techniques.

45. Distribute: $3\left(4x - 2.3y + \frac{2}{3}z\right)$
46. Simplify: $5x - x$
47. Evaluate $11 - 4x$ if x is -0.3.
48. Find 30% of 400.
49. Simplify: $4(3x - 7) - (8x - 2.7)$
50. Commute the x and the 3: $4 + x + 3$

4-4 EQUATIONS THAT INVOLVE DECIMALS

Until now the equations you have solved have "come out nicely." The answers were usually *integers*. As you recall from Section 2.2, the integers are the whole numbers 0, 1, 2, 3, . . . and their opposites, -1, -2, -3, ... They are used to mark the scale on the number line.

In most problems from the real world, the answers are *not* integers. For instance, if you drive for 258 mi between fill-ups and buy 13.8 gal of gas, then your mileage is

$$\frac{258}{13.8} \text{ miles per gallon (mpg).}$$

Dividing by calculator gives approximately

$$18.69565217 \text{ mpg.}$$

Normally, such numbers would be rounded, for example, to

$$18.7 \text{ mpg.}$$

In this section you will solve equations whose solutions turn out to be "untidy decimals" like this.

Objective

Be able to find approximate solutions for equations involving decimals.

Cover the answers as you work these examples.

EXAMPLE 1

Solve $17x + 38 = -24$. Round off to two decimal places. Check your answer.

- - - - - - - - - -

	Think These Reasons
$17x + 38 = -24$	Write the given equation.
$17x = -62$	Subtract 38 from both members.
$x = -\frac{62}{17}$	Divide each member by 17.
$x = -3.64705\ldots$	Use a calculator. (Save this value in memory for use in the check.)
$\underline{\underline{x \approx -3.65}}$	Round off to two decimal places.

Check:

$17(-3.647\ldots) + 38 \stackrel{?}{=} -24$	Recall the value of x from memory.
$-24 = -24$	Do the operations. The answer checks.

Notes:

1. The symbol $\approx$ means *is approximately equal to.*
2. The round off to two decimal places, you (mentally) put a mark after the *second* digit to the *right* of the decimal point, like this:

$$-3.64\,\vdots\,7058824.$$

Next, circle the two digits on either side of the mark.

$$-3.6\,(4\,\vdots\,7)\,058824$$

Then ask, "Is 47 closer to 40 or closer to 50?" Since it is closer to 50, you rounded off *upward,* getting

$$-3.65.$$

3. A number ending in 5 should be rounded off *upwards* unless there is a reason for doing otherwise. Thus

$$2.975,$$

when rounded off to two decimal places, becomes

$$2.98.$$

4. Because of round-off inside some calculators, the check may show a number only approximately equal to -24, such as -23.9997.

EXAMPLE 2

Solve $5.2x - 26.3 = 0.47x - 8$. Round off to two decimal places. Check your answer.

$5.2x - 26.3 = 0.47x - 8$	Write the given equation.
$5.2x - 0.47x = -8 + 26.3$	Add 26.3 to and subtract $0.47x$ from each member.
$4.73x = 18.3$	Combine like terms.
$x = \dfrac{18.3}{4.73}$	Divide each member by 4.73.
$x = 3.86892\ldots$	Use a calculator. (Save this value in memory for use in the check.)
$\underline{\underline{x \approx 3.87}}$	Round off to two decimal places.

Check: $5.2(3.868\ldots) - 26.3 \stackrel{?}{=} 0.47(3.868\ldots) - 8$

$$-6.1816\ldots = -6.1816\ldots \checkmark$$

Note: $0.47x$ could be written $.47x$. However, the leading zero helps you avoid losing the decimal point and thinking that the number is $47x$.

EXAMPLE 3

Solve $5.3x + 11.82 = 4.2(3.1x - 7.5)$. Round to two decimal places. Check your answer.

$5.3x + 11.82 = 4.2(3.1x - 7.5)$	Write the given equation.
$5.3x + 11.82 = 13.02x - 31.50$	Distribute 4.2.
$5.3x - 13.02x = -31.50 - 11.82$	Subtract 11.82 and $13.02x$ from each member.
$-7.72x = -43.32$	Combine like terms.
$x = \dfrac{-43.32}{-7.72}$	Divide each member by −7.72.
$x = 5.61139\ldots$	Use a calculator. (Save this value in memory for use in the check.)
$\underline{\underline{x \approx 5.61}}$	Round to two decimal places.

Check: $5.3(5.611\ldots) + 11.82 \stackrel{?}{=} 4.2(3.1(5.611\ldots) - 7.5)$

$41.5604\ldots = 41.5604\ldots$ ✓

Note: In checking, the entire calculation for each member can be done on the calculator *without* writing intermediate values! You should write down the *last* line of the check to show that the two members really are equal.

ORAL PRACTICE

Round off to two decimal places.

EXAMPLES

	Answers
i. 0.293	i. 0.29
ii. −5.407	ii. −5.41
iii. 3.698241	iii. 3.70

A. 3.127

B. 48.582

C. 0.587

D. −1.094

E. 3.52831

F. 6.497

G. -9.4308

H. 0.057

I. -99.699

J. 0.535

Use a calculator to find each quotient. Round off approximate answers to two decimal places.

K. $\frac{3.7}{1.3}$

L. $\frac{6.8}{1.4}$

M. $\frac{4.2}{9.7}$

N. $\frac{-5.4}{0.7}$

O. $\frac{0.7}{-3.7}$

P. $\frac{5.1}{1.7}$

Q. $\frac{4.03}{0.65}$

R. $\frac{3.76}{2.09}$

S. $\frac{0}{5.9}$

T. $\frac{3.8}{0}$

EXERCISE 4-4

For Problems 1 through 20, solve the equation. Round off the answer to two decimal places. Check and write the last line of the check.

1. $12x = 5x + 37$
2. $15x = 2x + 58$
3. $57 - 13x = 4x + 8$
4. $67 - 5x = 9x + 7$
5. $3.2x = 7.1x + 10.2$
6. $4.1x = 9.5x + 23.7$
7. $0.3c - 8.5 = 1 + 1.7c$
8. $0.2d - 7.3 = 2 + 3.6d$
9. $4.5 - 7.2x = 3.4x - 49.5$
10. $5.3 - 4.8x = 1.3x - 52.7$
11. $0.3x + 0.4 + 0.5x = 0.6x + 0.7$
12. $0.4x + 0.5 = 0.6x + 0.7 + 0.8x$
13. $3(2.4x + 5) = x + 2.7$
14. $2(3.7x + 8) = x + 1.9$
15. $6.3 + 1.2s = 4(7.1 - s)$
16. $5.9 - 1.7t = 3(4.1 - t)$
17. $2.4(3.1x + 4.9) = 75.9 + 0.87x$
18. $3.7(2.1x + 1.7) = 86.2 + 0.85x$
19. $0.72z - 19.7 = 0.3(0.2z + 1.8)$
20. $1.8 - 0.63y = 0.7(0.3y + 10.9)$

Problems 21 through 30 review other techniques.

21. Factor completely: $24x + 36y$

22. Add the fractions: $\frac{3}{4} + \frac{7}{8}$

23. Find 60% of 300.

24. Write the statement of the addition property of equality.

25. Associate the 4 and the y: $3x + 4 + y$

26. Simplify: $-(3 - 4x) + 17x$

27. Simplify the fraction: $\frac{27}{81}$

28. Simplify: $3(4x - 7) - 2(5x - 13)$

29. Write 64 as a power that has 4 as its base.

30. Bonnie starts working 3 hours after Clyde. Clyde has been working for x hours. Write an expression for the number of hours Bonnie has been working.

4-5 LITERAL EQUATIONS AND FORMULAS

You have been solving equations in which there is one variable and several constants, such as

$$3x + 91 = 44.$$

If a letter is used to stand for one or more of the constants, as in

$$3x + a = 44,$$

the equation is said to be a *literal equation*. The word "literal" comes from the Latin word "littera," which means "letter."

If you solve a literal equation, the value of x comes out in terms of the other letters. In the above equation, subtracting a from each member gives

$$3x = 44 - a.$$

Dividing by 3 gives

$$x = \left(\frac{1}{3}\right)(44 - a).$$

The result is called a *formula* for x in terms of a. In this section you will solve some literal equations, and evaluate formulas for given values of the literal constants.

Objectives

1. Given a literal equation, solve it for the variable.
2. Given a formula, evaluate it for various values of the literal constants.

Cover the answers as you work these examples.

EXAMPLE 1

Solve $5y + 3c = 17$ for y in terms of c.

	Think These Reasons
$5y + 3c = 17$	Write the given equation.
$5y = 17 - 3c$	Subtract $3c$ from each member.
$y = \frac{(17 - 3c)}{5}$	Divide each member by 5. (You could multiply by $\frac{1}{5}$).

EXAMPLE 2

Solve $A = LW$ for L in terms of W.

$A = LW$	Write the given equation.
$\frac{A}{W} = L$	Divide each member by W.
$L = \frac{A}{W}$	Use the symmetric axiom so that the desired variable is on the left.

EXAMPLE 3

The length, L, of a rectangle is given in terms of the area, A, and width, W, by the formula $L = \frac{A}{W}$. Find the length if:

a. A is 300 in^2 and W is 8 in.

b. A is 0.4 square miles, and W is 0.025 square miles.

a. $L = \frac{A}{W}$	Write the formula.
$L = \frac{300}{8}$	Substitute for A and W.
$L = 37.5$	Arithmetic
Length is 37.5 in.	Write the answer.

b. $L = \frac{A}{W}$ Write the formula.

$L = \frac{0.4}{0.025}$ Substitute for A and W.

$L = 16$ Arithmetic

16 mi Write the answer.

EXAMPLE 4

The definition of rate of speed is distance divided by time. Let r stand for rate, d stand for distance, and t stand for time.

a. Write a formula for r in terms of d and t.
b. Solve for d in terms of r and t.
c. Evaluate d when the speed is 55 miles per hour and the time is 4.2 hours.

- - - - -

a. $r = \frac{d}{t}$ Get the formula from the words.

- - - - -

b. $rt = d$ Multiply each member by t.

$d = rt$ Use the symmetric axiom to write the desired variable on the left.

- - - - -

c. $d = (55)(4.2)$ Substitute for r and t.

$d = 231$ Arithmetic. (Since the question just asked you to evaluate d, you do not need to write that the distance is 231 miles.)

ORAL PRACTICE

Evaluate the formula for the given value of the literal constant.

$x = 9g$:	A. $g = 5$	B. $g = 200$	C. $g = 0.7$
$y = 7p$:	D. $p = 8$	E. $p = -4$	F. $p = 1000$
$z = 3a + 4$:	G. $a = 2$	H. $a = 2.5$	I. $a = 0$

Solve the literal equation for x:

J. $5x = k$ K. $cx = 92$ L. $fx = t$

M. $x + e = 1$ N. $x - 7 = r$ O. $w + x = n$

P. $\frac{x}{3} = c$ Q. $\frac{u}{x} = 5$

R. What is the origin of the word "literal?"

EXERCISE 4-5

For Problems 1 through 20, solve the literal equation for x.

1. $5x + t = 17$
2. $7x - k = 8$
3. $4 - 2x = g$
4. $15 + 3x = u$
5. $a + 6x = c$
6. $b - 7x = n$
7. $ax - b = k$
8. $hx + j = r$
9. $2x = 4a + 2b$
10. $3x = 12c + 6d$
11. $x + 3v = 9v$
12. $x - 7f = f$
13. $pcx = 2p$
14. $0.25ax = 3ab$
15. $\frac{ax}{6} = 2b$
16. $\frac{mx}{r} = 4r$
17. $\frac{21w}{x} = 3$
18. $\frac{pc}{x} = \frac{c}{p}$
19. $16(x - a) = 4(2a - x)$
20. $13(x + 2g) - 3(4x + 5g) = 0$

For Problems 21 through 30, evaluate the formula for the given values of the literal constants.

21. $W = DV$, $D = 7$ and $V = 4$
22. $F = MA$, $M = 100$ and $A = 9.8$
23. $C = 2pr$, $p = 3.14$, $r = 20$
24. $A = pr^2$, $p = 3.14$, $r = 20$
25. $V = \left(\frac{4}{3}\right)pr^3$, $p = 3.14$, $r = 2$
26. $V = LWH$, $L = 5$, $W = 3$, $H = 2$
27. $r = \frac{d}{t}$, $d = 500$ and $t = 20$
28. $V = pr^2h$, $p = 3.14$, $r = 4$, $h = 7$
29. $A = 0.5bh$, $b = 22$, $h = 3$
30. $P = \frac{5000T}{V}$, $T = 300$, $V = 20$

31. *Force, Mass, and Acceleration Problem* If you pull or push an object with a certain force, the object can accelerate (go faster). Newton's second law of motion says that

$$F = MA,$$

where F stands for force, M stands for mass, and A stands for acceleration.

a. What force is required to give a 3 kilogram mass an acceleration of 5 meters per second^2? (The units of force in the metric system are Newtons.) Do you evaluate a formula or solve an equation?
b. Solve $F = MA$ for A in terms of F and M.
c. If a force of 200 Newtons acts on a mass of 30 kilograms, what will the acceleration be?

32. *Spike Heel Problem* The pressure exerted on the floor by a person's shoe heel depends on the weight of the person and the width of the heel. The formula is

$$P = \frac{1.2W}{H^2},$$

where P is pressure in pounds per square inch, W is weight in pounds, and H is heel width in inches.

a. How much pressure does a 270 pound wrestler exert on the floor if his heel is 3 inches wide?
b. How much pressure does a 120-pound model exert on the floor if she is wearing a spike heel $\frac{1}{4}$ inch wide? Surprising?!
c. Suppose that the floor in an airplane can stand pressures up to 40 pounds per square inch. What is the heaviest a person wearing a 3-inch heel could be without exceeding this pressure?

4-6 PROBLEMS THAT INVOLVE MORE THAN ONE EXPRESSION

Suppose that Butch Err starts peeling potatoes. Four minutes later his sister Janet joins him, and both peel potatoes. There are several variable quantities in this situation.

The number of minutes Butch has been peeling.

The number of minutes Janet has been peeling.

The number of potatoes Butch has peeled.

The number of potatoes Janet has peeled.

The total number of potatoes that have been peeled.

If you are given some information about how fast each one peels and you pick a variable to represent one of the variable quantities, you can write expressions for the other quantities. In this section you will work problems in which there is more than one expression involving the variable.

Objective

Be able to solve problems in which there are two or more variable expressions.

Cover the answers as you work the examples. Uncover the answer to one part to make sure you are right before going on to the next part.

EXAMPLE 1

Potato Peeling Problem Butch starts peeling potatoes at the rate of 3 potatoes per minute. Four minutes later Janet joins him and peels at the rate of 5 potatoes per minute. Butch continues at 3 per minute.

a. Define a variable for the number of minutes Butch has been peeling.

b. Write expressions for:
   i. the number of minutes Janet has been peeling;
   ii. the number of potatoes Butch has peeled;
   iii. the number of potatoes Janet has peeled;
   iv. the total number of potatoes that have been peeled.

c. Write an equation stating that they have peeled a total of 36 potatoes. Then solve the equation to find out how long Butch has been peeling when 36 have been peeled.

d. How many of the 36 potatoes did each one peel?

- - - - -

a. Let x = the number of minutes Butch has been peeling. (See Note 1.)

- - - - -

b. i. $\underline{\underline{x - 4}}$ = number of minutes Janet has been peeling. (See Note 2.)

ii. $\underline{\underline{3x}}$ = number of potatoes Butch has peeled. (See Note 3.)

iii. $\underline{\underline{5(x - 4)}}$ = number of potatoes Janet has peeled. (See Note 4.)

iv. $\underline{\underline{3x + 5(x - 4)}}$ = total number of potatoes.

- - - - -

		Think These Reasons
c.	$3x + 5(x - 4) = 36$	Set total number of potatoes equal to 36.
	$3x + 5x - 20 = 36$	Distribute the 5.
	$8x - 20 = 36$	Combine like terms.
	$8x = 56$	Add 20 to each member.
	$x = 7$	Divide each member by 8.
	Butch peeled for 7 min.	Answer the question.

- - - - -

d. *Butch*: *Janet*:

Butch:	*Janet*:	
$3(7)$	$5(7 - 4)$	Substitute 7 for x in the appropriate expressions and evaluate.
$= 21$	$= 5(3)$	
	$= 15$	

Butch peeled 21 potatoes.
Janet peeled 15 potatoes. — Answer the question. (See Note 5.)

Notes:

1. You should *always* write a definition of the variable, even if it is given in the problem. This way you will not forget which of the variable quantities it stands for.
2. Since Janet starts 4 minutes *after* Butch, she has been peeling for 4 *fewer* minutes. So her time is 4 *less* than x.
3. Three potatoes per minute for x minutes gives $3x$ potatoes.
4. Multiply Janet's rate, 5, by *her* time, $(x - 4)$.
5. You can check your answers by seeing that 21 and 15 have a sum of 36, the total number of potatoes peeled.

Some problems involve distances. For these problems, it is helpful to draw a diagram showing the distances. You can mark the expressions representing the distances on the diagram, much as you did in Section 1.2. Here is an example.

EXAMPLE 2

Worm and Snail Problem A worm starts at the oak tree and moves away, heading for the elm tree at a constant rate of 13 meters per hour (m/h). At the same time, a snail starts at the elm tree and moves toward the oak tree at a constant rate of 17 m/h. The two trees are 100 m apart. Let x be the number of hours the two creatures have been creeping.

a. Draw a diagram showing the two trees 100 m apart and the worm and snail somewhere between the trees. Draw arrows marking each creature's distance from the *oak* tree.
b. Write the definition of x. Then write an expression for each one's distance from the oak tree.
c. Who is closer to the oak tree after 2 hours? How much closer?
d. Who is closer to the oak tree after 4 hours? How much closer?
e. When do they pass each other?
f. How far are they from the oak tree when they pass each other?

- - - - -

a. (See Note 1.)

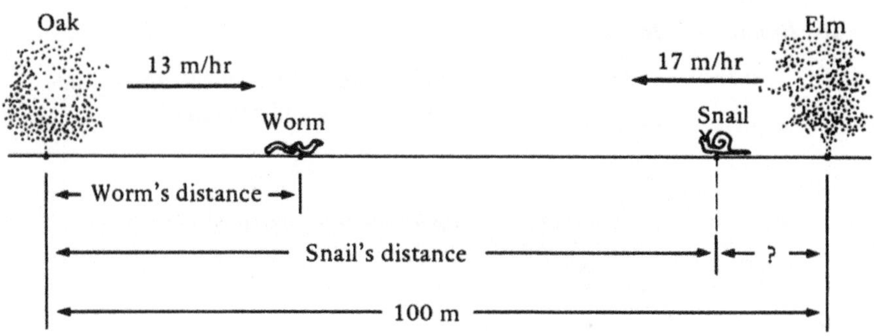

b. x = number of hours they have been going.

$13x$ = number of meters worm is from oak tree. (See Note 2.)

$100 - 17x$ = number of meters snail is from oak tree. (See Note 3.)

- - - - -

c. *Worm:*

$13x$
$= 13(2)$
$= 26$

Snail:

$100 - 17x$
$= 100 - 17(2)$
$= 66$

Worm is closer by 40 m.

- - - - -

d. *Worm:*

$13x$
$= 13(4)$
$= 52$

Snail:

$100 - 17x$
$= 100 - 17(4)$
$= 32$

Snail is closer by 20 m.

Think These Reasons

e. $13x = 100 - 17x$ Let the two distances be *equal*. (See Note 4.)

$30x = 100$ Add $17x$ to each member.

$x = 3\frac{1}{3}$ Divide each member by 30.

$3\frac{1}{3}$ hours Answer the question.

- - - - -

f. *Worm:* or *Snail:*

Worm:		*Snail:*
$13x$		$100 - 17x$
$= 13\left(3\frac{1}{3}\right)$		$= 100 - 17\left(3\frac{1}{3}\right)$
$= 13\left(\frac{10}{3}\right)$		$= 100 - \frac{170}{3}$
$= \frac{130}{3}$		$= 100 - 56\frac{2}{3}$
$= 43\frac{1}{3}$		$= 43\frac{1}{3}$
$43\frac{1}{3}$ meters		$43\frac{1}{3}$ meters (See Note 5.)

Notes:

1. Show enough information in the diagram to show clearly which distance is which.
2. 13 is the rate and x is the time; distance = rate × time.
3. The snail has *gone* a distance of $17x$ m (rate × time). So its *position* is $100 - 17x$ meters from the oak tree.
4. When they pass each other, each one is the *same* distance from the oak tree. So you let their distances equal each other.
5. You can find either the worm's distance or the snail's distance, since both are equal. Finding *both* distances gives you a check on the correctness of your answer.

EXERCISE 4-6

Work the following problems. For those problems in which the answers are not integers, express the answers either as mixed numbers or as decimals, rounded to two decimal places.

1. *Coal Shoveling Problem* Doug Upp can shovel coal at the rate of 16 tons per day. His brother, Sid, can shovel 10 tons per day.
   a. Define a variable for the number of days Doug has been shoveling. Then write an expression for the number of tons Doug has shoveled.
   b. Three days later Sid joins Doug, and both shovel together. Write an expression for the number of *days* Sid has been shoveling in terms of the variable in part (a). Then write an expression for the number of *tons* Sid has shoveled.
   c. Write an equation stating that the total number of tons Doug and Sid have shoveled is 100. Then solve the equation to find out how many days Doug dug when they have shoveled this much coal.
   d. How much of the 100 tons did Sid shovel?

2. *Dishwashing Problem* Moe Tell starts washing dishes at the Greasy Spoon Cafe. Fifteen minutes later Fran Tick joins Moe, and both wash until all the dishes are done.
   a. Define a variable for the number of minutes Moe has been washing dishes. Then write an expression in terms of that variable for the number of minutes Fran has been washing.
   b. Moe washes 9 dishes per minute and Fran washes 16 dishes per minute. Write expressions representing the number of dishes Moe has washed and the number of dishes Fran has washed.
   c. Write an equation stating that the total number of dishes washed is 760. Then solve it to find out how long Moe worked.
   d. How many dishes did each one wash?

3. *Money Problem* Phil T. Rich has \$100 and spends \$3.00 of it per day. Ernest Worker has only \$20 but is adding to it at the rate of \$5.00 per day. Let x be the number of days that have passed.
   a. Write the definition of x. Then write two expressions, one representing how much Phil has after x days and the other representing how much Ernest has after x days.
   b. Who has more money, and how much more, after:
      i. 1 week; ii. 2 weeks?
   c. After how many days will each have the *same* amount of money? Write and solve an equation to find this number of days. **After 10 days.**
   d. Show that each actually *does* have the same amount of money after the number of days you calculated in part (c).

4. *Another Money Problem* Les Moore now has \$100 and adds to it at \$5 per week. Lotta Spences now has \$300, but she is spending \$10 of it per week. Let x be the number of weeks that have passed.
   a. Write the definition of x. Then write expressions for the numbers of dollars each have after x weeks.

b. Write an equation stating that each has the same number of dollars. Solve it to find out when they have this number of dollars.
c. How many dollars will this be?

5. *Temperature Problem* The temperature in Scorpion Gulch is 38°C and is dropping at the rate of 1.7 degrees per hour. The temperature at Conn Junction is 25°C and is going up at 2.1 degrees per hour.
   a. Write expressions representing the temperature at each place after x hours.
   b. Write an equation stating that both places are at the same temperature. Solve it to find out *when* they are at the same temperature.
   c. What is the temperature when both are the same?

6. *Weight Change Problem* Fred weighs 187 pounds but is on a diet that makes him lose 1.7 pounds per week. Joe weighs only 93 pounds but is on a diet that makes him gain 0.9 pounds per week.
   a. Write an expression representing Fred's weight after x weeks and another expression representing Joe's weight after x weeks.
   b. What is each one's weight after:
      i. 10 weeks; ii. one year?
   c. After how many weeks will each be the *same* weight? Show your work.

7. *Equation-Solving Problem* Kay Oss can solve equations at the rate of 26 per hour. Her boy friend, Dan D. Lyons, can solve them at 20 per hour. When they start their homework assignments, Kay has already solved 3 equations in study hall, and Dan has already solved 8.
   a. Write two expressions, one each for the number of equations Kay and Dan will have solved.
   b. How many equations has each solved after 20 minutes?
   c. How long will it take until each has solved the *same* number? How many equations is this?
   d. There are 27 equations to be solved all together. Who finishes first? Show your work.

8. *Waitress and Cook Problem* The waitress at the Greasy Spoon Cafe makes wages of \$32 per day and the cook makes \$50 per day. In addition, they divide the tips received in such a way that the waitress gets 70% of the tip money and the cook gets 30% of it. ("70% of . . ." means "0.7 times . . . .") Let x be the number of dollar tips in a day.
   a. Write an expression representing the total amount of money (wages plus tips) the waitress makes and the total amount the cook makes a day.
   b. How much does each make if there are:
      i. \$20 in tips; ii. \$100 in tips?

c. What amount of tip money makes each person get the *same* total number of dollars per day?

9. *Plumber Problem* Nick O'Time, the plumber, charges $30 per hour. His brother, Ivan, the plumber's helper, charges $20 per hour. Nick starts working on a job. Four hours later, Ivan joins him and both work until the job is finished.
   a. If Nick has been working for x hours, how long has Ivan been working?
   b. Write expressions for the number of dollars Nick has earned and for the number of dollars Ivan has earned after x hours.
   c. The total bill for the job is $470. Write an equation stating this fact, and solve it to find out how long Nick worked.
   d. How much of the $470 does each one get?

10. *Bathtub Problem* Suppose that you turn on the hot water, which flows at 8.7 liters per minute into the bathtub. Two minutes later you also turn on the cold water, which flows at 13.2 liters per minute. Let x be the number of minutes since you turned on the *cold* water.
    a. Write expressions in terms of x for the number of minutes the hot water has been running, the number of liters the hot faucet has delivered, and the number of liters the cold faucet has delivered.
    b. Write an equation stating that the hot and cold faucets have delivered the *same* number of liters. Solve the equation to find out when this happens.
    c. The tub holds 100 liters. Will it have overflowed by the time the hot and cold faucets have delivered the same amounts? Justify your answer.

11. *Truck and Patrol Car Problem* A truck passes a highway patrol station going 70 kilometers per hour (km/h). When the truck is 10 kilometers past the station, a patrol car starts after it, going 100 km/h. Let t be the number of hours the patrol car has been going.
    a. Write the definition of t. Then write two expressions, one representing the patrol car's distance from the station and the other representing the truck's distance from the station after t hours.

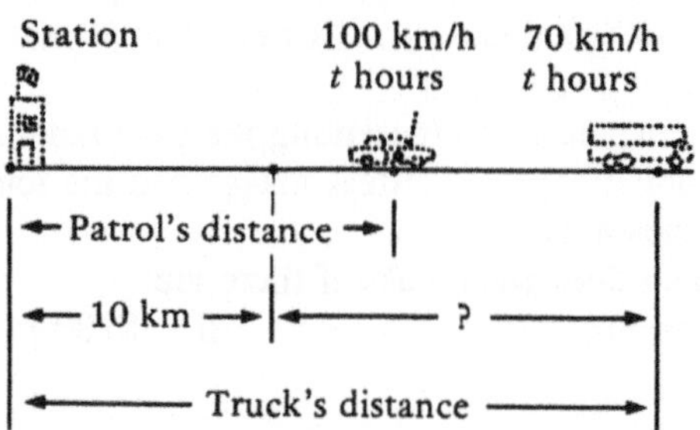

b. If they continue at the same speeds, who will be farther from the station, and how many kilometers farther, after:
   i. 10 minutes; ii. 30 minutes?

c. At what time t does the patrol car reach the truck?

d. Show that the two distances really *are* the same at the time you calculated in part (c).

12. *Cougar and Fawn Problem* A cougar spots a fawn 132 meters away. The cougar starts toward the fawn at a speed of 18 meters per second (m/sec). At the same instant, the fawn starts running away at 11 m/sec. Let x be the number of seconds they have been running.
   a. Write the definition of x. Then write expressions for the cougar's and fawn's distances from the *cougar's* starting point after x seconds.
   b. How far is the cougar from the fawn after 8 seconds?
   c. Write an equation stating that the distance between the cougar and the fawn (fawn's distance minus cougar's distance) equals 60 meters. Then solve the equation to find out *when* they are 60 meters apart.
   d. The cougar has enough energy to run for a total of 17 seconds. Will it catch the fawn before it runs out of energy? Justify your answer.

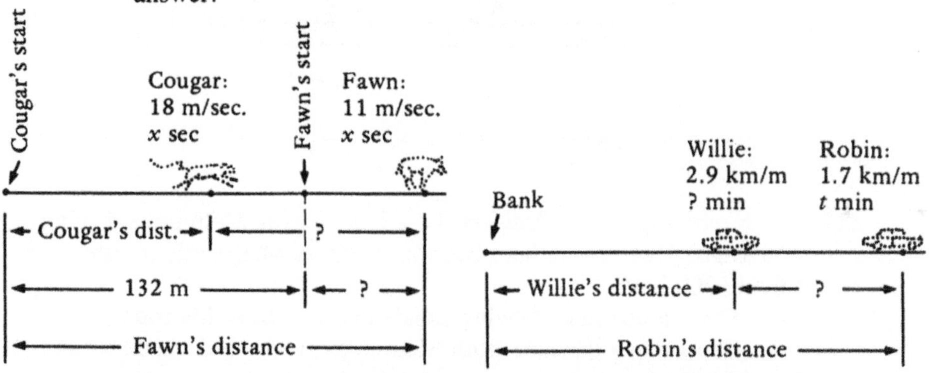

13. *Pursuit Problem* Robin Banks robs a bank and takes off in his get-away car at 1.7 kilometers per minute (km/m). 5 minutes later Willie Katchup leaves the bank and chases Robin at 2.9 km/m. Let t be the number of minutes Robin has been driving.
   a. Write the definition of t. Then write an expression representing Robin's distance from the bank in terms of t.
   b. In terms of t, how long has Willie been driving? Write an expression representing Willie's distance from the bank in terms of t.
   c. When Willie catches up with Robin, their distances from the bank are *equal*. Write an equation stating this fact and solve it to find out *when* Willie Katchup will catch up with Robin Banks.
   d. *Where* does Willie catch Robin?

14. ***Tunnel Problem*** Ornery and Sly Company has a contract to dig a tunnel through Bald Mountain. Crew A starts at the west end and digs at 9 meters per day. Let x be the number of days Crew A has been digging.
    a. Write an expression for the number of meters Crew A has dug after x days.
    b. Crew B starts at the east end two days after Crew A and digs at 12 meters per day. In terms of x, how many days has Crew B been digging? How many meters have they dug in this number of days?
    c. After how many days will both crews have dug the *same* number of meters?
    d. The total length of the tunnel is to be 2000 meters. Write an equation stating this fact. Then solve the equation to find out how many days it takes to dig the tunnel from the time Crew A starts.

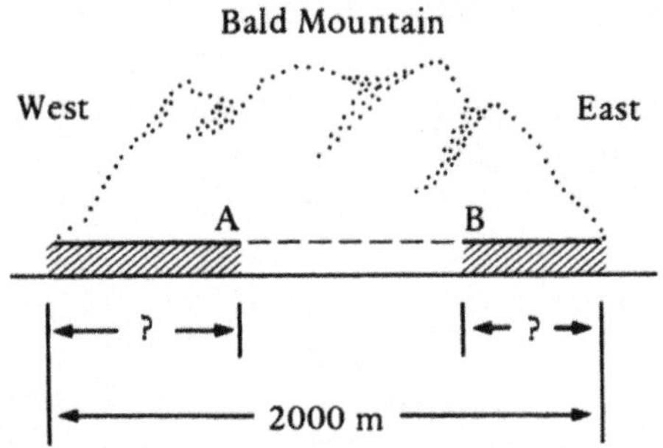

15. ***Lois and Superman Problem*** Lois Lane leaves Metropolis driving 50 km/h. Three hours later Superman leaves Metropolis to catch her, flying 300 km/h.
    a. Draw a diagram showing Lois's distance from Metropolis, Superman's distance from Metropolis, and the distance between them.
    b. Let x be the number of hours Lois has been driving. In terms of x, how far has she gone?
    c. In terms of x, how many hours has Superman been flying? How *far* has he flown in this number of hours?
    d. Write an equation involving x that is true when Superman catches up with Lois.
    e. When does Superman catch up with Lois? How far are they from Metropolis then?

16. ***Rescue Problem*** Phoebe Small is swimming in the ocean, 187 meters out from the beach. She screams for help and starts swimming for the beach at a speed of 0.7 meters per second (m/sec). Fifteen seconds later Calvin Butterball starts toward her in a rowboat, going 1.6 m/sec.

a. Draw a diagram showing the beach where Calvin starts and the point 187 m away where Phoebe starts. Show Calvin and Phoebe somewhere in between.
b. Let x be the number of seconds since Phoebe screamed. Write expressions for the distance she has gone and for her distance from the beach.
c. Write expressions for the number of seconds Calvin has been rowing and for his distance from the beach.
d. How far apart will they be 33 seconds after Phoebe screamed?
e. Phoebe has enough strength to swim for 1 min 40 sec. Will Calvin reach her before she runs out of strength? Justify your answer.

17. *Car and Bus Problem* A bus is 13 kilometers from town, going away at 80 kilometers per hour (km/h). At the same moment a car leaves town going the same direction as the bus, at the same speed.
 a. Draw a diagram showing town, the bus's starting point (13 kilometers from town), and the bus and car in appropriate places. Show the bus's distance from town and the car's distance from town.
 b. Let x be the number of hours the car and bus have been going. Write expressions for each vehicle's distance from town.
 c. After how long will the bus's distance from town be twice the car's distance?
 d. After how long will the car's distance from town be 90% of the bus's distance? ("90% of . . ." means "0.9 times . . . .")
 e. Write an equation stating that both are the same distance from town. Then show that the equation has *no* solutions. Why is this result reasonable?

18. *Age Problem* Janet Kim is now 13 years old. Her father, Jeong, is now 31.
 a. Write expressions for each person's age x years from now.
 b. Write an equation stating that Jeong is twice as old as Janet. Then solve it to find out *when* Jeong is twice as old.
 c. When is Jeong *three* times as old as Janet?
 d. Write an equation stating that Jeong is *exactly* as old as Janet. When will this be true?
 e. Write an equation stating that Janet's age is 18 years less than Jeong's age. When will this be true?
 f. When will the sum of their ages be:
 i. 85; ii. 36?

19. *Magazine Sales Problem* The student council of a high school arranges with a publisher to sell subscriptions to its magazines. The school will keep 40% of the subscription money and give the other 60% to the publisher. ("40% of . . ." means "0.4 times . . . .") As

an added incentive, the publisher will pay the school an additional \$100, regardless of how many subscriptions are sold. Let x be the total number of dollars worth of subscriptions sold.

a. Write an expression for the number of dollars the publisher makes and another expression for the number of dollars the school makes. Remember—if no magazines are sold, the school makes \$100 and the publisher makes −\$100.
b. For what amount of sales does the publisher "break even"? That is, when does the publisher make \$0?
c. How much does the school make when the publisher breaks even?
d. For what amount of sales do the school and the publisher make the *same* amount of money?

20. ***Airplane Engine Shutdown Problem*** A Fly-by-Night Airlines plane starts off on a trip with all engines running. It flies at 900 kilometers per hour (km/h). Then after it has been flying for x hours, the pilot shuts down one engine to conserve fuel. The speed is reduced to 700 km/h. The plane flies for a total of 3 hours.
    a. Draw a diagram showing the starting and ending points for the trip. Somewhere between, mark the point at which the engine was shut down. Show the distance flown at 900 km/h and the distance flown at 700 km/h.
    b. Write an expression for the time flown at 700 km/h, for the distance flown at 700 km/h, and for the distance flown at 900 km/h.
    c. If the plane flies 1.3 hours before shutting down one engine, how far does it fly all together in 3 hours?
    d. How long should the pilot fly before shutting down the engine in order to go a total distance of 2352 kilometers in 3 hours?
    e. How long should the pilot fly before shutting down the engine in order to go a total distance of 2970 kilometers in 3 hours?

21. ***Missile Problem*** A missile tracking station in the Pacific Ocean detects a ballistic missile coming straight toward it at 300 kilometers per minute from a test site in the continental United States.
    a. Let t be the number of minutes since the missile was detected. At time $t = 0$, the missile was 2800 kilometers from the tracking station. Write an expression in terms of t for the missile's distance from the station.
    b. Where is the missile:
        i. 6 minutes after it is detected;
        ii. 4 minutes *before* it is detected?
    c. At time $t = 7$, the tracking station fires an interceptor directly toward the oncoming missile. The interceptor travels at 431 kilometers per minute. Write an expression for the interceptor's

distance from the tracking station at time t. Think carefully about how many minutes the interceptor has been traveling!

d. Write an equation that is true when the interceptor *meets* the missile. At what value of t will they meet? How far from the tracking station will they be?

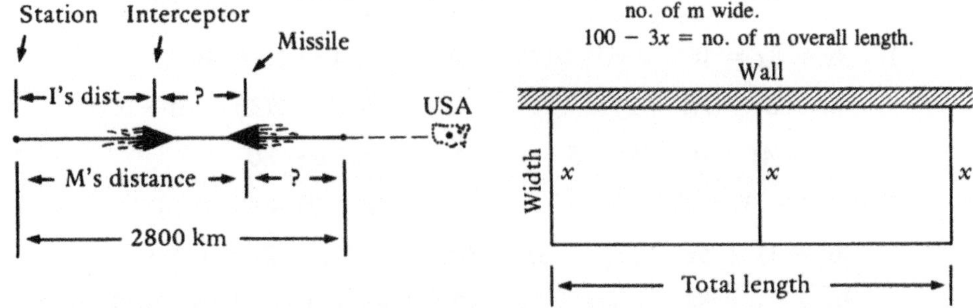

22. *Stock Pens Problem* Two stock pens are to be built next to each other, with one side of each being against an existing wall (see the figure). The width (perpendicular to the wall) is x meters. The total amount of fence material to be used is 100 meters.
    a. Write an expression for the total length, indicated in the diagram.
    b. What overall length will the pens be if they are 10 meters wide?
    c. How wide will the pens be if they are 30 meters long overall?
    d. How wide will the pens be if the width is one-third the overall length?

4-7 CHAPTER REVIEW AND TEST

In this chapter you learned how to solve equations like

$$3(x + 5) = 2x + 7,$$

in which the variable appears in more than one place. By using the distributive properties, adding appropriate numbers to each member, and combining like terms, you learned how to transform these equations to more familiar forms and solve them. Finally, you learned how to solve problems in which there was more than one expression involving the variable.

The Chapter Test below is fairly long. You should put yourself under pressure and see how much of it you can work in one, continuous session the length of a normal classroom test. Don't dawdle! Make yourself concentrate the whole time just as though you were actually taking a test!!

CHAPTER TEST

For Problems 1 through 15, solve the equation and check your answer. Round off approximate answers to two decimal places.

1. $3x + 8x = 165$
2. $7x + 4 - 2x = 49$
3. $4(t + 5) - 3(t + 2) = 14$
4. $31 = 5 - 2(3x + 4) - x$
5. $5(r + 4) - (r - 3) = 5$
6. $7x = 3x - 80$
7. $5(2x - 3) = 6x + 9$
8. $2(4c - 7) = 8c + 14$
9. $6x + 33 + 5x = 11(x + 3)$
10. $5 + 3(x - 2) = x + x - 13$
11. $9x = 2x + 58$
12. $7.4x + 3.8 = 5.9x - 9.7$
13. $7(2.3 - 0.4x) = x + 1.5$
14. $5.3 - 5.3d = 2.8 + 2.8d$
15. Juan Moore solves the equation

$$3(2x + 7) = 5x + 21 + x$$

and gets $x = 4$ for an answer.

a. Substitute 4 for x and show that it *is* a solution.
b. Is 4 the *only* solution? Explain.

16. Solve for x: $3x + 12y = 57$

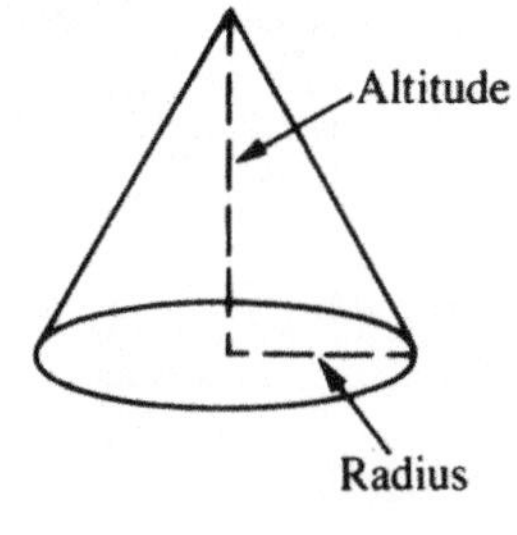

17. The volume of a cone is given by

$$V = \left(\frac{1}{3}\right)pr^2h,$$

where V is the volume, p is about 3.14, r is the radius of the cone's base, and h is the cone's altitude (see sketch). Find out how many cubic centimeters a conical drinking cup will hold if its radius is 4 cm and its altitude is 10 cm.

18. ***Bricklaying Problem*** A bricklayer's assistant starts building a wall, laying 50 bricks per hour. Two hours later the master bricklayer joins the assistant, and both lay bricks. The master bricklayer lays 80 bricks per hour.

a. Let x be the number of hours since the assistant started laying bricks. In terms of x, how many hours has the master been laying bricks?
b. Write expressions for the number of bricks the assistant has laid and the number of bricks the master has laid.

c. Write an equation stating that the assistant and the master have laid the *same* number of bricks. How long has each one worked when they have laid the same number?
d. They must lay a total of 1000 bricks. Will they finish before the assistant has worked 8 hours? Justify your answer.

19. *Marathon Problem* Mary Thon starts at a point 26 miles from school and runs toward school at 6 miles per hour (mph). Randy Miles starts from school 1.3 hours later and runs toward Mary at 8 mph.
a. Draw a diagram showing the school and Mary's starting point 26 miles apart. Show Mary and Randy somewhere in between. Mark each person's distance from school.
b. Let x be the number of hours Mary has been running. Write expressions for the distance she has run and for her distance from school.
c. In terms of x, how many hours has Randy been running? How far is he from school?
d. How long has Mary been running when she and Randy meet?
e. How far from school do they meet?

20. *Ceramic Sales Problem* Clay Potts owns a ceramics store. His brother, Jack, works for him, earning wages of \$50 per day plus 10% of the profits. All Clay gets is the other 90% of the profits. ("90% of . . ." means "0.9 times . . . .")
a. Let x be the number of dollars profit the store makes in a day. Write expressions for the total number of dollars Jack gets (wages plus profits) and for the total number of dollars Clay gets.
b. On Monday the store makes a profit of only \$30. How much does each one make?
c. Business is better on Tuesday, and the store makes a profit of \$100. Who makes more, Clay or Jack? How much more?
d. What number of dollars profit must the store make in a day for each one to get the *same* amount of money?

5

Some Operations with Polynomials and Radicals

In the first four chapters, you learned how to solve various kinds of equations. In this chapter and the next, you will learn ways to solve equations in which the variable is squared. *Expressions that appear in these equations are called* polynomials. *This chapter concentrates on operations with polynomials. In the next chapter you will learn the actual procedures for solving such* quadratic *equations.*

Expression:
$x^2 + 5x + 2$
A polynomial

Expression:
$\sqrt{1776}$
A radical

Equation:
$x^2 + 5x + 2 = 0$
A quadratic equation

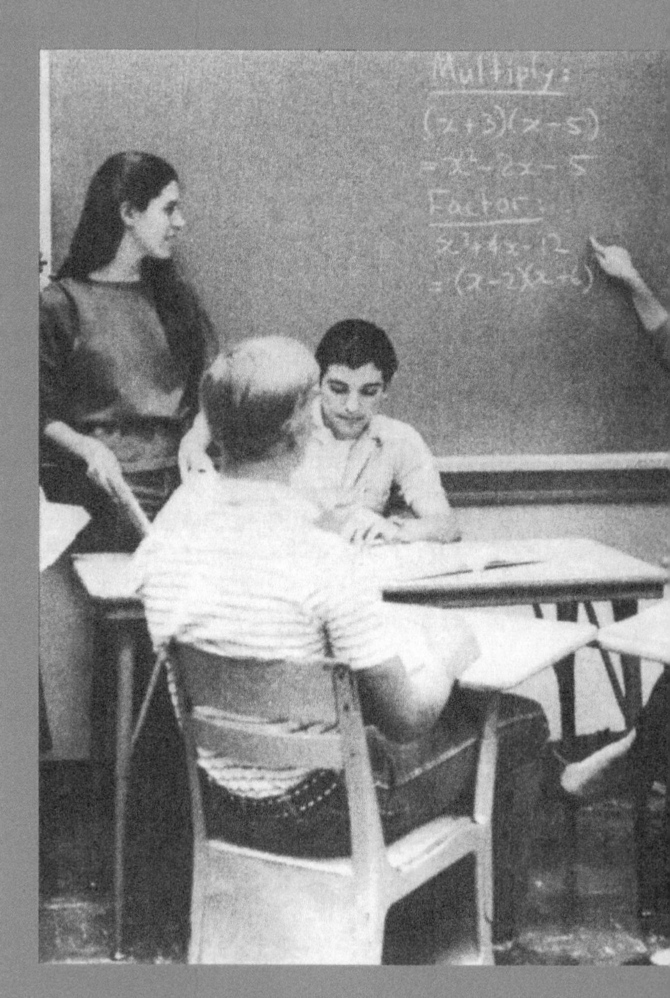

5-1 INTRODUCTION TO POLYNOMIALS

This section is meant for you to read and understand on your own. You should be able to do this and work the problems without help from your teacher.

The expressions below are polynomials.

$$3x^2 + 5x - 7$$

$$8x^4 - 11x + 2x^5 - x^2$$

$$5x^7 + 9x^4 - 3x^2 + 8$$

The polynomial $5x^7 + 9x^4 - 3x^2 + 8$ is arranged in *descending powers of x*, because the exponents of x in each term go *down* in value,

7, 4, 2, 0 (no variable),

as you go from left to right. The polynomial below is arranged in *ascending powers of y*.

$$9y - 7y^3 + y^5$$

As you go from term to term, the exponents go *up* in value: 1, 3, 5.

A polynomial is considered to be simpler if it is arranged in either ascending or descending powers of the variable.

Objective

Given a polynomial with several terms, arrange it in ascending or descending powers of the variable.

In order to accomplish this objective, all you need to do is commute terms so that the exponents either increase or decrease from term to term.

Cover the answers as you work these examples.

EXAMPLE 1

Arrange in descending powers of z: $5z - 6z^3 + 4z^2 - 11$.

	Think These Reasons
$5z - 6z^3 + 4z^2 - 11$	Write the given expression.
$= -6z^3 + 4z^2 + 5z - 11$	Commute terms so that the value of the exponents of z *decrease*: 3, 2, 1, no variable. (Remember that the − sign goes along with the term it precedes.)

EXAMPLE 2

Arrange in ascending powers of x: $4x^6 - 7x - 5x^3 + x^2$.

$4x^6 - 7x - 5x^3 + x^2$	Write the given expression.
$= -7x + x^2 - 5x^3 + 4x^6$	Commute terms so that the exponents of x *increase*: 1, 2, 3, 6. Note that x is equivalent to x^1.

Now, work the problems below to make sure you have the right idea. There are also some problems to renew your skills from previous chapters.

EXERCISE 5-1

You should work *all* these problems, not just the odds or just the evens.

For Problems 1 through 5, commute terms so that the polynomial is in
a. descending powers of the variable,
b. ascending powers of the variable.

1. $3x + 5x^2 + 4$
2. $6 + 4x^2 - 3x$
3. $x^3 + x^2 + x^5 + 9$
4. $x^4 - x^5 + x + 1$
5. $8x + 2x^5 - 9x^3 + 5x^4 + x^2$

Problems 6 through 12 reinforce concepts you have learned in earlier sections.

6. Solve and check: $3x + 9 = -21$.
7. Simplify $5x - 7 + 3x$.
8. Solve and check: $8x - 12 = 4x$.
9. Simplify $5(x + 4) - 3(2x - 7)$.
10. Solve and check: $2(4x - 3) = 5(2x - 12)$.
11. Evaluate $4x - 7(3x + 2)$ if x is -5.
12. Solve and check: $2.7x = 4(3.1x - 7.6)$.

5-2 NAMES OF POLYNOMIALS

In the last section you learned that an expression like

$$3x^2 + 5x - 7$$

is called a polynomial. The only operations that appear in a polynomial are *addition, subtraction,* and *multiplication.*

DEFINITION

POLYNOMIAL
A **polynomial** is an expression that has no operations other than addition, subtraction, and multiplication by or of the variable(s).

Notes:

1. Expressions such as

$$\frac{x - 2}{3x + 4} \quad \text{or} \quad |x - 5|,$$

which have *division* by a variable or the *absolute value* of a variable, are *not* polynomials.
2. Powers of variables, such as x^3, *are* permitted in polynomials because they imply *multiplication:* $x \cdot x \cdot x$.
3. Single terms like $2x$, $5y^2$, x, or even just a constant such as 7 are also called polynomials.

As a result of this definition, polynomials always consist of one or more terms, each of which looks something like the expression shown at the top of the next page.

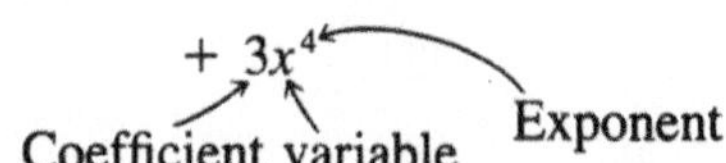

If the polynomial is just a power of the variable, then the coefficient is equal to 1.

x^4 equals $1 \cdot x^4$. — The coefficient is 1.

If the variable appears without an exponent, then the exponent is 1.

$3x$ equals $3x^1$. — The exponent is 1.

Just as $1 \cdot x$ equals x, x^1 also equals x. An expression is considered to be simpler when written with x rather than with $1x$ or x^1.

If there is no variable in a term, then that term is called the **constant** term.

$4x^2 + 2x + 5 \leftarrow$ 5 is the constant term.

If there is a $-$ sign in front of a term, as in $x^2 - 3x$, the coefficient is considered to be *negative*.

$x^2 - 3x$ equals $x^2 + (-3)x$. — The coefficient is -3.

$x^5 - x^2$ equals $x^5 + (-1)x^2$. — The coefficient is -1.

Polynomials with one, two, or three terms are given special names.

Number of Terms	*Example*	*Name*
One	$8x$	Monomial
Two	$13x - 4$	Binomial
Three	$5x^2 - 9x + 11$	Trinomial

As you can see, all these names end with *-nomial*. This suffix comes from the Latin word *nomens*, which means *name*. So binomial means, literally, *two names*. The prefix *poly-* means *many*, although the word polynomial can be used for any number of terms, including one, two, or three.

Polynomials with only one variable are also named according to the highest power of that variable that appears in the expression. This number is called the *degree* of the polynomial. For example,

$$5x^3 + 13x^2$$

is of *third* degree, because x^3 is the highest power of x.

DEFINITION

DEGREE
The **degree** of a polynomial with one variable is the exponent of the highest power of that variable.

First, second, and third degree polynomials have special names.

Degree	*Example*	*Name*
First	$17x - 4$	**Linear**
Second	$9x^2 - 2x + 11$	**Quadratic**
Third	x^3	**Cubic**

These words come from the fact that lines, squares (*quadrangles*), and cubes have 1, 2, and 3 dimensions, respectively.

By putting together the names for degree and number of terms, you can name various polynomials. For instance, $x^2 + 5x + 2$ is a *quadratic trinomial,* because it is of *second* degree and has *three* terms.

Objective

Given an expression, tell whether or not it is a polynomial. If it is, tell the coefficient of each term, and name the polynomial by degree and by number of terms.

Cover the answers as you work these examples.

EXAMPLE 1

Tell whether or not the expression is a polynomial. If it is, tell *why*. If it is not, tell why *not*.

a. $5x^3 - 4x + 1$

- - - - - - - - - -

Think These Reasons

Polynomial — No operations other than +, −, ×

b. $3x$

- - - - - - - - - -

Polynomial — No operations other than +, −, ×

c. $\frac{3}{x}$

- - - - - - - - - -

Not a polynomial — Division by a variable

d. $|x + 3|$

- - - - - - - - - -

Not a polynomial — Absolute value of a variable

EXAMPLE 2

Give the coefficient of each term in $5x^4 - 7x^3 + x^2 - x + 8$.

- - - - - - - - - -

$5; -7; 1; -1; 8$ — Read the explanation above.

EXAMPLE 3

Name each polynomial according to degree and number of terms.

a. $13x - 7$

- - - - - - - - - -

Linear binomial — First degree, two terms

b. $5x^3$

- - - - - - - - - -

Cubic monomial — Third degree, one term

c. $6x^2 + 11x - 8$

- - - - - - - - - -

Quadratic trinomial — Second degree, three terms

d. $5x^4 + x^7$

- - - - - - - - - -

Seventh-degree binomial — Two terms (No special name for seventh degree)

e. $x^3 + x^2 + x + 1$

- - - - - - - - - -

Cubic polynomial with four terms — Third degree (No special name for four terms)

EXERCISE 5-2

If your teacher prefers, part or all of this exercise may be done orally instead of in writing.

For Problems 1 though 12, tell whether or not the expression is a polynomial. If so, tell why. If not, tell why not.

1. $x^3 + 4x$
2. $x^4 - 5x$
3. $x^3 + \frac{4}{x}$
4. $x^4 - \frac{5}{x}$
5. y^5
6. z^6
7. x
8. 5
9. 3
10. $|x - 7|$
11. $|x + 4|$
12. $2x$

For Problems 13 through 20, give the coefficient of each term.

13. $3x^5 + 2x^3 - 4x + 7$
14. $5x^4 - 3x^2 + 6x - 9$
15. $z^3 - 5z^2 + 2z$
16. $y^5 + 4y^2 - 3y$
17. $4x^2 + x$
18. $3z^2 + z$
19. $x^3 - x + 5$
20. $c^4 - c^2 + 3$

For Problems 21 through 36, name the polynomial by degree and by number of terms.

21. $x^2 + 3x + 4$
22. $x^3 - 7$
23. $5x^3$
24. $5x^2 - 8x + 17$
25. $x^2 - 7$
26. x^2
27. x
28. $4x + 5$
29. x^5
30. $2431x$
31. $8x^4 + 7x^3$
32. $19x^6 - 4x + 7$
33. $2x^3 + 5x^2 + 11x - 1$
34. $x^7 - x^5 + x^3 - x + 9$
35. $5x + 2$
36. $8 - 7x - 6x^2$

For Problems 37 through 46, give an example of the polynomial described.

37. Linear binomial
38. Quadratic binomial
39. Quadratic trinomial
40. Linear monomial
41. Cubic trinomial
42. Cubic binomial
43. Quadratic monomial
44. Fourth-degree trinomial
45. Sixth-degree binomial
46. Cubic polynomial with four terms

For Problems 47 through 56, commute terms so that the polynomial is in descending powers of x. (See Section 5-1 for examples.)

47. $5x + 7x^2 + 2$
48. $6 + 3x^2 + 18x$
49. $x^5 + x^3 - x^7 + 11$
50. $4x + x^4 - x^2 - x^3$
51. $2x^3 + x^4 - 3 - x$
52. $5x^7 - 2 + x^5 - 5x$
53. $7x + x^5 - 9x^3 + 3x^4 + x^2$
54. $x + 3 + x^2 - 5x^3 + 2x^4$
55. $4^5 - x^5$
56. $3^8 + x^6$
57. The expression $\frac{7}{x-3}$ is *not* a polynomial, since it involves division by an expression containing a variable. For what value of x is the expression *not* equal to a real number? Explain.

Problems 58 through 61 review concepts and techniques from previous sections.

58. Simplify $9(x + 7) - 8x$.
59. Evaluate $14 - 2(4x + 7)$ if x is -3.
60. Solve and check: $5(x + 3) = 7(x - 4)$.
61. *Lawn Mowing Problem* Moe Delaune, who can mow the lawn at a rate of 10 square meters per minute, mows for x minutes. Dru Upp, who can mow at 12 square meters per minute, joins Moe 7 minutes after he started, and both mow the lawn together.
    a. Write expressions in terms of x for the numbers of square meters each has mowed.
    b. How long has Moe been mowing:
        i. when they have mowed a total of 202 square meters;
        ii. when they have mowed the *same* number of square meters?

5-3 PRODUCT OF TWO BINOMIALS

You know how to use the distributive properties to multiply a constant by a binomial. For example,

$$\begin{aligned} &4(x + 5) \\ &= 4 \cdot x + 4 \cdot 5 \\ &= 4x + 20. \end{aligned}$$

Suppose that instead of 4 times $x + 5$, you have another *binomial* times $(x + 5)$, such as

$$(x + 3)(x + 5).$$

You can still distribute $(x + 3)$ the same way you did 4. Both expressions simply stand for numbers! You get

Distribute!

$$(x + 3)(x + 5)$$
$$= (x + 3) \cdot x + (x + 3) \cdot 5.$$

This can be simplified by distributing x and 5, getting

$$x^2 + 3x + 5x + 15.$$

Combining like terms gives

$$x^2 + 8x + 15.$$

If you look at the next-to-the-last step, above,

$$(x + 3)(x + 5) = x^2 + 3x + 5x + 15,$$

you should see that each term in $x + 5$ is multiplied by each term in $(x + 3)$. This fact gives a *quick* way to multiply two binomials.

1. Multiply each term by x.

$$(x + 3)(x + 5) = x^2 + 5x \ldots$$

2. Multiply each term by 3.

$$(x + 3)(x + 5) = x^2 + 5x + 3x + 15$$

3. Combine like terms.

$$(x + 3)(x + 5) = x^2 + 8x + 15$$

With practice, you can combine the like terms mentally and write only the question and the answer, like this:

$$(x + 3)(x + 5) = \underline{\underline{x^2 + 8x + 15}}.$$

TECHNIQUE

MULTIPLYING TWO BINOMIALS

1. Multiply each term of one binomial by each term of the other.
2. Combine the like terms.

Objective

Be able to multiply two binomials *quickly*, by writing only the question and the answer, if possible.

Cover the answers as you work these examples.

EXAMPLE 1

Multiply $(x + 7)(x + 2)$.

- - - - - - - - - -

	Think These Reasons
$(x + 7)(x + 2)$	Write the given expression.
$= x^2 + 2x + 7x + 14$	Multiply each term in $(x + 2)$ by each term in $(x + 7)$.
$= \underline{\underline{x^2 + 9x + 14}}$	Combine like terms.

EXAMPLE 2

Multiply $(x + 5)(x + 8)$.

- - - - - - - - - -

$(x + 5)(x + 8)$	Write the given expression.
$= \underline{\underline{x^2 + 13x + 40}}$	The middle term is $8x + 5x$. (Try doing this in your head if you are brave!)

EXAMPLE 3

Multiply $(x - 3)(x + 8)$.

- - - - - - - - - -

$(x - 3)(x + 8)$	Write the given expression.
$= x^2 + 8x - 3x - 24$	$-3(x)$ is $-3x$ and $-3(8)$ is -24.
$= \underline{\underline{x^2 + 5x - 24}}$	Combine like terms.

EXAMPLE 4

Multiply $(x + 2)(x - 10)$.

- - - - - - - - - -

$(x + 2)(x - 10)$	Write the given expression.
$= x^2 - 10x + 2x - 20$	$x(-10)$ is $-10x$ and $2(-10)$ is -20.
$= \underline{\underline{x^2 - 8x - 20}}$	Combine like terms (in your head, if possible).

EXAMPLE 5

Multiply $(x - 7)(x - 9)$.

$(x - 7)(x - 9)$	Write the given expression.
$= x^2 - 9x - 7x + 63$	$(-7)(-9)$ is $+63$.
$= \underline{\underline{x^2 - 16x + 63}}$	Combine like terms (in your head, if possible).

EXAMPLE 6

Multiply $(3x - 5)(4x + 1)$.

$(3x - 5)(4x + 1)$	Write the given expression.
$= 12x^2 + 3x - 20x - 5$	The first term is $(3x)(4x)$, or $12x^2$.
$= \underline{\underline{12x^2 - 17x - 5}}$	Combine like terms.

EXAMPLE 7

Simplify $(x - 3)^2$.

$(x - 3)^2$	Write the given expression.
$= (x - 3)(x - 3)$	Definition of squaring
$= \underline{\underline{x^2 - 6x + 9}}$	Multiply, and combine like terms.

It is possible to check your answers to this kind of problem by substituting a simple value of x into both the original expression and into the answer. In Example 4, for instance, let $x = 3$.

$(x + 2)(x - 10)$		$x^2 - 8x - 20$
$= (5)(-7)$		$= 9 - 24 - 20$
$= -35$	⟵ Same! ⟶	$= -35$

If you get the same answer for both, you can be reasonably sure the expressions are equivalent.

ORAL PRACTICE

Give the middle term if these binomials are multiplied.

EXAMPLES

		Answers	
i.	$(x + 3)(x + 7)$	i.	$10x$
ii.	$(x - 4)(2x + 5)$	ii.	$-3x$
iii.	$(3x - 4)(2x + 5)$	iii.	$7x$
iv.	$(x - 8)(x + 8)$	iv.	0

A. $(x + 2)(x + 5)$

B. $(x - 3)(x - 4)$

C. $(x + 7)(x - 4)$

D. $(x + 3)(x - 8)$

E. $(x - 1)(x + 6)$

F. $(x - 10)(x + 10)$

G. $(3x + 2)(x + 4)$

H. $(x + 5)(2x - 3)$

I. $(3x - 5)(x - 2)$

J. $(2x + 5)(3x + 4)$

K. $(4x - 1)(3x - 2)$

L. $(5x - 2)(3x + 2)$

EXERCISE 5-3

For Problems 1 through 40, multiply the binomials. If possible, write down only the given expression and the answer, combining the middle terms in your head. It is advisable for you to check your answers.

1. $(x + 4)(x + 3)$
2. $(x + 7)(x + 9)$
3. $(x + 8)(x - 5)$
4. $(x + 6)(x - 2)$
5. $(x + 2)(x - 7)$
6. $(x + 3)(x - 9)$
7. $(r - 4)(r + 7)$
8. $(b - 3)(b + 8)$
9. $(s - 6)(s + 1)$
10. $(t - 5)(t + 2)$
11. $(x - 8)(x - 4)$
12. $(x - 7)(x - 6)$
13. $(x - 1)(x - 2)$
14. $(x - 5)(x - 8)$
15. $(2x + 3)(x + 4)$
16. $(4x + 5)(x + 2)$
17. $(3x + 1)(x - 2)$
18. $(2x + 1)(x - 4)$
19. $(x - 5)(2x - 1)$
20. $(x - 3)(3x - 2)$
21. $(x + 4)(3x + 5)$
22. $(x + 5)(2x + 6)$
23. $(2x - 3)(4x + 3)$
24. $(3x - 5)(2x + 3)$
25. $(5x + 4)(2x - 7)$
26. $(7x + 5)(2x - 4)$
27. $(4x + 3)(4x + 3)$
28. $(5x + 2)(5x + 2)$

29. $(4x + 3)(4x - 3)$

30. $(5x + 2)(5x - 2)$

31. $(2x - 7)(2x - 7)$

32. $(3x - 7)(3x - 7)$

33. $(2x - 7)(2x + 7)$

34. $(3x - 7)(3x + 7)$

35. $(x + 6)^2$

36. $(x + 8)^2$

37. $(x - 9)^2$

38. $(x - 4)^2$

39. $(3x + 5)^2$

40. $(4x - 5)^2$

For Problems 41 through 50 a binomial is multiplied by a trinomial. Find the product by multiplying each term in the trinomial by each term in the binomial and combining the like terms.

EXAMPLE

$(x + 3)(x^2 - 5x + 7)$

$= x^3 - 5x^2 + 7x + 3x^2 - 15x + 21$

$= \underline{\underline{x^3 - 2x^2 - 8x + 21}}$

41. $(x + 2)(x^2 + 3x + 5)$

42. $(x + 3)(x^2 + 2x + 6)$

43. $(x - 3)(x^2 + 4x + 2)$

44. $(x - 2)(x^2 + 5x + 3)$

45. $(x + 5)(x^2 - 2x + 3)$

46. $(x + 4)(x^2 - 3x + 5)$

47. $(x - 6)(x^2 - 4x - 5)$

48. $(x - 5)(x^2 - 4x - 6)$

49. $(2x + 3)(3x^2 - 4x + 5)$

50. $(3x - 2)(2x^2 + 5x - 4)$

For Problems 51 through 60 you are to multiply *three* binomials. You can do this by associating and multiplying two of them first.

EXAMPLE

$(x + 5)(x + 2)(x - 6)$

$= (x + 5)(x^2 - 4x - 12)$

$= x^3 - 4x^2 - 12x + 5x^2 - 20x - 60$

$= \underline{\underline{x^3 + x^2 - 32x - 60}}$

51. $(x + 2)(x + 3)(x + 4)$

52. $(x + 5)(x + 4)(x + 3)$

53. $(x - 5)(x + 2)(x + 1)$

54. $(x - 2)(x + 6)(x + 1)$

55. $(x + 6)(x - 3)(x - 5)$

56. $(x + 4)(x - 2)(x - 6)$

57. $(x - 1)(x + 2)(x - 7)$

58. $(x - 1)(x + 3)(x - 5)$

59. $(x - 2)(x - 6)(x - 4)$

60. $(x - 3)(x - 7)(x - 2)$

Problems 61 through 70 review skills previously learned.

61. Arrange in descending powers of x: $7x - 3x^2 + 4 - 8x^5$.

62. Name by degree and by number of terms:
a. $6x^5 + 11$; b. $x^3 + 9x^2 - 3x + 14$; c. $9 - 3x$.

63. Write an example of a linear monomial.

64. Write an example of a quadratic trinomial.

65. Tell whether or not these are polynomials. If so, tell *why*. If not, tell why *not*.
a. $x^5 + 2$ b. $\frac{1}{5}x - 7$ c. $\frac{5}{x} - 8$ d. $x^3 - 5x + 1$

66. Solve and check: $4x = 3(7 - 5x)$. Round off the answer to two decimal places.

67. Simplify $3x - 8(4 - 2x)$.

68. Evaluate this absolute value expression $|38 - 2x|$ if $x = 23$.

69. Evaluate $-x^2$ if x is 5.

70. ***Ice Worm Problem*** An ice worm lives at the South Pole in a hole that is 200 feet below the surface of the ice. The worm decides to come out and see what the weather is like, so it starts slithering up at 3 feet per minute.
   a. Define a variable for the number of minutes it has been slithering, then write an expression for how far it has left to go to reach the surface.
   b. How far from the surface will it be after 17 minutes?
   c. How long does it take the worm to get to a point 30 feet from the surface?

For Problems 71 and 72, multiply the binomials the "long" way, by distributing twice, as shown at the beginning of this section.

71. $(3x - 5)(2x + 4)$

72. $(4x - 3)(2x + 5)$

73. Check the answer to Problem 71 by substituting 3 for x in both the original expression and in your answer.

74. Check the answer to Problem 72 by substituting 3 for x in both the original expression and in your answer.

5-4 FACTORING QUADRATIC TRINOMIALS

In the last section you learned how to multiply two binomials together. For example,

$$(x + 3)(x + 5) = x^2 + 8x + 15.$$

In this section you learn how to *reverse* the process. You will start with a quadratic trinomial, such as $x^2 + 8x + 15$, and transform it into *factored form,* $(x + 3)(x + 5)$. The process is called *factoring* the polynomial.

DEFINITION

FACTORING A POLYNOMIAL
To factor a polynomial means to transform it to a *product* of two or more factors.

Objective

Given a quadratic trinomial with the x^2-coefficient equal to 1, factor it into a product of linear binomials (if possible).

The way to factor $x^2 + 8x + 15$ is to recall where the 8 and the 15 came from in the multiplication process. The 8 is 3 *plus* 5. The 15 is 3 *times* 5. See the following diagram.

Sum, 3 + 5

$$(x + 3)(x + 5) = x^2 + 8x + 15$$

Product, $3 \cdot 5$

To find the factors of $x^2 + 8x + 15$, you write

$$(x \quad)(x \quad).$$

Then you look for two *factors* of 15 whose *sum* is 8. The factors of 15 are

1, 15;

3, 5.

The 3 and 5 have a sum equal to 8. So you put the 3 and 8 in the spaces inside each pair of parentheses. The entire problem would look like this:

$$x^2 + 8x + 15$$
$$= \underline{\underline{(x + 3)(x + 5)}}.$$

Cover the answers as you work these examples.

EXAMPLE 1

Factor $x^2 + 7x + 10$.

- - - - - - - - - -

Think These Reasons

$x^2 + 7x + 10$	Write the given expression.
$= \underline{\underline{(x + 2)(x + 5)}}$	10 equals $2 \cdot 5$, and $2 + 5$ is 7. The factors can appear in either order, $(x + 2)(x + 5)$ or $(x + 5)(x + 2)$, since multiplication is a commutative operation.

EXAMPLE 2

Factor $x^2 + 9x + 20$.

- - - - - - - - - -

$x^2 + 9x + 20$	Write the given expression.
$= \underline{\underline{(x + 4)(x + 5)}}$	The factors of 20 are 1, 20; 2, 10; 4, 5. The sum of 4 and 5 is 9.

EXAMPLE 3

Factor $x^2 + 12x + 20$.

- - - - - - - - - -

Think These Reasons

$x^2 + 12x + 20$	
$= \underline{\underline{(x + 2)(x + 10)}}$	See Example 2. The sum of 2 and 10 is 12.

EXAMPLE 4

Factor $x^2 + 21x + 20$.

- - - - - - - - - -

$x^2 + 21x + 20$	
$= \underline{\underline{(x + 1)(x + 20)}}$	See Example 2. The sum of 1 and 20 is 21.

EXAMPLE 5

Factor $x^2 - 12x + 20$.

- - - - - - - - - -

$x^2 - 12x + 20$	Write the given expression.
$= \underline{\underline{(x - 2)(x - 10)}}$	$-12x$ is *negative*. So you need two factors of 20 whose sum is -12. They are -2 and -10.

EXAMPLE 6

Factor $x^2 + 15x + 20$.

$x^2 + 15x + 20$	Write the given expression.
Prime	$1 + 20 = 21$ $2 + 10 = 12$ ← Skips 15! $4 + 5 = 9$

DEFINITION

PRIME POLYNOMIAL
A **prime polynomial** is a polynomial whose only factors are 1 and the polynomial itself.

ORAL PRACTICE

For each trinomial, give two factors of the constant term whose sum equals the coefficient of the linear term.

EXAMPLES

	Answers
i. $x^2 + 9x + 20$	i. 4 and 5
ii. $c^2 - 7c + 6$	ii. -1 and -6

A. $x^2 + 5x + 6$

B. $x^2 + 6x + 5$

C. $t^2 + 8t + 15$

D. $y^2 - 6y + 8$

E. $x^2 - 5x + 4$

F. $b^2 - 8b + 12$

G. $z^2 + 11z + 10$

H. $x^2 - 7x + 10$

I. $x^2 + 7x + 12$

J. $x^2 + 5x + 8$

K. $x^2 - 8x + 7$

L. $x^2 - 9x + 12$

EXERCISE 5-4

Factor the following quadratic trinomials or write that they are prime. It is advisable for you to check your answers mentally by multiplying the factors together.

1. $x^2 + 7x + 6$

2. $x^2 + 11x + 10$

3. $x^2 + 6x + 5$
4. $x^2 + 8x + 7$
5. $x^2 - 26x + 25$
6. $x^2 - 17x + 16$
7. $r^2 - 8r + 12$
8. $s^2 - 7s + 12$
9. $z^2 + 5z + 6$
10. $y^2 + 6y + 8$
11. $x^2 + 6x + 9$
12. $x^2 + 4x + 4$
13. $x^2 + 10x + 9$
14. $x^2 + 5x + 4$
15. $x^2 - 10x + 21$
16. $x^2 - 15x + 26$
17. $a^2 - 13a + 40$
18. $c^2 - 16c + 15$
19. $x^2 + 16x + 48$
20. $x^2 + 19x + 60$
21. $x^2 + 14x + 48$
22. $x^2 + 16x + 60$
23. $x^2 - 19x + 48$
24. $x^2 - 17x + 60$
25. $x^2 - 20x + 48$
26. $x^2 - 23x + 60$
27. $x^2 - 26x + 48$
28. $x^2 - 30x + 60$
29. $m^2 + 11m + 18$
30. $h^2 + 11h + 24$
31. $x^2 - 52x + 100$
32. $x^2 - 43x + 120$
33. $x^2 + 45x + 120$
34. $x^2 + 39x + 140$
35. $b^2 + 25b + 150$
36. $z^2 + 30z + 160$
37. $y^2 - 37y + 300$
38. $u^2 + 77u + 360$
39. $x^2 - 90x + 1001$
40. $x^2 - 98x + 2001$

For Problems 41 through 50, multiply the binomials.

41. $(x + 4)(3x + 5)$
42. $(2x - 3)(4x + 3)$
43. $(5x + 4)(2x - 7)$
44. $(4x + 3)(4x + 3)$
45. $(2x - 7)(2x - 7)$
46. $(4x + 3)(4x - 3)$
47. $(2x - 7)(2x + 7)$
48. $(x + 6)^2$
49. $(x - 9)^2$
50. $(3x + 5)^2$
51. Solve and check: $5(x - 7) = x - 3$.
52. Evaluate $x^2 + 8$ if $x = 9$.
53. Simplify $4x - (7 - 9x)$.
54. Write an example of a sixth-degree binomial.
55. Arrange in descending powers of x: $x^2 - 2x^3 + 11 - 5x$.
56. *Tutoring Problem* Let x be the number of minutes Mally Factor has been working algebra problems. Her tutor, Val Ewing, joins her when Mally has been working for 20 minutes. Val charges \$.30 per

minute for tutoring services. Write an expression in terms of x for the number of dollars Val charges Mally. $0.30(x - 20)$

5-5 FACTORING QUADRATIC TRINOMIALS—THIRD TERM NEGATIVE

In the last section, you factored trinomials such as

$$x^2 + 8x + 15 = (x + 3)(x + 5).$$

Perhaps you noticed that, although the middle term was sometimes positive and sometimes negative, the last term was always *positive*. If the last term is *negative*, the two binomials will have *opposite* signs. For example, multiplying

$$(x - 4)(x + 7)$$

gives

$$x^2 + 3x - 28.$$

In this section, you will factor quadratic trinomials in which the last term is negative.

Objective

Be able to factor quadratic trinomials such as $x^2 + 3x - 28$, in which the constant term is *negative*.

The procedure is exactly the same as in the last section. This time you want two factors of -28 that add up to $+3$. Writing the factors of -28 shows which pair to pick.

Factors	*Sum*	
$-1, 28$	27	
$-2, 14$	12	
$-4, 7$	3	⟵ That's it!

So $x^2 + 3x - 28$ factors as follows:

$$x^2 + 3x - 28$$
$$= \underline{\underline{(x - 4)(x + 7)}}.$$

The answer can be checked by multiplying the binomials back together again.

$(x - 4)(x + 7)$	Write the answer.
$= x^2 + 7x - 4x - 28$	Multiply each term in one factor by each term in the other.
$= x^2 + 3x - 28$ ✔	Combine like terms.

Cover the answers as you work these examples.

EXAMPLE 1

Factor $x^2 + 3x - 10$.

Think These Reasons

$x^2 + 3x - 10$	Write the given expression.
$= \underline{\underline{(x - 2)(x + 5)}}$	The factors of -10 are: -1, 10 (Sum = 9. Not right.) -2, 5 (Sum = 3. That's it!)

EXAMPLE 2

Factor $x^2 - 3x - 10$.

$x^2 - 3x - 10$	Write the given expression.
$= \underline{\underline{(x + 2)(x - 5)}}$	$-3x$ is *negative*. So the two factors of -10 must be $+2$ and -5.

EXAMPLE 3

Factor $x^2 + x - 20$.

$x^2 + x - 20$	Write the given expression.
$= \underline{\underline{(x - 4)(x + 5)}}$	

Factors of -20	*Sum*	
-1, 20	19	
-2, 10	8	
-4, 5	1	⟵ That's it!

(You must realize that the coefficient of the middle term, x, is 1.)

EXAMPLE 4

Factor $x^2 - 8x - 20$.

$x^2 - 8x - 20$	Write the given expression.
$= \underline{\underline{(x + 2)(x - 10)}}$	See the factors of -20 in Example 3. This time the *larger* one must be negative since the sum is -8.

EXAMPLE 5

Factor $x^2 - 9x - 20$.

$x^2 - 9x - 20$	Write the given expression.

Prime

$1 + (-20) = -19$
$2 + (-10) = -8$ Skips -9.
$4 + (-5) = -1$

Therefore, *no* factors of -20 have a sum of -9.

ORAL PRACTICE

For each trinomial, give two factors of the constant term whose sum equals the coefficient of the linear term.

EXAMPLES

	Answers
i. $x^2 + 2x - 15$	i. -3 and 5
ii. $p^2 - 4p - 12$	ii. 2 and -6

A. $x^2 + 2x - 3$
B. $x^2 + 4x - 5$
C. $z^2 + 9z - 10$
D. $y^2 - 3y - 10$
E. $x^2 - 3x - 4$
F. $v^2 - 2v - 15$
G. $x^2 + x - 6$
H. $x^2 + x - 12$
I. $u^2 - u - 20$
J. $x^2 + 4x - 6$
K. $x^2 - 5x - 14$
L. $x^2 - 5x + 6$

EXERCISE 5-5

For Problems 1 through 40, factor the trinomial or state that it is prime. Check your answers by multiplication.

1. $x^2 + 3x - 10$
2. $x^2 + 4x - 12$
3. $x^2 + 2x - 8$
4. $x^2 + 3x - 4$
5. $x^2 + 8x - 9$
6. $x^2 + 9x - 10$
7. $r^2 - 4r - 12$
8. $s^2 - 2s - 15$
9. $a^2 - a - 30$
10. $b^2 - b - 20$
11. $x^2 + x - 20$
12. $x^2 + x - 6$
13. $x^2 - 5x - 50$
14. $x^2 - 7x - 30$
15. $x^2 - 23x - 50$
16. $x^2 - 13x - 30$
17. $x^2 - 20x - 50$
18. $x^2 - 12x - 30$
19. $u^2 - 71u - 72$
20. $t^2 - 8t - 48$

21. $u^2 + 20u - 72$
22. $t^2 + 2t - 48$
23. $u^2 - 14u - 72$
24. $t^2 + 16t - 48$
25. $u^2 + u - 72$
26. $t^2 - 13t - 48$
27. $x^2 - 13x + 42$
28. $x^2 - 17x + 42$
29. $x^2 + 5x - 6$
30. $x^2 + 13x - 30$
31. $x^2 - 5x + 6$
32. $x^2 - 13x + 30$
33. $x^2 + 26x + 120$
34. $x^2 - 17x + 60$
35. $x^2 + 26x - 120$
36. $x^2 - 17x - 60$
37. $x^2 - 21x + 98$
38. $x^2 + 24x + 63$
39. $x^2 + 14x - 51$
40. $x^2 - 9x - 52$

For Problems 41 through 46, multiply the binomials.

41. $(x + 2)(x - 7)$
42. $(x - 3)(x - 8)$
43. $(x - 2)(4x + 3)$
44. $(3x - 4)(x + 5)$
45. $(3x + 8)(7x + 4)$
46. $(5x + 3)(2x - 1)$

47. María Pasos and Jaime Peña factor a trinomial as follows:
María: $x^2 + 6x - 40 = (x + 10)(x - 4)$;
Jaime: $x^2 + 6x - 40 = (x - 10)(x + 4)$.
Who is right? Explain.

48. Oscar Gray and Alexis Smirnoff factor a trinominal as follows:
Oscar: $x^2 - 11x - 42 = (x - 14)(x + 3)$;
Alexis: $x^2 - 11x - 42 = (x + 3)(x - 14)$.
Who is right? Explain.

49. Here is one way to make up factoring problems. For example, if the last term is to be -12, you can write the factors as shown below.

Factors	*Sum*
$-1, 12$	11
$-2, 6$	4
$-3, 4$	1
$-4, 3$	-1
$-6, 2$	-4
$-12, 1$	-11

The possible trinomials are:

$$x^2 + 11x - 12 \qquad x^2 + 4x - 12 \qquad x^2 + x - 12$$

$$x^2 - 11x - 12 \qquad x^2 - 4x - 12 \qquad x^2 - x - 12.$$

Write all factorable quadratic trinomials whose first term is x^2 and whose last term is:

a. -6; b. -8; c. 10; d. 18; e. 25.

5-6 FACTORING QUADRATIC TRINOMIALS— FIRST COEFFICIENT NOT 1

In the factoring problems of the last two sections, the trinomials always looked like

$$x^2 - 6x + 8 \qquad \text{or} \qquad x^2 + 5x - 6.$$

The x^2-term always had a coefficient of 1 (although you did not *write* the 1). In this section you will learn how to factor quadratic trinomials like

$$3x^2 - 11x - 4,$$

in which the x^2-term has a coefficient *other* than 1. This coefficient is often called the **leading coefficient.**

Objective

Be able to factor quadratic trinomials in which the coefficient of the squared term is not equal to 1.

The procedure that you used for trinomials like $x^2 + 5x - 6$ no longer works for trinomials like $3x^2 - 11x - 4$. So you simply search for two binomials whose product is $3x^2 - 11x - 4$. Start by writing the given expression and two empty pairs of parentheses.

$$\begin{aligned} &3x^2 - 11x - 4 \\ &= (\qquad)(\qquad) \end{aligned}$$

You know that the first terms in the two factors must be $3x$ and x, so that you will get $3x^2$ when you multiply them together. You can fill in these terms.

$$\begin{aligned} &3x^2 - 11x - 4 \\ &= (3x \qquad)(x \qquad) \end{aligned}$$

The second terms must be one of the pairs

$$\begin{array}{ccc} -2 \text{ and } 2 & & 2 \text{ and } -2 \\ -1 \text{ and } 4 & & 4 \text{ and } -1 \\ 1 \text{ and } -4 & & -4 \text{ and } 1 \end{array}$$

so that their product will be -4. One way to find the right pair is to multiply the binomials and see which one gives the right middle term, $-11x$.

$(3x + 2)(x - 2) \rightarrow -6x + 2x \rightarrow -4x$ No

$(3x + 4)(x - 1) \rightarrow -3x + 4x \rightarrow +x$ No

$(3x - 1)(x + 4) \rightarrow +12x - x \rightarrow +11x$ Right number, wrong sign

$(3x + 1)(x - 4) \rightarrow -12x + x \rightarrow -11x$ That's it!

All of this trial-and-error work can be done on scratch paper or in your head. When you find the right factors, you simply write the final answer on your paper.

$$3x^2 - 11x - 4$$
$$= \underline{\underline{(3x + 1)(x - 4)}}$$

Cover the answers as you work these examples.

EXAMPLE 1

Factor $2x^2 + 7x + 5$.

- - - - -

Think These Reasons

$2x^2 + 7x + 5$	Write the given expression.
$= \underline{\underline{(2x + 5)(x + 1)}}$	Middle term is $2x + 5x = 7x$.

EXAMPLE 2

Factor $2x^2 + 11x + 5$.

- - - - -

$2x^2 + 11x + 5$	Write the given expression.
$= \underline{\underline{(2x + 1)(x + 5)}}$	Middle term is $10x + x = 11x$.

EXAMPLE 3

Factor $3a^2 + 5a - 2$.

- - - - -

$3a^2 + 5a - 2$	Write the given expression.
$= \underline{\underline{(3a - 1)(a + 2)}}$	Middle term is $6a - a = 5a$.

EXAMPLE 4

Factor $3x^2 - x - 2$.

- - - - -

$3x^2 - x - 2$	Write the given expression.
$= \underline{\underline{(3x + 2)(x - 1)}}$	Middle term is $-3x + 2x = -x$.

EXAMPLE 5

Factor $4x^2 - 7x - 2$.

$4x^2 - 7x - 2$	Write the given expression.
$= \underline{\underline{(4x + 1)(x - 2)}}$	Middle term is $-8x + x = -7x$.

ORAL PRACTICE

Tell what the middle term will be when the following factors are multiplied together.

EXAMPLES

	Answer
$(3x - 5)(2x + 7)$	$11x$

A. $(4x + 3)(2x + 5)$
B. $(6x + 1)(2x + 5)$
C. $(5x + 3)(3x + 4)$
D. $(2x - 7)(3x - 4)$
E. $(2x - 3)(2x - 3)$
F. $(2x - 3)(3x - 2)$
G. $(3x - 5)(2x + 4)$
H. $(4x - 2)(6x + 1)$
I. $(5x + 7)(2x - 3)$
J. $(x - 10)(2x - 3)$
K. $(x + 3)(5x - 3)$
L. $(5x + 3)(5x - 3)$

EXERCISE 5-6

For Problems 1–30, factor the trinomial.

1. $5x^2 + 8x + 3$
2. $7x^2 + 9x + 2$
3. $2x^2 + 5x + 2$
4. $3x^2 + 10x + 3$
5. $2y^2 + 7y + 3$
6. $3z^2 + 7z + 2$
7. $2x^2 + 9x + 4$
8. $3x^2 + 13x + 4$
9. $3x^2 - 16x + 5$
10. $2x^2 - 11x + 5$
11. $3x^2 - 5x + 2$
12. $2x^2 - 5x + 3$
13. $3p^2 - 8p + 4$
14. $3b^2 - 11b + 6$

15. $3x^2 - 8x - 3$

16. $2x^2 - 3x - 2$

17. $3v^2 + v - 2$

18. $5w^2 + 2w - 3$

19. $5x^2 - 8x - 4$

20. $3x^2 + 4x - 4$

21. $4x^2 + 8x + 3$

22. $4x^2 + 12x + 5$

23. $4x^2 + 7x + 3$

24. $4x^2 + 9x + 5$

25. $4u^2 + 8u - 5$

26. $4m^2 + 4m - 3$

27. $4x^2 + x - 5$

28. $4x^2 + x - 3$

29. $6x^2 + 17x + 12$

30. $10x^2 + 19x + 6$

For Problems 31 through 36, multiply the binomials.

31. $(x + 7)(x - 4)$

32. $(x - 9)(x + 2)$

33. $(3x - 5)(x + 8)$

34. $(x + 3)(7x + 8)$

35. $(2x - 1)(7x - 4)$

36. $(4x + 5)(6x - 7)$

37. Faye Doubt and her brother Peter factor a trinomial as follows:
Faye: $3x^2 - 2x - 8 = (3x + 4)(x - 2)$;
Peter: $3x^2 - 2x - 8 = (x - 2)(3x + 4)$.
Who is right? Explain.

38. Polly Nomial and Clara Fye factor a trinomial as follows:
Polly: $12x^2 + 7x - 12 = (3x + 4)(4x - 3)$;
Clara: $12x^2 + 7x - 12 = (x + 4)(x + 3)$.
Who is right? Explain.

39. Factor the following. This may require some cleverness!
a. $6 + 5x + x^2$
b. $1 + 5x + 6x^2$
c. $x^2 + 10x + 25$
d. $x^2 - 25$
e. $25x^2 + 10x + 1$
f. $4x^2 - 12x + 9$
g. $4x^2 - 9$
h. $(a + b)^2 + 7(a + b) + 6$
i. $(r - s)^2 + 3(r - s) + 2$
j. $(\text{number})^2 - 3(\text{number}) - 10$

40. *Binomials with Two Variables* If you multiply two binomials such as

$$(x + 3y)(x + 2y)$$

you get

$$x^2 + 5xy + 6y^2.$$

So if you factor $x^2 + 5xy + 6y^2$, the factors are binomials with *two* variables, $(x + 3y)(x + 2y)$. Otherwise, factoring $x^2 + 5xy + 6y^2$ is just like factoring $x^2 + 5x + 6$. Factor the following.
a. $x^2 + 11xy + 10y^2$
b. $x^2 + 3xy - 4y^2$
c. $a^2 - 7ab - 30b^2$
d. $2x^2 - 11xy + 5y^2$
e. $3c^2 + 4cd - 4d^2$
f. $x^2 + 7xy + 6y^2$
g. $x^2 + 2xy - 8y^2$
h. $a^2 - 5ab - 50b^2$
i. $3x^2 - 16xy + 5y^2$
j. $5c^2 - 8cd - 4d^2$

5-7 FACTORING A DIFFERENCE OF TWO SQUARES

In Section 5-5 you factored quadratic trinomials such as

$$x^2 + 5x - 36$$

by asking, "What two factors of -36 have a sum of 5?" The answer is 9 and -4. So you wrote

$$x^2 + 5x - 36 = (x + 9)(x - 4).$$

Suppose that you must factor $x^2 - 36$. The same reasoning can be used. Since there is no x-term, its coefficient must be *zero*. So you ask, "What two factors of -36 have a sum of 0?" The answer is 6 and -6. Thus you can write

$$x^2 - 36 = (x + 6)(x - 6).$$

Two binomials like $x + 6$ and $x - 6$, which are the same except for the sign between them, are called *conjugate binomials*.

DEFINITION

CONJUGATE BINOMIALS
Conjugate binomials are binomials that are the same except for the sign between the terms.

(For example, $3x + 5$ and $3x - 5$ are conjugate binomials.)

Whenever you multiply two conjugate binomials together, the middle term is zero (it "drops out"). For instance,

$$(x + 6)(x - 6) = x^2 - 6x + 6x - 36 = x^2 - 36.$$

The first and last terms of the answer are both squares of other numbers, and the sign between them is $-$. Therefore, $x^2 - 36$ is called a *difference of two squares*.

CONCLUSION

DIFFERENCE OF TWO SQUARES
The factors of a **difference of two squares** are conjugate binomials.

For instance, $a^2 - b^2 = (a + b)(a - b)$.

Beware! A *sum* of two squares does *not* factor. For instance, to factor

$$x^2 + 36,$$

you would need two factors of +36 whose sum is 0. Since they would have to be opposites of each other, their product could not possibly equal +36. Thus $x^2 + 36$ is *prime*.

Objective

Be able to factor a difference of two squares as a product of conjugate binomials.

To accomplish this objective, you should recognize certain numbers that are perfect squares. if you do not already know these, take some time to memorize them. The following problems will be easier if you do.

$0 = 0^2$	$1 = 1^2$	$4 = 2^2$	$9 = 3^2$	$16 = 4^2$	$25 = 5^2$
$36 = 6^2$	$49 = 7^2$	$64 = 8^2$	$81 = 9^2$	$100 = 10^2$	

Cover the answers as you work these examples.

EXAMPLE 1

Factor $x^2 - 9$.

- - - - -

Think These Reasons

$x^2 - 9$	Write the given expression.
$= \underline{\underline{(x + 3)(x - 3)}}$	$9 = 3^2$

EXAMPLE 2

Factor $r^2 - 49$.

- - - - -

$r^2 - 49$	Write the given expression.
$= \underline{\underline{(r + 7)(r - 7)}}$	$49 = 7^2$

EXAMPLE 3

Factor $4x^2 - 25$.

- - - - - - - - - -

$4x^2 - 25$	Write the given expression.
$= \underline{\underline{(2x + 5)(2x - 5)}}$	$4x^2 = (2x)^2$ and $25 = 5^2$

EXAMPLE 4

Factor $81b^2 - 1$.

- - - - - - - - - -

$81b^2 - 1$	Write the given expression.
$= \underline{\underline{(9b + 1)(9b - 1)}}$	$81b^2 = (9b)^2$ and $1 = 1^2$

EXAMPLE 5

Factor $x^2 - 12$.

- - - - - - - - - -

$x^2 - 12$	Write the given expression.
<u>Prime</u>	12 is *not* a perfect square.

EXAMPLE 6

Factor $x^2 + 16$.

- - - - - - - - - -

$x^2 + 16$	Write the given expression.
<u>Prime</u>	$x^2 + 16$ is a *sum* of two squares, not a difference.

ORAL PRACTICE

Tell whether or not the binomial is a difference of two squares. If it is, give its factors. If it is not, tell *why* not.

EXAMPLES

	Answers
i. $x^2 - 9$	i. Yes; $(x + 3)(x - 3)$.
ii. $a^3 - 16$	ii. No; a^3 is not a perfect square.
iii. $x^2 + 25$	iii. No; it is a *sum* of two squares.

A. $x^2 - 4$

B. $x^2 - 9$

C. $x^2 - 16$

D. $x^2 + 25$

E. $a^2 - 36$ F. $36 - x^2$
G. $b^2 - 49$ H. $x^2 - 1$
I. $x^2 - 10$ J. $u^2 - 100$
K. $81 - z^2$ L. $9x^2 - 4$

EXERCISE 5-7

For Problems 1 through 40, factor the polynomial or state that it is prime.

1. $x^2 - 16$
2. $x^2 - 4$
3. $x^2 - 64$
4. $x^2 - 25$
5. $a^2 - 4$
6. $a^2 - 64$
7. $c^2 - 9$
8. $d^2 - 49$
9. $x^2 - 1$
10. $p^2 - 1$
11. $4x^2 - 25$
12. $4x^2 - 9$
13. $9x^2 - 49$
14. $9x^2 - 16$
15. $25a^2 - 36$
16. $25j^2 - 81$
17. $81r^2 - 4$
18. $49x^2 - 36$
19. $9x^2 - 100$
20. $100x^2 - 9$
21. $4 - 25x^2$
22. $16 - 9x^2$
23. $100 - 9x^2$
24. $64 - 25x^2$
25. $15 - x^2$
26. $32 - x^2$
27. $1 - p^2$
28. $k^2 - 1$
29. $x^2 + 16$
30. $36 + x^2$

In Problems 31 through 40, a variable appears in *both* terms. Factor these binomials.

31. $4x^2 - 9y^2$
32. $9x^2 - 4y^2$
33. $25x^2 - 81y^2$
34. $25x^2 - 36y^2$
35. $x^2 - 49y^2$
36. $x^2 - 81y^2$
37. $36a^2 - b^2$
38. $49r^2 - p^2$
39. $c^2 - d^2$
40. $h^2 - m^2$

For Problems 41 through 50 you must recognize that an expression, no matter how complicated it looks, just stands for a *number*. Factor these.

41. $(a + b)^2 - 4$
42. $(x + y)^2 - 36$

43. $9x^2 - (c + d)^2$
44. $25x^2 - (m + c)^2$
45. $81 - 64(xy)^2$
46. $16(xy)^2 - 49$
47. $(x + 3)^2 - (x + 5)^2$
48. $(x - 4)^2 - (x - 6)^2$
49. $25(\text{number})^2 - 1$
50. $1 - 4(\text{number})^2$

Problems 51 through 62 review techniques from previous sections.

51. Multiply $(3x - 7)(4x + 2)$.
52. Multiply $(5x - 1)(4x - 7)$.
53. Factor $x^2 + 13x - 30$.
54. Factor $x^2 - 17x + 60$.
55. Factor $x^2 + 13x + 30$.
56. Factor $x^2 - 17x - 60$.
57. Solve and check $22 = 3x - 17$.
58. Solve and check $21 = 3(x - 17)$.
59. Simplify $34 - 5x + 7$.
60. Simplify $18x - 5 - 2x$.
61. Evaluate $(x - 7)(13 - 2x)$ if x is 9.
62. Evaluate $x^2 - 5x + 7$ if x is -3.

5-8 SQUARING A BINOMIAL

The expression $(x - 5)^2$ is the square of a binomial. Because $(x - 5)^2$ means $(x - 5)(x - 5)$, squaring a binomial involves the same process as multiplying two binomials together.

$$(x - 5)^2$$
$$= (x - 5)(x - 5)$$
$$= x^2 - 10x + 25$$

In this section you will practice squaring binomials. While doing so, you should look for a pattern that will allow you to square a binomial in *one* step, in your head!

Objective

Learn a pattern for squaring a binomial in one step.

Cover the answers as you work these examples.

EXAMPLE 1

Do the squaring: $(x + 3)^2$.

- - - - - - - - - -

Think These Reasons

$(x + 3)^2$	Write the given expression.
$= (x + 3)(x + 3)$	Definition of squaring.
$= \underline{\underline{x^2 + 6x + 9}}$	Middle term is $3x + 3x$.

EXAMPLE 2

Do the squaring: $(y - 7)^2$.

- - - - - - - - - -

$(y - 7)^2$	Write the given expression.
$= (y - 7)(y - 7)$	Definition of squaring.
$= \underline{\underline{y^2 - 14y + 49}}$	Middle term is $-7y - 7y$.

EXAMPLE 3

Do the squaring: $(3x + 5)^2$.

- - - - - - - - - -

$(3x + 5)^2$	Write the given expression.
$= (3x + 5)(3x + 5)$	Definition of squaring.
$= \underline{\underline{9x^2 + 30x + 25}}$	First term is $(3x)^2$, or $9x^2$. Middle term is $15x + 15x$.

In Example 3, the middle term is $30x$. This term comes from adding *two* terms, $15x + 15x$. The term $15x$ can be found easily from the original binomial, $3x + 5$. You just multiply the two terms together! This pattern can be used to get the middle term in *one* step.

$$(3x + 5)^2 = 9x^2 + 30x + 25$$

$$(3x)(5) = 15x; \qquad 2(15x) = 30x$$

The first and last terms in the answer are just the *squares* of the two terms in the binomial.

$$(3x)^2 = 9x^2$$

$$(3x + 5)^2 = 9x^2 + 30x + 25$$

$$5^2 = 25$$

CONCLUSION

BINOMIAL SQUARE PATTERN
To square a binomial quickly, you:

1. Square the first term.
2. Add *twice* the *product* of the two terms.
3. Add the square of the last term.

In the next examples you will practice using this shortcut.

EXAMPLE 4

Square using the pattern: $(x + 9)^2$.

Think These Reasons

$(x + 9)^2$	Write the given expression.
$= \underline{\underline{x^2 + 18x + 81}}$	Middle term is $2(x)(9)$.

EXAMPLE 5

Square using the pattern: $(x - 5)^2$.

$(x - 5)^2$	Write the given expression.
$= \underline{\underline{x^2 - 10x + 25}}$	Middle term is $2(x)(-5)$. Last term is $(-5)^2$.

EXAMPLE 6

Square using the pattern: $(7x - 3)^2$.

$(7x - 3)^2$	Write the given expression.
$= \underline{\underline{49x^2 - 42x + 9}}$	First term is $(7x)^2$. Middle term is $2(7x)(-3)$.

ORAL PRACTICE

Tell what the middle term will be when the squaring is done.

A. $(x + 5)^2$ B. $(p + 7)^2$ C. $(x - 11)^2$
D. $(h - 3)^2$ E. $(3x + 7)^2$ F. $(5x - 4)^2$
G. $(6b - 7)^2$ H. $(9c + 1)^2$ I. $(10 + x)^2$
J. $(7 - x)^2$ K. $(2x - 3y)^2$ L. $(a + b)^2$

EXERCISE 5-8

For Problems 1 through 10, write the binomial square as a product of two binomials, then multiply the binomials.

1. $(x + 9)^2$
2. $(x + 7)^2$
3. $(x - 10)^2$
4. $(x - 3)^2$
5. $(5x + 6)^2$
6. $(3x + 4)^2$
7. $(4x - 7)^2$
8. $(8x - 3)^2$
9. $(6 - x)^2$
10. $(9 - x)^2$

For Problems 11 through 50, square the binomial in *one* step, writing just the given expression and the answer.

11. $(x + 8)^2$
12. $(x + 6)^2$
13. $(x + 3)^2$
14. $(x + 5)^2$
15. $(h - 6)^2$
16. $(n - 4)^2$
17. $(x + 12)^2$
18. $(x + 10)^2$
19. $(k - 7)^2$
20. $(p - 8)^2$
21. $(4x + 3)^2$
22. $(5x + 4)^2$
23. $(5x - 2)^2$
24. $(3x - 5)^2$
25. $(7x - 1)^2$
26. $(9x - 1)^2$
27. $(6x + 7)^2$
28. $(5x + 8)^2$
29. $(3c - 7)^2$
30. $(6d - 3)^2$
31. $(5 + x)^2$
32. $(11 + x)^2$
33. $(9 - 4x)^2$
34. $(3 - 10x)^2$
35. $(t + 1)^2$
36. $(v - 1)^2$
37. $(x - 2)^2$
38. $(x + 2)^2$
39. $(9a - 7)^2$
40. $(8b - 9)^2$

In Problems 41 through 50, there is a variable in both terms. If you understand what you have been doing, these problems should be straightforward.

41. $(x + 4y)^2$
42. $(x + 3y)^2$
43. $(5a - b)^2$
44. $(3c - d)^2$
45. $(2y + 5z)^2$
46. $(6a + 2h)^2$
47. $(a + b)^2$
48. $(x + y)^2$
49. $(a - b)^2$
50. $(x - y)^2$

Problems 51 through 60 review techniques from previous sections.

51. Factor $x^2 + 8x + 15$.
52. Factor $x^2 - 3x - 28$.
53. Factor $5w^2 + 2w - 3$.
54. Factor $7k^2 + 9k + 2$.
55. Factor $d^2 - 49$.
56. Factor $a^2 - 64$.
57. Factor $100x^2 - 9$.
58. Factor $49x^2 - 36$.
59. Multiply $(x + 3)(4x - 7)$.
60. Multiply $(5x - 4)(x - 1)$.
61. Explain the error in the work below:
    $(x + 4)^2$
    $= x^2 + 16$.
62. Explain the error in the work below:
    $(x - 6)^2$
    $= x^2 - 12x - 36$.

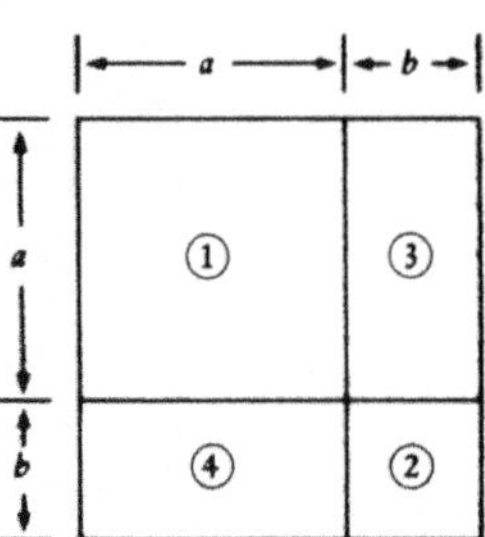

63. a. Do the squaring: $(x - 3)^2$.
    b. Do the squaring: $(3 - x)^2$.
    c. Are the answers equivalent? Explain.
64. These questions refer to the diagram.
    a. What are the dimensions of the entire square? What is its area?
    b. What is the area of square 1?
    c. What is the area of square 2?
    d. What are the areas of rectangles 3 and 4?
    e. Show that the sum of the areas of 1, 2, 3, and 4 equals the area of the entire square found in part (a).
65. *Cube of a Binomial Problem* There is a pattern for finding the *cube* of a binomial, such as $(x + y)^3$, in your head.
    a. Write $(x + y)^3$ as $(x + y)(x + y)(x + y)$.
    b. Associate and multiply the second and third factors.
    c. Multiply the first $(x + y)$ by the answer you got in part (b). To do this, multiply each term in one factor by each term in the other. Combine the like terms. Arrange in descending powers of x.
    d. Describe in words the patterns you observe in the answer to part (c).
    e. Use the pattern of part (c) to cube these binomials in one step.
       i. $(a + b)^3$ ii. $(r - s)^3$ iii. $(x + 2)^3$ iv. $(x - 5)^3$

66. *Square of a Trinomial Problem* If you square a trinomial such as

$$(x + y + z)^2,$$

a pattern appears. To discover this pattern, do the following.

a. Write $(x + y + z)^2$ as $(x + y + z)(x + y + z)$. What fact allows you to do this?
b. Multiply the x in the first factor by each term in the second.

$$(x + y + z)(x + y + z) = \ldots$$

c. Do the same with the y and z in the first factor. You should now have *nine* terms in the answer.
d. Combine like terms. Commute all the *squared* terms to the left.
e. The pattern you should see in part (d) is
   (1) Add the *squares* of each term.
   (2) Add *twice* the *product* of each possible *pair* of terms.
   Use this pattern to square each trinomial.
   i. $(a + b + c)^2$ ii. $(r + 3s + 5)^2$ iii. $(4x + 5y - 3z)^2$

5-9 FACTORING TRINOMIAL SQUARES

In the last section you learned a quick way to square a binomial. For instance,

$$(x - 5)^2 = x^2 - 10x + 25.$$

The answer, $x^2 - 10x + 25$, is called a **trinomial square.** Obviously, such a quadratic trinomial can be factored, as shown.

$$\begin{aligned} &x^2 - 10x + 25 \\ &= (x - 5)(x - 5) \\ &= (x - 5)^2 \end{aligned}$$

In this section you will learn how to go quickly from the first step to the last step, without writing the middle step.

Objective

Given a quadratic trinomial such as $x^2 - 10x + 25$, tell whether or not it is a trinomial square and, if so, transform it in *one* step to the square of a binomial (such as $(x - 5)^2$).

In order for a quadratic trinomial to be a trinomial square, the first and last terms must each be perfect squares. You can use the *square root* key on a calculator, usually marked $\sqrt{x}$, to tell whether or not a large number is a perfect square. For instance, if you press

49 $\boxed{\sqrt{x}}$,

you should get 7 for the answer. Because $7^2 = 49$, 7 is called a *square root* of 49. The number -7 is also a square root of 49, because $(-7)^2 = 49$.

If you press

157 $\boxed{\sqrt{x}}$,

you get 12.52996409. Since the square root of 157 is not an *integer*, 157 is *not* a perfect square.

The symbol $\sqrt{n}$ stands only for the *positive* square root of n. The symbol $-\sqrt{n}$ stands for the negative square root of n. For example,

$$\sqrt{25} = 5 \quad \text{and} \quad -\sqrt{25} = -5.$$

However, the symbol $\sqrt{-25}$ does not stand for a real number at all! Since $5^2 = +25$ and $(-5)^2$ also equals $+25$, there is *no* real number you could square to get -25.

Cover the answers as you work these examples.

EXAMPLE 1

Decide whether or not the number is a perfect square by finding its square root on a calculator.

a. 169

\- - - - - - - - - -

Yes $\sqrt{169} = 13$

b. 276,676

\- - - - - - - - - -

Yes $\sqrt{276676} = 526$

c. 3250

\- - - - - - - - - -

No $\sqrt{3250} \approx 57.00877125$

d. -64

\- - - - - - - - - -

No $\sqrt{-64}$ is not a real number. You should get an error message if you put this into a calculator.

Here is a formal definition of square root.

DEFINITION

SQUARE ROOT
A **square root** of a number n is a number that gives n for the answer when it is squared.

That is, $\sqrt{n}$ is the non-negative number for which

$$(\sqrt{n})^2 = n.$$

With this background in mind, you are ready to accomplish the objective—identifying and factoring trinomial squares. The first thing to do is check the *constant* term.

$$x^2 - 10x + 25$$

Is this a perfect square?
Yes! $\sqrt{25}$ is 5.

If the answer had been no, you would need to go no further. The trinomial would not be a trinomial square. Since the answer is yes, $\sqrt{25} = 5$, you must check the *middle* term.

$$x^2 - 10x + 25$$

Is this *twice* $\sqrt{25}$?
Yes!

Again, if the answer had been no, the expression would not be a trinomial square. Since the answer is yes, you can now conclude that it *is* a trinomial square. You write

$$x^2 - 10x + 25$$
$$= (x - 5)^2$$

Think: -5 is $\frac{1}{2}$ of -10.

EXAMPLE 2

Tell whether or not each of the following is a trinomial square. If it is, then transform it into the square of a binomial. If it is not, tell *why* not.

a. $x^2 + 12x + 36$

	Think These Reasons
$x^2 + 12x + 36$	Write the given expression.
$= \underline{\underline{(x + 6)^2}}$	$\sqrt{36} = 6$ and $2(6) = 12$, the correct middle coefficient.

b. $x^2 - 20x + 100$

- - - - -

$x^2 - 20x + 100$	Write the given expression.
$= \underline{\underline{(x - 10)^2}}$	$\sqrt{100} = 10$, so -10 is also a square root of 100. $2(-10) = -20$, the correct middle coefficient.

c. $x^2 + 10x + 64$

- - - - -

$= x^2 + 10x + 64$	Write the given expression.
Not a trinomial square	$\sqrt{64} = 8$, but $2(8) = 16$, not 10

d. $x^2 - 8x + 15$

- - - - -

$x^2 - 8x + 15$	Write the given expression.
Not a trinomial square	15 is not a perfect square.

ORAL PRACTICE

Give the following square roots from memory.

EXAMPLES

	Answers
i. $\sqrt{36}$	i. 6
ii. $-\sqrt{4}$	ii. -2
iii. $\sqrt{-25}$	iii. Not a real number

A. $\sqrt{49}$　B. $\sqrt{25}$　C. $\sqrt{81}$

D. $-\sqrt{64}$　E. $-\sqrt{16}$　F. $\sqrt{-9}$

G. $-\sqrt{9}$　H. $\sqrt{100}$　I. $\sqrt{1}$　J. $\sqrt{0}$

Use a calculator to find out whether or not these are perfect squares. If so, give the square root.

EXAMPLES

	Answers
i. 169	i. Yes. Square root of 169 is 13.
ii. 180	ii. No. (Calculator shows 13.4164. . . .)

K. 729
L. 8836
M. 1369
N. 5041
O. 1024
P. 484
Q. 125
R. 128881
S. 242164
T. 149769
U. 29716
V. 41209
W. 9801
X. 5908
Y. 788544

EXERCISE 5-9

For Problems 1 through 40, either write the trinomial as a square of a binomial or tell why it is not a trinomial square.

1. $x^2 + 6x + 9$
2. $x^2 - 12x + 36$
3. $x^2 - 10x + 25$
4. $x^2 + 8x + 16$
5. $x^2 + 16x + 64$
6. $x^2 - 14x + 49$
7. $x^2 - 4x + 4$
8. $x^2 - 6x + 9$
9. $x^2 - 2x + 1$
10. $x^2 + 2x + 1$
11. $x^2 - 8x + 20$
12. $x^2 - 10x + 25$
13. $x^2 - 8x + 16$
14. $x^2 - 10x + 36$
15. $x^2 - 8x - 16$
16. $x^2 - 10x + 40$
17. $a^2 + 20a + 81$
18. $t^2 + 18t + 81$
19. $a^2 + 20a + 100$
20. $t^2 + 18t + 64$
21. $x^2 - 30x + 225$
22. $x^2 + 50x + 625$
23. $x^2 + 62x + 961$
24. $x^2 + 102x + 2601$
25. $x^2 - 94x + 2209$
26. $x^2 - 74x + 1369$
27. $x^2 + 178x + 7921$
28. $x^2 + 198x + 9801$
29. $x^2 - 148x + 5476$
30. $x^2 - 66x + 4356$
31. $x^2 + 68x + 4624$
32. $x^2 + 70x + 1225$
33. $x^2 - 222x + 12{,}321$
34. $x^2 - 202x + 10{,}201$
35. $x^2 + 20x + 400$
36. $x^2 - 30x + 900$
37. $x^2 - 200x + 10{,}000$
38. $x^2 + 180x + 810$
39. $x^2 + 100x + 1000$
40. $x^2 - 180x - 8100$

Problems 41 through 50 review techniques from previous sections.

41. Multiply $(3x - 2)(x + 4)$.
42. Multiply $(5x + 2)(x - 7)$.
43. Multiply $(4x + 3)^2$.
44. Multiply $(3x - 5)^2$.

45. Factor $3x^2 - 22x + 7$.

46. Factor $2x^2 + 7x + 5$.

47. Solve and check:
$3(x + 2) = 5x - 19$.

48. Solve and check:
$4(2 - x) = 6x - 18$.

49. Evaluate $|13 - 4x|$ if $x = 7$.

50. Evaluate $|5 - 7x|$ if $x = -2$.

51. Evaluate the trinomial square for the given value of x and thus show that it *is* a perfect square.
a. $x^2 + 6x + 9$; $x = 4$
b. $x^2 - 10x + 25$; $x = 3$
c. $x^2 - 2x + 1$; $x = -5$
d. $9x^2 + 12x + 4$; $x = 2$

52. The following trinomials have squared terms whose coefficients are not equal to 1. All but two of these are trinomial squares. For those that are trinomial squares, factor into the square of a binomial. Tell which two are *not* trinomial squares.
a. $9x^2 + 24x + 16$
b. $25x^2 - 70x + 49$
c. $4x^2 + 10x + 25$
d. $4x^2 - 36x + 81$
e. $9x^2 + 16x + 24$
f. $64x^2 - 16x + 1$
g. $81x^2 - 36x + 4$
h. $49x^2 + 42x + 9$

53. Explain each statement.
a. 7 and -7 are *both* square roots of 49.
b. $\sqrt{49}$ equals only 7, not -7.
c. $-\sqrt{49}$ *is* a real number, but $\sqrt{-49}$ is *not* a real number.

54. Recall that the horizontal bar ("vinculum") over the top in $\sqrt{\text{expression}}$ means "Do what is underneath first." Answer these questions.
a. Evaluate $\sqrt{5^2}$.
b. Evaluate $\sqrt{(-5)^2}$.
c. What do you discover about the two answers?

5-10 RADICALS, IRRATIONAL NUMBERS, AND THE CLOSURE AXIOMS

In the last section you took square roots of numbers. An expression such as $\sqrt{49}$ is called a **radical**. The name comes from the Latin word *radix*, which means *root*. (The word *radish* has the same origin, since a radish is a root.)

You also learned that there is no real-number answer for the square root of a *negative* number. A radical such as $\sqrt{-9}$ does not represent a real number, because no real number squared gives a negative answer.

$$\sqrt{-9} \text{ is not } -3 \text{ because } (-3)^2 = +9.$$

$$\sqrt{-9} \text{ is not } +3 \text{ because } (+3)^2 = +9.$$

So there is *no* real number equal to $\sqrt{-9}$.

Because of this fact, the set of real numbers is said to be *not closed* under the operation of taking the square root. The set of real numbers *is* closed under addition, subtraction, and multiplication. You *always* get a real number for an answer when you do these operations on real numbers.

Addition:	$1\frac{1}{5} + 2\frac{3}{5} = 3\frac{4}{5}$	Real number
Subtraction:	$3 - 7 = -4$	Real number
Multiplication:	$(4.2)(3) = 12.6$	Real number

Other sets of numbers may or may not be closed under various operations. For instance, when you divide an integer by an integer, you do not always get an integer for the answer.

$$\frac{12}{4} = 3 \qquad \text{Integer}$$

$$\frac{13}{4} = 3\frac{1}{4} \qquad \textit{Not} \text{ an integer}$$

So the set of integers is *not* closed under division.

A fraction, such as $\frac{12}{4}$ or $\frac{13}{4}$, is called a **rational number.** The word *rational* is an adjective coming from the word *ratio,* which implies division. A ratio of two *integers* is a rational number.

DEFINITION

RATIONAL NUMBER
A **rational number** is a number that can be written as a ratio of two integers.

A radical such as $\sqrt{7}$ *cannot* be written as a ratio of two integers. The best you can do for such numbers is write them as nonending, nonrepeating decimals:

$$\sqrt{7} = 2.64575131. . . .$$

It is to be hoped that you will continue studying mathematics long enough to find out *why* this is true. Such numbers are called *irrational numbers.*

DEFINITION

IRRATIONAL NUMBER
An **irrational number** is a real number that *cannot* be written as a ratio of two integers.

Since the square root of a rational number is not always a rational number, the set of rational numbers is *not* closed under the operation of taking the square root.

$\sqrt{9} = 3 = \frac{3}{1}$ Rational

$\sqrt{10} = 3.16227766. . . .$ Irrational

The set of real numbers is closed under addition and multiplication. That is, when you add or multiply two real numbers, the answer is always a real number. These two facts are assumed to be true without proof—they are *axioms*.

CLOSURE AXIOMS

CLOSURE UNDER MULTIPLICATION
The set of real numbers is *closed under multiplication.*

That is, if x and y are any real numbers, then xy is a unique real number.

CLOSURE UNDER ADDITION
The set of real numbers is *closed under addition.*

That is, if x and y are any real numbers, then $x + y$ is a unique real number.

The word *unique* in these axioms means *only one*. For instance, 3 + 7 *always* equals 10, never equals any other number besides 10.

In this section you are to learn the meaning of closure. You do this by finding out whether or not certain sets of numbers are closed under various operations.

Objective

Given a set of numbers and an operation to be performed on these numbers, tell whether or not the set is closed under that operation.

Here is a formal definition of closure.

DEFINITION

CLOSURE

A given set of numbers is **closed** under an operation if there is just *one* answer, and that answer is *in* the given set whenever the operation is performed with numbers that are in that set.

That is,

(number in set)(operation)(number in set)
= (*unique* number *in* set)

Cover the answers as you work these examples.

EXAMPLE 1

Tell whether each set of numbers is closed under the given operation. If it is, give an example to show that you know what it means to be closed. If it is not, give an example that shows *why* not. (*Note*: The braces, {. . .}, mean *the set of*. . . or *the set containing* . . . .)

a. {integers}, subtraction

\- - - - - - - - - -

Think These Reasons

Closed — $5 - 7 = -2$, which is an integer.

b. {negative numbers}, multiplication

\- - - - - - - - - -

Not closed — $(-3)(-2) = +6$, and $+6$ is *not* a negative number.

c. {rational numbers}, addition

\- - - - - - - - - -

Closed — $\frac{2}{5} + \frac{1}{5} = \frac{3}{5}$, which is a rational number.

d. {0, 1}, addition

\- - - - - - - - - -

Not closed — $1 + 1 = 2$, and 2 is *not* in the set.

e. {rational numbers}, square root

\- - - - - - - - - -

Not closed — $\sqrt{10}$ is *not* a rational number.

Note: A counterexample is enough to prove that a set is *not* closed. However, an affirmative example is not enough to prove that it *is* closed. For instance, the set of integers is not closed under division, even though you sometimes do get an integer for an answer, such as $12 \div 6 = 2$.

EXAMPLE 2

Tell whether each radical represents a rational number, an irrational number, or neither.

a. $\sqrt{25}$

\- - - - - - - - - -

Rational — 25 is a perfect square.

b. $\sqrt{70}$

\- - - - - - - - - -

Irrational — 70 is *not* a perfect square.

c. $\sqrt{-36}$

\- - - - - - - - - -

Neither rational nor irrational — Square roots of negative numbers are not real numbers.

d. $-\sqrt{36}$

\- - - - - - - - - -

Rational — $-\sqrt{36} = -6$ and $-6 = \frac{-6}{1}$, which is a ratio of two integers.

EXERCISE 5-10

For Problems 1 through 30, tell whether or not the set is closed under the given operation. Give an example to show why or why not.

1. {real numbers}; multiplication
2. {real numbers}; addition
3. {negative numbers}; addition
4. {negative numbers}; subtraction
5. {positive integers}; division
6. {positive integers}; multiplication
7. {positive numbers}; division
8. {positive numbers}; subtraction

9. {negative integers}; multiplication
10. {negative integers}; addition
11. {real numbers}; subtraction
12. {real numbers}; division
13. {positive integers}; addition
14. {positive integers}; subtraction
15. {rational numbers}; multiplication
16. {rational numbers}; addition
17. {integers}; addition
18. {integers}; multiplication
19. {0, 1}; subtraction
20. {0, 1}; division
21. {0, 1}; multiplication
22. {0, 1}; addition
23. {negative numbers}; absolute value
24. {positive numbers}; absolute value
25. {positive integers}; raising to powers
26. {negative integers}; square root
27. {real numbers}; square root
28. {rational numbers}; square root
29. {0, 1}; square root
30. {perfect squares}; square root

For Problems 31 through 44, tell whether the radical represents a rational number, an irrational number, or neither.

31. $\sqrt{81}$
32. $\sqrt{64}$
33. $\sqrt{32}$
34. $\sqrt{20}$
35. $\sqrt{100}$
36. $\sqrt{9}$
37. $-\sqrt{49}$
38. $-\sqrt{36}$
39. $-\sqrt{60}$
40. $-\sqrt{10}$
41. $\sqrt{-16}$
42. $\sqrt{-4}$
43. $\sqrt{1}$
44. $\sqrt{0}$

Problems 45 through 54 review techniques from previous sections.

45. Multiply $(2x + 3)(4x + 5)$.
46. Multiply $(5x - 2)(6x - 2)$.
47. Factor $2x^2 - 5x - 12$.
48. Factor $3x^2 - 17x - 6$.
49. Write as a binomial squared: $c^2 - 18c + 81$.
50. Write as a binomial squared: $p^2 + 12p + 36$.
51. Solve and check: $3(x + 4) = 27$.
52. Solve and check: $4x + 50 = -6x$.

53. Simplify $3(x + 4) - 27$.

54. Simplify $4x + 50 - 6x$.

5-11 CHAPTER REVIEW AND TEST

In this chapter you have learned what a polynomial is. After learning their names, you concentrated on multiplying linear binomials and on the reverse process, factoring quadratic trinomials. As a special case, you learned how to *square* a binomial and to tell whether or not a quadratic trinomial *is* the square of a binomial. You also learned what a radical is and what it means for a set of numbers to be closed under an operation.

To make sure you know what this chapter is all about, skim through each section till you find the "Objective." Then *write it down*. The physical process of writing the words helps you remember it. If you don't understand what the objective means, turn to the exercise at the end of the section and look at some problems. Try to connect the words in the objective with what you are asked to do in the problems.

Before you try the Chapter Test on the following pages skim through the chapter again. This time, write a list of all words that "sound important." After you have finished the list, go back and think of a meaning or example for each word. If you are unsure of the meaning, look it up in the book or in your class notes.

After you have made the two lists above, doing the Chapter Test should be relatively straightforward. It may take you longer than a normal classroom test, though, if you work all of the problems.

CHAPTER TEST

1. What is the difference in meaning in each case?
   a. Expression that is a polynomial and one that is not
   b. Trinomial and cubic
   c. Second degree and two terms
   d. The square of 9 and the square root of 9
   e. $-\sqrt{25}$ and $\sqrt{-25}$

2. Write each of the following.
   a. Definition of degree
   b. Meaning of linear
   c. Coefficients in $x^3 - 5x^2 + 4x - 11$
   d. Example of a cubic monomial
   e. Example of a quadratic trinomial

3. a. Arrange in descending powers of x:
   $7x - 2 + 3x^5 - 4x^2 + x^4$

b. Arrange in ascending powers of x:
$x^3 - 3 - 5x + x^2$

4. Name the polynomials by degree and by number of terms.
a. $17x^3$
b. $13x + 5$
c. $7x^2 - 3x + 11$

5. Multiply.
a. $(x + 7)(x + 3)$
b. $(x - 2)(x - 11)$
c. $(y + 5)(y - 9)$
d. $(x - 6)(x + 1)$
e. $(3x + 4)(5x + 1)$
f. $(2z + 7)(3z - 4)$
g. $(4x - 5)(6x - 2)$
h. $(9m - 7)(2m + 3)$
i. $(x - 8)(x + 8)$
j. $(4x + 10)(4x - 10)$
k. $(x + 3)(x + 3)$
l. $(6x - 5)(6x - 5)$

6. Factor each expression or state that it is prime.
a. $x^2 + 6x + 8$
b. $x^2 - 11x + 30$
c. $a^2 + 2a - 3$
d. $v^2 - 5v - 14$
e. $x^2 + 13x + 40$
f. $x^2 - 14x + 40$
g. $x^2 - 22x - 40$
h. $x^2 - 23x - 50$
i. $3x^2 + 16x + 5$
j. $2x^2 + 5x - 7$
k. $5w^2 - 9w - 2$
l. $3x^2 - 5x + 2$
m. $x^2 - 16$
n. $25x^2 - 36$
o. $x^2 + 49$

7. Do the squaring.
a. $(x + 8)^2$
b. $(x - 7)^2$
c. $(2x + 5)^2$
d. $(3a - 4)^2$
e. $(7 - 3x)^2$
f. $(r + s)^2$

8. Transform to the square of a binomial, or tell why it is *not* a trinomial square.
a. $x^2 + 18x + 81$
b. $x^2 - 48x + 576$
c. $x^2 + 142x - 5041$
d. $x^2 - 210x + 11{,}025$
e. $x^2 - 174x + 7570$
f. $a^2 + 2ab + b^2$

9. Tell whether or not the set is closed under the given operation. If it is not, give an example that shows *why* not.
a. {positive integers}; subtraction
b. {integers}; division
c. {−1, 0, 1}; multiplication
d. {real numbers}; square root

10. Tell whether the following are rational numbers, irrational numbers, or neither.
a. $\sqrt{100}$
b. $\sqrt{80}$
c. $-\sqrt{49}$
d. $\sqrt{-1}$

6 Quadratic Equations

n the last chapter you learned hat quadratic *means second de- ree. In this chapter you will earn how to solve* quadratic equa- ions, *in which the variable is quared. Reducing such an equa- ion to one without squares of ariables requires taking the* quare root *of each member. Once ou have learned how to solve uadratic equations, you can use he techniques for such things as redicting the height of a football everal seconds after it is kicked*

Variable:

	Number of seconds since football was kicked

Expression:

$25t - 5t^2$	Number of meters it is above the ground

Equation:

$25t - 5t^2 = 20$	Says that the ball is 20 meters up

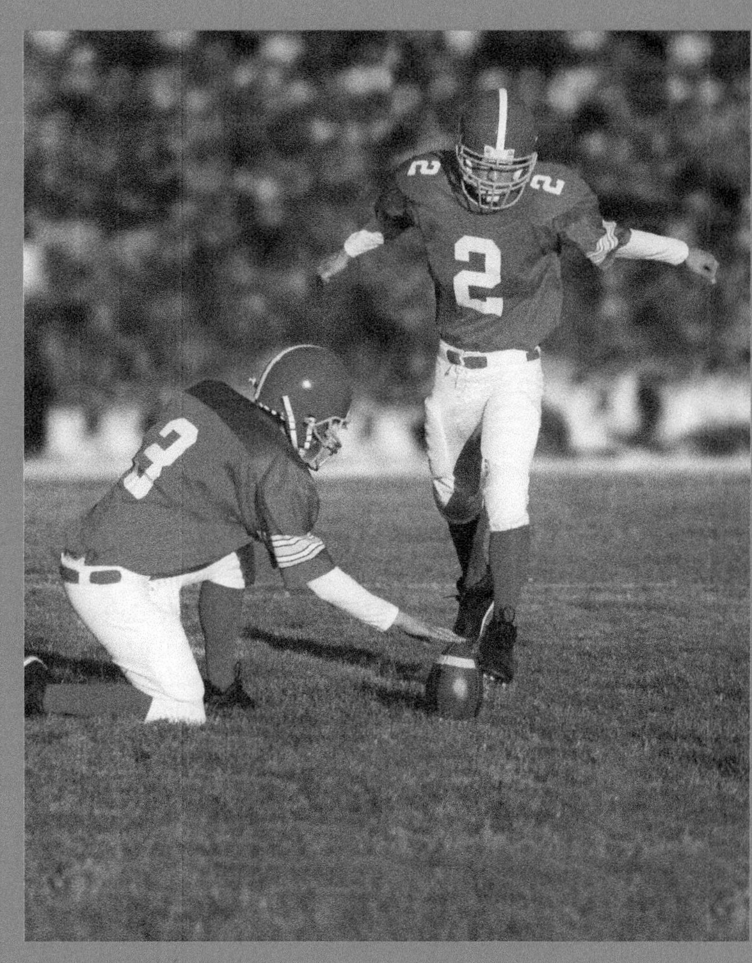

6-1 INTRODUCTION TO THE QUADRATIC FORMULA

The following equation is called the **Quadratic Formula**.

$$x = \frac{-b \pm \sqrt{b^2 - 4ac}}{2a}$$

It is read "x equals the opposite of b, plus or minus the square root of the quantity b squared minus $4ac$, all divided by $2a$." Later in this chapter you will learn for what the a, b, and c stand, for what the formula is used, and why the formula works. For the time being, you should just learn to say it.

Objective

Memorize the Quadratic Formula.

EXERCISE 6-1

1. Memorize the Quadratic Formula. You should be able to reproduce it from memory on a quiz. To assist you in doing this, you should learn to connect the *words* given above with various parts of the formula. Remember such things as the fact that the line of division starts below the − sign in front of b and goes all the way to the other side of the expression. However, it does *not* go under the = sign or the x.

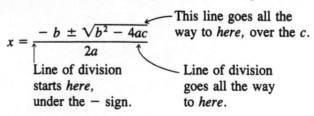

$$x = \frac{-\,b \pm \sqrt{b^2 - 4ac}}{2a}$$

This line goes all the way to *here*, over the c.

Line of division starts *here*, under the − sign.

Line of division goes all the way to *here*.

6-2 EVALUATING RADICAL EXPRESSIONS

In the last chapter, you learned that square roots of numbers, such as $\sqrt{9}$, are called radicals. Various parts of a radical have special names.

$\sqrt{9}$	A *radical*
$\sqrt{\ }$	The *radical sign*
9	The *radicand*
$\overline{\ \ }$	A symbol of inclusion, called a vinculum

In this section you will learn how to use a calculator to evaluate expressions containing radicals.

Objective

Given an expression containing a radical, evaluate the expression by calculator and round off the answer.

If you press 9 [$\sqrt{x}$] on a calculator, you get 3 for the answer. However, $\sqrt{11}$ gives 3.316624790. From Section 5.10 you should recall that 3 is a *rational* number, because it can be written as $\frac{3}{1}$, a ratio of two integers. But $\sqrt{11}$ is an irrational number. The value 3.316624790. . . is the first part of a nonending, nonrepeating decimal. For most problems in this book, you will round decimals like this to two decimal places. So you would say

$$\sqrt{11} \approx 3.32.$$

If the radical is part of a more complicated expression, you do all the calculator work *first*. You round off only the final answer. Otherwise your answer would not be as accurate. For the expression

$$\frac{5 + \sqrt{11}}{7},$$

you would press

5 [+] 11 [$\sqrt{x}$] [=] [÷] 7 [=]

The answer is 1.1880893. . . , which rounds to 1.19. You must press [=] *before* dividing if your calculator multiplies and divides before it adds and subtracts. Otherwise, only the $\sqrt{11}$ would be divided by 7.

Evaluating expressions by calculator is a skill that must be learned and practiced. If you press the buttons in the wrong order, you will probably get a wrong answer! Practice by working the following examples before you attempt Exercise 6-2. Cover the answers as you work the examples.

EXAMPLE 1

Evaluate $\sqrt{5 + 7}$. Round your answer to two decimal places.

- - - - - - - - - -

Think These Reasons

$\sqrt{5 + 7}$	Write the given expression.
$= \sqrt{12}$	Do the operations under the bar *first*.
$\approx \underline{\underline{3.46}}$	Press 12, $\boxed{\sqrt{x}}$. Then round.

EXAMPLE 2

Evaluate $\sqrt{5} + \sqrt{7}$. Round your answer to two decimal places.

- - - - - - - - - -

$\sqrt{5} + \sqrt{7}$	Write the given expression.
$\approx \underline{\underline{4.88}}$	Press 5, $\boxed{\sqrt{x}}$, $\boxed{+}$, 7, $\boxed{\sqrt{x}}$, $\boxed{=}$. (See the instruction manual for your calculator if it uses a different order of operations, such as reverse Polish.)

From the answers to Examples 1 and 2, you can see that $\sqrt{5 + 7}$ does *not* equal $\sqrt{5} + \sqrt{7}$.

EXAMPLE 3

Evaluate $\sqrt{(3.6)(5.7)}$. Round your answer to two decimal places.

- - - - - - - - - -

$\sqrt{(3.6)(5.7)}$	Write the given expression.
$\approx \underline{\underline{4.53}}$	Press 3.6, $\boxed{\times}$, 5.7, $\boxed{=}$, $\boxed{\sqrt{x}}$. (Try doing the whole computation on the calculator without writing down intermediate steps. Write just the given expression and the answer.)

EXAMPLE 4

- - - - - - - - - -

Evaluate $\sqrt{3.6} \times \sqrt{5.7}$. Round your answer to two decimal places.

$\sqrt{3.6} \times \sqrt{5.7}$	Write the given expression.

$\approx \underline{\underline{4.53}}$ Press 3.6, [√x], [×], 5.7, [√x], [=].

From the answers to Examples 3 and 4, you can see that $\sqrt{(3.6)(5.7)}$ *is* equal to $\sqrt{3.6} \times \sqrt{5.7}$.

EXAMPLE 5

Evaluate $\dfrac{-70 + \sqrt{384}}{12}$. Round your answer to two decimal places.

$\dfrac{-70 + \sqrt{384}}{12}$ Write the given expression.

$\approx \underline{\underline{-4.20}}$ Press 70, [+/−] to enter −70. Then press [+], 384, [√x], [=], [÷], 12, [=].
(The calculator should read −4.2003402. The final 0 in −4.20 *is* significant. If you had written only −4.2, the number could have been something like −4.23 or −4.18.)

ORAL PRACTICE

Evaluate the following radicals by calculator. Tell whether the answer is a rational number or an irrational number. Round irrational numbers to two decimal places.

EXAMPLES

	Answers
i. $\sqrt{37}$	i. 6.08, irrational
ii. $\sqrt{49}$	ii. 7, rational

A. $\sqrt{17}$	B. $\sqrt{60}$	C. $\sqrt{121}$
D. $\sqrt{2}$	E. $\sqrt{25}$	F. $-\sqrt{13}$
G. $-\sqrt{289}$	H. $\sqrt{-9}$	I. $\sqrt{56169}$
J. $\sqrt{265435}$	K. $\sqrt{5.29}$	L. $\sqrt{22.09}$
M. $\sqrt{42.73}$	N. $-\sqrt{1.44}$	O. $-\sqrt{50.51}$

EXERCISE 6-2

0. Write the Quadratic Formula. If you cannot do this from memory, go back to Section 6-1 and look it up.

For Problems 1 through 32, evaluate the expression. Round off irrational answers to two decimal places.

1. $\sqrt{(7)(9)}$
2. $\sqrt{(11)(25)}$
3. $\sqrt{7 + 9}$
4. $\sqrt{11 + 25}$
5. $\sqrt{7} + \sqrt{9}$
6. $\sqrt{11} + \sqrt{25}$
7. $7 + \sqrt{9}$
8. $11 + \sqrt{25}$
9. $7\sqrt{9}$
10. $11\sqrt{25}$
11. $\sqrt{\dfrac{7}{9}}$
12. $\sqrt{\dfrac{11}{25}}$
13. $\sqrt{7 - 9}$
14. $\sqrt{11 - 25}$
15. $8\sqrt{17 - 3}$
16. $6\sqrt{19 - 5}$
17. $\sqrt{(9.2)(7.5)}$
18. $\sqrt{(6.7)(8.9)}$
19. $\sqrt{4.2} \times \sqrt{3.5}$
20. $\sqrt{3.7} \times \sqrt{9.8}$
21. $3 + \sqrt{9 - 5}$
22. $5 - \sqrt{25 - 8}$
23. $-10 + \sqrt{67}$
24. $-6 + \sqrt{23}$
25. $\dfrac{5 - \sqrt{257}}{4}$
26. $\dfrac{7 - \sqrt{423}}{8}$
27. $\dfrac{-6 - \sqrt{21}}{2}$
28. $\dfrac{-9 - \sqrt{39}}{2}$
29. $-8 + \sqrt{64 - 4(3)(2)}$
30. $-3 + \sqrt{9 + 4(5)(7)}$
31. $\dfrac{17 - \sqrt{289 - 4(3)(5)}}{6}$
32. $\dfrac{13 - \sqrt{169 - 4(5)(6)}}{10}$
33. Demonstrate that the operation $\sqrt{}$ (taking the positive square root) *distributes* over multiplication by evaluating the two expressions and showing that they are equal.
    a. $\sqrt{4 \times 9}$ and $\sqrt{4} \times \sqrt{9}$
    b. $\sqrt{3 \times 7}$ and $\sqrt{3} \times \sqrt{7}$
    c. $\sqrt{12 \times 75}$ and $\sqrt{12} \times \sqrt{75}$
    d. $\sqrt{2.9 \times 7.3}$ and $\sqrt{2.9} \times \sqrt{7.3}$

34. Demonstrate that the operation $\sqrt{\ }$ (taking the positive square root) distributes over *division* by evaluating the two expressions and showing that they are equal.
a. $\sqrt{\frac{100}{4}}$ and $\frac{\sqrt{100}}{\sqrt{4}}$
b. $\sqrt{\frac{37}{2}}$ and $\frac{\sqrt{37}}{\sqrt{2}}$
c. $\sqrt{\frac{75}{3}}$ and $\frac{\sqrt{75}}{\sqrt{3}}$
d. $\sqrt{\frac{3.7}{8.5}}$ and $\frac{\sqrt{3.7}}{\sqrt{8.5}}$

35. Demonstrate that the operation $\sqrt{\ }$ does *not* distribute over addition or subtraction by showing:
a. $\sqrt{25 + 36}$ does *not* equal $\sqrt{25} + \sqrt{36}$;
b. $\sqrt{100 - 49}$ does *not* equal $\sqrt{100} - \sqrt{49}$.

36. Evaluate the following.
a. $\sqrt{(-5)^2}$
b. $\sqrt{(-7)^2}$
c. $\sqrt{(-9)^2}$
d. $\sqrt{6^2}$
e. $\sqrt{11^2}$
f. $\sqrt{(-123)^2}$
g. Explain why $\sqrt{n^2}$ equals $|n|$, the *absolute value of n*, and not n.

37. Phoebe Small must tell whether $\sqrt{289{,}329{,}955{,}237}$ is a rational number or an irrational number. Her calculator will not help, because it will not take 12-digit numbers. She is smart, though, and quickly reaches the right answer. Which is it? How did she tell?

6-3 EQUATIONS CONTAINING ABSOLUTE VALUES

In Section 2-2 you learned that the absolute value of a number is the distance between that number and the origin on a number line.

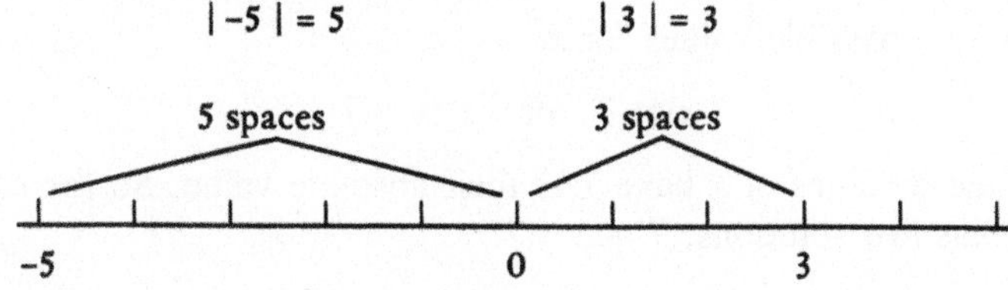

You are now ready to learn a formal definition of absolute value.

If the number inside the absolute value sign is *positive*, such as $|3|$, then its absolute value is just the number itself:

$$|3| = 3.$$

If the number inside the absolute value sign is *negative*, you take its *opposite*.

$$|-5| = 5 \qquad 5 \text{ is the } \textit{opposite} \text{ of } -5.$$

If the number inside the absolute value sign is 0, it does not matter *which* you do, because 0 and -0 are the same number:

$$|0| = 0.$$

DEFINITION

ABSOLUTE VALUE
The **absolute value** of a number is the number itself or the opposite of the number, whichever is *positive* (or zero).

That is,

$$|n| = n, \qquad \text{if } n \text{ is positive (or 0);}$$
$$|n| = -n, \qquad \text{if } n \text{ is negative.}$$

Note that $-n$ means the *opposite* of n. It does *not* necessarily stand for a negative number. For instance, the opposite of -9, written $-(-9)$, is 9. And 9 is a positive number.

A positive number, such as 7, has two different numbers with this as their absolute value.

$$|-7| = 7 \qquad |7| = 7$$

So if a *variable* appears inside the absolute value sign, as in

$$|x| = 7,$$

there are two possible values for x.

$$x = 7 \quad \text{or} \quad x = -7$$

Both of these values of x have 7 as their absolute value. So the equation $|x| = 7$ has *two* solutions, 7 and -7.

Since equations can have more than one solution, the solutions can be written in a *set*. For $|x| = 7$, the **solution set** is

$$S = \{7, -7\}.$$

The letter S stands for "solution set." As mentioned in Section 5-10, the braces, { }, are used as set symbols. The symbols $\{7, -7\}$ are read "The set containing 7 and -7." From now on, *solving an equation* will mean writing the solution set.

AGREEMENT

SOLVING AN EQUATION
Solving an equation means writing its solution set.

Objective

Given an equation involving the absolute value of a variable expression, find its solution set.

Cover the answers as you solve the following equations.

EXAMPLE 1

Find the solution set of $|x| = 15$.

	Think These Reasons
$|x| = 15$	Write the given equation.
$x = 15$ or $x = -15$	$|15|$ and $|-15|$ both equal 15.
$\therefore S = \{15, -15\}$	Write the solution set.

EXAMPLE 2

Find the solution set of $|5x - 7| = 62$.

$|5x - 7| = 62$	Write the given equation.
$5x - 7 = 62$ or $5x - 7 = -62$	The number in the absolute value sign must be 62 or -62.
$5x = 69$ or $5x = -55$	Add 7 to each member of both equations.
$x = 13.8$ or $x = -11$	Divide each member of both equations by 5.
$\therefore S = \{13.8, -11\}$	Write the solution set.

Note: There is a more compact way to write the transformed equation. The $\pm$ sign means plus or minus, or positive or negative. You saw this sign in the Quadratic Formula in Section 6-1. So you could write the following.

$\lvert 5x - 7 \rvert = 62$	Write the given equation.
$5x - 7 = \pm 62$	Use the $\pm$ sign.
$5x = 7 \pm 62$	Add 7 to each member.
$x = \dfrac{7 \pm 62}{5}$	Divide each member by 5.
$x = \dfrac{69}{5}$ or $\dfrac{-55}{5}$	$7 + 62 = 69$; $7 - 62 = -55$
$x = 13.8$ or -11	Do the division.
$\therefore S = \{13.8, -11\}$	Write the solution set.

Note: The step $x = \dfrac{7 \pm 62}{5}$ looks a little bit like the Quadratic Formula!

EXAMPLE 3

Find the solution set of $\lvert x + 5 \rvert = -7$.

- - - - - - - - - -

There are *no* solutions. Absolute values of numbers are always positive or zero. So the solution set has *no* numbers in it. It is called the **empty set.** There are two ways of writing the empty set:

$$S = \emptyset \quad \text{or} \quad S = \{\ \}.$$

In both cases you read "*S* equals the empty set" or "*S* equals the null set."

EXAMPLE 4

Find the solution set of $42 - \lvert x + 3 \rvert = 15$.

- - - - - - - - - -

$42 - \lvert x + 3 \rvert = 15$	Write the given equation.
$-\lvert x + 3 \rvert = -27$	Subtract 42 from each member.
$\lvert x + 3 \rvert = 27$	Multiply each member by -1. (From here on, the problem is just like those above.)
$x + 3 = \pm 27$	The number in the absolute value sign must be 27 or -27.
$x = -3 \pm 27$	Add -3 to each member.
$x = 24$ or -30	Do the arithmetic.
$\therefore S = \{24, -30\}$	Write the solution set.

ORAL PRACTICE

For Problems A through F give the result after the first step in solving the equation.

EXAMPLE

	Answer
$\lvert x - 7\rvert = 13$	$x - 7 = \pm 13$

A. $\lvert x - 3\rvert = 7$

B. $\lvert x + 4\rvert = 2$

C. $\lvert 3x - 8\rvert = 5$

D. $\lvert 4x + 3\rvert = 9$

E. $\lvert 7 - 5x\rvert = 4$

F. $\lvert x + 5\rvert = -6$

Tell the solution set of the equation.

EXAMPLE

	Answer
$x = 4 \pm 7$	$S = \{11, -3\}$

G. $x = 10 \pm 3$

H. $x = 4 \pm 6$

I. $x = -2 \pm 8$

J. $x = -7 \pm 3$

K. $x = \dfrac{5 \pm 9}{2}$

L. $x = \dfrac{8 \pm 7}{5}$

Give the first step in solving the equation.

EXAMPLE

	Answer
$\lvert x + 3\rvert - 7 = 15$	Add 7 to each member.

M. $\lvert x + 4\rvert - 6 = 5$

N. $\lvert x + 3\rvert + 7 = 22$

O. $\lvert 3x - 5\rvert - 8 = 2$

P. $6 - \lvert x + 4\rvert = 1$

EXERCISE 6-3

0. Write the Quadratic Formula. If you cannot do this from memory, look it up in Section 6-1.

For Problems 1 through 24, find the solution set of the equation.

1. $|x| = 15$
2. $|x| = 29$
3. $|x| = 132$
4. $|x| = 540$
5. $|x - 2| = 7$
6. $|x - 5| = 13$
7. $|x + 3| = 19$
8. $|x + 7| = 15$
9. $|x - 4| = -8$
10. $|x + 3| = -5$
11. $|5 - x| = 31$
12. $|4 - x| = 19$
13. $|2x - 5| = 29$
14. $|2x - 7| = 43$
15. $|4x + 7| = 45$
16. $|4x + 19| = 7$
17. $|5x - 33| = 22$
18. $|5x - 11| = 29$
19. $|7 - 10x| = 38$
20. $|18 - 10x| = 173$
21. $|3 + 4x| = -19$
22. $|3 + 8x| = -1$
23. $|x - 8| = 0$
24. $|x - 13| = 0$

For Problems 25 through 36, solve the equation. You may need to do a preliminary transformation before removing the absolute value signs.

25. $|x| - 9 = 21$
26. $|x| - 4 = 33$
27. $38 - |x| = 14$
28. $95 - |x| = 81$
29. $|2x + 3| - 5 = 17$
30. $|2x + 5| - 7 = 22$
31. $4 - |x - 1| = -5$
32. $5 - |x - 3| = 1$

*33. $|3x - 12| = x$

*34. $|4x - 6| = x$

*35. $|x| = x$

*36. $|x| = -x$

* These are tough. You must be very clever to solve them! You should remember *all parts* of the definition of absolute value.

37. You solve an equation like

$$|7x + 3| = 5$$

by transforming it to simpler forms. At one step in the process the equation looks a bit like the Quadratic Formula. Show this step.

38. Evaluate the following radicals. Remember, $\sqrt{n}$ stands for the *positive* square root of n. Then answer part (e).
    a. $\sqrt{(-6)^2}$ b. $\sqrt{(-5)^2}$ c. $\sqrt{7^2}$ d. $\sqrt{8^2}$
    e. $\sqrt{n^2}$ is *positive*, whether n is positive or negative. Explain why $\sqrt{n^2}$ can be written as $|n|$.

6-4 EQUATIONS WITH SQUARES

In the last section you solved equations such as

$$|x - 3| = 5.$$

In this section you will solve equations such as

$$(x - 3)^2 = 25.$$

The second equation can be transformed to the first one by taking the *square root* of each member. The fact that you can do this is called the square root property of equality.

SQUARE ROOT PROPERTY OF EQUALITY
If two positive numbers are equal, then their positive square roots are equal.

That is, if $a = b$, then $\sqrt{a} = \sqrt{b}$.

Objective

Be able to solve equations like $(x - 3)^2 = 25$, in which the square of a binomial equals a constant.

To see why the transformation can be done, you need to realize two things about the radical sign. Suppose you must evaluate

$$\sqrt{(-7)^2}.$$

First, the vinculum means to do what is underneath *first,* so you write

$$\sqrt{49},$$

because $(-7)^2$ equals $+49$. Second, $\sqrt{}$ means to take the *positive* square root, so you write

$$7.$$

The number you started with was -7. The answer is $+7$, which is the *absolute value* of -7, written $|-7|$. So

$$\sqrt{(-7)^2} = |-7| = 7.$$

This conclusion is summarized below.

SQUARE ROOT OF A PERFECT SQUARE

$$\sqrt{(\text{number})^2} = |\text{number}|$$

Using this conclusion you can solve equations like $(x - 3)^2 = 25$. Cover the answers as you work the examples on the next page.

EXAMPLE 1

Solve $(x - 3)^2 = 25$.

- - - - - - - - - -

	Think These Reasons
$(x - 3)^2 = 25$	Write the given equation.
$\sqrt{(x - 3)^2} = \sqrt{25}$	Take the positive square root of each member.
$\|x - 3\| = 5$	$\sqrt{(\text{number})^2} = \|\text{number}\|$, and $\sqrt{25} = 5$. (From here on this is just like the problems of Section 6-3. You have transformed a new problem into an old problem.)
$x - 3 = \pm 5$	Definition of absolute value
$x = 3 \pm 5$	Add 3 to each member.
$x = 8 \quad \text{or} \quad -2$	Do the arithmetic.
$S = \{8, -2\}$	Write the solution set.

Note: Recall that solving now means writing the solution set.

EXAMPLE 2

Solve $(0.3x + 1.9)^2 = 28.7$.

- - - - - - - - - -

$(0.3x + 1.9)^2 = 28.7$	Write the given equation.
$\sqrt{(0.3x + 1.9)^2} = \sqrt{28.7}$	Take the square root of each member.

$\lvert 0.3x + 1.9 \rvert = \sqrt{28.7}$	$\sqrt{n^2} = \lvert n \rvert$
$0.3x + 1.9 = \pm\sqrt{28.7}$	Definition of absolute value
$0.3x = -1.9 \pm \sqrt{28.7}$	Add -1.9 to each member.
$x = \dfrac{-1.9 \pm \sqrt{28.7}}{0.3}$	Divide each member by 0.3.
$x \approx 11.52$ or -24.19	Do the arithmetic.
$S = \{11.52, -24.19\}$	Write the solution set.

Because there are a lot of chances for error, it is advisable to check your answers. The best way is to store the answer in the calculator's memory *without* rounding off. The check of 11.52 . . . would look like this:

Check: $(0.3(11.52\ldots) + 1.9)^2 \stackrel{?}{=} 28.7$	Substitute 11.52. . . for x.
$28.7 = 28.7$ ✔	Answer checks. (The calculator may show an answer slightly different from 28.7.)

Note: Recall the Quadratic Formula from Section 6-1 and notice that

$$x = \frac{-1.9 \pm \sqrt{28.7}}{0.3}$$

in the solution of Example 2 looks very much like

$$x = \frac{-b \pm \sqrt{b^2 - 4ac}}{2a}.$$

EXAMPLE 3

Solve $(2x + 7)^2 = -64$.

$(2x + 7)^2 = -64$	Write the given equation.
$\sqrt{(2x + 7)^2} = \sqrt{-64}$	Take the square root of each member.
$S = \emptyset$	Since $\sqrt{-64}$ is *not* a real number, there are *no* real values of x that satisfy the equation. Therefore, the solution set is the *empty* set. You could tell that this is so before you take the square root. No real number squared could equal -64.

ORAL PRACTICE

Give the result after the first step in solving the equation.

EXAMPLES

		Answers
i.	$(x + 5)^2 = 81$	i. $\lvert x + 5 \rvert = 9$
ii.	$(x - 7)^2 = 34$	ii. $\lvert x - 7 \rvert = \sqrt{34}$

A. $(x + 4)^2 = 36$

B. $(x - 3)^2 = 64$

C. $(x + 2)^2 = 100$

D. $(x - 6)^2 = 49$

E. $(x + 8)^2 = 21$

F. $(x - 1)^2 = 79$

G. $(x + 7)^2 = 38.2$

H. $(x - 6.2)^2 = 9.71$

I. $(3x - 9)^2 = 16$

J. $(0.6x + 2.3)^2 = 1.7$

K. $(x + 10)^2 = -9$

L. $(x - 1)^2 = 0$

EXERCISE 6-4

0. Write the Quadratic Formula. If you cannot do this from memory, go back and look in Section 6-1.

For Problems 1 through 30, find the solution set of the equation. Round off irrational answers to two decimal places.

1. $(x - 5)^2 = 49$
2. $(x - 3)^2 = 64$
3. $(x + 3)^2 = 100$
4. $(x + 5)^2 = 81$
5. $(x + 2)^2 = 74$
6. $(x + 7)^2 = 95$
7. $(x - 8)^2 = 39$
8. $(x - 2)^2 = 53$
9. $(x - 7)^2 = 86.2$
10. $(x - 1)^2 = 73.5$
11. $(2x + 5)^2 = 81$
12. $(2x + 7)^2 = 25$
13. $(3x - 11)^2 = 19$
14. $(6x - 13)^2 = 29$
15. $(5x + 14)^2 = 6$
16. $(5x + 9)^2 = 7$
17. $(3x - 2)^2 = 0$
18. $(4x - 12)^2 = 0$
19. $(6 - x)^2 = 14$
20. $(10 - x)^2 = 39$
21. $(x + 4.1)^2 = 7.3$
22. $(x + 6.2)^2 = 9.7$
23. $(7x - 3.5)^2 = 88.9$
24. $(3x - 2.8)^2 = 44.2$
25. $(0.4x + 7.3)^2 = 242.5$
26. $(0.7x + 5.8)^2 = 46.31$
27. $(x - 8)^2 = 64$
28. $(x + 9)^2 = -36$
29. $(x + 2)^2 = -25$
30. $(x - 5)^2 = 25$

For Problems 31 through 40, solve the equation as you did in Section 6-3.

31. $|x + 4| = 25$
32. $|x + 3| = 81$
33. $|x - 6| = 7$
34. $|x - 8| = 10$
35. $|2x + 5| = 21$
36. $|3x + 6| = 30$
37. $|5 - 4x| = 49$
38. $|9 - 5x| = 64$
39. $|x + 2| = -1$
40. $|x + 7| = 0$
41. Explain why $\sqrt{(x - 3)^2}$ must be written $|x - 3|$, not $x - 3$.

6-5 EQUATIONS WITH TRINOMIAL SQUARES

This chapter is about solving quadratic equations. In some special cases, such as

$$x^2 - 10x + 25 = 70,$$

the left member may be a *trinomial square*. From Section 5-9 you should recall how to transform $x^2 - 10x + 25$ into the square of a binomial.

Is this $2 \times \sqrt{25}$? If so, make this $\frac{1}{2}(-10)$.

$$x^2 - 10x + 25 = (x - 5)^2$$

Thus the equation above can be written

$$(x - 5)^2 = 70.$$

From here, on, it is an *old* problem.

	Think These Reasons
$\sqrt{(x-5)^2} = \sqrt{70}$	Take the square root of each member.
$\lvert x - 5\rvert = \sqrt{70}$	$\sqrt{n^2} = \lvert n\rvert$
$x - 5 = \pm\sqrt{70}$	Definition of absolute value
$x = 5 \pm \sqrt{70}$	Add 5 to each member.
$x \approx 13.37$ or -3.37	Do the arithmetic.
$\therefore S = \{13.37, -3.37\}$	Write the solution set.

Objective

Be able to solve quadratic equations in which the left member is a trinomial square.

Cover the answers as you work the examples below.

EXAMPLE 1

Solve $x^2 + 6x + 9 = 113$.

- - - - - - - - - -

Think These Reasons

$x^2 + 6x + 9 = 113$	Write the given equation.
$(x + 3)^2 = 113$	Half of 6 is 3, and 3^2 is 9. So the left member is a trinomial square.
$\sqrt{(x + 3)^2} = \sqrt{113}$	Take the square root of each member.
$\lvert x + 3 \rvert = \sqrt{113}$	$\sqrt{(\text{number})^2} = \lvert\text{number}\rvert$
$x + 3 = \pm\sqrt{113}$	Definition of absolute value
$x = -3 \pm \sqrt{113}$	Add -3 to each member.
$\underline{\underline{S = \{7.63, -13.63\}}}$	Do the arithmetic and write the solution set.

Note: It is best *not* to use a calculator until you get to the step $x = \ldots$. Then you write the answers in the solution set as you find them on the calculator. You can also *check* the answers before you clear the calculator. Just store the answer—for instance, $-13.63\ldots$— in memory and recall it as needed in the check.

Check:

$(-13.63\ldots)^2 + 6(-13.63\ldots) + 9 \stackrel{?}{=} 113$	Substitute $-13.63\ldots$ for x.
$113 = 113$ ✔	Evaluate the expression. (The calculator may show a number slightly different from 113.)

EXAMPLE 2

Solve $x^2 - 7.4x + 13.69 = 8.3$.

- - - - - - - - - -

$x^2 - 7.4x + 13.69 = 8.3$	Write the given equation.
$(x - 3.7)^2 = 8.3$	$\frac{1}{2}(-7.4)$ is -3.7, and $(-3.7)^2$ is 13.69. So the left member *is* a trinomial square.
$\sqrt{(x - 3.7)^2} = \sqrt{8.3}$	Take the square root of each member.
$\lvert x - 3.7 \rvert = \sqrt{8.3}$	Square root of a perfect square
$x - 3.7 = \pm\sqrt{8.3}$	Definition of absolute value
$x = 3.7 \pm \sqrt{8.3}$	Add 3.7 to each member.
$S = \{6.58, 0.82\}$	Do the arithmetic and write the solution set.

Check (of 6.58):

$(6.58\ldots)^2 - 7.4(6.58\ldots) + 13.69 \stackrel{?}{=} 8.3$	Substitute 6.58 . . . for x.
$8.3 = 8.3$ ✔	Answer checks. (Your calculator may show a slightly different value.)

ORAL PRACTICE

Give the result after the first step in solving the equation.

EXAMPLE

	Answer
$x^2 - 10x + 25 = 41$	$(x - 5)^2 = 41$

A. $x^2 - 6x + 9 = 13$

B. $x^2 + 8x + 16 = 7$

C. $x^2 - 2x + 1 = 11$

D. $x^2 + 12x + 36 = 22$

E. $x^2 + 4x + 4 = 51$

F. $x^2 - 14x + 49 = 0$

G. $x^2 + 5x + 6.25 = 17$

H. $x^2 - 7x + 12.25 = 9.5$

I. $x^2 - 3.8x + 3.61 = 2.4$

J. $x^2 + 7.6x + 14.44 = 2$

EXERCISE 6-5

0. Write the Quadratic Formula. If you cannot do this from memory, reread Section 6-1.

For Problems 1 through 30, solve the equation by writing the left member as the square of a binomial. Write any irrational solutions as decimals, correct to two decimal places.

1. $x^2 + 6x + 9 = 16$
2. $x^2 - 10x + 25 = 81$
3. $x^2 - 4x + 4 = 25$
4. $x^2 + 6x + 9 = 49$
5. $x^2 + 2x + 1 = 42$
6. $x^2 + 4x + 4 = 73$
7. $x^2 - 18x + 81 = 2001$
8. $x^2 - 16x + 64 = 1776$
9. $x^2 + 8x + 16 = 98.6$
10. $x^2 - 14x + 49 = 74.3$
11. $x^2 - 12x + 36 = 29$
12. $x^2 - 2x + 1 = 57$
13. $x^2 - 20x + 100 = 8.6$
14. $x^2 + 18x + 81 = 20.3$
15. $x^2 - 6x + 9 = -4$
16. $x^2 - 8x + 16 = 0$
17. $x^2 + 14x + 49 = 49$
18. $x^2 + 12x + 36 = -25$
19. $x^2 + 10x + 25 = 0$
20. $x^2 + 20x + 100 = 100$
21. $x^2 + 5x + 6.25 = 49$
22. $x^2 + 3x + 2.25 = 81$
23. $x^2 - 7x + 12.25 = 9$
24. $x^2 - 5x + 6.25 = 36$
25. $x^2 - 9x + 20.25 = 73$
26. $x^2 - 13x + 42.25 = 19$
27. $x^2 + 2.6x + 1.69 = 5.7$
28. $x^2 - 8.6x + 18.49 = 7.1$
29. $x^2 - 1.4x + 0.49 = 0.35$
30. $x^2 + 1.8x + 0.81 = 0.47$

For Problems 31 through 40, solve the equation as you did in Section 6-3 or 6-4.

31. $|x - 5| = 36$
32. $|x - 11| = 81$
33. $|x + 300| = 2000$
34. $|x + 0.03| = 0.08$
35. $|5x - 1| = 14$
36. $|10x - 6| = 93$
37. $(x + 7)^2 = 100$
38. $(x + 4)^2 = 25$
39. $(x - 0.3)^2 = 0.49$
40. $(x - 20)^2 = 900$

For Problems 41 through 48, use the fact that "taking the positive square root" distributes over division. (See Problem 34, Section 6-2.) For example,

$$\sqrt{\frac{36}{49}} = \frac{\sqrt{36}}{\sqrt{49}} = \frac{6}{7}.$$

41. $x^2 + \frac{2}{3}x + \frac{1}{9} = \frac{4}{9}$

42. $x^2 + \frac{2}{9}x + \frac{1}{81} = \frac{64}{81}$

43. $x^2 - \frac{6}{5}x + \frac{9}{25} = \frac{81}{25}$

44. $x^2 - \frac{8}{5}x + \frac{16}{25} = \frac{9}{25}$

45. $x^2 + \frac{7}{3}x + \frac{49}{36} = \frac{25}{36}$

46. $x^2 + \frac{5}{3}x + \frac{25}{36} = \frac{1}{36}$

47. $x^2 - \frac{5}{4}x + \frac{25}{64} = \frac{121}{64}$

48. $x^2 - \frac{3}{4}x + \frac{9}{64} = \frac{121}{64}$

49. In the equation $x^2 + 10x + 13 = 47$, the left member is *not* a trinomial square since 13, the constant term, is not a perfect square.
    a. What would the constant term have to be in order for the left member to be a trinomial square?
    b. Add a number to each member of the equation to *make* the left member a trinomial square?
    c. Solve the equation.

6-6 COMPLETING THE SQUARE

You already know how to square a binomial. For example,

$(x + 5)^2$	
$= (x + 5)(x + 5)$	Definition of squaring
$= x^2 + 5x + 5x + 25$	Multiply each term of one binomial by each term of the other.
$= x^2 + 10x + 25$	Combine like terms.

Recall that the quick way to do this is as follows:

1. *Square* the first term of $(x + 5)$.

$$(x + 5)^2 = x^2 \ldots$$

2. Add *twice* the *product* of the two terms in $(x + 5)$.

$$(x + 5)^2 = x^2 + 10x \ldots$$

3. Add the square of the *last* term in $(x + 5)$.

$$(x + 5)^2 = x^2 + 10x + 25.$$

To make sure you can do this, work the example below, covering the answer till you have finished each part.

EXAMPLE 1

Do the squaring.

a. $(x + 7)^2$

- - - - - - - - - -

Think These Reasons

$(x + 7)^2$	Write the given expression.
$= \underline{\underline{x^2 + 14x + 49}}$	$14x$ is $2(x)(7)$ and 49 is 7^2.

b. $(x - 9)^2$

- - - - - - - - - -

$(x - 9)^2$	Write the given expression.
$= \underline{\underline{x^2 - 18x + 81}}$	$-18x$ is $2(x)(-9)$ and 81 is $(-9)^2$. Do not forget the $-$ sign.

If you know this pattern, you can *reverse* the process and find the constant term needed to make a trinomial a trinomial square. For instance, what number could you add to

$$x^2 + 6x$$

to make it a trinomial square? The thought process goes like this.

1. Write $x^2 + 6x$ and *part* of a binomial squared. Leave a blank space in the binomial.

$$x^2 + 6x$$
$$(x \quad)^2$$

2. Fill in the number in the binomial.

$$x^2 + 6\,x$$
$$(x + 3)^2$$

3 is $\frac{1}{2}(6)$.

3. Fill in the number in the trinomial.

$$x^2 + 6x + 9$$
$$(x + 3)^2$$

9 is 3^2.

The process of adding 9 to $x^2 + 6x$ is called *completing the square*. Once you see the pattern, it is easy to do in your head. The technique is given below.

TECHNIQUE

COMPLETING THE SQUARE
If the x^2-coefficient equals 1 (as in $x^2 + 6x$),
then to **complete the square** you do the following:

1. Take *half* the coefficient of x.
   ($\frac{1}{2}$ of 6, in this case)
2. Square it.
   ($3^2 = 9$, in this case)
3. Add the result.
   ($x^2 + 6x + 9$, in this case)

Objective

Be able to add a constant to a quadratic binomial, such as $x^2 + 6x$, to make the result a trinomial square.

EXAMPLE 2

Complete each square.

a. $x^2 + 8x + \cdots$

- - - - -   - - - - -

$\underline{\underline{x^2 + 8x + 16}}$ $\frac{1}{2}$ of 8 is 4, and 4^2 is 16. (Do *not* write an = sign, since the expression given does not *equal* the answer.)

b. $x^2 - 10x + \cdots$

- - - - -   - - - - -

$\underline{\underline{x^2 - 10x + 25}}$ $\frac{1}{2}$ of (-10) is -5, and $(-5)^2$ is 25.

c. $x^2 + 7x + \cdots$

- - - - -   - - - - -

$\underline{\underline{x^2 + 7x + 12.25}}$ $\frac{1}{2}$ of 7 is 3.5, and 3.5^2 is 12.25.

d. $x^2 - 2.7x + \cdots$

- - - - -   - - - - -

$\underline{\underline{x^2 - 2.7x + 1.8225}}$ $\frac{1}{2}$ of -2.7 is -1.35, and $(-1.35)^2$ is 1.8225.

EXERCISE 6-6

0. State the Quadratic Formula.

For Problems 1 through 10, square the binomial in *one* step.

1. $(x + 6)^2$
2. $(x + 8)^2$
3. $(x - 5)^2$
4. $(x - 3)^2$
5. $(x + 9)^2$
6. $(x + 4)^2$
7. $(x - 2)^2$
8. $(x - 1)^2$
9. $(x + 1)^2$
10. $(x + 2)^2$

For Problems 11 through 30, copy the expression and add a constant to complete the square.

11. $x^2 + 10x + \cdots$
12. $x^2 + 20x + \cdots$
13. $x^2 - 6x + \cdots$
14. $x^2 - 12x + \cdots$
15. $x^2 + 24x + \cdots$
16. $x^2 + 14x + \cdots$
17. $x^2 - 50x + \cdots$
18. $x^2 - 100x + \cdots$
19. $x^2 - 2x + \cdots$
20. $x^2 - 4x + \cdots$
21. $x^2 + 5x + \cdots$
22. $x^2 + 3x + \cdots$
23. $x^2 - 13x + \cdots$
24. $x^2 - 15x + \cdots$
25. $x^2 - 3.8x + \cdots$
26. $x^2 - 2.6x + \cdots$
27. $x^2 + 5.1x + \cdots$
28. $x^2 + 3.7x + \cdots$
29. $x^2 + 0.3x + \cdots$
30. $x^2 + 0.7x + \cdots$
31. The equation $x^2 + 10x + 17 = 21$ cannot be solved by the method of Section 6-5 since the left member is not a trinomial square. Now that you know how to *complete* the square, you should be able to figure out a way to solve this equation. First, subtract 17 from each member. Then, figure out what number to add to $x^2 + 10x$ to complete the square. Add this number to *each* member of the equation. Then solve it the way you learned in Section 6-5.

6-7 SOLVING QUADRATIC EQUATIONS BY COMPLETING THE SQUARE

Once you understand the process of completing the square, you can use the technique to solve quadratic equations such as

$$x^2 - 10x + 7 = 0.$$

If the left member were a trinomial square, you could solve the equation as in Section 5-5. Therefore, you *make* it a trinomial square by completing the square.

Objective

Be able to solve quadratic equations such as $x^2 - 10x + 7 = 0$ by completing the square and adding the same number to the other member.

Cover the answers as you work these examples.

EXAMPLE 1

Solve $x^2 - 10x + 7 = 0$ by completing the square.

- - - - -

Think These Reasons

$x^2 - 10x + 7 = 0$	Write the given equation.
$x^2 - 10x = -7$	Add -7 to each member, leaving a space in which to complete the square.
$x^2 - 10x + 25 = -7 + 25$	Add 25 to each member of the equation to complete the square on the left.
$(x - 5)^2 = 18$	Write the left member as a square. -5 is *half* of -10. Do the arithmetic on the right.

From here on, the problem is just like those in Section 6-4.

- - - - -

$\sqrt{(x-5)^2} = \sqrt{18}$	Take the square root of each member.
$\lvert x - 5\rvert = \sqrt{18}$	$\sqrt{(\text{number})^2} = \lvert\text{number}\rvert$
$x - 5 = \pm\sqrt{18}$	Definition of absolute value

$x = 5 \pm \sqrt{18}$	Add 5 to each member.
$\underline{\underline{S = \{9.24, 0.76\}}}$	Do the arithmetic and write the solution set.

Checking the answer may give a small surprise.

$$(9.24\ldots)^2 - 10(9.24\ldots) + 7 \stackrel{?}{=} 0$$

$$0 = 0 \quad \checkmark$$

The number on the left will probably be close to, but not equal to, zero. On a scientific calculator, it may look something like 2-08. This is how the calculator shows 2×10^{-8}, which equals 0.00000002. You will learn about this kind of number when you study scientific notation in Section 9-6.

The preceding method for completing the square does not work if the x^2-coefficient is not equal to 1. To solve an equation like

$$5x^2 + 13x + 8 = 0,$$

you simply divide each member by 5, getting

$$\frac{5x^2 + 13x + 8}{5} = \frac{0}{5}.$$

On the left, division distributes over addition. On the right, $\frac{0}{5}$ is 0. So the equation becomes

$$x^2 + 2.6x + 1.6 = 0.$$

From here on you would solve the equation as in Example 1.

EXAMPLE 2

Solve $4x^2 + 12x - 7 = 0$ by completing the square.

$4x^2 + 12x - 7 = 0$	Write the given equation.
$x^2 + 3x - 1.75 = 0$	Divide each member by 4.
$x^2 + 3x = 1.75$	Add 1.75 to each member.
$x^2 + 3x + 2.25 = 1.75 + 2.25$	Complete the square.
$(x + 1.5)^2 = 4$	Write the left member as a square. Do the arithmetic on the right.
$x + 1.5 = \pm 2$	Take the square root of each member.
$x = -1.5 \pm 2$	Add -1.5 to each member.
$\underline{\underline{S = \{0.5, -3.5\}}}$	Write the solution set.

Check (of −3.5):

$4(-3.5)^2 + 12(-3.5) - 7 \stackrel{?}{=} 0$ — Substitute $x = -3.5$.

$0 = 0$ ✓ — Check is *exact*.

ORAL PRACTICE

For Problems A through L on the next page, give the number that must be added to complete the square.

EXAMPLES

	Answers
i. $x^2 - 12x + \cdots$	i. 36
ii. $x^2 + 7x + \cdots$	ii. 12.25

A. $x^2 + 14x + \cdots$

B. $x^2 - 10x + \cdots$

C. $x^2 + 6x + \cdots$

D. $x^2 - 20x + \cdots$

E. $x^2 - 5x + \cdots$

F. $x^2 + 3x + \cdots$

G. $x^2 - 7x + \cdots$

H. $x^2 + 9x + \cdots$

I. $x^2 + 2x + \cdots$

J. $x^2 + x + \cdots$

K. $x^2 + 2.2x + \cdots$

L. $x^2 - 3.2x + \cdots$

EXERCISE 6-7

0. Write the Quadratic Formula.

For Problems 1 through 50, solve the equation by completing the square. Write any irrational answers as decimals, correct to two decimal places.

1. $x^2 + 6x + 4 = 0$
2. $x^2 + 8x + 3 = 0$
3. $x^2 - 8x + 3 = 0$
4. $x^2 + 10x + 21 = 0$
5. $x^2 - 16x - 17 = 0$
6. $x^2 - 12x - 34 = 0$
7. $x^2 + 14x - 43 = 0$
8. $x^2 - 4x - 77 = 0$
9. $x^2 - 10x + 21 = 0$
10. $x^2 + 16x + 20 = 0$

(Problems 11 through 20 have decimals in the equation or other surprises!)

11. $x^2 + 20x - 19.8 = 0$
12. $x^2 + 10x - 8.7 = 0$
13. $x^2 - 2x - 33.4 = 0$
14. $x^2 - 6x - 21.9 = 0$

15. $x^2 + 4x + 15 = 0$
16. $x^2 - 20x + 100 = 0$
17. $x^2 - 12x + 36 = 0$
18. $x^2 + 2x + 9 = 0$
19. $x^2 + 18x = 0$
20. $x^2 - 14x = 0$

(In Problems 21 through 30, the x-coefficient is not an even integer.)

21. $x^2 + 5x + 3 = 0$
22. $x^2 + 7x + 2 = 0$
23. $x^2 - 7x - 4 = 0$
24. $x^2 - 5x - 8 = 0$
25. $x^2 - 3x - 20 = 0$
26. $x^2 - 9x - 22 = 0$
27. $x^2 - 11x + 30 = 0$
28. $x^2 - 3x + 1 = 0$
29. $x^2 + 3.4x - 6 = 0$
30. $x^2 + 2.8x - 5 = 0$

(Problems 31 through 40 require other transformations before you complete the square.)

31. $x^2 - 6x + 13 = 29$
32. $x^2 + 8x + 7 = 27$
33. $x^2 = -8x - 7$
34. $x^2 = 14x - 33$
35. $x^2 + 0.65 = 1.8x$
36. $x^2 + 1.68 = -2.6x$
37. $9.8x = 2 - x^2$
38. $4.6x = 54 - x^2$
39. $x^2 + 5x = 2x + 5$
40. $x^2 - x = 4x - 2$
41. $2x^2 - 10x + 11 = 0$
42. $2x^2 - 14x + 13 = 0$
43. $5x^2 + 13x + 7 = 0$
44. $5x^2 + 24x + 21 = 0$
45. $0.2x^2 + 4.1x - 30 = 0$
46. $0.2x^2 + 3.7x - 1.9 = 0$
47. $-4x^2 + 20x + 39 = 0$
48. $-4x^2 - 22x + 31 = 0$
49. $5x^2 - 13x + 12 = 0$
50. $5x^2 + 8x + 9 = 0$

For Problems 51 through 60, solve the equation. These are like equations you have solved before this section. *Think* carefully about what you are doing!

51. $|x - 5| = 64$
52. $|x + 7| = 9$
53. $|3x + 21| = 9$
54. $|5x - 34| = 49$
55. $(x - 6)^2 = 100$
56. $(x + 8)^2 = 4$
57. $(x + 4.7)^2 = 81$
58. $(x - 2.3)^2 = 36$
59. $(x - 7) = 25$
60. $(x + 13) = 1$
61. The words *completing the square* can be illustrated by area. For instance, the diagram shows a square with side x, flanked by two rect-

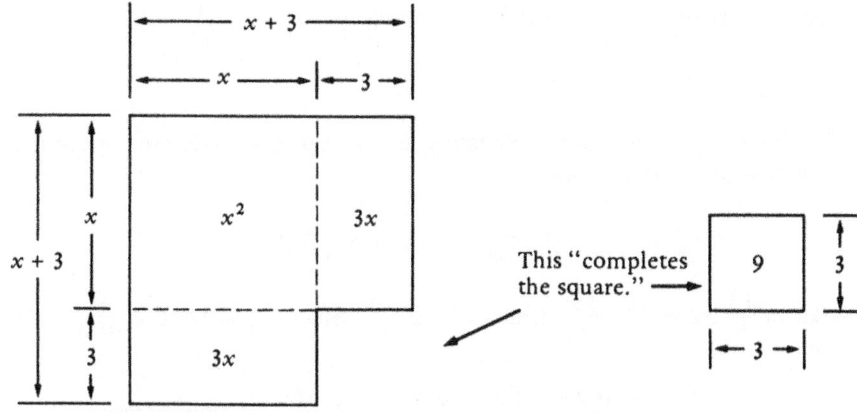

angles of dimension 3 by x. The total area is $x^2 + 3x + 3x$, or $x^2 + 6x$. As you can see, adding a 3-by-3 square (area 9) "completes" the big square! Draw pictures showing completing the square for the following expressions.

a. $x^2 + 10x$ b. $x^2 + 18x$ c. $x^2 - 12x$ (Be clever!)

62. It is possible to complete the square by adding a *middle* term. For instance, if $x^2 + 9$ were to be made into a trinomial square, the middle term would have to be $6x$. What would the middle term have to be to make these expressions trinomial squares?

a. $x^2 + \cdots + 16$ b. $x^2 + \cdots + 100$ c. $x^2 - \cdots + 81$
d. $x^2 - \cdots + 49$ e. $x^2 + \cdots + 53$

6-8 THE QUADRATIC FORMULA

You have learned what the Quadratic Formula *is*:

$$x = \frac{-b \pm \sqrt{b^2 - 4ac}}{2a}.$$

Now you are ready to learn:

1. what it *means*;
2. *why* it works.

After you have this knowledge, you will be able to:

3. *use* the formula to solve quadratic equations.

There is a pattern in the solution of a quadratic equation that shows up if you do *not* simplify as you go along. For instance, to solve

$$5x^2 + 13x + 7 = 0,$$

you first divide each member by 5, getting

$$x^2 + \frac{13}{5}x + \frac{7}{5} = 0.$$

The fractions $\frac{13}{5}$ and $\frac{7}{5}$ are deliberately left in that form. Clearing space to complete the square gives

$$x^2 + \frac{13}{5}x \qquad = -\frac{7}{5}. \qquad \text{Add } -\frac{7}{5} \text{ to each member.}$$

Half *of* $\frac{13}{5}$ means $\frac{1}{2} \cdot \frac{13}{5}$, which equals $\frac{13}{10}$. Since $\frac{13}{10}$ squared is $\frac{169}{100}$, you get

$$x^2 + \frac{13}{5}x + \frac{169}{100} = \frac{169}{100} - \frac{7}{5}. \qquad \text{Add } \frac{169}{100} \text{ to each member.}$$

The two fractions on the right can be added by finding a common denominator, as you have before. To find a common denominator, divide 5 into 100, getting 20, and then multiply $\frac{7}{5}$ by 1 in the form $\frac{20}{20}$.

$$x^2 + \frac{13}{5}x + \frac{169}{100} = \frac{169}{100} - \frac{20}{20} \cdot \frac{7}{5}$$

Writing the left member as a square and adding on the right gives

$$\left(x + \frac{13}{10}\right)^2 = \frac{169 - 20(7)}{100}.$$

Taking the square root of each member gives

$$x + \frac{13}{10} = \pm\sqrt{\frac{169 - 20(7)}{100}}.$$

The square root of a fraction equals the square root of the numerator divided by the square root of the denominator. For instance, $\sqrt{25/16} = \sqrt{25}/\sqrt{16}$, as you can check by doing the arithmetic. So the equation can be written

$$x + \frac{13}{10} = \pm\frac{\sqrt{169 - 20(7)}}{10}.$$

The denominator is 10, since $\sqrt{100} = 10$. The numerator is left as a radical. Its radicand is not a perfect square, as you can see by doing the arithmetic; you get $\sqrt{29}$.

Adding $-\frac{13}{10}$ to each member gives

$$x = -\frac{13}{10} \pm \frac{\sqrt{169 - 20(7)}}{10}.$$

Since these fractions have the same denominator, you can add and subtract their numerators, getting

$$x = \frac{-13 \pm \sqrt{169 - 20(7)}}{10}.$$

This looks very much like the Quadratic Formula! Comparing this with the original equation,

$$5x^2 + 13x + 7 = 0,$$

you can see 13 and 7 in the answer. The 169 is 13^2. The 5 also shows up after a bit of searching: 20 is 4(5) and 10 is 2(5). So the solutions can be written

$$x = \frac{-13 \pm \sqrt{13^2 - 4(5)(7)}}{2(5)}.$$

If the equation had been $ax^2 + bx + c = 0$, the answer would be the Quadratic Formula! The a, b, and c are the three coefficients in the quadratic equation. If you know the formula, you can write the solutions for *any* quadratic equation, without having to complete the square.

QUADRATIC FORMULA
If $ax^2 + bx + c = 0$, and $a \neq 0$ then

$$x = \frac{-b \pm \sqrt{b^2 - 4ac}}{2a}.$$

The restriction "a does not equal 0" is needed for two reasons. If a were 0, the equation would not be quadratic and you would not need the Quadratic Formula. Also, if a were 0 you could not *use* the formula because it would lead to division by 0.

Objective

Be able to solve a given quadratic equation using the Quadratic Formula.

Cover the answers as you work these examples.

EXAMPLE 1

Solve by the Quadratic Formula: $5x^2 + 12x + 3 = 0$.

	Think These Reasons
$5x^2 + 12x + 3 = 0$	Write the given equation.
$x = \frac{-12 \pm \sqrt{144 - 4(5)(3)}}{2(5)}$	Use the Quadratic Formula; $a = 5$, $b = 12$, $c = 3$.
$S = \{-0.28, -2.12\}$	Write the solution set. The radical is $\sqrt{84}$, which is approximately 9.16515390.

EXAMPLE 2

Solve by the Quadratic Formula: $3x^2 - 5x - 9 = 0$.

$3x^2 - 5x - 9 = 0$	Write the given equation.
$x = \dfrac{5 \pm \sqrt{25 - 4(3)(-9)}}{2(3)}$	Use the Quadratic Formula; $a = 3$, $b = -5$, $c = -9$.
$S = \{2.76, -1.09\}$	Write the solution set. The radical is $\sqrt{133}$, which is approximately 11.53256259.

EXAMPLE 3

Solve by the Quadratic Formula: $5x^2 + 13x - 6 = 0$.

$5x^2 + 13x - 6 = 0$	Write the given equation.
$x = \dfrac{-13 \pm \sqrt{169 - 4(5)(-6)}}{2(5)}$	Use the Quadratic Formula; $a = 5$, $b = 13$, $c = -6$.
$S = \{0.4, -3\}$	Write the solution set. The radical is $\sqrt{289}$, which is *exactly* 17. So the solutions are *rational* numbers. (This happens whenever $b^2 - 4ac$ is a *perfect square*.)

EXAMPLE 4

Solve by the Quadratic Formula: $7x^2 - 3x + 6 = 0$.

Think These Reasons

$7x^2 - 3x + 6 = 0$	Write the given equation.
$x = \dfrac{3 \pm \sqrt{9 - 4(7)(6)}}{2(7)}$	Use the Quadratic Formula; $a = 7$, $b = -3$, $c = 6$.
$S = \emptyset$	The radical is $\sqrt{-159}$, which is *not* a real number! (This happens whenever $b^2 - 4ac$ is *negative*.)

EXAMPLE 5

Solve by the Quadratic Formula: $(3x + 4)(x - 5) = 17$.

$(3x + 4)(x - 5) = 17$	Write the given equation.
$3x^2 - 11x - 20 = 17$	Multiply the binomials.

$3x^2 - 11x - 37 = 0$	Make the right member zero, since the Quadratic Formula begins: "If $ax^2 + bx + c = 0$. . ."
$x = \dfrac{11 \pm \sqrt{121 - 4(3)(-37)}}{2(3)}$	Use the Quadratic Formula; $a = 3$, $b = -11$, $c = -37$.
$S = \{5.79, -2.13\}$	The radical is $\sqrt{565}$, which is approximately 23.769729.

ORAL PRACTICE

Give the values of a, b, and c to use in the Quadratic Formula.

EXAMPLE

	Answer
$8x^2 - 9x + 1 = 0$	$a = 8$, $b = -9$, $c = 1$

A. $3x^2 + 5x + 7 = 0$

B. $2x^2 + 6x - 9 = 0$

C. $4x^2 - 3x - 8 = 0$

D. $-5x^2 - 4x + 1 = 0$

E. $x^2 + 10x - 1 = 0$

F. $6x^2 + x + 12 = 0$

G. $7x^2 - x + 5 = 0$

H. $-x^2 + x - 3 = 0$

I. $3x^2 + 7x = 0$

J. $4x^2 + 9 = 0$

K. $3x + 5 + 4x^2 = 0$

L. $2 - x^2 + 3x = 0$

EXERCISE 6-8

For Problems 1 through 20, solve the equation using the Quadratic Formula. Write irrational solutions as decimals, correct to two decimal places. Check each answer by storing it in the calculator's memory. Then evaluate the expression(s) in the equation using the stored value.

1. $3x^2 + 14x + 15 = 0$
2. $7x^2 + 10x + 3 = 0$
3. $7x^2 - 20x + 9 = 0$
4. $3x^2 - 24x + 17 = 0$
5. $9x^2 + 5x - 8 = 0$
6. $6x^2 + 7x - 9 = 0$
7. $-5x^2 - 18x + 79 = 0$
8. $-8x^2 + 5x + 21 = 0$
9. $5x^2 - 13x + 12 = 0$
10. $5x^2 - 13x - 6 = 0$
11. $6x^2 - 17x - 3 = 0$
12. $6x^2 + 9x + 10 = 0$

13. $0.5x^2 + 11x + 3.5 = 0$

14. $0.8x^2 + 3x + 2.1 = 0$

15. $0.2x^2 - 0.8x - 4.2 = 0$

16. $0.2x^2 - 6.7x - 10.5 = 0$

17. $x^2 + 7x - 13 = 0$

18. $x^2 - 6x + 3 = 0$

19. $-x^2 - x + 1 = 0$

20. $-x^2 + x + 1 = 0$

For Problems 21 through 30, solve the equation as above. Note that one term is missing.

EXAMPLES

i. $3x^2 + 7 = 0$ can be written $3x^2 + 0x + 7 = 0$; so $a = 3$, $b = 0$, and $c = 7$.
ii. $8x^2 - 5x = 0$ can be written $8x^2 - 5x + 0 = 0$; so $a = 8$, $b = -5$, and $c = 0$.

21. $5x^2 - 9 = 0$

22. $6x^2 - 18 = 0$

23. $6x^2 + 7 = 0$

24. $3x^2 + 8 = 0$

25. $3x^2 + 5x = 0$

26. $5x^2 + 7x = 0$

27. $x^2 - x = 0$

28. $x^2 + x = 0$

29. $4x - 10 = 0$ (Be clever!)

30. $2x - 11 = 0$ (Be clever!)

For Problems 31 through 50 solve the equation as above. You must first transform it to $ax^2 + bx + c = 0$ so that you can use the Quadratic Formula.

31. $3x^2 + 5x = -2$

32. $2x^2 + 7x = -3$

33. $3x^2 + 7x - 2 = 3x - 7x^2$

34. $x^2 + 4x - 1 = x - 4x^2$

35. $x(x - 3) = 7$

36. $x(x - 5) = 4$

37. $n(n + 1) = 30$

38. $z(z + 2) = 35$

39. $(x + 3)^2 + 2x = 2$

40. $(x + 5)^2 - x = 30$

41. $(x + 5)(x - 2) = 3$

42. $(x - 5)(x + 4) = 8$

43. $(3x - 2)(2x + 5) = 36$

44. $(4x - 1)(2x + 3) = 15$

45. $(x - 3)^2 + 25 = 0$

46. $(x + 5)^2 + 49 = 0$

47. $0.3(x - 5) = x^2 - 1.7$

48. $0.7(2 - x) = x^2 + 0.8$

49. $(x + 10)^2 + x = (x + 8)^2 + 6$

50. $(x - 7)^2 + 5x = (x + 3)^2 - 20$

For Problems 51 through 60, solve the equation using appropriate techniques from previous sections.

51. $|x + 2| = 2.3$
52. $|x - 5| = 7.1$
53. $|5x - 28| = 49$
54. $|2x + 13| = 64$
55. $(x + 7)^2 = 16$
56. $(x - 3)^2 = 81$
57. $x^2 + 2x - 15 = 0$ (Complete the square.)
58. $x^2 - 2x - 8 = 0$ (Complete the square.)
59. $x^2 - 5.4x + 7 = 0$ (Complete the square.)
60. $x^2 - 10.2x + 2 = 0$ (Complete the square.)
61. You have noticed that sometimes there are *no* real solutions to certain quadratic equations. This happens when the number under the radical sign is *negative*. From the Quadratic Formula, you know that this number is $b^2 - 4ac$. Without actually solving the following equations, find the value of $b^2 - 4ac$ and use the result to tell whether or not the equation has real-number solutions.
    a. $3x^2 + 2x + 5 = 0$
    b. $x^2 + 7x - 3 = 0$
    c. $5x^2 + x - 20 = 0$
    d. $2x^2 - 3x + 7 = 0$
62. *General Proof of Quadratic Formula* Starting with the equation $ax^2 + bx + c = 0$, derive the Quadratic Formula by completing the square.

6-9 VERTICAL MOTION PROBLEMS

You recall from Section 2-8 that distance equals rate multiplied by time—that is,

$$d = rt,$$

This formula works if the rate, r, is *constant*. When something is thrown upward into the air, the rate *varies*. The rate gets slower and slower as the object goes up, then becomes negative as it comes back down again. In physics you will learn that instead of d equaling rt, it is given approximately by

$$d = rt - 5t^2,$$

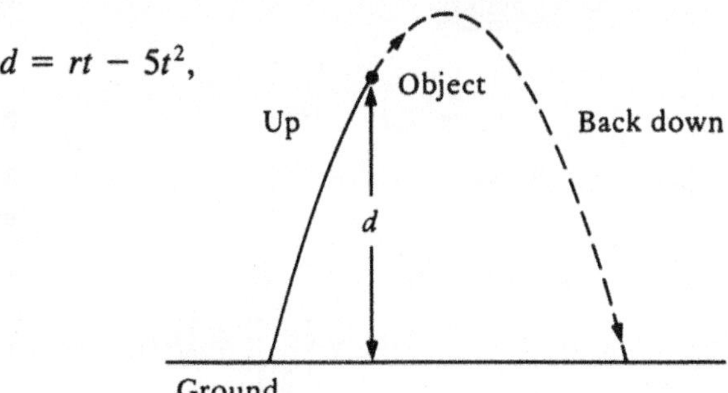

where t is the number of seconds since the object was thrown upward, d is its distance in meters above where it was thrown, and r is the rate when it was first thrown (the *initial upward velocity*) in meters per second.

Since the variable t is squared, this formula is a quadratic equation. In this section you use the formula to solve problems involving vertical motion.

Objective

For a known value of r, find d when t is given, or find t when d is given.

Put paper at the dotted lines. Uncover to the next dotted lines after you have worked that part of the example.

EXAMPLE

A ball is thrown upward with an initial velocity of 35 meters per second (m/sec).

a. Write an equation relating d and t.

b. How high is the ball after 3 sec?

c. After how many seconds will it be 50 m high?

d. When will it be 57 m high?

e. When will it be 70 m high?

f. When will the ball be back to the ground?

- - - - -

Think These Reasons

a. $d = 35t - 5t^2$ — Substitute 35 for r in $d = rt - 5t^2$.

- - - - -

b. $d = 35(3) - 5(3)^2$ — Substitute 3 for t.

$d = 60$ — Do the arithmetic.

60 meters — Write the answer.

- - - - -

c. $50 = 35t - 5t^2$ — Substitute 50 for d.

$5t^2 - 35t + 50 = 0$ — Make the right member equal zero.

$t^2 - 7t + 10 = 0$ — Divide each member by 5.

$t = \dfrac{7 \pm \sqrt{49 - 4(1)(10)}}{2(1)}$ — Use the Quadratic Formula.

$t = \dfrac{7 \pm 3}{2}$ Arithmetic

$t = 5 \quad \text{or} \quad 2$ Arithmetic

After 2 seconds, and after 5 seconds — Answer the question. (At 2 seconds the ball is going up. At 5 seconds it is coming back down.)

- - - - -

d. $57 = 35t - 5t^2$ Substitute 57 for *d*.

$5t^2 - 35t + 57 = 0$ Make the right member equal zero.

$t^2 - 7t + 11.4 = 0$ Divide each member by 5.

$t = \dfrac{7 \pm \sqrt{49 - 4(1)(11.4)}}{2(1)}$ Use the Quadratic Formula.

$t = \dfrac{7 \pm \sqrt{3.4}}{2}$ Arithmetic

$t \approx 4.42 \quad \text{or} \quad 2.58$ Arithmetic

2.58 seconds (going up);
4.42 seconds (coming down) — Answer the question. (Round off the answers, since they are approximate.)

- - - - -

e. $70 = 35t - 5t^2$ Substitute 70 for *d*.

$5t^2 - 35t + 70 = 0$ Make the right member equal zero.

$t^2 - 7t + 14 = 0$ Divide each member by 5.

$t = \dfrac{7 \pm \sqrt{49 - 4(1)(14)}}{2(1)}$ Use the Quadratic Formula.

$t = \dfrac{7 \pm \sqrt{-7}}{2}$ Arithmetic

Ball never reaches 70 m. — Answer the question. (Since $\sqrt{-7}$ is not a real number, there are *no* values of *t* at which the ball is 70 m high.)

- - - - -

f. $0 = 35t - 5t^2$ The ball is back on the ground when $d = 0$. So you substitute 0 for *d*.

$5t^2 - 35t = 0$ Subtract $35t$. Add $5t^2$.

$t^2 - 7t = 0$ Divide by 5.

$t = \frac{7 \pm \sqrt{49 - 4(1)(0)}}{2(1)}$ Use the Quadratic Formula.

$t = \frac{7 \pm 7}{2}$ Arithmetic; $\sqrt{49} = 7$

$t = 7$ or 0 Arithmetic

After 7 seconds Answer the question. (The value 0 represents the time at which the ball was thrown.)

The Vertical Motion Formula is repeated below.

VERTICAL MOTION FORMULA
If an object is thrown into the air with an initial upward velocity of r meters per second then its distance, d meters, above its starting point at time t seconds after it was thrown is approximately

$$d = rt - 5t^2.$$

ORAL PRACTICE

For Problems A through J, state an equation for distance above the starting point in terms of time if each object has the given initial upward velocity.

EXAMPLE

Spear, 30m/sec *Answer* $d = 30t - 5t^2$

A. Apple; 6 m/sec

B. Bullet, 700 m/sec

C. Cable; 3m/sec

D. Date, 7 m/sec

E. Eggplant; 2 m/sec

F. Flare, 100 m/sec

G. Gymnast; 13 m/sec

H. Horseshoe, 0.3 m/sec

I. Ice cube; 6.8 m/sec

J. Jumping bean, 0.04 m/sec

EXERCISE 6-9 1

1. *Football Problem* A football is kicked into the air with an initial upward velocity of 25 meters per second (m/sec).
   a. Calculate its height after:
      i. 2 seconds; ii. 3 seconds.
   b. When will it be 20 meters above the ground?
   c. Copy the diagram. Show the answers to part (a) in relationship to the 20 meters of part (b).
   d. When will the ball hit the ground?

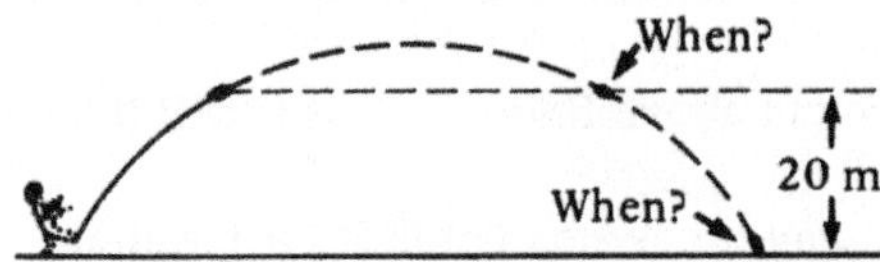

2. *Baton Problem* A twirler throws a baton with an initial upward velocity of 20 meters per second (m/sec).
   a. Calculate its height after 2 seconds.
   b. When will it be 15 meters above where it was thrown?
   c. Copy the diagram. Show the answer to part (a) in relationship to the 15 meters of part (b).
   d. When will the baton be back down at the twirler's level?

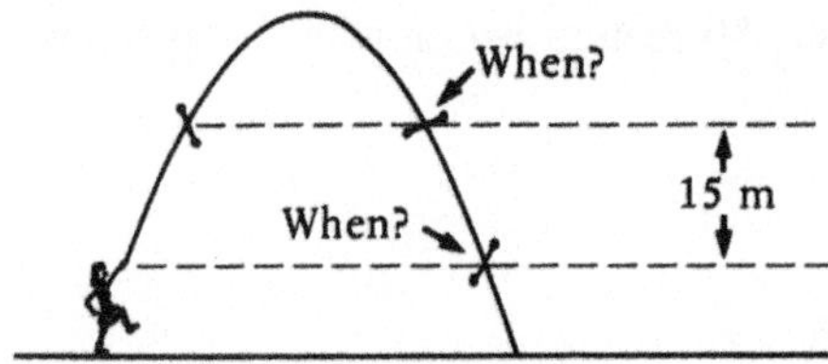

3. *Pop Fly Problem* Milt Famey, the baseball player, hits a pop fly to the infield. It goes upward with an initial velocity of 30 m/sec.
   a. What is its altitude after 2 seconds?
   b. When is it 25 meters above where it was hit?
   c. When is it back down?
   d. The ball is at its highest halfway between the time it is hit ($t = 0$) and the time it gets back down. (See part (c).)
      i. When is it at its highest?
      ii. What is its highest distance?
   e. Draw a diagram showing the positions of the ball in parts (a), (b), and (d).

4. *Cannonball Problem* A cannonball is fired with an initial upward velocity of 100 m/sec.
   a. Calculate its altitude after 3 seconds.
   b. At what time(s) will it be 480 meters high?
   c. When does it return to the ground?
   d. The cannonball reaches its highest point halfway between the time it was fired ($t = 0$) and the time it hits the ground.
      i. When is it at its highest?
      ii. How high is it at its highest?
   e. Draw a diagram showing the positions of the cannonball in parts (a), (b), and (d).

5. *Snoopy's Dogfight Problem* Snoopy is flying in his Sopwith Camel. He fires at the Red Baron. The bullet has an initial upward velocity of 120 m/sec.
   a. The Red Baron is 400 meters above Snoopy. When will the bullet first reach his altitude?
   b. The bullet misses on the way up. When could it hit the Red Baron on its way back down?
   c. If the bullet also misses the Red Baron on its way down, when will it be back at the level of Snoopy's Sopwith Camel?
   d. If it misses Snoopy on the way down, when will it hit the ground, 900 meters *below* where it was fired?

6. *Rock off the Cliff Problem* Suppose that you throw a rock into the air from the top of a cliff. The initial upward velocity is 15 m/sec.
   a. How high will the rock be above the cliff top after 2 seconds?
   b. Where will it be after 4 seconds? Think!
   c. When will it again be at the same level you threw it?
   d. When will it hit the water, 50 meters *below* where you threw it?

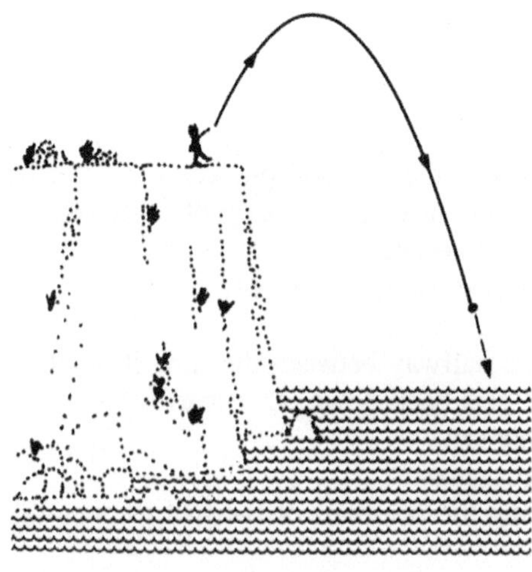

7. *Clown's Cannon Problem* At the circus, Art Tillery is fired into the air from a cannon on a platform. His initial upward velocity is 7 m/sec.
   a. How high is he above the firing point after 0.6 sec?
   b. When will he be 2 m above his firing point?
   c. When will he be back at the level of the cannon?
   d. When will he land in the tank of water, 20 m *below* his firing point?

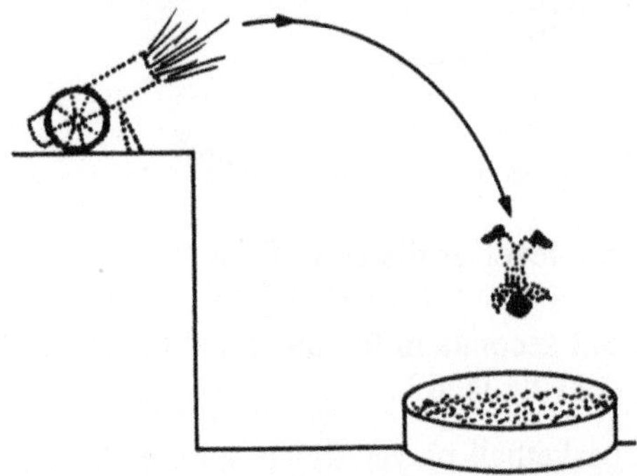

8. *Coyote and Roadrunner Problem* Wile E. Coyote is standing on a springboard atop a high cliff. Roadrunner drops a boulder on the other end of the springboard, sending Wile up with an initial velocity of 45 m/sec.
   a. How high will Wile be after 4 seconds?
   b. At what *other* time will he be at the same altitude as in part (a)?
   c. At 4 seconds, was Wile going *up* or *down?* Explain.
   d. When does he again reach the level of the springboard?
   e. On the way down, Wile misses the cliff! At what time does he land in the river, 120 meters *below* the top of the cliff?

9. *Chuck's Rock Problem* Chuck throws a rock with an initial upward velocity of 12 m/sec.
   a. How high is it after 0.7 sec?
   b. When will it be 7.2 meters up?
   c. At the time in part (b), is it going *up* or *down?* Explain.
   d. When does the rock get back to ground level?
   e. On the way back down, the rock goes straight down a well, splashing at the bottom 4 seconds after it was thrown. How deep is the well?

10. *Ski Jump Problem* As Al Pine jumps off the end of the ski jump, he has an initial upward velocity of 13 m/sec.
    a. How high will he be 2 seconds after he jumps?
    b. At what *other* time is he as high as in part (a)?

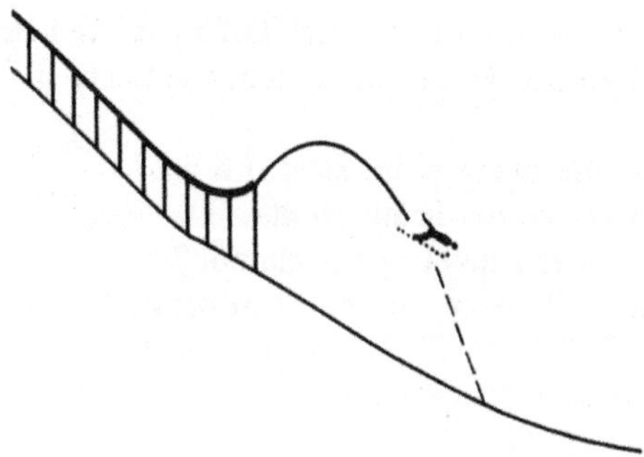

c. At 2 seconds, was Al going *up* or going *down*? Explain.
d. When is he again at the level of the end of the ski jump?
e. Al spends a total of 5.2 seconds in the air. How far below the end of the ski jump does he land?

11. *Basketball Problem* A basketball player shoots a long shot. The ball has an initial upward velocity of 6 m/sec. When it is released, the ball is at the same level as the basket.
    a. After 0.3 seconds, how high is the ball above the basket?
    b. The basket is 3 meters above the gym floor. After 0.3 seconds, how high is the ball above the gym floor?
    c. Assuming that the aim is good, when will the ball go in the basket?
    d. The ball is at its highest halfway between the time it is thrown and the time it goes in the basket. What time is this? How high is the ball above the gym floor?

12. *Volleyball Problem* In an underhanded volleyball serve, the ball leaves the server's hand 1 m above the floor. Suppose that its initial upward velocity is 7 m/sec.
    a. How high above the *floor* will it be after 0.3 seconds?
    b. If nobody else touches it, when will it be:
        i. back to the level where it was served;
        ii. down on the floor?
    c. The ball reaches its highest level halfway between the time it is served and the time it is back at the same level. What time is this? How high is it above the floor then?

13. *Golf Problem* A golf ball is hit high into the air with an initial upward velocity of 33 m/sec.
    a. How high is it after 3 seconds?
    b. When will it be 29 meters above the ground?
    c. Substitute 60 for d and try to solve for t. What does this tell you about when the ball will be 60 m up?
    d. Draw a diagram that illustrates your answer to part (c).

14. *Naval Gunnery Problem* Big guns on naval ships must fire projectiles many kilometers. To do this, the projectile must also go high into the air. Suppose that the initial upward velocity of a projectile is 300 m/sec.
    a. How high will the projectile be 20 seconds after it is fired?
    b. When will it reach 1 kilometer above where it was fired?
    c. Will it ever be 5000 meters above where it was fired? Explain.
    d. How long does it take to reach the target, which is at the same level as the projectile was fired?

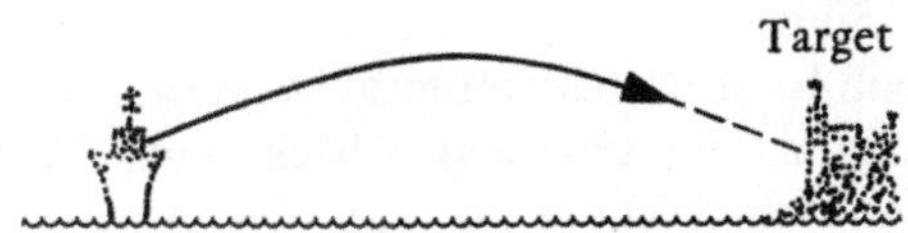

15. *Moon Jumping Problem* An astronaut on the earth practices jumping to the ground from a spaceship resting 3 meters above the ground. The initial upward velocity of the jump is 4 m/sec.
    a. When will the astronaut be back at the same level as the jump?
    b. At what time is the highest point reached? How high above the ground is that?

c. When does the astronaut reach the ground?

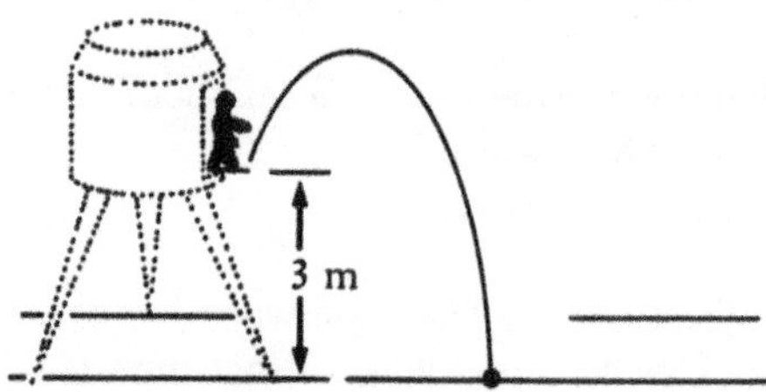

d. When the astronaut is on the moon, gravity is much weaker. The equation there is

$$d = rt - 0.8t^2.$$

Suppose the initial velocity of the jump is still 4 m/sec.

i. When will the astronaut be back at the same level as the jump?
ii. How high above the moon's surface does the astronaut go?
iii. When does the astronaut land on the moon's surface?

16. *Sports on the Moon Problem* Since gravity is much weaker on the moon, an object thrown upward from its surface reaches an altitude d given by

$$d = rt - 0.8t^2.$$

a. Find the time it takes for each of the following to return to the level from which they started.
   i. A high jumper, $r = 7$ m/sec.
   ii. A baseball, $r = 30$ m/sec.
   iii. A golf ball, $r = 33$ m/sec.
   iv. An arrow, $r = 50$ m/sec.
b. Each of the above will be at its maximum altitude halfway between the time it starts and the time it gets back down. Find the maximum altitude for each object in part (a).

17. *Rhoda's Motorcycle Problem* Rhoda Davidson prepares to jump her motorcycle from one ramp to another. Since precise calculations are essential to her safe landing, she uses the equation

$$d = rt - 4.893t^2,$$

in which 5 is replaced by the more precise value 4.893, which is the value at her latitude, 20 degrees.

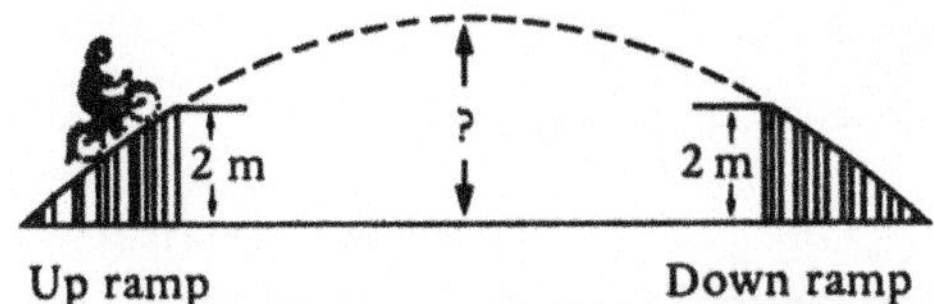

a. If she takes off with an upward initial velocity of $r = 13.7$ m/sec:
   i. when will she land on the down ramp;
   ii. what is the highest she goes above the *ground* (see figure)?

b. If her time of flight is to be precisely 3.7 seconds:
   i. what must her initial upward velocity be;
   ii. what is the highest she goes above the ground?

c. If her initial upward velocity is $r = 11$ m/sec, will she ever be 9 meters above the ground (7 m above the top of the ramp)? Justify your answer.

18. *Diving Board Problem* Suppose that you spring into the air from the 3-meter diving board. You hit the water, 3 meters *below* the board, at 1.6 seconds from the time you sprang.
    a. What was your initial upward velocity, r?
    b. When do you pass the board on your way back down?
    c. How high above the board did you go?
    d. If you spring from the 1-meter board with the same initial upward velocity as in part (a), when will you hit the water?
    e. If another diver *steps* off the 10-meter platform (initial velocity is $r = 0$) at the same time as you *spring* from the 3-meter board, as in part (a), who reaches the water sooner? How *much* sooner?

6-10 THE DISCRIMINANT

If you solve the equation

$$x^2 + 7x - 3 = 0$$

using the Quadratic Formula, you get

$$x = \frac{-7 \pm \sqrt{49 - 4(1)(-3)}}{2(1)}$$

$$= \frac{-7 \pm \sqrt{61}}{2}$$

$$\approx 0.41 \quad \text{or} \quad -7.41.$$

However, solving the equation

$$2x^2 - 3x + 7 = 0$$

gives

$$\begin{aligned} x &= \frac{3 \pm \sqrt{9 - 4(2)(7)}}{2(2)} \\ &= \frac{3 \pm \sqrt{-47}}{4}. \end{aligned}$$

There are *no* real solutions, because $\sqrt{-47}$ is *not* a real number.

The expression $b^2 - 4ac$ under the radical sign in the Quadratic Formula is called the *discriminant*. By looking at the value of this expression, you can discriminate between quadratic equations that *have* solutions and those that *do not*. You can also tell whether real solutions will be *rational* numbers or *irrational* numbers.

DEFINITION

DISCRIMINANT
The expression $b^2 - 4ac$, which appears in

$$x = \frac{-b \pm \sqrt{b^2 - 4ac}}{2a},$$

is called the **discriminant.**

Objective

Given a quadratic equation, use the discriminant to tell whether or not the equation has real solutions and, if so, whether they are rational numbers or irrational numbers.

Cover the answers as you work this example.

EXAMPLE

For each equation, evaluate the discriminant and use it to tell what kind of solutions the equation has.

a. $3x^2 + 5x + 7 = 0$

Think These Reasons

$b^2 - 4ac$	Write the discriminant.
$= 25 - 4(3)(7)$	Substitute for a, b, and c.
$= \underline{-59}$	Do the arithmetic.
No real solutions	$\sqrt{-59}$ is not a real number because -59 is *negative*.

Note: the radical sign is *not* part of the discriminant!

b. $5x^2 + 3x - 2 = 0$

$b^2 - 4ac$	Write the discriminant.
$= 9 - 4(5)(-2)$	Substitute for a, b, and c ($c = -2$).
$= \underline{49}$	Do the arithmetic.
Real solutions,	$\sqrt{49}$ is a real number because 49 is *positive*.
Rational numbers	$\sqrt{49}$ is a rational number because 49 is a *perfect square*.

c. $x^2 - 6x + 3 = 0$

$b^2 - 4ac$	Write the discriminant.
$= 36 - 4(1)(3)$	Substitute for a, b, and c ($a = 1$).
$= \underline{24}$	Do the arithmetic.
Real solutions,	$\sqrt{24}$ is a real number because 24 is *positive*.
Irrational numbers	$\sqrt{24}$ is an irrational number because 24 is *not* a perfect square.

From the above examples, you can see that the nature of the solutions of a quadratic equation can be found from the value of the discriminant. A positive discriminant means there *are* solutions. A negative discriminant means there are *no* solutions. A perfect square discriminant means the solutions are *rational* numbers.

CONCLUSION

SOLUTIONS OF A QUADRATIC EQUATION

1. If $b^2 - 4ac$ is *negative,* such as -25, there are no real solutions, because $\sqrt{-25}$ is *not* a real number.
2. If $b^2 - 4ac$ is *positive* or *zero,* such as 29, 81, or 0, there are real solutions, because $\sqrt{29}$, $\sqrt{81}$, and $\sqrt{0}$ are real numbers.
3. If $b^2 - 4ac$ is a *perfect square,* such as 49, the solutions are *rational* numbers, because $\sqrt{49}$ is 7, a rational number.

ORAL PRACTICE

Assume that the following numbers are discriminants of quadratic equations. Tell whether or not the equation has real solutions. If so, tell whether those solutions are rational numbers or irrational numbers.

EXAMPLES

	Answers
i. 23	i. Real solutions, irrational numbers
ii. 36	ii. Real solutions, rational numbers
iii. -9	iii. No real solutions

A. 37

B. 49

C. 100

D. -25

E. 56

F. -10

G. 81

H. 12

I. -16

J. -3

K. 1

L. 0

EXERCISE 6-10

For Problems 1 through 20, evaluate and write the discriminant. Then use the answer to tell whether or not the equation has real solutions, and, if so, whether they are rational numbers or irrational numbers.

1. $3x^2 + 10x + 2 = 0$
2. $5x^2 + 10x + 2 = 0$
3. $7x^2 + 8x + 5 = 0$
4. $2x^2 + 6x - 5 = 0$
5. $5x^2 + 6x - 7 = 0$
6. $2x^2 + 6x + 5 = 0$
7. $6x^2 - 5x - 21 = 0$
8. $9x^2 - 42x + 49 = 0$
9. $4x^2 + 20x + 25 = 0$
10. $9x^2 - 85x + 49 = 0$
11. $x^2 + 3x - 5 = 0$
12. $x^2 + 5x - 14 = 0$
13. $3x^2 - x + 2 = 0$
14. $x^2 + 5x + 14 = 0$
15. $x^2 - x - 6 = 0$
16. $x^2 - x - 30 = 0$
17. $x^2 + x + 1 = 0$
18. $x^2 + x - 3 = 0$
19. $x^2 + x - 1 = 0$
20. $x^2 + x + 3 = 0$

For Problems 21 through 34, first transform the equation to the form $ax^2 + bx + c = 0$, making the right member equal zero. Then use the discriminant to tell the nature of the solutions, as in Problems 1 through 20.

21. $3x^2 + 11x + 6 = 5$
22. $10x^2 + 11x + 4 = 10$
23. $x^2 - 5x - 10 = -2x$
24. $x^2 - 2x - 8 = 3x$
25. $13x + 6x^2 - 5 = 0$
26. $5x + 12x^2 + 7 = 0$
27. $2x^2 - 6x = x - 10$
28. $12x^2 - 20x = 5 - 3x$
29. $0.6x^2 + 2.1x = 1.9$
30. $0.6x^2 + 6.4x = 7$
31. $2.86 + 1.51x = 0.3x^2$
32. $1 = 0.8x - 1.6x^2$
33. $x^2 = 1.8x - 0.81$
34. $0.7x^2 = -1.3 + 2.3x$

For Problems 35 through 40, recall that when an object is thrown into the air, its vertical distance, d, above where it was thrown is given by

$$d = rt - 5t^2,$$

where d is in meters, r is the initial upward velocity in meters per second, and t is the time in seconds since it was thrown. To find out whether d ever equals a certain given value, substitute that value for d. Transform the equation so that the right member is zero. Then use the discriminant to find out whether or not there are any real values of t satisfying the equation.

35. *Antiaircraft Problem* A target plane flies at 2100 meters. An antiaircraft gun fires a projectile with an initial upward velocity of 200 m/sec. Will the projectile ever reach the altitude of the target plane? Justify your answer.

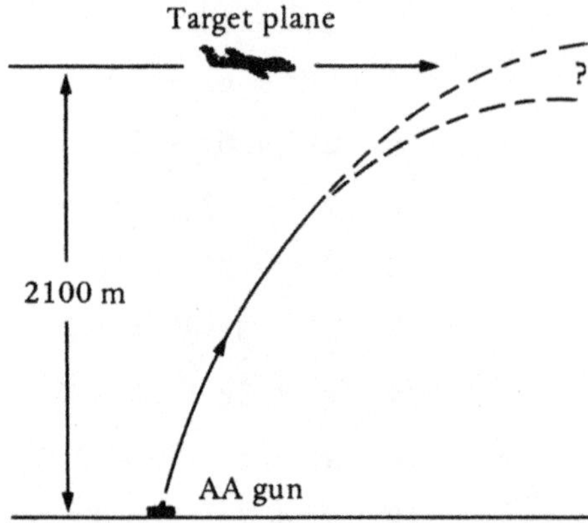

36. *Flea Jump Problem* A flea on the floor wishes to jump up on a dog's back, 0.9 meters above. The flea can jump with an initial velocity of 4.3 meters per second. Can the flea jump as high as the dog's back? Justify your answer.

37. *Basketball Dunking Problem* In order to dunk a basketball, Jim Shortz must jump 1.2 meters above the floor. He can jump up with an initial velocity of 5.1 m/sec. Can Jim dunk the ball? Justify your answer.

38. *Ball over the House Problem* Sally Forth and Stan Back stand on opposite sides of a house. They plan to throw a ball back and forth over the house. Stan can throw the ball with an initial upward velocity of 16 m/sec, and Sally can throw it with an initial upward velocity of 15 m/sec. The house is 10 meters high. Will they be able to play the game? Justify your answer.

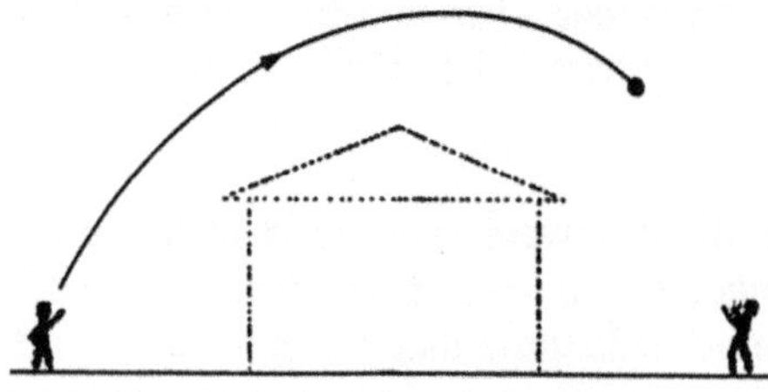

39. *Escape by Knight Problem* Sir Mount is trapped in Dracula's castle. To escape, he must jump up 1.7 meters so that his hands will reach the top of the wall. Sir Mount is a good athlete and can jump with an initial upward velocity of 5.8 m/sec. Will he be able to reach the top of the wall? Justify your answer.

40. ***Rescue Problem*** A rescue party approaches a mountain climber stranded on a ledge 15 meters above. The rescuers can throw a rope upward with an initial velocity of 16 m/sec. Will they be able to reach the stranded climber with the rope? Justify your answer.

6-11 CHAPTER REVIEW AND TEST

This chapter ties together almost everything you have learned in algebra so far. In order to solve quadratic equations, you had to complete the square, factor trinomial squares, find square roots, solve absolute value equations, and write solution sets. You learned that quadratic expressions such as $13t - 5t^2$ can represent things in the real world such as distance above the ground. You evaluated such expressions for given values of t and solved for t if you knew the value of the expression.

To get the most benefit from the Chapter Test, you should put yourself under pressure and try to finish as much as possible in the time of a normal classroom test.

CHAPTER TEST

1. What is the difference in each case?
   a. $\sqrt{-36}$ and $|-36|$
   b. Radical and radicand
   c. Quadratic equation and Quadratic Formula
   d. When $d = rt$ applies and when $d = rt - 5t^2$ applies
   e. Quadratic equation with a positive discriminant and one with a negative discriminant
2. Write each of the following.
   a. The Quadratic Formula
   b. A radical that is a rational number
   c. What $\sqrt{n^2}$ equals
   d. The coefficient in the expression x^2
   e. The number to add to $x^2 + 7x$ to complete the square
3. Evaluate the following radicals by calculator. Tell whether each represents a *rational* number, an *irrational* number, or neither.
   a. $\sqrt{85}$
   b. $-\sqrt{15{,}129}$
   c. $\sqrt{-1369}$
   d. $\sqrt{817.96}$

4. Solve *without* using the Quadratic Formula.
   a. $(x + 6)^2 = 81$ b. $(0.3x - 2.7)^2 = 17.8$
   c. $x^2 + 10x + 25 = 9$ d. $x^2 - 4x + 4 = -9$
   e. $|5x - 7| = 49$ f. $|3x + 2| = -25$

5. What number can be added to complete the square?
   a. $x^2 + 12x$ b. $x^2 - 5x$ c. $x^2 + 2.6x$

6. For the equation $5x^2 + 7x - 3 = 0$
   a. Solve using the Quadratic Formula.
   b. Solve by first dividing each member by 5 and then completing the square.
   c. Show that both solution sets are the same.

7. Solve.
   a. $0.2x^2 + 4.3x - 8.6 = 0$ b. $11x^2 - 5x = 0$
   c. $(3x - 2)(x - 5) = 17$ d. $(x + 6)^2 - 5x = x^2 + 1$

8. Find the discriminant. Use it to tell whether or not the equation has real-number solutions and, if so, whether they are rational or irrational numbers.
   a. $5x^2 - 3x - 7 = 0$ b. $x^2 + 6x + 10 = 0$
   c. $3x^2 + 10x - 8 = 0$

9. A soccer player kicks the ball, giving it an initial upward velocity of 17 meters per second.
   a. How high will it be after 1.2 seconds?
   b. When will it be 10 meters above the ground?
   c. Use the discriminant to show that it will *never* be 20 m high.
   d. Draw a sketch showing the results of parts (a), (b), and (c).

6-12 CUMULATIVE REVIEW, CHAPTERS 1 THROUGH 6

In the first part of this book you learned to evaluate expressions and to solve equations. Along the way you learned such words as *commute, associate,* and *distribute,* which describe ways you can transform an expression without actually evaluating it. You also learned some things that can be done to each member of an equation, such as adding the same number or reversing the two members. Some of these properties are called *axioms*. Others can be proved using the axioms. You should know the names listed below and what they mean.

AXIOMS FOR ADDITION AND MULTIPLICATION OF REAL NUMBERS

1. Commutative axiom for addition
2. Commutative axiom for multiplication
3. Associative axiom for addition
4. Associative axiom for multiplication
5. Distributive axiom for multiplication over addition
6. Closure under addition
7. Closure under multiplication
8. Additive identity
9. Multiplicative identity
10. Additive inverses
11. Multiplicative inverses

the axioms for equality are as follows:

AXIOMS OF EQUALITY

1. Transitive axiom
2. Symmetric axiom
3. Reflexive axiom

some properties that can be proved from the axioms are as follows:

MULTIPLICATION PROPERTY OF −1
For any real number x, $-1 \cdot x = -x$.

MULTIPLICATION PROPERTY OF 0
For any real number x, $0 \cdot x = 0$.

OTHER DISTRIBUTIVE PROPERTIES
(See Section 3-3.)

ADDITION PROPERTY OF EQUALITY
For real numbers x, y, and z, if $x = y$, then $x + z = y + z$. (That is, you can add the same number to each member of an equation.)

MULTIPLICATION PROPERTY OF EQUALITY
For real numbers x, y, and z, if $x = y$, then $xz = yz$. (That is, you can multiply each member of an equation by the same number.)

These axioms and properties can be used to accomplish the three major things done in algebra.

THREE MAJOR THINGS DONE IN ALGEBRA

- Write an expression representing something in the real world.
- Find the value of the expression when you know what x equals.
- Find the value of x when you know what the expression equals.

As you review, you should make a list of words you have learned, such as

commute
equation
solve
linear
evaluate
factor
.
.
.

For each item on your list you should try to tell which of the three major things applies. For instance, "combining like terms" makes expressions easier to *evaluate* and makes equations easier to *solve*.

After you have done the reviewing, try working the following exercise. This should be roughly equivalent to a 2-hour semester exam. You may want to try working on it several days before your own semester exam so that you will have time to learn things you have forgotten.

EXERCISE 6-12

1. Name the three major things one does in algebra.
2. Write a definition of each of the following.
   a. Variable b. Power c. Rational number
   d. Subtraction e. Commute f. Axiom
   g. Negative number h. Integer i. Quadratic
   j. Discriminant

3. What is the difference in each case?
   a. Equation and expression
   b. Real number and integer
   c. Term and factor
   d. Trinomial and cubic expression
   e. Coefficient and exponent

4. Write a statement of the following properties or axioms.
   a. Multiplication property of -1
   b. Distributive axiom
   c. Associative axiom for multiplication
   d. Closure axiom for addition
   e. Additive identity axiom
   f. Multiplicative inverse axiom
   g. Addition property of equality
   h. Multiplication property of zero
   i. Reflexive axiom of equality
   j. Square root property of equality

5. Tell what axiom was used.
   a. $x + (y + z) = (x + y) + z$
   b. $x(y + z) = xy + xz$
   c. $x(y + z) = x(z + y)$
   d. If $6 = x$, then $x = 6$.
   e. If $6 = x$ and $x = y$, then $6 = y$.

6. Evaluate the following *constant* expressions:
   a. $4 + 2 \cdot 3 + 5$
   b. $(4 + 2) \cdot 3 + 5$
   c. $4 + 2 \cdot (3 + 5)$
   d. $3 \cdot 2^5$
   e. -3^4
   f. $47 - 7(30 \div 5 \times 2)$

7. Write an expression representing each.
   a. The seventh power of x
   b. Seven times x
   c. Seven more than x
   d. The sum of seven x's
   e. Seven less than twice x
   f. The sum of the squares of seven and x
   g. The square of the sum of seven and x
   h. 128 as a power with 2 as its base
   i. A seventh-degree trinomial
   j. The length marked "?"

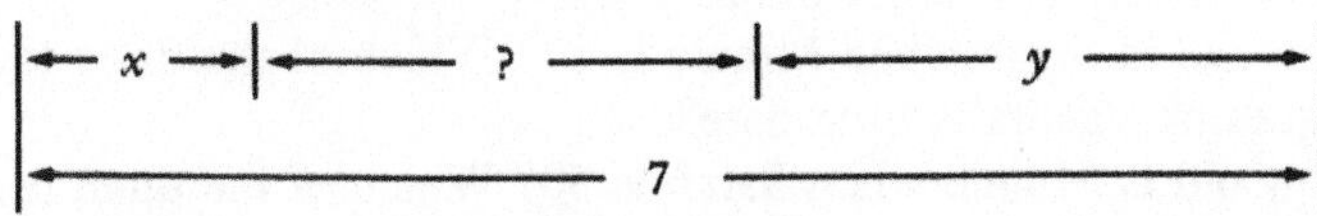

8. Transform the expression as indicated.
   a. Distribute: $4x(x^2 - 3x + 5)$
   b. Multiply: $(3a - 2b)(a + 4b)$
   c. Multiply: $(4x + 7)(4x - 7)$
   d. Square: $(x - 3.5)^2$
   e. Factor: $x^2 - 13x + 12$
   f. Factor: $v^2 - 5v - 24$
   g. Factor: $x^2 + 10x + 25$
   h. Factor: $b^2 - 1$
   i. Factor: $2x^2 - 9x - 5$
   j. Simplify: $3(x^2 - 2x - 1) - 4(x^2 - 3x + 2)$

k. Simplify: $\dfrac{9x^2 - 15x + 21}{3}$

l. Complete the square: $x^2 - 5x + \cdots$.

9. For the *linear* expression $3x + 17$:
   a. tell what the name *linear* means;
   b. evaluate the expression if x is -9;
   c. find x if the expression is equal to 52;
   d. find x if the expression is equal to $8x - 12$.

10. For the *absolute value* expression $|9 - 5x|$:
   a. evaluate it if x is 7;
   b. evaluate it if x is 1;
   c. find x if the expression is equal to 31;
   d. find x if the expression is equal to -4.

11. For the *quadratic* expression $5x^2 - 7x + 12$:
   a. evaluate it if x is -3;
   b. find x if the expression is equal to 18;
   c. find x if the expression is equal to 3;
   d. find the discriminant of the original expression.

12. You have seen a few *radical* expressions. In this problem you will apply what you know to a new situation. For the expression $\sqrt{4x - 13}$:
   a. evaluate it if x is 8;
   b. evaluate it if x is 2;
   c. find x if the expression is 5. You can do this by setting the expression equal to 5, then solving the resulting equation by *squaring* each member.

13. For parts (a) through (d), solve the equation *without* using the Quadratic Formula.
   a. $|x - 7| = 5$
   b. $(x - 7)^2 = 25$
   c. $x^2 - 14x + 49 = 25$
   d. $x^2 - 14x + 24 = 0$
   e. Explain how parts (a), (b), and (c) relate to part (d).

14. *Age Problem* Sarah Sota is 4 years older than her sister Minnie. Let x be Minnie's age.
   a. Write an expression for Sarah's age.
   b. How old is Sarah when Minnie is 17? Which of the three techniques of algebra is used here?
   c. How old is Minnie when Sarah is 50? Which of the three techniques of algebra is used here?
   d. How old are they when the sum of the squares of their ages is 208?

15. *Eggs Problem* A restaurant lets customers order any number of eggs for breakfast. They charge 65 cents per egg plus a one-time charge of 85 cents for cooking, service, and so on.
   a. Define a variable for the number of eggs ordered, and write an expression for the number of cents a customer must pay for this number of eggs.

b. How much must one pay for a dozen eggs?
c. Juanita Lott has $5.40. How many eggs could she order for this amount?

16. *Cross-Country Runners Problem* Art and Bob are cross-country runners. Art starts running at 200 meters per minute. Three minutes later, Bob starts from the same point, going in the same direction at 215 meters per minute.
    a. Draw a diagram showing the starting point, Art, and Bob, with Art farther from the start than Bob.
    b. How far has Art gone in x minutes? Write this expression on your diagram from part (a).
    c. How far has Bob gone when Art has been running for x minutes? Write this expression on your diagram from part (a).
    d. If they keep running at the same rates, will Bob have overtaken Art before x is 30? Justify your answer.

17. *Shotput Problem* Ann Athlete throws the shot with an initial upward velocity of 7 meters per second.
    a. How high is it above where she threw it after 0.4 second?
    b. When will it hit the ground, 1.3 meters *below* where she threw it?

18. *Semester Average Problem* Nita B. Topaz has an average of 75 for the semester so far, before her semester exam. She learns that her final grade will be 80% of this average, plus 20% of the semester exam grade. ("80% of . . ." means "0.8 times . . . .")
    a. Define a variable for Nita's exam grade. Then write an expression for her final grade.
    b. If Nita makes 90 on her exam, what will be her final grade?
    c. What does Nita need to make on the exam to have a final grade of 80?
    d. If passing is 60 or above, could Nita possibly have a failing final grade? Explain.

7

Expressions and Equations Containing Two Variables

ı many situations from the real orld there are two variable uantities. For instance, if x *is ıe width of a rectangular field ıd* y *is its length, then an ex- ression for its area is* xy*. The ength of fence needed to enclose he field is equal to its perimeter,* x + 2y*. In this chapter you will o the normal things with such xpressions, evaluate them, and olve equations containing them.*

ariables:

	Number of feet wide
	Number of feet long

xpressions:

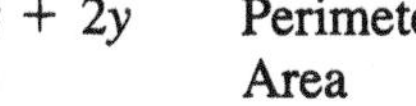

$x + 2y$	Perimeter
y	Area

7-1 EVALUATING EXPRESSIONS CONTAINING TWO VARIABLES

This section is meant for you to read and work on your own, without help from your teacher. If you succeed, you will have gotten a good overview of the content of this chapter.

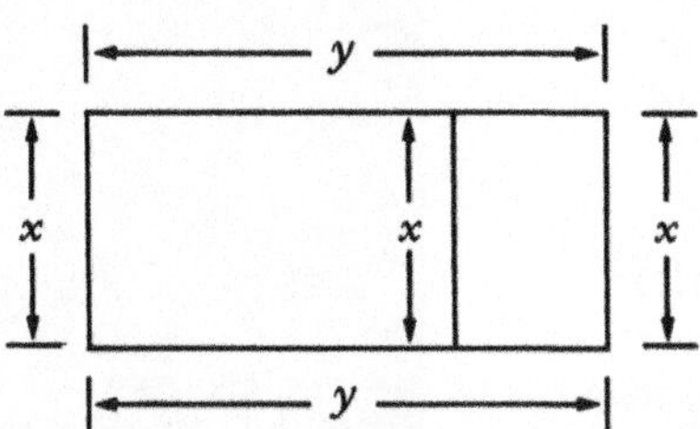

The diagram shows a rectangle x units by y units that is divided into two parts. If this were the plan for a cattle pen, the total of the lengths of the sides would be the length of fence needed to build the pen. This length would be

$$x + x + x + y + y,$$

or more simply

$$3x + 2y.$$

If x is 50 and y is 70, the total length would be

$$\begin{aligned} &3(50) + 2(70) \\ &= 150 + 140 \\ &= \underline{\underline{290.}} \end{aligned}$$

If x is 70 and y is 50, the total length would be

$$\begin{aligned} &3(70) + 2(50) \\ &= 210 + 100 \\ &= \underline{\underline{310.}} \end{aligned}$$

Obviously, it makes a difference which number you substitute for x and which you substitute for y! In this section you will evaluate expressions like this for various values of x and y.

Objective:

Given an expression with two variables, evaluate it for different values of the variables.

Cover the answers as you work the following examples.

EXAMPLE 1

For the expression $5x + 9y$:

a. Evaluate it if $x = 3$ and $y = -2$.
b. Find x if $y = 10$ and the expression equals 120.
c. Find y if $x = -7$ and the expression equals 1.

Think These Reasons

a.	$5x + 9y$	Write the given expression.
	$= 5(3) + 9(-2)$	Substitute for x and y.
	$= \underline{\underline{-3}}$	Do the computation.
b.	$5x + 9(10) = 120$	Set the expression equal to 120, and substitute 10 for y.
	$5x = 30$	Subtract 90 from each member.
	$\underline{\underline{x = 6}}$	Divide by 5.
c.	$5(-7) + 9y = 1$	Set the expression equal to q, and substitute -7 for x.
	$9y = 36$	Add 35 to each member.
	$\underline{\underline{y = 4}}$	Divide by 9.

EXAMPLE 2

Evaluate $3x^2 - 5y^2$ if $x = -9$ and $y = 20$.

$3x^2 - 5y^2$	Write the given expression.
$= 3(-9)^2 - 5(20)^2$	Substitute -9 for x and 20 for y.
$= 243 - 2000$	Do the computation.
$= \underline{\underline{-1757}}$	Do the computation.

EXERCISE 7-1

1. For the expression $8x + 5y$:
   a. Evaluate it if $x = 2$ and $y = 3$.
   b. Evaluate it if $x = 7$ and $y = -3$.
   c. Find x if the expression equals 61 and $y = -9$.
   d. Find y if the expression equals -50 and $x = 0$.
2. For the expression $6x + 10y$:
   a. Evaluate it if $x = 4$ and $y = 3$.
   b. Evaluate it if $x = -9$ and $y = 13$.
   c. Find x if the expression equals -38 and $y = -8$.
   d. Find y if the expression equals 12 and $x = 2$.
3. For the expression $10x - 7y$:
   a. Evaluate it if $x = 3$ and $y = 2$.
   b. Evaluate it if $x = 2$ and $y = 3$.
   c. Find x if the expression equals 67.7 and $y = -3.1$.
   d. Find y if the expression equals 86.9 and $x = -0.55$.
4. For the expression $-3.8x + 10y$:
   a. Evaluate it if $x = 3$ and $y = 7$.
   b. Evaluate it if $x = 7$ and $y = 3$.
   c. Find x if the expression equals -6 and $y = -2.5$.
   d. Find y if the expression equals 18.6 and $x = -0.3$.
5. Evaluate $7 - 3(x + 2y)$ if:
   a. $x = 9$ and $y = 7$;
   b. $x = 18$ and $y = -9$;
   c. $x = -4$ and $y = -11$.
6. Evaluate $8 - 5(4x - y)$ if:
   a. $x = 3$ and $y = 5$;
   b. $x = 2$ and $y = 8$;
   c. $x = -5$ and $y = 3$.
7. Evaluate $x^2 + 6y^2$ if:
   a. $x = 5$ and $y = 3$;
   b. $x = -7$ and $y = 10$;
   c. $x = 100$ and $y = -20$;
   d. $x = -8$ and $y = -1$.
8. Evaluate $4x^2 + y^2$ if:
   a. $x = 6$ and $y = 8$;
   b. $x = -3$ and $y = 30$;
   c. $x = 50$ and $y = -100$;
   d. $x = -6$ and $y = -12$.

7-2 THE CARTESIAN COORDINATE SYSTEM

A number line is used to plot values of a variable. If an expression has two variables, such as $3x + 2y$, it takes *two* number lines, one for x and the other for y. The values $x = 4$ and $y = 7$ could be shown as follows.

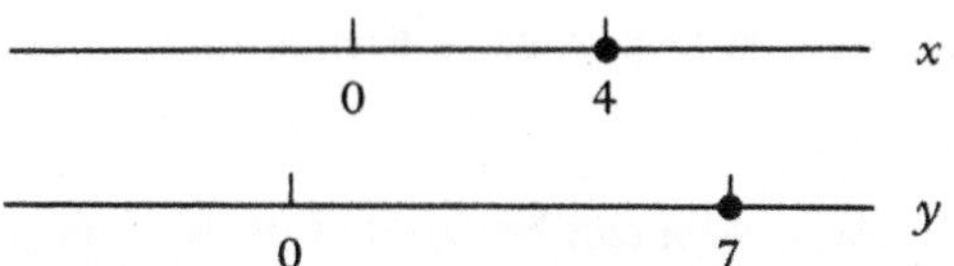

The usual way to show both values in the same diagram is to cross the two number lines at their origins (see the graph). To plot a point, you start at the origin and move across 4 units in the x-direction. Then you move up 7 units in the y-direction. The point in the plane is called the **graph** of $x = 4$ and $y = 7$. The two number lines are called the ***x*-axis** and the ***y*-axis.**

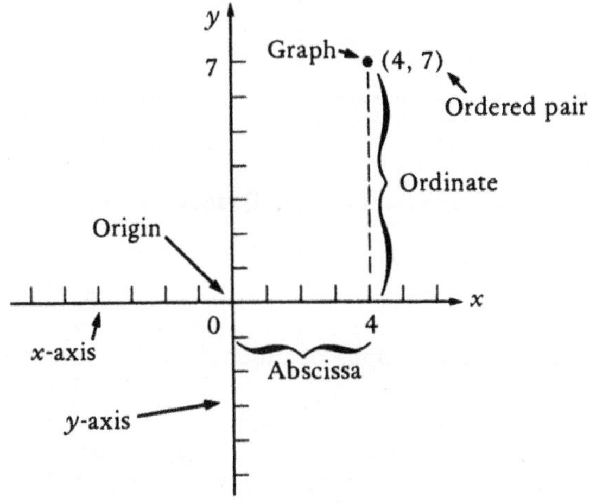

Cartesian coordinate system
(The Cartesian plane)

To shorten things, $x = 4$ and $y = 7$ is written $(4, 7)$. This symbol is called an **ordered pair** of numbers. The order in which the numbers occur tells which number goes with which variable. Unless you are told otherwise, the variables in an ordered pair come in alphabetical order, as in (x, y). People commonly use the idea of ordered pair for such things as time of day (three thirty), balls and strikes (a count of 3 and 2), and men's shirt sizes $(15\frac{1}{2}, 35)$.

The first number in an ordered pair is called the **abscissa.** The word comes from the same Latin root as the word *scissors*. This number tells you where to "cut off" as you run along the x-axis. The second number in an ordered pair is called the **ordinate.** This word comes from *order*. Together, the two numbers $(4, 7)$ are called the **coordinates** of a point in a plane.

The whole system—x-axis, y-axis, points in the plane—is called a **Cartesian coordinate system.** Cartesian is capitalized because it comes from the proper name René Descartes, a French mathematician who lived from 1596 to 1650.

A Cartesian coordinate system can be thought of as a piece of graph paper with two axes drawn on it. The axes divide the graph paper into four regions called **quadrants.** The quadrants are numbered counterclockwise, starting at the upper right (where both variables are positive), as shown in the figure.

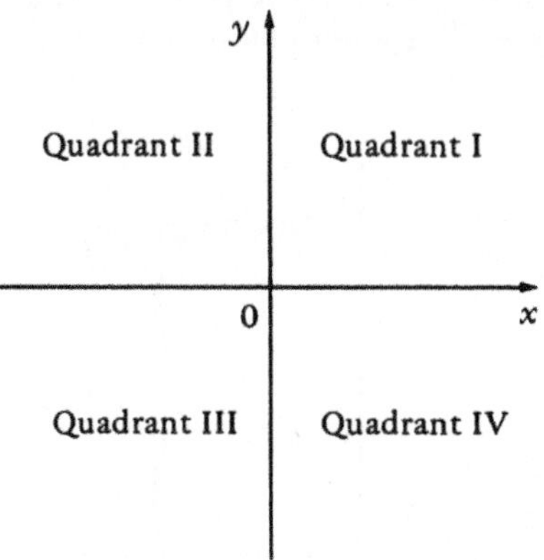

In this section you will plot graphs of ordered pairs and read coordinates of a given point.

Objective:

Given an ordered pair, plot its graph; or given a point in a Cartesian coordinate system, read its coordinates correct to the nearest 0.1 unit.

Cover the answer with paper until you have worked the example.

EXAMPLE 1

Plot $(2, 5)$ and $(-3, 1)$ in a Cartesian coordinate system.

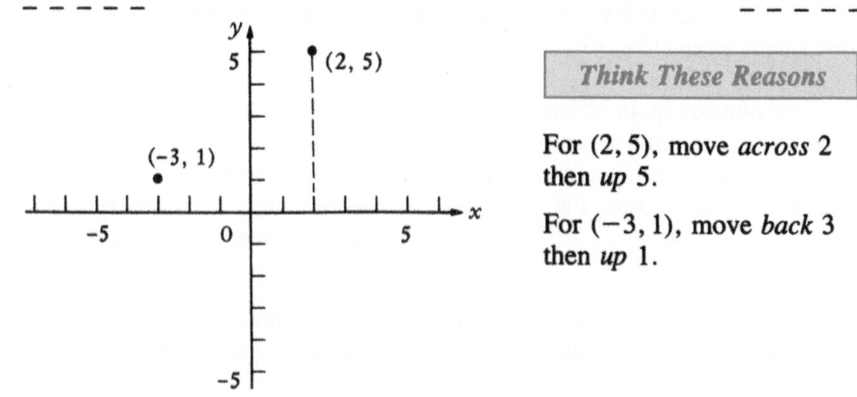

Think These Reasons

For $(2, 5)$, move *across* 2 then *up* 5.

For $(-3, 1)$, move *back* 3 then *up* 1.

Note: Be sure you label the x-axis and y-axis as shown, with arrow heads and the letters x and y. Also, show the **scale** on the two axes. For instance, you might put a number every 5 units, as shown above.

EXAMPLE 2

Write the coordinates of points A and B. Estimate noninteger coordinates to the nearest 0.1 unit.

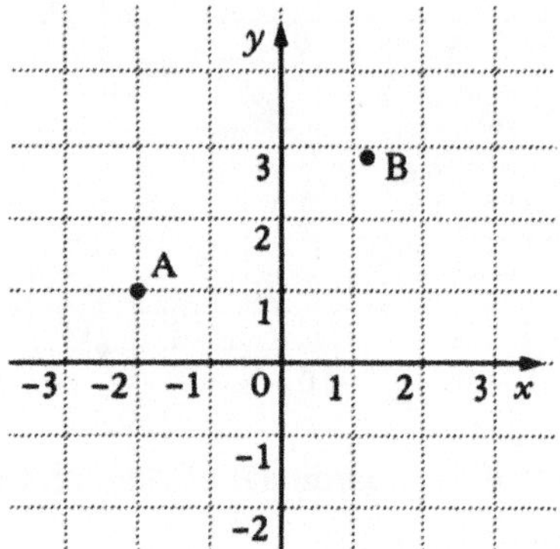

$\underline{A(-2, 1)}$ You move -2 in the x-direction, and then move up 1 in the y-direction to get to the point. So the ordered pair is $(-2, 1)$. The name of the point and the ordered pair are written together as $A(-2, 1)$.

$\underline{B(1.2, 2.9)}$ The abscissa is *between* 1 and 2. Since it is *less* than halfway, it is either $1.1, 1.2, 1.3$, or 1.4. Because the abscissa is not close to 1 or 1.5, rule out 1.1 and 1.4. So you pick either 1.2 or 1.3; in this case, 1.2 looks *best*. Your answer will be counted correct if it is within ± 0.1 of the "right" answer. So $1.1, 1.2$, or 1.3 would be acceptable values for x.

The ordinate is between 2 and 3. Since it is more than halfway, it is either $2.6, 2.7, 2.8$, or 2.9. Pick 2.9, because the point is so close to 3. Again, $2.8, 2.9$, or 3.0 would be acceptable since they are within ± 0.1 unit of the "right" answer.

ORAL PRACTICE

For A through T, give the coordinates of the point.

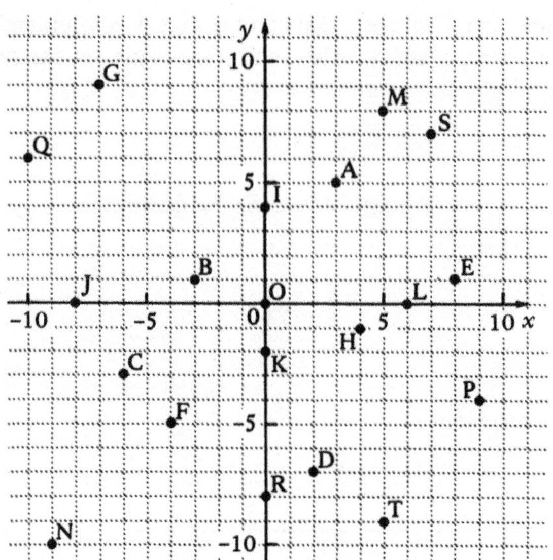

For U through DD, give the coordinate of the point correct to the nearest 0.1 unit.

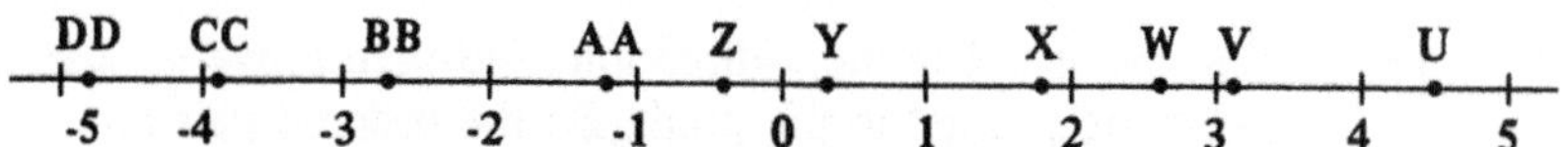

Give the quadrant in which the following points are found.

EE. $(5, 3)$

FF. $(6, -2)$

GG. $(-7.2, 1)$

HH. $(-3.4, -2.8)$

EXERCISE 7-2

For Problems 1 and 2, write the coordinates of each point as an ordered pair. All points have integer coordinates.

1. 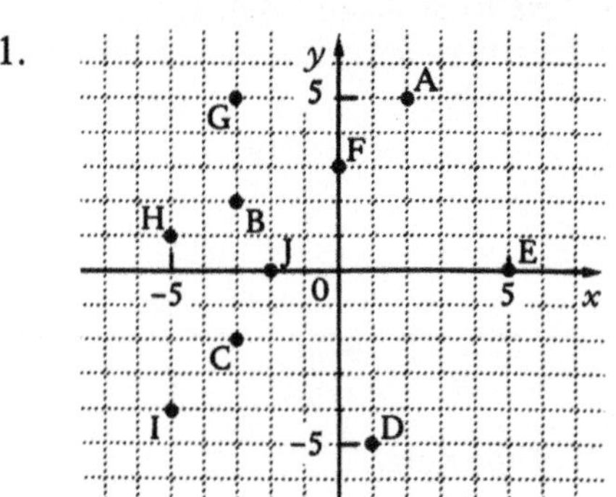

2. 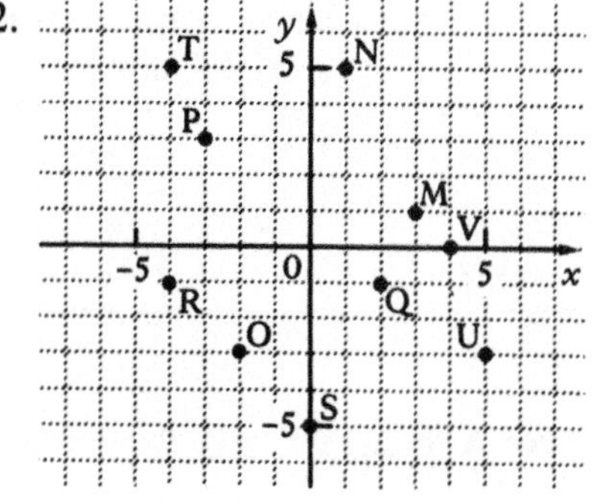

For Problems 3 and 4, draw a Cartesian coordinate system on graph paper. Then plot the points. Be sure to indicate which is which!

3. a. $(5, 2)$
   b. $(-3, 7)$
   c. $(4, -6)$
   d. $(-2, -1)$
   e. $(0, 3)$

4. a. $(1, 3)$
   b. $(-2, 5)$
   c. $(-4, -7)$
   d. $(3, -8)$
   e. $(5, 0)$

5. Estimate the coordinates of points A, B, C, and D, below, to the nearest 0.1 unit.

6. Estimate the coordinates of points R, S, T, and U, below, to the nearest 0.1 unit.

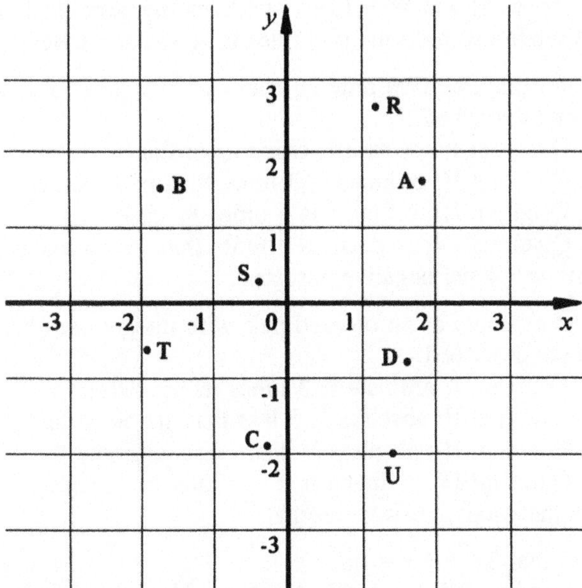

7. Plot points $A(7, 10)$ and $B(1, -2)$ on graph paper. Use a ruler to connect them with a straight line. Then write the coordinates of each point.
   a. The point midway between A and B
   b. The point $\frac{1}{3}$ of the way from A to B
   c. The point $\frac{2}{3}$ of the way from A to B
   d. The point where the line crosses the x-axis.

8. Plot points $R(-2, 7)$ and $S(6, 3)$ on graph paper. Use a ruler to connect them with a straight line. Then write the coordinates of each point.
   a. The point midway between R and S
   b. The point $\frac{1}{4}$ of the way from R to S
   c. The point $\frac{3}{4}$ of the way from R to S
   d. The point where the graph crosses the y-axis.

9. Connect points $A(-3, 1)$ and $B(5, 4)$ with a straight line. Connect points $C(1, 5)$ and $D(3, -1)$ with another straight line. Then estimate to the nearest 0.1 unit the coordinates of the point where the two lines intersect.

10. Connect points $R(-2, 4)$ and $S(4, 1)$ with a straight line. Connect points $T(-1, -2)$ and $U(3, 4)$ with another straight line. Then estimate to the nearest 0.1 unit the coordinates of the point where the two lines intersect.

11. Connect points $E(-4, -2)$ and $F(1, 1)$ with a straight line. Connect points $G(-3, 1)$ and $H(2, 4)$ with another straight line. What special relationship do the two lines have to each other?

12. Connect points $P(-4, 1)$ and $J(2, 5)$ with a staight line. Connect points $U(-5, 5)$ and $W(-1, -1)$ with another straight line. What special relationship do the two lines have to each other?

13. Write an example of an ordered pair with integer coordinates for each point described.
    a. In Quadrant I; abscissa is twice its ordinate.
    b. In Quadrant II; ordinate is 3 more than its abscissa.
    c. In Quadrant III; ordinate is 5 times its abscissa.
    d. In Quadrant IV; abscissa is 4 more than its ordinate.
    e. On the x-axis; negative abscissa

14. Write an example of an ordered pair with integer coordinates for each point described.
    a. In Quadrant I; ordinate is 3 times its abscissa.
    b. In Quadrant II; abscissa is 5 less than its ordinate.
    c. In Quadrant III; abscissa is 4 times its ordinate.
    d. In Quadrant IV; ordinate is 6 less than its abscissa.
    e. On the y-axis; positive ordinate

15. Suppose that $3x + 5y = 60$.
    a. Substitute 10 for x in this equation. Then solve for y. Write the values of x and y as an ordered pair. Then repeat the procedure for $x = 15$ and for $x = -5$.
    b. Plot the three ordered pairs on a Cartesian coordinate system. If your work is correct, all three points should lie on a straight line.

16. Suppose that $5x - 2y = 30$.
    a. Substitute 4 for x in this equation. Then solve for y. Write the values of x and y as an ordered pair. Then repeat the procedure for $x = 8$ and for $x = -2$.
    b. Plot the three ordered pairs on a Cartesian coordinate system. If your work is correct, all three points should lie on a straight line.

7-3 GRAPHS OF EQUATIONS CONTAINING TWO VARIABLES

Algebra is the study of expressions with variables. One thing you do with such expressions is to set them equal to some number and find the value of the variable. If the expression has *two* variables, there may be many values that satisfy the equation. For example,

$$2x + 5y = 30$$

is a true statement for ordered pairs (0, 6), (5, 4), and (13, 0.8), as well as many others. For instance, for (5, 4), 2(5) + 5(4) equals 10 + 20, which *does* equal 30.

Such ordered pairs are called *solutions* of the equation.

DEFINITION

> **SOLUTION, EQUATION CONTAINING TWO VARIABLES**
> A **solution** of an equation with two variables is an ordered pair that makes the equation a *true* statement.

The set of *all* such ordered pairs is called the *solution set.*

Since the solution set contains so many ordered pairs, you usually draw a graph of it rather than trying to write the pairs. To plot the graph of an equation such as

$$2x + 5y = 30,$$

you must find some ordered pairs. One way is to pick a value of one variable, substitute it into the equation, then calculate the value of the other variable. For instance, choose $x = 7$.

$2(7) + 5y = 30$	Substitute 7 for x.
$14 + 5y = 30$	Do the computation.
$5y = 16$	Subtract 14 from each member.
$y = \underline{\underline{3.2}}$	Divide each member by 5.

So one ordered pair would be (7, 3.2).

An efficient way to calculate *many* ordered pairs is to get one variable by itself on the left side and everything else on the right. Starting with $2x + 5y = 30$ and isolating y, you would write the following.

$$2x + 5y = 30$$

$$5y = -2x + 30 \qquad \text{Add } -2x \text{ to each member.}$$

$$y = -\frac{2}{5}x + 6 \qquad \text{Divide each member by 5.}$$

In the last equation, y is said to be written *in terms of* x. This procedure is the same as for solving the literal equations in Section 4-5. Finding values of y is now the familiar process of evaluating an expression. For instance,

$x = 10$:

$$y = -\frac{2}{5}(10) + 6 = -4 + 6 = 2;$$

$x = -5$:

$$y = -\frac{2}{5}(-5) + 6 = 2 + 6 = 8.$$

To keep track of all these values of x and y, it is convenient to make a table of values. These values can then be plotted as ordered pairs, as shown next.

x	y
0	6
5	4
10	2
15	0
−5	8
−10	10

Make a table of values.

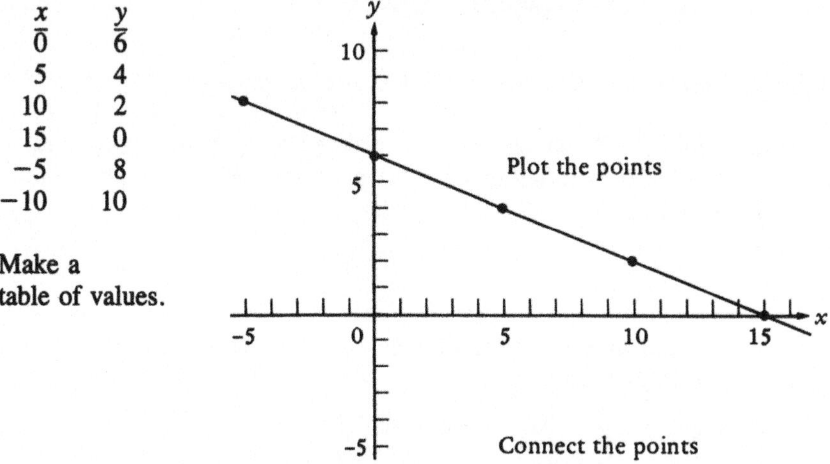

A pattern shows up when you plot the ordered pairs from this table. The points are in a straight line! Later in this chapter you will learn why all linear equations have straight-line graphs. To complete this graph, you can simply connect the points. The second figure shows the finished graph. Any point on this line represents an ordered pair in the solution set of this equation.

Objective:

Given a linear equation with two variables (such as $2x + 5y = 30$), transform it so that y is written in terms of x. Then evaluate y for various values of x and use the resulting ordered pairs to plot the graph.

Cover the answers as you work this example.

EXAMPLE

For the equation $x - 2y = 6$:

a. transform the equation so that y is given in terms of x;

b. pick four values of x, and evaluate y;

c. plot the graph.

Think These Reasons

a. $x - 2y = 6$	Write the given equation.
$-2y = -x + 6$	Add $-x$ to each member.
$y = \frac{1}{2}x - 3$	Multiply each member by $-\frac{1}{2}$.

b. Make a table of values.

x	y
0	−3
2	−2
4	−1
6	0

c. Plot the graph.

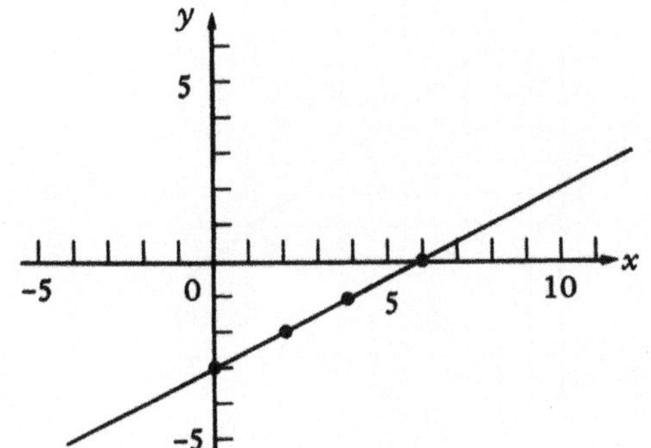

ORAL PRACTICE

For A through L, give the coordinates of the ordered pairs.

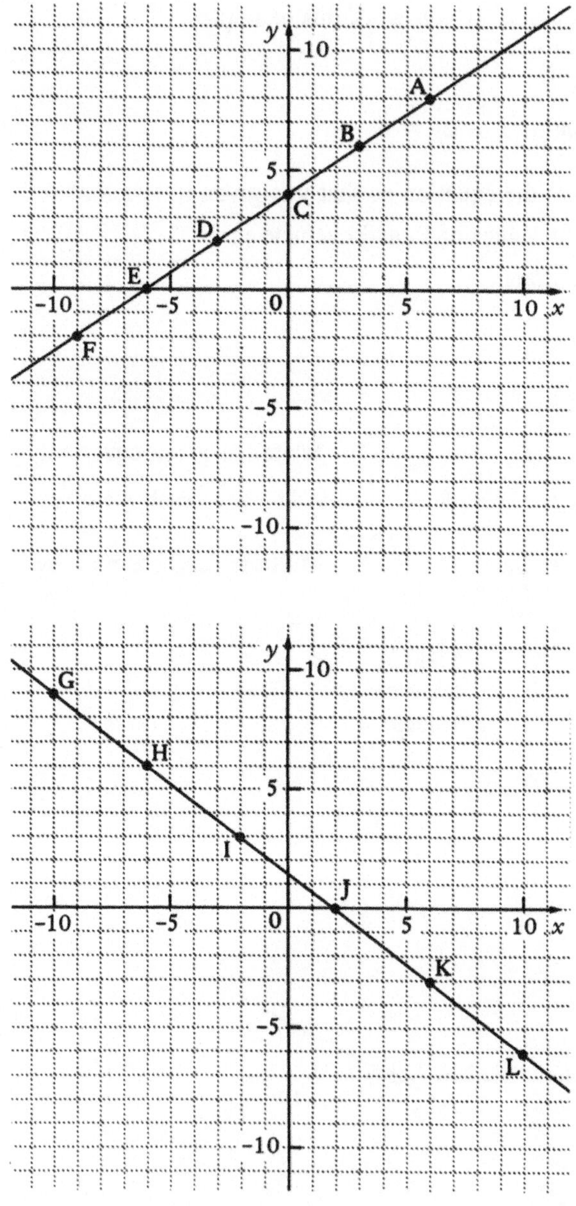

Transform the equation so that y is given in terms of x.

M.	$4x + y = 9$	N.	$7x + y = -10$	O.	$8x - y = 6$
P.	$5x - y = -7$	Q.	$3x + 2y = 5$	R.	$6x + 2y = -10$
S.	$7x - 3y = 4$	T.	$12x - 3y = -15$	U.	$x + 4y = -11$
V.	$x - 5y = 20$	W.	$x + y = 6$	X.	$x - y = -9$

EXERCISE 7-3

For Problems 1 through 8, draw a graph of the indicated set of points. Connect the points with a straight line.

1.

(x, y)
$(5, 8)$
$(3, 5)$
$(1, 2)$
$(-1, -1)$

2.

(x, y)
$(7, 5)$
$(4, 3)$
$(1, 1)$
$(-2, -1)$

3.

(x, y)
$(-3, 7)$
$(0, 4)$
$(3, 1)$
$(6, -2)$

4.

(x, y)
$(-2, 7)$
$(0, 3)$
$(2, -1)$
$(4, -5)$

5.

x	y
−5	3
−1	1
3	−1
7	−3

6.

x	y
−5	7
−2	2
1	−3
4	−8

7.

x	y
−5	−7
0	−4
5	−1
10	2

8.

x	y
−1	−5
0	−2
1	1
2	4

For Problems 9 through 20:

a. transform the equation so that y is given in terms of x;
b. pick four numbers, substitute them for x, and evaluate y.
c. plot the graph of the equation.

9. $3x + y = 12$
10. $2x + y = 10$
11. $2x - y = 6$
12. $3x - y = 6$
13. $4x + 5y = 40$
14. $3x + 5y = 30$
15. $3x - 2y = -18$
16. $2x - 3y = -12$
17. $x + y = 7$
18. $x - y = 4$
19. $x - 3y = 0$
20. $x + 2y = 0$

7-4 INTERCEPTS AND RAPID GRAPHING

In the last section you observed that equations such as

$$3x + 2y = 12$$

have graphs that turn out to be straight lines. You can use this fact to draw these graphs with very little work! All you need to do is find *two* points and draw the line.

The easiest two points to find are usually the points where the graph crosses the two coordinate axes. A graph crosses the y-axis where $x = 0$. Substituting 0 for x in $3x + 2y = 12$ gives

$$0 + 2y = 12$$
$$y = 6.$$

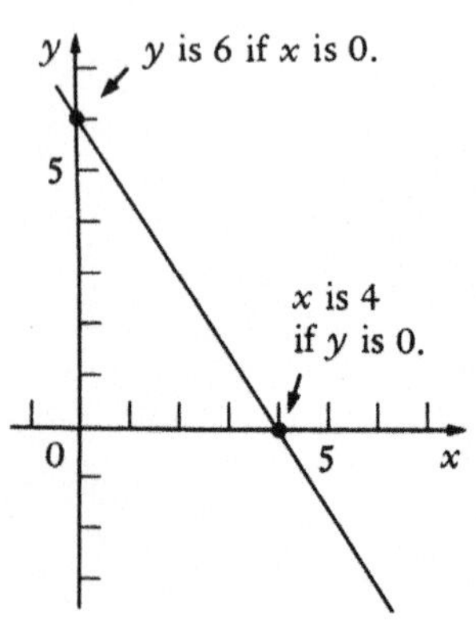

Similarly, substituting 0 for y gives

$$3x + 0 = 12$$
$$x = 4.$$

You can plot the two ordered pairs $(0, 6)$ and $(4, 0)$ and draw the line, as shown in the figure.

The numbers 6 and 4 have special names. The 6 is called the *y-intercept*. The 4 is called the *x-intercept*. These names come from the fact that the graph "intercepts" the two axes at these values.

DEFINITION

> **INTERCEPTS**
> The **y-intercept** is the value of y when x is 0.
> The **x-intercept** is the value of x when y is 0.

Objective:

Given an equation of a line, find the x- and y-intercepts, and use these to draw the graph *quickly*.

Cover the answers as you work this example.

EXAMPLE

For the equation $5x - 3y = -30$:
a. find the x- and y-intercepts;
b. plot the graph.

a. Let $x = 0$.

$0 - 3y = -30$

$y = 10$

y-intercept is 10.

Let $y = 0$.

$5x - 0 = -30$

$x = -6$

x-intercept is -6.

b.

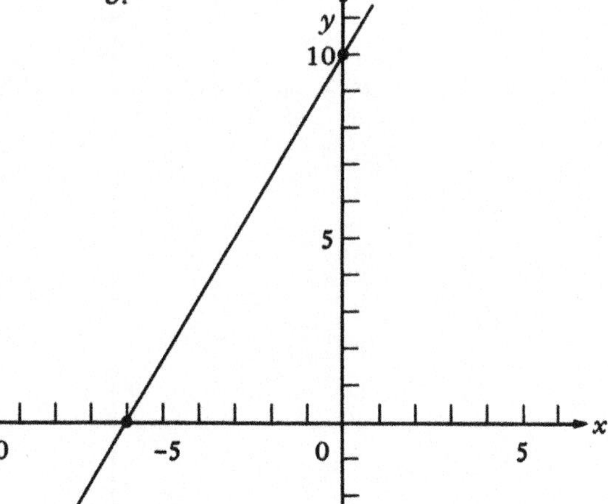

ORAL PRACTICE

Give the y-intercept.

EXAMPLE

	Answer
$3x - 2y = 18$	-9

A. $4x + 3y = 24$

B. $2x + 5y = -100$

C. $3x - 4y = 36$

D. $5x - 8y = -80$

E. $2x + y = 10$

F. $6x - y = -18$

Tell the x-intercept.

G. $4x + 3y = 24$

H. $2x + 5y = -100$

I. $3x - 4y = 36$

J. $5x - 8y = -80$

K. $x + 2y = 10$

L. $x - 6y = -18$

Give the x- and y-intercepts of each line.

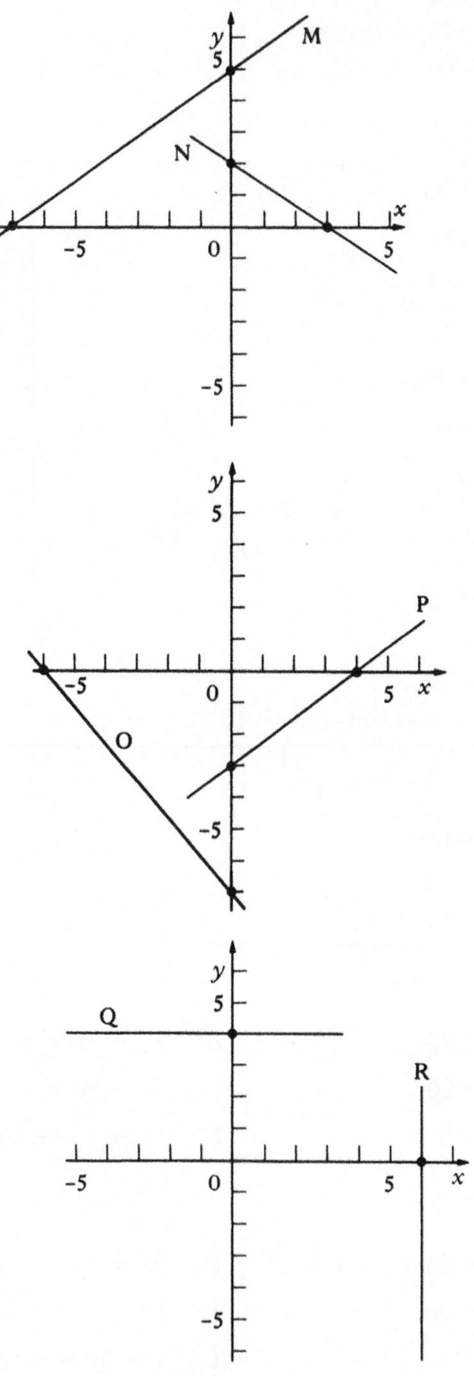

EXERCISE 7-4

For Problems 1 through 20, calculate the x- and y-intercepts. Use them to plot the graph.

1. $4x + 3y = 24$
2. $3x + 4y = 36$
3. $2x + 5y = -20$
4. $5x + 3y = -15$
5. $3x - 4y = 36$
6. $4x - 3y = 24$
7. $5x - 8y = -40$
8. $6x - 5y = -30$
9. $2x + y = 10$
10. $3x + y = 6$
11. $6x - y = -12$
12. $4x - y = -8$
13. $x + 3y = 6$
14. $x + 5y = 10$
15. $x + y = 4$
16. $x + y = -7$
17. $x - y = -3$
18. $x - y = 5$
19. $2x + 3y = 15$
20. $3x + 2y = 9$

For Problems 21 through 24, plot the two points carefully on graph paper. Connect the points with a straight line, using a ruler and a *sharp* pencil. Then read the x- and y-intercepts, correct to the nearest 0.1 unit, from the graph. Your answer will be considered to be correct if it is no more than ± 0.1 unit from the correct answer.

21. $(-3, 9)$ and $(10, -2)$
22. $(-5, -1)$ and $(3, 6)$
23. $(7, 1)$ and $(-2, -4)$
24. $(-3, 3)$ and $(2, -5)$
25. *Tickets Problem* Reserved tickets for the basketball game cost \$3 each and general admission tickets cost \$2 each. Let x be the number of reserved tickets a person sells and let y be the number of general admission tickets that person sells.

TICKET SALES	
Reserved:	
x @ \$3 . . .	______
Gen. Admission:	
y @ \$2 . . .	______
Total . . .	======

a. Write an expression for the total number of dollars the person gets for tickets sold.
b. How much money is received for:
   i. 8 reserved, 10 general admission;
   ii. 10 reserved, 8 general admission?
c. A member of the pep squad must sell $30 worth of tickets. Write an equation stating this.
d. Find the intercepts of the equation in part (c) and use these to plot the graph of the equation.
e. Since only whole numbers of tickets can be sold, x and y must be integers. From your graph, find all possible ordered pairs (x, y) that have nonnegative integer coordinates.

26. *Socks and Scarves Problem* Socks cost $3 a pair and scarves cost $5 each. Natalie Attired buys some of each. Let x be the number of pairs of socks and let y be the number of scarves she buys.

NATALIE'S BILL

Socks:
x pr. @ $3 . . _____

Scarves:
y @ $5 . . . _____

Total . . . _____

a. Write an expression for the total number of dollars she pays.
b. How much would she pay for:
   i. 7 pairs of socks, 4 scarves;
   ii. 4 pairs of socks, 7 scarves?
c. Write an equation stating that Natalie spends a total of $60 for socks and scarves.
d. Find the intercepts for the equation in part (c) and use these to plot the graph of the equation.
e. You can buy only a whole number of pairs of socks and a whole number of scarves. Use your graph to find all possible numbers of pairs of socks and scarves Natalie could have bought for $60 total.

27. *Walking and Cycling Problem* Ida Clare can walk at a rate of 100 yards per minute and can ride her bike at 300 yards per minute. Let x be the number of minutes she walks and let y by the number of minutes she rides.
a. Write an expression for the total number of yards she goes.
b. How far does she go if she:
   i. walks for 7 minutes and rides for 3 minutes;
   ii. walks for 3 minutes and rides for 7 minutes?

c. Ida must deliver a package to a destination 6000 yards away. Write an equation stating this.
d. Find the intercepts for the equation in part (c). Use these numbers to plot the graph of the equation.
e. If Ida walks for 12 minutes on her 6000-yard delivery, how many minutes must she ride her bike? Show that this ordered pair is *on* your graph in part (d).

28. *Train and Bus Problem* A train averages 80 miles per hour (mi/h), and a bus averages 50 mi/h. Let x be the number of hours you ride the train and let y be the number of hours you ride the bus.
   a. Write an expression for the total number of miles you ride.
   b. How far do you go if you ride:
      i. 3 hours on the train and 6 hours on the bus;
      ii. 6 hours on the train and 3 hours on the bus?
   c. You make a 400-mile trip, part by train and part by bus. Write an equation stating this fact.
   d. Find the intercepts of the equation and use them to plot the graph of the equation.
   e. If you go for 2 hours on the train, how many hours must you ride the bus to complete the 400-mile trip? Show that this ordered pair is *on* your graph in part (d).

7-5 SLOPE AND RAPID GRAPHING

If you go from the point (2, 1) to the point (7, 3), as in the figure, you must run across 5 units in the x-direction and rise up 2 units in the y-direction. These distances are given the (obvious!) names *run* and *rise*.

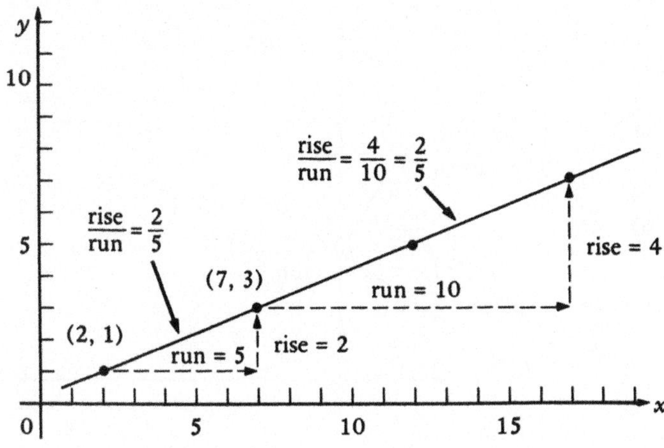

DEFINITION

> **RUN AND RISE**
> In going from one point to another in a Cartesian coordinate system, the **run** is the change in x and the **rise** is the change in y.

For any two points on the same straight line, the ratio

$$\frac{\text{rise}}{\text{run}}$$

is *constant*. For the line in the figure, the ratio rise/run is always equal to $\frac{2}{5}$, no matter what pair of points you pick. Since this number indicates how "steep" the line is, it is called the *slope* of the line.

DEFINITION

> **SLOPE**
> The slope of a line is the ratio
> $$\frac{\text{rise}}{\text{run}}.$$

The slope shows up in the equation of a line if you write the equation so that y is in terms of x. Suppose that you plot

$$y = \frac{2}{3}x + 4.$$

as you did in Section 7-3. By substituting various values for x, you can evaluate y and make a table.

x	y
−6	0
−3	2
0	4
3	6
6	8
9	10

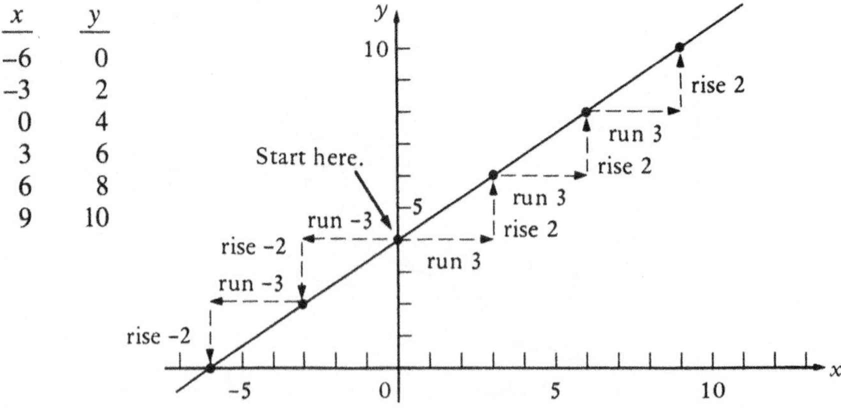

For each pair of points, the slope is $\frac{2}{3}$. And this number is the coefficient of x in the equation! From the table or the graph, you can see that this is true; each time x increases by 3, y increases by 2.

This fact reveals the reason a linear equation has a straight-line graph. It also provides a quick way to draw the graph. You start at any point on the graph, run 3 and rise 2, and you will be at another point on the graph.

All you need is a convenient starting point. The y-intercept is easy to find. Substituting 0 for x in the equation gives

$$y = \frac{2}{3}(0) + 4 = 4.$$

So the y-intercept is 4. Note that this number also shows up in the equation.

$$y = \underbrace{\frac{2}{3}}_{\text{slope}}x + \underbrace{4}_{y\text{-intercept}}$$

Any linear equation with y by itself on the left and a linear binomial on the right is said to be in *slope-intercept form*. The letter m is usually used for the slope and b is used for the y-intercept.

CONCLUSION

> **SLOPE-INTERCEPT FORM**
> An equation of the form $y = mx + b$, where m and b are constants, is in **slope-intercept form.**
> The constant m is the *slope*.
> The constant b is the y-intercept.

For the equation $y = \frac{2}{3}x + 4$, $m = \frac{2}{3}$ and $b = 4$.

Objectives:

1. Given two points in a Cartesian coordinate system, find the slope of the line connecting them.
2. Given a linear equation with two variables, find the slope and the y-intercept and use these numbers to plot the graph quickly.

Cover the answers as you work these examples.

EXAMPLE 1

Find the slope of each line.

a. Line A b. Line B c. Line C d. Line D

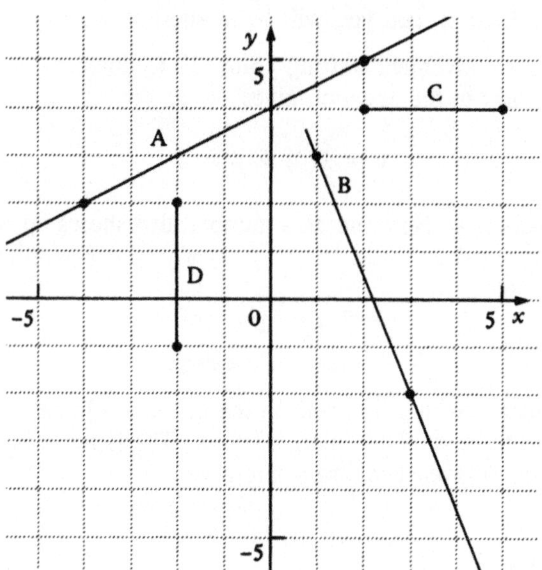

Think These Reasons

a. $m = \frac{\text{rise}}{\text{run}}$ Definition of slope

$= \frac{3}{6}$ Count squares. Rise is *up* 3. Run is 6.

$= \frac{1}{2}$ Simplify the fraction, if possible.

b. $m = \frac{\text{rise}}{\text{run}}$ Definition of slope

$= \frac{-5}{2}$ Rise is *down* 5. Run is 2.

$= -\frac{5}{2}$ Negative divided by positive is negative.

c. $m = \frac{\text{rise}}{\text{run}}$ Definition of slope

$= \frac{0}{3}$	Zero squares up or down, 3 squares across
$= \underline{\underline{0}}$	Arithmetic

- - - - -

d. $m = \frac{\text{rise}}{\text{run}}$	Definition of slope
$= \frac{3}{0}$	3 squares up. Zero squares across
No value!	No answer for division by zero!

The line in part (c) is *horizontal*. The line in part (d) is *vertical*. From the answers to these examples you can draw the conclusion shown.

CONCLUSION

SLOPES OF HORIZONTAL AND VERTICAL LINES

Horizontal lines have 0 for a slope.

Vertical lines do not *have* a slope!!

EXAMPLE 2

Write the slope and y-intercept and plot the graph.

$$y = -\frac{3}{5}x + 7$$

- - - - -

$m = -\frac{3}{5}$	$\left(\text{Also equals } \frac{-3}{5} \text{ and } \frac{3}{-5}.\right)$
$b = 7$	Let $x = 0$. Find y.

For the graph, start at the y-intercept. Count *across* 5 and *down* 3. Or count *back* 5 and *up* 3. Repeat until you have enough points to draw the graph.

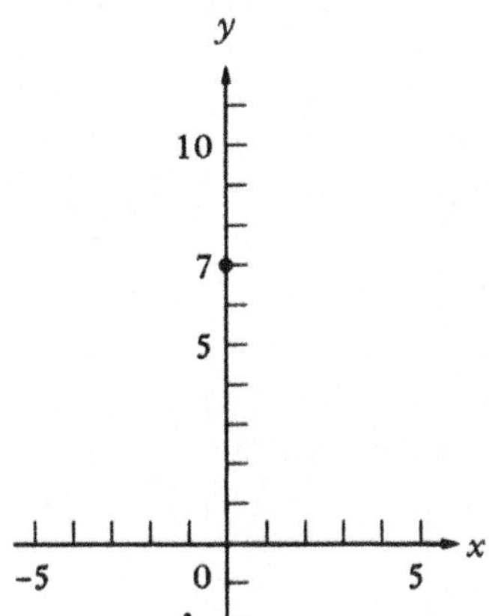

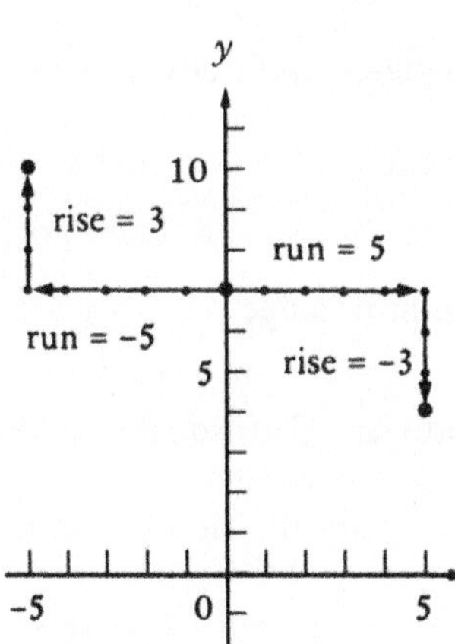

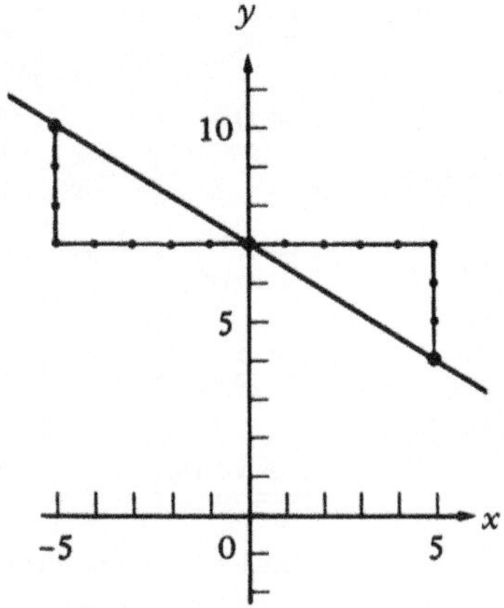

ORAL PRACTICE

Give the slope.

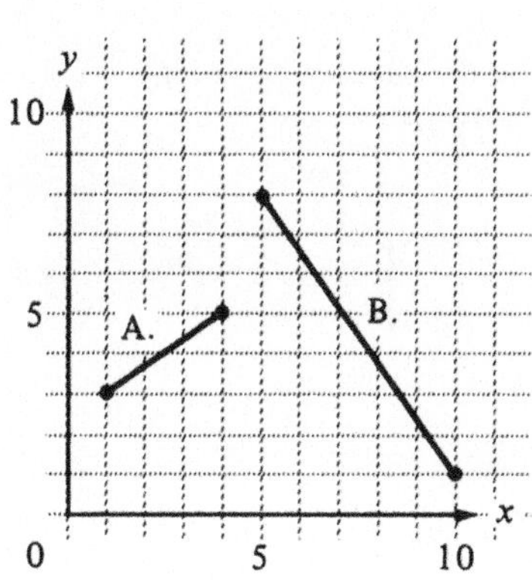

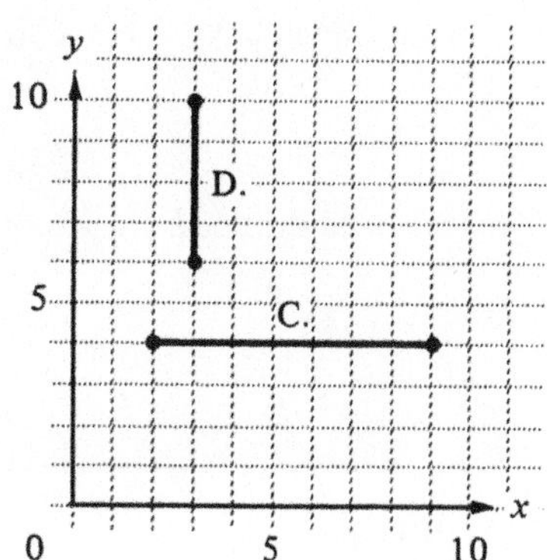

Give the slope.

E. $y = \frac{3}{4}x + 7$ F. $y = \frac{9}{5}x - 4$ G. $y = -\frac{3}{2}x + 8$

H. $y = -4x + 9$ I. $y = x + 6$ J. $y = -x + 2$

Give the y-intercept.

K. $y = \frac{3}{4}x + 7$ L. $y = \frac{9}{5}x - 4$ M. $y = -\frac{3}{2}x + 8$

N. $y = -4x + 9$ O. $y = x - 6$ P. $y = 3x$

Transform to slope-intercept form.

EXAMPLE

	Answer
$3x + 4y = 24$	$y = -\frac{3}{4}x + 6$

Q. $3x + y = 7$

R. $5x - y = 8$

S. $6x + 5y = 20$

T. $2x - 3y = 15$

U. $x + 2y = 6$

V. $-x + 3y = -12$

EXERCISE 7-5

For Problems 1 and 2, find the slope of each line. Simplify as much as possible.

1.

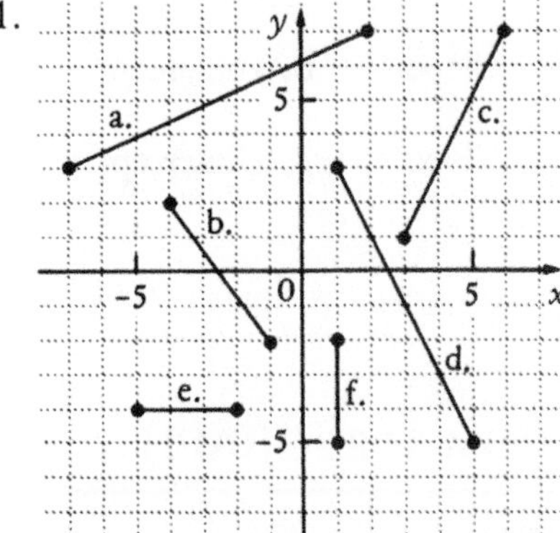

2.

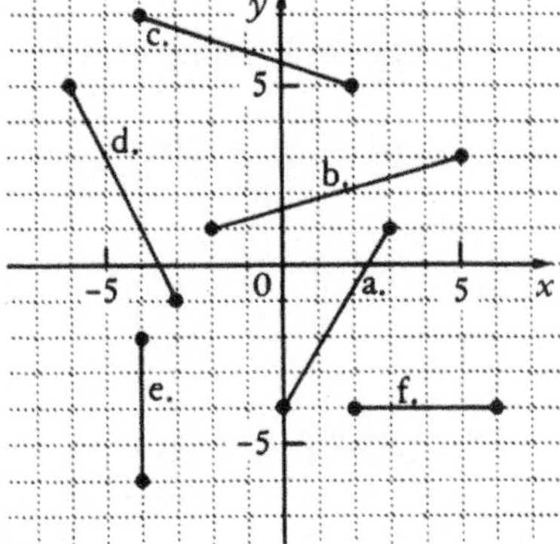

For Problems 3 through 10, plot the points on a Cartesian coordinate system and connect them with a straight line. Find the slope and simplify it if possible.

3. $(-2, 4)$ and $(5, -1)$.

4. $(-2, 1)$ and $(3, 5)$.

5. $(-2, 1)$ and $(1, -3)$.

6. $(-1, 4)$ and $(3, -4)$.

7. $(-1, 2)$ and $(-4, -6)$.

8. $(-3, -4)$ and $(3, -1)$.

9. $(-6, 1)$ and $(1, -3)$.

10. $(-3, 3)$ and $(-1, -2)$.

For Problems 11 through 22, plot the graph using the slope and the y-intercept. Label the axes and show the scale.

11. $y = \frac{3}{5}x + 3$ 12. $y = \frac{5}{2}x - 1$ 13. $y = -\frac{3}{2}x - 4$

14. $y = -\frac{1}{4}x + 3$ 15. $y = 2x - 5$ 16. $y = 3x - 2$

17. $y = -3x + 1$ 18. $y = -2x + 6$ 19. $y = 3x$

20. $y = -2x$ 21. $y = -x + 4$ 22. $y = x - 5$

In Problems 23 through 30, transform the equation to the slope-intercept form ($y = mx + b$). Then give the slope and the y-intercept. Finally, plot the graph.

23. $7x + 2y = 10$ 24. $3x + 5y = 10$

25. $x - 4y = 12$ 26. $2x - 5y = 15$

27. $y - 3 = \frac{2}{3}(x - 6)$ 28. $y - 5 = \frac{3}{7}(x - 7)$

29. $y + 2 = -\frac{1}{4}(x + 8)$ 30. $y + 3 = -\frac{5}{2}(x - 4)$

For Problems 31 through 34, find the equation of the line described. To do this, you need to recall where the slope and y-intercept appear in the equation $y = mx + b$.

31. Slope = 3, y-intercept = 5 32. Slope = −6, y-intercept = 9

33. Slope = $\frac{2}{3}$, y-intercept = −1 34. Slope = −7, y-intercept = 0

7-6 FINDING AN EQUATION FROM THE GRAPH

In the last section you plotted graphs of lines using the y-intercept and slope. Suppose someone says, "Find an equation of the line shown in Figure 7-6a." "That's easy!" you reply. "The y-intercept is −4. Counting squares, the run is 2 and rise is 3. So the slope is $\frac{3}{2}$." You can then just substitute these numbers for the literal constants in

$$y = mx + b$$

and get

$$y = \frac{3}{2}x - 4.$$

In this section you will learn how to get an equation of a line either from the graph or from information about the graph.

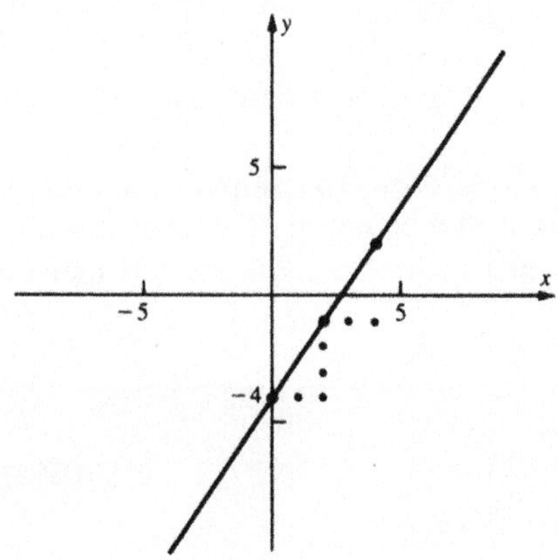

Figure 7-6a

Objective:

Given the graph of a line, or information about the graph, write an equation for the line.

There is another form of the equation of a line that helps when the y-intercept is not known. Think about the equation

$$y - 4 = \frac{2}{5}(x - 3).$$

If y is 4, the left member of the equation is zero. If x is 3, the right member is 0. So the ordered pair $(x, y) = (3, 4)$ satisfies the equation. This fact means that the point $(3, 4)$ is on the graph. If you distribute the $\frac{2}{5}$ on the right, it becomes the coefficient of x. So $\frac{2}{3}$ is the slope of the line. The graph is shown in Figure 7-6b.

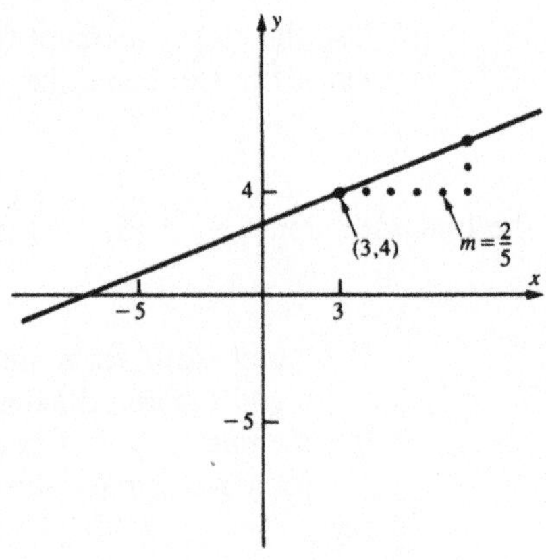

Figure 7-6b

An equation written in the form

$$y - 4 = \frac{2}{5}(x - 3)$$

is said to be in *point-slope form*. The slope, $\frac{2}{5}$, and the coordinates of a point, (3, 4), show up in the equation. The coordinates of the point are the values of x and y that make the right and left members equal zero.

POINT-SLOPE FORM OF A LINEAR EQUATION
An equation in the form

$$y - y_1 = m(x - x_1)$$

is said to be in **point-slope form.** The slope is m, and a fixed point on the line is (x_1, y_1). The variables x and y stand for coordinates of a variable point on the line.

Armed with the point-slope form, you can find an equation of a line, as long as you know the value of the slope and the coordinates of one point.

Cover the answers as you work these examples.

EXAMPLE 1

Write an equation of a line with slope -3 and y-intercept 5.

- - - - - - - - - -

Think These Reasons

$y = -3x + 5$ — Use the slope-intercept form since you know the slope and the y-intercept.

EXAMPLE 2

Write an equation of the line with slope $-\frac{3}{4}$ if $(5, -1)$ is on the line.

- - - - - - - - - -

$y + 1 = -\frac{3}{4}(x - 5)$ — Use point-slope form since you know the slope and the coordinates of a point. The left member is $y + 1$ because substituting -1 for y must make the left member equal zero.

EXAMPLE 3

Write an equation of the line containing (3, 7) and (5, 1).

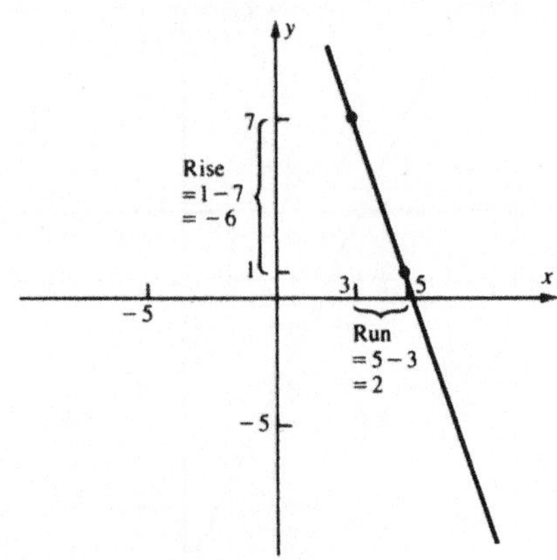

Figure 7-6c

Draw the two points, as shown in Figure 7-6c. For the points (3, 7) and (5, 1),

$$\text{run} = 5 - 3 = 2$$

$$\text{rise} = 1 - 7 = -6.$$

So the slope is

$$m = \frac{-6}{2} = -3.$$

Using the point-slope form with either point gives

$$\underline{\underline{y - 7 = -3(x - 3)}} \quad \text{or}$$

$$\underline{\underline{y - 1 = -3(x - 5)}}.$$

EXAMPLE 4

Show that the two answers in Example 3 are equivalent equations.

Transform each equation to slope-intercept form, and compare.

$$y - 7 = -3(x - 3) \qquad y - 1 = -3(x - 5)$$

$$y - 7 = -3x + 9 \qquad y - 1 = -3x + 15$$

$$y = -3x + 16 \longleftarrow \text{same!} \longrightarrow y = -3x + 16$$

EXAMPLE 5

Find an equation of each line shown in Figure 7-6d.

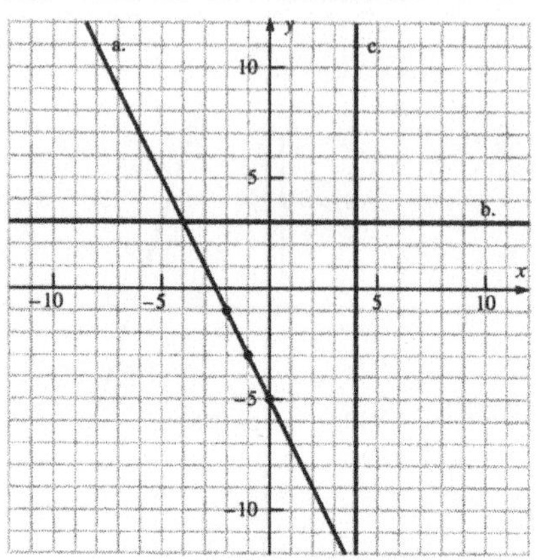

Figure 7-6d

a. The y-intercept is -5. — y is -5 when x is 0.

The slope is -2. — Run 1, rise -2

Equation is $y = -2x - 5$. — Use slope-intercept form.

b. The y-intercept is 3. — The graph crosses the y-axis at 3.

The slope is 0. — No matter what the run equals, the rise is zero.

Equation is $y = 0x + 3$. — Use slope-intercept form.

$y = 3$ — Simplify.

Note: The final equation, $y = 3$, says, "No matter what x is, y is always 3." This fact is useful in part (c), below.

c. There is no number for the y-intercept. — The graph is parallel to the y-axis.

There is no number for the slope. — The run is zero. If you run at all, you will be off the line no matter how high or low you rise.

Equation is $x = 4$. — Observe that no matter what y is, x is always 4. Since there is no number for the slope, you cannot use either point-slope or slope-intercept form.

The last two parts of Example 5 lead to the following conclusions about equations of horizontal and vertical lines.

EQUATIONS OF HORIZONTAL AND VERTICAL LINES
If y = constant, the graph is a **horizontal line.**
If x = constant, the graph is a **vertical line.**

ORAL PRACTICE

Name a point on the line.

A. $y - 8 = 5(x - 11)$
B. $y + 5 = -4(x - 2)$
C. $y - 3 = 6(x + 4)$
D. $y + 1 = 0.17(x + 9)$
E. $y - 2 = x - 5$
F. $y - 0 = 4(x - 7)$
G. $y + 0.3 = 15(x - 0)$
H. $y = \left(\frac{2}{3}\right)(x + 1)$
I. $y - \frac{3}{5} = 4x$
J. $y = 4.5x$
K. $y = 3$
L. $x = 17$

Tell the slope of the line containing the two points. Simplify any fractions.

M. (3, 7) and (5, 16)
N. (8, 2) and (1, 5)
O. (200, 300) and (500, 400)
P. (5, −1) and (2, 6)
Q. (−4, 3) and (2, 13)
R. (−8, 7) and (4, −9)
S. (5, −3) and (0, −11)
T. (3, 8) and (7, 8)
U. (5, 1) and (5, 3)
V. (0, 0) and (−4, 8)

EXERCISE 7-6

For Problems 1 through 8,
a. Write the slope and a point on the graph,
b. Plot the graph.

1. $y - 4 = \frac{2}{5}(x - 1)$
2. $y - 2 = \frac{3}{5}(x - 4)$
3. $y + 2 = 4(x - 3)$
4. $y - 3 = 2(x + 4)$
5. $y - 5 = -\frac{1}{3}(x + 4)$
6. $y + 5 = \frac{1}{4}(x - 3)$
7. $y + 1 = \frac{3}{2}(x + 5)$
8. $y + 4 = -\frac{5}{3}(x + 1)$

For Problems 9 through 38, write an equation of the line described.

9. Has y-intercept 5 and slope 2.
10. Has y-intercept -2 and slope 6.
11. Has y-intercept $\frac{2}{3}$ and slope -5.
12. Has y-intercept 0.3 and slope -1.9.
13. Has slope -3 and contains (4, 9).
14. Has slope 7 and contains (3, 18).
15. Has slope $\frac{4}{9}$ and contains (2, 5).
16. Has slope $-\frac{2}{7}$ and contains (5, 6).
17. Has slope -13 and contains $(-7, 2)$.
18. Has slope 15 and contains $(14, -3.7)$.
19. Has slope $\frac{1}{8}$ and contains $(-2, -4)$,
20. Has slope -0.007 and contains $(-0.8, -0.3)$.
21. Contains (4, 5) and (6, 12).
22. Contains (8, 3) and (11, 5).
23. Contains $(-1, 2)$ and $(5, -4)$.
24. Contains $(6, -3)$ and $(-5, 4)$.
25. Contains $(-8, -1)$ and $(4, -5)$.
26. Contains $(-6, 4)$ and $(-2, 1)$.
27. Is vertical, and contains (3, 8).
28. Is horizontal, and contains $(-4, 1)$.
29. Is horizontal, and contains $(2, -7)$.
30. Is vertical, and contains $(-5, -6)$.

31.
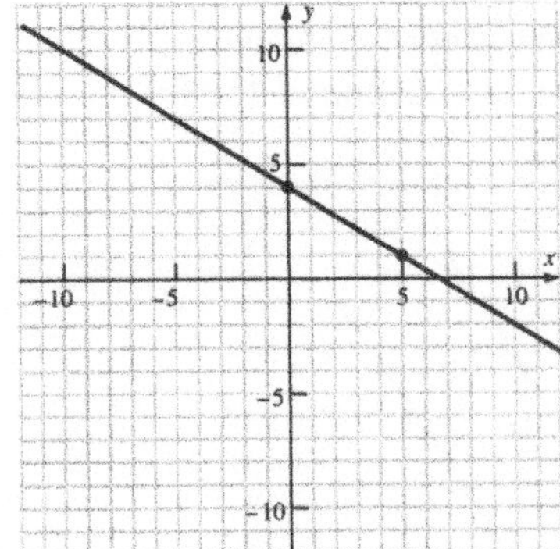

32.
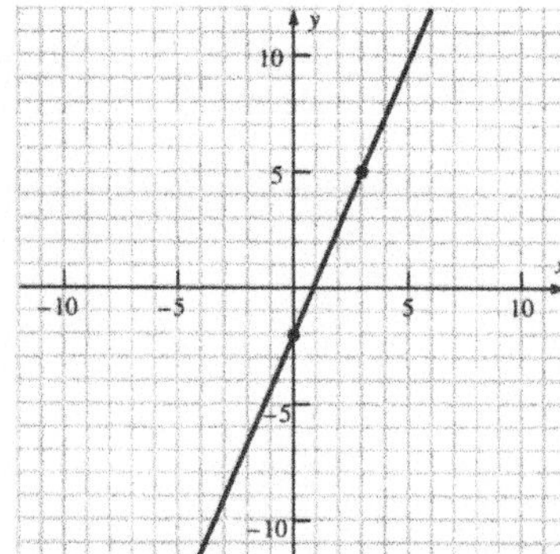

33.
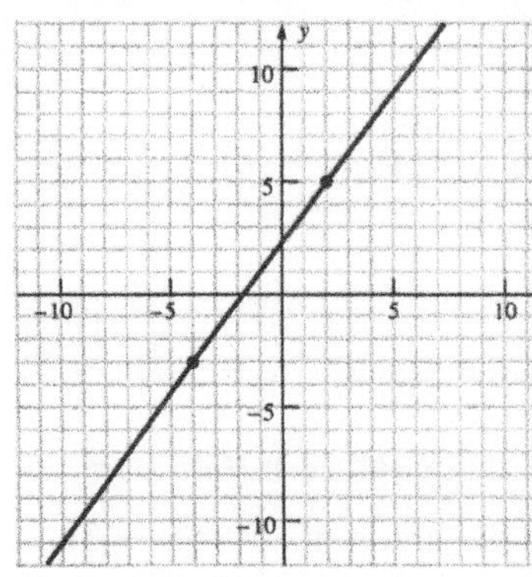

34.
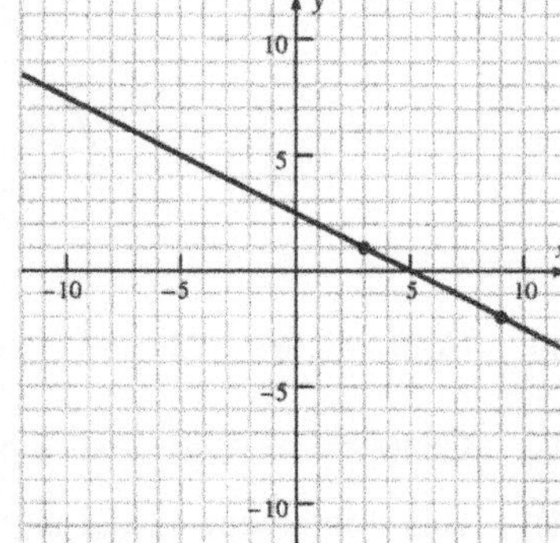

35.
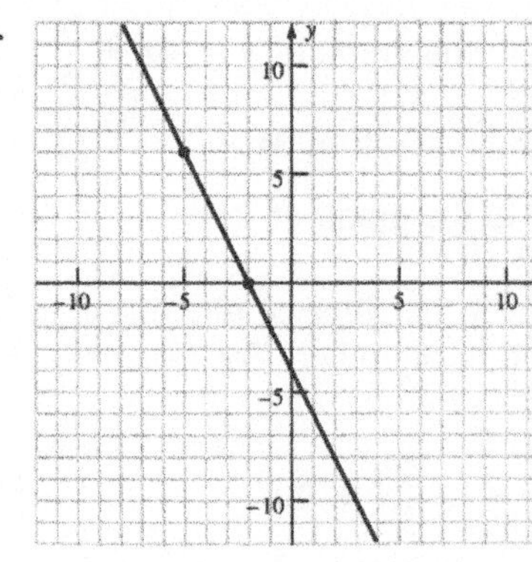

36.
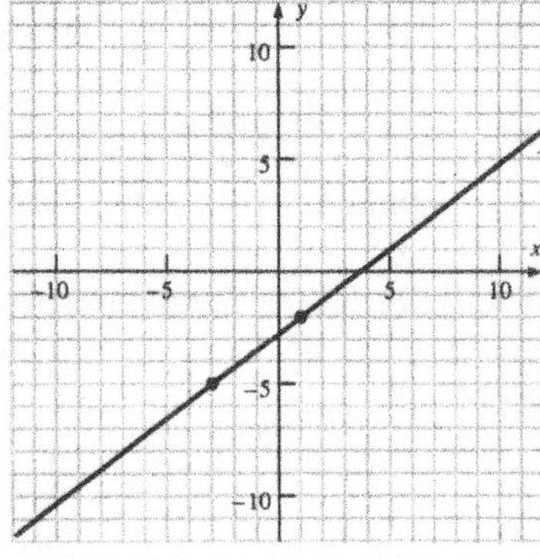

37.
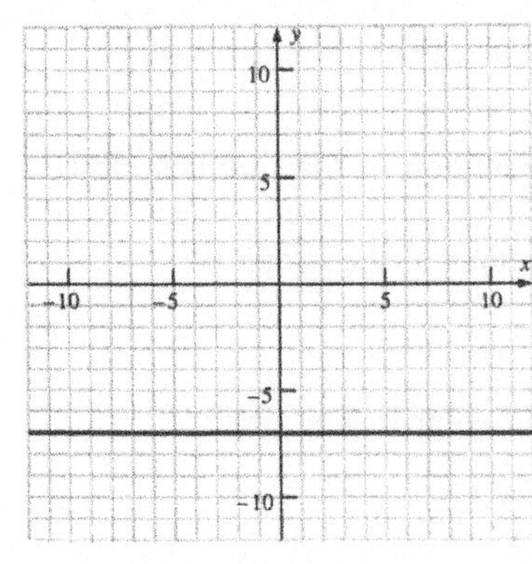

38.
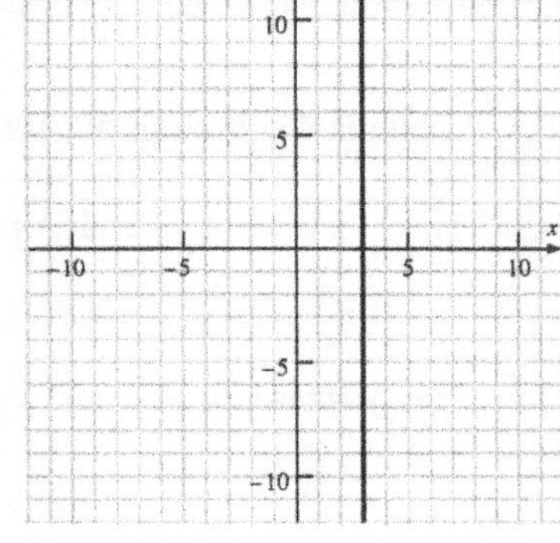

Two lines are *parallel* to each other if their slopes are equal. See Figure 7-6e. For Problems 39 through 44, write an equation of the line described.

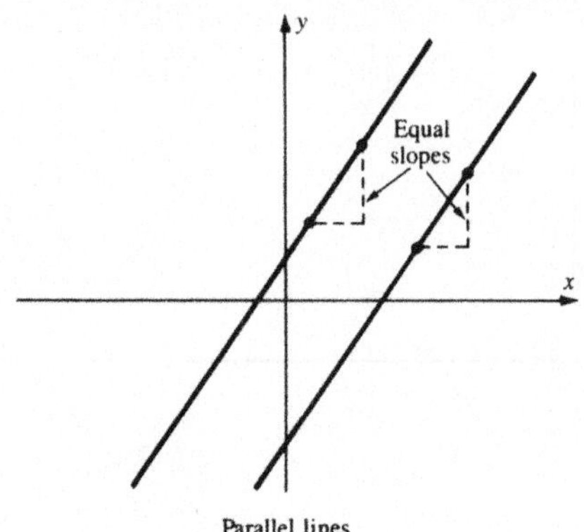

Figure 7-6e

39. Contains $(6, -1)$, and is parallel to the graph of $y = \left(\frac{2}{7}\right)x + 3$.

40. Contains $(-3, 8)$, and is parallel to the graph of $y = 0.8x - 7$.

41. Has y-intercept 4, and is parallel to the graph of $y = 7x - 3$.

42. Has y-intercept -2, and is parallel to the graph of $y = 4x + \frac{3}{8}$.

43. Has y-intercept 5, and is parallel to the graph of $3x + 7y = 42$.

44. Contains $(-4, -3)$, and is parallel to the graph of $2x - 5y = 40$.

Two lines are *perpendicular* to each other if the slope of one line equals the *opposite* of the *reciprocal* of the slope of the other. For instance, the graphs of

$$y = \frac{3}{5}x + 7 \quad \text{and} \quad y = -\frac{5}{3}x + 20$$

are perpendicular since $-\frac{5}{3}$ is the opposite of the reciprocal of $\frac{3}{5}$.

For Problems 45 through 50, write an equation of the line described.

45. Has y-intercept 4, and is perpendicular to the graph of $y = \left(\frac{5}{7}\right)x - 2$.

46. Has y-intercept -1, and is perpendicular to the graph of $y = \left(-\frac{4}{9}\right)x + 11$.

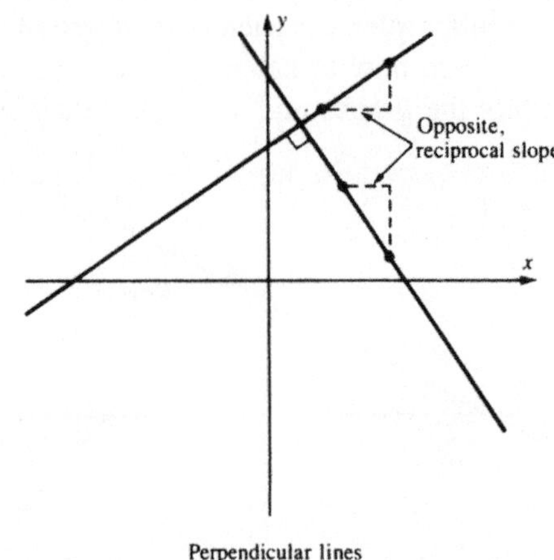

Figure 7-6f

47. Contains (4, 9), and is perpendicular to the graph of $y = 7x + \frac{3}{8}$.

48. Contains (−6, 1), and is perpendicular to the graph of $y = -2x + 0.83$.

49. Contains (−3, −10), and is perpendicular to the graph of $4x - 5y = 1$.

50. Has y-intercept −4, and is perpendicular to the graph of $8x + 7y = 112$.

The following are intended to make you think hard! Find an equation of the line described.

51. Has x-intercept 5 and slope 4.

52. Has x-intercept 2 and y-intercept 5.

53. Has x-intercept 3, and is horizontal.

54. Has y-intercept 8, and is vertical.

55. Has x-intercept 0 and y-intercept 0.

7-7 FINDING THE INTERSECTION OF TWO GRAPHS BY ACCURATE PLOTTING

This section ties together what you have been learning and prepares you for the rest of the chapter. You should be able to read it and work the problems without help from your teacher.

If you draw the graphs of two linear equations on the same coordinate system, they will probably intersect each other somewhere. In the next few sections you will learn how to calculate this point of intersection. For now, you will just plot the graphs and *see* where they intersect.

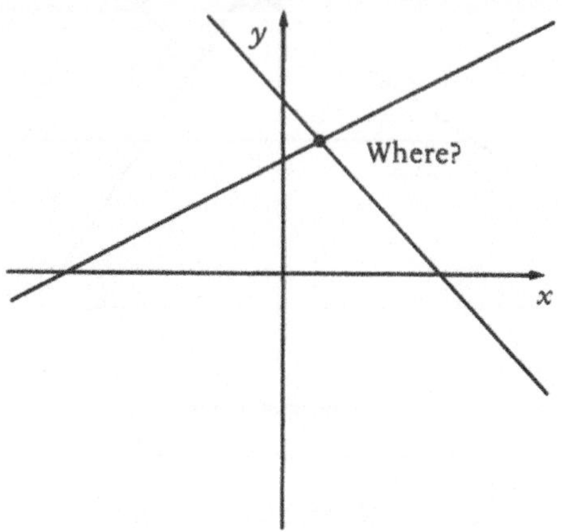

Objective:

Given two linear equations in two variables, to plot the graphs accurately enough to read the coordinates of the point of intersection correct to 0.1 unit.

Cover the answers as you work this example.

EXAMPLE

Plot the graphs and read the coordinates of the point of intersection correct to 0.1 unit.

$$x + 2y = 4$$
$$4x - 5y = -20$$

Find the intercepts.

For $x + 2y = 4$:

x-intercept:

$$x + 0 = 4$$
$$x = 4$$

y-intercept:

$$0 + 2y = 4$$
$$y = 2$$

Plot the graphs.

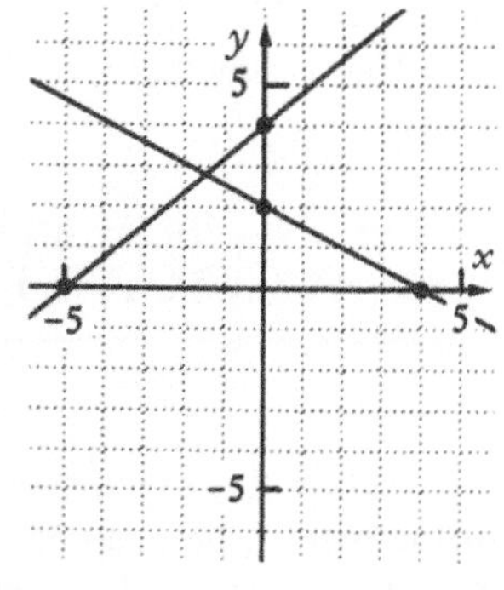

For $4x - 5y = -20$:

x-intercept:

$$4x - 0 = -20$$
$$x = -5$$

y-intercept:

$$0 - 5y = -20$$
$$y = 4$$

Read the point of intersection.

$(-1.5, 2.8)$

Note: In order to get accurate answers, you must draw accurate graphs! So sharpen your pencil, use a good ruler, and be careful. Your answers will be considered to be right if they are no more than ± 0.1 unit from the correct answer. For instance, the y-coordinate could be 2.7, 2.8, or 2.9 and still be counted right.

EXERCISE 7-7

For each pair of equations, find the intercepts and draw both graphs on the same set of axes. Then read the coordinates of the point where the two graphs intersect. Write the answer to the nearest 0.1 unit. Your answer will be counted correct if it is no more than ± 0.1 unit from the right answer.

1. $2x + 3y = 18$
   $x - y = 5$
2. $x - 2y = -10$
   $4x + 3y = 24$
3. $2x + y = 8$
   $5x - 3y = 15$
4. $3x + 4y = 12$
   $2x - 3y = -6$
5. $8x - 5y = -40$
   $2x + y = -6$
6. $2x - y = -6$
   $x + 2y = 4$
7. $3x + 2y = -12$
   $x - y = -2$
8. $5x + 7y = -35$
   $3x - 2y = 6$
9. $2x + 3y = -12$
   $8x - 5y = 40$
10. $5x + 2y = 20$
    $3x - 7y = 21$
11. $3x + 5y = 15$
    $3x + 5y = 30$
    (Surprising?)
12. $x - 3y = 6$
    $x - 3y = -3$
    (Surprising?)

7-8 SOLVING SYSTEMS OF EQUATIONS BY SUBSTITUTION

In the last section you learned how to plot graphs of two equations and find their intersection point. For instance, if you plot

$$2x + 5y = -10$$

and

$$3x - y = 4$$

on the same Cartesian plane, the graphs intersect at approximately

$$(0.6, -2.2),$$

as shown in the figure.

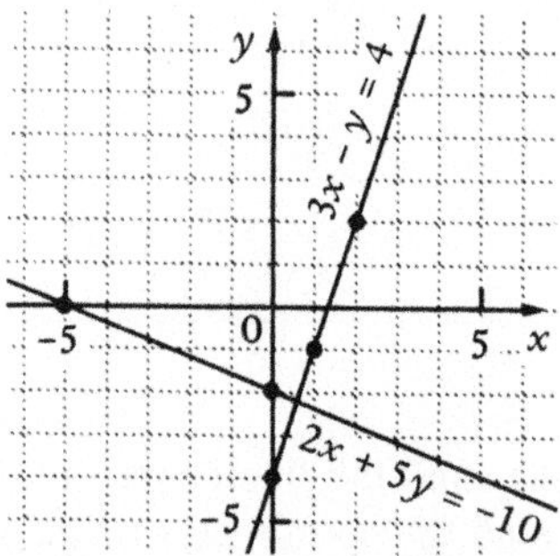

Finding intersection points by actual graphing has two disadvantages. It is tedious, and it is of limited accuracy. In this section you will learn how to *calculate* such intersection points.

A pair of equations with the same two variables is called a *system* of equations. The ordered pair where the graphs intersect each other makes *both* equations true. It is called the *solution* of the system. For future reference, here are definitions of these words.

DEFINITIONS

SYSTEM OF EQUATIONS
A **system of equations** is two or more equations with the same variables.

SOLUTION OF A SYSTEM
A **solution** of a system of equations is an ordered pair that satisfies *all* the equations in the system.

To solve the system

$$2x + 5y = -10 \qquad (1)$$

$$3x - y = 4 \qquad (2)$$

you can transform one equation so that a variable is *by itself*. Solving Equation (2) for y in terms of x gives

$-y = -3x + 4$ Add $-3x$ to each member.

$y = 3x - 4$ Multiply each member by -1. (3)

Where the graphs intersect, the y in one equation stands for the *same* number as the y in the other. So you may *substitute* $(3x - 4)$ for the y in Equation (1).

$$2x + 5(3x - 4) = -10$$

The result is an equation with only *one* variable. Solve it for x.

$2x + 15x - 20 = -10$ Distribute the 5.

$17x = 10$ Combine like terms; add 20 to each member.

$x = \frac{10}{17}$ Divide each member by 17.

$x = 0.5882\ldots$ Save this in memory.

Substituting $0.5882\ldots$ for x in Equation (3) gives

$$y = 3(0.5882\ldots) - 4$$

$$y = -2.2352\ldots$$

Rounding the values of x and y gives the approximate solution

$$(0.59, -2.24).$$

As you can see, the $(0.6, -2.2)$ from the graph is quite close to this more accurate value.

The process above is called solving a system by **substitution.** Sometimes the equations in a system are called **simultaneous equations** because you solve both equations at the same time.

Objective:

Be able to solve a system of two linear equations with two variables by the substitution method.

Cover the answer as you work the example.

EXAMPLE

Solve.

$$5x + 3y = 17$$
$$x - 2y = 6$$

- - - - -   - - - - -

		Think These Reasons
$5x + 3y = 17$	(1)	Write the given system. Number each equation for future reference.
$x - 2y = 6$	(2)	
$x = 2y + 6$	(3)	Solve (2) for x in terms of y. This is the easiest way, since x has a coefficient of 1.
$5(2y + 6) + 3y = 17$		Substitute $2y + 6$ for x in (1). (*Do not* substitute it back in (2)!)
$10y + 30 + 3y = 17$		Distribute 5.
$13y = -13$		Combine like terms; add -30.
$y = -1$		Divide each member by 13.
$x = 2(-1) + 6$		Substitute -1 for y in (3).
$x = 4$		Do the computation.
Solution: $\underline{\underline{(4, -1)}}$		Write the answer.

Note: Checking the answer requires substituting it into *both* equations. It is possible for an ordered pair to satisfy one equation but not the other.

Check: $5(4) + 3(-1) \stackrel{?}{=} 17$ $4 - 2(-1) \stackrel{?}{=} 6$

$20 - 3 \stackrel{?}{=} 17$ $4 + 2 \stackrel{?}{=} 6$

$17 = 17$ ✓ $6 = 6$ ✓

ORAL PRACTICE

Solve for x in terms of y or for y in terms of x, whichever is easier.

EXAMPLES

	Answers
i. $x + 3y = 7$	i. $x = 7 - 3y$
ii. $4x - y = 9$	ii. $y = 4x - 9$

A. $x + 2y = 5$

B. $x - 6y = 8$

C. $2x + y = 10$

D. $6x - y = 12$

E. $x - 5y = -15$

F. $6x + y = -24$

G. $x - 3y = 30$

H. $10x - y = 70$

I. $x - y = 8$

J. $x + y = 6$

K. $x - 2y = 0$

L. $x + 3(y + 2) = 10$

EXERCISE 7-8

For Problems 1 through 30, solve the system by substitution.

1. $y = 2x$
   $3x + y = 10$

2. $y = 3x$
   $2x - y = 2$

3. $y = 3x$
   $5x - 2y = 1$

4. $y = 2x$
   $4x + 3y = 30$

5. $y = x + 4$
   $3x + y = 16$

6. $y = x - 3$
   $4x + y = 32$

7. $x = y - 5$
   $3x + 2y = 3$

8. $x = y + 8$
   $5x + 3y = 12$

9. $4x + 3y = 31$
   $y = 2x + 7$

10. $4x + 5y = 48$
    $y = 3x + 2$

11. $x + 2y = 2$
    $5x - 3y = -29$

12. $3x + y = 13$
    $2x - 4y = 18$

13. $6x - y = 31$
    $4x + 3y = 17$

14. $x - 7y = -22$
    $5x + 2y = 1$

15. $7x - 6y = -30$
    $x - 4y = -20$

16. $2x - 9y = 14$
    $6x - y = 42$

17. $x + y = 23$
    $9x - 8y = 27$

18. $x - y = 6$
    $10x + 11y = 149$

19. $x - 3y = 13$
    $5x + 3y = 2$

20. $7x - 3y = -23$
    $x + 5y = 32$

21. $3(x - 2) + y = -4$
$4x - 7y = 36$

22. $4(x - 3) + y = -11$
$6x - 2y = -16$

23. $x + 6y = 19$
$5(x - 7) + 2y = -24$

24. $x + 5y = 22$
$3(x - 9) + 4y = -5$

25. $2(x + 3) - y = 7$
$7x - 3(y - 1) = 9$

26. $6(x + 2) - y = 31$
$5x - 2(y - 3) = 23$

For Problems 27 through 30, find the solution correct to two decimal places for each coordinate.

27. $x = 0.6(300 + y)$
$y = 0.2(300 + x)$

28. $x = 0.8(500 + y)$
$y = 0.7(500 + x)$

29. $x = 0.9(1000 - y)$
$y = 0.7(1000 - x)$

30. $x = 0.3(200 - y)$
$y = 0.2(200 - x)$

For Problems 31 through 34, solve the system by substitution. Then plot the graphs of the two equations, using the rise-and-run technique of Section 7-5 or the two-intercept technique of Section 7-4. Show that the two graphs do intersect at the point you calculated.

31. $2x - y = -3$
$x + y = 9$

32. $3x + y = 1$
$x - y = 7$

33. $x - 3y = -18$
$2x + 3y = 9$

34. $2x - y = -6$
$5x + 3y = -15$

7-9 SOLVING SYSTEMS BY THE LINEAR COMBINATION METHOD

Suppose that you must solve the system

$$5x + 3y = 25 \qquad (1)$$

$$7x - 3y = -1 \qquad (2)$$

None of the variable terms has a coefficient of 1. Thus to solve for y in terms of x or for x in terms of y, you must divide by a coefficient. The resulting fractions would make the substitution method of the last section tedious to use.

There is another method that works very easily for this system. Observe that the coefficients of y in the two equations are *opposites* of each other. If you add $7x - 3y$ to the left member of Equation (1) and add -1 to the right member, the y-terms have a sum of *zero*. (They "cancel out!")

$$(5x + 3y) + (7x - 3y) = 25 + (-1)$$
$$12x = 24$$

An efficient way to do this addition is simply to draw a line under the two equations and add like terms.

$$\begin{array}{rl} 5x + 3y = 25 & \\ \underline{7x - 3y = -1} & \\ 12x \qquad = 24 & \text{Add the two equations.} \\ x = 2 & \text{Divide each member by 12.} \end{array}$$

Substituting 2 for x in either equation lets you find y. Using the first one, you get the following value.

$$\begin{array}{rl} 5(2) + 3y = 25 & \text{Substitute 2 for } x. \\ 3y = 15 & \text{Subtract 10 from each member.} \\ y = 5 & \text{Divide each member by 3.} \\ \textit{Solution: } \underline{\underline{(2, 5)}} & \text{Write the answer.} \end{array}$$

If neither variable has opposite coefficients, you can *transform* each equation first so that they will. Here's how you would solve the following system.

$$5x + 3y = 9$$
$$2x - 4y = 40$$

Multiplying each member of the first by 2 makes the coefficient of x equal 10. Multiplying each member of the second by -5 makes its x-coefficient equal -10. The terms $10x$ and $-10x$ are opposites of each other. You can draw arrows from each equation with the symbols m 2 and m -5 to indicate what you are doing. The entire solution looks like this:

$$\begin{array}{lcrl} 5x + 3y = 9 & \xrightarrow{\text{m } 2} & 10x + 6y = 18 & \text{Multiply by 2.} \\ 2x - 4y = 40 & \xrightarrow{\text{m } -5} & \underline{-10x + 20y = -200} & \text{Multiply by } -5. \\ & & 26y = -182 & \text{Add the equations.} \\ & & y = -7 & \text{Divide by 26.} \\ 5x + 3(-7) = 9 & & & \text{Substitute } -7 \text{ for } y \text{ in the first equation.} \\ 5x = 30 & & & \text{Add 21 to each member.} \\ x = 6 & & & \text{Divide by 5.} \\ \textit{Solution: } \underline{\underline{(6, -7)}} & & & \text{Write the answer.} \end{array}$$

To check the solution, you must substitute (6, −7) into *each* equation. It is possible for an ordered pair to satisfy one of the equations but not the other.

Check:

$$5(6) + 3(-7) \stackrel{?}{=} 9 \qquad\qquad 2(6) - 4(-7) \stackrel{?}{=} 40$$

$$30 - 21 \stackrel{?}{=} 9 \qquad\qquad 12 + 28 \stackrel{?}{=} 40$$

$$9 = 9 \ \checkmark \qquad\qquad 40 = 40 \ \checkmark$$

Note that you could have eliminated y first, instead of x. You would multiply the first equation by 4 and the second by 3, getting the following:

$$\begin{array}{lcr} 5x + 3y = 9 & \xrightarrow{\text{m } 4} & 20x + 12y = 36 \\ 2x - 4y = 40 & \xrightarrow{\text{m } 3} & \underline{6x - 12y = 120} \\ & & 26x \qquad = 156 \\ & & x = 6 \end{array}$$

Then y would be found by substituting 6 for x in the first or second equation.

This method is called the **linear combination** method for solving a system of equations. A linear combination of two quantities is what you get by multiplying each quantity by a constant, then adding the results. The method is also called **addition-subtraction.**

Objective:

Given a system of two linear equations with two variables, solve it by the linear combination method, transforming the equations first as needed.

Cover the answers as you work the examples.

EXAMPLE 1

Solve:

$4x + 9y = 75$

$4x + 3y = 33$

- - - - -

Think These Reasons

$$\begin{array}{lcrl} 4x + 9y = 75 & \longrightarrow & 4x + 9y = 75 & \text{Write an equation.} \\ 4x + 3y = 33 & \xrightarrow{\text{m } -1} & \underline{-\ 4x - 3y = -33} & \text{Multiply by } -1. \\ & & 6y = 42 & \text{Add the equations.} \\ & & y = 7 & \text{Divide by 6.} \end{array}$$

$4x + 3(7) = 33$	Substitute 7 for y in the second equation.
$4x = 12$	Subtract 21 from each member.
$x = 3$	Divide each member by 4.
Solution: $\underline{\underline{(3, 7)}}$	Write the solution.

EXAMPLE 2

Solve:

$2x - 3y = -8$

$11x + 5y = -1$

- - - - -

$2x - 3y = -8$	$\xrightarrow{\text{m } 5}$	$10x - 15y = -40$	Multiply by 5.
$11x + 5y = -1$	$\xrightarrow{\text{m } 3}$	$33x + 15y = -3$	Multiply by 3.
		$43x \quad = -43$	Add the equations.
		$x = -1$	Divide by 43.

$2(-1) - 3y = -8$	Substitute -1 for x in the first equation.
$-3y = -6$	Add 2 to each member.
$y = 2$	Divide each member by -3.
Solution: $\underline{\underline{(-1, 2)}}$	Write the solution.

Note: There are other ways you could have started. To eliminate x instead of y, you could multiply the first equation by 11 and the second by -2, making the x-coefficients 22 and -22. Then you would eliminate x by adding the equations.

ORAL PRACTICE

Give the equation that results after you add to eliminate a variable.

EXAMPLE

	Answer
$3x + 2y = 2$ $5x - 2y = 9$	$8x = 11$

A. $2x + 3y = 7$
$4x - 3y = 5$

B. $7x - 4y = 9$
$2x + 4y = 3$

C. $2x + 8y = -3$
$-2x + 5y = 10$

D. $3x + 4y = 8$
$-3x + 5y = -1$

E. $4x - 5y = 9$
$-3x + 5y = -7$

F. $-4x - 3y = -1$
$4x + 8y = 5$

Tell the number by which each equation should be multiplied to eliminate x by linear combination.

EXAMPLE

	Answer
$5x + 3y = 9$	m 2
$2x - 8y = 4$	m -5

G. $2x + 5y = 7$
$3x + 4y = 9$

H. $4x - 3y = 2$
$-5x + 8y = 1$

I. $2x + 10y = 9$
$8x + 5y = 7$

Tell the number by which each equation should be multiplied to eliminate y by linear combination.

J. $2x + 5y = 7$
$3x + 4y = 9$

K. $4x - 3y = 2$
$-5x + 8y = 1$

L. $2x + 10y = 9$
$8x + 5y = 7$

EXERCISE 7-9

For Problems 1 through 20, solve the system by the linear combination method.

1. $3x - y = 5$
$2x + y = 15$

2. $4x + y = 10$
$6x - y = 20$

3. $x + 4y = 17$
$-x + 7y = 38$

4. $-x + 5y = 6$
$x + 3y = 18$

5. $8x + y = 21$
$3x + y = 13$

6. $7x + y = 47$
$2x + y = 19$

7. $x - 4y = 23$
$x + 5y = -4$

8. $x - 6y = 13$
$x + 2y = 5$

9. $5x + 3y = 27$
$7x - 3y = 45$

10. $2x + 5y = 14$
$7x - 5y = -41$

11. $-2x + 7y = 8.7$
$2x + 3y = 18.3$

12. $-4x + 8y = -3.6$
$4x - 3y = 13.1$

13. $10x + 7y = -30$
$8x + 7y = -24$

14. $6x + 11y = -48$
$x + 11y = -8$

15. $5x - y = 22$
$5x + 4y = -63$

16. $3x - 5y = 61$
$3x - y = 17$

17. $2.3x - 1.7y = 3.5$
$4.7x - 1.7y = 10.7$

18. $4.1x - 1.3y = 7.1$
$2.9x - 1.3y = 3.5$

19. $10x - 4y = 35$
$3x + 4y = 21$

20. $9x + 2y = 59$
$-2x - 2y = -8$

For Problems 21 through 40, first transform the equations so that either the x-coefficients or the y-coefficients are opposite. Then solve by the linear combination method.

21. $3x + 5y = 17$
$2x + 3y = 11$

22. $5x + 2y = 24$
$4x + 3y = 29$

23. $4x - 5y = -19$
$3x + 7y = 18$

24. $6x - 5y = 28$
$4x + 9y = -6$

25. $6a - 7b = 12$
$5a - 4b = 10$

26. $8r - 3s = 15$
$7r - 4s = 20$

27. $2x + 9y = 12.5$
$6x + 5y = 8.9$

28. $3x + 5y = 4.7$
$6x + 2y = 6.2$

29. $7u + 8v = 23$
$3u - 2v = -1$

30. $7c + 10d = -13$
$3c - 2d = 7$

31. $4x - 3y = 2.7$
$8x + 5y = 13.1$

32. $5x - 6y = 2.7$
$10x + 7y = 1.6$

33. $3x - 5y = -29$
$2x - 10y = -42$

34. $7x - 2y = -26$
$5x - 12y = -45$

35. $4x + y = 42$
$6x - 5y = 50$

36. $2x + 9y = 39$
$5x - y = -20$

37. $x + 12y = -8$
$8x - 5y = 37$

38. $7x - 8y = 51$
$x + 10y = -15$

39. $5x + 7y = 18.9$
$2x - 3y = -8.1$

40. $6x + 5y = 5.1$
$4x - 2y = -1.4$

For Problems 41 through 44, find an equation of the line connecting the two given points. You can find the slope by first finding the rise and run. The y-intercept can be found from $y = mx + b$ by substituting the slope for m, and one of the ordered pairs for x and y.

41. (3, 4) and (6, 10)

42. (1, 7) and (−3, −5)

43. (8, 5) and (−4, 2)

44. (3, 9) and (15, 1)

7-10 PROBLEMS INVOLVING TWO VARIABLES

Suppose that hamburgers cost \$2.00 each and hot dogs cost \$1.50 each. The amount of money you spend on burgers and dogs depends on how many of each you buy.

Let x = the number of burgers.

Let y = the number of hot dogs.

The amount of money spent is

$$2x + 1.5y.$$

This two-variable expression represents a number of dollars. If you know values of x and y, you can easily find the cost. For instance, if x is 5 and y is 3, then

$$\begin{aligned} &2x + 1.5y \\ &= 2(5) + 1.5(3) \\ &= 14.50. \end{aligned}$$

But the reverse problem is not so simple. If you know that the total spent is \$14.50, you can write the equation

$$2x + 1.5y = 14.50. \tag{1}$$

But you cannot say for sure that x is 5 and y is 3. It is possible that x is 2 and y is 7, because

$$\begin{aligned} &2(2) + 1.5(7) \\ &= 14.50. \end{aligned}$$

You need a second equation to form a *system* that can be solved for both variables. For instance, if you know that the total number of burgers and hot dogs is 8, the second equation would be

$$x + y = 8. \tag{2}$$

You solve this system as follows.

$$\begin{array}{rcr} 2x + 1.5y = 14.5 & \longrightarrow & 2x + 1.5y = 14.5 \\ x + y = 8 & \xrightarrow{m\ -2} & -2x - 2y = -16 \\ \hline \end{array}$$

$$\begin{array}{r} 2x + 1.5y = 14.5 \\ 2x + 2y = 16 \\ \hline -0.5y = -1.5 \end{array}$$

$-0.5y = -1.5$ Add.

$y = 3$ Divide by -0.5

$x + 3 = 8$ Substitute 3 for y in the second equation.

$x = 5$

5 hamburgers and 3 hot dogs

In this section you will solve similar problems involving expressions with two variables.

Objective:

Given a problem involving two variables, write and solve a system of two equations and answer the question asked.

Cover the answers as you work the examples.

EXAMPLE 1

Swiss and Limburger Cheese Problem Swiss cheese and Limburger cheese cost different amounts per kilogram, but you do not know how much. A box containing 3 kilograms (kg) of Swiss and 2 kg of Limburger costs \$24.40. Another box containing 4 kg of Swiss and 5 kg of Limburger costs \$47.70. Assuming that these figures are for cheese only (not for the box), how much is each kind of cheese worth per kilogram?

Think These Reasons

Let x = number of dollars per kilogram for Swiss.
Let y = number of dollars per kilogram for Limburger. — Define the variables.

First write two equations involving x and y. Then solve the system.

$$3x + 2y = 24.40 \xrightarrow{\text{m } 5} 15x + 10y = 122.00$$

$$4x + 5y = 47.70 \xrightarrow{\text{m } -2} -8x - 10y = -95.40$$

$$7x = 26.60 \quad \text{Add.}$$

$$x = 3.80 \quad \text{Divide by 7.}$$

$3(3.80) + 2y = 24.40$	Substitute 3.80 for x in the first equation.
$11.40 + 2y = 24.40$	Do the arithmetic.
$2y = 13.00$	Subtract 11.40.
$y = 6.50$	Divide by 2.
\$3.80/kg for Swiss, \$6.50/kg for Limburger	Answer the question.

EXAMPLE 2

Cereal Sugar Problem According to information on the labels, cereal A contains about 38% sugar. Cereal B contains about 46% sugar.

a. What percent sugar would there be in a mixture of 100 g of cereal A and 200 g of cereal B?

b. How many grams of each cereal would be needed to make a kilogram of a mixture containing 40% sugar?

- - - - - - - - - -

a. Let x = number of grams of cereal A.
Let y = number of grams of cereal B. — Define the variables.

$0.38x + 0.46y$ = number of grams of sugar. — Write an expression.

If $x = 100$ and $y = 200$, then — Evaluate the expression.

$$0.38x + 0.46y$$
$$= 38 + 92$$
$$= 130$$

130 g of sugar

Total mass is 100 + 200, or 300 g.

Percent of sugar is $\frac{130}{300} \times 100$ — $\text{Percent} = \frac{\text{number}}{\text{total}} \times 100.$

$$\approx 43.3$$

43.3% sugar. — Answer the question.

b. First, write two equations.

$$x + y = 1000 \qquad \text{Total is 1000 g (1 kg).}$$
$$0.38x + 0.46y = 0.4(1000) \qquad \text{Sugar is 40\% of 1000 g.}$$

Then simplify and linearly combine.

$$\begin{array}{rcr} x + y = 1000 & \xrightarrow{\text{m } -0.38} & -0.38x - 0.38y = -380 \\ 0.38x + 0.46y = 400 & \longrightarrow & 0.38x + 0.46y = 400 \\ \hline & & 0.08y = 20 \\ & & y = 250 \end{array}$$

$x + 250 = 1000$ — Substitute 250 for y in the first equation.

$x = 750$ — Subtract 250.

Cereal A: 750 g,
cereal B: 250 g — Answer the question.

EXAMPLE 3

Submarine Problem A submarine sails submerged for a distance of 150 nautical miles against a current of unknown speed, taking a total of 10 hours. It returns to the starting point, going with the current, in 6 hours.

For both trips it moves the same speed through the water. How many knots (nautical miles per hour) does the sub travel through the water, and how many knots is the current?

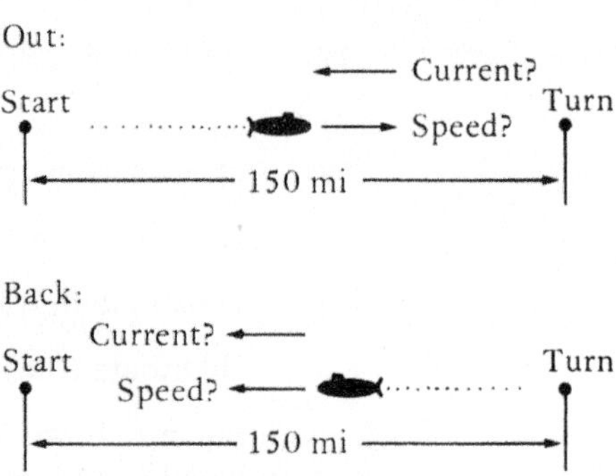

Let x = number of knots sub goes. Let y = number of knots current flows.	Define variables.
$x - y$ = net rate *against* the current.	Subtract the speeds when the motions oppose each other.
$x + y$ = net rate *with* the current.	Add the speeds when the motions help each other.
$(x - y)(10) = 150$ $(x + y)(6) = 150$	Rate × time = distance.
$x - y = 15$	Divide each member by 10.
$x + y = 25$	Divide each member by 6.
$2x = 40$	Add the two equations.
$x = 20$	Divide each member by 2.
$20 + y = 25$	Substitute 20 for x in $x + y = 25$.
$y = 5$	Subtract 5 from each member.
Sub goes at 20 knots. Current is 5 knots.	Answer the question.

EXAMPLE 4

Insurance Problem The Joneses have two insurance policies. The first one pays 80% of those expenses not covered by the second. The second pays 70% of those expenses not covered by the first. Mrs. Jones has an operation that costs $3000 and is covered by *both* policies. How much do the Joneses get from each policy? Is the total more than 100% of the $3000?

Let x = number of dollars paid by the first policy.
Let y = number of dollars paid by the second policy.

$3000 - x$ = number of dollars *not* paid by the first policy.
$3000 - y$ = number of dollars *not* paid by the second policy.

$x = 0.8(3000 - y)$	(1)	Because x is 80% of what is *not*
$y = 0.7(3000 - x)$	(2)	paid by the second and y is 70% of what is *not* paid by the first.
$x = 2400 - 0.8y$		Distribute 0.8 in (1).
$x = 2400 - 0.8[0.7(3000 - x)]$		Substitute $0.7(3000 - x)$ for y.
$x = 2400 - 1680 + 0.56x$		Distribute (0.8)(0.7), or 0.56.
$0.44x = 720$		Subtract $0.56x$ from each member and do the arithmetic.
$x = 1636.3636...$		Divide by 0.44.
$y = 0.7(3000 - 1636.36...)$		Substitute 1636.36... for x in (2).
$y = 954.5454...$		Do the arithmetic.
First policy pays \$1636.36. Second policy pays \$954.55.		Answer the question.

The total paid is \$2590.91, which is *less* than 100% of \$3000.

Note: The substitution technique is better for this system, since you already have x in terms of y and y in terms of x.

EXERCISE 7-10

Problems 1 through 10 involve finding unknown prices or rates. The first two problems lead you step by step through the problem. For the others, *you* must think of the steps.

1. ***Mexican Dinner Problem*** Suppose that you are helping set the prices for the menu at a new Mexican restaurant. The regular dinner contains 2 tacos and 3 enchiladas. The special dinner contains 4 tacos and 5 enchiladas.
   a. Let x be the number of cents charged for each taco and let y be the number of cents charged for each enchilada. Write two expressions, one for the price of a regular dinner and the other for the price of a special dinner.

b. How much would each dinner cost if:
   i. tacos are 35¢ each and enchiladas are 60¢ each?
   ii. tacos are 45¢ each and enchiladas are 50¢ each?

c. The boss sets prices of $2.39 for the regular dinner and $4.23 for the special dinner. How many cents did she assume per taco and how many cents per enchilada?

RESTAURANTE
LAS PALMAS

Regular . . . $ ____
2 tacos
3 enchiladas

Special . . . $ ____
4 tacos
5 enchiladas

2. *Scuba Diving Problem* A scuba diving resort hotel offers divers two plans. Plan A gives 3 nights' lodging and 4 dives. Plan B gives 5 nights' lodging and 8 dives.

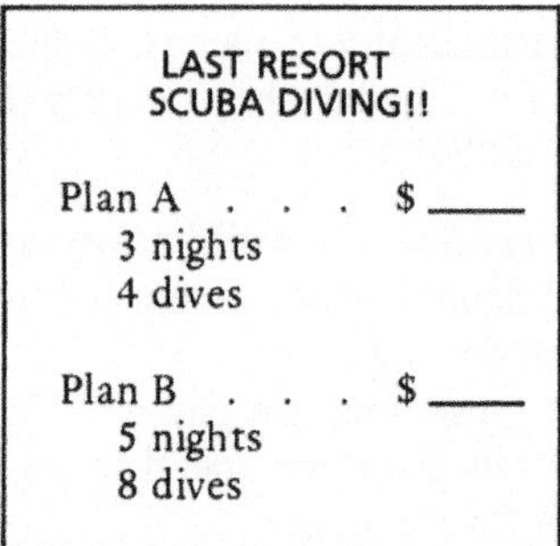

LAST RESORT
SCUBA DIVING!!
Plan A . . . $
3 nights
4 dives
Plan B . . . $
5 nights
8 dives

a. Let x be the number of dollars they charge per night and let y be the number of dollars per dive. Write two expressions, one for the amount you would pay for plan A and the other for plan B.

b. Evaluate the expressions in part (a) if lodging is $50 per night and dives are $40 each.

c. If lodging is increased to $80 per night and dives are reduced to $20 each, do the two plans increase or decrease in cost? By how much?

d. A new price list comes out in which plan A costs $440 and plan B costs $780. What prices are now being assumed per night and per dive?

3. ***Eggs and Sausage Problem*** A breakfast menu lists 2 eggs with 1 sausage patty for \$2.23 and 3 eggs with 2 sausage patties for \$3.76.
   a. Assuming that these amounts pay only for the eggs and sausage, how much do you pay for an egg and how much do you pay for a sausage?
   b. How much would you expect to pay for the Glutton's Breakfast of 5 eggs and 7 sausage patties?

4. ***Artist's Kit Problem*** A beginner's artist kit costs \$6.35 and contains 2 brushes and 5 jars of paint. The standard kit has 4 brushes and 12 jars of paint and costs \$13.20.
   a. Assuming that all brushes cost the same and that all jars of paint cost the same, what are the prices of a brush and of a jar of paint?
   b. How much would you expect to pay for a deluxe kit containing 7 brushes and 20 jars of paint?

5. ***Regular and Unleaded Gas Problem 1*** Regular gas and unleaded gas sell for different prices per liter. Suppose that 2 liters of regular and 3 liters of unleaded cost a total of 252 cents. Five liters of regular and 4 liters of unleaded cost a total of 448 cents. What is the price per liter for each kind of gas?

6. ***Worm and Snail Relay Problem*** A worm and a snail enter the relay races. If the worm goes for 5 hours and then the snail goes for 4 hours, they cover a total of 448 inches. If the worm goes for 2 hours and the snail goes for 3 hours, they cover a total of 252 inches. How fast does each one slither?

7. ***Ice Cream Cone Problem*** A well-known chain of ice cream stores sells a cone with 3 scoops of ice cream for \$1.28 and a cone with 2 scoops of ice cream for \$.87.
   a. Assuming that these amounts pay only for the ice cream and for the cone, how much do you spend for each scoop of ice cream, and how much for the cone?
   b. How much would you expect to pay for a cone with 4 scoops of ice cream?

8. ***Firewood Problem*** It costs \$140 to buy a cord of firewood, delivered to your house, and \$80 to buy one-half cord, delivered. Assume that you pay a certain number of dollars per cord for the wood, plus a fixed number of dollars for delivery.
   a. How much do you pay per cord and how much for delivery?
   b. How much would you expect to pay to buy $1\frac{1}{2}$ cords, delivered? (The answer is *not* \$220!)

9. ***Regular and Unleaded Gas Problem 2*** A gas station has just raised its prices. The attendant resets the pump but forgets to record the old prices. Rather than revealing her forgetfulness by asking her boss, she

consults yesterday's sales report. She finds that 450 liters of regular and 320 liters of unleaded were sold, for a total of \$384.83. Regular was 5 cents per liter cheaper than unleaded. What were the two prices per liter yesterday?

10. *Regular and Unleaded Gas Problem 3* Unleaded gas costs 5¢ per liter more than regular gas. A dealer buys 1000 liters of unleaded and 3000 liters of regular, for a total of \$1870. How many cents per liter does each kind of gas cost?

Problems 11 through 16 involve finding various numbers of items for which the prices are known. The first two lead you step by step through the problem. For the others, *you* must think of the steps.

11. *Carwash Problem* The Math Club raised money for its summer trip by washing cars. They charged \$3 for a car and \$5 for a truck.

CARWASH ACCOUNTING			
Kind	Price	No.	\$
Cars	\$3	_____	_____
Trucks	\$5	_____	_____
Totals . .		_____	_____

a. Define variables for the number of cars washed and for the number of trucks washed. Then write an expression for the total number of dollars received.
b. Evaluate the expression in part (a) for:
   i. 27 cars and 13 trucks;
   ii. 41 cars and 8 trucks;
   iii. 16 cars and 23 trucks. (Surprising?)
c. Suppose the club earned a total of \$181 for washing a total of 49 vehicles. Write a system of two equations stating these facts, and solve the system to find out how many of each kind of vehicle they washed.

12. *Yogurt Problem* Mel Ting sells half-gallons of frozen yogurt for \$4 each and gallons for \$7 each.

MEL'S FROZEN YOGURT			
Size	Price	No.	\$
½ gal.	\$4	_____	_____
1 gal.	\$7	_____	_____
Totals . .		_____	_____

a. Define variables for the number of half-gallons and for the number of gallons sold. Then write an expression for the total number of dollars received.
b. Evaluate the expression in part (a) for:
   i. 33 half-gallons and 19 gallons;
   ii. 57 half-gallons and 30 gallons;
   iii. 36 half-gallons and 42 gallons. (Surprising?)
c. One day Mel sells a total of 50 containers of yogurt, for a total of $287. Write a system of equations expressing these facts. Then solve the system to find out how many of each kind of container he sold.

13. ***Football Tickets Problem*** Suppose that you are collecting tickets at a football game. Reserved seat tickets cost $4.00 each and general admission tickets costs $3.00 each. After the game is over, the turnstile count shows that 1787 people paid admission. You count a total of $5792 from the sale of tickets. You are just about ready to leave for your postgame date when your boss says, "By the way, how many of each kind of ticket were there?" Rather than spending half an hour sorting and counting all the ticket stubs, you decide to use algebra. What do you tell your boss?

14. ***Basketball Tickets Problem*** At a professional basketball game, the turnstile count showed that 17,406 people paid admission. The total cash received for tickets was $133,372. Without actually counting the ticket stubs, find out how many paid for reserved seats ($10.00 each) and how many paid general admission ($6.00 each).

15. ***Cars and Trucks Problem*** A trainload of cars and trucks is en route to an automobile dealer for whom you work. Before they arrive, the dealer receives an invoice showing a total of 160 vehicles. But the part of the invoice showing how many of each kind of vehicle has been torn off and lost. Your boss desperately needs to know how many of each there are before they arrive. Since you know algebra, she comes to you for aid. The invoice shows a total mass of 182,800 kilograms of vehicles, and each truck is 1400 kg and each car is 1000 kg. How many of each kind are there?

16. In the 1970s the government held down the price of oil from old wells but allowed a higher price for oil from new wells. One month the oil company that was producing from a particular field was paid $28,832.10 for a total of 1395 barrels of oil. But there was no indication of how many of these barrels were "new" oil and how many were "old" oil. Figure out these numbers using the fact that new oil sold for $23.70 per barrel and old oil sold for $12.30 per barrel.

Problems 17 through 22 involve mixtures of varying quantities of substances with known compositions. The first two problems lead you step by step through the problem. For the others, *you* must think of what to do.

17. ***Exhaust Gas Problem*** Carbon monoxide is a gas that is 43% carbon. Carbon dioxide is only 27% carbon. Suppose that the Environmental Protection Agency (EPA) analyzes exhaust from cars, a mixture of carbon monoxide and carbon dioxide.

EPA EXHAUST REPORT

Gas	%C	mg gas	mg C
CO	43%	______	______
CO_2	27%	______	______
Totals		______	______

Percent C = ____ × 100 = ____

   a. Define variables for the number of milligrams (mg) of each gas in a sample. Then write an expression for the number of mg of carbon in the sample.
   b. Evaluate the expression in part (a) if one mixes 2000 mg of carbon monoxide and 3000 mg of carbon dioxide.
   c. What is the percent of carbon in the mixture of part (b)?
   d. If the EPA finds that a 1600-mg sample of exhaust gas has 32% carbon, how many mg of the sample were carbon monoxide, and how many were carbon dioxide?

18. ***Gasoline Octane Problem*** The *octane number* of gasoline can be thought of as the percent of the compound octane in the gasoline. For instance, 89-octane gas would be 89% octane and 11% something else. Suppose that a wholesaler has 84-octane gas and 91-octane gas.
   a. The wholesaler mixes x gallons of 84-octane gas and y gallons of 91-octane gas. Write an expression for the number of gallons of octane in the mixture.
   b. Evaluate the expression in part (a) if 1000 gallons of 84-octane gas is mixed with 2000 gallons of 91-octane gas.
   c. What will be the octane number of the mixture in part (b)?
   d. If the wholesaler receives an order for 15,000 gallons of 89.7-octane gas, how much of each kind should be mixed to fill the order?

19. ***Silver Alloy Problem*** Old silver coins contain 90% silver. Silver solder contains 63% silver. If you wanted to make 200 kilograms of

an alloy containing 82% silver, how many kilograms of old coins and how many kilograms of silver solder could you melt together to do this?

20. *Brass Alloy Problem* Suppose that you operate a junk yard. You have vast quantities of yellow brass (67% copper, 33% zinc) and red brass (85% copper, 15% zinc) on hand. Al Oye sends an order for 500 tons of brass containing 80% copper and 20% zinc. How many tons of each kind of brass would you have to melt together to fill Al's order?

21. *Regular and Advanced Students' Test Problem* Assume that advanced students would average 93% on an achievement test and that regular students would average 75% on it.
    a. If 100 advanced students and 300 regular students took the test, what would you expect the average to be?
    b. How many of each kind of student would be needed to get a group of 90 students who would average 87% on the test?

22. *Pitcher and Catcher's Batting Problem* Carl Catcher has a batting average of .370, meaning that he makes a hit 37% of the times he is at bat. Pete Pitcher has a batting average of only .110. Let x be the number of times Carl comes to bat and let y be the number of times Pete comes to bat.
    a. If Carl bats 7 times and Pete bats 3 times, what should their overall batting average be?
    b. In a total of 50 times at bat, how many times may Pete bat in order for their combined average to be as close as possible to .300?

Problems 23 through 32 involve motion with and against a current. The first two lead you step by step through the problem. For others, you must think of what to do.

23. *Shark Problem* A shark takes 20 minutes to swim with the current from its cave to the feeding grounds. Later, it returns against the current, taking 30 minutes.

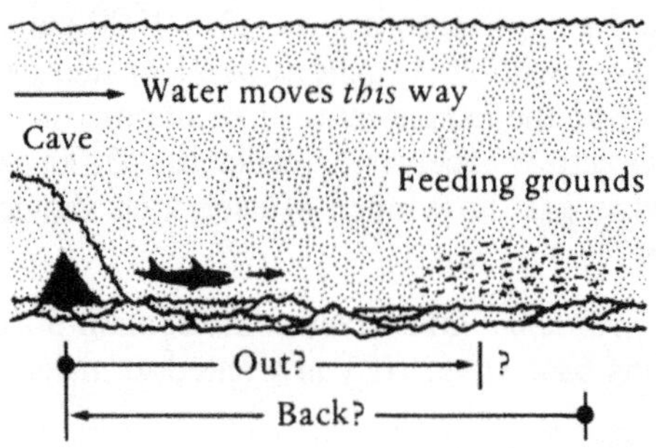

a. Define variables for the shark's speed through the water and for the speed of the current (the speed at which the water is moving). Use feet per minute (ft/min). Then write two expressions, one for the distance the shark swims out and the other for the distance it swims back.
b. Evaluate the expression in part (a) if:
   i. the shark swims 400 ft/min and the current is 100 ft/min;
   ii. the shark swims 80 ft/min and the current is 50 ft/min.
c. How fast does the shark swim and how fast is the current if both the trip out and the trip back are 2100 feet?

24. ***Bee Problem*** The wind blows the smell of a field of flowers to the beehive. A bee flies out to get pollen and then returns to the hive. The outgoing trip takes 70 seconds and the return trip takes 40 seconds.

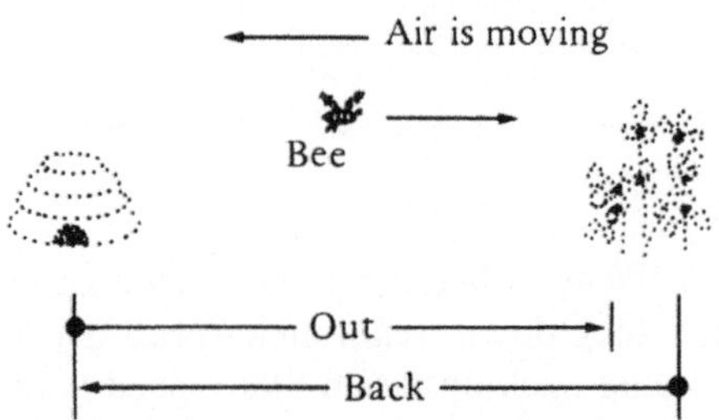

a. Define variables for the rate at which the bee flies through the (still) air and for the rate at which the air is moving (the wind speed) in feet per second. Then write two expressions, one for the distance the bee flew to reach the flower bed and the other for the distance she flies to return to the hive.
b. How far did the bee fly out and how far back if:
   i. she flies 20 ft/sec and the wind is 5 ft/sec;
   ii. she flies 30 ft/sec and the wind is 20 ft/sec?
c. How fast does the bee fly and what is the wind speed if both the trip out and the return trip are 560 feet?

25. ***Snoopy's Dogflight Problem*** Snoopy flies his Sopwith Camel the 120 kilometers from London to Calais in 12 hours, flying into a headwind. The return trip, with the same wind as a tailwind, takes only 2 hours. How fast does Snoopy fly through the air? How fast is the wind blowing?

26. ***A. T. Miles's Flight Problem*** A. T. Miles flies his small plane from Tampa to Orlando, a distance of 80 miles, against a headwind. The trip takes 32 minutes. Later, he returns to Tampa with the wind at his back, making the return trip in 20 minutes. How fast does he fly through the air? How fast is the wind blowing?

27. ***Escalator Problem*** Ann Tick runs up the "down" escalator in 12 seconds and back down again in 8 seconds. The escalator is 48 feet long. How fast does Ann run? How fast does the escalator move?

28. ***Conveyor Belt Problem*** A conveyor belt 420 feet long is moving coal in a strip mine. A rabbit hops on at one end and runs in the same direction the belt is moving. When it gets to the other end, the rabbit turns and runs back, against the motion of the conveyor. The first trip takes 60 seconds and the return trip takes 210 seconds. How fast does the rabbit run and how fast does the conveyor belt move?

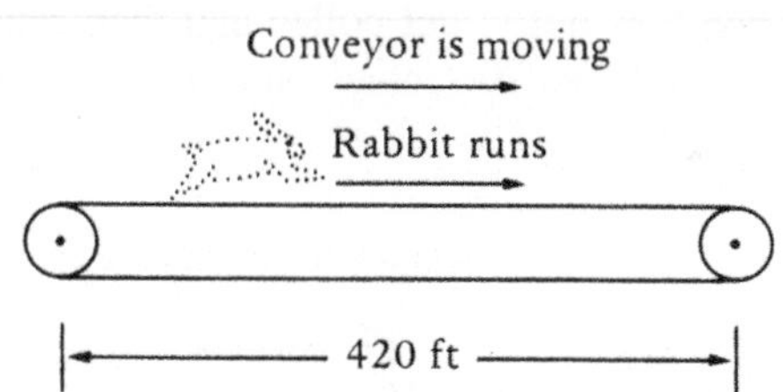

29. ***Pedalboat Problem*** Eb and Flo are pedalboating on the San Antonio River. Going downstream their speed is 40 meters per minute (m/min). Coming back upstream their speed is only 26 m/min. How fast do they move through the water? How fast is the current going?

30. ***Mississippi River Tug Problem*** Going downstream a tugboat averages 17 kilometers per hour (km/h). Coming back upstream its average speed is only 6 km/h. How fast does the current flow? How fast does the tugboat move through the water?

31. ***Aquaman Problem*** Aquaman swims into a storm drain, from which water is flowing at an unknown rate. He swims 200 meters against the flow in 3 min. Then he returns 150 meters with the flow in 0.7 min, before emerging through a manhole in the top of the drain. How fast does Aquaman swim through the water, and how fast does the water flow in the drain?

32. ***Niagara Falls Problem*** Miss Hapse is sailing a remote controlled model boat downstream in the Niagara River. She discovers that at full speed the model can cover 1128 feet in 2 minutes. Suddenly she realizes that the boat is only 240 feet from the falls! She turns it around and runs it at top speed in the other direction. But it is a losing battle. As the boat goes over the falls, she observes that 5 minutes passed since it was turned around. How fast did the boat move through the water? How fast was the water flowing?

Problems 33 through 36 involve equations in which y is in terms of x and x is in terms of y.

33. ***Calvin's Vacation Problem*** Calvin Butterball earns \$400 working at the supermarket to help pay his share of a vacation trip with Phoebe Small's family. To supplement his earnings, Calvin's mother will give him an additional 20% of what he earns and his father will give him an additional 30% of what he earns.
   a. How much will he get from each parent?
   b. Calvin is good at business deals and asks if his mother will give him 20% of the *total* he gets from working and from his father. He also asks if his father will give 30% of the total he gets from working and from his mother. His parents agree, provided Calvin can figure out the right amounts. How much will Calvin get from each parent under these conditions?
   c. How much more will Calvin get in part (b) than in part (a)?

34. ***Fund-Raising Problem*** The Student Council conducts a fund-raising project for needy families. The School Board agrees to give an additional amount equal to 70% of what is raised. The Chamber of Commerce agrees to give an additional amount equal to 60% of what is raised. Here is the catch! The Board will pay 70% of the *total* from the project and from the Chamber of Commerce. The Chamber will pay 60% of the *total* from the project and from the School Board. The project makes \$2000.
   a. How much will the School Board give, and how much will the Chamber of Commerce give?
   b. How much more money will the Student Council get under this plan than they would if the Board and the Chamber just paid 70% and 60%, respectively, of the \$2000?

35. ***Income Tax Problem 1*** If a family pays state income tax, they can deduct this amount from their income for federal tax purposes. For instance, if the income is \$50,000, and the state tax is \$4000, then they pay federal tax on only the remaining \$46,000. A mathematical difficulty arises in states that let you deduct the *federal* tax from the income before figuring *state* tax. You need to know each amount of tax before you can figure out the other! Here's how they get around this difficulty. Suppose that the income is \$50,000.
   a. Let f be the number of dollars of federal tax and let s be the number of dollars of state tax. Write two equations, one saying that the state tax is 10% of what is left after paying federal tax and the other saying that the federal tax is 20% of what is left after paying state tax.
   b. How much state and federal tax does the family pay?
   c. How much does the family save over what they would pay if the 10% and 20% tax rates applied to the entire \$50,000?

36. ***Income Tax Problem 2*** Repeat Problem 35 if the family's income is \$200,000 and the state and federal tax rates are 40% and 60%, respectively. Explain why this family would be in trouble if the 40% and 60% tax rates were applied to the entire \$200,000.

For Problems 37 through 40, you must use the concepts of this chapter in clever ways!

37. ***Uphill and Downhill Running Problem*** Suppose that you can run 240 meters per minute (m/min) going downhill, but only 160 m/min going uphill.
    a. One day you run 2672 meters in a total of 13 min. How many minutes did you run uphill and how many minutes down?
    b. Another day you run 2184 meters in a total of 10 min. How far did you run uphill and how far down?

38. ***Test Problems Problem*** A test is to contain some questions worth 7 points each and some worth 5 points each. Let x be the number of 7-point questions and let y be the number of 5-point questions.
    a. Write an equation stating that the total number of points on the test is to be 100.
    b. Figure out how many of each kind of question there could be. (There is more than one correct answer. Drawing a graph may help you find them.)

B P B P B   P P
B

39. ***Marching Formation Problem*** The marching band and the pep squad do a combined routine in which they divide into 5-member and 3-member groups, as shown in the figure. If the band has a total of 100 members and the pep squad has a total of 80 members, how many of each kind of group can be formed so that no one is left over?

40. ***Scattered Data Problem*** In Section 7-6 you found the equation of a line from two points on the graph. In the real world, two variables are often related by a linear graph. When you measure values of x and y, there can be inaccuracies. The points might not quite lie in a straight line. Your purpose is to find the "best" line to represent the data. Suppose the following values of x and y have been measured.

x:	2	4	5	6	8
y:	8	11	12	14	20

    a. Plot all six points on graph paper.
    b. The line that fits best goes through the point whose x-coordinate is the average of the x-values, and whose y-coordinate is the average of the y-values. Calculate these average values, and plot the point on your graph. Is it the same as one of the data points?
    c. With a ruler, draw the line through the point in part (b) that you think best fits the six data points.
    d. Approximately what is the slope of the line in part (c)?
    e. Write an equation of the line in part (d). Transform it to the slope-intercept form, $y = mx + b$.
    f. The equation in part (e) can be used to predict other values of x and y. Predict what y would be if $x = 3$, if $x = 7$, and if $x = 30$. Predict the value of x that would make $y = 100$.

41. ***Shoe Size Experiment Problem*** Tall people have longer feet than short people. It seems reasonable to assume that there is a linear relationship between height and shoe size. In this problem you will conduct an experiment to try to determine such a relationship.
   a. Select a group of people, such as the students in your class. Have each person record height and shoe size on an index card. You may want to measure height in inches or in centimeters rather than in feet and inches. Separate the cards into boys and girls, because shoe sizes are determined differently for each sex.
   b. Plot two graphs of all the data points, one for boys and one for girls. Use x for height and y for shoe size. Then draw the best-fitting line as in Problem 40. Find the equation of each line.
   c. Bob Lanier was a professional basketball player. He wears a size 22 shoe. Based on your equation, how tall do you predict he is?
   d. Tell at least two ways you could change the way you get data for this problem that would make the line better represent the relationship between shoe size and height.

7-11 CHAPTER REVIEW AND TEST

In this chapter you have studied expressions that have two variables, such as $5x + 7y$. To evaluate such expressions, you need to know values for both x and y. Setting such an expression equal to some number gives an equation with two variables, like

$$5x + 7y = 35.$$

These equations have *many* solutions, and you learned how to plot a graph of these solutions on a *Cartesian plane* (see the figures). *Slopes* and *intercepts* helped you plot these graphs quickly. By reversing the graphing process, you found an equation when information about the graph was given.

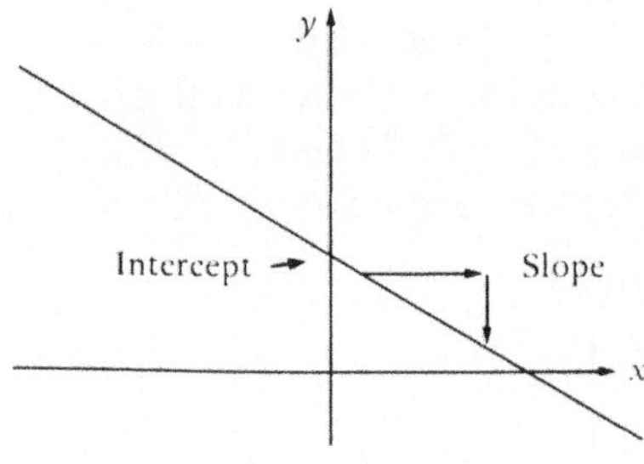

Equation with two variables

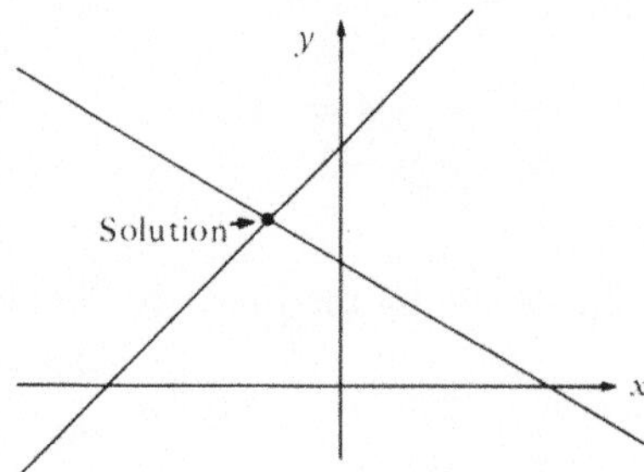

System of equations

Two such equations form a *system of equations*. The *solution* of a system satisfies both equations and is represented by the point where the graphs cross. You learned how to calculate this ordered pair either by *substitution* or by *linear combination*.

In preparation for the Chapter Test below, go back and make a list of the objectives of each section. If you do not understand what the objective means, rework enough of the examples in that section to refresh your memory. The test itself is a good review but should be tried only after you have looked through your notes. The test may take you longer than a normal classroom test.

CHAPTER TEST

1. What is the difference in each case?
   a. Ordinate and abscissa.
   b. Rise and run.
   c. Slope and intercept.
   d. x-intercept and y-intercept.
   e. Slope of a horizontal line and slope of a vertical line.
2. a. Who is credited with inventing the xy-coordinate system?
   b. Draw a coordinate system and show the names of the quadrants.
   c. What is a system of equations?
   d. Find the x-intercept of $5x + 3y = 90$.
   e. Write an example of an equation in slope-intercept form.
3. For the expression $2x + 7y$:
   a. evaluate it if x is 13 and y is -8;
   b. find x if the expression equals 73 and y is 5;
   c. find y if the expression equals -1 and x is 10.
4. Plot the points $(1, 2)$ and $(5, -1)$ on a Cartesian coordinate system. Connect the points with a straight line. Find the slope of the line.
5. Plot the graph:
   a. $y = -\frac{3}{7}x$
   b. $y - 4 = 3(x + 2)$
   c. $y = -3$
6. Find an equation of the line.
   a. Has slope $\frac{2}{7}$ and y-intercept 8.
   b. Contains $(4, -3)$ and has slope $-\frac{5}{2}$.
   c. Contains $(-2, 7)$ and $(3, -1)$.
   d. Is vertical, and contains $(4, 6)$.
7. Solve by the linear combination method.

$$2x + 3y = 8.1$$
$$5x - 2y = -1.6$$

8. Solve by substitution.

$$5x - y = -3$$
$$3x + 8y = 24$$

9. Solve by either method.

a. $x + 4y = 19$
$6x + 5y = 38$

b. $x = 0.7(300 - y)$
$y = 0.8(300 - x)$

10. Use the system

$$x + 2y = 8$$
$$5x - 2y = 6.$$

a. Plot the graph of the first equation by finding the two intercepts.
b. Transform the second equation to slope-intercept form. Use the slope and intercept to plot the graph on the *same* coordinate system as part (a).
c. Read the intersection point of the two graphs correct to 0.1 unit.
d. Solve the system of equations either by addition-subtraction or by substitution. Show that the answer agrees with the one you found by graphing in part (c).

11. ***Hamburger and Hot Dog Problem*** As junior employee in your office, you are sent out to get hamburgers and hot dogs for the 23 people who work there. On the way, you forget how many of each to buy. So you decide to figure it out by algebra. Each person gets one burger or one dog (not both!). You have collected a total of \$32.10. Burgers cost \$1.50 each and dogs cost \$1.10 each. How many of each should you buy?

12. ***Crow's Flight Problem*** A. Crow flies 10.5 miles against the wind and returns with the wind. The first flight takes 35 minutes and the return flight takes 15 minutes. How many miles per minute does A. Crow fly? How fast is the wind blowing?

13. ***Antifreeze Problem*** Brand A antifreeze is 85% ethylene glycol. Brand B is 60% ethylene glycol. The two brands are to be mixed.

a. Define variables for the numbers of gallons of each kind used. Then write an expression for the number of gallons of ethylene glycol in the mixture.
b. If 100 gallons of brand A is mixed with 150 gallons of brand B, find:
   i. the number of gallons of ethylene glycol in the mixture;
   ii. the percent of ethylene glycol in the mixture.
c. If 1000 gallons of mixture is to have 78% ethylene glycol, how many gallons of each brand should be used?

8

Linear Functions, Scattered Data, and Probability

In the last chapter you learned how to graph linear equations with two variables. Now you will use two variables in real-world situations where the value of one variable depends on the value of the other. For instance, the length of each vertical girder on a bridge depends on the distance of that girder from the end of the bridge. You will find an equation that fits a set of points, then use that equation to make predictions about such things as how high your grade could be if you studied for 5 hours. You will also fit linear functions to data that is "scattered." For instance, the height of an oak tree is a function of how old it is. But data gathered from many oak trees will not follow a perfectly smooth line. Figuring out something about the real world by analyzing data is a problem in statistics. The reverse problem, using knowledge of the real world to predict how the data will come out, is called probability. You will use both probability and statistics in this chapter.

8-1 LINEAR FUNCTIONS

Sometimes in the real world two variable quantities are related in such a way that the graph is a straight line. As an example, suppose that a plumber charges $35 to make a house call, plus $25 an hour for the actual work.

Let x be the number of hours the plumber works.

Let y be the total number of dollars charged.

An expression for the number of dollars charged is $25x + 35$. So an equation for y in terms of x is

$$y = 25x + 35.$$

From your work in Chapter 7 you should recognize that this is the equation of a straight line. The slope is 25 and the y-intercept is 35. The figure shows a graph of this equation. Different scales are used on the two axes to make the graph have reasonable proportions.

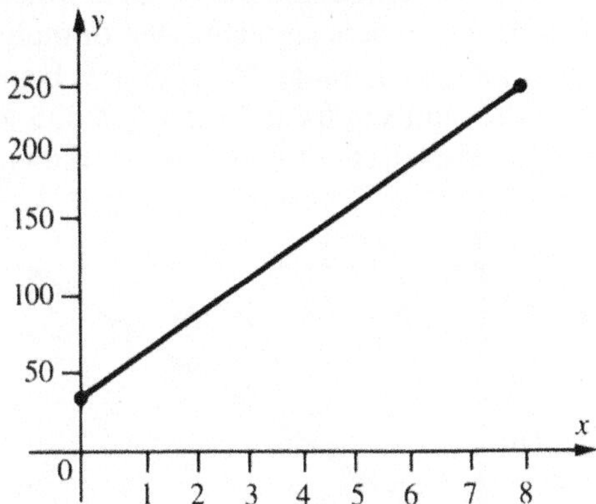

If x and y are related by a linear equation, such as $y = 25x + 35$, then y is said to be a *linear function* of x. The following is a formal definition of linear function.

DEFINITION

LINEAR FUNCTION
A **linear function** is a set of ordered pairs (x, y) that are related by an equation of the form

$$y = mx + b,$$

where m and b stand for constants.

The value of one variable in a function often depends on the value of the other. For instance, the number of dollars the plumber makes depends on the number of hours worked. The variable that depends on the other is called the **dependent variable.** The variable it depends on is called the **independent variable.** The dependent variable is usually plotted on the vertical axis, as in the sketch.

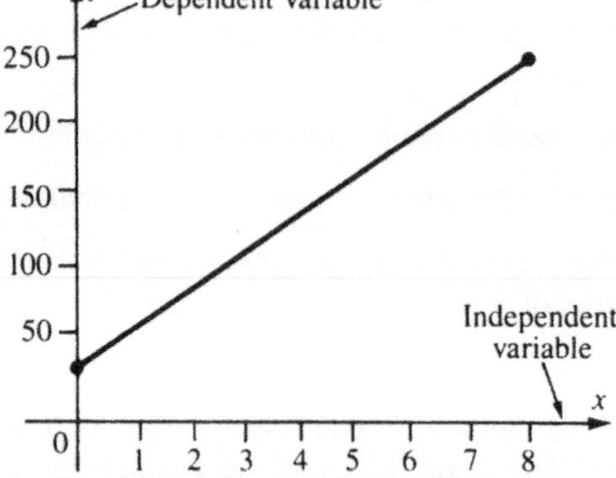

In the plumber example, above, the number of hours worked cannot be negative. If you assume that the plumber would not work more than 8 hours on any one call, the permissible values of x would be all numbers from 0 through 8. These numbers are called the **domain** of the function. The total number of dollars can range from 35 at 0 hours worked to 235 at 8 hours worked. The numbers from 35 through 235 are called the **range** of the function. These sets of numbers are shown in the sketch.

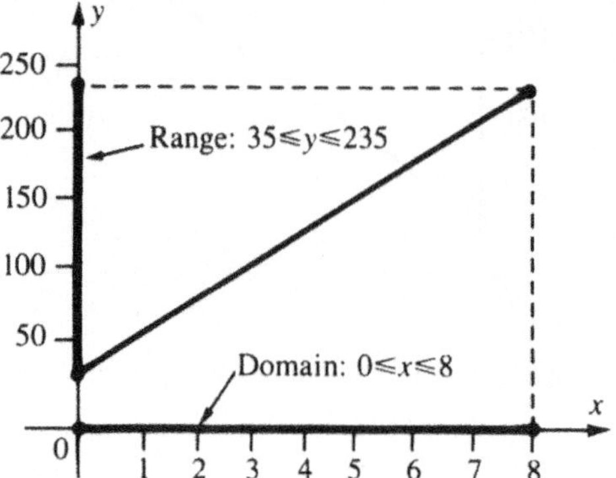

DEFINITION

> **DOMAIN AND RANGE**
> The **domain** of a function is the set of permissible values of the **independent variable.**
>
> The **range** of a function is the set of values of the **dependent variable** corresponding to all values of the independent variable in the domain.

Objective:

Given a situation from the real world in which two variables are related by a linear function, find the equation and use it to predict values of the variables.

EXAMPLE

For the plumber problem, above:

a. Find the total charge for 5 hours 15 minutes.
b. How long could the plumber work without exceeding a total bill of \$120?

Think These Reasons

a. The equation is $y = 25x + 35$.	From the first part of this section.
5 hours 15 minutes is 5.25 hours.	60 minutes in an hour.
$y = 25(5.25) + 35$	Substitute 5.25 for x.
$y = 166.25$	Do the computations.
\$166.25	Answer the question.
b. $120 = 25x + 35$	Substitute 120 for y.
$85 = 25x$	Subtract 35.
$3.4 = x$	Divide by 25.
3 hours 24 minutes	Answer the question.

ORAL PRACTICE

State the domain and range of the linear function.

A.

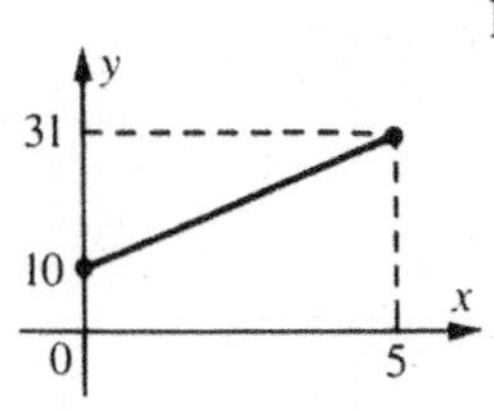

B.

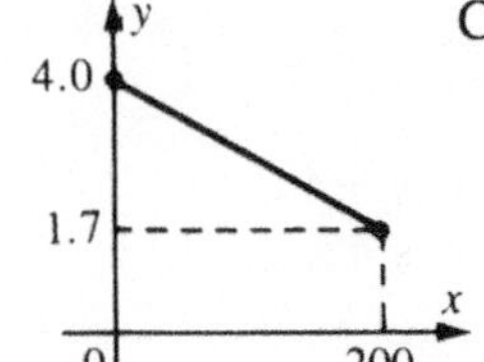

C.

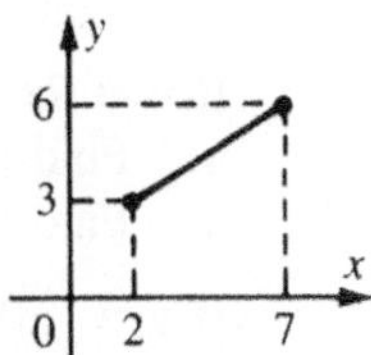

D.

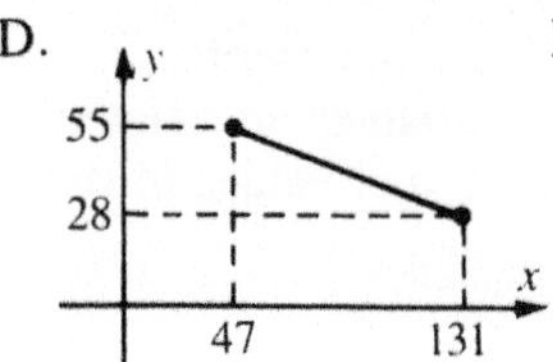

E.

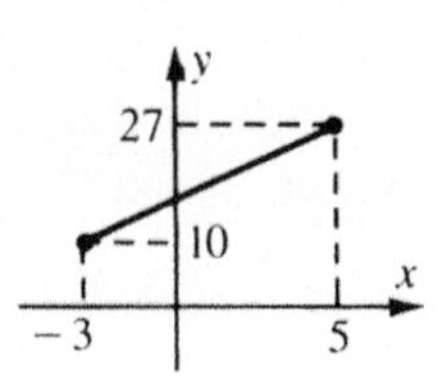

F.

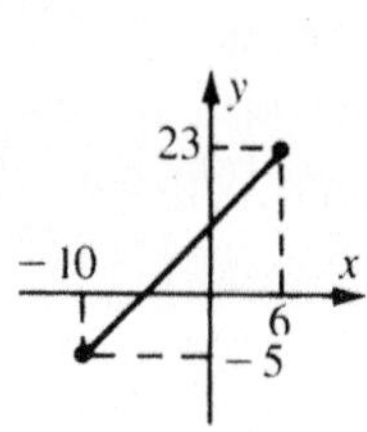

G.

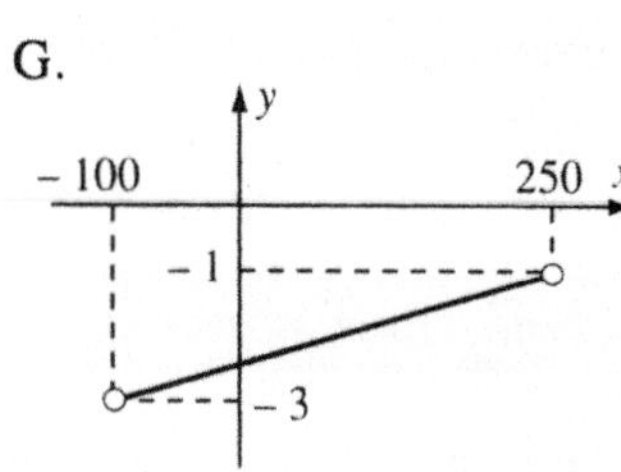

H.

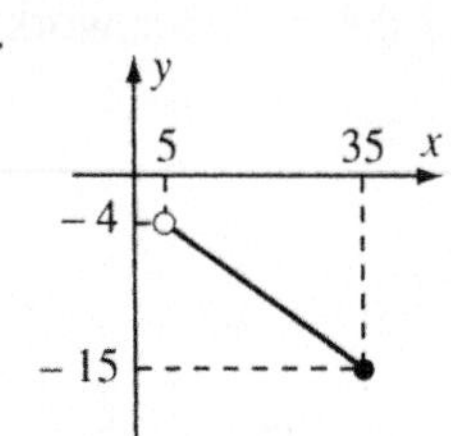

Tell which variable is independent and which is dependent.

I.

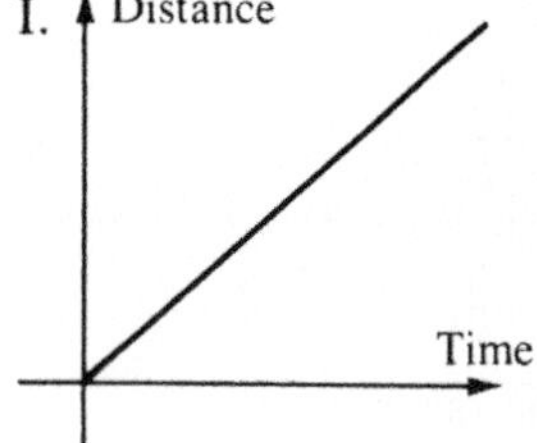

J.

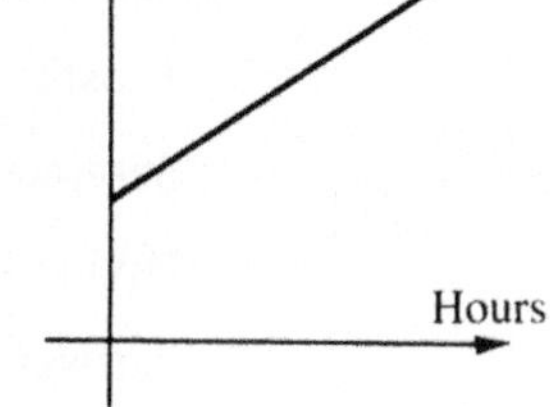

K.

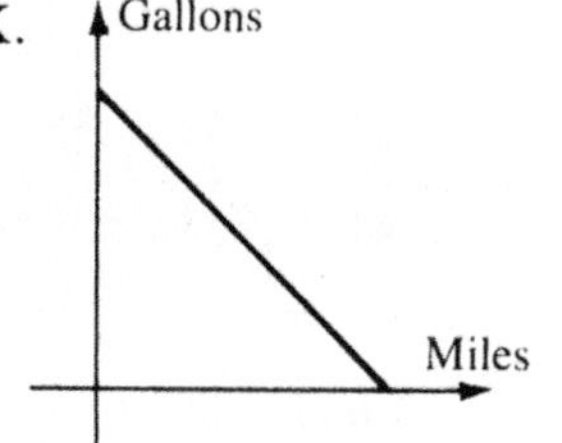

EXERCISE 8-1

1. If $y = 7x + 3$,
   a. Find y when x is -4.
   b. Find x when y is 45.
2. If $y = -0.4x + 170$,
   a. Find y when x is 200.
   b. Find x when y is 87.

For Problems 3–6, sketch the graph of the linear function described.

3. Slope is positive and y-intercept is negative.
4. Slope is negative and y-intercept is positive.
5. Domain: $2 \le x \le 7$, range: $3 \le y \le 6$
6. Domain: $0 \le x \le 8$, range: $1 \le y \le 9$
7. ***House-Building Problem*** The cost of building a new house depends on the number of square feet of floor space. Suppose that the builder will charge $60 per square foot, and that the lot on which the house is to be built costs $40,000.
   a. Write an equation expressing total cost as a function of square feet of floor space.
   b. What will the total cost be for a 2500-square-foot house?
   c. The new owners can afford to pay as much as $220,000 for the house and lot. What is the largest house they could build?
   d. Sketch the graph of this function and show domain and range.
8. ***Owning a Car Problem*** Lisa Carr figures that it costs her 22 cents a mile to drive her car, plus a fixed monthly cost of $230 for car payments, etc. So her total monthly cost for owning the car is a function of the number of miles a month she drives it.
   a. Write an equation expressing total monthly cost in terms of number of miles driven that month.
   b. How much will it cost Lisa if she drives 1000 miles a month?
   c. Lisa can afford no more than $500 a month, total, for car expenses. About how far can she drive each month?
   d. Sketch the graph of this function and show domain and range.
9. ***Tip Money Problem*** Suppose that a waiter makes $40 a day, plus 70% of the tip money he receives.
   a. Write an equation expressing total daily pay as a function of tip money received.
   b. How much tip money would be needed for the waiter to earn $100 in a day?
   c. How much would the waiter make in a day if he received $57 in tip money?
   d. Sketch the graph of this function and show domain and range.
10. ***Commission Problem*** Suppose that an insurance agent makes $700 a month base pay. In addition, she makes a commission of 8% of the value of the insurance policies she sells.
    a. Write an equation expressing total monthly pay as a function of number of dollars worth of policies sold.
    b. How many dollars worth of insurance must she sell to make $2000 in a month?
    c. How many dollars will she get, total, if she sells $1 million worth of insurance in a month?
    d. Sketch the graph of this function. Show domain and range.

11. ***Highway Painting Problem*** The Highway Department estimates that it takes 2.3 hours to paint a mile of center stripe on the highway. In addition, it takes about 45 minutes for the crew to get ready to paint.
    a. Write an equation expressing total time it will take as a function of number of miles to be painted.
    b. How long will it take, total, for the crew to paint 2 miles?
    c. What is the maximum number of miles a crew can paint in a day if they may spend no more than 8 hours, total, that day?
    d. Sketch the graph of this linear function. Show clearly the range and domain.

12. ***Elevator Cable Problem*** The number of feet of cable needed for an elevator in a building is 40 times the number of stories tall the building is, plus 50 feet (used to go into and out of the machinery).
    a. Write an equation expressing total number of feet of cable as a function of number of stories.
    b. How much cable would be needed for a 7-story building?
    c. A reel of elevator cable contains 1000 feet of cable. What is the tallest building that could be equipped with an elevator without having to splice together pieces of cable?
    d. What is the domain of this linear function if the building codes do not allow spliced cable? (Think hard about your answer!)
    e. Sketch the graph of this linear function. Use the domain in part (d).

13. ***Corn Flakes Problem*** A 24-ounce box of corn flakes costs $1.95. An 18-ounce box costs only $1.49. Assume that the cost of a box of corn flakes is a linear function of the number of ounces in the box.
    a. Define variables for the number of ounces and the number of dollars. Write the given information as ordered pairs.
    b. Find the slope of this linear function.
    c. Use the point-slope form to write an equation for this function.
    d. How would you find out what they assume as the fixed cost for the box, etc.? What is this fixed cost?

14. ***Haircut Problem*** Dan Druff shaved off all his hair some time ago. At present, his hair is 6 cm long. Three weeks ago it was only 4.8 cm long. Let x be the number of weeks that have elapsed after the present, and let y be the number of centimeters long his hair is.
    a. Write the pieces of information about hair length and time as ordered pairs. You must decide in which order to write the variables. (Think carefully about the correct values of x!)
    b. Find the slope of this linear function.
    c. Write an equation for this function.
    d. How long ago did Dan shave off his hair?
    e. Sketch the graph of this linear function. Show the domain.

8-2

SCATTERED DATA AND LINEAR REGRESSION

In the last section you fitted a linear equation to two given points. If you measure many data points for two variables that should be linearly related, you usually find that the points are "scattered." Figure 8-2a, below, shows the number of pushups (y) various elementary school children can do versus the number of days (x) since they started training to do pushups.

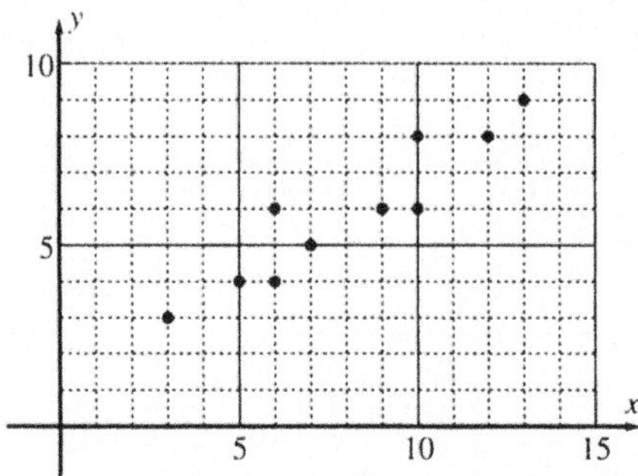

Figure 8-2a

Objective:

Given scattered data that is linearly related, find the equation of the linear function that best fits the data, and use the equation to make predictions.

A graph such as Figure 8-2a is called a **scatter plot.** The data may be scattered for several reasons. First, several people are doing the pushups, so there may be several data points for the same day. Second, the same person might improve more, or not as much, one day as on the previous day.

If the general trend of the data is linear it is possible to find the linear function that fits the data *best*. The best-fitting graph is called the **regression line,** and its equation is called the **regression equation.** The process of finding the best-fitting linear function is called **linear regression.**

In the example below you will see how you can fit a regression line to given data. Cover the answers as you work the example.

EXAMPLE

Pushups Problem This problem relates to the data in Figure 8-2a.

a. Find the average value of x (x_{av}) and the average value of y (y_{av}).
b. Photocopy the scatter plot in Figure 8-2a or copy it onto a piece of graph paper. Draw the line you think best fits the data. This line should go through the point (x_{av}, y_{av}).
c. Write an equation for the line you drew in part (b).

d. Based on your equation, how many pushups would you expect a child to be able to do after 50 days?
e. Based on your equation, how many days would you expect a child to have to train before being able to do 100 pushups?
f. Use a calculator or computer that does linear regression to find the actual regression equation. How close did your equation in part (c) come to it?

- - - - -

a. $x_{av} = \dfrac{3+5+6+6+7+9+10+10+12+13}{10}$ Add the values. Divide by 10.

$= \underline{\underline{8.1}}$

$y_{av} = \dfrac{3+4+4+6+5+6+6+8+8+9}{10} = \underline{\underline{5.9}}$

- - - - -

b.

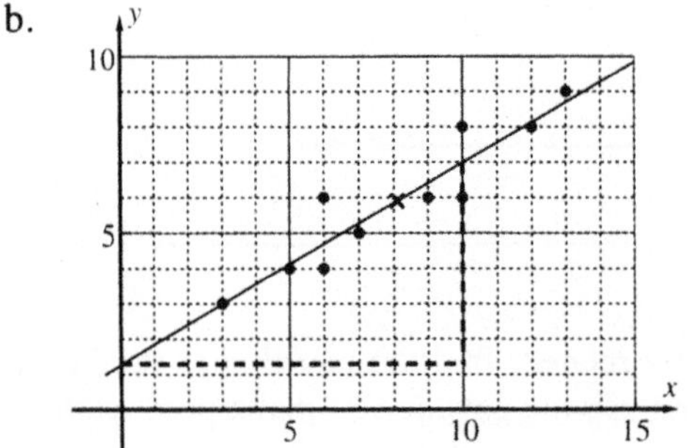

Mark $(x_{av}, y_{av}) = (8.1, 5.9)$ with an $\times$. Pivot your ruler back and forth around this point until as many points as possible are as close to the line as possible. The result will approximate the line of best fit.

- - - - -

c. y-intercept ≈ 1.3	Read the graph, above.
Slope $\approx \dfrac{7 - 1.3}{10} = 0.57$	Draw dotted lines on the graph.
Equation is $\underline{\underline{y = 0.57x + 1.3}}$	Use $y = mx + b$.

- - - - -

d. $y = 0.57(50) + 1.3 = 29.8$	Substitute 50 for x and compute.
About 30 pushups.	Write a real-world answer.

- - - - -

e. $100 = 0.57x + 1.3$	Substitute 100 for y.
$98.7 = 0.57x$	Solve the equation.
$173.1578... = x$	
About 173 days.	Write a real-world answer.

f. The graph below shows what the calculator display might look like. The best-fit regression equation is

$$y = 0.5715283x + 1.270183,$$

so the equation in part (c) is close to the best fit.

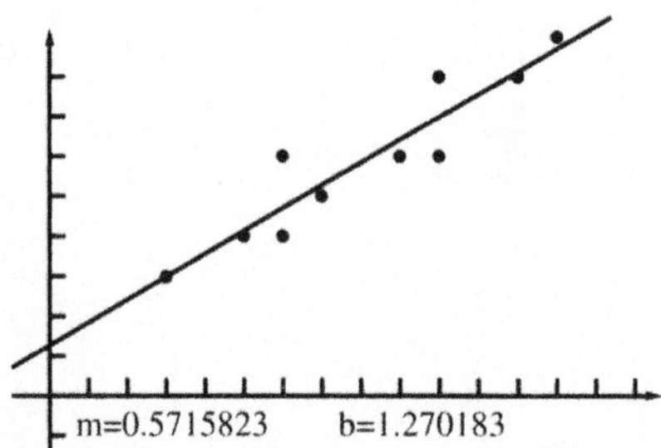

There are actually *several* kinds of "averages" for any set of numbers. If you add up the numbers and divide by how many numbers there are in the set, you are finding the *mean* of the set. You did this to get x_{av} and y_{av} in this section. There are two other averages of a set of numbers in statistics, the *mode* and the *median*. The mode is the number in the set that occurs most frequently. The median is the middle number in the set—the one that is in the middle of the list when all the numbers are arranged in numerical order.

ORAL PRACTICE

For each graph:

a. Tell whether or not there is a pattern in the data.
b. If there is a pattern, tell whether or not the pattern is linear.
c. If the pattern is linear, tell whether the slope is positive or negative.

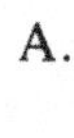

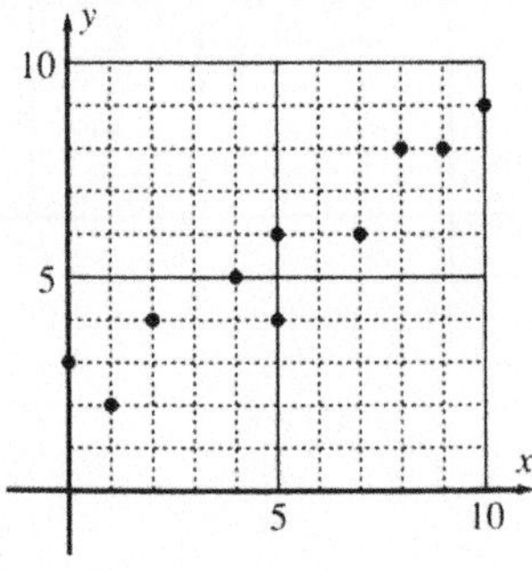

B.

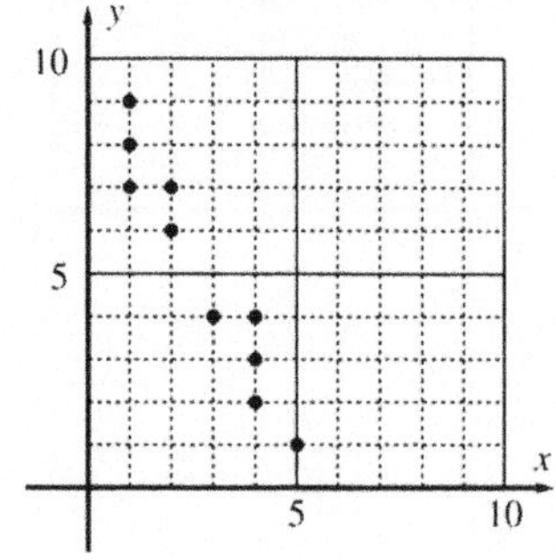

C.

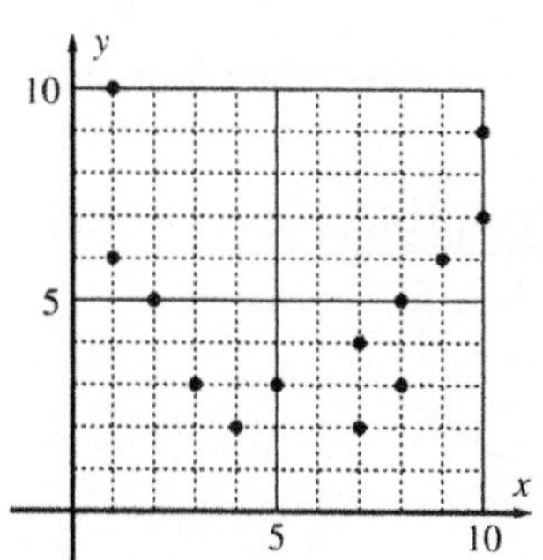

D.

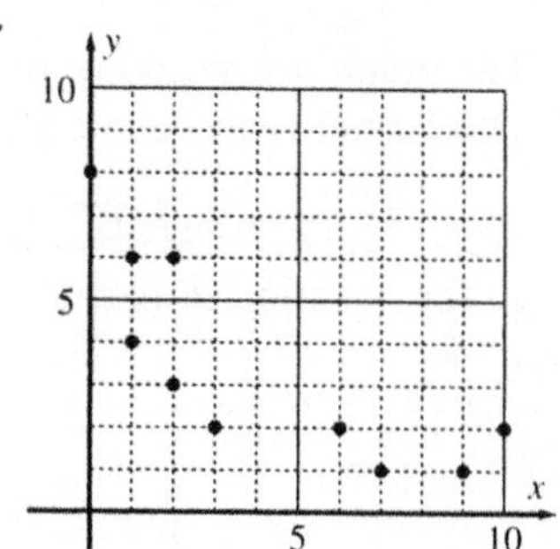

E.

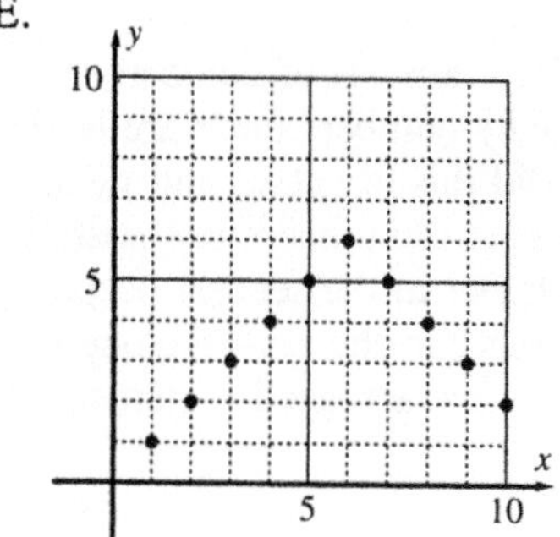

F.

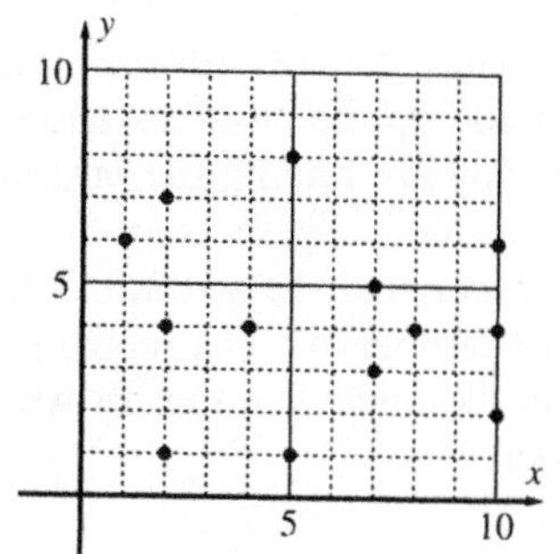

G.

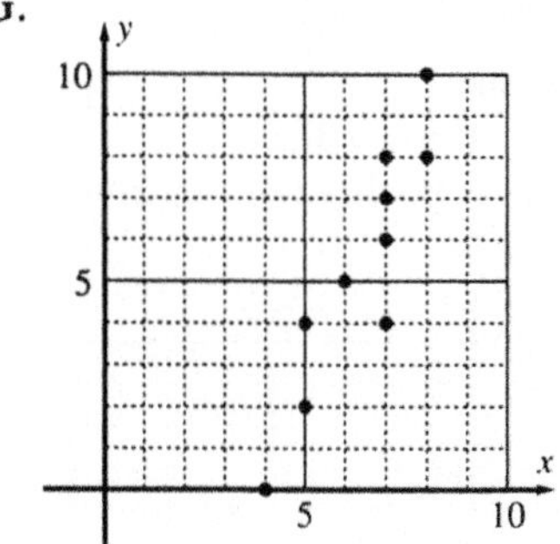

H.

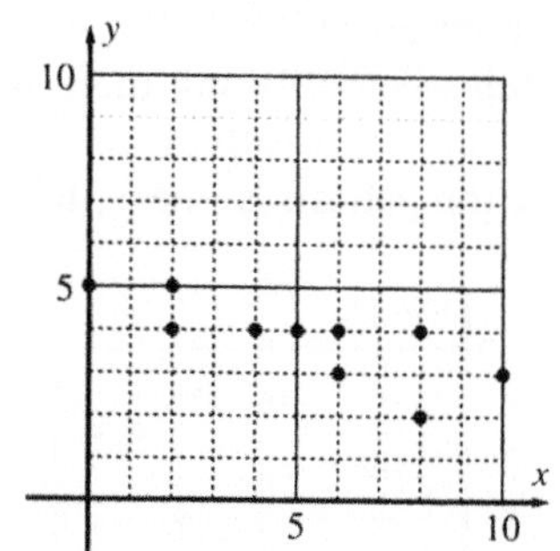

EXERCISE 8-2

For Problems 1 through 6, photocopy the scatter plot or copy it on graph paper. Then draw the best-fitting line through the data points and write an equation for the line you have drawn. The averages of x and y are given for some sets of data.

1.

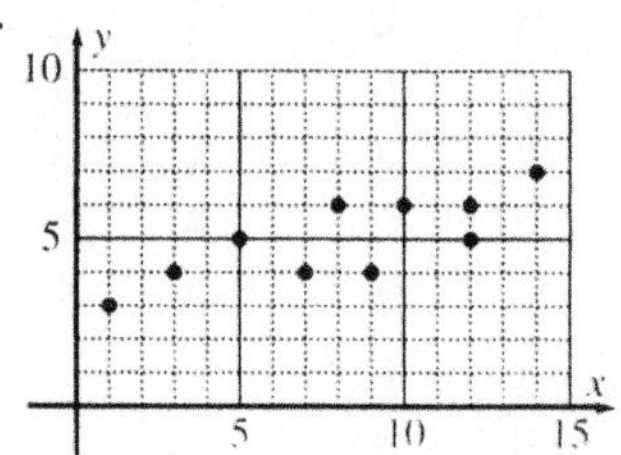

$X_{av} = 8.1$
$Y_{av} = 5.0$

2.

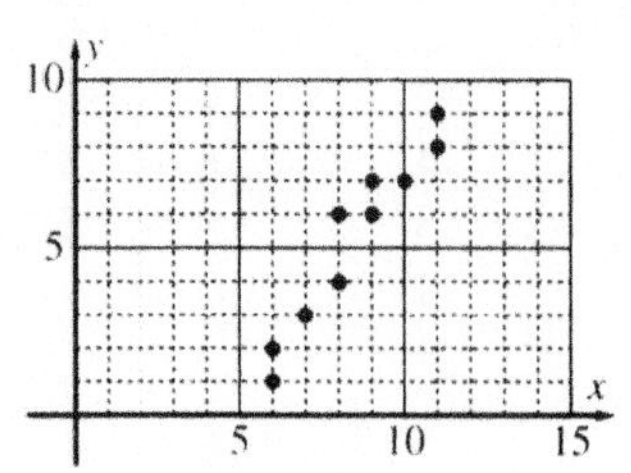

$X_{av} = 8.5$
$Y_{av} = 5.3$

3.

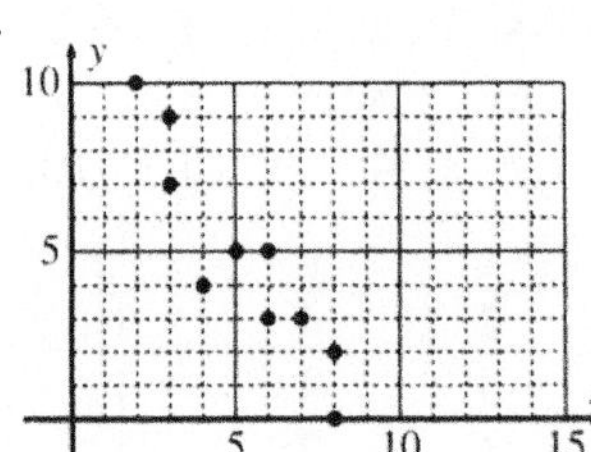

4.

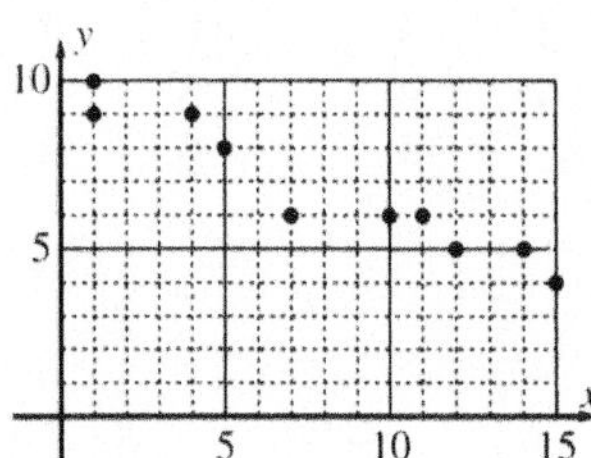

5.

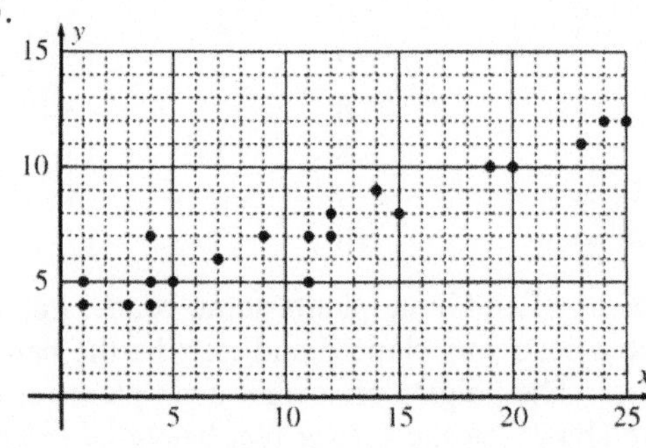

$X_{av} = 11.2$
$Y_{av} = 7.3$

6.

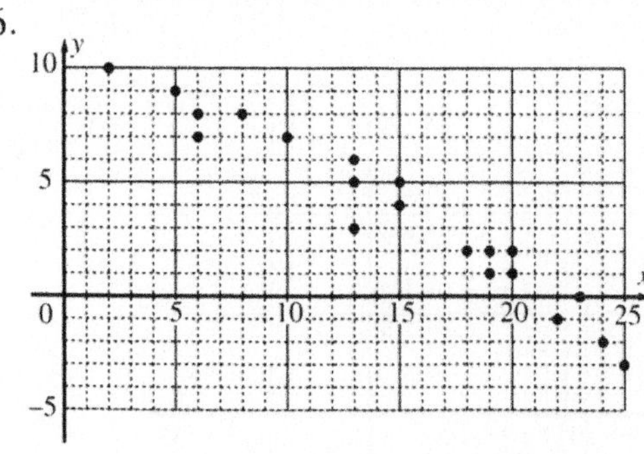

For Problems 7 through 12:

a. Make a scatter plot of the data.
b. Find x_{av} and y_{av}, and graph the linear function that best fits the data.
c. Write an equation for the linear function you graphed in part (b).
d. Use a graphing calculator or computer to find by linear regression the equation of the linear function that actually fits the data best.
e. Tell how your graph in part (b) differs from the best-fit graph.

7.

x	y	x	y
0	3	5	6
1	2	7	6
2	4	8	8
4	5	9	8
5	4	10	9

8.

x	y	x	y
1	9	3	4
1	8	4	4
1	7	4	3
2	6	4	2
3	4	5	1

9.

x	y	x	y
0	5	6	4
2	5	6	3
2	4	8	4
4	4	8	2
5	4	9	3

10.

x	y	x	y
4	0	7	6
5	2	7	7
5	4	7	8
6	5	8	8
7	4	8	10

11.

x	y	x	y
−2	−7	2	−3
−2	−6	3	−3
−1	−7	5	0
−1	−6	5	2
1	−6	5	2
0	−7	5	3
1	−5	6	1
1	−5	6	2
1	−4	6	4
2	−4	8	4

12.

x	y	x	y
2	4	10	−1
3	3	11	−4
4	2	11	−4
7	0	12	−4
7	1	12	−4
7	2	12	−3
8	−2	13	−4
8	1	13	−3
9	−1	14	−5
10	−3	17	−7

13. ***Lee Gume's Bean Problem*** Lee Gume plants some beans. Let x be the number of days since a bean was planted and let y be the height of the bean plant in inches. The heights of several bean plants at various numbers of days are shown on the scatter plot below.

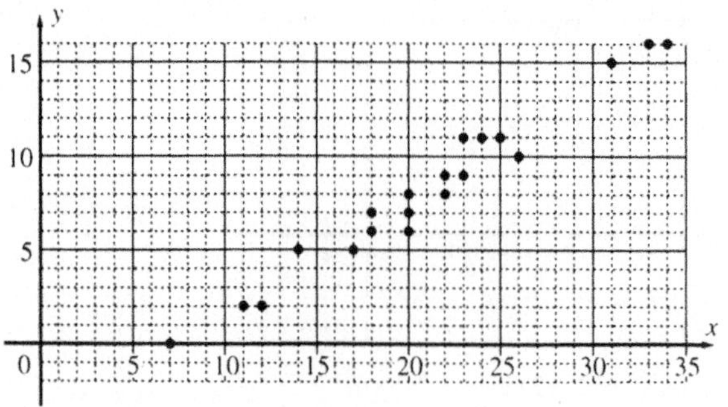

a. Photocopy this scatter plot, or draw it on your own graph paper.
b. The average values of x and y are 21 and 8.2, respectively. Draw the line that best fits the given data.
c. What is the slope of the line you drew?
d. Write an equation of the line you drew.
e. How tall should Lee expect a bean plant to be 100 days after it is planted? Show your work.

14. ***Piano Solo Problem*** You decide to examine the effects of repeated practice on a person's ability to play a piano piece without mistakes. From data you collect at the local junior high school you find that various students make the numbers of mistakes shown below (y) on a given piece on the xth practice session.

x	y	x	y	x	y	x	y
1	25	8	17	13	14	17	11
4	20	9	18	13	11	19	10
7	19	9	17	14	14	19	8
8	20	9	17	15	13	21	10
8	19	9	17	16	12	23	6

a. On graph paper, make a scatter plot of the above data. Figure out a good way to show repeated data. Does the data seem to be linearly related?
b. Find the average values, x_{av} and y_{av}. Plot the point on your graph from part (a).
c. Draw the graph of the best-fitting linear function.
d. Write the equation of the best-fitting line from part (c).
e. Based on your equation, find out, on the average, how many times a junior high school student would be expected to have to practice this piece in order to make *no* mistakes.
f. The data above were really generated by computer using random values of x and y, with the y-values picked to cluster around a given linear function. If you actually measured mistakes versus number of practice sessions for junior high school students, in what ways would you expect the data to differ from this linear data?

15. ***Sports Record Problem*** If you examine world or Olympic records for various races such as the mile or the 100 meters, you will find that over the years the length of time has decreased. Although the data is scattered, it often seems to follow a *linear* trend. Suppose somebody tried to tell you that this kind of data really *is* linear. What reasoning would you use to show that it could not possibly be so?

8-3 PROBABILITY

In the last section you looked for patterns in data gathered in some kind of real-world experiment. From the data you reached conclusions such as "The data are linearly related." In this section and the next you will study the *converse* of this problem. From analysis of possible outcomes of a real-world experiment, you will predict the likelihood that a certain result will occur. This likelihood is called the probability of the result.

Suppose that 20 pieces of paper are marked with the integers 1 through 20. The papers are placed in a hat and you draw one at random. You win if the number you draw is a prime.

To find out how likely you are to win, write out all possible outcomes:

1 2 3 4 5 6 7 8 9 10 11 12 13 14 15 16 17 18 19 20

These are the primes in this set of numbers (note that 1 is not a prime):

2 3 5 7 11 13 17 19

Since there are 8 successful outcomes out of the 20, and each outcome is equally likely, it is reasonable to expect that you would draw a prime roughly 8/20 of the time. This fraction, 8/20, is called the **probability** of drawing a prime. The act of drawing a number is called a **random experiment.** Each number that could be drawn is called an **outcome** of the random experiment. The desired result of a random experiment, such as "The number is prime," is called an **event.** The set of all successful outcomes for the experiment is called the **event space.** The set of all possible outcomes, successful or not, is called the **sample space.**

Objective:

Given a description of a random experiment, calculate the probability that a certain event will happen.

Cover the answers as you work these examples.

EXAMPLE 1

A piece of paper with a number between 1 and 20 is drawn from a hat, as described above.

a. What is the special name given to this set?
{1, 2, 3, 4, 5, 6, 7, 8, 9, 10, 11, 12, 13, 14, 15, 16, 17, 18, 19, 20}
b. What is the name given to this set? {2, 3, 5, 7, 11, 13, 17, 19}
c. What is the name of each element of the set in part (a)?
d. What name is given to "The result is a prime"?

e. What name is given to the act of drawing one of the numbers?

f. What is the ratio $\dfrac{\text{number of successful outcomes}}{\text{total number of outcomes}}$ called?

g. What must be true of each outcome for the probability of an event to equal the ratio in part (f)?

h. What is the probability of the event "The number selected is evenly divisible by 3"?

i. What is the percent probability that the number selected is evenly divisible by 3?

Think These Reasons

- - - - -

a. Sample space. — Read the text above.

- - - - -

b. Event space. — Read the text above.

- - - - -

c. Outcome. — Read the text above.

- - - - -

d. Event. — Read the text above.

- - - - -

e. Random experiment. — Read the text above.

- - - - -

f. Probability of an event. — Read the text above.

- - - - -

g. They must be equally likely. — Read the text above.

- - - - -

h. The successful outcomes are:
3, 6, 9, 12, 15, 18 — These are divisible by 3.
There are 20 possible outcomes.
Probability = 6/20 = $\underline{\underline{3/10}}$ — (number successful)/(total number)

- - - - -

i. (6/20)(100) = $\underline{\underline{30\%}}$

Sometimes you can find the probability of an event by using geometry. The next example shows you how to find a **geometric probability.**

EXAMPLE 2

Figure 8-3a shows a square, 10 units by 10 units, on a Cartesian coordinate system. Inside the square is a quarter-circle of radius 10 units. If a point is picked at random inside the square, what is the probability that it is also inside the quarter-circle?

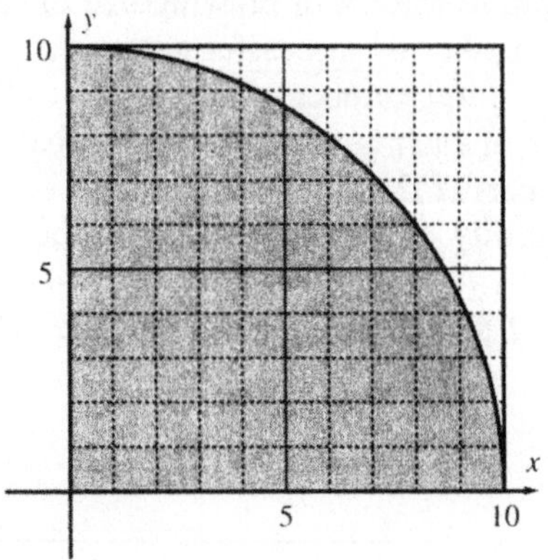

Figure 8-3a

The sample space is all points in the square.

The event space is all points in the quarter-circle.

Since any point is equally likely to be picked, the probability equals the area of the quarter-circle divided by the area of the square.

Probability	$= \dfrac{\pi(10^2) \times (1/4)}{10^2}$	$\dfrac{\text{area of event space}}{\text{area of sample space}}$
	$= \underline{\underline{\pi/4}}$	Simplify.
	$= \underline{\underline{0.78539\ldots}}$	Write as a decimal, if desired.
	$\approx \underline{\underline{78.5\%}}$	Write as a percent, if desired.

TERMS ASSOCIATED WITH PROBABILITY

Random experiment: an action in which there is no way to tell beforehand just which of several possible things will happen.

Outcomes: equally likely results of a random experiment.

Sample space: the set of all possible outcomes for a random experiment.

Event: a favorable outcome of a random experiment.

Event space: the set of all favorable outcomes for an event.

Probability: $\dfrac{\text{number of favorable outcomes}}{\text{total number of outcomes}}$

$$= \frac{\text{number of elements in the event space}}{\text{number of elements in the sample space}}$$

The following box summarizes the difference between probability and statistics.

> **Probability:** Given information about something in the real world, predict the results of a random experiment.
>
> **Statistics:** Given data resulting from a random experiment, predict something about the real-world situation from which the data comes.

ORAL PRACTICE

Find the probability for each of the following random experiments:

A. Pick an even number from {1, 2, 3, 4, 5, 6, 7, 8, 9}.
B. Pick an odd number from {1, 2, 3, 4, 5, 6, 7, 8, 9}.
C. Pick a prime number from {1, 2, 3, 4, 5, 6, 7, 8, 9}. (1 is *not* a prime.)
D. Pick 7 from {1, 2, 3, 4, 5, 6, 7, 8, 9}.
E. Pick a single-digit number from {1, 2, 3, 4, 5, 6, 7, 8, 9}.
F. Pick a two-digit number from {1, 2, 3, 4, 5, 6, 7, 8, 9}.
G. Pick an outcome in an event space with 200 elements if the sample space has 1000 elements.
H. Pick an outcome that cannot happen from a sample space of 10 elements.
I. Pick an outcome that is bound to happen from a sample space of 3000 elements.
J. Draw a 2 card from a normal 52-card deck.

EXERCISE 8-3

1. *Number Line Problem No. 1* The diagram shows the integers 0 through 10 on a number line.

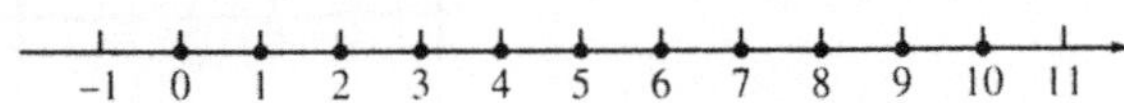

If an integer is selected at random from these, find the probability that:

a. It is 6
b. It is 4 or 7.
c. It is even.
d. It is evenly divisible by 3.
e. It is at least 2.
f. It is less than 10.
g. It is positive.
h. It has three digits.

2. ***Number Line Problem No. 2*** The segment shaded on the number line represents all real numbers from 0 through 10.

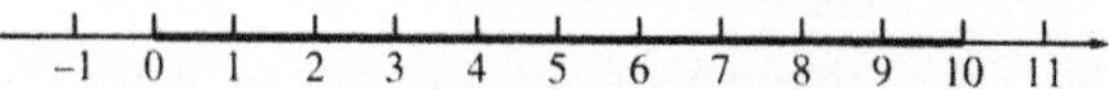

If a number is selected at random from these, find the probability that:

a. It is 4 or more.
b. It is at most 8.
c. It is between 5 and 7.
d. It is non-negative.
e. It is greater than 11.
f. It is between 7 and 11.
g. The next lower integer is even and the next higher integer is odd.

3. ***Area Problem*** The diagram below at left shows a lightly shaded rectangle of width 6 units and height 4 units. Values of $x = w$ and $y = h$ are picked between 0 and 6, and between 0 and 4, respectively. A darker rectangle is drawn with width w and height h.

a. If $w = 4$ and $h = 3$, what fraction of the lighter rectangle lies within the darker rectangle?
b. If an ordered pair (x, y) is selected within the lighter rectangle, what is the probability that it is also in the darker rectangle?
c. If w and h are picked at random, what is the probability that $w \leq 4$?
   What is the probability that $h \leq 3$?
d. What do you suppose the probability is that both $w \leq 4$ and $h \leq 3$?
e. How does your answer to part (d) relate to the answers to parts (a) and (b)?
f. If w and h are selected at random, what is the probability that the perimeter of the darker rectangle is no more than 14?

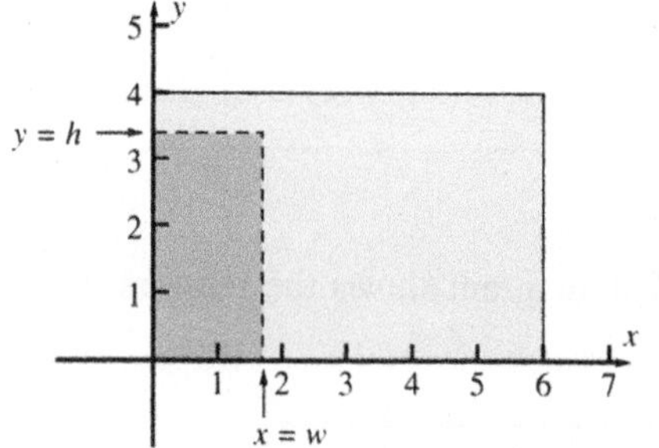

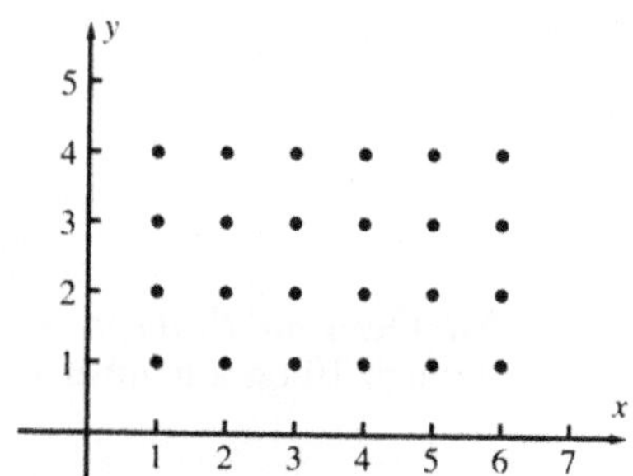

4. ***Rectangular Array Problem***The diagram above at right shows ordered pairs (x, y) with integer coordinates. The values of x are 1 through 6 and the values of y are 1 through 4. An ordered pair (x, y) is selected at random.

a. What is the probability that $x \geq 3$?
b. What is the probability that $y > 1$?
c. Sketch the above diagram on your paper. Show the points that have $x \geq 3$ and $y > 1$.
d. What is the probability that a point selected at random has $x \geq 3$ and $y > 1$?
e. How could you calculate the probability that $x \geq 3$ and $y > 1$ from the answers to parts (a) and (b) *without* drawing a diagram?
f. What is the probability that $x + y > 4$?
g. What is the probability that $xy < 7$?
h. What is the probability that $x = 5$ or $y = 2$? (Be careful!)
i. Suppose that an array of dots is made as shown above, but with x and y both from 1 through 1000. What would be the probability that a dot picked at random would have $x \geq 567$ and $y > 341$?

5. ***Archery Problem*** An archery target is circular, with a diameter of 48 inches (see diagram). The five concentric rings have radii of 4.8", 9.6", 14.4", 19.2", and 24". You recall that the area of a circle is given by $A = \pi r^2$, where A is the area, r is the radius, and $\pi = 3.14159\ldots$.

a. What fraction of the area of the entire target is inside the "bull's-eye" (4.8" radius)?
b. If arrows hitting the target fall at random, what is the percent probability that one will hit the bull's-eye?
c. What is the probability that an arrow hitting the target at random will land in the darkest band, between the 14.4" radius and the 19.2" radius?
d. Ann Archer shoots a National Round for women, consisting of a total of 72 arrows. Suppose that 10 of the arrows hit the bull's-eye. Does her actual probability of hitting the bull's-eye agree with the random probability you calculated in part (b)? How might you account for any difference between the two answers?

6. ***The Gnat and Screen Problem*** A gnat attempts to fly through a window screen without hitting one of the screen wires. The wires are spaced 2 mm apart, and the gnat has a diameter of 1 mm. An expanded view of the screen and gnat is shown in the diagram.

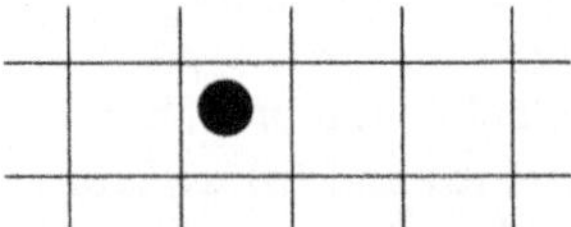

   a. Sketch a diagram showing the part of one grid square at which the gnat could aim its center and pass through the screen without touching a wire.
   b. What fraction of the area of a grid square is the area of the rectangle you drew in part (a)?
   c. If the gnat flies at the screen at random, what is the probability that it will get through without hitting a wire?
   d. What is the probability that the gnat *will* hit a wire?
   e. Annie Cologist observes hundreds of gnats flying at the screen. About 70% of them get through it without touching a wire. Does this result suggest that the gnats are flying at random, or that they are able to "aim" for a clear space?

7. ***Sample Space and Event Space Problem***
   What is the sample space for each of the following?
   a. Selecting points on the number line in Problem 1.
   b. Selecting points on the number line in Problem 2.
   c. Selecting ordered pairs in Problem 3.
   d. Selecting ordered pairs in Problem 4.
   e. Shooting arrows in Problem 5.
   f. Flying through the screen in Problem 6.
   What is the event space for each of the following?
   g. Selecting an integer in Problem 1.d.
   h. Selecting a number in Problem 2.a.
   i. Selecting an ordered pair in Problem 3.b.
   j. Selecting an ordered pair in Problem 4.g.
   k. Shooting an arrow in Problem 5.c.
   l. Flying through the screen in Problem 6.

8. ***Comprehension Problem*** Show that you understand the meaning of sample space and event space by answering the following questions.
   a. If you try to draw a card that is hearts from a normal 52-card deck, what is the sample space? What is the event space? What is the probability of success? What is the probability of failure?
   b. If you flip a coin three times, it could fall in various sequences of heads and tails. These ways could be listed as HTH, HHT, etc. Write all outcomes in the sample space. Write all the outcomes in the event "There are at least two heads." What is the probability that there will be at least two heads? Surprising?

9. *Counting Problem* In this problem you are to find the probability that a five-digit positive integer has all different digits.
   a. What is the lowest possible positive integer? What is the highest possible? How many positive integers are in the sample space?
   b. How many different ways could the first digit (the digit on the left) of the positive integer be picked?
   c. After the first digit is picked, only nine different digits remain for the second digit. In how many ways could you pick the first digit and then the second so that the two are not the same?
   d. In how many ways could you pick the third digit? In how many ways could you pick the first, then the second, then the third digit so that none of the three are the same?
   e. Calculate the number of positive integers in the event space for the event "None of the five digits is the same."
   f. What is the probability that a five-digit positive integer picked at random has no two digits the same?

10. *Lottery Problem* In one state's lottery fifty balls, numbered 1 through 50, are placed in a container and six are drawn at random.
    a. There are 50 different ways the first number could be picked. For each way the first number is picked, there are 49 ways the second could be picked. For each way of picking the first and second numbers, there are 48 ways to pick the third, etc. In how many different ways could all six numbers be picked?
    b. A winning combination is all six numbers correct (in any order). Show that there are 720 outcomes in part (a) for each winning combination.
    c. What is the probability of getting a winning combination?
    d. How much would you have to spend to buy a $1.00 lottery ticket for *every* possible winning combination? If the prize is $10 million, would you come out with a profit or a loss this way?

11. *Factorial Problem* In Problems 9 and 10 you encountered strings of consecutive digits multiplied together, such as

$$9 \cdot 8 \cdot 7 \cdot 6 \quad \text{and} \quad 50 \cdot 49 \cdot 48 \cdot 47 \cdot 46 \cdot 45.$$

Such continued products are called *factorials*. If the first factor (or last factor) is 1, then the factorial is given a special name. For instance, "five factorial," abbreviated 5!, is equal to $5 \cdot 4 \cdot 3 \cdot 2 \cdot 1$. Thus $5! = 120$. (You may have seen a factorial key on your calculator. It is usually marked $x!$.) Evaluate the following expressions:

a. 4! b. 7! c. 9! d. 10!
e. 60! (Use a calculator.) f. 12!/4!
g. (3!)(4!)

True or false?

h. 12!/3! is equal to 4!. i. (3!)(4!) is equal to 7!.
j. (3!)(4!) is equal to 12!. k. 24!/6! is equal to 23!.

8-4 EXPERIMENTAL PROBABILITY

In the last section you calculated the probability that the results of a random experiment would come out a particular way. In this section you will predict the probability of a certain event, then do the random experiment to see how close the experimental results come to the predicted results.

Objective:

Given a description of a random experiment, calculate a probability for a certain event. Then do the experiment and compare the actual and predicted results.

Suppose you flip eight coins. Since the probability of the event "The result is heads" is 50% for each coin, you would expect four of the eight coins to come up heads. But there is no guarantee that this will be the result.

The diagram on the left shows the theoretically expected results of doing this random experiment 100 times. The graph on the right shows actual results. The number of heads is plotted horizontally, and the number of times the experiment ended with this number of heads is plotted vertically. This kind of diagram is called a **bar graph** or a **histogram.** The numbers on the horizontal axis are written in the spaces instead of at the grid lines.

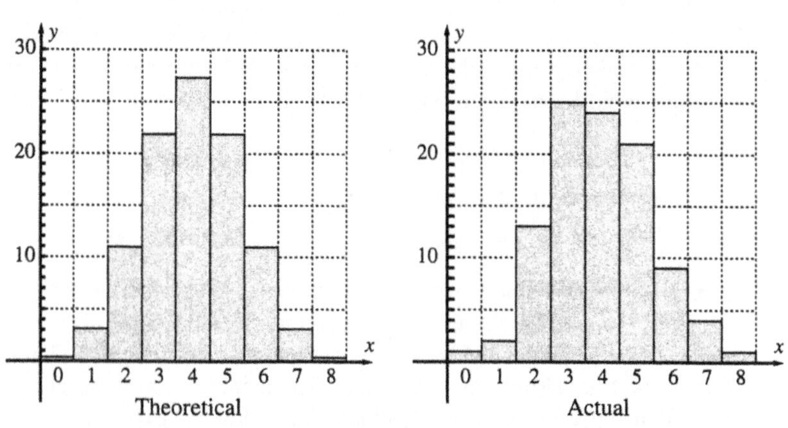

Figure 8-4a

The two histograms show that the results of an experiment match the theoretical results only approximately. In the following exercises you will find theoretical results, then do an experiment to find actual results.

ORAL PRACTICE

If you draw a card from a normal 52-card deck, what is the theoretical probability that:

A. It is black.
B. It is an ace.
C. It is a face card.
D. It is a black face card.
E. It is a red 10.
F. It is the 3 of spades.
G. It is a joker.
H. It is black or red.

Suppose that you randomly select 20 cards from a standard deck. Then you draw a card from those 20, record its color, and return the card to your stack of 20. You repeat this experiment until you have drawn a total of 50 cards, getting black only 10 times. True or false:

I. The experimental probability of "black" is 10/50.
J. The experimental probability of "black" is 20%.
K. The experimental probability of "red" is 80%.
L. There are probably fewer black cards than red among the 20.
M. There are definitely fewer black cards than red among the 20.
N. If you draw 50 times again, you will get exactly 10 blacks again.
O. If you draw 50 times again, you might get more reds than blacks.
P. If you draw 50 times again, you might get all blacks.

EXERCISE 8-4

1. *Coin Flip Experiment No. 1*
   a. If a fair coin is flipped once, what is the theoretical probability that it will come up tails?
   b. Flip a coin 10 times. Based on your random experiment, what is the experimental probability that the coin will come up tails?
   c. If you are working in groups, combine the results of the 10 flips of each member of your group to find the experimental probability that a flipped coin will come up tails.
   d. Combine the results of the 10 flips of all groups to find the experimental probability that a flipped coin will come up tails.
   e. If there are 30 students in the class and each flipped a coin 10 times, you would expect 150 of the 300 results to be tails. How many tails would you expect for the experiment you have just done in your class? How many tails were there actually?
   f. One of the "laws" of random events is that *total* numbers of outcomes tend to get *farther* from the theoretical value as the number of trials increases, but *averages* tend to get *closer* to the theoretical value. Do your results confirm this law? Explain.

2. *Coin Flip Experiment No. 2* If you flip a coin once, there are two equally likely outcomes: "heads" and "tails" (H and T). If you flip it twice, there are *four* equally likely outcomes: HH, HT, TH, and TT. The histograms below show the number of outcomes with exactly x tails for various numbers of flips.

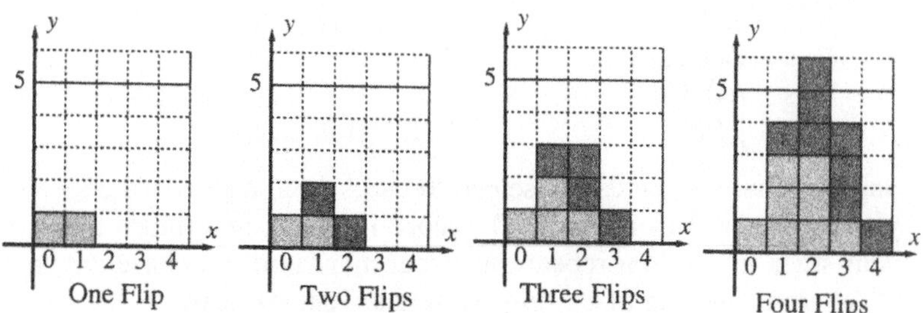

   a. If you flip the coin three times there are *eight* equally likely outcomes. Write these outcomes using H and T. Confirm that there are three outcomes that have tails exactly twice.
   b. If you flip the coin four times there are *sixteen* equally likely outcomes. Write these outcomes using H and T. Explain how there can be four different outcomes that have tails exactly once.
   c. Flipping four coins once is equivalent to flipping one coin four times. Flip four coins and record the number of tails by darkening the appropriate square on graph paper as in the diagram above. Do this experiment 16 times. How is your histogram similar to the one shown above, and how does it differ?
   d. Compare your histogram with those of other students in your group or class. Are most of the histograms exactly like the theoretical one, or do most of them differ from it?
   e. The darker squares in each graph above show how that histogram can be constructed from the one before it. Use this pattern to construct a theoretical histogram for five flips. How many different outcomes are there? What is the probability that there will be exactly three tails? How can you calculate the total number of outcomes from the number of flips? How many different outcomes would there be for 10 flips?

3. *Dice Roll Experiment No. 1* If you roll a die (singular of "dice") there are six equally likely outcomes for the number of spots on the top face: 1, 2, 3, 4, 5, and 6.
   a. Since there are six equally likely outcomes, you would expect that rolling a die 30 times would give 1 five times, 2 five times, etc. Draw a histogram on graph paper, as in Problem 2, showing the theoretical number of 1's, 2's, etc.
   b. Roll a die 30 times. As you do the rolling, construct a histogram by marking an X in the appropriate column for the result of each roll. In what ways is the experimental histogram like the theoretical one in part (a), and in what ways does it differ?

4. *Dice Roll Experiment No. 2* If you roll a pair of dice there are 36 equally likely outcomes for the numbers of spots on the top faces. For instance, the first could be 5 and the second 3. The *sum* of the numbers is what people are usually interested in. In this problem you will investigate what actually happens when you roll two dice.
   a. Write an ordered pair for each possible outcome. For instance, (5, 3) would represent 5 on the first die and 3 on the second die. It will help if you arrange the ordered pairs systematically.
   b. Figure out how many outcomes produce a total of 2, how many produce a total of 3, and so forth, all the way to a total of 12. Present the results in a histogram as in Problem 1, where x is the total and y is the number of outcomes that give this total.
   c. If you roll a die 36 times you might "expect" each of the 36 outcomes to occur once. (They won't, of course, but that's what you'd expect theoretically.) Roll a pair of dice 36 times. As you do the rolling, construct a histogram. Use the ordered pairs from part (a) as your list of possible outcomes and mark an X in the appropriate column for the result of each roll. In what ways is the experimental histogram like the theoretical one in part (b), and in what ways does it differ?

5. *Thumbtack Experiment* If you flip a thumbtack, it can land either "point up" or "point down."

   However, for a thumbtack, unlike a coin, "up" and "down" are probably *not* equally likely. In this problem you will try to find experimentally the probability of "up" and "down" for your thumbtack.
   a. Before you do any flipping, write down which you *think* is more probable, "up" (U) or "down" (D). If you are working in groups, compare your answers. You need not all have the same answer. Then survey the entire class. Based on your preconceived ideas, what is the probability of U?
   b. Flip a tack 10 times (or 10 identical tacks once). Based on this one experiment, what is the probability of U?
   c. Get the results of the 10 flips from the entire class. Record the number of U's in 10 flips by making a histogram as in Problem 2. There will be *eleven* columns, for 0 through 10 U's.
   d. Based on the histogram, which seems more likely, U or D?
   e. Repeat the 10-flip experiment until it has been done a total of 100 times. You may share data with other students in the class. Extend your histogram in part (c) to include the new data. Does the added data confirm your answer to part (d) or refute it?
   f. By appropriate computation, calculate the experimental probability that the kind of thumbtack you have been using will land U.

8-5 CHAPTER REVIEW AND TEST

In this chapter you have reversed the process of graphing a line from a given equation. First you found an equation for the line whose graph goes through two given points. Then you found an equation for the line that best fits *many* (possibly scattered) points. That equation can be used to make predictions, such as how tall a plant will be at various times after the seed is planted. The scattered data you analyzed is typical of events that happen at random. This fact led us to look at probability, both theoretically and experimentally.

CHAPTER TEST

1. ***House-Building Problem*** Bill Ding constructs quality homes. He figures that a house built on a particular lot should be sold for \$373,000 if it has a floor space of 3000 square feet. A 4000-square-foot house constructed on the same lot should be sold for \$483,000. The selling price is the sum of the construction cost, at a fixed number of dollars per square foot, and the cost of the lot.
   a. Figure out the number of dollars per square foot it costs to construct the house, and the cost of the lot.
   b. Write an equation for price as a function of square feet.
   c. How big a house on this lot could be sold for \$1 million?
   d. Zoning restrictions specify that a house on this lot can have a floor space of no less than 2000 square feet. Mr. Ding wants the selling cost to be less than \$1 million. Write the domain and range.
   e. Sketch the graph of this linear function, showing clearly the domain and range.

2. ***Scattered Data Problem*** Copy the scatter plot shown below onto your graph paper. Draw the graph of the linear function you think best fits this data. Write an equation of this linear function. Then use the equation to predict y when x is 100. Note: $x_{av} = 10.3$ and $y_{av} = 3.6$.

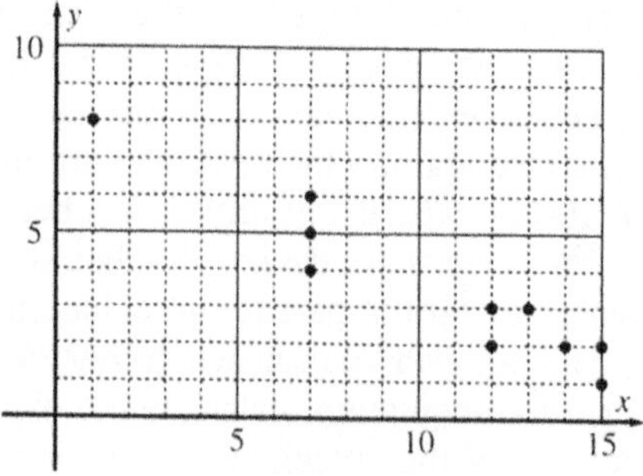

3. *Spilled Ice Cream Problem* Chris Cross is 14 months old, and is just learning how to walk. He zigzags across the 12-by-15-foot room shown in the figure, eventually falling down. The ice cream cone he is carrying spills either on the 9-by-12-foot rug or on the floor around the rug.

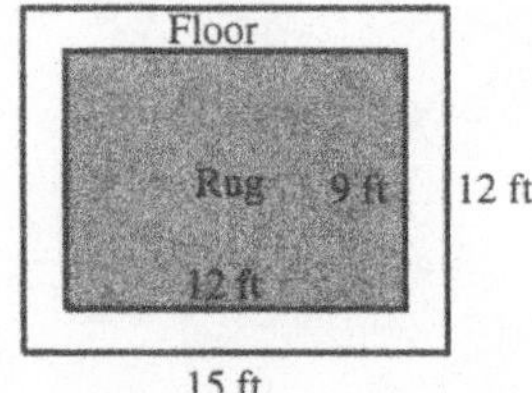

   a. How many square feet are in the sample space? How many square feet are in the event space "The ice cream lands on the rug"?
   b. What is the probability that the ice cream will land on the rug?
   c. What is the probability that the ice cream will land on the floor?

4. *Coin Flip Experiment* This problem concerns the random experiment of flipping a coin twice.
   a. List the *four* possible equally likely outcomes. Use the letters H and T.
   b. If you do the experiment 20 times, how many times would you expect to get no heads? Exactly one head? Two heads? Present your answers in a histogram on graph paper.
   c. Do this experiment 20 times. As you go, record the number of heads in a histogram on graph paper.
   d. In what ways is your experimental histogram from part (c) similar to the theoretical one from part (b), and in what ways is it different?

9 Properties of Exponents

In Chapter 1 you learned about powers and exponents. For instance, 2^5 *means five 2s multiplied together. In this chapter you will learn how to multiply and divide powers quickly by operating with their exponents. For instance, when you divide two powers that have equal bases, you can subtract their exponents. The result leads to a definition of negative exponents. Positive and negative exponents can be used to simplify operations with very large or very small numbers by writing them in* scientific notation. *For example, the* 8,000,000,000 *neurons in a person's brain could be written as* 8×10^9.

Expression:
x^5 means $x \cdot x \cdot x \cdot x \cdot x$.
Operation:
$\frac{x^5}{x^7} = x^{-2}$
Application:
8 billion equals 8,000,000,000, which equals 8×10^9.

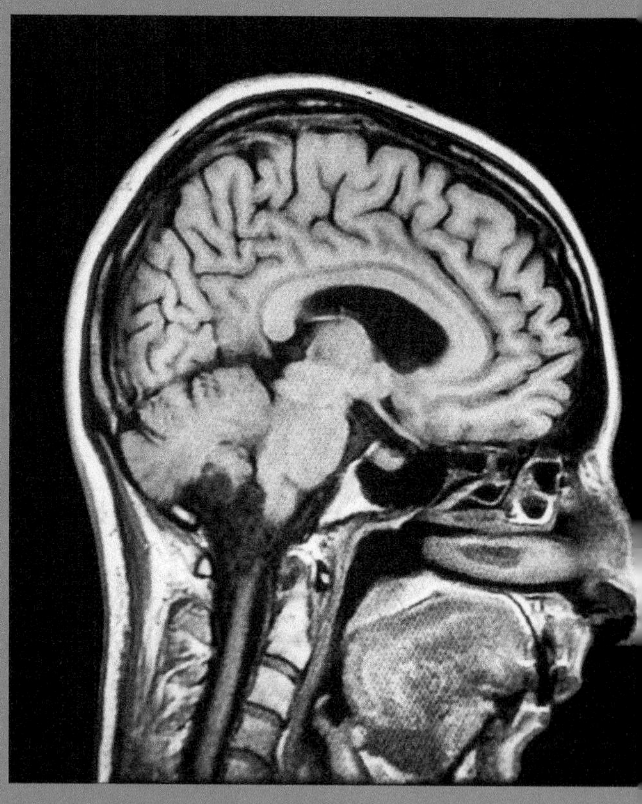

9-1 PRIME NUMBERS AND PRIME FACTORS

This section reviews information you have probably encountered in earlier mathematics courses. So you should be able to read it and work the problems without help.

The numbers

$$2, 3, 5, 7, 11, 13, \ldots$$

are called *prime* numbers. A prime has only two factors, 1 and itself.

$$\begin{aligned} 2 &= 1 \cdot 2 \\ 3 &= 1 \cdot 3 \\ 5 &= 1 \cdot 5 \\ 7 &= 1 \cdot 7 \\ 11 &= 1 \cdot 11 \\ 13 &= 1 \cdot 13 \end{aligned}$$

DEFINITION

PRIME NUMBER
A **prime number** is a positive integer that has *no* positive integers as factors other than 1 and itself.
The number 1 is *not* considered to be a prime.

A number such as 144 is called a **composite** number, because it can be factored into a product composed of several primes. For example,

$$144 = 2 \cdot 2 \cdot 2 \cdot 2 \cdot 3 \cdot 3.$$

These primes can be found by using the "upside-down, short-division" process explained in Section 1-3.

Prime factors of 144

$$\begin{array}{r} 2\underline{)144} \\ 2\underline{)72} \\ 2\underline{)36} \\ 2\underline{)18} \\ 3\underline{)9} \\ 3 \end{array}$$

Ask yourself, "What prime goes into 144?", then, "What prime goes into 72?", and so forth.

The product $2 \cdot 2 \cdot 2 \cdot 2 \cdot 3 \cdot 3$ can be written using *powers*. Since 2^4 means $2 \cdot 2 \cdot 2 \cdot 2$ and 3^2 means $3 \cdot 3$, you can write

$$144 = 2^4 \cdot 3^2.$$

In the next few sections you will learn some properties of powers. In this section, you concentrate on factoring integers into primes.

Objective:

Be able to factor a given integer into a product of primes. If a prime occurs more than once, write the product in terms of powers.

Cover the answers as you work these examples.

EXAMPLE 1

Write 1125 as a product of powers of primes.

- - - - -

$$\begin{aligned} &1125 \\ &= 3 \cdot 3 \cdot 5 \cdot 5 \cdot 5 \\ &= \underline{\underline{3^2 \cdot 5^3}} \end{aligned}$$

Work:

$$\begin{array}{r} 3\underline{)1125} \\ 3\underline{)375} \\ 5\underline{)125} \\ 5\underline{)25} \\ 5 \end{array}$$

- - - - -

EXAMPLE 2

Write 7007 as a product of powers of primes.

- - - - -

$$\begin{aligned} &7007 \\ &= 7 \cdot 7 \cdot 11 \cdot 13 \\ &= \underline{\underline{7^2 \cdot 11 \cdot 13}} \end{aligned}$$

Work:

$$\begin{array}{r} 7\underline{)7007} \\ 7\underline{)1001} \\ 11\underline{)143} \\ 13 \end{array}$$

- - - - -

Note: You may want to use a calculator to do the actual division and then write the results in the upside-down, short-division form.

EXERCISE 9-1

For Problems 1 through 20, write as a product of powers of primes.

1. 40
2. 63
3. 225
4. 351
5. 252
6. 360
7. 784
8. 500
9. 891
10. 800
11. 2057
12. 3211
13. 2700
14. 3528
15. 6125
16. 8575
17. 15,379
18. 12,005
19. 30,030
20. 75,600
21. *1 is Not a Prime Problem* The number 1 fits the definition of prime numbers, because

$$1 = 1 \cdot 1.$$

That is, 1 has no other factors besides 1 and itself. Yet the definition includes the restriction that the number 1 is *not* considered to be a prime. The reason for this restriction is the following conclusion, called the *fundamental theorem of arithmetic*.

> **FUNDAMENTAL THEOREM OF ARITHMETIC**
> Each positive integer has exactly *one* set of prime factors.

a. Write the set of prime factors of 12.
b. Explain why 12 would have *other* sets of prime factors if 1 were considered to be a prime.
c. What is the set of prime factors of 1 itself?

9-2 THE OPERATION EXPONENTIATION

You recall that a power is an expression involving repeated multiplication. For instance, 5^3 means three 5s multiplied together.

$$5^3 = 5 \times 5 \times 5$$

The operation *raising to powers* is called *exponentiation*.

DEFINITION

EXPONENTIATION
x^a means a x's multiplied together. That is, for any real number x and for any positive integer a,

$$x^a = x \cdot x \cdot x \cdot \cdot \cdot x \qquad (a \text{ factors}).$$

In this section you use this definition to evaluate and operate with powers. For instance, x^4 means four x's multiplied together. If x is 6, you would evaluate x^4 as follows.

$$x^4$$
$$= 6^4$$
$$= 6 \times 6 \times 6 \times 6$$
$$= 1296$$

The operations are straightforward. A calculator will help when the numbers are large.

Objective:
Given an expression involving a power of a variable, use the definition of exponentiation to evaluate or simplify the expression.

Cover the answers as you work these examples.

EXAMPLE 1

Evaluate x^4y^2 if $x = 3$ and $y = -5$.

- - - - -

	Think These Reasons
x^4y^2	Write the given expression.
$= 3^4 \times (-5)^2$	Substitute for x and y.
$= 3 \times 3 \times 3 \times 3 \times (-5) \times (-5)$	Use the definition of exponentiation.
$= \underline{\underline{2025}}$	Do the arithmetic. (Negative times negative is *positive*.)

EXAMPLE 2

Write x^5x^2 as a single power of x.

x^5x^2	Write the given expression.
$= x \cdot x \cdot x \cdot x \cdot x \cdot x \cdot x$	Use the definition of exponentiation.
$= \underline{\underline{x^7}}$	There are seven x's multiplied together.

EXAMPLE 3

Write $(x^4)^3$ as a single power of x.

$(x^4)^3$	Write the given expression.
$= x^4 \cdot x^4 \cdot x^4$	Use the definition of exponentiation.
$= x \cdot x \cdot x \cdot x \cdot x \cdot x \cdot x \cdot x \cdot x \cdot x \cdot x \cdot x$	Use the definition again.
$= \underline{\underline{x^{12}}}$	There are 12 x's multiplied together.

EXAMPLE 4

Write $(5x)^3$ without parentheses.

$(5x)^3$	Write the given expression.
$= 5x \cdot 5x \cdot 5x$	Use the definition of exponentiation.
$= (5 \cdot 5 \cdot 5)(x \cdot x \cdot x)$	Commute and associate.
$= \underline{\underline{125x^3}}$	$5 \cdot 5 \cdot 5 = 125$; $x \cdot x \cdot x = x^3$.

ORAL PRACTICE

Tell what the expression would be if written using powers.

A. $x \cdot x \cdot x \cdot x$

B. $y \cdot y \cdot y$

C. $z \cdot z \cdot z \cdot z \cdot z$

D. $x \cdot x \cdot x \cdot y \cdot y$

E. $a \cdot a \cdot b \cdot b \cdot c \cdot c$

F. $x \cdot x \cdot x \cdot x \cdot y$

G. $r \cdot c \cdot c \cdot c$

H. $7 \cdot a \cdot a \cdot a \cdot a$

I. $5 \cdot x \cdot x \cdot y \cdot y \cdot y$

J. $3 \cdot x \cdot x \cdot x \cdot x \cdot y \cdot y \cdot y \cdot y \cdot y \cdot z \cdot z \cdot z \cdot z \cdot z \cdot z \cdot z$

Evaluate these powers.

K. 2^3

L. 3^2

M. 3^3

N. 2^2

O. 4^2

P. 2^4

Q. $(-2)^3$

R. $(-2)^4$

S. 3^1

T. 1^3

U. 0^3

V. $(-1)^5$

EXERCISE 9-2

For Problems 1 through 10, evaluate the power for the given values of the variable.

1. x^3
   a. $x = 2$
   b. $x = 5$
   c. $x = -3$

2. x^4
   a. $x = 2$
   b. $x = 3$
   c. $x = -4$

3. x^6
   a. $x = 2$
   b. $x = 4$
   c. $x = -1$

4. x^5
   a. $x = 2$
   b. $x = 4$
   c. $x = -1$

5. $3x^4$
   a. $x = 2$
   b. $x = 6$
   c. $x = 10$

6. $5x^3$
   a. $x = 2$
   b. $x = 4$
   c. $x = 10$

7. x^2y^3
   a. $x = 4, y = 5$
   b. $x = -1, y = 2$
   c. $x = 3, y = -2$

8. x^3y^4
   a. $x = 2, y = 5$
   b. $x = -1, y = 2$
   c. $x = 5, y = -2$

9. $(x^2)^5$
   a. $x = 3$
   b. $x = -2$
   c. $x = 4$

10. $(x^3)^2$
    a. $x = 4$
    b. $x = -5$
    c. $x = 10$

For Problems 11 through 20, write the expression as a single power of x.

11. x^3x^4
12. x^5x^3
13. x^2x^7
14. x^4x^6
15. x^5x^8
16. x^2x^9
17. $(x^2)^4$
18. $(x^3)^2$
19. $(x^3)^5$
20. $(x^5)^3$

For Problems 21 through 30, write the expression without parentheses.

21. $(xy)^3$
22. $(xy)^4$
23. $(ab)^6$
24. $(rt)^5$
25. $(3x)^4$
26. $(2x)^5$
27. $(5x)^2$
28. $(3x)^3$
29. $(x^2y)^4$
30. $(xy^2)^3$

31. *Definition of Exponentiation Problem* I. Neuitt loses points on a test for saying, "5^3 means 5 multiplied by itself 3 times." Explain the error.

32. *Using a Calculator to Evaluate Powers* It is important to know how to evaluate powers by hand and to be familiar with the powers of base 2, 3, and 10. To evaluate exponential expressions with large bases and/or exponents, however, it is usually more convenient to use a calculator.

    a. Locate the $\boxed{x^y}$ key on your calculator. Evaluate 3^4 by entering 3, pressing the $\boxed{x^y}$ key, and then entering 4 and pressing =. (If your calculator has a $\boxed{y^x}$ key instead, you may have to enter the power first, then press $\boxed{y^x}$, then enter the base. If you do not have either key, you can multiply out $3 \times 3 \times 3 \times 3$. In any case, be sure you are finding that $3^4 = 81$.)
    b. Use your calculator to evaluate:
       i. 8^5 ii. 5^8 iii. 7^9 iv. 9^7 v. 10^7
    c. Which is bigger, 7^8 or 8^7?
    d. Evaluate 6^4 and 6^5. Do you think that $6^{4.5}$ has a value? Assuming that it does, estimate its value. Then use your calculator to find $6^{4.5}$.
    e. The real-world meaning of $6^{4.5}$ is probably not clear. (How can you multiply something 4.5 times?) To get an idea of the *mathematical* meaning of a decimal exponent, find:
       i. $4^{0.5}$ ii. $9^{0.5}$ iii. $49^{0.5}$ iv. $81^{0.5}$
    f. What does the 0.5 power of a number represent?

9-3 EXPONENTS, PRODUCTS, AND POWERS

In the last section you learned the formal definition of exponentiation as repeated multiplication. For instance, 5^3 means three 5s multiplied together, as shown.

$$5^3 = 5 \times 5 \times 5.$$

Because of this definition, there are some interesting things that happen to exponents when you multiply or divide two powers. In this section you will learn three properties of exponentiation, and in the next section you will learn two more.

PRODUCT OF TWO POWERS

The expressions 5^3 and 5^4 are two powers that have equal bases, 5, and different exponents, 3 and 4. If you multiply these two powers together, you get

$$\begin{aligned} &(5^3)(5^4) \\ &= (5 \times 5 \times 5)(5 \times 5 \times 5 \times 5) \\ &= 5 \times 5 \times 5 \times 5 \times 5 \times 5 \times 5 \\ &= 5^7. \end{aligned}$$

The last step is true because there are seven 5s multiplied together, which is what 5^7 really means. A quick way to get the answer is to *add* the exponents.

$$(5^3)(5^4) = 5^{3+4} = 5^7$$

This shortcut will work as long as the two powers have equal bases. If the bases are different, such as in $(5^3)(6^4)$, there is no way to simplify the expression (other than to evaluate it); $(5^3)(6^4)$ equals $5 \times 5 \times 5 \times 6 \times 6 \times 6 \times 6$, which is neither a power of 5 nor a power of 6.

PRODUCT OF TWO POWERS WITH EQUAL BASES

If you multiply two powers, and both bases are equal, then you can *add* the exponents (and use the same base). That is, for any real number x and for any positive integers a and b,

$$(x^a)(x^b) = x^{a+b}.$$

POWER OF A PRODUCT

The parentheses in the expression $(3 \times 5)^4$ mean to multiply 3 by 5 first, then raise the answer to the fourth power.

$$(3 \times 5)^4 = 15^4 = 50{,}625$$

However, you can use the definition of exponentiation first and write

$$(3 \times 5)^4 = (3 \times 5)(3 \times 5)(3 \times 5)(3 \times 5).$$

Commuting and associating factors gives

$$(3 \times 3 \times 3 \times 3)(5 \times 5 \times 5 \times 5),$$

which results in

$$3^4 \times 5^4.$$

The exponent has been *distributed* to each factor, 3 and 5. In other words, exponentiation distributes over multiplication. Carrying out the multiplication shows that you really do get the same answer.

$$3^4 \times 5^4 = 81 \times 625 = 50{,}625$$

POWER OF A PRODUCT
Exponentiation distributes over multiplication. That is, for any real numbers x and y, and for any positive integer a,

$$(xy)^a = x^a y^a.$$

Be careful that you do not try to distribute exponentiation over addition or subtraction! Recall from Section 5.8 that

$$(x + y)^2 = x^2 + 2xy + y^2.$$

There are middle terms when you raise *sums* to powers.

POWER OF A POWER

The parentheses in the expression $(2^3)^4$ mean to raise 2 to the third power first, then raise the answer to the fourth power.

$$(2^3)^4 = 8^4 = 4096$$

Again, the definition of exponentiation could be used to write

$$(2^3)^4$$
$$= (2^3)(2^3)(2^3)(2^3)$$

$$= (2 \times 2 \times 2)(2 \times 2 \times 2)(2 \times 2 \times 2)(2 \times 2 \times 2)$$
$$= 2 \times 2 \times 2 \times 2 \times 2 \times 2 \times 2 \times 2 \times 2 \times 2 \times 2 \times 2$$
$$= 2^{12}.$$

The last step is true because there are 12 2s multiplied together, which is what 2^{12} means. A quick way to get the answer is to *multiply* the exponents.

$$(2^3)^4 = 2^{3 \cdot 4} = 2^{12}$$

This property is summarized as follows.

POWER OF A POWER
If you raise a power to a power, then you can *multiply* the exponents. That is, for any real number x and for any positive integers a and b,

$$(x^a)^b = x^{ab}.$$

If the expressions with which you are dealing contain only constants, these three properties are not really needed. However, if the expressions contain *variables*, the properties allow you to *simplify* the expressions. What you must learn is when to *add* the exponents, when to *multiply* them, and when to *distribute* them.

Objective:

Given an expression containing powers and variables, simplify the expression using the three properties of exponentiation.

Cover the answers as you work these examples.

EXAMPLE 1

Simplify $(x^8)(x^{20})$.

- - - - -   - - - - -

	Think These Reasons
$(x^8)(x^{20})$	Write the given expression.
$= x^{8+20}$	Add the exponents. Use x as the base.
$= \underline{\underline{x^{28}}}$	Do the arithmetic.

Note: You can probably do the whole problem in your head and just write

$$(x^8)(x^{20}) = x^{28}.$$

EXAMPLE 2

Simplify $(5r^7)(6r^2)$.

$(5r^7)(6r^2)$	Write the given expression.
$= \underline{\underline{30r^9}}$	Commute, associate, and multiply the coefficients. Add the exponents and use r as the base.

EXAMPLE 3

Simplify $(5xy^7)^3$.

$(5xy^7)^3$	Write the given expression.
$= (5)^3(x)^3(y^7)^3$	Distribute the exponentiation to *all three* factors. Do not forget the coefficient, 5.
$= \underline{\underline{125x^3y^{21}}}$	$5^3 = 125$; multiply the exponents since a power is raised to a power.

EXAMPLE 4

Simplify $3x^5 + 9x^5$.

$3x^5 + 9x^5$	Write the given expression.
$= \underline{\underline{12x^5}}$	Combine like terms. (There are *no* operations performed on the exponents.)

EXAMPLE 5

Simplify $5x^3 + 4x^9$.

Cannot be simplified.	The powers are *added*, not multiplied. There are no properties for a *sum* of two powers, even if the bases are equal.

ORAL PRACTICE

Simplify each expression.

A. $(x^3)(x^2)$ B. $(x^3)^2$

C. $(x^4)(x^5)$ D. $(x^4)^5$

E. $(x^5)^4$ F. $(xy)^3$

G. $(ab)^7$ H. $(3x)^2$

I. $(2x)^3$ J. $(x^2y)^3$

K. $(xy^2)^3$ L. $(x^2y^3)^4$

M. $(x)(x^3)$ N. $x^3 + x^3$

O. $x^3 + x^4$ P. $4x^5 - x^5$

EXERCISE 9-3

For Problems 1 through 6, evaluate the expression two ways:
a. by doing what is in parentheses first;
b. by using the appropriate property of exponentiation first.
Use a calculator (if necessary) to do the final operations, and thus show that the two answers are the same.

1. $(2^4)(2^2)$
2. $(3^4)(3^5)$
3. $(4 \times 5)^3$
4. $(2 \times 5)^3$
5. $(3^2)^5$
6. $(2^4)^3$

For Problems 7 through 60, simplify the expression.

7. $(x^5)(x^{13})$
8. $(x^8)(x^{12})$
9. $(y^{30})(y^{50})$
10. $(z^{40})(z^{60})$
11. $(z)(z^7)$
12. $(r^5)(r)$
13. $(a^{41})(a^{29})(a^{17})$
14. $(y^{70})(y^{17})(y^{13})$
15. $(3x^6)(5x^7)$
16. $(2x^8)(9x^3)$
17. $(9r^{20})(7r^{32})$
18. $(8s^{30})(7s^{20})$
19. $(-8s^{12})(6s^{47})$
20. $(-5x^9)(11x^{21})$
21. $(-10x^8)(-20x^{80})$
22. $(-30a^{19})(-10a^{17})$
23. $(5x^7)(2x^9)(3x^{11})$
24. $(6x^5)(2x^{10})(7x^{13})$
25. $(7b^{10})(-11b^{20})(13b)$
26. $(3y)(-23y^8)(-29y^{31})$
27. $(x^9)^6$
28. $(x^7)^8$

29. $(p^{12})^5$
30. $(y^{10})^5$
31. $(y^2)^7$
32. $(s^4)^8$
33. $(5r^6)^3$
34. $(3x^5)^4$
35. $(-2x^{10})^5$
36. $(-7x^8)^2$
37. $(-3x^7)^4$
38. $(-2y^6)^3$
39. $[(x^5)^7]^4$
40. $[(x^6)^7]^{10}$
41. $(xy)^9$
42. $(ab)^{10}$
43. $(ab)^{17}$
44. $(pj)^{52}$
45. $(3rs)^5$
46. $(2xy)^5$
47. $(0.1x^3y^5)^3$
48. $(0.1r^2s^6)^4$
49. $(-6c^5d^6)^2$
50. $(-9m^3n^8)^2$
51. $(-2x^6y^7)^3$
52. $(-5x^4y^{11})^3$
53. $(10xy^{10})^4$
54. $(10cd^6)^3$
55. $(3^x5^y)^z$
56. $(4^a7^b)^c$
57. $8x^6 + 3x^6$
58. $7x^9 + 11x^9$
59. $13y^7 - 21y^7$
60. $14a^3 - 50a^3$

For Problems 61 through 100, either simplify the expression or state that it cannot be simplified.

61. $(3x^9)(3x^5)$
62. $(4x^7)(4x^9)$
63. $(9x^3)(5x^3)$
64. $(7x^4)(9x^4)$
65. $9x^3 + 5x^3$
66. $7x^4 + 9x^4$
67. $x^5 \cdot y^7$
68. $x^8 \cdot y^3$
69. $x^5 \cdot x^7$
70. $x^8 \cdot x^3$
71. $x^5 + x^7$
72. $x^8 + x^3$
73. $x^5 + x^5$
74. $x^8 + x^8$
75. $x^5 - x^5$
76. $x^8 - x^8$
77. $3x^5 - x^5$
78. $5x^8 - x^8$
79. $(x^5)^2$
80. $(x^8)^3$
81. $(-2x)^3$
82. $(-4x)^3$
83. $(-2x)^4$
84. $(-3x)^4$
85. $-(2x)^4$
86. $-(3x)^4$

87. $(x^2)^4$

88. $(x^3)^4$

89. $(xy)^4$

90. $(xy)^5$

91. $(2x^2y^3)^4$

92. $(2x^3y^2)^5$

93. $(x^4y^2)^6(x^2y^3)^4$

94. $(x^5y^6)^2(x^3y^2)^5$

95. $5x^3 - x^3$

96. $7x^5 - x^5$

97. $3x^5 - x^3$

98. $5x^7 - x^5$

99. $3x^5(x^2 - y^3)$

100. $4x^9(x^7 + y^5)$

9-4 EXPONENTS AND QUOTIENTS

Recall from earlier work in mathematics that you multiply fractions by multiplying their numerators together and multiplying their denominators together. For instance,

$$\frac{3}{7} \times \frac{4}{5} = \frac{3 \times 4}{7 \times 5} = \frac{12}{35}.$$

Later in your mathematical career you will learn how to prove this multiplication property of fractions.

MULTIPLICATION PROPERTY OF FRACTIONS
To multiply two fractions, multiply their numerators and multiply their denominators. That is, for any real numbers a, b, x, and y, with $b \neq 0$ and $y \neq 0$,

$$\frac{a}{b} \cdot \frac{x}{y} = \frac{ax}{by}.$$

This property gives a way to transform a quotient that is raised to a power, such as

$$\left(\frac{2}{3}\right)^5.$$

Using the definition of exponentiation, you can write this as

$$\left(\frac{2}{3}\right)^5 = \left(\frac{2}{3}\right)\left(\frac{2}{3}\right)\left(\frac{2}{3}\right)\left(\frac{2}{3}\right)\left(\frac{2}{3}\right).$$

Using the multiplication property of fractions (repeatedly) gives

$$\frac{2 \times 2 \times 2 \times 2 \times 2}{3 \times 3 \times 3 \times 3 \times 3},$$

which equals

$$\frac{2^5}{3^5}.$$

As you can see, the exponent, 5, has been *distributed* to the 2 in the numerator and to the 3 in the denominator.

POWER OF A QUOTIENT
Exponentiation *distributes* over division. That is, for any real numbers x and y ($y \neq 0$), and for any integer a,

$$\left(\frac{x}{y}\right)^a = \frac{x^a}{y^a}.$$

The multiplication property of fractions can be used in the other direction to simplify fractions. For instance, to simplify $\frac{24}{36}$, you could write the following.

$\frac{24}{36}$	
$= \frac{12 \times 2}{12 \times 3}$	24 equals 12 times 2. 36 equals 12 times 3.
$= \frac{12}{12} \times \frac{2}{3}$	Multiplication property of fractions
$= 1 \times \frac{2}{3}$	A number divided by itself equals 1.
$= \frac{2}{3}$	1 times a number equals that number.

The same technique can be used to simplify quotients with *variables* in the numerator or denominator. For instance, $\frac{x^7}{x^4}$ can be simplified as follows.

$\frac{x^7}{x^4}$	
$= \frac{x \cdot x \cdot x \cdot x \cdot x \cdot x \cdot x}{x \cdot x \cdot x \cdot x}$	Use the definition of exponentiation.

$= \dfrac{x \cdot x \cdot x \cdot x}{x \cdot x \cdot x \cdot x} \times \dfrac{x \cdot x \cdot x}{1}$ Use the multiplication property of fractions.

$= 1 \times \dfrac{x \cdot x \cdot x}{1}$ A number divided by itself equals 1.

$= \underline{\underline{x^3}}$ Multiplying or dividing by 1 leaves the number unchanged, and $x \cdot x \cdot x$ equals x^3.

From this example you should see a *quick* way to get the answer. The exponent in the answer, 3, is the *difference* between 7 and 4. Once you know this, you can write simply

$$\frac{x^7}{x^4} = x^{7-4} = \underline{\underline{x^3}}.$$

In fact, the middle step can be done in your head. The general property is as follows.

QUOTIENT OF TWO POWERS WITH EQUAL BASES
If you divide two powers, and they have equal bases, then you can *subtract* the exponents (numerator minus denominator) and use that same base. That is, for any nonzero number x and for any positive integers a and b,

$$\frac{x^a}{x^b} = x^{a-b}.$$

The fact that 1 times a number equals that number is an axiom. It is sometimes called the *multiplication property of 1*. Another name for this property is the *multiplicative identity axiom*. The answer after multiplying a number by 1 is identical to the original number.

MULTIPLICATIVE IDENTITY AXIOM
(or **Multiplication Property of 1**)
Multiplying a number by 1 does not change its value. That is, for any real number x,

$$x \cdot 1 = x.$$

In this section you will use these properties to simplify expressions involving powers and division.

Objective:

Be able to simplify powers of quotients and quotients of powers using the properties of exponentiation.

Cover the answers as you work these examples.

EXAMPLE 1

Transform to remove the parentheses: $\left(\frac{x}{y}\right)^7$.

	Think These Reasons
$\left(\frac{x}{y}\right)^7$	Write the given expression.
$= \frac{x^7}{y^7}$	Power of a quotient property

EXAMPLE 2

Simplify $\frac{x^{10}}{x^4}$.

$\frac{x^{10}}{x^4}$	Write the given expression.
$= x^6$	Subtract the exponents.

EXAMPLE 3

Simplify $\frac{15x^6y^7}{5x^2y^4}$.

$\frac{15x^6y^7}{5x^2y^4}$	Write the given expression.
$= \frac{15}{5} \times \frac{x^6}{x^2} \times \frac{y^7}{y^4}$	Use the multiplication property of fractions to separate the x's, y's, and constants.
$= 3x^4y^3$	Simplify the coefficient. Subtract exponents of powers with equal bases.

EXAMPLE 4

Simplify $\frac{x^9}{y^3}\left(\frac{y}{x}\right)^5$.

$\frac{x^9}{y^3}\left(\frac{y}{x}\right)^5$ Write the given expression.

$= \frac{x^9}{y^3} \times \frac{y^5}{x^5}$ Distribute exponentiation over division.

$= \frac{x^9y^5}{y^3x^5}$ Use the multiplication property of fractions to make *one* fraction.

$= \frac{x^9y^5}{x^5y^3}$ Commute the multiplication in the denominator.

$= \frac{x^9}{x^5} \times \frac{y^5}{y^3}$ Use the multiplication property of fractions to separate the x's and y's.

$= \underline{\underline{x^4y^2}}$ Subtract the exponents of powers with equal bases.

Note: Once you understand the reasons in this example, you can shorten the work, as follows.

$\frac{x^9}{y^3}\left(\frac{y}{x}\right)^5$ Write the given expression.

$= \frac{x^9y^5}{y^3x^5}$ Distribute the exponentiation. Combine the fractions.

$= \underline{\underline{x^4y^2}}$ Subtract the exponents of powers with *equal* bases.

EXAMPLE 5

Simplify $\frac{x^7}{y^5}$.

$\frac{x^7}{y^5}$ Write the given expression.

Cannot be simplified. The bases are not *equal*.

ORAL PRACTICE

Give the expression as a *single* power.

A. $\frac{2^7}{2^3}$ B. $\frac{3^9}{3^4}$

C. $\frac{5^8}{5^2}$ D. $\frac{7^5}{7^4}$

E. $\frac{6^8}{6}$ F. $\frac{x^8}{x^3}$

G. $\frac{y^9}{y^7}$ H. $\frac{z^5}{z^2}$

I. $\frac{a^3}{a^2}$ J. $\frac{b^7}{b}$

Transform to remove the parentheses.

K. $\left(\frac{x}{y}\right)^5$ L. $\left(\frac{a}{b}\right)^3$

M. $\left(\frac{c}{d}\right)^8$ N. $\left(\frac{4}{5}\right)^2$

O. $\left(\frac{3}{7}\right)^1$

Do the following.

P. Evaluate 2^7. Q. Evaluate 2^4.

R. Evaluate $\frac{2^7}{2^4}$ by dividing the answers to P and Q.

S. Simplify $\frac{2^7}{2^4}$ using the properties of exponentiation.

T. Evaluate the answer to S.

U. Tell one reason why people transform expressions using the properties of exponentiation.

EXERCISE 9-4

For Problems 1 through 40, simplify the expression.

1. $\frac{x^{11}}{x^7}$
2. $\frac{x^{15}}{x^8}$
3. $\frac{s^{22}}{s^8}$
4. $\frac{r^{31}}{r^{19}}$

5. $\frac{3x^6}{x^2}$

6. $\frac{5x^7}{x^5}$

7. $\frac{6c^9}{2c^4}$

8. $\frac{10p^8}{5p^4}$

9. $\frac{x^9}{x^8}$

10. $\frac{x^5}{x^4}$

11. $\frac{y^5}{y}$

12. $\frac{z^7}{z}$

13. $\frac{x^5}{x^5}$

14. $\frac{x^7}{x^7}$

15. $\frac{3z^8}{z^8}$

16. $\frac{4y^9}{y^9}$

17. $\frac{-8x^9}{4x^3}$

18. $\frac{-12x^8}{3x^2}$

19. $\frac{20x^{12}}{-5x^3}$

20. $\frac{32x^{10}}{-8x^5}$

21. $\frac{x^5y^7}{x^2y^5}$

22. $\frac{x^9y^5}{x^5y^2}$

23. $\frac{a^{12}b^8}{a^4b^4}$

24. $\frac{c^9d^{15}}{c^3d^3}$

25. $\frac{40x^9y^8}{10x^4y^7}$

26. $\frac{70x^5y^{11}}{7x^3y^9}$

27. $\frac{24x^{10}y^{15}}{8x^2y^5}$

28. $\frac{36x^{15}y^{20}}{12x^3y^5}$

29. $\frac{56x^4y^6}{8x^4}$

30. $\frac{72x^2y^5}{9y^5}$

31. $\frac{28x^3y^7}{7y^6}$

32. $\frac{54x^8y^4}{6x^7}$

33. $\frac{x^{10}}{y^5}\left(\frac{y}{x}\right)^8$

34. $\frac{x^8}{y^3}\left(\frac{y}{x}\right)^4$

35. $\frac{r^7}{t^4}\left(\frac{t}{r}\right)^5$

36. $\frac{p^9}{f^3}\left(\frac{f}{p}\right)^6$

37. $\frac{x^5}{4}\left(\frac{2}{x}\right)^3$

38. $\frac{x^7}{9}\left(\frac{3}{x}\right)^4$

39. $\frac{5^8}{3^4}\left(\frac{3}{5}\right)^7$

40. $\frac{2^{10}}{3^6}\left(\frac{3}{2}\right)^7$

For Problems 41 through 60, simplify the expression using the properties of exponentiation in this section and the last.

41. $\left(\frac{x^5}{y^4}\right)^2$

42. $\left(\frac{x^7}{y^5}\right)^3$

43. $\left(\frac{a^4}{b^2}\right)^3$

44. $\left(\frac{c^{10}}{d^5}\right)^2$

45. $\frac{(xy)^5}{x^3}$

46. $\frac{(xy)^7}{y^5}$

47. $\frac{(xy)^9}{x^2y^3}$

48. $\frac{(xy)^8}{x^4y^5}$

49. $\frac{(2x)^5}{2x^5}$

50. $\frac{(3x)^4}{3x^4}$

51. $\frac{(x^3y)^2}{x^2y}$

52. $\frac{(xy^5)^3}{x^2y}$

53. $\frac{(x^2y^3)^4}{x^5y^6}$

54. $\frac{(x^3y^4)^2}{x^2y^5}$

55. $\frac{x^{11}y^{13}}{(xy^3)^2}$

56. $\frac{x^{10}y^{12}}{(x^2y)^3}$

57. $\frac{(3x^6)^4}{(3x^2)^3}$

58. $\frac{(2x^4)^5}{(2x^3)^2}$

59. $\frac{(5ab^2)^6}{(5a^2b)^3}$

60. $\frac{(3c^2d)^{10}}{(3cd^5)^2}$

9-5 NEGATIVE AND ZERO EXPONENTS

In the last section you learned that when you divide two powers with equal bases, you can subtract their exponents. For instance,

$$\frac{x^5}{x^3} = x^{5-3} = x^2.$$

This property leads to difficulties if the exponent of the denominator is larger than the exponent of the numerator. What would $\frac{x^4}{x^7}$ equal? Using the property, you would get

$$\frac{x^4}{x^7} = x^{4-7} = x^{-3}.$$

The answer has a *negative* exponent, which does not make sense in terms of repeated multiplication of x's. However, you can find an answer by going back to the definition of exponentiation.

$$\frac{x^4}{x^7}$$

$= \dfrac{x \cdot x \cdot x \cdot x}{x \cdot x \cdot x \cdot x \cdot x \cdot x \cdot x}$	Use the definition of exponentiation.
$= \dfrac{x \cdot x \cdot x \cdot x \cdot 1}{x \cdot x \cdot x \cdot x \cdot x \cdot x \cdot x}$	Use the multiplicative identity axiom to multiply by 1.
$= \dfrac{x \cdot x \cdot x \cdot x}{x \cdot x \cdot x \cdot x} \cdot \dfrac{1}{x \cdot x \cdot x}$	Use the multiplication property of fractions to get *two* fractions
$= 1 \cdot \dfrac{1}{x \cdot x \cdot x}$	A number divided by itself equals 1.
$= \dfrac{1}{x^3}$	Use the multiplicative identity axiom and the definition of exponentiation.

In order to subtract exponents, you must *define* x^{-3} to be the same thing as $\frac{1}{x^3}$.

DEFINITION

> **NEGATIVE EXPONENTS**
> For any nonzero number x and for any integer n,
>
> $$x^{-n} = \frac{1}{x^n}.$$

A similar difficulty arises with a power divided by itself.

$$\frac{x^5}{x^5} = x^{5-5} = x^0$$

Since any nonzero number divided by itself equals 1, x^0 must be defined to be 1.

DEFINITION

> **ZERO EXPONENT**
> For any nonzero number x,
>
> $$x^0 = 1.$$

In this section you will use positive and negative exponents along with the properties of exponentiation to simplify expressions involving powers.

Objective:

Be able to simplify expressions involving powers with positive, negative, and zero exponents.

Cover the answers as you work the examples.

EXAMPLE 1

Simplify $\frac{x^5}{x^7}$.

- - - - -

Think These Reasons

$\frac{x^5}{x^7}$ Write the given expression.

$= \underline{\underline{x^{-2}}}$ Subtract the exponents: $5 - 7 = -2$.

EXAMPLE 2

Simplify $\frac{r^{-3}}{r^4}$.

- - - - -

$\frac{r^{-3}}{r^4}$ Write the given expression.

$= \underline{\underline{r^{-7}}}$ Subtract the exponents: $-3 - 4 = -7$.

EXAMPLE 3

Simplify $x^{-7}x^4$.

- - - - -

$x^{-7}x^4$ Write the given expression.

$= \underline{\underline{x^{-3}}}$ *Add* the exponents: $-7 + 4 = -3$.

EXAMPLE 4

Simplify $(3x^{-5})^2$.

- - - - -

$(3x^{-5})^2$ Write the given expression.

$= \underline{\underline{9x^{-10}}}$ Distribute exponentiation over multiplication; multiply the exponents.

EXAMPLE 5

Simplify $\frac{x^7}{y^5}\left(\frac{x^3}{y}\right)^{-2}$.

- - - - -

$\frac{x^7}{y^5}\left(\frac{x^3}{y}\right)^{-2}$	Write the given expression.
$= \frac{x^7x^{-6}}{y^5y^{-2}}$	Distribute exponentiation over division. Combine the resulting fractions.
$= \frac{x}{y^3}$	Add the exponents in the numerator and denominator.
$= \underline{\underline{xy^{-3}}}$	Dividing by y^3 is equivalent to multiplying by its reciprocal, y^{-3}.

ORAL PRACTICE

Evaluate each expression.

EXAMPLES

	Answers
i. 2^{-3}	i. $\frac{1}{8}$
ii. 5^0	ii. 1

A. 3^{-2}

B. 5^{-3}

C. 4^{-3}

D. 7^0

E. 0^7

Transform to a single power with a positive or negative exponent.

F. $\frac{x^4}{x^9}$

G. $\frac{a^5}{a^7}$

H. $\frac{y^{-3}}{y^5}$

I. $\frac{z^6}{z^{-4}}$

J. $\frac{p^{-8}}{p^{-11}}$

K. $\frac{x^3}{x^{-3}}$

L. $\frac{x^{-5}}{x^5}$

M. $\frac{x^{-7}}{x^{-7}}$

N. $\frac{x^0}{x^4}$

O. $\frac{x^{-5}}{x^0}$

P. x^5x^{-7}

Q. $x^{-2}x^5$

R. $x^{-6}x^{-7}$

S. x^0x^{-4}

T. x^8x^{-8}

U. $(x^{-3})^2$

V. $(x^2)^{-3}$

W. $(x^{-5})^{-2}$

X. $(x^3y^{-2})^4$

Y. $(2x^{-4}y)^{-3}$

EXERCISE 9-5

For Problems 1 through 10, evaluate the expression *without* using a calculator.

1. 3^{-2}
2. 2^{-3}
3. 4^{-3}
4. 4^{-2}
5. 5^{-2}
6. 7^{-3}
7. 1^{-5}
8. 1^{-8}
9. $(-2)^{-3}$
10. $(3)^{-2}$

For Problems 11 through 40, a. write powers with positive or negative exponents, leaving no powers in denominators; b. write the powers *without* negative exponents.

11. $\frac{x^3}{x^8}$
12. $\frac{x^5}{x^7}$
13. $\frac{y^5}{y^9}$
14. $\frac{z^6}{z^8}$
15. $\frac{a}{a^5}$
16. $\frac{b}{b^4}$
17. $\frac{c^5}{c^6}$
18. $\frac{d^7}{d^8}$
19. $\frac{x^5}{x^0}$
20. $\frac{x^0}{x^7}$
21. $\frac{x^{-3}}{x^{-3}}$
22. $\frac{x^4}{x^4}$

23. x^5x^{-3}

24. x^7x^{-2}

25. $x^{-8}x^2$

26. $x^{-6}x^2$

27. $x^{-6}x^{-7}$

28. $x^{-3}x^{-5}$

29. x^7y^{-3}

30. x^5y^{-2}

31. x^5x^0

32. x^0x^6

33. x^0x^{-7}

34. $x^{-3}x^0$

35. $\dfrac{r^2s^3}{r^6s^9}$

36. $\dfrac{a^5b^2}{a^8b^6}$

37. $\dfrac{a^5b^6}{a^7b^6}$

38. $\dfrac{m^9k^7}{m^4k^7}$

39. $\dfrac{c^5d^0}{c^2d^7}$

40. $\dfrac{r^6s^0}{r^4s^8}$

For Problems 41 through 110, simplify the expression. Use negative exponents, and leave no variables in denominators.

41. $\dfrac{t^{15}v^7}{t^0v^{10}}$

42. $\dfrac{c^{19}d^{13}}{c^0d^{18}}$

43. $\dfrac{x^7y}{xy^5}$

44. $\dfrac{x^6z}{xz^9}$

45. $\dfrac{x^7y}{(xy)^5}$

46. $\dfrac{(xy)^6}{x^5y}$

47. $(x^2y^{-3})^5$

48. $(x^{-2}y^4)^6$

49. $(2x^{-3})^4$

50. $(3x^{-5})^2$

51. $(x^{-3}y^4)^{-2}$

52. $(x^5y^{-2})^{-3}$

53. $(3x^{-4})^{-2}$

54. $(2x^{-6})^{-3}$

55. $\dfrac{x^{-8}}{x^2}$

56. $\dfrac{x^{-7}}{x^3}$

57. $\dfrac{a^3}{a^{-10}}$

58. $\dfrac{y^4}{y^{-13}}$

59. $\dfrac{h^{-4}}{h^{-6}}$

60. $\dfrac{z^{-2}}{z^{-7}}$

61. $\dfrac{p^0}{p^{-5}}$

62. $\dfrac{a^0}{a^{-3}}$

63. $\dfrac{y^7}{y^0}$

64. $\dfrac{b^{11}}{b^0}$

65. $\dfrac{x^5y^{-7}}{x^3y^9}$

66. $\dfrac{x^6y^{-3}}{x^2y^8}$

67. $\dfrac{r^{-2}y^5}{r^{10}y^7}$

68. $\dfrac{t^{-3}u^7}{t^9u^{12}}$

69. $\dfrac{c^{-3}d^{-7}}{c^5d^{-7}}$

70. $\dfrac{y^{-5}z^{-9}}{y^{-5}z^3}$

71. $\dfrac{15x^9}{3x^7}$

72. $\dfrac{20x^7}{5x^2}$

73. $\dfrac{12a^{10}}{15a^7}$

74. $\dfrac{18y^{12}}{12y^4}$

75. $\dfrac{6r^9}{12r^{-4}}$

76. $\dfrac{5z^2}{10z^{-3}}$

77. $\dfrac{51m^6p}{17m^4p^{-9}}$

78. $\dfrac{57k^7p}{19k^3p^{-5}}$

79. $\dfrac{2t^5v^{-7}}{10t^6v^{-8}}$

80. $\dfrac{4r^8s^{-6}}{40r^7s^{-7}}$

81. $\dfrac{x^5}{y^4}\left(\dfrac{y}{x}\right)^3$

82. $\dfrac{x^9}{y^5}\left(\dfrac{y}{x}\right)^4$

83. $\left(\dfrac{m}{x}\right)^5 \times \dfrac{x^6}{m^{-11}}$

84. $\left(\dfrac{n}{d}\right)^5 \times \dfrac{d^7}{n^{-4}}$

85. $\left(\dfrac{a}{b}\right)^{-5} \times \dfrac{a^5}{b^7}$

86. $\left(\dfrac{x}{y}\right)^{-7} \times \dfrac{x^7}{y^5}$

87. $\dfrac{r^{-3}}{s^5}\left(\dfrac{r}{s}\right)^7$

88. $\dfrac{k^{-2}}{r^4}\left(\dfrac{k}{r}\right)^8$

89. $\left(\dfrac{x}{y}\right)^0 \times \dfrac{1}{x^3}$

90. $\left(\dfrac{a}{b}\right)^0 \times \dfrac{1}{a^5}$

91. $\left(\dfrac{x^5}{y^4}\right)^2$

92. $\left(\dfrac{x^7}{y^5}\right)^3$

93. $\left(\dfrac{x^{-2}}{y^5}\right)^3$

94. $\left(\dfrac{x^{-4}}{y^3}\right)^2$

95. $\left(\dfrac{x^2}{y^3}\right)^4\left(\dfrac{y^5}{x^3}\right)^2$

96. $\left(\dfrac{x^4}{y^5}\right)^2\left(\dfrac{y^2}{x^3}\right)^5$

97. $\left(\frac{a^{-2}}{b^3}\right)^5\left(\frac{b^{-3}}{a^4}\right)^{-2}$

98. $\left(\frac{t^{-3}}{u^4}\right)^3\left(\frac{u^{-4}}{t^6}\right)^{-5}$

99. $\frac{(x^6y^2)^3}{(x^4y^3)^5}$

100. $\frac{(x^4y^3)^2}{(x^5y^2)^4}$

101. $\frac{(r^{-3}s^4)^2}{(r^5s^{-2})^3}$

102. $\frac{(m^{-2}p^5)^2}{(m^4p^{-3})^3}$

103. $\frac{(3x^6)^4}{(3x^{-2})^3}$

104. $\frac{(2x^4)^5}{(2x^{-1})^3}$

105. $\frac{(2tp^2)^3}{(2t^2p)^4}$

106. $\frac{(3ab^3)^2}{(3a^2b)^4}$

107. $\frac{(5rs^{-2})^6}{(5r^3s)^2}$

108. $\frac{(5cd^{-3})^5}{(5c^2d)^3}$

109. $\frac{(3r^6)^3}{9r^6}$

110. $\frac{(4a^5)^3}{4a^{15}}$

9-6 POWERS OF 10 AND SCIENTIFIC NOTATION

Multiplying or dividing a number by 10 is easy. For instance,

$$37.29 \times 10 = 372.9 \quad \text{and} \quad 37.29 \div 10 = 3.729.$$

All you need do is move the decimal point one place. To tell which way to move it, remember that *multiplying* by 10 makes a number *bigger* and *dividing* by 10 makes a number *smaller*.

It is just as easy to multiply or divide by a *power* of 10. For instance, multiplying a number by 10^3 moves the decimal point *three* places.

$$9.2153 \times 10^3 = 9215.3$$

$$13.7 \times 10^3 = 13{,}700$$

$$0.000025 \times 10^3 = 0.025$$

Dividing by a power of 10 moves the decimal point in the other direction. Again, the number of places it moves is equal to the exponent of 10. For instance,

$413.2 \div 10^2 = 4.132$ Moves 2 places.

$6.1 \div 10^5 = 0.000061$ Moves 5 places.

$300{,}000 \div 10^4 = 30.$ Moves 4 places.

In each case, dividing by a power of 10 makes the number *smaller*.

Suppose that you multiply a number by 10^{-2}, which has a *negative* exponent. To figure out what happens, use the following reasoning.

21.584×10^{-2}	
$= 21.584 \times \frac{1}{10^2}$	Definition of negative exponents
$= 21.584 \div 10^2$	Definition of division
$= 0.21584$	Dividing by 10^2 makes the number *smaller*.

When you multiply a number by 10^{-2}, the decimal point moves *two* places and the number gets *smaller*. Using this observation, the answer to such a problem can be written in one step. For instance,

$$98.74 \times 10^{-3} = 0.09874.$$

Your thought process should be: Move the decimal point *three* places in the direction that makes the number *smaller*.

Powers of 10 provide a compact way to write very large or very small numbers. It is hard to read a number such as

$$5380000000$$

because it is impossible for the human brain to comprehend this many digits without actually counting them. It is much easier to read this number if it is written as 5.38 times the appropriate power of 10.

$$5380000000 = 5.38 \times 10^9$$

To find out what the exponent should be, you must count how far the decimal point moves.

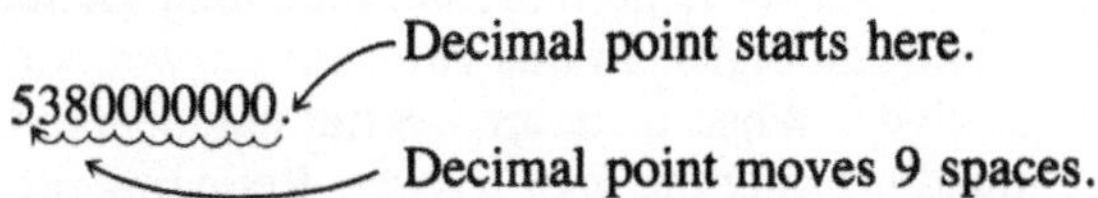
Decimal point starts here.
5380000000.
Decimal point moves 9 spaces.

Very small numbers (close to zero) can be treated the same way. For instance, 0.000002345 can be written as 2.345 times a power of 10. Again, the exponent is found by counting how far the decimal point moves.

$$0.000002345 = 2.345 \times 10^{-6}$$

Decimal point moves 6 spaces.

The most reliable way to tell whether the exponent will be positive or negative is to realize that large numbers (absolute value larger than 10) will have *positive* exponents, and small numbers, or decimals (absolute value less than 1), will have *negative* exponents.

Numbers such as 5.38×10^9 and 2.345×10^{-6} are said to be in **scientific notation.** The factor on the left has the decimal point after the *first* (nonzero) digit. This factor is called the **mantissa.** The factor on the right is a power of 10. Its exponent is called the **characteristic.**

Characteristic

$5.38 \times 10^9 \qquad 2.345 \times 10^{-6}$

Mantissa

Numbers too great or too small to put into a calculator can be multiplied or divided easily if they are first transformed to scientific notation. For instance,

$(5380000000)(0.000002345)$	
$= (5.38 \times 10^9)(2.345 \times 10^{-6})$	Transform to scientific notation.
$= (5.38 \times 2.345)(10^9 \times 10^{-6})$	Commute and associate the mantissas and the powers of 10.
$= 12.6161 \times 10^3$	Multiply.
$= 1.26161 \times 10^4$	Move the decimal point so the number is in scientific notation.
$\approx 1.26 \times 10^4.$	Round the answer.

The next-to-last step is taken so that the mantissa will have the decimal point after the *first* digit—12.6161 equals 1.26161×10^1, and $10^1 \times 10^3 = 10^4$.

The answer is rounded off because the given numbers are only approximate. The number of digits in the mantissa is called the number of **significant digits.** The answer is no more accurate than the factor with the *least* number of significant digits. In this case, the answer is rounded off to three significant digits. When there are several numbers to be multiplied or divided, you round off only the *final* answer. Rounding off at intermediate steps would make the final answer less precise.

Dividing numbers in scientific notation is also relatively easy. For instance,

$\dfrac{5.38 \times 10^9}{2.345 \times 10^{-6}}$	
$= \dfrac{5.38}{2.345} \times \dfrac{10^9}{10^{-6}}$	Use the multiplication property of fractions.
$\approx 2.29 \times 10^{15}.$	Divide the mantissas and round off to three significant digits. Subtract the exponents: $9 - (-6) = 9 + 6 = 15$.

Objective:

Given large or small numbers, transform them to scientific notation (and vice versa), and multiply or divide them.

Cover the answers as you work the examples.

EXAMPLE 1

Transform to decimal form.

a. 8.49×10^6

- - - - -

8.49×10^6

$= \underline{\underline{8{,}490{,}000}}$

b. 6.291×10^{-4}

- - - - -

6.291×10^{-4}

$= \underline{\underline{0.0006291}}$

EXAMPLE 2

Transform to scientific notation.

a. 374,100

- - - - -

374,100

$= \underline{\underline{3.741 \times 10^5}}$

b. 0.0029

- - - - -

0.0029

$= \underline{\underline{2.9 \times 10^{-3}}}$

c. 34 billion

- - - - -

34 billion

$= 34{,}000{,}000{,}000$

$= \underline{\underline{3.4 \times 10^{10}}}$

In the United States, the following numbers are named as shown.

NAMES FOR LARGE NUMBERS

10^3	thousand
10^6	million
10^9	billion
10^{12}	trillion
10^{15}	quadrillion
10^{18}	quintillion

Each number is 1000 times the previous one. In Europe, a million is also 10^6, but a billion is 10^{12}, a trillion is 10^{18}, and so forth. There, each named number is 1,000,000 times the previous one.

EXAMPLE 3

Multiply $(7.82 \times 10^4)(3.4 \times 10^{-9})$. Round your answer to the appropriate number of significant digits.

	Think These Reasons
$(7.82 \times 10^4)(3.4 \times 10^{-9})$	Write the given expression.
$= 26.588 \times 10^{-5}$	Multiply the mantissas. Add the exponents.
$= 2.6588 \times 10^{-4}$	Write the answer with the decimal point after the first digit.
$\approx \underline{\underline{2.7 \times 10^{-4}}}$	Round off to two significant digits.

Note: The whole computation can be done in one step. The minimum you should write is

$$(7.82 \times 10^4)(3.4 \times 10^{-9}) \approx \underline{\underline{2.7 \times 10^{-4}}}.$$

EXAMPLE 4

Divide: $\dfrac{4.378 \times 10^{13}}{7.91 \times 10^4}$. Round your answer.

$\dfrac{4.378 \times 10^{13}}{7.91 \times 10^4}$	Write the given expression.
$\approx 0.553 \times 10^9$	Divide the mantissas and round off to three significant digits. Subtract the exponents.

$= \underline{\underline{5.53 \times 10^8}}$ — Write the answer with the decimal point after the first nonzero digit.

Note: The last sign is = rather than ≈ because it connects 0.553×10^9 and 5.53×10^8. These two numbers are *exactly* equal, not just approximately equal.

EXAMPLE 5

Find the reciprocal of 3.49×10^{-7}. Round your answer.

- - - - -

$\dfrac{1}{3.49 \times 10^{-7}}$ — Write the *reciprocal* of the given expression.

$= \dfrac{1 \times 10^0}{3.49 \times 10^{-7}}$ — Write the numerator in scientific notation. 10^0 is equal to 1.

- - - - -

Think These Reasons

$= \dfrac{1}{3.49} \times \dfrac{10^0}{10^{-7}}$ — Use the multiplication property of fractions to separate the mantissas and the powers.

$\approx 0.287 \times 10^7$ — $1 \div 3.49 \approx 0.287$. Subtract the exponents: $0 - (-7) = 7$.

$= \underline{\underline{2.87 \times 10^6}}$ — Write the answer in scientific notation.

EXAMPLE 6

Evaluate $(9.43 \times 10^{-4})^3$. Round your answer.

- - - - -

$(9.43 \times 10^{-4})^3$ — Write the given expression.

$= 9.43^3 \times (10^{-4})^3$ — Distribute exponentiation over multiplication.

$\approx 839 \times 10^{-12}$ — $9.43 \times 9.43 \times 9.43 \approx 839$. Multiply the exponents.

$= \underline{\underline{8.39 \times 10^{-10}}}$ — Write the answer in scientific notation.

ORAL PRACTICE

Give the number in scientific notation.

A. 358

B. 7290

C. 0.0743

D. 0.000045

E. 23×10^5

F. 42×10^{-7}

G. 0.51×10^8

H. 0.19×10^{-3}

Give the number in words.

EXAMPLES

	Answers
i. 48,500,000	i. 48.5 million
ii. 6.3×10^{11}	ii. 630 billion

I. 294,000

J. 1,500,000

K. 32,000,000

L. 413×10^5

M. 5×10^9

N. 8.2×10^{13}

O. 7.2×10^{14}

P. 6.8×10^0

Evaluate. Give the answer in scientific notation.

Q. $(2 \times 10^4)(3 \times 10^2)$

R. $(4 \times 10^{-3})(2 \times 10^7)$

S. $(1 \times 10^4)(8 \times 10^{-9})$

T. $(3 \times 10^{-5})(2 \times 10^{-6})$

U. $(4 \times 10^3)(5 \times 10^6)$

V. $(6 \times 10^{-4})(3 \times 10^{-2})$

W. $\dfrac{6 \times 10^8}{2 \times 10^5}$

X. $\dfrac{8 \times 10^3}{4 \times 10^9}$

Y. $(3 \times 10^7)^2$

Z. $(2 \times 10^4)^3$

EXERCISE 9-6

1. Write a number that is 10 times as large as
   a. 5.73
   b. 29.1
   c. 304
   d. 0.068
   e. 0.00907

2. Write a number that is 10 times as large as
   a. 6.03
   b. 427.9
   c. 2214
   d. 0.53
   e. 0.000998

3. Write a number that is $\frac{1}{10}$ as large as
   a. 63.9
   b. 7.91
   c. 82
   d. 0.48
   e. 0.00014

4. Write a number that is $\frac{1}{10}$ as large as
   a. 47.2
   b. 6.85
   c. 943
   d. 0.025
   e. 3

For Problems 5 through 14, transform the number to decimal form.

5. 7.1×10^3
6. 3.6×10^4
7. 4.65×10^5
8. 9.24×10^5
9. 3.8×10^{-4}
10. 4.83×10^{-6}
11. 8.6×10^1
12. 7.4×10^{-1}
13. 9.8×10^{-1}
14. 6.02×10^1

For Problems 15 through 36, transform the number to scientific notation.

15. 43,800
16. 715,200
17. 291.7
18. 49.63
19. 34,500,000
20. 517,000
21. 0.00739
22. 0.000281
23. 0.00000114
24. 0.0000000192
25. 27.5 million
26. 44.2 thousand
27. 200 thousand
28. 30 billion
29. 62.4×10^3
30. 73.6×10^5
31. 548×10^{-7}
32. 295×10^{-8}
33. 0.07×10^8
34. 0.0034×10^9
35. 97.1×10^{-4}
36. 84.6×10^{-2}

For Problems 37 through 60, do the operations in your *head,* without using a calculator. Write the answer in scientific notation.

37. $(2 \times 10^7)(3 \times 10^8)$
38. $(2 \times 10^5)(4 \times 10^8)$
39. $(4 \times 10^9)(2 \times 10^{-3})$
40. $(3 \times 10^{-4})(2 \times 10^{11})$
41. $(7 \times 10^4)(5 \times 10^{11})$
42. $(5 \times 10^7)(9 \times 10^8)$

43. $(6 \times 10^3)(7 \times 10^{-8})$

44. $(9 \times 10^6)(7 \times 10^{-13})$

45. $(9 \times 10^{-5})(6 \times 10^5)$

46. $(8 \times 10^{-7})(6 \times 10^7)$

47. $(8 \times 10^{-4})(7 \times 10^{-20})$

48. $(4 \times 10^{-5})(7 \times 10^{-10})$

49. $\dfrac{8 \times 10^{15}}{2 \times 10^4}$

50. $\dfrac{8 \times 10^{17}}{4 \times 10^8}$

51. $\dfrac{6 \times 10^4}{3 \times 10^{11}}$

52. $\dfrac{6 \times 10^5}{2 \times 10^{12}}$

53. $\dfrac{5 \times 10^{-2}}{1 \times 10^4}$

54. $\dfrac{7 \times 10^{-3}}{1 \times 10^5}$

55. $\dfrac{7 \times 10^5}{2 \times 10^{-3}}$

56. $\dfrac{9 \times 10^3}{2 \times 10^{-7}}$

57. $\dfrac{2 \times 10^{-3}}{4 \times 10^{-12}}$

58. $\dfrac{2 \times 10^{-9}}{8 \times 10^{-7}}$

59. $\dfrac{4 \times 10^{-8}}{5 \times 10^8}$

60. $\dfrac{3 \times 10^{-4}}{6 \times 10^4}$

For Problems 61 through 76, use a calculator to multiply or divide the mantissas. Write the answer in scientific notation, with the appropriate number of significant digits.

61. $(2.05 \times 10^6)(3.12 \times 10^7)$

62. $(3.52 \times 10^4)(2.11 \times 10^7)$

63. $(4.9 \times 10^{17})(1.345 \times 10^{-5})$

64. $(1.3 \times 10^{-5})(4.253 \times 10^{12})$

65. $(8.65 \times 10^3)(2.296 \times 10^{-18})$

66. $(9.06 \times 10^{-9})(5.224 \times 10^3)$

67. $(1.79 \times 10^{-4})(9.7 \times 10^{-9})$

68. $(1.72 \times 10^{-5})(3.6 \times 10^{-11})$

69. $\dfrac{3.75 \times 10^8}{2.93 \times 10^5}$

70. $\dfrac{4.28 \times 10^6}{1.94 \times 10^2}$

71. $\dfrac{4.976 \times 10^{-8}}{8.2 \times 10^5}$

72. $\dfrac{7.732 \times 10^{-7}}{9.63 \times 10^3}$

73. $\dfrac{7.6 \times 10^4}{9.83 \times 10^{-9}}$

74. $\dfrac{1.07 \times 10^4}{8.3 \times 10^{-2}}$

75. $\dfrac{6.802 \times 10^{-7}}{5.1996 \times 10^{-11}}$

76. $\dfrac{7.41 \times 10^{-12}}{6.94 \times 10^{-5}}$

For Problems 77 through 80, find the reciprocal of the given number.

77. 5.87×10^4

78. 2.93×10^5

79. 1.62×10^{-7}

80. 7.8×10^{-9}

For Problems 81 through 86, raise the number to the indicated power.

81. $(2.34 \times 10^5)^2$

82. $(1.29 \times 10^7)^2$

83. $(4.08 \times 10^{-5})^2$

84. $(6.13 \times 10^{-6})^2$

85. $(8.97 \times 10^4)^3$

86. $(7.21 \times 10^5)^3$

9-7 PROBLEMS INVOLVING NUMBERS IN SCIENTIFIC NOTATION

As you might expect from the name, numbers in scientific notation occur in problems from science! More generally, they occur in problems from the real world. In this section you work problems involving arithmetic performed on very large or very small numbers. As in the previous section, the properties of exponentiation are the key to operating with such numbers.

Objective:

Given a problem from the real world involving very large or very small constants, do the arithmetic using scientific notation.

Cover the answer as you work the example.

EXAMPLE

Louisiana Purchase Problem In 1803, when Thomas Jefferson was president, the United States purchased about 5×10^8 acres of land from the French for 15 million dollars. About how much per acre did the land cost?

- - - - - - - - - -

	Think These Reasons
15 million $= 1.5 \times 10^7$	1 million $= 10^6$
\$ per acre $= \dfrac{1.5 \times 10^7}{5 \times 10^8}$	*Per* means *divided by*. So \$ per acre = \$ ÷ acres.
$= 0.3 \times 10^{-1}$	Divide the mantissas. Subtract the exponents.
$= 3 \times 10^{-2}$	Write in scientific notation.
About 3 cents per acre	Answer the question.

EXERCISE 9-7

1. *National Debt Problem* In 1980 the national debt of the United States was about 970 billion dollars. The 1980 census showed 226,504,825 people. About how many dollars per person was the national debt?

2. *Average Ocean Depth Problem* The total area of the world's oceans is about 360.928 million square kilometers. The total volume of water in the oceans is about 1.32 billion cubic kilometers. The average depth equals the volume divided by the area. What is the average depth? How many meters is this?

3. *Continental Drift Problem* Measurements show that Europe and Africa are separating from the Americas at a rate of about 1 inch per year. The continents are presently about 4000 miles apart. Assuming that the rate has remained constant, how many years has it been since the continents split apart and started drifting?

They used to *fit!*

4. *Clothing Industry Problem* There are about 230 million people in the United States. Assume that each person buys 6 pairs of socks a year and that socks cost about $4 a pair. How much money can the clothing industry expect to take in each year from selling socks? Give the answer in words.

5. *Automotive Batteries Problem* There are about 120 million cars and trucks in the United States. Each one uses a battery, which needs replacing about once every 3 years. If an average battery costs $80, how much money can the battery manufacturing industry expect to make each year?

6. *Brain Cell Problem* The brain of a normal adult weighs about 3 pounds. It has about 8 billion neurons (brain cells). How many pounds per neuron is that? Answer in scientific notation.

7. *Earth's Land Area Problem* The total area of the earth's surface is about 5.1007×10^8 square kilometers. The area of all land is about 1.49141×10^8 square kilometers. What percent of the earth's sur-

face is land? (Divide land area by total area and multiply by 100.)

8. *Gold Plated Pinhead Problem* An atom of gold has an area of about 6.6×10^{-16} square centimeter. How many atoms would it take to cover the head of a pin of area 3.2×10^{-2} square centimeter, with a layer of gold 1 atom thick?

9. *Glacier Problem* A typical glacier moves downhill at about 5 inches per day. Suppose that the glacier is 4 miles long.
   a. Recalling that 1 mile is 5280 feet, how many days will it take for snow that falls at the top of the glacier to move downhill to the bottom?
   b. How many years is this?

10. *Numbers on a Calculator Problem* A normal calculator can handle numbers as big as 9.99×10^{99}. To see how big a number this is, answer the following questions.
   a. The volume of the earth is 2.59×10^{11} cubic miles. One cubic mile is 5280^3 cubic feet. What is the volume of the earth in cubic feet?
   b. One grain of sand has a volume of about 1.3×10^{-9} cubic feet. Divide the answer in part (a) by 1.3×10^{-9} to find the number of grains of sand the earth could hold.
   c. Which is bigger, the number of grains of sand the earth could hold or the largest number a calculator can hold?

11. *Paper Consumption Problem* A school uses 150 cartons of paper in a year. Each carton has 10 reams, and each ream has 500 sheets.
   a. How many sheets of paper does the school use in a year?
   b. If there are 2000 students in the school, how many sheets of paper per student is this?

12. *Speed of Light Problem* Light travels at a speed of 299,792 kilometers per second. How long does it take light to get from:
   a. New York to Los Angeles, 3900 km;
   b. the sun to the earth, 150 million km;
   c. Earth to Pluto at its closest point of approach, 4.44 billion km? Answer in hours.

13. *Light-Year Problem* Light travels 299,792 kilometers per second. How far does light travel in a year? This distance is called a **light-year.** Answer in words.

14. *Life in Seconds Problem* The average life expectancy in the United States is about 71 years. About how many seconds is this? Answer in words.

15. *Leaky Faucet Problem* A leaking faucet drips 1 drop per second.
   a. How many drops does it leak in a year?
   b. There are about 76,000 drops of water in a gallon. How many gallons per year would be leaked at one drop per second?

16. *Water Bill Problem* The Dupp family goes on vacation. They are gone for a month. Near the end, Fess admits that he left the water running in the back yard. Phil estimates that the faucet runs at 4 gallons per minute. Mae knows that water costs about 0.1 cent per gallon. Bill gets more and more worried about how much the water bill will be. How much *will* it be?

17. *Power Consumption Problem* Suppose that a house has 12 100-watt light bulbs.
    a. A *kilowatt* (kw) of electrical power is 1000 watts. How many kilowatts do the 12 bulbs require in all?
    b. If the lights stay on an average of 8 hours a day, how many hours in all will they be on in a year?
    c. The amount of energy used by the lights is measured in *kilowatt-hours,* abbreviated kwh. This number is found by multiplying the number of kilowatts by the number of hours. How many kilowatt-hours in all will the bulbs use in a year?
    d. Suppose that electricity costs 7.8 cents per kwh. How much would be spent on lighting in a year?
    e. How much could be saved by:
        i. using 60-watt bulbs instead of 100-watt;
        ii. burning the lights (100-watt) 6 hours a day instead of 8?

18. *Computer Calculations Problems* A popular brand of personal computer can do a computation in 5×10^{-7} second.
    a. How many computations can it do in one second? Answer in words.
    b. How long would it take the computer to do a billion computations?
    c. If a program takes 30 seconds to run, how many computations were done?

19. *Sahara Desert Problem* The Sahara Desert covers about 3 million square miles.
    a. Write this number in scientific notation.
    b. One square mile is 5280^2 square feet. About how many square feet is the Sahara Desert?
    c. Assume that the Sahara Desert is covered with sand to an average depth of 200 feet. The volume of this sand in cubic feet is the area in square feet times the depth in feet. How many cubic feet of sand are there?
    d. A grain of sand has a volume of about 1.3×10^{-9} cubic foot. Divide the volume in cubic feet by 1.3×10^{-9} to find out approximately how many grains of sand there are in the Sahara Desert.

20. *Ocean Water Molecules Problem* According to the World Book Encyclopedia, there are about 326 million cubic miles of water on the earth.

a. Write this number in scientific notation.
b. One cubic mile is 5280^3 cubic feet. About how many cubic feet of water are there on the earth?
c. A thimble holds about 5×10^{-4} cubic foot of water. Divide the answer to part (b) by 5×10^{-4} to find out how many thimblefuls of water there are on the earth.
d. A cubic foot of water has about 9.47×10^{26} water molecules. Which is greater, the number of water molecules in a thimbleful of water or the number of thimblefuls of water on the earth? How many *times* as great?

9-8 CHAPTER REVIEW AND TEST

In this chapter you have returned to an old concept, raising numbers to powers (*exponentiation*). Based on the definition of exponentiation, there are properties that allow you to operate on powers by operating on their exponents. These properties are useful for operating on numbers in scientific notation.

There are four operations you do with exponents.

1. Add.
2. Subtract.
3. Multiply.
4. Distribute.

Your main task is to remember which thing you do at which time. There is a memory aid that may help. List the operations according to the order of operations.

Exponentiation
Multiplication
Addition
Nothing

When you do an operation to a *power*, you do the operation *below* to its exponent! For instance,

Exponentiation: $(2^3)^4 = 2^{3 \cdot 4} \longleftarrow$ *Multiply* the exponents.

Addition: $x^3 + y^4 \longleftarrow$ Do *nothing* to the exponents.

If you understand the concepts of this chapter, you should be able to work the following test in a length of time equal to one class period.

CHAPTER TEST

1. What is the difference in each case?
   a. A prime number and a composite number.
   b. A power and an exponent.
   c. 3^0 and 0^3.
   d. 2^3 and 2^{-3}.
   e. A mantissa and a characteristic.

2. State each.
   a. The definition of zero exponent.
   b. The definition of negative exponents.
   c. The property of a product of two powers with equal bases.
   d. The property of a power of a quotient.
   e. The property of a power of a power.

3. Calvin Butterball and Phoebe Small give the following answers on an algebra test. Who is right? Write *Calvin, Phoebe, both,* or *neither.*

Problem	*Calvin's answer*	*Phoebe's answer*
a. Simplify x^6x^8.	x^{48}	x^{14}
b. Simplify $(x^6)^8$.	x^{48}	x^{14}
c. Simplify $(2y^3)^5$.	$2y^{15}$	$10y^{15}$
d. Simplify $\left(\frac{3x^5}{y^4}\right)^3$.	$\frac{27x^{15}}{y^{12}}$	$27x^{15}y^{-12}$
e. Simplify $\frac{x^5y}{x^3y^7}$.	x^2y^{-7}	$\frac{x^2}{y^6}$
f. Simplify x^0.	1	x
g. Significant digits in 7.89×10^5.	2	3
h. One trillionth.	0.000,000,001	10^{-9}

4. Simplify, or state that the expression cannot be simplified.
   a. $(5x^8)(7x^9)$
   b. $(5a^7)^3$
   c. $\frac{r^5s^{-2}}{r^8s^5}$
   d. $\left(\frac{x^{13}y^0}{x^8y^{-5}}\right)^2$
   e. $\frac{1}{a^2b^{-6}}$
   f. $\frac{81b^5}{27c^3}$
   g. $\frac{x^5}{x}$
   h. $\frac{5x}{x}$
   i. $3x^7 \cdot 3x^9$
   j. $3x^7 + 3x^9$
   k. $7x^3 + 9x^3$
   l. $7x^3 - 7x^3$
   m. $7x^3 - x^3$

5. Do the following operations. Write the answers in scientific notation, rounded off to the appropriate number of significant digits.
   a. (32.4 billion)(5.7 million)
   b. $(7.91 \times 10^{-7})(6.43 \times 10^{25})$
   c. $\dfrac{1.873 \times 10^{5}}{7.64 \times 10^{-7}}$
   d. $\dfrac{4.73 \times 10^{-17}}{6.02 \times 10^{-8}}$
   e. $(7.46 \times 10^{9})^{2}$
   f. $\dfrac{1}{2.5 \times 10^{-7}}$ (*Exact* answer)

6. ***Government Spending Rate Problem*** The United States Government's budget for 1981 called for spending about 635 billion dollars. There are 5.256×10^{5} minutes in a year. About how many dollars per minute did the Government spend that year?

10

More Operations With Polynomials

In Chapter 5 you learned how to multiply two binomials and how to factor quadratic trinomials. In this chapter you will learn some more ways to factor polynomials. You will also find out a quick way to solve certain quadratic equations by factoring. The speed you gain will help you do better on standardized tests or in contest mathematics. On that kind of test you might do such things as finding the exact time at which the hands of a clock coincide.

Expression:
$15x^2 - 6ax - 2cx + 8ac$
Factored form:
$(5x - 2a)(3x - 4c)$
Equation:
$2x^2 - x - 3 = 0$
Factored form:
$(2x - 3)(x + 1) = 0$
Solution:
$S = \{\frac{3}{2}, -1\}$

10-1 REVIEW OF MULTIPLYING AND FACTORING POLYNOMIALS

Since this section is a review of things you learned in Chapter 5, you should be able to read it quickly and work the problems without prior classroom discussion. If you are rusty on the techniques, go back to Chapter 5 and look things up!

You should remember how to multiply two binomials. To find

$$(3x + 2)(x - 7),$$

you multiply each term of the first binomial by each term of the second one.

$(3x + 2)(x - 7)$

$= 3x^2 - 21x + 2x - 14$ Multiply $3x$ by x and by -7. Multiply 2 by x and by -7.

$= \underline{\underline{3x^2 - 19x - 14}}$ Combine like terms.

To factor a quadratic trinomial, you reverse this process. For example, to factor $3x^2 - 19x - 14$ you first write

$3x^2 - 19x - 14$

$= (\quad)(\quad)$. Write empty parentheses.

The first terms in the binomials must be $3x$ and x, because their product is $3x^2$. So you fill in these numbers.

$3x^2 - 19x - 14$

$= (3x \quad)(x \quad)$ Fill in the first terms.

The other terms in the binomials must have a product equal to -14. The possibilities are as follows.

$+1, -14 \qquad +7, \ -2$

$-1, +14 \qquad -7, \ +2$

$+2, -7 \qquad +14, -1$

$-2, +7 \qquad -14, +1$

You simply *try* these possibilities until you find one that works. The correct pair is the one that gives $-19x$ for the middle term when the binomials are multiplied together again. That pair turns out to be $+2, -7$. So you finish by filling in these numbers. The complete problem looks like this:

$3x^2 - 19x - 14$

$= \underline{\underline{(3x + 2)(x - 7)}}$ Fill in the constants that give $-19x$ for the middle term and -14 for the last term.

Objective

Recall how to multiply two binomials and how to factor quadratic trinomials.

The following problems give you practice doing this.

EXERCISE 10-1

For Problems 1 through 10, multiply the binomials.

1. $(x + 3)(x + 11)$
2. $(x + 5)(x + 9)$
3. $(2x + 5)(x - 4)$
4. $(3x - 7)(x + 2)$
5. $(3x - 8)(2x - 7)$
6. $(5x - 3)(7x - 4)$
7. $(x + 5)(x - 5)$
8. $(3x - 4)(3x + 4)$
9. $(3x + 4)(3x + 4)$
10. $(x - 6)(x - 6)$

For Problems 11 through 20, factor the polynomial.

11. $x^2 + 14x + 45$
12. $x^2 + 14x + 33$
13. $x^2 - 4x - 21$
14. $x^2 + 6x - 16$
15. $x^2 - 12x + 20$
16. $x^2 - 13x + 36$
17. $4x^2 - 49$
18. $x^2 + 14x + 49$
19. $2x^2 + 9x - 5$
20. $3x^2 - 20x - 7$

21. The answer to a factoring problem is

$$x^2 - 2x - 15 = (x + 3)(x - 5).$$

a. Show that the answer is correct by evaluating both $x^2 - 2x - 15$ and $(x + 3)(x - 5)$ if:
i. $x = 3$; ii. $x = -4$.

b. Which expression is easier to evaluate?

22. The answer to a multiplication problem is

$$(3x + 2)(x + 1) = 3x^2 + 5x + 2.$$

a. Show that the answer is correct by evaluating both $(3x + 2)(x + 1)$ and $3x^2 + 5x + 2$ if:
i. $x = 4$; ii. $x = -1$.

b. Which expression is easier to evaluate?

10-2 THE GREATEST COMMON FACTOR

In Section 10.1 you factored integers as products of primes. For instance,

$$108 = 2 \cdot 2 \cdot 3 \cdot 3 \cdot 3$$

$$120 = 2 \cdot 2 \cdot 2 \cdot 3 \cdot 5.$$

Since 2 is a factor of both 108 and 120, it is called a **common factor** of these two numbers. So are 3 and 6, as you can check by dividing 108 and 120 by 3 and by 6.

$$\frac{108}{3} = 36 \qquad \frac{108}{6} = 18$$

$$\frac{120}{3} = 40 \qquad \frac{120}{6} = 20$$

(18 and 20: The quotient is an *integer*.)

For what you will be doing next in algebra, it is important to find the *greatest* common factor (GCF) of two numbers.

DEFINITION

GREATEST COMMON FACTOR
The **greatest common factor** (GCF) of two positive integers a and b is the greatest integer for which

$$a/\text{GCF} = \text{integer},$$

and

$$b/\text{GCF} = \text{integer}.$$

The GCF of two integers can be found by factoring them into primes. For 108 and 120 you would think

$$108 = 2 \cdot 2 \cdot 3 \cdot 3 \cdot 3$$

$$120 = 2 \cdot 2 \cdot 2 \cdot 3 \cdot 5$$

$$\therefore \text{GCF} = 2 \cdot 2 \cdot 3 = 12$$

The GCF is formed by multiplying all common prime factors as many times as they occur.

If two integers have *no* common prime factors, their GCF is 1. Such numbers are said to be **relatively prime.** For example,

$$10 = 2 \cdot 5$$

$$21 = 3 \cdot 7.$$

Both 10 and 21 are composite. But they have no *common* prime factors. Their GCF is 1.

Expressions with variables can have common factors, too. For instance,

$$x^5 = x \cdot x \cdot x \cdot x \cdot x$$

$$x^3 = x \cdot x \cdot x$$

$$\text{GCF} = x \cdot x \cdot x = x^3.$$

In this section you will practice finding the greatest common factor of given pairs of expressions.

Objective

Given two integers or two expressions with powers of variables, write the greatest common factor of the expressions.

Cover the answers as you work these examples.

EXAMPLE 1

Find the GCF of 12 and 15.

Think These Reasons

GCF = 3	$12 = 2 \cdot 2 \cdot 3$	The 3s are common factors.
	$15 = 3 \cdot 5$	

EXAMPLE 2

Find the GCF of 540 and 2250.

$540 = 2 \cdot 2 \cdot 3 \cdot 3 \cdot 3 \cdot 5$

$2250 = 2 \cdot 3 \cdot 3 \cdot 5 \cdot 5 \cdot 5$

$\text{GCF} = 2 \cdot 3 \cdot 3 \cdot 5$

$= \underline{\underline{90}}$

540	2250
2)540	2)2250
2)270	3)1125
3)135	3)375
3)45	5)125
3)15	5)25
5	5

EXAMPLE 3

Find the GCF of 32 and 45.

$32 = 2 \cdot 2 \cdot 2 \cdot 2 \cdot 2$

$45 = 3 \cdot 3 \cdot 5$

$\underline{\underline{\text{GCF} = 1}}$

32 and 45 are relatively prime.

EXAMPLE 4

Find the GCF of y^7 and y^4.

$y^7 = y \cdot y \cdot y \cdot y \cdot y \cdot y \cdot y$

$y^4 = y \cdot y \cdot y \cdot y$

$\underline{\underline{\text{GCF} = y^4}}$

Note: You could do this problem more quickly by observing that the GCF always contains the power with the *smaller* exponent.

EXAMPLE 5

Find the GCF of x^4y^7 and x^5y^3.

$\underline{\underline{\text{GCF} = x^4y^3}}$

$x^4y^7 = x \cdot x \cdot x \cdot x \cdot y \cdot y \cdot y \cdot y \cdot y \cdot y \cdot y$

$x^5y^3 = x \cdot x \cdot x \cdot x \cdot x \cdot y \cdot y \cdot y$

There are 4 common x-factors and 3 common y-factors.

EXAMPLE 6

Find the GCF of x^7y^5 and x^2z^4.

- - - - -

GCF $= x^2$

There are 2 common x-factors.
The y and z are not *common* factors.

EXAMPLE 7

Find the GCF of $24x^3y^5$ and $36x^4y$.

- - - - -

GCF $= 12x^3y$

The GCF of 24 and 36 is 12.
There are 3 common x-factors and 1 common y-factor.

EXAMPLE 8

Find the GCF of the two terms in $12x^3 - 18xy^2$.

- - - - -

GCF $= 6x$

The GCF of 12 and 18 is 6.
There is one common x-factor.
y is not a common factor.

ORAL PRACTICE

Give the GCF of these numbers. If the GCF is 1, also give *relatively prime*.

A. 8 and 12

B. 9 and 15

C. 10 and 15

D. 12 and 15

E. 12 and 16

F. 9 and 16

G. 4 and 10

H. 5 and 10

I. 6 and 10

J. 6 and 12

K. 6 and 15

L. 8 and 15

EXERCISE 10-2

1. Write from memory the definition of greatest common factor.
2. Tell what it means for two numbers to be relatively prime. Explain why two composite numbers can be relatively prime to each other.

For Problems 3 through 20, write the GCF of the given pair of numbers. Do the work mentally wherever possible. If the GCF equals 1, also write *relatively prime*.

3. 12 and 18
4. 16 and 20
5. 20 and 24
6. 24 and 30
7. 22 and 33
8. 18 and 21
9. 35 and 12
10. 22 and 9
11. 54 and 36
12. 56 and 32
13. 600 and 450
14. 252 and 588
15. 270 and 225
16. 315 and 189
17. 189 and 220
18. 225 and 308
19. 1000 and 1500
20. 2000 and 2100

For Problems 21 through 40, write the GCF of the two expressions.

21. x^5 and x^3
22. x^6 and x^5
23. a^7 and a^9
24. r^3 and r^7
25. b^6 and b^9
26. c^8 and c^{12}
27. x^2y^3 and x^5y^2
28. x^4y^2 and x^3y^7
29. $r^{10}s^{11}$ and r^9s^{13}
30. $a^{12}h^{13}$ and a^9h^7
31. $10x^6$ and $5x^4$
32. $12x^5$ and $6x^8$
33. $16m^2$ and $20m^3$
34. $20m^4$ and $24m^3$
35. $18a^3b^8$ and $21ab^6$
36. $18c^3d^4$ and $12c^6d$
37. $56c^3d^2$ and $32c^3e^2$
38. $54x^4z^2$ and $36y^2z^3$
39. $24x^2y^3z^4$ and $30x^5y^4z^3$
40. $22a^3b^5c$ and $55ab^4c^7$

For Problems 41 through 50, find the GCF of the two terms in the expression.

41. $6x^3 + 9x^2$
42. $10x^2 + 15x^3$
43. $4a^2 - 8a^5$
44. $7b^5 - 14b^6$
45. $3c^8 - 12c^5$
46. $7d^9 - 21d^4$
47. $10x^2y^4 + 15x^3y$
48. $8x^5y^2 + 12xy^3$
49. $x^{12} - x^8$
50. $y^{15} - y^{10}$

For Problems 51 through 60, find the GCF of the three numbers. In order to be a common factor, a number must be a factor of all three given numbers. If there are no factors common to all three, also write *relatively prime*.

51. 24, 18, and 42
52. 24, 32, and 40
53. 50, 75, and 60
54. 36, 54, and 60
55. 12, 15, and 35.
56. 50, 65, and 39
57. 100, 120, and 150
58. 200, 300, and 250
59. 720, 108, and 1800
60. 324, 540, and 1080

10-3 FACTORING POLYNOMIALS THAT HAVE COMMON FACTORS

Suppose you had to factor $4x^2 + 40x + 84$. The x^2-coefficient does not equal 1. So you might start by writing $(4x + \quad)(x + \quad)$ or $(2x + \quad)(2x + \quad)$ and looking for the right factors of 84 to fill in the spaces.

However, if you *think* before you start to work, you will see that each term of $4x^2 + 40x + 84$ has 4 as a common factor. Using the distributive axiom, you can factor 4 from each term, as you did in Section 3.4.

$$4x^2 + 40x + 84$$
$$= 4(x^2 + 10x + 21)$$

The trinomial $x^2 + 10x + 21$ is much easier to factor than the original polynomial. You get

$$4(x + 3)(x + 7).$$

In this form the polynomial is said to be *completely factored*. The operations with fractions in the next chapter rely upon factoring polynomials completely.

TECHNIQUE

FIRST STEP IN FACTORING
The first step in factoring any polynomial is to factor the GCF of the terms from the polynomial.

Objective

Given a polynomial whose terms have common factors, be able to factor the polynomial completely.

Cover the answers as you work these examples.

EXAMPLE 1

Factor completely: $3x^2 + 30x + 48$.

Think These Reasons

$3x^2 + 30x + 48$	Write the given expression.
$= 3(x^2 + 10x + 16)$	Factor out the GCF of the three terms.
$= \underline{3(x + 2)(x + 8)}$	2 and 8 are the two *factors* of 16 whose *sum* is 10.

EXAMPLE 2

Factor completely: $15x^2 - 5x - 10$.

$15x^2 - 5x - 10$	Write the given expression.
$= 5(3x^2 - x - 2)$	Factor out 5.
$= \underline{5(3x + 2)(x - 1)}$	First terms are $3x$ and x. Last terms, 2 and -1, give $-x$ and -2 when the binomials are multiplied.

EXAMPLE 3

Factor completely: $7x^2 - 63$.

$7x^2 - 63$	Write the given expression.
$= 7(x^2 - 9)$	Factor out 7.
$= \underline{7(x + 3)(x - 3)}$	Factor a difference of two squares. (See Section 5-7.)

EXAMPLE 4

Factor completely: $3x^5 + 6x^4y - 45x^3y^2$.

$3x^5 + 6x^4y - 45x^3y^2$	Write the given expression.
$= 3x^3(x^2 + 2xy - 15y^2)$	Factor out the GCF, $3x^3$. (The GCF may contain a variable!)
$= \underline{\underline{3x^3(x - 3y)(x + 5y)}}$	-3 and 5 are two factors of -15 whose sum is 2. (Do not forget y in the second terms.)

ORAL PRACTICE

Give the result of factoring out the GCF.

EXAMPLE

	Answer
$2x^3 + 6x^2 - 8x$	$2x$ times the quantity $x^2 + 3x - 4$.

A. $3x^2 + 12x + 9$

B. $4x^2 + 8x + 20$

C. $4x^2 + 10x + 20$

D. $6x^2 + 9x + 30$

E. $6x^2 + 8x + 30$

F. $7x^2 - 14x + 28$

G. $x^3 - 4x^2 + 3x$

H. $y^3 + 8y^2 - 7y$

I. $x^5 + 7x^4 + 9x^3$

J. $a^8 - 5a^7 - 4a^6$

K. $x^3y^3 - xy$

L. $x^3y - xy^3$

EXERCISE 10-3

Factor completely.

1. $2x^2 + 16x + 30$
2. $3x^2 + 21x + 30$
3. $3x^2 + 30x + 72$
4. $4x^2 + 28x + 48$
5. $4x^2 + 4x - 24$
6. $5x^2 + 35x - 40$
7. $5r^2 - 10r - 175$
8. $10s^2 - 40s - 210$
9. $2x^2 + 14xy + 24y^2$
10. $2x^2 + 12xy + 16y^2$
11. $6x^2 - 24x + 18$
12. $6x^2 - 54x + 120$
13. $10s^2 + 110s - 120$
14. $8p^2 + 32p - 96$
15. $8a^2 - 16ab - 120b^2$
16. $7r^2 - 42rs - 112s^2$

17. $x^4 - 8x^3 + 12x^2$
18. $x^6 - 9x^5 + 18x^4$
19. $2c^5 + 6c^4 - 8c^3$
20. $3a^5 + 12a^4 - 15a^3$
21. $4x^2 - 100$
22. $2x^2 - 98$
23. $5x^2 - 180$
24. $10x^2 - 250$
25. $7x^3 - 7x$
26. $11a^3 - 11a$
27. $10x^2 - 90y^2$
28. $3x^2 - 27y^2$
29. $x^3y - xy^3$
30. $r^3s - rs^3$
31. $6x^2 - 48x + 96$
32. $7x^2 - 70x + 175$
33. $2m^2 + 20mp + 50p^2$
34. $9b^2 + 72bc + 144c^2$
35. $3ax^2 + 36ax + 60a$
36. $5dx^2 + 50dx + 80d$
37. $6c^2x^2 - 600d^2x^2$
38. $8p^2x^2 - 392p^2s^2$
39. $2x^4y^3 - 18x^3y^4 - 72x^2y^5$
40. $3x^6y^2 - 15x^5y^3 - 150x^4y^4$
41. $6x^2 + 21x + 15$
42. $6x^2 + 44x + 14$
43. $15x^2 + 40x - 15$
44. $12x^2 + 18x - 30$
45. $20e^2 - 28e + 8$
46. $15c^2 - 48c + 9$
47. $18x^2 - 24xy - 24y^2$
48. $16x^2 - 24xy - 72y^2$
49. $4y^6 - 18y^5 + 8y^4$
50. $15z^5 - 65z^4 + 20z^3$

10-4 COMMON BINOMIAL FACTORS

You have learned how to use the distributive properties to factor out common factors. For instance,

$$3x + 12 = 3(x + 4).$$

The number 3 is a common factor of each term. Sometimes, terms of an expression have common factors that are binomials, such as in

$$(x - 5)x + (x - 5)(4).$$

In this case the binomial $(x - 5)$ is a common factor of each term. It can be factored out in the same way 3 was in the first example.

$$(x - 5)x + (x - 5)(4)$$
$$= (x - 5)(x + 4).$$

Factoring $(x - 5)$ out of the first term leaves x and factoring $(x - 5)$ out of the second term leaves 4. So the other factor is $(x + 4)$, just as it was in the first example.

Objective

Be able to factor a polynomial that has common binomial factors.

Cover the answers as you work these examples.

EXAMPLE 1

Factor $(x + 7)x - (x + 7)(12)$.

- - - - -

Think These Reasons

$(x + 7)x - (x + 7)(12)$ — Write the given expression.

$= \underline{\underline{(x + 7)(x - 12)}}$ — Factor out $(x + 7)$ from each term. x remains from one term and -12 remains from the other.

EXAMPLE 2

Factor $x(x - 2) + 6(x - 2)$.

- - - - -

$x(x - 2) + 6(x - 2)$ — Write the given expression.

$= \underline{\underline{(x - 2)(x + 6)}}$ — Factor out $(x - 2)$ from each term. x remains from one term and 6 remains from the other.

EXAMPLE 3

Factor $2a(3r + 5) - 7b(3r + 5)$.

- - - - -

$2a(3r + 5) - 7b(3r + 5)$ — Write the given expression.

$= \underline{\underline{(3r + 5)(2a - 7b)}}$ — Factor out $(3r + 5)$. $2a$ remains from one term and $-7b$ remains from the other.

EXAMPLE 4

Factor $3x(5x - 8) - (5x - 8)$.

- - - - -

$3x(5x - 8) - (5x - 8)$ — Write the given expression.

$= \underline{\underline{(5x - 8)(3x - 1)}}$ — Factor out $(5x - 8)$. $3x$ remains from one term. -1 remains from the other, because $-(5x - 8) \div (5x - 8)$ equals -1.

EXAMPLE 5

Factor completely: $x^2(2x + 5) - 36(2x + 5)$.

$x^2(2x + 5) - 36(2x + 5)$	Write the given expression.
$= (2x + 5)(x^2 - 36)$	Factor out $(2x + 5)$.
$= \underline{\underline{(2x + 5)(x + 6)(x - 6)}}$	Factor $x^2 - 36$ as a difference of two squares. Each factor is now prime, so the expression is factored completely.

ORAL PRACTICE

Give the common binomial factor.

EXAMPLES

	Answers
i. $(x + 5)x + (x + 5)y$	ii. The quantity $x + 5$.
ii. $(x + 6)x + (x + 5)y$	ii. No common factors.

A. $(x + 3)x + (x + 3)y$

B. $(x - 7)x + (x - 7)y$

C. $a(x + 2) - b(x + 2)$

D. $c(x - 4) - d(x - 4)$

E. $k(x - 6) + (x - 6)p$

F. $(x + 9)j - k(x + 9)$

G. $(x - 3)y + (x - 4)z$

H. $(x + 5)r - (x - 5)s$

I. $x(x - 1) + 6(x - 1)$

J. $x(x + 8) - 7(x + 8)$

K. $(x + 2)(x + 3) + 5(x + 2)$

L. $(x - 4)(x - 1) - 6(x - 1)$

EXERCISE 10-4

For Problems 1 through 30, factor the polynomial completely.

1. $(x + 2)x + (x + 2)(10)$
2. $(x + 3)x + (x + 3)(5)$
3. $(x - 5)x - (x - 5)(8)$
4. $(x - 7)x + (x - 7)(9)$
5. $x(x + 4) - 7(x + 4)$
6. $x(x + 8) - 2(x + 8)$
7. $3x(x - 21) + 4(x - 21)$
8. $5x(x - 6) + 3(x - 6)$
9. $6r(2r - 9) - 3(2r - 9)$
10. $6b(3s - 2) - 4(3s - 2)$
11. $7a(4a + b) - 6(4a + b)$
12. $4p(3p + j) - 7(3p + j)$

13. $12(3x - 1) + x(3x - 1)$
14. $13(2x - 5) + x(2x - 5)$
15. $6x(x + 3) + (x + 3)$
16. $3x(x - 4) + (x - 4)$
17. $m(8m - 5) - (8m - 5)$
18. $k(6k - 1) - (6k - 1)$
19. $(3x - 7) + 2x(3x - 7)$
20. $(4x - 5) + 3x(4x - 5)$
21. $p(x - j) - k(x - j)$
22. $y(r + c) - k(r + c)$
23. $x^2(x + 4) - 9(x + 4)$
24. $x^2(x - 7) - 49(x - 7)$
25. $a^2(r - 5) - b^2(r - 5)$
26. $c^2(s - 2) - d^2(s - 2)$
27. $x^2(a^2 - 4) - y^2(a^2 - 4)$
28. $x^2(y^2 - 25) - z^2(y^2 - 25)$
29. $x^2(16 - r^2) - (16 - r^2)$
30. $x^2(9 - v^2) - (9 - v^2)$

For Problems 31 through 50, factor out the common polynomial factor and simplify the result as much as possible. Factor further, if possible.

31. $x(x + 3) + (x - 5)(x + 3)$
32. $x(x + 2) + (x - 3)(x + 2)$
33. $x(2x - 7) + (2x - 7)(x + 6)$
34. $x(3x - 5) + (3x - 5)(x + 4)$
35. $(3a + 4)(5x - 2) - (3a + 4)$
36. $(2r + 11)(x - 3) - (2r + 11)$
37. $x^2(x + 7) + (5x + 6)(x + 7)$
38. $x^2(x - 4) + (9x + 14)(x - 4)$
39. $x^2(2x - 1) - (2x - 1)(3x + 4)$
40. $x^2(5x + 1) - (5x + 1)(3x - 2)$
41. $x^2(5y - z) - (12x - 20)(5y - z)$
42. $x^2(a - 2b) - (7x - 10)(a - 2b)$
43. $x(x^2 + 6x + 5) + 2(x^2 + 6x + 5)$
44. $x(x^2 - 3x - 28) - 3(x^2 - 3x - 28)$
45. $x(x^2 - 6x + 9) - 3(x^2 - 6x + 9)$
46. $x(x^2 + 4x + 4) + 2(x^2 + 4x + 4)$
47. $x^3(x + 3) - 25x(x + 3)$
48. $x^5(x - 7) - 9x^3(x - 7)$
49. $(x + 2)(x^2 + x + 1) - (x + 2)$
50. $(x - 3)(x^2 + 3x + 1) - (x - 3)$

For Problems 51 through 60, factor the polynomials (if necessary). Then give the greatest common factor (GCF) of the two polynomials.

EXAMPLE

$(x + 4)(x - 1)$ and $(x - 1)(x + 2)$
GCF $= (x - 1)$

51. $x^2 + 3x + 2$ and $x + 1$

52. $x^2 + 5x + 6$ and $x + 3$

53. $x^2 + 2x - 8$ and $x^2 - 3x + 2$

54. $x^2 - 7x + 10$ and $x^2 - x - 2$

55. $x^2 - x - 6$ and $x^2 + x - 6$

56. $x^2 - 7x + 12$ and $x^2 + 3x - 4$

57. $x^2 - 9$ and $x^2 + 2x - 15$

58. $x^2 - 25$ and $x^2 - 8x + 15$

59. $(x + 1)(x - 2)(x + 3)$ and $(x + 1)(x + 3)(x - 5)$

60. $(x + 2)(x - 2)(x - 7)$ and $(x - 7)(x + 7)(x - 2)$

10-5 FACTORING BY GROUPING (ASSOCIATING)

In the last section you learned how to factor polynomials that have common binomial factors, such as

$$2a(3r + 5) - 7b(3r + 5)$$
$$= (3r + 5)(2a - 7b).$$

Suppose that you are asked to factor

$$6ar + 10a - 21br - 35b.$$

The first two terms have $2a$ as a common factor. The last two terms have $-7b$ as a common factor. Associating terms and then doing the factoring gives

$6ar + 10a - 21br - 35b$	Given expression.
$= (6ar + 10a) + (-21br - 35b)$	Associate terms.
$= 2a(3r + 5) - 7b(3r + 5)$	Factor out $2a$ and $-7b$.
$= (3r + 5)(2a - 7b).$	Factor out $(3r + 5)$.

As you can see, the next-to-last line is the same as the first example. All that is new is associating pairs of terms and factoring out their greatest common factor. This technique is called **factoring by grouping,** or **factoring by associating**.

Objective

Given a polynomial with four terms, be able to factor it by grouping (associating).

Cover the answers as you work these examples.

EXAMPLE 1

Factor completely: $x^2 + 2x + xy + 2y$.

– – – – –　　　　– – – – –

	Think These Reasons
$x^2 + 2x + xy + 2y$	Write the given expression.
$= x(x + 2) + y(x + 2)$	Factor x from $x^2 + 2x$ and factor y from $xy + 2y$.
$= \underline{\underline{(x + 2)(x + y)}}$	Factor out $(x + 2)$.

EXAMPLE 2

Factor completely: $15x^2 - 6ax - 20cx + 8ac$.

– – – – – – – – – –

$15x^2 - 6ax - 20cx + 8ac$	Write the given expression.
$= 3x(5x - 2a) - 4c(5x - 2a)$	Factor $3x$ from $15x^2 - 6ax$ and factor $-4c$ from $-20cx + 8ac$. (When you factor $-4c$ out of $+8ac$, you get $-2a$, not $+2a$!)
$= \underline{\underline{(5x - 2a)(3x - 4c)}}$	Factor out $(5x - 2a)$.

EXAMPLE 3

Factor completely: $ax + 3a + x + 3$.

– – – – – – – – – –

$ax + 3a + x + 3$	Write the given expression.
$= a(x + 3) + 1(x + 3)$	Factor a from $ax + 3a$ and factor 1 from $x + 3$.
$= \underline{\underline{(x + 3)(a + 1)}}$	Factor out $(x + 3)$.

EXAMPLE 4

Factor completely: $x^3 - 5x^2 - 9x + 45$.

– – – – – – – – – –

$x^3 - 5x^2 - 9x + 45$	Write the given expression.
$= x^2(x - 5) - 9(x - 5)$	Factor x^2 from $x^3 - 5x^2$ and factor -9 from $-9x + 45$.
$= (x - 5)(x^2 - 9)$	Factor out $(x - 5)$.
$= \underline{\underline{(x - 5)(x + 3)(x - 3)}}$	To factor completely, factor $x^2 - 9$ as a difference of two squares.

EXAMPLE 5

Factor completely: $15x^2 - 12x + 10x - 8$.

– – – – – – – – – –

$15x^2 - 12x + 10x - 8$	Write the given expression.
$= 3x(5x - 4) + 2(5x - 4)$	Factor $3x$ from $15x^2 - 12x$ and factor 2 from $10x - 8$. Do *not* combine like terms.
$= \underline{\underline{(5x - 4)(3x + 2)}}$	Factor out $(5x - 4)$.

ORAL PRACTICE

Tell what you would factor out of the first two terms and what you would factor out of the last two terms to factor by grouping.

EXAMPLES

	Answers
i. $3ax + ab - 6x - 2b$	i. $a, -2$
ii. $6x - 2c - 3x + c$	ii. $2, -1$

A. $ax + bx + ay + by$

B. $x^2 + xy + xz + yz$

C. $ax - 2x + ay - 2y$

D. $3x - 3y - ax + ay$

E. $ac + bc - a^2 - ab$

F. $a^2c + a^2d + b^2c + b^2d$

G. $x^3 + 3x^2 + 2x + 6$

H. $x^3 - 5x^2 - 3x + 15$

I. $2a + ax - 2x^2 - x^3$

J. $x^2 - 2x + xy - 2y$

K. $5ax + 10a - x - 2$

L. $6a^2 + 5ab + 6a + 5b$

EXERCISE 10-5

In Problems 1 through 34, factor the polynomial completely.

1. $a^2 + 3a + ab + 3b$
2. $r^2 + 7r + rc + 7c$
3. $8x^2 + 12xy + 10xz + 15yz$
4. $15x^2 + 20xy + 18nx + 24ny$
5. $bx + 3cx - 2br - 6cr$
6. $ax + 4ex - 3ad - 12de$
7. $6ax - 14x + 15a - 35$
8. $9hx - 21x + 6h - 14$
9. $mc - 6cv - 5m + 30v$
10. $rv - 2vx - 6r + 12x$
11. $x^2 + 5xy + x + 5y$
12. $x^2 + 8xz + x + 8z$
13. $5rz + 2sz - 5r - 2s$
14. $6dt + 5ct - 6d - 5c$

15. $30ab + 36a + 70b + 84$

16. $24mx + 36m + 30x + 45$

17. $2x^3 - 3x^2 - 4x + 6$

18. $10x^3 - 15x^2 + 2x - 3$

19. $12x^3 + 45x^2 + 32x + 120$

20. $2x^3 - 7x^2 - 10x + 35$

21. $24x^3 - 18x^2 + 60x - 45$

22. $64x^3 - 160x^2 + 24x - 60$

23. $2x^3 + x^2 - 18x - 9$

24. $3x^3 + x^2 - 75x - 25$

25. $5x^3 - 10x^2 - 80x + 160$

26. $6x^3 - 6x^2 - 24x + 24$

27. $12x^2 + 18x + 10x + 15$

28. $15x^2 + 21x + 25x + 35$

29. $2x^2 - 3x + 14x - 21$

30. $8x^2 - 6x + 12x - 9$

31. $15x^2 - 6x + 5x - 2$

32. $16x^2 - 10x + 8x - 5$

33. $8x^2 - 3x - 8x + 3$

34. $10x^2 - 7x - 10x + 7$

In Problems 35 through 54, some of the polynomials can be arranged in groups of three terms and one term, or one term and three terms. For instance,

$$x^2 + 6x + 9 - y^2 = (x + 3)^2 - y^2,$$

which is a difference of two squares. Other polynomials have more than four terms. For instance,

$$x^2 + 5x + 6 - ax - 3a = (x + 3)(x + 2) - a(x + 3),$$

which has $(x + 3)$ as a common binomial factor. Factor each of these polynomials completely.

35. $x^2 + 6x + 9 - y^2$

36. $x^2 + 8x + 16 - c^2$

37. $x^2 - 10x + 25 - 9a^2$

38. $x^2 - 14x + 49 - 16y^2$

39. $x^2 - (y^2 + 8y + 16)$

40. $x^2 - (a^2 + 10a + 25)$

41. $25x^2 - a^2 + 4a - 4$

42. $100x^2 - y^2 + 6y - 9$

43. $x^2 - 10x + 25 - 49c^2$

44. $x^2 - 8x + 16 - 25b^2$

45. $x^2 + 5x + 6 - ax - 3a$

46. $x^2 + 9x + 20 - rx - 4r$

47. $x^2 + 2x - 3 + rx + 3r$

48. $x^2 + 4x - 5 + sx + 5s$

49. $3sx + 15s + x^2 + 3x - 10$

50. $2mx + 6m + x^2 + x - 6$

51. $x^4 - 2x^3 + x^2 + 3x - 10$

52. $x^4 - 5x^3 + x^2 + x - 30$

53. $cx^2 + 8cx + 15c + dx^2 - 2dx - 35d$

54. $ux^2 + 9ux + 14u + zx^2 - 3zx - 10z$

10-6 FACTORING HARDER QUADRATIC TRINOMIALS

Suppose you have to factor

$$6x^2 + 31x + 35.$$

There are so many possible factors to try that you could spend a whole evening on one set of problems! What you need is a systematic way to factor these harder quadratic trinomials.

In Problems 27 through 34 of the last section, you factored polynomials like

$$6x^2 + 10x + 21x + 35$$

by grouping. Associating the first two terms and the last two terms gives

$$(6x^2 + 10x) + (21x + 35).$$

Factoring out $2x$ from $6x^2 + 10x$ and 7 from $21x + 35$ gives

$$2x(3x + 5) + 7(3x + 5).$$

Now, $(3x + 5)$ is a common binomial factor and can be factored out, giving

$$(3x + 5)(2x + 7).$$

Suppose that you have to factor the quadratic trinomial

$$6x^2 + 31x + 35.$$

If you could split the middle term, $31x$, into $10x + 21x$, you could factor as above. Observe that (10)(21) equals 210, and that (6)(35) also equals 210. This is true because when you multiply $(3x + 5)(2x + 7)$, you get

$$(3x + 5)(2x + 7) = (3 \cdot 2)x^2 + (5 \cdot 2)x + (3 \cdot 7)x + (5 \cdot 7).$$

5, 2, 3, 7

3, 2, 5, 7

All four coefficients—3, 2, 5, and 7—appear in the 6 and 35. All four also appear in the 10 and 21. So 10 and 21 are two *factors* of 210 that *add* up to 31. To factor

$$6x^2 + 31x + 35$$

from scratch, you would first *multiply* (6)(35), getting 210. Then you would look for *other* factors of 210—specifically, factors that add up to 31. A systematic way of looking for these factors is to make a table.

Factors	Sum	31?
1, 210	211	No.
2, 105	107	No.
3, 70	73	No.
5, 42	47	No.
6, 35	41	No.
7,30	37	No.
10, 21	31	Yes!

So you split the middle term, $31x$, into $10x + 21x$, write

$$6x^2 + 10x + 21x + 35,$$

and factor by grouping as shown above.

TECHNIQUE

SPLITTING THE MIDDLE TERM
To factor a quadratic trinomial of the form

$$ax^2 + bx + c:$$

1. Multiply a by c.
2. Look for two factors of ac whose sum is b.
3. Split the middle term and factor by grouping.

(If there are *no* factors of ac whose sum is b, then $ax^2 + bx + c$ is *prime*.)

You should always be alert for easier ways of working problems. For instance,

$$3x^2 + 5x + 2$$

is easy to factor by inspection, without splitting the middle term. You just write empty parentheses and then fill in the binomials that give $3x^2 + 5x + 2$ when they are multiplied back together.

$$3x^2 + 5x + 2$$
$$= (3x + 2)(x + 1)$$

Objective

Given a quadratic trinomial, such as $6x^2 + 31x + 35$, factor it by inspection or by splitting the middle term.

Cover the answers as you work the examples.

EXAMPLE 1

Factor $8x^2 + 26x + 15$.

- - - - -

Think These Reasons

$(8)(15) = 120$ — Multiply the x^2-coefficient by the constant term.

$1 + 120 = 121$ — Seek two factors of 120 whose sum is 26.
$2 + 60 = 62$
$3 + 40 = 43$
$4 + 30 = 34$
$5 + 24 = 29$
$6 + 20 = 26$ This is it!

$8x^2 + 26x + 15$ — Write the given expression.

$= 8x^2 + 6x + 20x + 15$ — Split the middle term.

$= 2x(4x + 3) + 5(4x + 3)$ — Factor $2x$ from $8x^2 + 6x$ and factor 5 from $20x + 15$.

$= \underline{\underline{(4x + 3)(2x + 5)}}$ — Factor out $(4x + 3)$.

EXAMPLE 2

Factor $18x^2 - 23x - 6$.

- - - - -

$(18)(-6) = -108$ — Multiply the x^2-coefficient by the constant term.

$1 - 108 = -107$ — Seek two factors of -108 whose sum is -23.
$2 - 54 = -52$
$3 - 36 = -33$
$4 - 27 = -23$ This is it!

$18x^2 - 23x - 6$ — Write the given expression.

$= 18x^2 + 4x - 27x - 6$ — Split the middle term

$= 2x(9x + 2) - 3(9x + 2)$ — Factor out $2x$ and -3.

$= \underline{\underline{(9x + 2)(2x - 3)}}$ — Factor out $(9x + 2)$.

EXAMPLE 3

Factor $3x^2 - 19x + 16$.

- - - - -

$(3)(16) = 48$	Multiply the x^2-coefficient by the constant term.
$-1 - 48 = -49$ $-2 - 24 = -26$ $-3 - 16 = -19$ This is it!	Seek two factors of $+48$ whose sum is -19. Both must be *negative.*
$3x^2 - 19x + 16$	Write the given expression.
$= 3x^2 - 3x - 16x + 16$	Split the middle term.
$= 3x(x - 1) - 16(x - 1)$	Factor out $3x$ and -16.
$= \underline{\underline{(x - 1)(3x - 16)}}$	Factor out $x - 1$.

EXAMPLE 4

Factor $10x^2 + 21x + 6$.

\- - - - -

$(10)(6) = 60$	Multiply the x^2-coefficient by the constant term.
$1 + 60 = 61$	Seek two factors of 60 whose sum is 21.
$2 + 30 = 32$ $3 + 20 = 23$ $4 + 15 = 19$ Skips 21!	
$\therefore$ $\underline{\underline{10x^2 + 21x + 6 \text{ is prime.}}}$	*No* integer factors of 60 add up to 21.

Note: This is how to use the technique of splitting the middle term to tell whether or not a quadratic trinomial will factor.

EXAMPLE 5

Factor $2x^2 + 9x - 5$.

\- - - - -

$2x^2 + 9x - 5$	Write the given expression.
$= \underline{\underline{(2x - 1)(x + 5)}}$	Factor by inspection. This one is easy to do without splitting the middle term.

EXAMPLE 6

Factor $20x^2 + 30x - 200$.

\- - - - -

$20x^2 + 30x - 200$	Write the given expression.

$= 10(2x^2 + 3x - 20)$ — Factor out 10, the GCF of the terms. (Remember, factor out *common* factors *first*!)

$= \underline{\underline{10(2x - 5)(x + 4)}}$ — Factor $2x^2 + 3x - 20$ by inspection.

ORAL PRACTICE

Are these middle terms split correctly? Explain.

EXAMPLES

i. $2x^2 - 5x + 3 = 2x^2 - 3x - 2x + 3$
Yes; $(2)(3) = 6$, $(-3)(-2) = 6$, and $-3 - 2 = -5$.

ii. $2x^2 - 5x + 3 = 2x^2 - 3x + 2x + 3$
No; $(2)(3) = 6$, but $(-3)(2) = -6$, or
no; $-3 + 2$ equals -1, not -5.

A. $3x^2 + 7x + 2 = 3x^2 + x + 6x + 2$

B. $3x^2 + 7x + 2 = 3x^2 + 6x + x + 2$

C. $2x^2 + 11x + 15 = 2x^2 + 5x + 6x + 15$

D. $3x^2 + 10x - 8 = 3x^2 - 2x + 12x - 8$

E. $3x^2 - 10x - 8 = 3x^2 + 2x + 12x - 8$

F. $6x^2 + 11x + 5 = 6x^2 + 5x + 6x + 5$

G. $6x^2 + 13x + 5 = 6x^2 + 10x + 3x + 5$

H. $6x^2 + 17x + 5 = 6x^2 + 10x + 3x + 5$

I. $6x^2 + 17x + 5 = 6x^2 + 3x + 14x + 5$

J. $6x^2 + 17x + 5 = 6x^2 + 2x + 15x + 5$

EXERCISE 10-6

For Problems 1 through 20, use the technique of splitting the middle term to factor the polynomial completely or show it is prime.

1. $3x^2 + 16x + 16$
2. $2x^2 + 15x + 18$
3. $6x^2 + 23x + 20$
4. $6x^2 + 25x + 25$
5. $2x^2 + 11x - 90$
6. $3x^2 + 20x + 40$

7. $20x^2 - 43x - 12$
8. $30x^2 - 67x - 12$
9. $9x^2 - 39x + 40$
10. $3x^2 + 37x - 70$
11. $4x^2 + 7x + 18$
12. $10x^2 - 51x + 54$
13. $24x^2 + 19xy + 2y^2$
14. $12x^2 + 145xy + 12y^2$
15. $4r^2 - 9rs + 5s^2$
16. $8p^2 - 17pj + 9j^2$
17. $48x^2 - 40x - 48$
18. $24x^2 - 66x - 18$
19. $-12x^2 - 33x + 45$
20. $-80x^2 - 290x + 120$

For Problems 21 through 50, factor the polynomial completely, either by inspection (preferably) or by splitting the middle term.

21. $2x^2 + 7x + 3$
22. $3x^2 + 7x + 2$
23. $3x^2 + 10x + 8$
24. $3x^2 + 11x + 8$
25. $5x^2 - 21x + 4$
26. $7x^2 - 16x + 4$
27. $6x^2 + 7x - 5$
28. $6x^2 + 5x - 4$
29. $6x^2 - x - 5$
30. $6x^2 - 17x - 3$
31. $6r^2 + 13rs + 6s^2$
32. $6a^2 + 11ab + 4b^2$
33. $15a^2 + 16ab + 4b^2$
34. $6x^2 + 19xy + 15y^2$
35. $6m^2 - 25m + 4$
36. $4r^2 - 25r + 6$
37. $2m^2 + 15m - 50$
38. $5p^2 - 8p - 4$
39. $4x^2 + 36x + 32$
40. $6x^2 + 36x + 48$
41. $7x^2 - 6xy - y^2$
42. $9c^2 - 8cd - d^2$
43. $8x^5 + 2x^4 - 3x^3$
44. $18x^7 - 9x^6 - 2x^5$
45. $2a^3x - 13a^2x^2 + 15ax^3$
46. $4u^3v - 12u^2v^2 + 9uv^3$
47. $27ru^2 + 36ru + 12r$
48. $10sn^2 - 75sn - 135s$
49. $12(x + 3)x^2 - 2(x + 3)x - 4(x + 3)$
50. $12(x - 2)x^2 - 21(x - 2)x - 6(x - 2)$

10-7 SOLVING QUADRATIC EQUATIONS BY FACTORING

In Chapter 6 you learned how to use the Quadratic Formula to solve equations like

$$x^2 - x - 2 = 0.$$

You also know how to factor quadratic trinomials like

$$x^2 - x - 2.$$

It is time to put these two ideas together and come up with a quick way to solve certain kinds of quadratic equations.

Starting with

$$x^2 - x - 2 = 0,$$

you can factor the left member to get

$$(x - 2)(x + 1) = 0.$$

In this form, the equation says that a *product* of two numbers equals *zero*. But the only way a product can equal zero is for one of its *factors* to be zero. So the equation can be transformed to

$$x - 2 = 0 \quad \text{or} \quad x + 1 = 0.$$

This transformation changes one hard problem into two easy problems. Adding 2 in the first clause and subtracting 1 in the second gives

$$x = 2 \quad \text{or} \quad x = -1.$$

$$\therefore S = \{2, -1\}$$

The fact that zero times a number equals zero is called the *multiplication property of zero*.

MULTIPLICATION PROPERTY OF ZERO
If one factor of a product is 0, then the product equals 0. That is, for any real number n,

$$n \cdot 0 = 0 \quad \text{or} \quad 0 \cdot n = 0.$$

The fact that a product can be zero *only* if one of its factors is zero is called the *converse of the multiplication property of zero*.

CONVERSE OF THE MULTIPLICATION PROPERTY OF ZERO
If a product of real numbers equals zero, then one of its factors equals zero. That is, for real numbers n and p, if $np = 0$, then $n = 0$ or $p = 0$.

Unfortunately, the factoring scheme above does not work if the trinomial cannot be factored. There is a quick way to tell whether or not it will factor. You recall that for the equation

$$ax^2 + bx + c = 0,$$

the Quadratic Formula says that

$$x = \frac{-b \pm \sqrt{b^2 - 4ac}}{2a}.$$

You recall that $b^2 - 4ac$ under the radical sign is called the *discriminant*. For $x^2 - x - 2$, the discriminant is

$$(-1)^2 - 4(1)(-2) = 9.$$

The number 9 happens to be a *perfect square*, 3^2. So $\sqrt{9} = 3$, and the solutions for x will not involve any radicals. This is also the case whenever a trinomial $ax^2 + bx + c$ can be factored.

CONCLUSION

DISCRIMINANT TEST FOR FACTORABILITY
A quadratic trinomial $ax^2 + bx + c$ can be factored if and only if the discriminant, $b^2 - 4ac$, is a perfect square.

Objective

Given a quadratic equation, solve it by factoring, if practical. Otherwise, solve it by the Quadratic Formula.

Cover the answers as you work these examples.

EXAMPLE 1

Solve $(7x - 3)(2x + 5) = 0$.

Think These Reasons

$(7x - 3)(2x + 5) = 0$	Write the given equation.
$7x - 3 = 0$ or $2x + 5 = 0$	A product is 0 only if a factor is 0.
$7x = 3$ or $2x = -5$	Add 3 and add -5.
$x = \frac{3}{7}$ or $x = -\frac{5}{2}$	Divide by 7 and divide by 2.

$\therefore S = \left\{\frac{3}{7}, -\frac{5}{2}\right\}$ Write the solution set.

EXAMPLE 2

Solve $2x^2 - x - 3 = 0$.

- - - - -

$2x^2 - x - 3 = 0$	Write the given equation.
$(2x - 3)(x + 1) = 0$	Factor (by inspection, if you can).
$2x - 3 = 0$ or $x + 1 = 0$	A product is 0 only if a factor is 0.
$2x = 3$ or $x = -1$	Add 3 and add -1.
$x = \frac{3}{2}$ or $x = -1$	Divide by 2.
$\therefore S = \left\{\frac{3}{2}, -1\right\}$	Write the solution set.

EXAMPLE 3

Solve $2x^2 + 15x + 12 = 0$.

- - - - -

$2x^2 + 15x + 12 = 0$	Write the given expression.
$b^2 - 4ac = 15^2 - 4(2)(12)$	Calculate the discriminant.
$= 129$	129 is not a perfect square, so the trinomial cannot be factored.
$x = \frac{-15 \pm \sqrt{129}}{2(2)}$	Use the Quadratic Formula.
$x \approx -0.91$ or -6.59	Do the arithmetic.
$\therefore S = \{-0.91, -6.59\}$	Write the solution set.

EXAMPLE 4

Solve $10x^2 - 83x + 24 = 0$.

- - - - -

$10x^2 - 83x + 24 = 0$	Write the given equation.
$x = \frac{83 \pm \sqrt{6889 - 4(10)(24)}}{2(10)}$	Use the Quadratic Formula. (It would be impractical to factor a trinomial with such big coefficients!)
$x = \frac{83 \pm \sqrt{5929}}{20}$	Do the computation.

$x = \dfrac{83 \pm 77}{20}$	Take the square root. (The trinomial *would* have factored, since 5929 is a perfect square.)
$x = 8 \quad \text{or} \quad \dfrac{3}{10}$	Finish the computation.
$\therefore S = \left\{8, \dfrac{3}{10}\right\}$	Write the solution set.

ORAL PRACTICE

Can the equation be solved by factoring? Explain.

EXAMPLES

	Answers.
i. $3x^2 - 10x - 8 = 0$	i. Yes; $b^2 - 4ac = 196$, a perfect square.
ii. $5x^2 - 11x + 3 = 0$	ii. No; $b^2 - 4ac = 61$, not a perfect square.

A. $x^2 + 8x + 15 = 0$

B. $x^2 - x - 6 = 0$

C. $x^2 + 5x + 3 = 0$

D. $x^2 + 3x + 5 = 0$

E. $x^2 + 3x - 10 = 0$

F. $x^2 + 3x + 10 = 0$

G. $2x^2 + 7x + 6 = 0$

H. $3x^2 - 8x + 5 = 0$

I. $3x^2 + 10x - 8 = 0$

J. $2x^2 + 5x - 10 = 0$

K. $x^2 + 6x + 10 = 0$

L. $4x^2 - 12x + 9 = 0$

EXERCISE 10-7

1. State the multiplication property of zero.
2. State the converse of the multiplication property of zero.

For Problems 3 through 16, solve the equation.

3. $(x - 3)(x - 7) = 0$
4. $(x - 9)(x - 2) = 0$
5. $(3x - 5)(x + 4) = 0$
6. $(4x - 7)(x + 3) = 0$

7. $(7x + 8)(2x - 11) = 0$
8. $(11x + 17)(2x - 13) = 0$
9. $(5x + 13)(4x + 21) = 0$
10. $(5x + 24)(4x + 37) = 0$
11. $(x - 3)(x + 4)(x - 5) = 0$
12. $(x - 6)(x - 5)(x + 1) = 0$
13. $(6x - 5)(x + 7)(2x - 9) = 0$
14. $(2x - 9)(x + 8)(6x - 7) = 0$
15. $(x - 1)(x + 2)(x + 3)(x - 4) = 0$
16. $(x + 6)(x - 7)(x - 8)(x + 9) = 0$

For Problems 17 through 40, solve by factoring, if practical. Otherwise, solve by the Quadratic Formula. Round off irrational solutions to two decimal places.

17. $x^2 + 7x + 10 = 0$
18. $x^2 + 10x + 21 = 0$
19. $x^2 - x - 12 = 0$
20. $x^2 - 3x - 10 = 0$
21. $x^2 + 4x - 5 = 0$
22. $x^2 + 5x - 6 = 0$
23. $x^2 - 5x + 6 = 0$
24. $x^2 - 6x + 8 = 0$
25. $x^2 + 7x + 5 = 0$
26. $x^2 + 9x + 7 = 0$
27. $2x^2 + 5x + 3 = 0$
28. $2x^2 + 11x + 5 = 0$
29. $3x^2 + 2x - 8 = 0$
30. $3x^2 + 7x - 20 = 0$
31. $5x^2 - 7x - 6 = 0$
32. $5x^2 - 8x - 4 = 0$
33. $6x^2 - 11x + 5 = 0$
34. $5x^2 - 24x + 16 = 0$
35. $5x^2 - 14x - 6 = 0$
36. $2x^2 - 15x - 5 = 0$
37. $6x^2 - 5x - 6 = 0$
38. $6x^2 - 7x - 20 = 0$
39. $16x^2 - 46x + 15 = 0$
40. $12x^2 - 20x + 7 = 0$

For Problems 41 through 46, the left member can be factored as a product of *three* linear binomials. Solve the equations. Each has three solutions.

41. $x^3 - 3x^2 - 4x + 12 = 0$
42. $x^3 - 2x^2 - 9x + 18 = 0$
43. $x^3 + 4x^2 - 25x - 100 = 0$
44. $x^3 + 5x^2 - 36x - 180 = 0$
45. $3x^3 + 4x^2 - 3x - 4 = 0$
46. $4x^3 + 24x^2 - x - 6 = 0$

For Problems 47 through 50, each equation has three solutions. However, you must be very clever to find all three. Try factoring, first!

47. $x^3 + 6x^2 - 5x - 30 = 0$
48. $x^3 + 2x^2 - 7x - 14 = 0$
49. $6x^3 - 3x^2 - 8x + 4 = 0$
50. $5x^3 - 20x^2 - 3x + 12 = 0$

10-8 CONTEST AND STANDARDIZED TEST PROBLEMS

Problems on contests, aptitude tests, and achievement tests are designed to measure your understanding of numbers rather than to show how mathematics is applied in realistic situations. Sometimes you can work these problems in your head without writing expressions and equations. Sometimes there are clever shortcuts you may be able to think up! You can always use algebra if no easier ways come to mind.

Suppose a question asks you to find two consecutive integers whose product is 56. You might choose 7 and 8, because you remember that $7 \times 8 = 56$, and 7 and 8 are consecutive. You might just *try* some possibilities.

$3 \times 4 = 12$	No
$4 \times 5 = 20$	No
$5 \times 6 = 30$	No
$6 \times 7 = 42$	No
$7 \times 8 = 56$	Yes!

This process is called *trial and error*. It is the process you have used to factor quadratic trinomials.

Trial and error is tedious if the numbers are big. But there may be other shortcuts. Faced with the problem of finding two consecutive integers whose product is 5402, Pamela Duke thought, "They must be about the same size. So I will find $\sqrt{5402}$ by calculator; it is 73.498299 . . . . The answer must be 73 and 74, the integers on either side." Upon multiplying, she found $73 \times 74 = 5402$, so her answer was right.

This problem could also be worked by algebra.

	Think These Reasons
Let x = smaller integer. Let y = larger integer.	Define variables.
$xy = 5402$	The product is 5402.
$y = x + 1$	The integers are consecutive.
$x(x + 1) = 5402$	Substitute $x + 1$ for y.
$x^2 + x = 5402$	Distribute x.

$x^2 + x - 5402 = 0$	Subtract 5402 from each member.
$x = \dfrac{-1 \pm \sqrt{1 - 4(1)(5402)}}{2(1)}$	Use the Quadratic Formula.
$x = \dfrac{-1 \pm 147}{2}$	Do the arithmetic.
$x = 73$ or -74	Finish the arithmetic.
$y = 74$ or -73	Substitute into $y = x + 1$.
$73, 74$ or $-74, -73$	Answer the question.

The algebraic solution takes a fairly long time. But it is *reliable*. Also, it uncovers another possible answer, -74 and -73, which you might otherwise miss. Finally, algebra will tell you if there is *no* answer. Had the values of x and y turned out not to be integers, then there would have been no such numbers.

The main purpose of this section is to make you familiar with some kinds of problems that appear on contests and standardized tests so that you can score higher on these tests. There are also some problems that are more realistic.

Objective

Be able to work problems involving ages, consecutive integers, digits, coins, relative rates, and rectangles.

The following examples show an algebraic solution as well as some shortcuts that might be used.

EXAMPLE 1

Age Problem R is 4 years younger than S. The product of their ages is 96. Find each one's age.

\- - - - -   - - - - -

Think These Reasons

Trial and error:

$5 \times 9 = 45$	No
$6 \times 10 = 60$	No
$7 \times 11 = 77$	No
$8 \times 12 = 96$	Yes!

R is 8, S is 12 because 8×12 is 96 and 8 is 4 less than 12.	Answer the question. This is all you need to write! *Justify* your answer to show why it is right.

Algebraic method:

Let r = R's age. Let s = S's age.		Define the variables.
$r = s - 4$ [R] [is] [4 years younger than S.]	(1)	Write an equation using one given piece of information.
$rs = 96$ [Product of ages] [is] [96.]	(2)	Write another equation using the other piece of given information.
$(s - 4)(s) = 96$		Substitute $s - 4$ for r in (2).
$s^2 - 4s - 96 = 0$		Distribute s. Subtract 96.
$(s + 8)(s - 12) = 0$		Factor.
$s + 8 = 0$ or $s - 12 = 0$		Set each factor equal to 0.
~~$s = -8$~~ or $s = 12$ Impossible.		Solve the equations. Discard any meaningless answers.
$r = 12 - 4$		Substitute 12 for s in (1).
$= 8$		Do the arithmetic.
R is 8, S is 12.		Answer the question.

EXAMPLE 2

Digits Problem The units digit of a two-digit number is 2 more than the tens digit. If the digits are reversed, the new number is 39 less than twice the original number. Find the original number.

Think These Reasons

Algebraic method:

Let t = tens digit. Let u = units digit.		Define the variables.
$u = t + 2$ [Units digit] [is] [2 more than tens digit.]	(1)	Write one equation using one known fact.
$10t + u$ is original number. $10u + t$ is reversed number.		(For instance, 39 means 30 + 9.)
$10u + t = 2(10t + u) - 39$ [Reversed number] [is] [39 less than twice the number.]	(2)	Write another equation using the other known fact.

$10u + t = 20t + 2u - 39$	Distribute 2.
$8u - 19t = -39$	Subtract $20t$ and $2u$.
$8(t + 2) - 19t = -39$	Substitute $t + 2$ for u.
$8t + 16 - 19t = -39$	Distribute 8.
$-11t = -55$	Combine like terms; subtract 16.
$t = 5$	Divide by -11.
$u = 5 + 2$	Substitute 5 for t in (1).
$u = 7$	Add.
Number is 57.	Write the answer.

\- - - - -   - - - - -

Trial and error:

Possible Numbers	×2	Reverse	Difference	
13	26	31	-5	
24	48	42	6	
35	70	53	17	
46	92	64	28	
→ 57	114	75	39	This is it!
68	136	86	50	
79	158	97	61	

Number is 57 because 7 is 2 more than 5 and 114 is 39 more than 75. — Answer the question. Justify your answer.

In Example 2, the trial-and-error method takes a bit of work. But it *is* practical because there are only seven possible two-digit numbers that have a units digit two more than the tens digit.

EXAMPLE 3

Coin (Total Value) Problem Eleven dimes and quarters have a total value of \$2.15. How many of each are there?
Algebraic method:

\- - - - -   - - - - -

Let d = number of dimes.
Let q = number of quarters. — Define the variables. Use letters that sound like what they represent.

$d + q = 11$ (1)   There are 11 coins in all.

$10d + 25q = 215$ (2)   Total value is \$2.15.

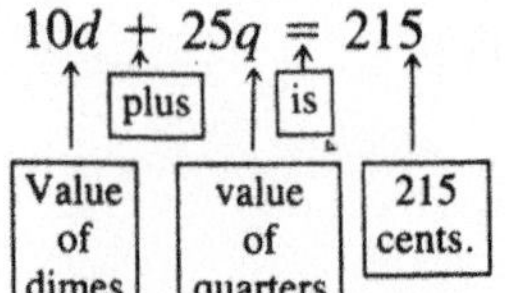

$2d + 5q = 43$	Divide (2) by 5.
$2d + 2q = 22$	Multiply (1) by 2.
$3q = 21$	Subtract.
$q = 7$	Divide each member by 3.
$d + 7 = 11$	Substitute 7 for q in (1).
$d = 4$	Subtract 4 from each member.
4 dimes, 7 quarters.	Answer the question.

- - - - -

Trial and error:

Dimes	*Quarters*	*Value*
0	11	2.75
1	10	2.60
2	9	2.45
3	8	2.30
4	7	2.15

4 dimes, 7 quarters, because 4×10 plus 7×25 is 215 and $4 + 7$ is 11.

- - - - -

Pattern method: If all 11 are quarters, the total is \$2.75. Each time you substitute a dime for a quarter, the total goes *down* by 15¢. The total has to go down 60¢ to get from \$2.75 to \$2.15. So there must be 4 dimes because 4×15 is 60.

4 dimes, 7 quarters, because 4×10 plus 7×25 is 215 and $4 + 7$ is 11.

EXAMPLE 4

Train Problem A freight train leaves point A going 50 km/h. Two hours later, a passenger train leaves A going in the same direction at 80 km/h. How long will it take the passenger train to catch the freight train?

- - - - -

This is a *relative rate* problem.

Let t = number of hours for the passenger train to catch up.

In two hours, the freight train has gone $2 \times 50 = 100$ km.
The passenger train *catches up* at a rate of $80 - 50 = 30$ km/h.
So the passenger train must catch up 100 km at 30 km/h.

$$\text{distance} = \text{rate} \times \text{time}$$

$$100 = 30t$$

$$3\tfrac{1}{3} = t$$

$$\underline{\underline{3 \text{ h } 20 \text{ min.}}}$$

This example shows a shortcut, using the concept of relative rate. The passenger train catches up 100 kilometers at a relative rate of 30 km/h. There are other algebraic ways to do this problem, but the relative rate technique is far superior.

EXAMPLE 5

Rectangle Problem A 7-inch by 10-inch rectangle has a strip of uniform width, x inches, around its outside. If the area of the strip is 50 square inches, what is the width of the strip?

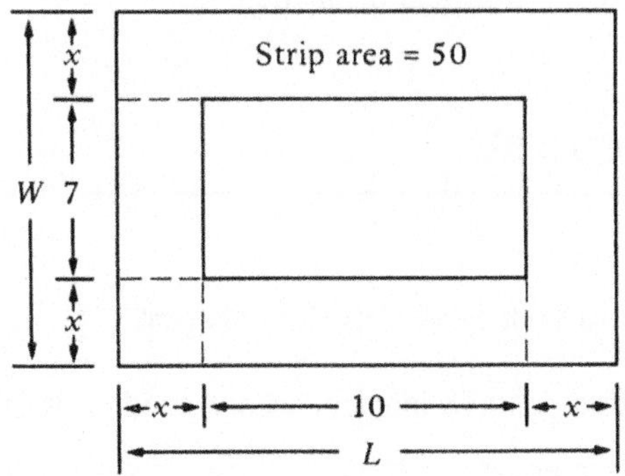

\- - - - -   - - - - -

Think These Reasons

Algebraic method:

x = number of inches of strip width.	Rewrite the definition of x.
Let L = number of inches in total length.	Define variables for length and width.
Let W = number of inches in total width.	
Area of inner rectangle $= 7(10) = 70$.	Area = length × width.
Total area $= 70 + 50 = 120$	Add the area of the strip.
$\therefore LW = 120$	Area = length × width.
$L = 10 + 2x$ $W = 7 + 2x$	See the diagram. For example, $L = x + 10 + x = 10 + 2x$.
$\therefore (10 + 2x)(7 + 2x) = 120$	Substitute for L and W.
$70 + 34x + 4x^2 = 120$	Multiply the binomials.

$4x^2 + 34x - 50 = 0$	Commute terms. Subtract 120 from each member.
$x = \dfrac{-34 \pm \sqrt{1156 - 4(4)(-50)}}{2(4)}$	Use the Quadratic Formula.
$x = \dfrac{-34 \pm \sqrt{1956}}{8}$	Do the computation.
$x \approx 1.28$ or ~~-9.78~~ (Impossible)	Discard any irrelevant answers.
About 1.28 in. wide	Answer the question.

Since the answer to this problem is not an integer, the problem would be impractical to do by the trial-and-error method.

ORAL PRACTICE

Do these problems in your head. Give the answer.

A. Two consecutive positive integers whose product is 20.

B. Two consecutive negative integers whose product is 20.

C. Two consecutive positive integers whose product is 42.

D. Two odd consecutive positive integers whose product is 35.

E. Two even consecutive positive integers whose product is 48.

F. Two even consecutive negative integers whose product is 80.

G. Two positive integers that differ by 3 and whose product is 70.

H. Two negative integers that differ by 3 and whose product is 54.

I. Two consecutive positive integers whose squares have a sum of 25.

J. Two consecutive negative integers whose squares have a sum of 13.

EXERCISE 10-8

Age Problems

1. A is 4 years older than B. The product of their ages is 45. How old is each?

2. C is 3 years younger than D. The product of their ages is 88. How old is each?

3. E is twice as old as F. The product of their ages is 72. How old is each?

4. G is 4 times as old as H. The product of their ages is 1600. How old is each?

5. J is 3 years older than K. If you square K's age and add twice J's age, the result is 69. What are their ages?

6. L is 2 years younger than M. The difference between the squares of their ages is 28. How old is each?

7. N's age is 70% of M's age. Four years ago M was 1.6 times as old as N. What are their ages now?

8. Q's age is 80% of R's age. Five years from now Q's age will be 90% of R's age. How old is each now?

9. Olivia, Newt, and John were each born 3 years apart, with Olivia the youngest and John the oldest. The sum of the squares of their ages is 606. How old is each?

10. April, Mae, June, and Julie were born in consecutive years, in that order, with April being the oldest. All they will tell you is that the sum of the squares of their ages is 534. How old are they?

11. Manny Moore is 5 years older than his brother, Les. All they will tell you is that the sum of the squares of their ages is 773. How old are they?

12. Mr. Rhee is 4 years older than Ms. Rhee, but their actual ages are a mystery. If they tell you that the sum of the squares of their ages is 3706, how old are they?

Consecutive Integers Problems

13. Find two consecutive integers whose product is 72.

14. Find two consecutive integers whose product is 90.

15. Find two consecutive integers whose product is 3422.

16. Find two consecutive integers whose product is 9312.

17. Find two consecutive positive integers if the sum of their squares is 3445.

18. Find two consecutive negative integers if the sum of their squares is 1513.

19. Find three consecutive negative integers if the sum of their squares is 12,290.

20. Find three consecutive positive integers if the sum of their squares is 1454.
21. Find two consecutive odd integers whose product is 7055.
22. Find two consecutive odd integers whose product is 1443.
23. Find three consecutive odd integers if the sum of their squares is 7211.
24. Find three consecutive odd integers if the sum of their squares is 15,995.
25. Find two consecutive odd integers if the sum of their squares is 510.
26. Find two consecutive odd integers if the sum of their squares is 1060.
27. Find two consecutive even negative integers whose product is 6888.
28. Find two consecutive even positive integers whose product is 2808.
29. Find three consecutive even negative integers if the sum of their squares is 5300.
30. Find three consecutive even integers if the sum of their squares is 1208.
31. Find two consecutive even integers if the square of the larger minus the square of the smaller is 348.
32. Find two consecutive even integers if the sum of their squares is 2200.
33. Find two consecutive even integers if the sum of their squares is 164.
34. Find two consecutive odd integers if the difference between their squares is 16.

Digits Problems

35. The units digit of a two-digit number is 40% of the tens digit. If the digits are reversed, the resulting number is 27 less than the original number. Find the original number.
36. A two-digit number is five times its units digit. If the digits are reversed, the resulting number is 27 more than the original number. Find the original number.
37. The sum of the digits of a two-digit number is 9. If the digits are reversed, the new number is 9 less than three times the original number. Find the original number.

38. The sum of the digits of a two-digit number is 6. If the digits are reversed, the new number is 9 less than four times the original number. Find the original number.

39. The units digit of a two-digit number is 1 less than twice the tens digit. The square of the tens digit is 9 more than the units digit. Find the number.

40. The tens digit of a two-digit number is 1 less than five times the units digit. The square of the units digit is 5 less than the tens digit. Find the number.

41. The tens digit of a two-digit number is 3 less than the square of the units digit. If 27 is subtracted from the number, the result is the number with the digits reversed. Find the original number.

42. The units digit of a two-digit number is 2 less than the square of the tens digit. If 36 is added to the number, the result is the number with the digits reversed. Find the original number.

43. The tens digit of a two-digit number is 7 times the units digit. What is the number? (Think!)

44. The units digit of a two-digit number is $\frac{3}{8}$ of the tens digit. What is the number? (Think!)

Coin and Total Value Problems

45. Twelve dimes and quarters have a total value of $1.95. How many of each are there?

46. Ten nickels and quarters have a total value of $1.70. How many of each are there?

47. Eighteen pennies and nickels have a total value of 38 cents. How many of each are there?

48. Twelve pennies and quarters have a total value of $2.52. How many of each are there?

49. *Bank Teller Problem* A bank teller has $10,000 in $20 bills and $50 bills. If the teller has a total of 320 bills, how many of each kind are there?

50. *Courier Problem* A courier picks up 1000 small, unmarked bills, some $20 bills and some $50 bills. The total value is $41,000. How many of each kind are there?

51. *Sandwich Problem* Ten sandwiches are purchased at a total cost of $18.50. Some are tuna sandwiches at $2.00 each, and the rest are cheese sandwiches at $1.50 each. How many of each kind are there?

52. *City Vehicle Problem* the city spent \$120,000 buying 10 new vehicles. Trucks cost \$14,000 each and cars cost \$9000 each. How many of each kind were bought?

53. *Plumbers' Wages Problem* Plumbers earn \$160 a day, and plumbers' helpers earn \$100 a day. Twenty plumbers and helpers earn a total of \$2600 in a day. How many of each are there?

54. *Carnival Problem* In a carnival game, you gain \$2 if you win and lose \$1 if you do not win. If someone plays 30 times and has a net loss of \$6, how many wins were there?

Relative Rate Problems

55. A leaves home going 30 kilometers per hour (km/h). Half an hour later, B starts from the same place and goes after A at 50 km/h. How long does it take B to catch up with A?

56. C leaves home going 40 kilometers per hour (km/h). When C is 9 km from home, D starts after C from the same place, going 58 km/h. How long does it take D to catch up with C?

57. E is approaching F at 20 km/h. When E is 30 km away, F starts out to meet E, going 40 km/h. How long does it take F to meet E?

58. G and H are 370 km apart. At the same instant they start toward each other, G going 50 km/h and H going 60 km/h. How long is it before they meet?

59. J and K start from 600 km apart and approach each other at constant, but different, rates. It takes 12 hours for them to meet. If J goes 10 km/h faster than K, how fast does each one travel?

60. *Clock Hands Problem* At exactly what time between 4:00 and 5:00 will the minute hand of a clock be directly over the hour hand? (*Note:* The minute hand's rate is 60 minutes per hour and the hour hand's rate is 5 minutes per hour. Find out their *relative* rate and then figure out how long it takes the minute hand to catch up the 20 minutes they are apart at 4:00.)

Rectangle Problems

61. A rectangle of area 63 has a length 2 more than its width. Find the length and width.

62. A rectangle of area 90 has a width 9 less than its length. Find the length and width.

63. The area of a rectangle is 96 square kilometers. Its width is 4 km less than its length. Find its dimensions.

64. The area of a rectangle is 567 square centimeters. Its length is 6 cm more than its width. Find its dimensions.

65. The area of a rectangle is 52.7 square meters. Its length is 2 meters more than its width. Find its dimensions.

66. The area of a rectangle is 3247 square millimeters. Its width is 51 mm less than its length. Find its dimensions.

67. A rectangle has a perimeter of 34 and an area of 60. Find its dimensions.

68. A rectangle has a perimeter of 32 and an area of 60. Find its dimensions.

69. ***Larger Field Problem*** Terry Torrey has a rectangular field 3 kilometers by 7 kilometers. He desires to purchase 24 square kilometers more, thus increasing the length and the width by equal amounts (see sketch). Find x, the number of kilometers by which length and width are increased.

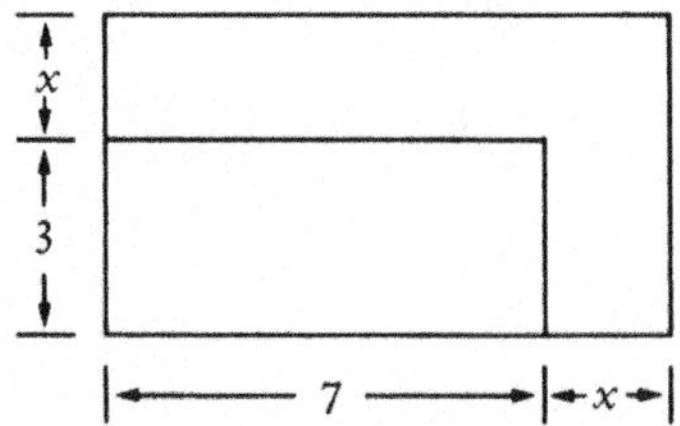

70. ***Road and Field Problem*** A rectangular tract of land 20 m by 30 m has part of its area covered by an L-shaped road, which goes around two sides. The road is the same width on both sides, and its area is 184 square meters. What are the dimensions of the part of the tract *not* covered by the road?

71. ***Patio Painting Problem*** Patty O'Cover paints a rectangle in one corner of a 24-ft by 18-ft patio. Her instructions are to cover $\frac{1}{6}$ of the area of the patio. The unpainted strip is to be the same width on both sides. What are the dimensions of the painted rectangle?

72. ***Rug Problem*** A rug 4 m by 5 m covers $\frac{2}{3}$ of the floor area in a room. The rug touches two walls, leaving a strip of uniform width around the other two walls. How wide is the strip?

73. How wide a strip could be added to all four sides of a 9-by-12 rectangle to form a new rectangle of area 180?

74. How wide a strip could be cut from all four sides of a 20-by-30 rectangle to form a new rectangle one less than half the original area?

75. *Picture Frame Problem* Matt Cutter makes a cardboard frame to go around the edges of an 8 cm by 10 cm photograph. The frame has an area of 63 square centimeters and is of equal width all the way around. What is this width?

76. *Lawn Problem* A landscape architect plans a rectangular back yard with flower beds of equal width completely surrounding a rectangular lawn. The yard has dimensions of 47 m by 39 m. The lawn is to occupy 90% of the total area. How wide are the flower beds?

77. *Swimming Pool Problem* A rectangular tract of land 40 m by 46 m is to have a rectangular swimming pool built in the middle of it. The pool is to occupy 60% of the area of the tract. The edges of the pool are all to be the *same* distance from the edges of the tract. What are the dimensions of the pool?

78. *Oil Lease Problem* Earl Wells leases a rectangular tract of land 5.3 km by 4.1 km. He can drill for oil on the inner 70% of the tract but must leave a strip of land of uniform width around the edges containing the other 30% of the land. How close can the wells come to the boundaries of the tract?

10-9 CHAPTER REVIEW AND TEST

In this chapter you have learned how to operate with polynomials that are more complicated than before. You found the greatest common factor (GCF) for pairs of integers, for pairs of polynomials, and for terms within a polynomial. Next you worked with polynomials with common binomial factors. The factoring-by-grouping technique allowed you to factor harder quadratic trinomials by splitting the middle term. Factoring gave an alternate way to solve quadratic equations without using the Quadratic Formula. This technique gave you a quick way to solve word problems of the type found on standardized tests and on contests.

Try working the following test quickly enough to finish it in the time normally allowed for a classroom test.

CHAPTER TEST

1. What is the:
   a. definition of greatest common factor;
   b. meaning of *relatively prime;*
   c. first step in factoring any polynomial;
   d. converse of the multiplication property of zero;
   e. discriminant test for factorability?

2. Factor completely.
   a. $8x^2 - 16x - 280$
   b. $x^5 + 13x^4 + 30x^3$
   c. $2x^3 - 50x$
   d. $r^2(x + 11) - s^2(x + 11)$
   e. $ab - 3ax + 2bx - 6x^2$
   f. $7x^2 - 15xy + 2y^2$

3. Use splitting the middle term to factor the polynomial completely or to show that it is prime.
   a. $10x^2 + 7x - 12$
   b. $9x^2 - 56x + 12$
   c. $15x^2 + 80x + 24$

4. Solve by factoring.
   a. $x^2 - 2x - 15 = 0$
   b. $2x^2 - 13x + 20 = 0$
   c. $3x^2 + 4x + 1 = 0$

5. Factor (if necessary). Then find the GCF.
   a. $x^2 - 4,\ x + 2$
   b. $x^2 + 6x + 9,\ x^2 + x - 6$
   c. $(x - 2)(x + 3),\ (x + 2)(x - 4)$

6. *Age Problem* A is 5 years older than B. The product of their ages is 84. How old is each?

7. *Consecutive Integers Problem* Find two consecutive odd integers if their product is 63.

8. *Digits Problem* The units digit of a two-digit number is 1 less than the square of the tens digit. The number with the digits reversed is 7 more than twice the original number. Find the original number.

9. *Coin Problem* Twelve dimes and quarters have a total value of $1.65. How many of each are there?

10. ***Relative Rate Problem*** C starts out going 40 miles per hour (mi/h). Three hours later, D starts out after C from the same point, going 60 mi/h. How long does it take D to catch up with C?

11. ***Rectangle Problem*** A rectangle 8 feet by 6 feet has a border of uniform width around the inside of all four edges. If the border has area 33 square feet, how wide is the border?

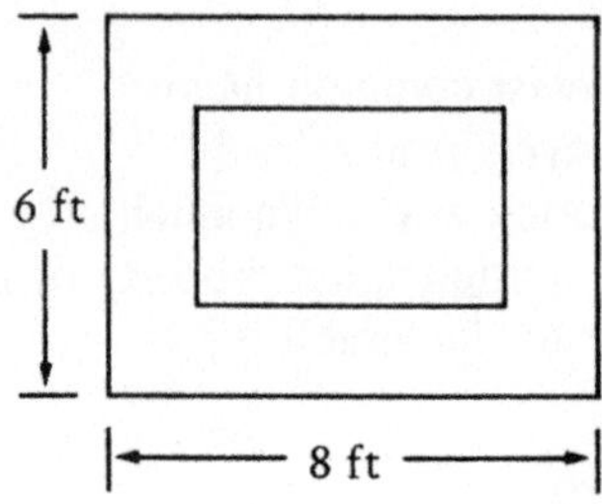

11

Rational Algebraic Expressions

know how to add, multiply,
simplify fractions. In this
pter you will do these things
fractions that contain vari-
es. You will evaluate them for
n values of the variable or
e equations to find the value
he variable. A good example is
roblem involving motion with
against a current, where time
als distance divided by rate.
rate is a sum or difference of
boat's rate and the current's
.

riable:
Speed of tugboat in water

pressions:
8 Speeds of tugboat with
8 respect to land, upstream
and downstream

$\frac{0}{8} + \frac{50}{x + 8}$ Total time for 200 miles upstream, 50 miles downstream

uation:

$\frac{0}{8} + \frac{50}{x + 8} = 52.5$

Total time is 52.5 hours.

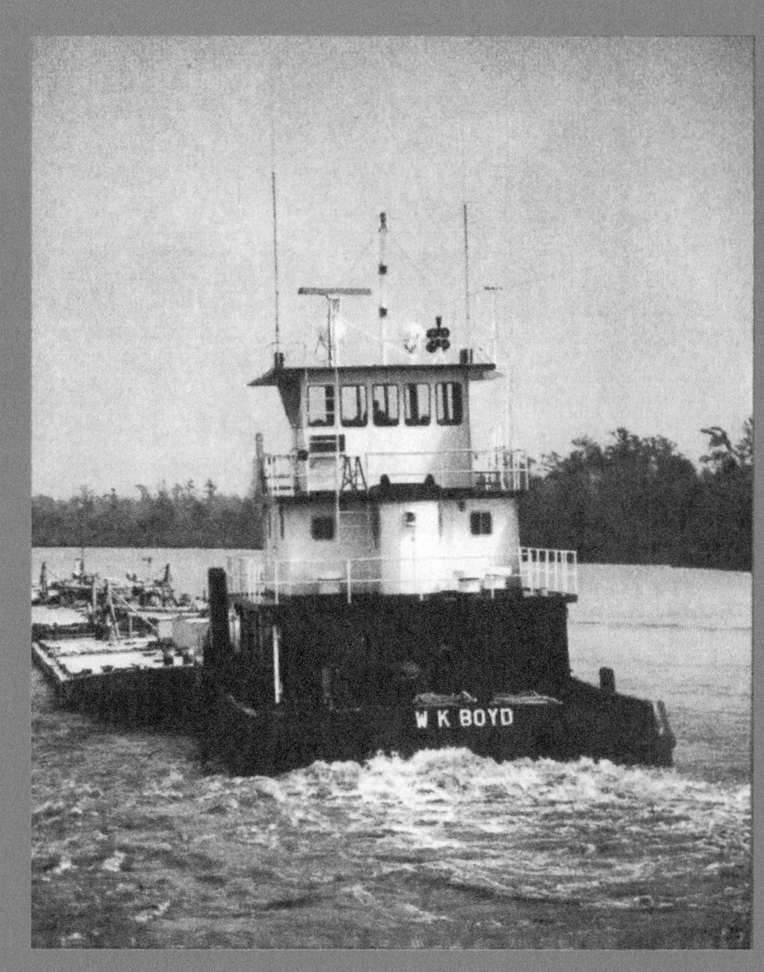

11-1 INTRODUCTION TO RATIONAL ALGEBRAIC EXPRESSIONS AND EQUATIONS

A rational algebraic expression is an expression that has a polynomial for its numerator and a polynomial for its denominator. Two rational expressions are

$$\frac{x + 3}{x - 2} \quad \text{and} \quad \frac{x^2 - 3x + 2}{x - 5}.$$

DEFINITION

RATIONAL ALGEBRAIC EXPRESSION
A **rational algebraic expression** is an expression that can be written as a ratio of two polynomials,

$$\frac{\text{polynomial}}{\text{polynomial}}.$$

(The denominator polynomial cannot be 0.)

It is easy to evaluate a rational expression such as

$$\frac{x - 5}{x + 4}.$$

All you need to do is substitute a given value of x and do the arithmetic. For instance, if x is 3, then

$$\frac{x - 5}{x + 4}$$

$$= \frac{3 - 5}{3 + 4}$$

$$= \frac{-2}{7}.$$

Finding x when you know the value of the expression takes a bit more work. For instance, if the expression above equals 9, you write

$$\frac{x - 5}{x + 4} = 9.$$

This equation is called a **fractional equation.** It can be transformed to a simpler one by getting rid of the fraction. To do this, you multiply each member by $(x + 4)$.

$$(x + 4) \cdot \frac{x - 5}{x + 4} = (x + 4)(9)$$

The left member becomes $x - 5$. The 9 can be distributed in the right member. The result is

$$x - 5 = 9x + 36.$$

From here on the problem is easy.

$$-8x = 41$$

$$x = -\frac{41}{8}$$

If you want a decimal answer, you can divide and get

$$\underline{\underline{x = -5.125}}$$

The result can be checked by substituting -5.125 for x and doing the arithmetic.

$$\frac{x - 5}{x + 4}$$

$$= \frac{-5.125 - 5}{-5.125 + 4}$$

$$= \frac{-10.125}{-1.125}$$

$$= 9 \checkmark$$

Objective

Given a rational algebraic expression, find its value when you know what x equals, and find out what x equals when you know the value of the expression.

Cover the answers as you work the examples on the next page.

EXAMPLE 1

Evaluate $\frac{x+7}{x-2}$ if:

a. x is 5; b. x is -7; c. x is 2.

Think These Reasons

a. $\frac{x+7}{x-2}$ Write the given expression.

$= \frac{5+7}{5-2}$ Substitute 5 for x.

$= \frac{12}{3}$ Do the computation.

$= \underline{4}$ Divide.

b. $\frac{x+7}{x-2}$ Write the given expression.

$= \frac{-7+7}{-7-2}$ Substitute -7 for x.

$= \frac{0}{-9}$ Do the computation.

$= \underline{0}$ Divide.

c. $\frac{x+7}{x-2}$ Write the given expression.

$= \frac{2+7}{2-2}$ Substitute 2 for x.

$= \frac{9}{0}$ Do the computation.

No value — $\frac{9}{0}$ is not a real number.

EXAMPLE 2

Find x if $\frac{x+7}{x-2}$ equals 3. Check your answer.

$\frac{x+7}{x-2} = 3$ Write an equation.

$x + 7 = 3(x - 2)$	Multiply each member by $x - 2$.
$x + 7 = 3x - 6$	Distribute 3.
$-2x = -13$	Subtract $3x$ and subtract 7.
$x = 6.5$	Divide by -2.

Check: $\dfrac{x + 7}{x - 2}$

$= \dfrac{6.5 + 7}{6.5 - 2}$ Substitute 6.5 for x.

$= \dfrac{13.5}{4.5}$ Do the computation.

$= 3$ ✓ Divide. The answer checks.

The following exercise has more problems like these.

EXERCISE 11-1

1. Evaluate $\dfrac{x - 9}{x + 4}$ if:
   a. x is 6;
   b. x is -5;
   c. x is 9.

2. Evaluate $\dfrac{x - 10}{x + 3}$ if:
   a. x is 2;
   b. x is -5;
   c. x is -3.

3. Evaluate $\dfrac{2x + 7}{x - 5}$ if:
   a. x is 8;
   b. x is -3;
   c. x is 5.

4. Evaluate $\dfrac{3x + 6}{x - 4}$ if:
   a. x is 7;
   b. x is -2;
   c. x is 4.

5. Evaluate $\dfrac{x^2 + 5x + 6}{x^2 + 7x + 10}$ if:
   a. x is 5;
   b. x is -3;
   c. x is 0.

6. Evaluate $\dfrac{x^2 + 6x + 8}{x^2 + 9x + 20}$ if:
   a. x is 3;
   b. x is -5;
   c. x is 0.

7. For $\dfrac{x - 9}{x + 4}$, find x if:
   a. the expression equals 3;
   b. the expression equals -4.

8. For $\dfrac{x - 10}{x + 3}$, find x if:
   a. the expression equals 5;
   b. the expression equals -4.

9. For $\frac{2x + 7}{x - 5}$, find x if:
   a. the expression equals 10;
   b. the expression equals 2. (Surprising?)

10. For $\frac{3x + 6}{x - 4}$, find x if:
   a. the expression equals 8;
   b. the expression equals 3. (Surprising?)

11-2 SIMPLIFYING RATIONAL ALGEBRAIC EXPRESSIONS

In Section 9-4, you used the multiplication property of fractions to simplify fractions.

$\frac{24}{36}$

$= \frac{12 \cdot 2}{12 \cdot 3}$ 12 is the GCF of 24 and 36.

$= \frac{12}{12} \cdot \frac{2}{3}$ Use the multiplication property of fractions.

$= \frac{2}{3}$ Use the multiplication property of 1. $\frac{12}{12}$ equals 1.

The same procedure is used to simplify fractions that contain variables. You factor the numerator and denominator and then get rid of the common factors.

$\frac{x^2 - 2x - 35}{x^2 + 7x + 10}$

$= \frac{(x + 5)(x - 7)}{(x + 5)(x + 2)}$ Factor the numerator and denominator.

$= \frac{x + 5}{x + 5} \cdot \frac{x - 7}{x + 2}$ Use the multiplication property of fractions.

$= \frac{x - 7}{x + 2}$ Use the multiplication property of 1: $\frac{x + 5}{x + 5}$ equals 1.

The next-to-last line looks like the step in making fractions have common denominators in which you multiplied by an appropriate form of 1. The line above can be thought of as: Multiply the numerator and denominator by the same number. With this in mind, you can go directly from

$$\frac{(x + 5)(x - 7)}{(x + 5)(x + 2)} \text{ to } \frac{x - 7}{x + 2}.$$

Your thought process should be: *Divide* the numerator and denominator by the same number. This process is called *canceling,* because the common factor in the numerator and the denominator seems to cancel out.

DEFINITION

CANCELING
To **cancel** in a fraction means to *divide* the numerator and denominator by the same common factor. That is, for real numbers a, b, and c, with $a \neq 0$ and $c \neq 0$,

$$\frac{ab}{ac} = \frac{b}{c}.$$

Do not read more into the definition of canceling than is there! For instance, in

$$\frac{x-7}{x+2},$$

you *cannot* cancel the x's. Since canceling is a *division* process, dividing the numerator and denominator by x would give

$$\frac{1 - \frac{7}{x}}{1 + \frac{2}{x}},$$

which is not simpler than the original fraction. Canceling can be done only when the numerator and denominator each consists of *one* term with common *factors* or can be written in that form.

Objective

Be able to cancel common factors from the numerator and denominator of a rational algebraic expression.

Cover the answers as you work these examples.

EXAMPLE 1

Simplify: $\frac{15x^8}{25x^2}$.

- - - - - - - - - -

Think These Reasons

$\dfrac{15x^8}{25x^2}$ — Write the given expression.

$= \dfrac{3x^6}{5}$ — Cancel 5 for the coefficients. Subtract exponents for the powers.

EXAMPLE 2

Simplify: $\dfrac{(x + 5)(x - 4)}{(x + 5)(x + 4)}$.

$\dfrac{(x + 5)(x - 4)}{(x + 5)(x + 4)}$ — Write the given expression.

$= \dfrac{x - 4}{x + 4}$ — Cancel the $(x + 5)$ factors. There are *no* other common factors. Do not cancel the *terms* x or 4!

EXAMPLE 3

Simplify: $\dfrac{2x^2 - 4x - 30}{2x^2 - 7x - 15}$.

$\dfrac{2x^2 - 4x - 30}{2x^2 - 7x - 15}$ — Write the given expression.

$= \dfrac{2(x^2 - 2x - 15)}{2x^2 - 7x - 15}$ — Factor out any *common* factors *first*.

$= \dfrac{2(x - 5)(x + 3)}{(2x + 3)(x - 5)}$ — Factor the trinomials.

$= \dfrac{2(x + 3)}{2x + 3}$ or $\dfrac{2x + 6}{2x + 3}$ — Cancel the $(x - 5)$ factors. Nothing else cancels.

ORAL PRACTICE

Can canceling be done? If so, *what* can be canceled?

A. $\dfrac{2(x + 3)}{3(x + 3)}$ B. $\dfrac{3(x + 4)}{3(x + 5)}$ C. $\dfrac{4(x + 4)}{6(x + 3)}$

D. $\frac{2(x + 3)}{2(y + 3)}$ E. $\frac{2(x + 3)}{2x + 3}$ F. $\frac{8x}{12x}$

G. $\frac{(x + 4)(3)}{12(x + 4)}$ H. $\frac{x + 3}{x - 3}$ I. $\frac{(x + 3)(x + 4)}{(x + 3)(x - 4)}$

J. $\frac{(x - 2)(x + 3)}{(x + 3)(x - 2)}$ K. $\frac{x^2 - 9}{x + 3}$

EXERCISE 11-2

For Problems 1 through 30, simplify the expression.

1. $\frac{12x^3}{18x^5}$
2. $\frac{24x^2}{36x^6}$
3. $\frac{25x^2y^8}{10x^3y^5}$
4. $\frac{35x^7y^4}{21x^2y^7}$
5. $\frac{(x + 3)(x - 2)}{(x + 5)(x - 2)}$
6. $\frac{(x - 7)(x + 4)}{(x - 6)(x + 4)}$
7. $\frac{(x - 8)(x + 2)}{(x + 4)(x - 8)}$
8. $\frac{(x - 12)(x + 6)}{(x + 6)(x - 3)}$
9. $\frac{(2x + 5)(x + 1)}{(2x - 5)(x + 1)}$
10. $\frac{(3x - 7)(x - 4)}{(3x - 7)(x + 4)}$
11. $\frac{x^2 + x - 6}{x^2 - 4}$
12. $\frac{x^2 - 3x - 18}{x^2 - 36}$
13. $\frac{x^2 + 2x - 3}{x^2 + 7x + 12}$
14. $\frac{x^2 + 2x - 8}{x^2 - 5x + 6}$
15. $\frac{x^2 + 2x - 35}{x^2 + x - 30}$
16. $\frac{x^2 + 9x + 8}{x^2 - 6x - 7}$
17. $\frac{3x^3 + 5x^2}{6x + 10}$
18. $\frac{3x^2 + 12x}{x^4 + 4x^3}$
19. $\frac{5x^2 - 20}{x^2 + 5x + 6}$
20. $\frac{7x^2 - 63}{x^2 + 7x + 12}$
21. $\frac{2x^2 - 5x - 3}{2x^2 - 3x - 2}$
22. $\frac{3x^2 - 5x - 2}{3x^2 + 7x + 2}$
23. $\frac{4x^2 - x - 3}{3x^2 + x - 4}$
24. $\frac{5x^2 - 9x - 2}{4x^2 - 7x - 2}$

25. $\dfrac{10x^2 - 19x + 6}{10x^2 - 21x + 9}$

26. $\dfrac{8x^2 + 10x + 3}{8x^2 + 2x - 3}$

27. $\dfrac{3x^2 + 27x + 60}{3x^2 + 12x - 15}$

28. $\dfrac{5x^2 + 10x - 40}{5x^2 + 15x - 20}$

29. $\dfrac{12x^2 - 27}{4x^2 - 2x - 12}$

30. $\dfrac{45x^2 - 20}{9x^2 + 6x - 8}$

31. Find x if $\dfrac{x + 6}{x + 9} = 4$.

32. Find x if $\dfrac{x + 7}{x - 5} = 2$.

33. For what value of x is $\dfrac{x - 3}{x + 5}$
   a. equal to zero?
   b. undefined?

34. For what value of x is $\dfrac{x - 6}{x - 7}$
   a. equal to zero?
   b. undefined?

11-3 MULTIPLYING AND DIVIDING RATIONAL EXPRESSIONS

You should recall that to multiply two fractions you multiply numerator by numerator and denominator by denominator. For instance,

$$\frac{2}{5} \cdot \frac{3}{7} = \frac{2 \cdot 3}{5 \cdot 7} = \frac{6}{35}.$$

Dividing fractions is done by multiplying the first fraction by the reciprocal of the second. For instance,

$$\frac{2}{5} \div \frac{3}{7} = \frac{2}{5} \cdot \frac{7}{3} = \frac{2 \cdot 7}{5 \cdot 3} = \frac{14}{15}.$$

In this section you will do the same thing with algebraic fractions (that is, with rational algebraic expressions).

Objective

Given two rational expressions, multiply them or divide them, and simplify the answer.

Cover the answers as you work these examples.

EXAMPLE 1

Given $\dfrac{12x}{15}$ and $\dfrac{20x}{18}$:

a. multiply them;
b. divide the first by the second.

Think These Reasons

a. $\frac{12x}{15} \cdot \frac{20x}{18}$ — Multiply the given expressions.

$= \frac{12 \cdot 20x^2}{15 \cdot 18}$ — Multiply numerator by numerator and denominator by denominator.

$= \frac{8}{9}x^2$ — Do the canceling.

b. $\frac{12x}{15} \div \frac{20x}{18}$ — Divide the first by the second.

$= \frac{12x}{15} \cdot \frac{18}{20x}$ — Change dividing to multiplying by the reciprocal.

$= \frac{12 \cdot 18x}{15 \cdot 20x}$ — Multiply.

$= \frac{18}{25}$ — Do the canceling.

EXAMPLE 2

Divide and simplify: $\frac{x^2 - 2x - 15}{4x^2 + 8x} \div \frac{x + 3}{4x - 20}$

$\frac{x^2 - 2x - 15}{4x^2 + 8x} \div \frac{x + 3}{4x - 20}$ — Write the given expression.

$= \frac{x^2 - 2x - 15}{4x^2 + 8x} \cdot \frac{4x - 20}{x + 3}$ — Write dividing as multiplying by the reciprocal.

$= \frac{(x - 5)(x + 3)}{4x(x + 2)} \cdot \frac{4(x - 5)}{x + 3}$ — Factor.

$= \frac{(x - 5)(x + 3)(4)(x - 5)}{4x(x + 2)(x + 3)}$ — Multiply.

$= \frac{(x - 5)(x - 5)}{x(x + 2)}$ — Cancel.

$= \frac{x^2 - 10x + 25}{x^2 + 2x}$ — Multiply.

ORAL PRACTICE

Multiply or divide, and simplify.

A. $\frac{2}{3x} \cdot \frac{6}{3x}$ B. $\frac{2}{3x} \div \frac{6}{3x}$ C. $\frac{5}{6a} \cdot \frac{3a}{2}$

D. $\frac{5}{6a} \div \frac{3a}{2}$ E. $\frac{C}{3} \cdot \frac{5}{C}$ F. $\frac{C}{3} \div \frac{5}{C}$

G. $\frac{x^3}{4} \cdot \frac{8}{x}$ H. $\frac{3}{4p} \div \frac{1}{12p^4}$ I. $\frac{3}{2} \cdot \frac{x+5}{12}$

J. $\frac{4}{x+1} \div \frac{5}{x+1}$ K. $\frac{2}{x-7} \cdot \frac{x-7}{8}$ L. $\frac{2}{3} \div \frac{3}{x-2}$

EXERCISE 11-3

For Problems 1 through 10:

a. multiply the two expressions;
b. divide the first expression by the second.

1. $\frac{8}{5x}, \frac{7}{9x}$ 2. $\frac{7}{6x}, \frac{2}{11x}$ 3. $\frac{5}{12x}, \frac{11}{18x}$

4. $\frac{8}{9x}, \frac{7}{6x}$ 5. $\frac{x}{12}, \frac{x+3}{4}$ 6. $\frac{x}{10}, \frac{x-3}{5}$

7. $\frac{x-6}{x+3}, \frac{x-5}{x-7}$ 8. $\frac{x+4}{x+7}, \frac{x-3}{x+6}$ 9. $\frac{2x+3}{3x-1}, \frac{4x+5}{x+2}$

10. $\frac{3x-4}{2x-1}, \frac{5x-2}{x-8}$

For Problems 11 through 50, do the multiplication and division and simplify.

11. $\frac{6x}{5y} \cdot \frac{10y}{8x}$ 12. $\frac{8x}{3y} \cdot \frac{12y}{16x}$

13. $\frac{5a}{7b} \div \frac{25a}{21b}$ 14. $\frac{9c}{14d} \div \frac{12c}{21d}$

15. $\frac{20p}{49s} \cdot \frac{42p}{10s}$

16. $\frac{24r}{55k} \cdot \frac{66r}{8k}$

17. $\frac{30m}{13t} \div \frac{15t}{52m}$

18. $\frac{40e}{17f} \div \frac{30f}{51e}$

19. $\frac{6ab^2}{35b} \cdot \frac{42a}{18ab}$

20. $\frac{32xy^3}{9x} \cdot \frac{15x}{16xy}$

21. $\frac{3p^2c^3}{5c^6} \div \frac{12p^4c}{10c^2}$

22. $\frac{22xyz}{27x} \div \frac{33xz}{5y}$

23. $\frac{5r}{4s} \cdot \frac{6r}{10s} \cdot \frac{8t}{12t}$

24. $\frac{10m}{11p} \cdot \frac{44p}{20k} \cdot \frac{15k}{8m}$

25. $\frac{6x + 12}{3x - 9} \cdot \frac{5x - 15}{4x + 8}$

26. $\frac{3x - 12}{8x + 12} \cdot \frac{12x + 18}{5x - 20}$

27. $\frac{c^2 - d^2}{4c} \cdot \frac{6c^3}{(c + d)^2}$

28. $\frac{3h^4}{(h - p)^2} \cdot \frac{h^2 - p^2}{12h}$

29. $\frac{4u^2 - 1}{u^3 - 16u} \cdot \frac{u^2 + 4u}{2u - 1}$

30. $\frac{v^2 - 9}{v^2 + 3v} \cdot \frac{v^3}{v^3 - 3v^2}$

31. $\frac{7x - 14y}{x + 6y} \div \frac{21}{3x + 9y}$

32. $\frac{24}{a + 4b} \div \frac{8a + 12b}{2a + 8b}$

33. $\frac{5a + 15}{a^2 - 9} \div \frac{5a - 15}{(a - 3)^2}$

34. $\frac{12 - 4x}{10 + 5x} \div \frac{9 - x^2}{4 - x^2}$

35. $\frac{x^2 + 2x - 35}{6x^3} \cdot \frac{2x^2 - 6x}{x^2 + 4x - 21}$

36. $\frac{d^2 + 4d - 45}{4d - 20} \cdot \frac{3d - 3}{d^2 - 81}$

37. $\frac{y^2 + 3y - 18}{y^2 - 8y + 12} \cdot \frac{2y - 4}{y^2 - 36}$

38. $\frac{x^2 - x - 2}{x^2 - 2x + 1} \cdot \frac{x - 1}{x + 1}$

39. $\frac{2c^2 + 5c + 2}{2c^2 + c - 6} \div \frac{6c + 3}{2c - 3}$

40. $\frac{3x^2 + 6x + 9}{4x + 6} \div \frac{4x^2 + 8x + 12}{2x + 3}$

41. $\frac{a^3 + ab^2}{a^3 - 2a^2b} \div \frac{a^2 + b^2}{(a - 2b)^2}$

42. $\frac{k^2v - 5k^2}{v^2 - 4} \div \frac{kv - 5k}{v + 2}$

43. $\frac{6x + 12}{8x - 4} \cdot \frac{3x - 9}{12x + 6} \div \frac{3x^2 - 12}{8x^2 - 2}$

44. $\frac{5a^2 - 5a}{4a^3} \cdot \frac{a^2 - 9a - 10}{4a - 40} \div \frac{2a^2 - 2}{a}$

45. $\frac{x^3 - 9x}{8} \div \frac{x + 3}{2} \cdot \frac{4}{3x - 9}$

46. $\dfrac{b^2 - 7b + 10}{b^2 - 6b + 5} \div \dfrac{1}{b - 2} \cdot \dfrac{b + 1}{b^2 - 4b + 4}$

47. $\dfrac{t^2 + 2t - 8}{t + 4} \cdot (t - 2)^{-1}$

48. $\dfrac{x^2 - 2x - 3}{x + 1} \cdot 5(x - 3)^{-1}$

49. $\dfrac{2x + 3}{4x + 5} \div \dfrac{4x + 5}{2x + 3} \cdot \dfrac{8x + 10}{2x + 3}$

50. $(x^2 + 4x - 12)^{-1} \div \dfrac{x + 6}{x - 4}$

51. Find x if $\dfrac{x + 3}{x - 2} = 5$.

52. Find x if $\dfrac{2x + 5}{x - 11} = 2$.

53. For what value of x is $\dfrac{x - 7}{x + 2}$

a. equal to zero?
b. undefined?

54. For what value of x is $\dfrac{2x + 7}{x - 4}$

a. equal to zero?
b. undefined?

11-4 LEAST COMMON MULTIPLE

In order to add two fractions, their denominators must be equal. For instance

$$\frac{2}{5} + \frac{3}{7} = \frac{14}{35} + \frac{15}{35} = \frac{29}{35}$$

The 35 is called a common denominator. It is a special case of a more general idea.

A **multiple** of a given number is an integer multiplied by that number. For instance, 12, 30, and 6000 are multiples of 6. Also, 32, 80, and 88 are multiples of 8. Listing the multiples of 6 and 8 in order shows something interesting.

Common multiples

6: 6 12 18 (24) 30 36 42 (48) 54 60 66 . . .

8: 8 16 (24) 32 40 (48) 56 64 72 80 88 . . .

Some multiples of 6 are also multiples of 8. These are called **common multiples** of 6 and 8. The number 24 is the smallest of the common multiples. It is called the **least common multiple.** This number is abbreviated LCM. When you add two fractions, you use the LCM of the denominators as the common denominator.

DEFINITION

LEAST COMMON MULTIPLE (LCM)
A **common multiple** of integers a and b is a number that equals

$$\text{integer} \times a \quad \text{and} \quad \text{integer} \times b.$$

The **least common multiple** (LCM) of integers a and b is the *smallest* positive number that is a common multiple of a and b.

The LCM of two integers can be found by factoring them into primes. For instance,

$$6 = 2 \cdot 3$$
$$8 = 2 \cdot 2 \cdot 2$$

To be a multiple of 6, a number must have at least one 2 and at least one 3 as factors. To be a multiple of 8, a number must have at least three 2's as factors. So the least common multiple of 6 and 8 has three 2's and one 3.

$$\text{LCM} = 2 \cdot 2 \cdot 2 \cdot 3 = 24$$

The diagram shows the set of factors of 6 and set of factors of 8. The overlapping region has factors of both 6 and 8, the *common* factors. The other regions have the rest of the factors of 6 and 8. From the diagram you should be able to see that the set of factors of the LCM is the *union* of the two sets of prime factors.

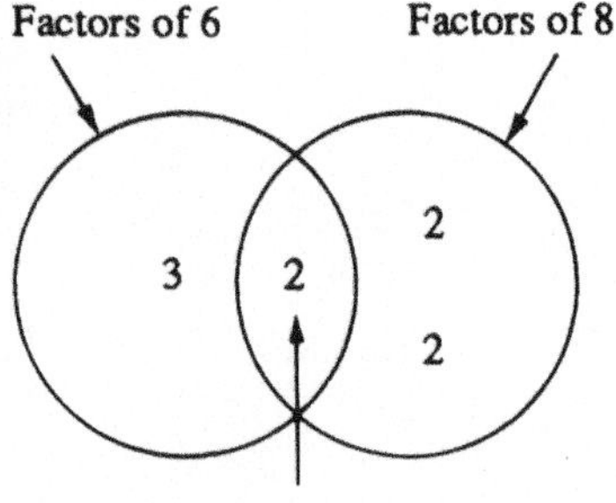

LCM of 6 and 8 is $2 \cdot 2 \cdot 2 \cdot 3$

In this section you will practice getting LCMs of two polynomials so that you will be prepared to find common denominators for adding rational expressions.

Objective

Given two polynomials, find their LCM.

Cover the answers as you work the examples.

EXAMPLE 1

Find the LCM of $12a^2b^5$, and $18a^3bc$.

- - - - - - - - - -

Think These Reasons

$12a^2b^5 = 2 \cdot 2 \cdot 3 \cdot a \cdot a \cdot b \cdot b \cdot b \cdot b \cdot b$	Factor.
$18a^3bc = 2 \cdot 3 \cdot 3 \cdot a \cdot a \cdot a \cdot b \cdot c$	Factor.
$\text{LCM} = 2 \cdot 2 \cdot 3 \cdot 3 \cdot a \cdot a \cdot a \cdot b \cdot b \cdot b \cdot b \cdot b \cdot c$	Pick the least number of factors that are needed to cover all of each expression.
$\text{LCM} = 36a^3b^5c$	Simplify.

From this example you may be able to see a short cut! Just take each factor with the *highest* exponent in either of the two expressions.

EXAMPLE 2

Find the LCM of $9x^4$ and $6x(x + 5)^3$.

- - - - - - - - - -

$\text{LCM} = 18x^4(x + 5)^3$	LCM of 9 and 6 is 18. Take the highest exponent of x and the highest exponent of $(x + 5)$.

EXAMPLE 3

Find the LCM of $x^2 - 2x - 15$ and $x^2 - 4x - 5$.

- - - - - - - - - -

$x^2 - 2x - 15 = (x + 3)(x - 5)$ $x^2 - 4x - 5 = (x - 5)(x + 1)$	Factor the two expressions.
$\text{LCM} = (x + 3)(x - 5)(x + 1)$	Write the LCM. The $(x - 5)$ is a common factor, so it appears only *once*.

ORAL PRACTICE

Find the LCM of the given pair of integers.

A. 6, 8 B. 12, 15 C. 12, 9 D. 8, 18 E. 7, 21

F. 4, 12 G. 5, 4 H. 9, 10 I. 4, 30 J. 24, 36

EXERCISE 11-4

For Problems 1 through 40, find the LCM of the two expressions.

1. a^2bc, ab^2c
2. $ax^2, 4a^2x$
3. $4x^3, 6x^5$
4. $6pc^2, 15p^2c$
5. $42a^3b, 49b^2c$
6. $56r^5t, 54r^3z^2$
7. $4x, 4(a - x)$
8. $a^2, a(a - b)$
9. $2(a - x), 3(a + x)$
10. $5(x + 3), 6(x - 3)$
11. $3(a + x), 7(a + x)$
12. $9(x - 3), 11(x - 3)$
13. $c^2m(c - m), cm^2(c - m)$
14. $p^3f(p + f), p^2f^4(p + f)$
15. $xyz(x - y), xy$
16. $a^2b, a^3b^2(a - b)$
17. $2a - 2b, 4a - 4b$
18. $4a^2 - 9, 6a^2 - 9a$
19. $j^2 - 9, j^2 + 3j$
20. $6r + 12t, 8r + 16t$
21. $(x - y)^2, x^2 - y^2$
22. $(c + 5)^2, c^2 - 25$
23. $(x - 3)(x + 2), (x + 2)(x - 7)$
24. $(x + 4)(x - 5), (x - 1)(x + 4)$
25. $(x - 2)^5(x + 3)^2, (x + 2)^4(x + 3)^3$
26. $(x + 1)^7(x - 7)^6, (x - 7)^4(x + 5)$
27. $x^2 + 6x + 8, x^2 + 7x + 12$
28. $x^2 - 7x + 12, x^2 - 9x + 20$
29. $2x^2 + x - 3, x^2 + 4x - 5$
30. $3x^2 + 5x - 2, x^2 + 6x + 8$
31. $12x^2 + 36x + 24, 18x^2 - 18$
32. $24x^2 - 96, 18x^2 + 18x - 36$
33. $x^3 - 2x^2 - x + 2, x^2 - 3x + 2$
34. $x^3 + x^2 - 9x - 9, x^2 - 4x + 3$

35. $x^2 - 4, 4x - 8$

36. $9x^2 - 1, 18x + 6$

37. $x^2 + 5x + 6, x^2 - 6x + 8$

38. $2x^2 + 7x + 3, 2x^2 + 7x - 4$

39. $x^5 + 2x^4 + x^3, x^7 - x^5$

40. $4x^3 - 16x, 6x^4 - 6x^3 - 12x^2$

For Problems 41 through 46, find the LCM of the *three* expressions.

41. x^3, a^2x^2, a^4

42. j^5, j^3w, jw^2

43. $10v^4, 12v^2c^2, 4vc^3$

44. $15r^3, 21r^2s^3, 35s^4$

45. $6x^3y^2z^4, 4xy^3z^2, 9x^2y^4z$

46. $9x^4y, 12x^3y^2, 54x^2y^3$

47. Write all the integral multiples of 2 and all the integral multiples of 3 that are between 1 and 20. Circle the pairs of *common* multiples. Put a box around the *least* common multiple.

48. Write all the integral multiples of 12 and all the integral multiples of 18 that are between 1 and 100. Circle the pairs of *common* multiples. Put a box around the *least* common multiple.

49. Find the LCM of 24 and 36. Find the GCF of 24 and 36. Show that (LCM)(GCF) = 24 × 36.

50. Find the LCM of 48 and 49. Find the GCF of 48 and 49. Is it possible for two integers like 48 and 49 that are just 1 apart to have any common factors other than 1? If so, *find* two such integers. If not, tell *why* not.

Problems 51 through 62 give you a brief review of adding and subtracting fractions before you go on to Section 11-5. Add or subtract. Simplify the answer, if possible.

51. $\frac{3}{5} + \frac{1}{5}$

52. $\frac{2}{7} + \frac{4}{7}$

53. $\frac{5}{8} - \frac{7}{8}$

54. $\frac{3}{10} - \frac{9}{10}$

55. $\frac{2}{3} + \frac{1}{2}$

56. $\frac{1}{3} + \frac{5}{2}$

57. $\frac{3}{5} - \frac{2}{7}$

58. $\frac{3}{5} - \frac{4}{11}$

59. $\frac{5}{6} + \frac{3}{4}$

60. $\frac{1}{6} + \frac{5}{4}$

61. $\frac{5}{8} - \frac{7}{12}$

62. $\frac{3}{8} - \frac{5}{12}$

11-5 ADDING AND SUBTRACTING RATIONAL EXPRESSIONS

In order to add two fractions, their denominators must be equal. In the last section, the example given was

$$\frac{2}{5} + \frac{3}{7} = \frac{14}{35} + \frac{15}{35} = \frac{29}{35}$$

In this section you will add rational algebraic expressions. The fractions will have variables in the numerator, denominator, or both. For instance, suppose you must add

$$\frac{7}{6x} + \frac{3}{4}.$$

The easiest common denominator to use is the least common multiple (LCM) of the two denominators. For $6x$ and 4, the LCM is:

$$\text{LCM} = 12x.$$

Multiplying $\frac{7}{6x}$ by $\frac{2}{2}$ (which equals 1) and $\frac{3}{4}$ by $\frac{3x}{3x}$ (which also equals 1) gives

$$\frac{7}{6x} \cdot \frac{2}{2} + \frac{3}{4} \cdot \frac{3x}{3x}$$

$$= \frac{14}{12x} + \frac{9x}{12x}$$

$$= \frac{14 + 9x}{12x}$$

Since $12x$ is the LCM of two denominators, it is called the *least common denominator*, or LCD.

DEFINITION

LEAST COMMON DENOMINATOR (LCD)
The **least common denominator** (LCD) of two fractions is the LCM of the two denominators.

Objective

Given two rational algebraic expressions, be able to find their LCD, and use the result to add or subtract the two expressions.

Cover the answers as you work these examples.

EXAMPLE 1

Do the addition:

Add: $\frac{5}{3x} + \frac{9}{4x}$.

- - - - -

Think These Reasons

$\frac{5}{3x} + \frac{9}{4x}$	Write the given expression.
$= \frac{5}{3x} \cdot \frac{4}{4} + \frac{9}{4x} \cdot \frac{3}{3}$	Write each fraction with the LCD, $12x$.
$= \frac{20}{12x} + \frac{27}{12x}$	Multiply the fractions.
$= \frac{47}{12x}$	Add the fractions.

EXAMPLE 2

Subtract: $\frac{5x}{x-y} - \frac{5y}{x-y}$

- - - - -

$\frac{5x}{x-y} - \frac{5y}{x-y}$	Write the given expression.
$= \frac{5x - 5y}{x-y}$	Denominators are already common.
$= \frac{5(x-y)}{x-y}$	Factor the numerator.
$= 5$	Cancel the $(x - y)$'s.

EXAMPLE 3

Add: $\frac{x+3}{x-7} + \frac{x-2}{x-1}$

- - - - -

$= \frac{x+3}{x-7} \cdot \frac{x-1}{x-1} + \frac{x-2}{x-1} \cdot \frac{x-7}{x-7}$	Multiply by suitable forms of 1.

$= \frac{x^2 + 2x - 3}{x^2 - 8x + 7} + \frac{x^2 - 9x + 14}{x^2 - 8x + 7}$ Multiply the numerators and the denominators.

$= \frac{(x^2 + 2x - 3) + (x^2 - 9x + 14)}{x^2 - 8x + 7}$ Add the numerators; use the common denominator.

$= \frac{2x^2 - 7x + 11}{x^2 - 8x + 7}$ Combine like terms.

EXAMPLE 4

Subtract: $\frac{x + 5}{x + 6} - \frac{x - 2}{x + 4}$.

$\frac{x + 5}{x + 6} - \frac{x - 2}{x + 4}$ Write the given expression.

$= \frac{x + 5}{x + 6} \cdot \frac{x + 4}{x + 4} - \frac{x - 2}{x + 4} \cdot \frac{x + 6}{x + 6}$ Write the fractions with the common denominator.

$= \frac{x^2 + 9x + 20}{x^2 + 10x + 24} - \frac{x^2 + 4x - 12}{x^2 + 10x + 24}$ Simplify each fraction.

$= \frac{(x^2 + 9x + 20) - (x^2 + 4x - 12)}{x^2 + 10x + 24}$ Subtract the numerators; use the common denominator.

$= \frac{x^2 + 9x + 20 - x^2 - 4x + 12}{x^2 + 10x + 24}$ Distribute -1.

$= \frac{5x + 32}{x^2 + 10x + 24}$ Combine like terms.

ORAL PRACTICE

Do the indicated operation and give the answer.

A. $\frac{2}{3x} + \frac{6}{3x}$ B. $\frac{2}{3x} - \frac{6}{3x}$ C. $\frac{x}{6} - \frac{x}{3}$

D. $\frac{x}{6} + \frac{x}{3}$ E. $\frac{5}{6x} + \frac{2}{3x}$ F. $\frac{5}{6x} - \frac{2}{3x}$

G. $\frac{1}{8} - \frac{5x + 3}{8}$ H. $\frac{2}{7} - \frac{3x - 4}{7}$ I. $\frac{4}{9} - \frac{x + 1}{9}$

J. $\frac{2}{3} + \frac{5x - 2}{3}$ K. $\frac{2}{3} - \frac{5x - 2}{3}$

EXERCISE 11-5

For Problems 1 through 10:

a. add the two expressions;
b. subtract the second expression from the first.

1. $\frac{8}{5x}, \frac{7}{9x}$
2. $\frac{7}{6x}, \frac{2}{11x}$
3. $\frac{5}{12x}, \frac{11}{18x}$
4. $\frac{8}{9x}, \frac{7}{6x}$
5. $\frac{x}{12}, \frac{x+3}{4}$
6. $\frac{x}{10}, \frac{x-3}{5}$
7. $\frac{x-6}{x+3}, \frac{x-5}{x-7}$
8. $\frac{x+4}{x+7}, \frac{x-3}{x+6}$
9. $\frac{2x+3}{3x-1}, \frac{4x+5}{x+2}$
10. $\frac{3x-4}{2x-1}, \frac{5x-2}{x-8}$

For Problems 11 through 70, do the indicated operations and simplify.

11. $\frac{5}{x} + \frac{3}{x}$
12. $\frac{7}{y} + \frac{4}{y}$
13. $\frac{2x}{3y} - \frac{5x}{3y}$
14. $\frac{a}{4b} - \frac{5a}{4b}$
15. $\frac{x}{8} + \frac{3x}{8}$
16. $\frac{c}{9} + \frac{5c}{9}$
17. $\frac{2}{a} + \frac{3}{b}$
18. $\frac{4}{d} + \frac{7}{j}$
19. $\frac{3}{r} - \frac{4}{s}$
20. $\frac{6}{x} - \frac{5}{x}$
21. $\frac{3}{2a} + \frac{1}{4a}$
22. $\frac{5}{6z} + \frac{2}{3z}$
23. $\frac{7}{10p} - \frac{3}{5p}$
24. $\frac{8}{9x} - \frac{2}{3x}$
25. $\frac{4}{5a} + \frac{2}{3a}$
26. $\frac{4}{7m} + \frac{3}{2m}$
27. $\frac{5}{4x} - \frac{2}{3x}$
28. $\frac{8}{3b} - \frac{2}{5b}$

29. $\frac{5}{6x} - \frac{1}{4x}$

30. $\frac{2}{9y} - \frac{5}{6y}$

31. $\frac{3}{ax} + \frac{2}{ay}$

32. $\frac{2}{rc} + \frac{4}{rd}$

33. $\frac{x-1}{3} + \frac{x+1}{6}$

34. $\frac{p+2}{6} + \frac{p-3}{8}$

35. $\frac{2c-3}{4} - \frac{c+2}{6}$

36. $\frac{3t+4}{8} - \frac{t+2}{3}$

37. $\frac{2a-b}{4} - \frac{a+4b}{10}$

38. $\frac{2x-1}{2} + \frac{x+2}{4}$

39. $\frac{5m-1}{6} - \frac{3m+2}{9}$

40. $\frac{3k+4}{3} - \frac{5k-1}{5}$

41. $\frac{a}{3} - \frac{3a}{7} + \frac{a}{21}$

42. $\frac{5a}{9} - \frac{3a}{2} + \frac{a}{6}$

43. $\frac{1}{4x} + \frac{1}{2x} - \frac{2}{3x}$

44. $\frac{2}{xy} + \frac{4}{xz} - \frac{3}{yz}$

45. $\frac{a}{2a+2b} + \frac{b}{2a+2b}$

46. $\frac{2a}{a+n} + \frac{2n}{a+n}$

47. $\frac{x}{3x-3y} - \frac{y}{3x-3y}$

48. $\frac{p}{3p-6} - \frac{2}{3p-6}$

49. $\frac{5}{6r-6s} - \frac{3}{4r-4s}$

50. $\frac{5}{6x-2y} - \frac{3}{9x-3y}$

51. $\frac{1}{2a-2b} + \frac{1}{4a-4b}$

52. $\frac{1}{3a+3b} + \frac{1}{12a+12b}$

53. $\frac{1}{x-1} + \frac{1}{x+1}$

54. $\frac{2}{x+3} + \frac{2}{x-3}$

55. $\frac{x}{x+y} - \frac{y}{x-y}$

56. $\frac{r}{r+7} - \frac{r}{r-7}$

57. $\frac{x}{x+3} - \frac{2}{x+4}$

58. $\frac{x}{x-1} - \frac{3}{x+5}$

59. $\frac{x-2}{x+4} + \frac{x+1}{x-2}$

60. $\frac{x+6}{x+3} + \frac{x+3}{x+6}$

61. $\frac{x+7}{x-1} - \frac{x+2}{x+3}$

62. $\frac{x-4}{x-2} - \frac{x-7}{x+1}$

63. $\frac{x-5}{x-10} - \frac{x-4}{x-2}$

64. $\frac{x-6}{x-1} - \frac{x-9}{x-3}$

65. $x + \dfrac{x+2}{x-2}$

66. $\dfrac{x-3}{x+4} + x$

67. $\dfrac{x^2 - 3x + 4}{x+2} - x$

68. $\dfrac{x^2 + 4x + 1}{x-3} - x$

69. $\dfrac{x-3}{x+5} \cdot \dfrac{x+5}{x-1}$

70. $\dfrac{x+8}{x-1} \cdot \dfrac{x+8}{x+2}$

11-6 COMBINED OPERATIONS AND SPECIAL CASES

There are some special cases you should know about when you simplify rational expressions, such as

$$\frac{5-x}{x-5}.$$

Here, the numerator and denominator are *opposites* of each other, as you can see by factoring -1 from the numerator.

$$\frac{5-x}{x-5} = \frac{-1(-5+x)}{x-5} = \frac{-1(x-5)}{x-5} = -1$$

The quick way to get this answer is to reason:

Any number divided by its opposite equals -1.

Caution is required here because some expressions *look* like opposites but really are *not*. For instance,

$$x - 5 \quad \text{and} \quad x + 5$$

are *conjugates*, not opposites. Nothing special happens when you divide two conjugates.

SPECIAL CASES

$\dfrac{x-5}{5-x} = -1$	A number divided by its opposite equals -1.
$\dfrac{x+5}{5+x} = 1$	A number divided by itself equals 1. ($x + 5$ and $5 + x$ are *equal*.)
$\dfrac{x-5}{x+5} = \dfrac{x-5}{x+5}$	A number divided by its conjugate is nothing special!

Another special case concerns the *opposite* of a fraction, such as

$$-\frac{7}{9}, \quad \frac{-7}{9}, \quad \text{and} \quad \frac{7}{-9}.$$

The expression $\frac{7}{9}$ means 7 divided by 9. Because negative divided by positive is negative and positive divided by negative is also negative, all three of these fractions are *equal*.

$$-\frac{7}{9} = \frac{-7}{9} = \frac{7}{-9}$$

The − sign can be associated with the numerator, the denominator, or the entire fraction. This fact is called the property of the opposite of a fraction.

PROPERTY

OPPOSITE OF A FRACTION

For any fraction $\frac{a}{b}$, $b \neq 0$,

$$-\frac{a}{b} = \frac{-a}{b} = \frac{a}{-b}.$$

Note that $\frac{-a}{-b}$ equals $+\frac{a}{b}$, since negative divided by negative is *positive*.

Objective

Be able to add, subtract, multiply, and divide rational algebraic expressions, and simplify the answer.

Cover the answers as you work these examples.

EXAMPLE 1

Simplify: $\dfrac{(x+2)(x-3)(x-4)}{(x+3)(4-x)(x+2)}$.

- - - - -   - - - - -

Think These Reasons

$\dfrac{(x+2)(x-3)(x-4)}{(x+3)(4-x)(x+2)}$ Write the given expression.

$= \dfrac{(x-3)(x-4)}{(x+3)(4-x)}$ Cancel the $(x + 2)$ factors.

$= -\dfrac{x-3}{x+3}$ $\dfrac{(x-4)}{(4-x)}$ equals -1. $(x - 3)$ and $(x + 3)$ are conjugates and do *not* cancel.

EXAMPLE 2

Perform the operations and simplify: $\dfrac{2x}{3x} - \dfrac{4}{5x} \div \dfrac{3}{10x}$.

- - - - -

$\dfrac{2x}{3x} - \dfrac{4}{5x} \div \dfrac{3}{10x}$ Write the given expression.

$= \dfrac{2x}{3x} - \dfrac{4}{5x} \cdot \dfrac{10x}{3}$ Multiply by the reciprocal.

$= \dfrac{2x}{3x} - \dfrac{40x}{15x}$ Multiply *before* subtracting.

$= \dfrac{2}{3} - \dfrac{8}{3}$ Cancel the x factors. Cancel 5.

$= -\dfrac{6}{3}$ Subtract the fractions.

$= -2$ Simplify.

EXAMPLE 3

Perform the operations and simplify: $\dfrac{2}{x+7} - \dfrac{1}{x-7}$.

- - - - -

$\dfrac{2}{x+7} - \dfrac{1}{x-7}$ Write the given expression.

$= \dfrac{2}{x+7} \cdot \dfrac{x-7}{x-7} - \dfrac{1}{x-7} \cdot \dfrac{x+7}{x+7}$ Write the fractions with common denominators.

$= \dfrac{2(x-7)-(x+7)}{(x+7)(x-7)}$ Add the numerators. Use the common denominator.

$= \dfrac{2x-14-x-7}{(x+7)(x-7)}$ Distribute 2 and -1 in the numerator.

$= \dfrac{x-21}{(x+7)(x-7)}$ Combine like terms in the numerator.

$= \dfrac{x-21}{x^2-49}$ Multiply the denominator factors. (This step is *optional*.)

EXAMPLE 4

Multiply and simplify: $\dfrac{x^2 - 10x + 9}{x^2 + x - 6} \cdot \dfrac{x^2 - 4}{1 - x^2}$.

$$\frac{x^2 - 10x + 9}{x^2 + x - 6} \cdot \frac{x^2 - 4}{1 - x^2}$$ Write the given expression.

$$= \frac{(x - 9)(x - 1)}{(x + 3)(x - 2)} \cdot \frac{(x + 2)(x - 2)}{(1 - x)(1 + x)}$$ Factor each numerator and denominator *first!* (If you multiply first, you get a *mess*.)

$$= \frac{(x - 9)(x - 1)(x + 2)(x - 2)}{(x + 3)(x - 2)(1 - x)(1 + x)}$$ Use the multiplication property of fractions.

$$= -\frac{(x - 9)(x + 2)}{(x + 3)(1 + x)}$$ Cancel the $(x - 2)$ factors. $\dfrac{x - 1}{1 - x}$ equals -1.

$$= -\frac{x^2 - 7x - 18}{x^2 + 4x + 3}$$ Do the indicated multiplication.

EXAMPLE 5

Subtract and simplify: $\dfrac{3x - 1}{x^2 + 2x - 15} - \dfrac{2}{x + 5}$.

$$\frac{3x - 1}{x^2 + 2x - 15} - \frac{2}{x + 5}$$ Write the given expression.

$$= \frac{3x - 1}{(x + 5)(x - 3)} - \frac{2}{x + 5}$$ Factor the denominator.

$$= \frac{3x - 1}{(x + 5)(x - 3)} - \frac{2}{x + 5} \cdot \frac{x - 3}{x - 3}$$ Write the fractions with common denominators. (You need transform only the *second* fraction.)

$$= \frac{3x - 1 - 2(x - 3)}{(x + 5)(x - 3)}$$ Subtract the numerators. Use the common denominator.

$$= \frac{3x - 1 - 2x + 6}{(x + 5)(x - 3)}$$ Distribute -2. (Be careful not to lose the $-$ sign!)

$$= \frac{x + 5}{(x + 5)(x - 3)}$$ Combine like terms.

$$= \frac{1}{x - 3}$$ Cancel the $(x + 5)$ factors. Do not lose the 1 in the numerator. Also, keep the denominator in *factored* form until the very end to see if any canceling can be done.

ORAL PRACTICE

Tell what each of the following fractions equals.

EXAMPLES

	Answers
i. $\dfrac{x-5}{5-x}$	i. -1
ii. $\dfrac{x-5}{x+5}$	ii. $\dfrac{x-5}{x+5}$
iii. $\dfrac{3}{-x}$	iii. $-\dfrac{3}{x}$

A. $\dfrac{x-7}{x-7}$ B. $\dfrac{x-7}{x+7}$ C. $\dfrac{x-7}{7-x}$

D. $\dfrac{x+7}{7+x}$ E. $\dfrac{2x+3}{2x-3}$ F. $\dfrac{3+2x}{2x+3}$

G. $\dfrac{2x-3}{3-2x}$ H. $\dfrac{2x+3}{3x+2}$ I. $\dfrac{-4}{x}$

J. $\dfrac{-x}{5}$ K. $\dfrac{x}{-y}$ L. $\dfrac{-x}{-y}$

M. $\dfrac{-(x+3)}{x+3}$ N. $-\dfrac{-(x+2)}{x+2}$ O. $\dfrac{x-5}{-(x-5)}$

P. $\dfrac{-(x+4)}{-(x+4)}$ Q. $\dfrac{-(x+4)}{-(4+x)}$ R. $\dfrac{-(3-x)}{x-3}$

S. $\dfrac{-x+3}{3-x}$ T. $-\dfrac{-(x-6)}{-(x-6)}$

EXERCISE 11-6

For Problems 1 through 10, simplify the expression.

1. $\dfrac{(x+7)(x-2)}{(x-7)(x-2)}$

2. $\dfrac{(x-8)(x+3)}{(x+8)(3+x)}$

3. $\dfrac{(x+3)(x-6)}{(x+3)(6-x)}$

4. $\dfrac{(x+5)(x-9)}{(x-5)(9-x)}$

5. $\dfrac{(a+4)(a-3)(2a-1)}{(4+a)(1-2a)(a+3)}$

6. $\dfrac{(r+6)(r-2)(2r+5)}{(6+r)(2r+5)(2-r)}$

7. $\dfrac{4-x^2}{x^2-4x+4}$

8. $\dfrac{x^2-6x+9}{9-x^2}$

9. $\dfrac{x^2-x-12}{6-x-x^2}$

10. $\dfrac{10+3x-x^2}{x^2+3x+2}$

For Problems 11 through 56, perform the indicated operations and simplify the answer.

11. $\dfrac{5}{7x}+\dfrac{4}{7x}-\dfrac{2}{7x}$

12. $\dfrac{4}{3x}-\dfrac{2}{3x}+\dfrac{7}{3x}$

13. $\dfrac{x}{5x}+\dfrac{2}{3x}\cdot\dfrac{6x}{5}$

14. $\dfrac{4x}{3x}-\dfrac{14}{9x}\cdot\dfrac{3x}{7}$

15. $\dfrac{3r}{r+s}+\dfrac{3s}{r+s}$

16. $\dfrac{5b}{a+b}+\dfrac{5a}{a+b}$

17. $\dfrac{c^2}{c-d}-\dfrac{d^2}{c-d}$

18. $\dfrac{h^2}{h-5}-\dfrac{25}{h-5}$

19. $\dfrac{36}{x-6}-\dfrac{x^2}{x-6}$

20. $\dfrac{64}{y-8}-\dfrac{y^2}{y-8}$

21. $\dfrac{2}{a}-\dfrac{3}{a^2}+\dfrac{4}{a^3}$

22. $\dfrac{5}{z^3}-\dfrac{6}{z^2}+\dfrac{7}{z}$

23. $\dfrac{6}{x^2}\cdot\dfrac{5}{2x^3}\div\dfrac{3x^4}{-4}$

24. $\dfrac{10}{x^5}\div\dfrac{5x^4}{6}\cdot\dfrac{1}{3x^2}$

25. $\dfrac{6u+12}{5}\cdot\dfrac{15u}{11u+22}$

26. $\dfrac{3v-15}{9v}\cdot\dfrac{v}{6v-30}$

27. $\dfrac{13x}{x-2}-\dfrac{26}{x-2}$

28. $\dfrac{7x}{x+5}+\dfrac{35}{x+5}$

29. $\dfrac{25-p^2}{12}\cdot\dfrac{6}{p-5}$

30. $\dfrac{4}{1-k^2}\cdot\dfrac{k+1}{4}$

31. $\dfrac{3}{x+4}+\dfrac{3}{x-4}$

32. $\dfrac{5}{x-3}+\dfrac{5}{x+3}$

33. $\dfrac{2}{x-5}-\dfrac{2}{x+5}$

34. $\dfrac{7}{x-8}-\dfrac{7}{x+8}$

35. $\dfrac{7}{x-3}+\dfrac{4}{3-x}$

36. $\dfrac{10}{x-4}+\dfrac{6}{4-x}$

37. $\dfrac{a}{a+3} \cdot \dfrac{3+a}{a^2+2a}$

38. $\dfrac{m-2}{m^2+5m} \cdot \dfrac{m}{2-m}$

39. $\dfrac{r}{r+5} - \dfrac{r^2-2}{r^2+5r}$

40. $\dfrac{c}{c-2} - \dfrac{c^2-1}{c^2-2c}$

41. $\dfrac{y}{y+1} \cdot (2y+2) - 2y$

42. $(3z-6) \cdot \dfrac{2z}{z-2} - 5z$

43. $\dfrac{x^2-x-12}{x^2-x-30} \cdot \dfrac{x^2-36}{9-x^2}$

44. $\dfrac{x^2-6x+5}{x^2-x-20} \cdot \dfrac{x^2-16}{1-x^2}$

45. $\dfrac{x^2+5x-14}{x^2-49} \div \dfrac{4-x^2}{x^2+9x+14}$

46. $\dfrac{36-x^2}{x^2-4x-12} \div \dfrac{x^2+10x+24}{x^2-4}$

47. $\dfrac{2x-11}{x^2-7x+12} + \dfrac{3}{(x-4)}$

48. $\dfrac{2x-36}{x^2-4x-12} + \dfrac{3}{x-6}$

49. $\dfrac{3x+35}{x^2-25} + \dfrac{2}{x+5}$

50. $\dfrac{5x-27}{x^2-9} + \dfrac{2}{x-3}$

51. $\dfrac{5x+17}{x^2+8x+7} - \dfrac{3}{x+7}$

52. $\dfrac{9x+35}{x^2-49} - \dfrac{7}{x-7}$

53. $\dfrac{2}{x-1} - \dfrac{x+9}{x^2+3x-4}$

54. $\dfrac{2}{x-3} - \dfrac{7x-3}{x^2+3x-18}$

55. $\dfrac{2}{x+6} - \dfrac{5x+28}{x^2+11x+30}$

56. $\dfrac{3}{x-5} - \dfrac{5x-16}{x^2-7x+10}$

57. ***The Density Property*** The diagram shows a number line. Between 3 and 4 there are many other numbers such as 3.5, 3.79, 3.22861154. . . , etc. If a set of numbers has the property that between any two of them there is another number of that kind, then the set of numbers is said to be *dense*. The work you have been doing with fractions allows you to tell whether or not certain sets of numbers are dense.

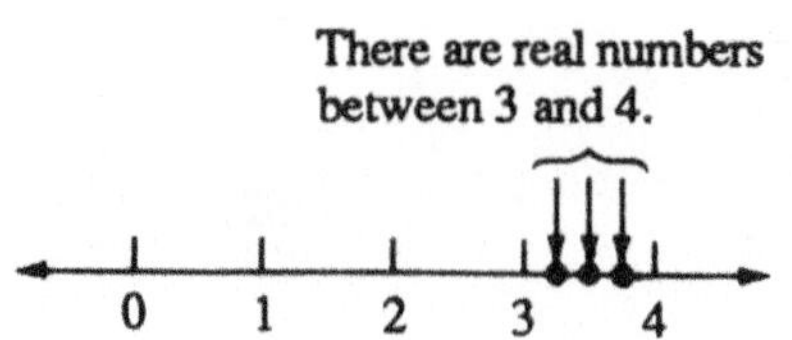
There are real numbers
between 3 and 4.
0
1
2
3
4

Answer the following questions.
a. Find a real number between 4.8 and 4.9.
b. Find five real numbers between 7.83 and 7.84.

c. Find the *average* of 378 and 381. Is the average ***between*** the two numbers, or somewhere else?
d. Explain why the set of real numbers is *dense* by telling how to find a number that is between any two given numbers x and y.
e. Find the average of $\frac{2}{7}$ and $\frac{3}{4}$. Is the answer between $\frac{2}{7}$ and $\frac{3}{4}$?
f. Let $x = \frac{a}{b}$ and let $y = \frac{c}{d}$, where a, b, c, and d stand for integers, and b and d are not zero. Why are x and y *rational* numbers?
g. Prove that the set of rational numbers is dense by showing that there is a rational number between any two given rational numbers.
h. Is there an *integer* between 73 and 76? Does this mean that the set of integers is dense? Explain your answer.

11-7 LONG DIVISION OF POLYNOMIALS

You know how to transform an improper fraction such as $\frac{747}{21}$ into a mixed number. First you long divide 747 by 21.

$$\begin{array}{r} 35 \\ 21\overline{)747} \\ \underline{63} \\ 117 \\ \underline{105} \\ 12 \end{array}$$

The answer is the sum of an integer and a proper fraction:

$$\frac{747}{21} = 35\frac{12}{21}.$$

A rational algebraic expression such as

$$\frac{3x^2 + 5x - 9}{x + 2}$$

can be thought of as an improper fraction, too, since its numerator is of higher degree than its denominator. The same long-division process can be used to transform this expression to the sum of a polynomial and a proper fraction. Here, step by step, is how it works.

First, write the fraction in long-division form.

$$x + 2\overline{)3x^2 + 5x - 9}$$

Divide $3x^2$ by x, getting $3x$. Write the $3x$ over the x-term in $3x^2 + 5x - 9$.

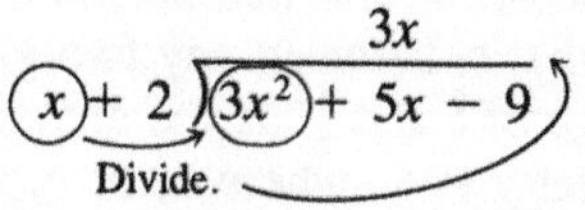

$$x + 2\overline{)3x^2 + 5x - 9}\quad\text{quotient: } 3x$$

Divide.

Now, multiply $3x$ by $x + 2$, getting $3x^2 + 6x$. Write this answer under the like terms in $3x^2 + 5x - 9$.

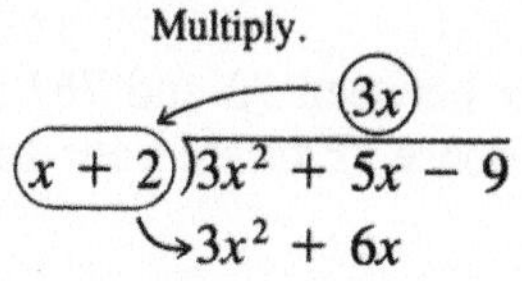

Multiply.

$$\begin{array}{r} 3x \\ x + 2\overline{)3x^2 + 5x - 9} \\ 3x^2 + 6x \end{array}$$

Subtract $3x^2 + 6x$ from $3x^2 + 5x - 9$.

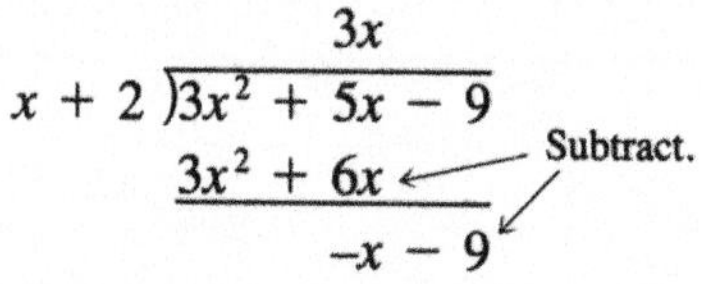

$$\begin{array}{r} 3x \\ x + 2\overline{)3x^2 + 5x - 9} \\ \underline{3x^2 + 6x} \\ -x - 9 \end{array}$$

Subtract.

Then you repeat the process, first dividing $-x$ by x, getting -1.

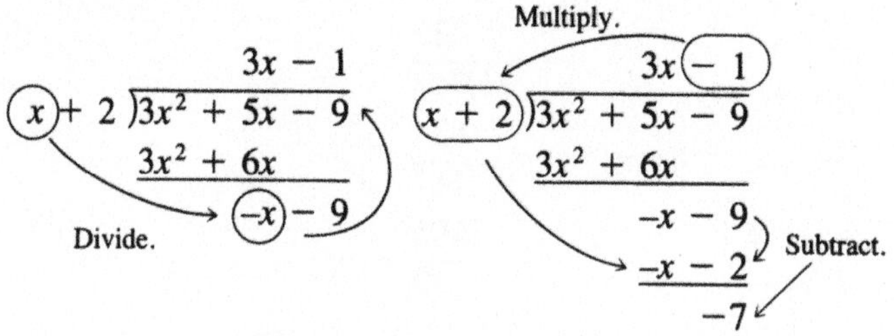

$$\begin{array}{r} 3x - 1 \\ x + 2\overline{)3x^2 + 5x - 9} \\ \underline{3x^2 + 6x} \\ -x - 9 \end{array}\qquad\begin{array}{r} 3x - 1 \\ x + 2\overline{)3x^2 + 5x - 9} \\ \underline{3x^2 + 6x} \\ -x - 9 \\ \underline{-x - 2} \\ -7 \end{array}$$

Divide. Multiply. Subtract.

So the answer is

$$\frac{3x^2 + 5x - 9}{x + 2} = 3x - 1 + \frac{-7}{x + 2}.$$

The polynomial $3x - 1$ is called the **quotient.** The number -7 is called the **remainder.**

The answer can be checked by multiplication.

$$(x + 2)\left(3x - 1 + \frac{-7}{x + 2}\right)$$

$= (x + 2)(3x - 1) + (-7)$	Distribute $x + 2$.
$= 3x^2 + 5x - 2 - 7$	Multiply the binomials.
$= 3x^2 + 5x - 9$	Combine like terms.

This yields the original numerator.

Objective

Given a rational algebraic expression in which a higher-degree polynomial is divided by a lower-degree polynomial, use long division to transform to mixed-number form—polynomial plus proper fraction.

The following examples help you master this technique. They also show you some tricky special cases. Cover the answer until you have worked the example.

EXAMPLE 1

Express $\dfrac{6x^2 + 8x - 4}{3x - 5}$ in mixed-number form.

$$\frac{6x^2 + 8x - 4}{3x - 5} = 2x + 6 + \frac{26}{3x - 5}$$

$$\begin{array}{r} 2x + 6 \\ 3x - 5 \overline{)\,6x^2 + 8x - 4} \\ \underline{6x^2 - 10x} \\ 18x - 4 \\ \underline{18x - 30} \\ 26 \end{array}$$

Check: $(3x - 5)(2x + 6) + 26$

$= 6x^2 + 8x - 30 + 26$

$= 6x^2 + 8x - 4$ ✓

Note: In the long division, $8x - (-10x)$ is $18x$ and $-4 - (-30)$ is 26.

EXAMPLE 2

Express $\dfrac{5x^3 + 7x^2 - 3x + 8}{x + 4}$ in mixed-number form.

$$\frac{5x^3 + 7x^2 - 3x + 8}{x + 4} = 5x^2 - 13x + 49 + \frac{-188}{x + 4}$$

$$\begin{array}{r} 5x^2 - 13x + 49 \\ x + 4 \overline{)\,5x^3 + 7x^2 - 3x + 8} \\ \underline{5x^3 + 20x^2} \\ -13x^2 - 3x + 8 \\ \underline{-13x^2 - 52x} \\ 49x + 8 \\ \underline{49x + 196} \\ -188 \end{array}$$

Check: $(x + 4)(5x^2 - 13x + 49) - 188$

$= 5x^3 - 13x^2 + 49x + 20x^2 - 52x + 196 - 188$

$= 5x^3 + 7x^2 - 3x + 8$ ✓

Note: In the check, multiply each term of $x + 4$ by each term of $5x^2 - 13x + 49$. Then combine like terms.

EXAMPLE 3

Express $\dfrac{x^3 - 3x^2 - 23x + 30}{x - 6}$ in mixed-number form.

- - - - -

$$\frac{x^3 - 3x^2 - 23x + 30}{x - 6}$$

$$\begin{array}{r} x^2 + 3x - 5 \\ x - 6 \overline{) x^3 - 3x^2 - 23x + 30} \\ \underline{x^3 - 6x^2 } \\ 3x^2 - 23x + 30 \\ \underline{3x^2 - 18x } \\ -5x + 30 \\ \underline{-5x + 30} \\ 0 \end{array}$$

Remainder is zero!

$$= \underline{\underline{x^2 + 3x - 5}}$$

Check: $(x - 6)(x^2 + 3x - 5)$

$= x^3 + 3x^2 - 5x - 6x^2 - 18x + 30$

$= x^3 - 3x^2 - 23x + 30$ ✔

Note: Since the remainder is *zero*, you can conclude that $x - 6$ is a *factor* of $x^3 - 3x^2 - 23x + 30$. As you can see in the check, $x^3 - 3x^2 - 23x + 30$ equals $(x - 6)(x^2 + 3x - 5)$.

EXAMPLE 4

Divide $x^3 + 27$ by $x + 3$, and write the quotient.

- - - - -

$$\frac{x^3 + 27}{x + 3}$$

$$\begin{array}{r} x^2 - 3x + 9 \\ x + 3 \overline{) x^3 + 0x^2 + 0x + 27} \\ \underline{x^3 + 3x^2 } \\ -3x^2 + 0x + 27 \\ \underline{-3x^2 - 9x } \\ 9x + 27 \\ \underline{9x + 27} \\ 0 \end{array}$$

Fill in the missing terms.

$$= \underline{\underline{x^2 - 3x + 9}}$$

Check: $(x + 3)(x^2 - 3x + 9)$

$= x^3 - 3x^2 + 9x + 3x^2 - 9x + 27$

$= x^3 + 27$ ✔

Note: In $x^3 + 27$, the x^2-term and the x-term are missing. Before you do the long division, you should put in these missing terms with zeros as their coefficients.

EXAMPLE 5

Express $\dfrac{2x^3 + 7x^2 - 8x - 11}{2x^2 + x - 5}$ in mixed-number form.

- - - - -

$$\frac{2x^3 + 7x^2 - 8x - 11}{2x^2 + x - 5}$$

$$\begin{array}{r} x + 3 \\ 2x^2 + x - 5 \overline{)2x^3 + 7x^2 - 8x - 11} \\ \underline{2x^3 + x^2 - 5x } \\ 6x^2 - 3x - 11 \\ \underline{6x^2 + 3x - 15} \\ -6x + 4 \end{array}$$

$$= x + 3 + \frac{-6x + 4}{2x^2 + x - 5}$$

Check: $(2x^2 + x - 5)(x + 3) + (-6x + 4)$

$= 2x^3 + 6x^2 + x^2 + 3x - 5x - 15 - 6x + 4$

$= 2x^3 + 7x^2 - 8x - 11$ ✓

Note: You can stop dividing when the degree of the remainder is less than the degree of the divisor.

EXERCISE 11-7

For Problems 1 through 24, write the expression in mixed-number form if the remainder is not 0 or as a single polynomial if the remainder is 0. It is advisable to check your answers as shown in the examples.

1. $\dfrac{x^2 + 5x - 11}{x + 3}$

2. $\dfrac{x^2 + 6x - 17}{x + 4}$

3. $\dfrac{6x^2 - 7x + 5}{2x - 1}$

4. $\dfrac{10x^2 - 9x + 7}{2x - 3}$

5. $\dfrac{12x^2 + 13x - 14}{3x - 2}$

6. $\dfrac{6x^2 + 11x - 35}{2x + 7}$

7. $\dfrac{x^3 - 2x^2 - 3x + 12}{x + 2}$

8. $\dfrac{x^3 - 4x^2 - 19x + 9}{x + 3}$

9. $\dfrac{x^3 - 7x^2 + 14x - 8}{x - 4}$

10. $\dfrac{x^3 - 9x^2 + 23x - 15}{x - 5}$

11. $\dfrac{8x^3 + 10x^2 - 13x - 20}{2x + 3}$

12. $\dfrac{12x^3 - 19x^2 - 25x - 10}{4x + 3}$

13. $\dfrac{x^3 + 7x^2 - 49}{x + 5}$

14. $\dfrac{x^3 + 5x^2 - 20}{x + 3}$

15. $\dfrac{4x^3 - 200x + 28}{x - 7}$

16. $\dfrac{5x^3 + 3x - 8}{x - 1}$

17. $\dfrac{x^3 - 729}{x - 9}$

18. $\dfrac{x^3 + 125}{x + 5}$

19. $\dfrac{x^3 - 4x^2 - x - 1}{x^2 - 2x - 5}$

20. $\dfrac{x^3 - 7x^2 + 10x + 9}{x^2 - 3x - 2}$

21. $\dfrac{2x^3 - 30x - 8}{x^2 + 4x + 1}$

22. $\dfrac{3x^3 - 5x^2 + 20}{x^2 - 3x + 4}$

23. $\dfrac{x^4 + 7x^3 + 5x^2 - 8x - 14}{x + 6}$

24. $\dfrac{x^4 + x^3 - 7x^2 - 2x + 8}{x - 2}$

25. ***Remainders Problem*** In this problem you will learn something about the remainder in a polynomial division problem.
    a. Divide $x^3 - 4x^2 + 9x - 10$ by $x - 3$. What is the remainder?
    b. Evaluate $x^3 - 4x^2 + 9x - 10$ if x is 3. How does the answer compare with the remainder in part (a)?
    c. Write the polynomial $x^3 - 4x^2 + 9x - 10$ in the form

    $$(x - 3)(\text{quotient}) + \text{remainder},$$

    using the results of parts (a) and (b). Based on the multiplication property of zero, explain why substituting 3 for x leaves only the remainder.
    d. Show that the polynomial $x^3 - 4x^2 + 9x - 10$ is zero if x is 2. What would you expect the remainder to be if the polynomial is divided by $x - 2$?

26. ***Factor Theorem and the Computer*** From Problem 25 you saw that if you substitute a number n for x in a polynomial such as $x^3 - 4x^2 + 9x - 10$, the *value* of the polynomial equals the *remainder* when the polynomial is divided by $x - n$. If this remainder is 0, then $x - n$ is a *factor* of the polynomial. This conclusion is called the **factor theorem.**

FACTOR THEOREM

$x - n$ is a *factor* of a polynomial if and only if the polynomial equals 0 when n is substituted for x.

The following computer program evaluates polynomials.

```
 10  PRINT "TYPE VALUES OF A, B, C, D"
 20  INPUT A,B,C,D
 30  PRINT " X      Y"
 40  PRINT "---    ---"
 50  FOR X =  -  ABS (D) TO ABS (D)
 60  LET Y =A * X * X * X + B * X * X + C * X + D
 70  PRINT X,Y
 80  IF Y <  > 0 THEN 100
 90  PRINT "***********"
100  NEXT X
110  END
```

For instance, to evaluate $x^3 - 4x^2 + 9x - 10$, you would type in

$$1, -4, 9, -10$$

for A, B, C, and D. Then the computer would evaluate the polynomial for each integer value of x, starting at -10 and ending at 10. The computer would print the value of x and the value of the polynomial. It would also print a row of asterisks, ***********, if the value of the polynomial is 0.

a. Run the program using the polynomial $x^3 - 4x^2 + x + 6$. Use the resulting output to find all factors of the form $x - n$ (such as $x - 3$), where n is a value of x that makes the polynomial equal 0.
b. Run the program again using $x^3 - 5x^2 + 11x - 15$. Write the *one* factor you discover. Then divide the factor into the polynomial to find the other factor.
c. Run the program again to show that there are *no* integer values of x that make $x^3 - 4x^2 + x + 5$ equal 0.

1-8 FRACTIONAL EQUATIONS AND EXTRANEOUS SOLUTIONS

In Section 12.1 you found values of x when you knew the value of a rational expression. For instance, you found x when

$$\frac{x - 5}{x + 4} = 9.$$

Equations like this that have a variable in a denominator are called *fractional equations*.

DEFINITION

> **FRACTIONAL EQUATION**
> A **fractional equation** is an equation that has a variable in at least one denominator.

Now that you know how to operate with rational expressions, you are prepared to solve more complicated fractional equations, such as

$$\frac{3}{x} + \frac{5}{6} = \frac{1}{4x}.$$

The way to work a new problem is to transform it into an old problem. For fractional equations, this means getting rid of the fractions. The technique is to *multiply* each member of the equation by the LCM of the denominators. The LCM of x, 6, and $4x$ is $12x$. So you write

$$12x\left(\frac{3}{x} + \frac{5}{6}\right) = 12x\left(\frac{1}{4x}\right).$$

On the right, $4x$ divided into $12x$ is 3. On the left, you distribute $12x$ to each term.

$$12x\left(\frac{3}{x}\right) + 12x\left(\frac{5}{6}\right) = 3(1)$$

Canceling can now be done in each term on the left, giving

$$12(3) + 2x(5) = 3(1).$$

Multiplying gives

$$36 + 10x = 3.$$

$$10x = -33$$

$$x = -3.3$$

$$\therefore S = \{-3.3\}$$

Check:
$$\frac{3}{-3.3} + \frac{5}{6} \stackrel{?}{=} \frac{1}{4(-3.3)}$$

$$-0.90909\ldots + 0.83333\ldots \stackrel{?}{=} -0.07575\ldots$$

$$-0.07575\ldots = -0.07575\ldots \quad ✓$$

Sometimes there are surprises when you solve a fractional equation. For

$$\frac{3}{x-2} - \frac{6}{x^2 - 2x} = 1,$$

the LCM of the denominators (the LCD) is found by factoring.

$$\frac{3}{x-2} - \frac{6}{x(x-2)} = 1,$$

so the LCD is $x(x - 2)$. Multiplying each member by this number gives

$$x(x-2)\left(\frac{3}{x-2} - \frac{6}{x(x-2)}\right) = x(x-2)(1).$$

Distributing on the left and right gives

$$x(x-2) \cdot \frac{3}{x-2} - x(x-2) \cdot \frac{6}{x(x-2)} = x^2 - 2x.$$

Canceling on the left leaves

$$3x - 6 = x^2 - 2x.$$

Subtracting $3x$ and adding 6 gives

$$0 = x^2 - 5x + 6.$$

This is now a familiar quadratic equation. In this case the right member *factors*, giving

$$0 = (x-2)(x-3).$$

Setting each factor equal to 0 gives

$$x - 2 = 0 \quad \text{or} \quad x - 3 = 0$$

$$x = 2 \quad \text{or} \quad x = 3.$$

The surprise comes when you check the answers.

$x = 2$:

$$\frac{3}{2-2} - \frac{6}{4-4} \stackrel{?}{=} 1$$

$$\frac{3}{0} - \frac{6}{0} \stackrel{?}{=} 1 \quad \text{Does not check!}$$

$x = 3$:

$$\frac{3}{3-2} - \frac{6}{9-6} \stackrel{?}{=} 1$$

$$1 = 1 \ \checkmark$$

In this example, 2 satisfies the *transformed* equation, $0 = x^2 - 5x + 6$. But it does *not* satisfy the original equation. Such a number is called an *extraneous solution*.

DEFINITION

EXTRANEOUS SOLUTION

An **extraneous solution** is a value of the variable that satisfies the *transformed* equation, but *not* the original one.

The difficulty arises because x cannot equal 2 in the original equation. Fractions are *undefined* if their denominators are zero. As soon as you find out that the LCD is $x(x - 2)$, you should state that $x \neq 0$ and $x \neq 2$. These numbers are said to be out of the *domain* of the variable.

DEFINITION

DOMAIN
The **domain** of a variable is the set of numbers that can be values of the variable.

Note: The domain of the variable must exclude all numbers that make a denominator equal zero.

When you find the LCD for the above equation, you should write

LCD: $x(x - 2)$
Domain exclusions: $x \neq 0$ and $x \neq 2$.

At the end of the problem you should *cross out* any extraneous solutions before you write the solution set.

Extraneous.

$\cancel{x = 2}$ or $x = 3$

$\therefore S = \{3\}$

Objective

Be able to solve a fractional equation, discarding any extraneous solutions.

Cover the answers as you work these examples.

EXAMPLE 1

Solve: $\dfrac{7}{2x} - \dfrac{3}{5} = \dfrac{1}{10}$.

		Think These Reasons
$\dfrac{7}{2x} - \dfrac{3}{5} = \dfrac{1}{10}$	LCD: $10x$ Domain exclusion: $x \neq 0$	Write the given equation. Write the LCD and domain exclusion.

$10x\left(\frac{7}{2x} - \frac{3}{5}\right) = 10x\left(\frac{1}{10}\right)$	Multiply each member by the LCD.
$5(7) - 2x(3) = x(1)$	Distribute $10x$ and cancel.
$35 - 6x = x$	Multiply.
$-7x = -35$	Subtract 35 and subtract x.
$x = 5$	Divide by -7.
$\therefore S = \{5\}$	Write the solution set. (5 is *not* excluded from the domain. So it *is* a solution.)

EXAMPLE 2

Solve: $\frac{3}{x-5} + \frac{3}{x+5} = 7$.

- - - - -

$\frac{3}{x-5} + \frac{3}{x+5} = 7$	LCD: $(x-5)(x+5)$ Domain exclusions: $x \neq 5, x \neq -5$.	Write the given equation. Write the LCD and domain exclusions.

$\left(\frac{3}{x-5} + \frac{3}{x+5}\right)(x-5)(x+5) = 7(x-5)(x+5)$	Multiply each member by the LCD.
$3(x+5) + 3(x-5) = 7(x^2 - 25)$	Distribute and cancel on the left. Multiply on the right.
$3x + 15 + 3x - 15 = 7x^2 - 175$	Distribute.
$6x = 7x^2 - 175$	Combine like terms.
$0 = 7x^2 - 6x - 175$	Make one member equal zero.
$x = \frac{6 \pm \sqrt{36 - 4(7)(-175)}}{2(7)}$	Use the Quadratic Formula.
$x = \frac{6 \pm \sqrt{4936}}{14}$	Do the computation.
$x \approx 5.45$ or $x \approx -4.59$	Round to two decimal places.
$\therefore S = \{5.45, -4.59\}$	Write the solution set. (Neither value of x is excluded from the domain, so both values are solutions.)

EXAMPLE 3

Solve: $\frac{2x}{x-3} - \frac{6}{x-3} = 9$.

- - - - -

$\dfrac{2x}{x-3} - \dfrac{6}{x-3} = 9$	LCD: $x - 3$ Domain exclusion: $x \neq 3$	Write the given equation. Write the LCD and domain exclusion.
$\left(\dfrac{2x}{x-3} - \dfrac{6}{x-3}\right)(x-3) = 9(x-3)$		Multiply each member by the LCD.
$2x - 6 = 9x - 27$		Distribute and cancel.
$-7x = -21$		Add 6: subtract $9x$.
$x = 3$ Extraneous.		Divide by -7. Discard the extraneous solution.
$\therefore S = \emptyset$		Write the solution set. (Since the only possible solution is out of the domain, the solution set is empty.)

ORAL PRACTICE

Give the LCD and the restrictions on the domain of x.

EXAMPLE

$\dfrac{3}{x+5} = \dfrac{7}{x-2}$

Answers
LCD = $(x + 5)(x - 2)$.
Domain: $x \neq -5, x \neq 2$.

A. $\dfrac{x-4}{x} = \dfrac{5}{x}$

B. $\dfrac{x}{x-4} = \dfrac{x}{5}$

C. $\dfrac{x-7}{2x} = \dfrac{9}{2x}$

D. $\dfrac{2x}{x-7} = \dfrac{2x}{9}$

E. $\dfrac{x+3}{x+4} = 5$

F. $\dfrac{x-2}{x+3} = \dfrac{x-5}{x-3}$

G. $\dfrac{x+3}{x} = \dfrac{6}{x-2}$

H. $\dfrac{x+3}{5} = \dfrac{6}{x-2}$

I. $\dfrac{1}{x} + \dfrac{1}{3x} = \dfrac{1}{4}$

EXERCISE 11-8

For Problems 1 through 24, solve the equation, discarding any extraneous solutions.

1. $\dfrac{4x-3}{x}=\dfrac{17}{x}$

2. $\dfrac{3x-8}{x}=\dfrac{13}{x}$

3. $\dfrac{11}{r}=\dfrac{7r+5}{3r}$

4. $\dfrac{7}{s}=\dfrac{4s-1}{5s}$

5. $\dfrac{x-2}{x}-\dfrac{7}{3x}=\dfrac{3}{4x}$

6. $\dfrac{x-3}{x}-\dfrac{6}{5x}=\dfrac{7}{2x}$

7. $\dfrac{1}{7}+\dfrac{1}{x}=\dfrac{1}{5}$

8. $\dfrac{1}{50}+\dfrac{1}{x}=\dfrac{1}{30}$

9. $\dfrac{1}{5}-\dfrac{1}{20}=\dfrac{1}{x}$

10. $\dfrac{1}{3}-\dfrac{1}{4}=\dfrac{1}{x}$

11. $\dfrac{b}{b+2}=\dfrac{3}{7}$

12. $\dfrac{a}{a+4}=\dfrac{8}{3}$

13. $\dfrac{3}{2x}=\dfrac{5}{x-7}$

14. $\dfrac{7}{3x}=\dfrac{4}{x-2}$

15. $\dfrac{x}{x-3}-\dfrac{3}{x-3}=8$

16. $\dfrac{8}{x-2}-\dfrac{x}{x-2}=5$

17. $\dfrac{4}{x+2}-\dfrac{x}{x+2}=3$

18. $\dfrac{x}{x+6}+\dfrac{6}{x+6}=11$

19. $\dfrac{8}{x+6}+\dfrac{8}{x-6}=1$

20. $\dfrac{3}{x-4}+\dfrac{3}{x+4}=1$

21. $\dfrac{2}{x+5}-\dfrac{1}{x-3}=3$

22. $\dfrac{3}{x-1}-\dfrac{2}{x+4}=5$

23. $\dfrac{x}{x+2}-\dfrac{7}{x+4}=2$

24. $\dfrac{3}{x-4}-\dfrac{5}{x+3}=2$

For Problems 25 through 34, add or subtract the fractions and simplify the answer. Remember that these are *expressions,* not equations. You cannot get rid of the denominators by multiplying each term by the LCD.

25. $\dfrac{8}{5x}+\dfrac{7}{10x}$

26. $\dfrac{7}{6x}+\dfrac{5}{3x}$

27. $\dfrac{2}{x+1}+\dfrac{3}{x+4}$

28. $\dfrac{5}{x+3}+\dfrac{2}{x+1}$

29. $\dfrac{4}{x+3} + \dfrac{4}{x-3}$

30. $\dfrac{6}{x+2} + \dfrac{6}{x-2}$

31. $\dfrac{x^2}{x-5} - \dfrac{25}{x-5}$

32. $\dfrac{x^2}{x-4} - \dfrac{16}{x-4}$

33. $\dfrac{5}{x-2} - \dfrac{4}{2-x}$

34. $\dfrac{7}{x-5} - \dfrac{4}{5-x}$

35. *General Proof of the Quadratic Formula*—In Section 6.8 you derived the Quadratic Formula by using a specific example, $5x^2 + 13x + 7 = 0$. Now that you have studied operations with algebraic fractions, you should be able to derive the formula in general. Starting with $ax^2 + bx + c = 0$, derive the Quadratic Formula.

11-9 PROBLEMS INVOLVING RATIO AND PROPORTION

If somebody says that men and women are in a 3-to-8 ratio, it means that

$$\frac{\text{number of men}}{\text{number of women}} = \frac{3}{8}.$$

There are many ways this equation could be true. For instance, there could be 3 men and 8 women. Or there could be 6 men and 16 women because

$$\frac{6}{16} = \frac{(3)(2)}{(8)(2)} = \frac{3}{8}.$$

The number of men must be a multiple of 3, and the number of women must be the *same* multiple of 8. This means that there is a number x such that

$$3x = \text{number of men},$$

$$8x = \text{number of women}.$$

The number x is a *common factor* of the number of men and the number of women. Suppose that in addition to knowing the ratio 3 : 8 (a short way of writing the ratio 3 to 8), you also know that there is a total of 407 people in the group. How many of each would there be?

Since $3x$ is the number of men and $8x$ is the number of women, you can write

$$3x + 8x = 407$$

$$11x = 407$$

$$x = 37.$$

So there are (3)(37), or 111, men and (8)(37), or 296, women.

In this section you will work more problems involving ratios of two integers.

Objective:

Given two integers, find their ratio in lowest terms; or given information about two integers including their ratio, find the integers.

Cover the answers as you work the examples.

EXAMPLE 1

Fish Problem Naturalists estimate that there are 3000 fish in Lake Muchimuck. Some are perch and the rest are bass. They drag a fishing net through the lake and catch 24 perch and 21 bass.

a. What is the ratio of perch to bass caught? Express the answer in lowest terms.

b. Assuming that the entire lake has this ratio, how many of each kind of fish were there (including those caught)?

- - - - -

a. $$\frac{\text{number of perch}}{\text{number of bass}} = \frac{24}{21} = \frac{8}{7}$$

Ratio is 8 : 7.

- - - - -

	Think These Reasons
b. Let x = common factor.	Define a variable.
$8x$ = Number of perch. $7x$ = Number of bass.	Write expressions for the numbers of fish.
$8x + 7x = 3000$ (Total number of fish) (is) (3000.)	Write an equation
$15x = 3000$	
$x = 200$	Solve the equation.
$\therefore 8x = 1600, \quad 7x = 1400$	Evaluate the expressions.
1600 perch, 1400 bass.	Answer the question.

Check: $1600 + 1400 = 3000$, and $\frac{1600}{1400} = \frac{8}{7}$, which checks.

EXAMPLE 2

Triangle Problem The sides of a triangle have lengths in the ratio 3 : 5 : 7. The perimeter of the triangle is 90 centimeters. Find the lengths of the sides.

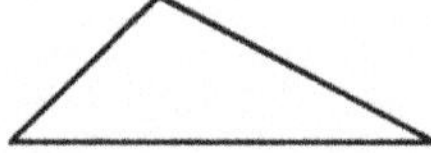

Note: The numbers 3 : 5 : 7 mean that sides 1 and 2 are in the ratio 3 : 5, sides 2 and 3 are in the ratio 5 : 7, and sides 1 and 3 are in the ratio 3 : 7.

Let x = common factor.
$\therefore$ $3x$, $5x$, and $7x$ are the lengths of the sides.

$$\underbrace{3x + 5x + 7x}_{\text{The perimeter}} \underbrace{=}_{\text{is}} \underbrace{90}_{90.}$$

$$15x = 90$$

$$x = 6$$

$$3x = 18, \qquad 5x = 30, \qquad 7x = 42.$$

$\therefore$ Sides are 18 cm, 30 cm, and 42 cm.

Check: $18 + 30 + 42 = 90$; $18 : 30 = 3 : 5$, $30 : 42 = 5 : 7$, $18 : 42 = 3 : 7$.

EXAMPLE 3

Freshmen and Sophomores Problem The freshmen at Scorpion Gulch High School outnumber the sophomores 7 : 5. If there are 231 freshmen, how many sophomores are there?

Let x = number of sophomores. — Define a variable.

$$\therefore \frac{231}{x} = \frac{7}{5}$$ — Write an equation.

(The ratio of freshmen to sophomores) (is) (7 : 5.)

$$5x\left(\frac{231}{x}\right) = 5x\left(\frac{7}{5}\right)$$ — Multiply each member by the LCD.

$$5(231) = 7x$$ — Cancel.

$$1155 = 7x$$ — Multiply.

$$165 = x$$ — Divide each member by 7.

165 sophomores. — Answer the question.

Check: $\frac{231}{165} = 1.4$, which equals $\frac{7}{5}$.

Note: In this problem you already *know* one of the two integers. So it is easier to define the variable to be the *other* integer rather than the common factor.

The equation in Example 3,

$$\frac{231}{x} = \frac{7}{5}$$

is called a **proportion.** It says that two ratios are equal. There is an easy way to solve a proportion. If you look at the third step in the example you see

$$(5)(231) = 7x.$$

This step can be reached by **cross multiplication.**

$$\frac{231}{x} \times \frac{7}{5}$$ Cross multiply.

To find a way to describe cross multiplication, write the fractions in ratio form.

$$231 : x = 7 : 5$$

This equation is read "231 is to x as 7 is to 5." The 231 and 5 are called **extremes** since they are at the two ends of the proportion. The x and 7 are called **means,** since they are in the middle of the proportion.

Means.

$$231 : x = 7 : 5$$ ← A proportion.

Extremes.

Since this equation is equivalent to $7x = (231)(5)$, you can say that the product of the means equals the product of the extremes. It may be easier for you to remember the cross-multiplying technique, but you should at least remember the words so that you will know what they mean.

DEFINITION

CROSS MULTIPLICATION
In a proportion such as $a : b = c : d$, the product of the means equals the product of the extremes.

That is, if $\frac{a}{b} = \frac{c}{d}$,

then $ad = bc$.

ORAL PRACTICE

Tell what the ratio would be in lowest terms.

EXAMPLES

	Answers
i. 15 : 25	i. 3 to 5
ii. 15 : 22	ii. Already in lowest terms.

A. 14 : 35　B. 24 : 36　C. 12 : 4　D. 8 : 48

E. 9 : 48　F. 10 : 48　G. 28 : 21　H. 21 : 14

I. 21 : 12　J. 21 : 10

Tell the result of cross multiplication.

EXAMPLE

	Answer
$\frac{2}{3} = \frac{10}{x}$	$2x = 30$

K. $\frac{5}{7} = \frac{9}{x}$　L. $\frac{3}{8} = \frac{4}{x}$　M. $\frac{5}{x} = \frac{10}{27}$　N. $\frac{7}{x} = \frac{1}{2}$　O. $\frac{x}{5} = \frac{2}{x}$

EXERCISE 11-9

1. *Ratio Problem 1* The ratio of two integers is 13 : 6. The smaller integer is 54. Find the larger integer.
2. *Ratio Problem 2* The ratio of two integers is 7 : 11. The larger integer is 187. Find the smaller integer.
3. *Ratio Problem 3* The ratio of two integers is 9 : 7. Their sum is 1024. Find the two integers.
4. *Ratio Problem 4* The ratio of two integers is 17 : 13. Their sum is 390. Find the integers.
5. *Grandchildren Problem* Mae Berry has 18 grandchildren on her son's side and 12 grandchildren on her daughter's side.

a. What is the ratio of these numbers, in lowest terms?
b. The elder Berry divides 7200 acres of land into two tracts, whose areas are in this ratio. How many acres are in each tract?

6. *Will Problem* A. Mann regularly gives $300 a month to charity and $800 a month to his grandchildren.
   a. What is the ratio of these two numbers, in lowest terms?
   b. Mr. Mann's will specifies that his estate will be divided in the same ratio. If his estate contains $104,500, how much will go to charity and how much will go to his grandchildren?

7. *Price-to-Earnings Ratio Problem* The stock of a certain company is priced at $18.20 per share. The company's earnings for one year amounted to $2.80 per share.
   a. Find the price-to-earnings ratio. Express it both as a ratio of two integers in lowest terms and as a ratio ___ : 1 (as it appears in newspapers), where the second number is 1 and the first number is not necessarily an integer.
   b. If the company earned $3,360,000 in that year, what was the total value of its stock?

8. *Commission-to-Selling-Price Ratio Problem* A real estate agent sold a house for $84,000. The agent's commission was $5040.
   a. What was the commission-to-selling-price ratio? Express the answer both as a ratio of two integers in lowest terms and as a *percent*.
   b. What would the commission be for a house that sells for $278,000 if the commission-to-selling-price ratio is the same?

9. *Basketball Tickets Problem* You are called upon to estimate how many of the 12,000 people who attend a professional basketball game are women. From a small sample, you determine that the ratio of men to women is about 3 : 2. About how many of the people attending are women?

10. *Peanut Contest Problem* A large jar contains 8400 nuts. You will receive a prize if you guess closest to the number of peanuts in the jar. From a small sample, you find that the ratio of peanuts to other nuts is about 3 : 4. Based on this information, about how many peanuts are in the jar?

11. *Milk Stock Problem* Suppose that you work in a supermarket. The milk display case can hold a total of 160 one-gallon containers of milk. Sales figures show that the cheaper generic milk outsells the national brand milk by 7 : 3. How many containers of each kind should you put in the case in order to have this ratio?

12. *Two Grades of Gasoline Problem* A local filling station finds that unleaded gas outsells regular gas in the ratio 9 : 4. The station's monthly quota is a total of 26,000 liters. How many liters of each kind should be ordered so that the quota will have this ratio?

13. ***Three Grades of Gasoline Problem*** A local filling station sells regular, unleaded, and super-unleaded gasoline in the ratio 5 : 7 : 2. Their total monthly quota is 28,000 liters of gasoline. How many liters of each kind should be ordered so that the quota will have this ratio?

14. ***Cereal Stock Problem*** A supermarket's cereal shelves have room for 510 boxes of cereal. Sales figures show that corn flakes, wheat flakes, and other cereals sell in the ratio of 5 : 3 : 9. How many boxes of each kind of cereal should be put on the shelves so that when the shelves are full the numbers of boxes will be in this ratio?

15. ***Triangle Problem 1*** The sides of a triangle are in the ratio 7 : 10 : 11. Its perimeter is 112 meters. How long is each side?

16. ***Triangle Problem 2*** The sides of a triangle are in the ratio 6 : 7 : 10. The perimeter is 184 furlongs. How long is each side?

17. ***Rectangle Problem 1*** The length and width of a rectangle are in the ratio 3 : 2. The perimeter is 73 centimeters. Find the length and the width.

18. ***Rectangle Problem 2*** The length and width of a rectangle are in the ratio 5 : 3. The perimeter is 56 feet. Find the length and the width.

19. ***Fish in the Lake Problem*** Ecologists are trying to determine how many fish there are in a particular lake. They catch 100 fish from the lake, put small tags on their tails, and put them back into the lake. Several days later they catch 15 fish. They find that 2 are tagged and the other 13 are not. Assuming that the tagged to untagged fish are in the ratio 2 : 13, how many fish are in the lake (counting the 15)?

20. ***Radioactive Blood Problem*** Researchers are trying to determine how much blood a particular animal has in its body. Since actually draining out the blood to measure it would kill the animal, they withdraw 100 milliliters (ml) of blood and replace it with 100 ml of slightly radioactive blood. They later withdraw a sample and find that the ratio of radioactive to nonradioactive blood is 2 : 34. About how many milliliters of blood does the animal have?

21. ***Age Problem 1*** Clara Fye is 31 years old. Her sister Molly is 47. When will their ages be in the ratio 4 : 5?

22. ***Age Problem 2*** Juan Ting is 23 years old. His sister Tess is 20. When will their ages be in the ratio 3 : 2? Surprising?

23. ***Clock Face Problem*** A clock reads 5:00.
    a. What is the ratio of the area on the clock's face between the two hands to the rest of the area?
    b. If the total area is 132 square centimeters, what is the area between the hands?

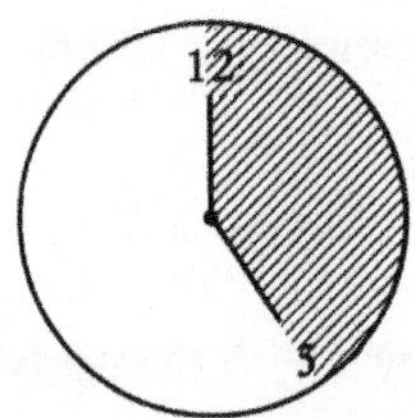

24. *Similar Rectangles Problem* The ratio of length to width is 3 : 2 for each of the two rectangles. The length of the larger rectangle is in the ratio 7 : 5 to that of the smaller one. What is the ratio of the *areas* of the two rectangles?

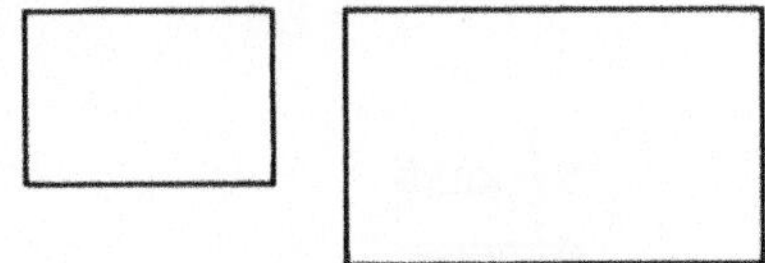

-10 PROBLEMS INVOLVING PROBABILITY AND OTHER RATIONAL EXPRESSIONS

The expressions you have been studying in this chapter have variables in their denominators. Such expressions can represent quantities in the real world. For instance, you recall that

$$\text{rate} \times \text{time} = \text{distance}.$$

Dividing each member of this equation by rate or by time gives

$$\text{rate} = \frac{\text{distance}}{\text{time}} \quad \text{or} \quad \text{time} = \frac{\text{distance}}{\text{rate}}.$$

If time or rate are variables, then these expressions will have variables in their denominators. For instance, suppose you travel through the water at x km/h against a current of 5 km/h. Your net speed is

$$x - 5.$$

If you travel a total distance of 10 km at this speed, the time it takes you will be

$$\text{time} = \frac{10}{x - 5}.$$

If x is 7, then

$$\text{time} = \frac{10}{7 - 5} = \frac{10}{2} = 5 \text{ hours}.$$

If x is 25, then

$$\text{time} = \frac{10}{25 - 5} = \frac{10}{20} = \frac{1}{2} \text{ hour}.$$

Suppose that you want to complete a 10-km trip in 3 h. You would write the *equation*

$$3 = \frac{10}{x - 5}.$$

Multiplying each member by $x - 5$ then solving for x gives

$$3(x - 5) = 10$$
$$3x - 15 = 10$$
$$3x = 25$$
$$x = 8\frac{1}{3}$$

$8\frac{1}{3}$ km/h

In this section you will work more problems in which variables appear in denominators. Some problems will relate to the real world. Others will be contest-type problems designed only to see if you can do the algebra.

Objective

Be able to write rational expressions involving quantities from the real world, and evaluate these expressions or solve for their variables.

The following examples show you how to do these things. You may like to try them on your own before you uncover the solutions.

EXAMPLE 1

Upstream-Downstream Problem A boat moves through the water at x km/h. It makes a journey 20 km upstream against a current of 3 km/h and then returns with the current.

a. Write an expression for the total time for the round trip.
b. How long will the round trip take if the boat goes 10 km/h through the water?
c. How fast must the boat travel through the water in order to complete the round trip in 5 hours?

- - - - - - - - - -

Think These Reasons

a. x = number of km/h the boat goes.	Restate the variable.
$\therefore x - 3$ = number of km/h upstream.	boat speed − current speed.

$x + 3$ = number of km/h downstream. — boat speed + current speed.

$\dfrac{20}{x-3}$ = number of hours upstream. — time = distance/rate.

$\dfrac{20}{x+3}$ = number of hours downstream.

$\dfrac{20}{x-3} + \dfrac{20}{x+3}$ = total time for round trip.

- - - - -

b. If $x = 10$, then

$$\frac{20}{x-3} + \frac{20}{x+3}$$ Write the expression.

$$= \frac{20}{10-3} + \frac{20}{10+3}$$ Substitute 10 for x.

$$\approx 2.857 + 1.539$$ Do the arithmetic.

$$= 4.396.$$

About 4.4 hours. — Answer the question.

- - - - -

c. If the time is 5 hours, then

$$\frac{20}{x-3} + \frac{20}{x+3} = 5$$ Write an equation.

$$(x-3)(x+3)\left(\frac{20}{x-3} + \frac{20}{x+3}\right) = 5(x-3)(x+3)$$ Multiply each member by LCD.

$$(x+3)(20) + (x-3)(20) = 5(x^2 - 9)$$ Distribute on the left; multiply on the right.

$$20x + 60 + 20x - 60 = 5x^2 - 45$$ Distribute.

Think These Reasons

$$0 = 5x^2 - 40x - 45$$ Make one member equal 0.

$$0 = x^2 - 8x - 9$$ Simplify (if possible).

$$x = \frac{8 \pm \sqrt{64 - 4(1)(-9)}}{2(1)}$$ Use the Quadratic Formula.

$$x = \frac{8 \pm \sqrt{100}}{2}$$ Simplify.

$x = 9$ or ~~-1~~ ↗ Out of domain. — Do the computation. Discard meaningless solutions.

9 km/h — Answer the question.

Note: In this case, you could also have solved the equation by factoring. Here's how.

$$0 = (x - 9)(x + 1)$$

$$x - 9 = 0 \quad \text{or} \quad x + 1 = 0$$

$$x = 9 \quad \text{or} \quad x = -1$$

EXAMPLE 2

Swimming Pool Problem The fill pipe can fill an empty swimming pool in 5 h. With the fill pipe and the garden hose both running, it takes only 3 h to fill an empty pool. How long would it take to fill the pool with just the hose?

- - - - -

Let x = number of hours for hose alone.	Define a variable.
Work = rate × time.	(Similar to $d = rt$.)
$\therefore$ Rate $= \dfrac{\text{work}}{\text{time}}$.	Divide by time.
Fill pipe's rate is $\dfrac{1}{5}$ pool per hour.	Rate = work/time.
Hose's rate is $\dfrac{1}{x}$ pool per hour.	In this case, the work is 1 pool.
$\therefore$ Combined rate is $\dfrac{1}{5} + \dfrac{1}{x}$.	Add the rates.
Combined time is 3 h.	Given
$\underbrace{\left(\dfrac{1}{5} + \dfrac{1}{x}\right)}_{\text{rate}}\underbrace{(3)}_{\text{time}} = \underbrace{1}_{\text{work}}$	Rate × time = work.
$\dfrac{3}{5} + \dfrac{3}{x} = 1$	Distribute 3.
$5x\left(\dfrac{3}{5} + \dfrac{3}{x}\right) = 5x(1)$	Multiply by the LCD.
$3x + 15 = 5x$	Distribute $5x$.
$15 = 2x$	
$7.5 = x$	

7.5 h — Answer the question.

EXAMPLE 3

Integer Quotient Problem When a certain large positive integer is divided by a smaller positive integer, the integer part of the quotient is 2 and the remainder is 9. The sum of the integers is 48. Find the two integers.

Let x = larger integer. Let y = smaller integer. — Define variables.

$$\frac{x}{y} = 2 + \frac{9}{y} \quad (1)$$ Write an equation.

$$x + y = 48 \quad (2)$$ Write another equation.

(Sum) (is) (48)

$$x = 48 - y \quad (3)$$ From equation (2).

$$\frac{48 - y}{y} = 2 + \frac{9}{y}$$ Substitute $48 - y$ for x in (1).

$$48 - y = 2y + 9$$ Multiply each member by y.

$$39 = 3y$$ Add y; subtract 9.

$$13 = y$$ Divide by 3.

$$\therefore x = 48 - 13$$ Substitute 13 for y in (3).

$$x = 35$$ Do the subtraction.

Integers are 35 and 13. — Answer the question.

EXAMPLE 4

Soup Can Probability Problem A flood washes all the labels off the soup cans in a grocery store. Inventory records show that there were 300 cans of tomato soup and 500 cans of beef-barley soup before the flood.

a. If a can is picked at random, what is the probability that it is tomato soup? What is the probability that it is beef-barley?
b. If 100 cans are picked at random, how many cans of beef-barley soup would you expect to get?
c. How many cans, total, would you have to take in order for the expected number of cans of tomato soup to be 60?

- - - - -

a. Total number of cans is
$300 + 500 = 800$.

Probability for tomato:

$\frac{300}{800} = \frac{3}{8}$

Probability equals number of favorable outcomes divided by total number of outcomes.

Probability for beef-barley:

$\frac{500}{800} = \frac{5}{8}$

- - - - -

b. Expected number of beef-barley:

$\left(\frac{5}{8}\right)(100) = 62.5$

Expected number of favorable outcomes equals probability times total number of outcomes.

About 62 or 63

Round off to an integer.

- - - - -

c. Let x be the total number of cans.

Define a variable.

$\left(\frac{3}{8}x\right) = 60$

Write an equation saying the expected number of favorable outcomes equals probability times total number of outcomes.

$\left(\frac{8}{3}\right)\left(\frac{3}{8}\right)x = \left(\frac{8}{3}\right)(60)$

Multiply by $\frac{8}{3}$.

$x = 160$

Do the computations.

About 160 cans

Answer the question.

ORAL PRACTICE

Tell the quantity asked for.

EXAMPLE

Distance = 50 mi, time = $x - 5$ min, rate = ?

Answer
50 over the quantity $x - 5$ mi/min

A. Distance = 30 ft, time = x sec, rate = ?

B. Distance = 20 km, rate = x km/h, time = ?

C. Distance = 100 yd, rate = $x - 2$ yd/day, time = ?

D. Distance = 300 in., time = $x + 5$ min, rate = ?.

E. Speed through water = 8 ft/sec, current = x ft/sec, speed upstream = ?.

F. Speed through water = 7 mi/h, current = x mi/h, speed downstream = ?.

G. Speed through water = x mi/h, current = 4 mi/h, speed upstream = ?.

H. Work = 1 job, time = 3 h, rate = ?.

I. Work = 1 lawn, time = x h, rate = ?.

J. Work = 1 tank, time = $x - 3$ min, rate = ?.

K. Work = 1 sink, rate = $\frac{1}{5}$ sink per min, time = ?.

L. Work = 1 tub, rate = $\frac{1}{x}$ tub per min, time = ?.

EXERCISE 11-10

1. *Blimp Problem 1* A blimp flies through the air at a speed of 120 kilometers per hour (km/h).
   a. How fast does it fly with respect to the ground if it flies:
      i. with a tail wind of 30 km/h;
      ii. into a head wind of 20 km/h;
      iii. into a head wind of x km/h;
      iv. with a tail wind of y km/h?
   b. How long does the blimp take to fly 60 km:
      i. with no wind blowing;
      ii. against a head wind of 20 km/h;
      iii. with a tail wind of 30 km/h;
      iv. with a tail wind of y km/h?

2. *Helicopter Problem 1* A helicopter flies through the air at a speed of 100 km/h.
   a. How fast does it go with respect to the ground if it flies:
      i. into a head wind of 40 km/h;
      ii. with a tail wind of 50 km/h;
      iii. with a tail wind of x km/h;
      iv. into a head wind of y km/h?
   b. How long does it take the helicopter to fly 45 km:
      i. with no wind blowing;
      ii. into a head wind of 40 km/h;
      iii. into a head wind of y km/h;
      iv. with a tail wind of x km/h?

3. *Blimp Problem 2* A blimp flies 120 km/h through the air. It goes 60 km into a head wind of x km/h. Later it returns the 60 km with a tail wind of y km/h.
   a. Write an expression for the total time taken for the round trip.
   b. How long will the round trip take if the head wind going is 40 km/h and the tail wind returning is 10 km/h?
   c. If the head wind and the tail wind are equal to x for both parts of the trip and the round trip takes 1.3 hours, how fast is the wind blowing?

4. *Helicopter Problem 2* A helicopter moves through the air at 100 km/h. It flies 200 km with a tail wind of x km/h. On the return trip it flies the 200 km with a head wind of y km/h.
   a. Write an expression for the total time taken for the round trip.
   b. If the tail wind is 20 km/h and the head wind is 30 km/h, how long will the round trip take?
   c. If the tail wind and the head wind both equal x for both parts of the trip and the round trip takes 5 hours, how fast is the wind blowing?

5. *Blimp Problem 3* A blimp moves through the air at 120 km/h. It goes 60 km into a head wind of x km/h and returns with the same wind as a tail wind.
   a. Write an expression for the total time for the round trip.
   b. How much longer does the round trip take when the wind is blowing 30 km/h than it does when there is no wind?

6. *Helicopter Problem 3* A helicopter flies through the air at 100 km/h. It goes 200 km with a tail wind of x km/h and returns with the same wind as a head wind.
   a. Write an expression for the total time for the round trip.
   b. It sounds reasonable that the wind should make no difference in the round trip time, since the speed you gain on the way there is lost on the way back. Show that this conclusion is *false* and that the time with wind blowing is actually *longer* than the time if there is no wind.

7. *Speedboat Problem* A speedboat race requires the boat to go 1000 meters down a swiftly moving river and then return upstream to the starting point. The current in the river is known to be 2 meters per second (m/sec).
   a. One boat goes through the water at 5 m/sec. How long will it take for the round trip?
   b. Another boat takes 300 seconds for the round trip. How fast does it go through the water?
   c. A rowboat enters the race. It can go only 1 m/sec through the water. What does the algebra tell you about its time to complete the race? What *really* happens to the rowboat?

8. *River Swimming Problem* A race is held, in which swimmers go 100 meters upstream in Rapid River and return downstream to the starting point. The current in the river is known to be 1 meter per second (m/sec).
   a. Flo Tilla swims through the water at 2 m/sec. How long will she take for the round trip?
   b. Olympia Poole makes the round trip in 80 seconds. How fast does she go through the water?
   c. Phoebe Small takes 5 minutes for the round trip. How fast does she go through the water?
   d. Mae Dupp can swim only 0.5 m/sec, but she enters the race anyway. What does the algebra say her time will be? What *actually* happens to Mae? What must the *domain* of the swimmer's speed variable be in order for the algebra to give reasonable answers to this problem?

9. *Escalator Problem* Gawain Upp runs up the down escalator! After he has gone 13 meters he realizes his mistake, turns around, and runs back down, still going the same speed. The escalator moves at 0.7 meters per second, and the round trip takes a total of 10 seconds. How fast does Gawain run?

10. *Popeye and Spinach Can Problem* Bluto puts a spinach can onto a conveyor belt headed toward a large circular saw at 0.8 meters per second. Popeye jumps on the end of the conveyor belt and runs along it, grabbing the can in the nick of time. He runs back along the conveyor belt 30 meters to its beginning. Popeye makes the round trip in 17 seconds. How fast does he run?

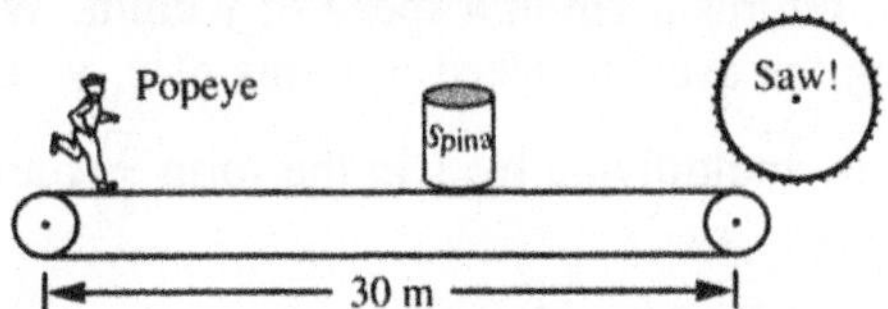

11. *Pedalboat Problem* A couple on a picnic rents a pedalboat. They go upstream 600 m, moving 30 m/min through the water. After the picnic they travel back downstream to the starting point. But they are tired and only go 20 m/min through the water. The total time spent pedaling is 75 min. How fast is the current flowing?

12. *Tugboat Problem* A tugboat pushes a string of barges 200 km up the Mississippi River against a current of 8 km/h. The tug then comes back downstream 50 km, going the same speed through the water. The total time for the two parts of the trip is 52.5 h. How fast does the tug go through the water?

13. *Average Speed Problem 1* A cyclist rides 5 km at a speed of 20 km/h. She returns at a speed of 10 km/h.

a. What is the total time for the round trip?
b. The *average speed* is defined as follows.

DEFINITION

AVERAGE SPEED

The **average speed** for a trip is $\dfrac{\text{total distance}}{\text{total time}}$.

Find her average speed for the round trip.
c. The average of 20 and 10 is 15. Is the average speed equal to 15, more than 15, or less than 15?

14. *Average Speed Problem 2* A cyclist rides 5 km at a speed of 20 km/h. How fast must she ride on the return trip to make her average speed equal:
 a. 15 km/h;
 b. 30 km/h;
 c. 40 km/h; (Surprising?);
 d. 50 km/h? (More surprising?)

15. *Average Speed Problem 3* A cyclist rides d km at a speed of x km/h and returns d km at a speed of y km/h. Write an expression representing the average speed in terms of x, y, and d. Simplify the expression by multiplying by 1 in the form $\frac{xy}{xy}$, and thus show that d drops out!

16. *Average Speed Problem 4*
 a. Use the simplified expression in Problem 15 to find *quickly* the average speed for the following round trips.
  i. Going: 70 km/h; returning: 90 km/h.
  ii. Going: 1000 km/h; returning: 800 km/h.
  iii. Going: 2 km/h; returning: 4 km/h.
 b. Show that in each case above, the average speed is *less* than the average of the speeds.

17. *River Rescue Problem* Susan is stranded in the river near the waterfall. David jumps in and swims 300 feet downstream to rescue her, moving 4 feet per second through the water. With Susan in tow, David manages to move only 2 feet per second through the water on the return trip. They arrive at the starting point, taking a total of 380 seconds for the round trip. How fast is the current?

18. *Airplane Problem* Two airplanes start at the same time from airports 500 km apart. Each one flies with an airspeed of 200 km/h directly toward the other airport. But one reaches its airport half an hour before the other plane reaches the other airport. How fast is the wind blowing?

19. *Envelope Problem* Cora Spondence can stuff a pile of letters into envelopes in 3 hours. N. V. Lopes takes 4 hours to do the same job. How many hours would it take to do the job if both of them worked together?

20. *Lawn Mowing Problem 1* John and Fred must mow the lawn before they can go swimming. By themselves, John would take 30 minutes and Fred would take 45 minutes. How long would it take to mow the lawn with both working together (using two mowers, of course!)?

21. *Lawn Mowing Problem 2* Marsha must mow the lawn before she can go swimming. She realizes that it would take her 50 minutes to do it by herself. So she gets Fran to help her. The job is completed in 30 minutes. How long would it have taken Fran to do the job alone?

22. *Bathtub Problem* The cold-water faucet can fill the bathtub in 7 minutes. When both the hot and cold faucets are running, the tub is filled in only 5 minutes. How long would it take the hot faucet to fill the tub by itself?

23. *Tank Draining Problem* The inlet valve on a storage tank in a chemical plant sticks in the open position. The tank is just about to overflow when workmen open the drain valve. To their relief, the liquid level in the tank starts dropping. Company records show that the inlet pipe can fill an empty tank in 7 hours and the drain can empty a full tank in 5 hours. How long will it be until the tank is empty with both inlet and drain open?

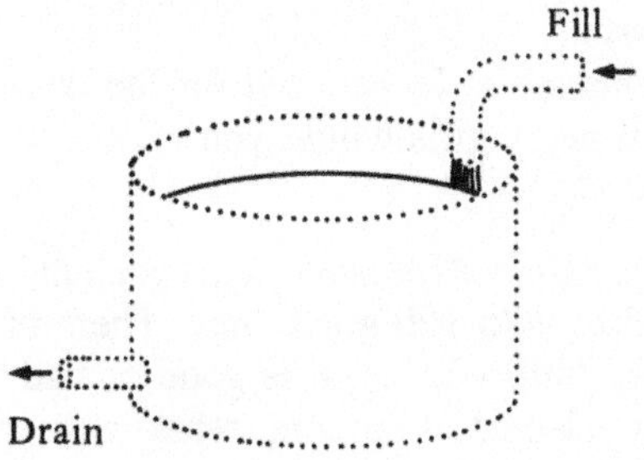

24. *Flood Control Problem* A torrential rain can fill the basin behind a flood control dam in 5 hours. With the dam's floodgates open, a full basin will drain in 20 hours. How long would it take to fill the basin in a torrential rain with the floodgates open?

25. *Sink Draining Problem* The drain can empty the water from a full sink in 3 minutes. If the water is running while the drain is open, it takes 8 minutes to empty a full sink. How long would it take to fill an empty sink with the drain closed?

26. *Cupcake Problem* Ellen Hsu has baked a large batch of cupcakes for a bake sale. She ices them and sets them on a tray. She knows that it would normally take her 10 minutes to fill the tray with cupcakes. However, students are buying the cupcakes on the tray while she is icing new ones. Ellen ices and the students buy at constant rates. The tray is finally full after 25 minutes. If the students continue to buy at the same rate, how long will it take to sell a tray of cupcakes after Ellen stops icing?

27. *Integer Quotient Problem 1* When a large positive integer is divided by a smaller one, the integer part of the quotient is 3 and the remainder is 2. The sum of the integers is 70. Find the two integers.

28. *Integer Quotient Problem 2* When a large positive integer is divided by a smaller one, the integer part of the quotient is 3 and the remainder is 1. The sum of the integers is 29. Find the two integers.

29. *Integer Quotient Problem 3* Two positive integers have a sum of 58. If 3 is added to each and then the larger divided by the smaller, the integer part of the quotient is 1 and the remainder is 16. Find the original integers.

30. *Integer Quotient Problem 4* Two positive integers have a sum of 56. If 6 is subtracted from each and then the larger divided by the smaller, the integer part of the quotient is 43 and the remainder is 0. Find the original integers.

31. *Probability Committee Selection Problem* A committee is to be selected at random from the freshman class. The class has 346 girls and 278 boys.
    a. If a student is picked at random, what is the probability that it is a girl? a boy?
    b. If 12 students are to be selected for the committee, approximately how many girls would you expect to be on the committee?

32. *Probability Light Bulb Problem* By accident, 100 defective light bulbs get mixed in with 900 good ones. There is no way to tell just by looking at the bulb whether it is good or bad.
    a. If a bulb is selected at random, what is the probability that it is bad? that it is good?
    b. If a sample of 20 bulbs is selected, what number would you expect to be bad?

33. *Probability Dice Problem*
   a. If you roll a die (singular of "dice"), what is the probability that the number comes up 1? What is the probability that the number comes up 5?
   b. If you roll a die 30 times, about how many times would you expect it to come up 1?
   c. Get a die and roll it 30 times. Record the number of times it comes up 1. Were the actual results the same as you expected?

34. *Probability Coin Flip Problem*
   a. If you flip a coin, what is the probability that it lands heads up? Tails up?
   b. If you flip a coin 50 times, how many times would you expect it to land heads up?
   c. Flip a coin 50 times. Record the number of times it lands heads up. Were the actual results the same as you expected?

11-11 CHAPTER REVIEW AND TEST

In this chapter you have refreshed your memory about fractions. If a fraction has a variable in it, then it stands for different numbers depending on the value of that variable. You learned how to evaluate these rational expressions for given values of x, and how to find x when you know the value of the expression. You also learned how to add, subtract, multiply, and simplify rational expressions without actually evaluating them. Finally you worked problems involving ratios and variable rates, in which variables appear in denominators.

Glance through your notes looking for names and definitions before you try the test below. The test may be longer than you would be expected to do in a normal class period.

CHAPTER TEST

1. What is the difference in each case?
   a. A polynomial and a rational algebraic expression.
   b. The way you add fractions and the way you multiply them.
   c. 3 : 5 and 3/5.
   d. A ratio and a proportion.
   e. Net speed upstream and net speed downstream.

2. Write each of the following.
   a. Definition of least common multiple.
   b. Definition of canceling.
   c. Property of the opposite of a fraction.
   d. Definition of extraneous solution.
   e. Definition of domain of a variable.

3. For the expressions $\dfrac{x+3}{x-1}$ and $\dfrac{x+1}{x-3}$:
   a. evaluate each expression for $x = 0, 1, 2, 3, -1$, and -3.
   b. find x if the first expression equals 2.
   c. find the product of the two expressions. Simplify if possible.
   d. find the first expression minus the second expression. Simplify if possible.
   e. find x if the first expression equals the second one.
   f. find x if the sum of the expressions equals.
      i. 2
      ii. 1
      iii. 3.
   g. find x if the product of the expressions equals 2.

4. Simplify.
   a. $\dfrac{24x^4}{32x^7}$
   b. $\dfrac{(x+7)(x-5)(x-3)}{(7+x)(5-x)(x+3)}$
   c. $\dfrac{x^2+7x+10}{x^2-25}$
   d. $\dfrac{2x^2+x-3}{3x^2-x-2}$

5. Do the indicated operations and simplify.
   a. $\dfrac{7}{5x} - \dfrac{3}{5x} + \dfrac{1}{5x}$
   b. $\dfrac{7}{5x} \cdot \dfrac{3}{5x} \cdot \dfrac{1}{5x}$
   c. $\dfrac{6a}{2a-b} - \dfrac{3b}{2a-b}$
   d. $\dfrac{9}{x-3} - \dfrac{x^2}{x-3}$
   e. $\dfrac{4}{x} + \dfrac{7}{x^2} - \dfrac{2}{x^3}$
   f. $\dfrac{x^2+x-6}{x^2+3x-10} \cdot \dfrac{x^2-8x+15}{9-x^2}$

6. Use long division, and express your answer in mixed-number form.

$$\frac{5x^3 - 13x^2 - 10x + 7}{x-3}$$

7. ***Television Manufacturing Problem*** The sales department of a television set manufacturing company finds that portables and console models sell in the ratio 7 : 3. The manufacturing department can make 570 sets each week. How many of each kind should be made in a week to have this desired ratio?

8. *Ditch Digging Problem* Doug Upp can dig a ditch in 3 hours. His brother Phil could dig the same ditch in 5 hours. How long would it take to dig the ditch if both work together?

9. *Superman Problem* Superman flies through the air at 3 miles per second, going 40 miles from Metropolis to Gotham against a head wind of unknown speed. He flies back to Metropolis, moving through the air at 2 miles per second with the same wind as a tail wind. The round trip takes 60 seconds. How fast is the wind blowing?

10. *Integer Quotient Problem* Two positive integers have a sum of 92. If the larger integer is divided by the smaller one, the quotient is 3 and the remainder is 12. What are the two integers?

11. *Peanuts and Popcorn Problem* A vendor carries 80 bags, total, of peanuts and popcorn. How many of each should she carry for the peanuts-to-popcorn ratio to be 3 : 7?

12. *Probability Problem:* The probability of rain is 20% on any one day.
    a. On how many days would you expect it to rain in a total of five weeks?
    b. How long, total, would you expect it to be until it has rained on 40 days?

12 Radical Algebraic Expressions

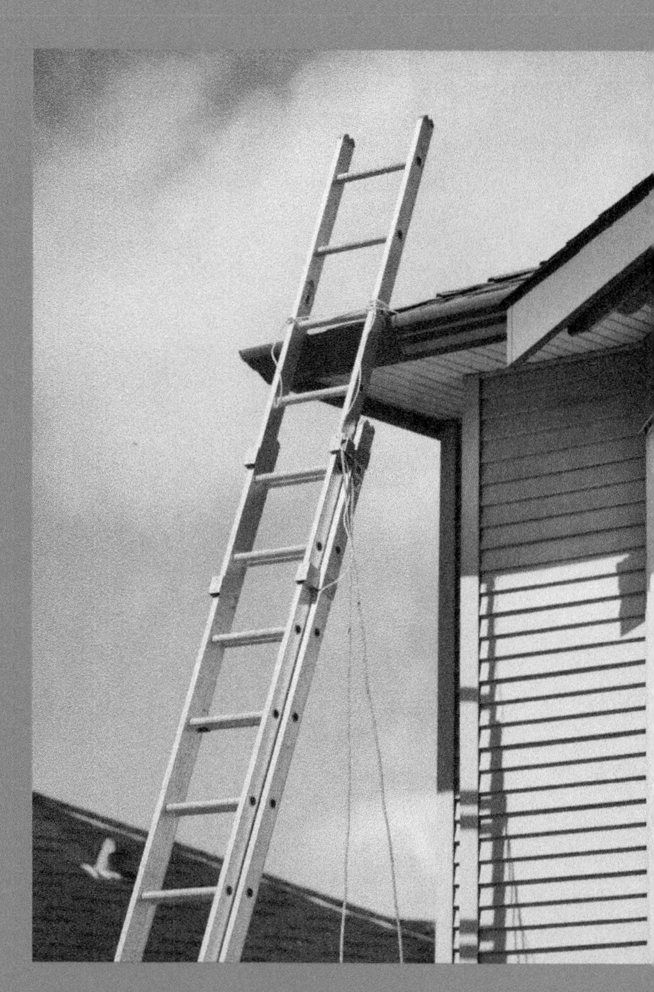

You have already learned how to evaluate radicals by calculator. In this chapter you will learn how to operate with square roots of expressions that have variables. *You will evaluate these expressions for given values of the variable and solve equations to find the value of the variable. You will also learn about other kinds of roots such as cube roots and fourth roots. Applications include predicting the weight of a shark from its length and finding the length of the third side of a right triangle when you know the lengths of the other two.*

Variables:
H and L
Side lengths in a right triangle

Expression:
$\sqrt{H^2 - L^2}$
Length of third side

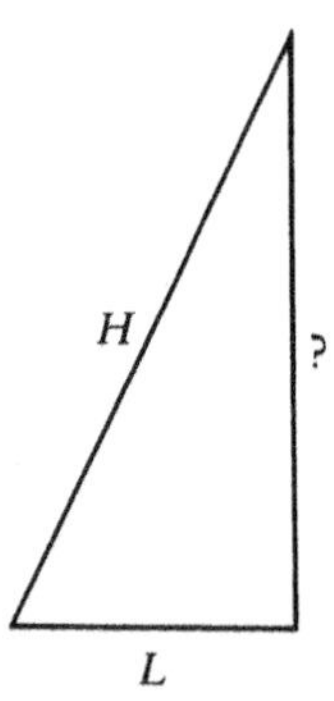

2-1 INTRODUCTION TO RADICAL ALGEBRAIC EXPRESSIONS

An expression such as $\sqrt{x - 16}$ is called a **radical algebraic expression.** In this section you will learn to evaluate expressions like this when you know what x equals, and vice versa.

Objective

For radical algebraic expressions such as $\sqrt{x - 16}$, evaluate the expression if x is given, and find x if a value of the expression is given.

Cover the answers as you work the examples.

EXAMPLE 1

Evaluate $\sqrt{x - 16}$ if x is 27.

Think These Reasons

$\sqrt{x - 16}$	Write the given expression.
$= \sqrt{27 - 16}$	Substitute 27 for x.
$= \sqrt{11}$	Do the arithmetic under the vinculum.
$\approx \underline{\underline{3.32}}$	Find the square root.

Note: The vinculum ("bar") means "Do what is underneath *first,*" just like a pair of parentheses.

EXAMPLE 2

Evaluate $\sqrt{x - 16}$ if x is 7.

$\sqrt{x - 16}$ Write the given expression.

$= \sqrt{7 - 16}$ Substitute 7 for x.

$= \sqrt{-9}$ Do the subtraction.

No value There are *no* real numbers that are square roots of negative numbers.

EXAMPLE 3

Find x if $\sqrt{x - 16}$ is 9.

$\sqrt{x - 16} = 9$ Write an equation.

$(\sqrt{x - 16})^2 = 9^2$ Square each member.

$x - 16 = 81$ Squaring a square root removes the radical sign. Recall from Section 5.9 that $(\sqrt{n})^2$ equals n.

$x = 97$ Add 16 to each member.

In the following exercise you will work more problems like these.

EXERCISE 12-1

For Problems 1 through 6, evaluate the expression for the given values of x. Use a calculator if necessary.

1. Evaluate $\sqrt{3x}$ if:
   a. x is 7;
   b. x is 27.
2. Evaluate $\sqrt{5x}$ if:
   a. x is 8;
   b. x is 125.
3. Evaluate $\sqrt{15 - x}$ if:
   a. x is 6;
   b. x is 15;
   c. x is 20.
4. Evaluate $\sqrt{x - 11}$ if:
   a. x is 47;
   b. x is 11;
   c. x is 2.
5. Evaluate $\dfrac{10}{\sqrt{x + 4}}$ if:
   a. x is 96;
   b. x is 0;
6. Evaluate $\dfrac{24}{\sqrt{x + 9}}$ if:
   a. x is 91;
   b. x is 0;

c. x is -3;
d. x is -4.

c. x is -5;
d. x is -9.

For Problems 7 through 10, find x for the given values.

7. Find x if $\sqrt{2x}$ is:
   a. 10;
   b. 3.

8. Find x if $\sqrt{3x}$ is:
   a. 12;
   b. 4.

9. Find x if $\sqrt{x + 5}$ is:
   a. 12;
   b. 2;
   c. 0.

10. Find x if $\sqrt{x + 11}$ is:
   a. 5;
   b. 3;
   c. 0.

12-2 SUMS, DIFFERENCES, AND PRODUCTS OF RADICALS

For some uses of radicals it is better *not* to evaluate them on a calculator. In this section you will learn ways to operate on radicals.

There is an easy way to multiply two square roots. For instance,

$$\sqrt{9} \times \sqrt{4} = 3 \times 2 = 6.$$

But 9×4 is 36, and $\sqrt{36}$ is also equal to 6. Thus

$$\sqrt{9} \times \sqrt{4} = \sqrt{9 \times 4}.$$

This example illustrates the fact that the operation square root *distributes* over multiplication.

PROPERTY

SQUARE ROOT OF A PRODUCT
The square root of a product of two nonnegative numbers equals the product of the square roots of the two numbers. That is, for nonnegative numbers x and y,

$$\boxed{\sqrt{xy} = \sqrt{x}\sqrt{y}}$$

In other words, square root distributes over multiplication.

In Problem 61 of the exercise, you will prove this property.

The property is useful in simplifying radicals.

$\sqrt{75}$	
$= \sqrt{25 \times 3}$	Factor 75.
$= \sqrt{25} \times \sqrt{3}$	Square root of a product property.
$= 5\sqrt{3}$	$\sqrt{25}$ is 5.

The answer, $5\sqrt{3}$, is considered to be simpler than $\sqrt{75}$, because the radicand 3 is *less* than the radicand 75. Note that $5\sqrt{3}$ means 5 *times* $\sqrt{3}$.

Unfortunately, there is *no* similar property for the square root of a sum. For instance,

$$\sqrt{9 + 16} \quad \text{but} \quad \sqrt{9} + \sqrt{16}$$
$$= \sqrt{25} \qquad = 3 + 4$$
$$= 5 \qquad = 7.$$

The only way for two square roots to be combined by addition is for the radicands to be equal. Thus

$$5\sqrt{3} + 7\sqrt{3} = 12\sqrt{3}.$$

The process is the same as adding like terms: $5x + 7x = 12x$.

Objective

Be able to simplify expressions involving sums, differences, and products of square roots, and check by evaluating by calculator.

Cover the answers as you work these examples.

EXAMPLE 1

Simplify: $\sqrt{72}$.

- - - - - - - - - -

	Think These Reasons
$\sqrt{72}$	Write the given expression.
$= \sqrt{36 \times 2}$	Factor so that at least one of the factors is a perfect square.
$= \underline{\underline{6\sqrt{2}}}$	Take the square root of 36.

Note: The answer can be checked by calculator.

$$\sqrt{72} \approx 8.4852814$$
$$6\sqrt{2} \approx 8.4852814$$

EXAMPLE 2

Multiply: $\sqrt{15} \times 7\sqrt{20}$.

$\sqrt{15} \times 7\sqrt{20}$	Write the given expression.
$= 7\sqrt{3 \times 5 \times 5 \times 4}$	Factor and multiply the radicands.
$= \underline{\underline{70\sqrt{3}}}$	Take the square roots of 5×5 and 4.

EXAMPLE 3

Simplify: $4\sqrt{6} - 7\sqrt{6} + \sqrt{6}$.

$4\sqrt{6} - 7\sqrt{6} + \sqrt{6}$	Write the given expression.
$= \underline{\underline{-2\sqrt{6}}}$	Combine like terms.

EXAMPLE 4

Simplify: $\sqrt{75} + \sqrt{48}$.

$\sqrt{75} + \sqrt{48}$	Write the given expression.
$= 5\sqrt{3} + 4\sqrt{3}$	Simplify $\sqrt{75}$ and $\sqrt{48}$.
$= \underline{\underline{9\sqrt{3}}}$	Combine like terms.

ORAL PRACTICE

Give the expression in simple radical form.

A. $\sqrt{12}$ B. $\sqrt{8}$ C. $\sqrt{20}$

D. $\sqrt{9}$ E. $\sqrt{18}$ F. $\sqrt{50}$

G. $\sqrt{2} \times \sqrt{3}$ H. $\sqrt{5} \times \sqrt{7}$ I. $\sqrt{6} \times \sqrt{3}$

J. $\sqrt{5} \times \sqrt{15}$ K. $6\sqrt{5} + 2\sqrt{5}$ L. $5\sqrt{3} - 2\sqrt{3}$

M. $5\sqrt{3} - \sqrt{3}$ N. $\sqrt{3} - 7\sqrt{3}$

EXERCISE 12-2

1. Evaluate both expressions to show each of the following.

   a. $\sqrt{4 \times 49} = \sqrt{4} \times \sqrt{49}$ b. $\sqrt{3 \times 7} = \sqrt{3} \times \sqrt{7}$
   c. $\sqrt{9 + 16} \neq \sqrt{9} + \sqrt{16}$
   d. $\sqrt{169 - 144} \neq \sqrt{169} - \sqrt{144}$

2. Evaluate both expressions to show each of the following.

   a. $\sqrt{81 \times 4} = \sqrt{81} \times \sqrt{4}$
   b. $\sqrt{6 \times 11} = \sqrt{6} \times \sqrt{11}$
   c. $\sqrt{225 + 64} \neq \sqrt{225} + \sqrt{64}$
   d. $\sqrt{25 - 16} \neq \sqrt{25} - \sqrt{16}$

For Problems 3 through 20, simplify the expression as much as possible. Leave the answer in *radical* form. You may check by getting a decimal approximation.

3. $\sqrt{12}$ 4. $\sqrt{20}$ 5. $\sqrt{40}$ 6. $\sqrt{18}$
7. $\sqrt{27}$ 8. $\sqrt{24}$ 9. $\sqrt{45}$ 10. $\sqrt{8}$
11. $\sqrt{32}$ 12. $\sqrt{162}$ 13. $\sqrt{108}$ 14. $\sqrt{80}$
15. $\sqrt{200}$ 16. $\sqrt{300}$ 17. $\sqrt{147}$ 18. $\sqrt{98}$
19. $\sqrt{405}$ 20. $\sqrt{448}$

For Problems 21 through 40, multiply the expressions and simplify the answer. Leave the answer in *integer* or *radical* form.

21. $\sqrt{3} \times \sqrt{15}$ 22. $\sqrt{5} \times \sqrt{30}$ 23. $\sqrt{21} \times \sqrt{7}$
24. $\sqrt{22} \times \sqrt{11}$ 25. $\sqrt{8} \times \sqrt{2}$ 26. $\sqrt{27} \times \sqrt{3}$
27. $\sqrt{3} \times \sqrt{12}$ 28. $\sqrt{7} \times \sqrt{28}$
29. $\sqrt{5} \times \sqrt{30} \times \sqrt{3}$ 30. $\sqrt{35} \times \sqrt{7} \times \sqrt{10}$
31. $7\sqrt{6} \times 3\sqrt{10}$ 32. $3\sqrt{14} \times 5\sqrt{2}$ 33. $8\sqrt{2} \times 5\sqrt{12}$
34. $10\sqrt{3} \times 7\sqrt{15}$ 35. $5\sqrt{9} \times 4\sqrt{11}$ 36. $2\sqrt{25} \times 3\sqrt{6}$
37. $6\sqrt{18} \times 5\sqrt{14}$ 38. $4\sqrt{12} \times 9\sqrt{6}$
39. $7\sqrt{6} \times \sqrt{15} \times 5\sqrt{10}$ 40. $3\sqrt{14} \times 2\sqrt{21} \times 5$

For Problems 41 through 60, simplify each term, if necessary. Then add or subtract. Leave the answer in *integer* or *radical* form.

41. $2\sqrt{5} + 7\sqrt{5}$

42. $6\sqrt{3} + 8\sqrt{3}$

43. $8\sqrt{7} - 3\sqrt{7}$

44. $5\sqrt{11} - 2\sqrt{11}$

45. $13\sqrt{6} - \sqrt{6}$

46. $9\sqrt{5} - \sqrt{5}$

47. $\sqrt{12} + 5\sqrt{3}$

48. $\sqrt{18} + 5\sqrt{2}$

49. $7\sqrt{5} + \sqrt{45}$

50. $5\sqrt{2} + \sqrt{72}$

51. $\sqrt{18} + \sqrt{50}$

52. $\sqrt{12} + \sqrt{75}$

53. $6\sqrt{12} - \sqrt{75}$

54. $4\sqrt{18} - \sqrt{50}$

55. $3\sqrt{7} - \sqrt{175}$

56. $2\sqrt{5} - \sqrt{125}$

57. $3\sqrt{5} - \sqrt{80} + \sqrt{20}$

58. $4\sqrt{6} - \sqrt{150} + \sqrt{24}$

59. $\sqrt{50} - \sqrt{18} - 2\sqrt{12}$

60. $\sqrt{75} - \sqrt{12} - 2\sqrt{8}$

61. ***Radicals with Variables Problem*** Square roots containing variables can be simplified by the techniques of this section. For instance, for non-negative values of x,

$$\sqrt{x^7} = \sqrt{x^2 \cdot x^2 \cdot x^2 \cdot x} = x \cdot x \cdot x \cdot \sqrt{x} = x^3\sqrt{x}$$

Simplify the following. Assume non-negative variables.

a. $\sqrt{x^5}$ b. $\sqrt{y^9}$ c. $\sqrt{x^6}$ d. $\sqrt{x^8y^3}$ e. $\sqrt{x^2y^{10}}$

62. ***Proof of the Square Root of a Product Property*** Prove that if $z = \sqrt{x}\sqrt{y}$, where x and y are nonnegative numbers, then z is also equal to $\sqrt{xy}$. Do this by squaring each member of the given equation, then distributing the exponentiation over the multiplication.

12-3 QUOTIENTS OF RADICALS

By calculator you can show that

$$\frac{\sqrt{13}}{\sqrt{2}} \approx 2.549509757 \text{ and } \sqrt{\frac{13}{2}} = \sqrt{6.5} \approx 2.549509757$$

The results are the same! So

$$\sqrt{\frac{13}{2}} = \frac{\sqrt{13}}{\sqrt{2}}.$$

This example illustrates that the operation square root distributes over division, just as it does over multiplication.

PROPERTY

SQUARE ROOT OF A QUOTIENT
The square root of a quotient of two positive numbers equals the quotient of the square roots of the numbers. That is, for positive numbers x and y,

$$\sqrt{\frac{x}{y}} = \frac{\sqrt{x}}{\sqrt{y}}$$

In other words, square root distributes over division.

You will prove this property in Problem 49 of the following exercise. The property can be used from right to left to divide two radicals. For instance,

$$\frac{\sqrt{51}}{\sqrt{3}} = \sqrt{\frac{51}{3}} = \sqrt{17}.$$

The answer, $\sqrt{17}$, is simpler than the original expression. However, this technique does not always give a simpler answer. For instance,

$$\frac{\sqrt{2}}{\sqrt{7}} = \sqrt{\frac{2}{7}} = \sqrt{0.285714285\ldots}.$$

If the denominator does not divide the numerator, there is another way to simplify the expression. You can eliminate the radical from either the numerator or the denominator by multiplying the fraction by an appropriate form of 1.

$$\frac{\sqrt{2}}{\sqrt{7}} \qquad \text{or} \qquad \frac{\sqrt{2}}{\sqrt{7}}$$

$$= \frac{\sqrt{2}}{\sqrt{7}} \times \frac{\sqrt{7}}{\sqrt{7}} \qquad = \frac{\sqrt{2}}{\sqrt{7}} \times \frac{\sqrt{2}}{\sqrt{2}}$$

$$= \frac{\sqrt{14}}{7} \qquad = \frac{2}{\sqrt{14}}$$

The expressions $\frac{\sqrt{14}}{7}$ and $\frac{2}{\sqrt{14}}$ are considered to be simpler than $\frac{\sqrt{2}}{\sqrt{7}}$ since they have only *one* radical.

The process of eliminating the radical from the denominator or from the numerator is called *rationalizing the denominator* or *rationalizing the numerator*. For most things you will be doing with radicals it is more convenient to have no radicals in the denominator. So the following definition is made.

DEFINITION

SIMPLE RADICAL FORM
A radical is said to be in **simple radical form** if:

1. There are no radicals in the denominator.
2. The radicand(s) in the numerator are as small as possible.

Objective

Given an expression involving quotients of radicals, transform it to simple radical form, and check by calculator.

Cover the answers as you work these examples.

EXAMPLE 1

Write in simple radical form: $\dfrac{\sqrt{5}}{\sqrt{7}}$.

\- - - - -   - - - - -

Think These Reasons

$\dfrac{\sqrt{5}}{\sqrt{7}}$	Write the given expression.
$= \dfrac{\sqrt{5}}{\sqrt{7}} \times \dfrac{\sqrt{7}}{\sqrt{7}}$	Multiply by a form of 1 to rationalize the denominator.
$= \dfrac{\sqrt{35}}{7}$	Do the multiplication.

Note: The answer can be checked by calculator.

$$\frac{\sqrt{5}}{\sqrt{7}} \approx 0.8451542$$

$$\frac{\sqrt{35}}{7} \approx 0.8451542$$

EXAMPLE 2

Write in simple radical form: $\dfrac{8}{\sqrt{24}}$.

\- - - - -   - - - - -

$\dfrac{8}{\sqrt{24}}$	Write the given expression.
$= \dfrac{8}{2\sqrt{6}} \times \dfrac{\sqrt{6}}{\sqrt{6}}$	Simplify $\sqrt{24}$. Then rationalize the denominator.
$= \dfrac{4\sqrt{6}}{6}$	Cancel. Multiply $\sqrt{6}\sqrt{6}$.
$= \dfrac{2\sqrt{6}}{3}$	Cancel.

Note: Although the given expression has only one radical already, simple radical form requires that any radicals be in the *numerator,* not the denominator.

EXAMPLE 3

Write in simple radical form: $\sqrt{\dfrac{75}{8}}$.

$\sqrt{\dfrac{75}{8}}$	Write the given expression.
$= \dfrac{\sqrt{75}}{\sqrt{8}}$	Square root distributes over division.
$= \dfrac{5\sqrt{3}}{2\sqrt{2}} \times \dfrac{\sqrt{2}}{\sqrt{2}}$	Simplify $\sqrt{75}$ and $\sqrt{8}$. Then rationalize the denominator.
$= \dfrac{5\sqrt{6}}{4}$	Multiply the radicals.

Note: The square root of a fraction is considered to have a radical in the *denominator*. To be in simple radical form, the expression must have a *rational* denominator.

EXAMPLE 4

Do the operations and write the answer in simple radical form: $\dfrac{\sqrt{24}}{\sqrt{50}} \div \dfrac{\sqrt{27}}{\sqrt{8}}$.

$\dfrac{\sqrt{24}}{\sqrt{50}} \div \dfrac{\sqrt{27}}{\sqrt{8}}$	Write the given expression.
$= \dfrac{\sqrt{24}}{\sqrt{50}} \times \dfrac{\sqrt{8}}{\sqrt{27}}$	Use the definition of division to change to multiplication.
$= \dfrac{2\sqrt{6} \times 2\sqrt{2}}{5\sqrt{2} \times 3\sqrt{3}}$	Multiply the fractions. Simplify the radicals.

$= \dfrac{4\sqrt{2}\sqrt{3}}{15\sqrt{3}}$ Multiply, and cancel $\sqrt{2}$. Split $\sqrt{6}$ into $\sqrt{2}\sqrt{3}$.

$= \dfrac{4\sqrt{2}}{15}$ Cancel $\sqrt{3}$.

EXAMPLE 5

Do the operations and write the answer in simple radical form: $\dfrac{\sqrt{12}}{\sqrt{50}} - \dfrac{\sqrt{27}}{\sqrt{8}}$.

- - - - - - - - - -

$\dfrac{\sqrt{12}}{\sqrt{50}} - \dfrac{\sqrt{27}}{\sqrt{8}}$ Write the given expression.

$= \dfrac{2\sqrt{3}}{5\sqrt{2}} - \dfrac{3\sqrt{3}}{2\sqrt{2}}$ Simplify the radicals.

$= \dfrac{2\sqrt{6}}{10} - \dfrac{3\sqrt{6}}{4}$ Rationalize the denominators.

$= \dfrac{4\sqrt{6}}{20} - \dfrac{15\sqrt{6}}{20}$ Write the fractions with a common denominator.

$= -\dfrac{11\sqrt{6}}{20}$ Subtract the numerators.

Note: When you are adding or subtracting radical fractions, it is usually easier to *rationalize* the denominators before finding a *common* denominator.

ORAL PRACTICE

Give the expression in simple radical form.

A. $\dfrac{2}{\sqrt{3}}$ B. $\dfrac{5}{\sqrt{2}}$ C. $\dfrac{1}{\sqrt{5}}$ D. $\dfrac{3}{\sqrt{7}}$ E. $\dfrac{6}{\sqrt{3}}$ F. $\dfrac{10}{\sqrt{5}}$

G. $\dfrac{\sqrt{2}}{3} \times \dfrac{4}{\sqrt{2}}$ H. $\dfrac{5}{\sqrt{3}} \div \dfrac{10}{\sqrt{3}}$ I. $\dfrac{2}{\sqrt{3}} \times \dfrac{10}{\sqrt{3}}$

J. $\dfrac{\sqrt{5}}{2} \div \dfrac{1}{\sqrt{20}}$ K. $\dfrac{2}{\sqrt{5}} + \dfrac{3}{\sqrt{5}}$ L. $\dfrac{4\sqrt{5}}{7} + \dfrac{3\sqrt{5}}{7}$

M. $\dfrac{8}{\sqrt{7}} - \dfrac{1}{\sqrt{7}}$ N. $\dfrac{3}{\sqrt{4}} - \dfrac{5}{\sqrt{4}}$

EXERCISE 12-3

For Problems 1 through 20, rationalize the denominator and simplify. Leave the answer in *integer, rational,* or *radical* form. You can check your answers by calculator.

1. $\dfrac{\sqrt{3}}{\sqrt{11}}$
2. $\dfrac{\sqrt{13}}{\sqrt{5}}$
3. $\dfrac{\sqrt{12}}{\sqrt{5}}$
4. $\dfrac{\sqrt{24}}{\sqrt{7}}$
5. $\dfrac{\sqrt{30}}{\sqrt{6}}$
6. $\dfrac{\sqrt{15}}{\sqrt{3}}$
7. $\sqrt{\dfrac{3}{13}}$
8. $\sqrt{\dfrac{2}{11}}$
9. $\sqrt{\dfrac{175}{24}}$
10. $\sqrt{\dfrac{63}{50}}$
11. $\dfrac{20}{\sqrt{10}}$
12. $\dfrac{40}{\sqrt{20}}$
13. $\dfrac{2\sqrt{5}}{3\sqrt{12}}$
14. $\dfrac{6\sqrt{8}}{5\sqrt{72}}$
15. $\dfrac{42\sqrt{15}}{3\sqrt{20}}$
16. $\dfrac{56\sqrt{30}}{7\sqrt{40}}$
17. $\dfrac{150}{\sqrt{300}}$
18. $\dfrac{63}{\sqrt{216}}$
19. $\dfrac{3\sqrt{35}}{\sqrt{7}\sqrt{45}}$
20. $\dfrac{3\sqrt{22}\sqrt{28}}{\sqrt{8}\sqrt{77}}$

For Problems 21 through 40, do the indicated operations and write the answer in simple radical form.

21. $\dfrac{\sqrt{3}}{\sqrt{5}} \times \dfrac{\sqrt{15}}{\sqrt{8}}$
22. $\dfrac{\sqrt{7}}{\sqrt{2}} \times \dfrac{\sqrt{14}}{\sqrt{27}}$
23. $\dfrac{\sqrt{18}}{\sqrt{7}} \times \sqrt{\dfrac{14}{5}}$
24. $\sqrt{\dfrac{75}{2}} \times \dfrac{\sqrt{15}}{\sqrt{6}}$
25. $\dfrac{\sqrt{30}}{\sqrt{14}} \div \dfrac{\sqrt{15}}{\sqrt{32}}$
26. $\dfrac{\sqrt{32}}{\sqrt{24}} \div \dfrac{\sqrt{22}}{\sqrt{3}}$
27. $\sqrt{\dfrac{27}{5}} \div \dfrac{\sqrt{10}}{\sqrt{3}}$
28. $\dfrac{\sqrt{10}}{\sqrt{6}} \div \sqrt{\dfrac{2}{15}}$
29. $\dfrac{3}{\sqrt{3}} + \dfrac{18}{\sqrt{27}}$
30. $\dfrac{2}{\sqrt{2}} + \dfrac{12}{\sqrt{8}}$
31. $\sqrt{45} - \dfrac{10}{\sqrt{5}}$
32. $\sqrt{28} - \dfrac{21}{\sqrt{7}}$

33. $6\sqrt{\frac{2}{3}} + 6\sqrt{\frac{3}{2}}$

34. $10\sqrt{\frac{2}{5}} + 10\sqrt{\frac{5}{2}}$

35. $3\sqrt{3} - \sqrt{48} + 3\sqrt{\frac{1}{3}}$

36. $5\sqrt{5} - \sqrt{45} + 10\sqrt{\frac{1}{5}}$

37. $6\sqrt{\frac{7}{4}} - 14\sqrt{\frac{1}{7}} + 3\sqrt{28}$

38. $6\sqrt{\frac{5}{3}} - 3\sqrt{60} + 10\sqrt{\frac{3}{5}}$

39. $\sqrt{6}\left(\sqrt{3} - \frac{1}{\sqrt{3}}\right)$

40. $\sqrt{15}\left(\frac{4}{\sqrt{5}} - \sqrt{5}\right)$

For Problems 41 through 44, rationalize the *numerator*.

41. $\frac{\sqrt{3}}{\sqrt{7}}$

42. $\frac{\sqrt{7}}{\sqrt{2}}$

43. $\frac{\sqrt{6}}{12}$

44. $\frac{\sqrt{15}}{30}$

45. ***Radicals with Variables Problem*** Square roots containing variables can be simplified by the techniques of this section. For instance, for positive values of x,

$$\frac{\sqrt{x^6}}{\sqrt{x^5}} = \sqrt{\frac{x^6}{x^5}} = \underline{\underline{\sqrt{x}}}.$$

Simplify the following. Assume positive values of variables.

a. $\frac{\sqrt{x^6}}{\sqrt{x^3}}$ b. $\frac{\sqrt{z^5}}{\sqrt{z^8}}$ c. $\frac{\sqrt{x^2y^5}}{\sqrt{x^3y}}$ d. $\frac{1}{\sqrt{x^4y^{10}}}$ e. $\frac{\sqrt{n^7}}{\sqrt{n^{11}}}$

46. ***Proof of the Square Root of a Quotient Property*** Prove that if

$$z = \frac{\sqrt{x}}{\sqrt{y}}, \quad \text{then} \quad z = \sqrt{\frac{x}{y}},$$

where x is nonnegative and y is positive. Do this by first squaring each member of the given equation and then distributing the exponentiation over the division.

12-4 BINOMIALS WITH RADICALS

So far you have multiplied and divided radical expressions with only one term, such as

$$\sqrt{12} \times \sqrt{18} \quad \text{or} \quad \frac{\sqrt{12}}{\sqrt{18}}.$$

In this section you do the same operations with *binomial* radical expressions. Multiply each term of one by each term of the other.

$$\begin{aligned}&(\sqrt{15} + \sqrt{3})(4\sqrt{15} - \sqrt{3})\\ &= 4(15) - \sqrt{45} + 4\sqrt{45} - 3\\ &= 57 + 3\sqrt{45}\\ &= \underline{\underline{57 + 9\sqrt{5}}}\end{aligned}$$

An important thing happens when you multiply two binomials that are *conjugates* of each other. For instance,

$$\begin{aligned}&(\sqrt{13} + \sqrt{7})(\sqrt{13} - \sqrt{7})\\ &= 13 - \sqrt{91} + \sqrt{91} - 7\\ &= \underline{\underline{6}}.\end{aligned}$$

The answer is a *rational* number! The two radical terms are *opposites* of each other and thus "drop out."

PROPERTY

PRODUCT OF CONJUGATE RADICAL BINOMIALS
For any nonnegative rational numbers x and y,

$$\boxed{(\sqrt{x} + \sqrt{y})(\sqrt{x} - \sqrt{y}) = x - y}$$

which is a rational number.

Note: This property corresponds to $(a + b)(a - b) = a^2 - b^2$.

This result gives a way to simplify radical expressions involving division by a binomial. For instance, you can rationalize the denominator of

$$\frac{35}{\sqrt{8} - \sqrt{3}}$$

by multiplying by 1 in the form $\dfrac{\sqrt{8} + \sqrt{3}}{\sqrt{8} + \sqrt{3}}$.

$$\frac{35}{\sqrt{8} - \sqrt{3}} \times \frac{\sqrt{8} + \sqrt{3}}{\sqrt{8} + \sqrt{3}}$$ Rationalize the denominator—$\sqrt{8} + \sqrt{3}$ is the *conjugate* of the denominator.

$$= \frac{35(\sqrt{8} + \sqrt{3})}{8 - 3}$$ Do the multiplication. Leave the 35 factored out in the numerator.

$$= \frac{35(2\sqrt{2} + \sqrt{3})}{5}$$ Do the arithmetic. Simplify $\sqrt{8}$.

$= 7(2\sqrt{2} + \sqrt{3})$ Cancel.

$= \underline{\underline{14\sqrt{2} + 7\sqrt{3}}}$ Distribute 7.

Objective

Be able to multiply or divide binomials containing square roots of constants.

Cover the answers as you work the examples.

EXAMPLE 1

Multiply and simplify: $(\sqrt{12} - 5)(\sqrt{12} + 7)$.

\- - - - -   - - - - -

	Think These Reasons
$(\sqrt{12} - 5)(\sqrt{12} + 7)$	Write the given expression.
$= 12 + 7\sqrt{12} - 5\sqrt{12} - 35$	Multiply the binomials.
$= 2\sqrt{12} - 23$	Combine like terms.
$= \underline{\underline{4\sqrt{3} - 23}}$	Simplify $\sqrt{12}$.

EXAMPLE 2

Multiply and simplify: $(\sqrt{11} - \sqrt{3})^2$.

\- - - - -   - - - - -

$(\sqrt{11} - \sqrt{3})^2$	Write the given expression.
$= (\sqrt{11} - \sqrt{3})(\sqrt{11} - \sqrt{3})$	Definition of squaring.
$= 11 - 2\sqrt{33} + 3$	Multiply the binomials.
$= \underline{\underline{14 - 2\sqrt{33}}}$	Combine like terms.

EXAMPLE 3

Multiply and simplify: $(3\sqrt{5} + 4)(3\sqrt{5} - 4)$.

\- - - - -   - - - - -

$(3\sqrt{5} + 4)(3\sqrt{5} - 4)$	Write the given expression.
$= 9(5) - 16$	Multiply conjugate binomials.
$= \underline{\underline{29}}$	Do the computations.

EXAMPLE 4

Rationalize the denominator and simplify: $\dfrac{\sqrt{3} - 2\sqrt{5}}{\sqrt{5} - \sqrt{3}}$.

$\dfrac{\sqrt{3} - 2\sqrt{5}}{\sqrt{5} - \sqrt{3}}$ — Write the given expression.

$= \dfrac{\sqrt{3} - 2\sqrt{5}}{\sqrt{5} - \sqrt{3}} \times \dfrac{\sqrt{5} + \sqrt{3}}{\sqrt{5} + \sqrt{3}}$ — Rationalize the denominator. $\sqrt{5} + \sqrt{3}$ is the *conjugate* of the denominator.

$= \dfrac{\sqrt{15} + 3 - 2(5) - 2\sqrt{15}}{5 - 3}$ — Do the multiplication.

$= \dfrac{-\sqrt{15} - 7}{2}$ or $-\dfrac{\sqrt{15} + 7}{2}$ — Combine like terms.

ORAL PRACTICE

Give the conjugate.

A. $\sqrt{3} + \sqrt{2}$ B. $\sqrt{5} - \sqrt{7}$ C. $\sqrt{11} - 4$ D. $9 + \sqrt{6}$

Give the result of multiplying these conjugates.

E. $(\sqrt{3} + \sqrt{2})(\sqrt{3} - \sqrt{2})$ F. $(\sqrt{7} - \sqrt{5})(\sqrt{7} + \sqrt{5})$

G. $(\sqrt{2} + \sqrt{10})(\sqrt{2} - \sqrt{10})$ H. $(\sqrt{5} + 3)(\sqrt{5} - 3)$

I. $(4 - \sqrt{3})(4 + \sqrt{3})$ J. $(\sqrt{7} + 2)(\sqrt{7} - 2)$

Give the result of squaring these binomials.

K. $(\sqrt{5} + \sqrt{2})^2$ L. $(\sqrt{3} - \sqrt{2})^2$

M. $(\sqrt{3} + 2)^2$ N. $(3 - \sqrt{2})^2$

EXERCISE 12-4

For Problems 1 through 40, do the multiplication and simplify the answer.

1. $\sqrt{5}(\sqrt{10} + 7)$
2. $\sqrt{3}(\sqrt{15} + 8)$

3. $\sqrt{7}(6 + \sqrt{28})$
4. $\sqrt{5}(13 + \sqrt{45})$
5. $\sqrt{15}(\sqrt{5} - \sqrt{3})$
6. $\sqrt{6}(\sqrt{2} - \sqrt{3})$
7. $\sqrt{3}(\sqrt{12} - \sqrt{75})$
8. $\sqrt{7}(\sqrt{28} - \sqrt{175})$
9. $\sqrt{10}(8\sqrt{5} + 7\sqrt{6})$
10. $\sqrt{15}(7\sqrt{3} + 4\sqrt{5})$
11. $(\sqrt{3} + 5)(\sqrt{3} + 2)$
12. $(\sqrt{5} + 7)(\sqrt{5} + 3)$
13. $(\sqrt{6} - 7)(\sqrt{6} + 4)$
14. $(\sqrt{10} - 6)(\sqrt{10} + 2)$
15. $(\sqrt{7} + 8)(\sqrt{7} - 3)$
16. $(\sqrt{11} + 2)(\sqrt{11} - 9)$
17. $(2 - \sqrt{5})(6 - \sqrt{5})$
18. $(4 - \sqrt{3})(11 - \sqrt{3})$
19. $(\sqrt{5} + \sqrt{2})(\sqrt{5} + 3\sqrt{2})$
20. $(\sqrt{2} + 4\sqrt{3})(\sqrt{2} + \sqrt{3})$
21. $(\sqrt{6} - 2\sqrt{3})(3\sqrt{6} + \sqrt{3})$
22. $(\sqrt{15} - 4\sqrt{5})(2\sqrt{15} + \sqrt{5})$
23. $(2\sqrt{15} - 4\sqrt{5})(6\sqrt{15} - 3\sqrt{5})$
24. $(3\sqrt{10} - 4\sqrt{2})(5\sqrt{10} - 6\sqrt{2})$
25. $(\sqrt{3} - 7)^2$
26. $(\sqrt{7} - 5)^2$
27. $(\sqrt{6} + \sqrt{3})^2$
28. $(\sqrt{10} + \sqrt{5})^2$
29. $(5\sqrt{2} - 3\sqrt{7})^2$
30. $(4\sqrt{2} - 5\sqrt{3})^2$
31. $(\sqrt{5} + 3)(\sqrt{5} - 3)$
32. $(\sqrt{7} + 8)(\sqrt{7} - 8)$
33. $(\sqrt{13} - \sqrt{2})(\sqrt{13} + \sqrt{2})$
34. $(\sqrt{3} - \sqrt{17})(\sqrt{3} + \sqrt{17})$
35. $(5\sqrt{3} - 1)(5\sqrt{3} + 1)$
36. $(1 - 3\sqrt{7})(1 + 3\sqrt{7})$
37. $(3\sqrt{2} + 5\sqrt{3})(3\sqrt{2} - 5\sqrt{3})$
38. $(4\sqrt{5} + 3\sqrt{7})(4\sqrt{5} - 3\sqrt{7})$
39. $(\sqrt{1001} + \sqrt{2001})(\sqrt{1001} - \sqrt{2001})$
40. $(\sqrt{1066} - \sqrt{1776})(\sqrt{1066} + \sqrt{1776})$

For Problems 41 through 60, simplify by first rationalizing the denominator.

41. $\dfrac{20}{\sqrt{6} + 2}$
42. $\dfrac{26}{\sqrt{10} + 3}$
43. $\dfrac{24}{\sqrt{15} - 3}$
44. $\dfrac{50}{\sqrt{30} - 5}$
45. $\dfrac{26}{4 - \sqrt{3}}$
46. $\dfrac{30}{6 - \sqrt{26}}$
47. $\dfrac{45}{\sqrt{2} + \sqrt{7}}$
48. $\dfrac{48}{\sqrt{3} + \sqrt{5}}$
49. $\dfrac{48}{\sqrt{11} - \sqrt{5}}$
50. $\dfrac{36}{\sqrt{19} - \sqrt{10}}$

51. $\dfrac{\sqrt{13} + 3}{5 - \sqrt{13}}$

52. $\dfrac{\sqrt{31} + 3}{6 - \sqrt{31}}$

53. $\dfrac{\sqrt{3} + 6}{\sqrt{3} + 5}$

54. $\dfrac{\sqrt{5} + 7}{\sqrt{5} + 3}$

55. $\dfrac{\sqrt{7} + \sqrt{5}}{\sqrt{7} - \sqrt{5}}$

56. $\dfrac{\sqrt{5} + \sqrt{3}}{\sqrt{5} - \sqrt{3}}$

57. $\dfrac{\sqrt{10} - \sqrt{6}}{\sqrt{10} + \sqrt{6}}$

58. $\dfrac{\sqrt{12} - \sqrt{3}}{\sqrt{12} + \sqrt{3}}$

59. $\dfrac{\sqrt{1776} + \sqrt{1066}}{\sqrt{1776} - \sqrt{1066}}$

60. $\dfrac{\sqrt{2001} + \sqrt{1001}}{\sqrt{2001} - \sqrt{1001}}$

12-5 SQUARE ROOTS OF VARIABLE EXPRESSIONS

Most of the simplifying you have done so far in this chapter has been for radicals with only constants. In this section you will do the same thing with square roots of expressions containing variables.

You recall that the square root of a perfect square is the absolute value of the base. For instance,

$$\sqrt{5^2} = |5| = 5, \quad \text{and} \quad \sqrt{(-7)^2} = |-7| = 7.$$

If the base is a variable, and you do not know beforehand whether it is positive or negative, you must leave in the absolute value sign.

$$\sqrt{x^2} = |x|.$$

Apart from this difficulty, simplifying expressions with variables is done the same way as with only constants.

Objective

Given an expression containing square roots of variables, simplify it, including rationalizing any denominators.

EXAMPLE 1

Simplify $\sqrt{x^7}$ if x is a positive number.

- - - - -

	Think These Reasons
$\sqrt{x^7}$	Write the given expression.

$= \sqrt{x \cdot x \cdot x \cdot x \cdot x \cdot x \cdot x}$ Definition of x^7

$= \sqrt{(x^2)(x^2)(x^2)(x)}$ Associate the factors in pairs.

$= |x|\,|x|\,|x|\sqrt{x}$ Distribute the square root over multiplication.

$= x \cdot x \cdot x\sqrt{x}$ x is stated to be positive.

$= \underline{\underline{x^3\sqrt{x}}}$ Definition of x^3

EXAMPLE 2

Simplify $\dfrac{\sqrt{xy^5}}{\sqrt{y}}$. Assume that x and y are positive.

$\dfrac{\sqrt{xy^5}}{\sqrt{y}}$ Write the given expression.

$= \dfrac{\sqrt{xy^5}}{\sqrt{y}} \cdot \dfrac{\sqrt{y}}{\sqrt{y}}$ Multiply by 1 to rationalize the denominator.

$= \dfrac{\sqrt{xy^6}}{y}$ Distribute square root over multiplication.

$= \dfrac{y^3\sqrt{x}}{y}$ Take $\sqrt{y^6}$.

$= \underline{\underline{y^2\sqrt{x}}}$ Cancel.

EXAMPLE 3

Simplify $\sqrt{x^2 + 12x + 36}$. Assume that the radicand is a positive number.

$\sqrt{x^2 + 12x + 36}$ Write the given expression.

$= \sqrt{(x + 6)^2}$ Factor the radicand.

$= \underline{\underline{|x + 6|}}$ Take the square root. Note that although the radicand is stated to be positive, $x + 6$ could be negative. So the absolute value sign is needed.

EXERCISE 12-5

For Problems 1 through 16, simplify the expression. Assume that all variables stand for positive numbers.

1. $\sqrt{x^6}$
2. $\sqrt{y^4}$
3. $\sqrt{9a^8}$

4. $\sqrt{25c^2}$
5. $\sqrt{a^7}$
6. $\sqrt{z^5}$
7. $\sqrt{12r^9}$
8. $\sqrt{48p^2}$
9. $\dfrac{\sqrt{x^3}}{\sqrt{y}}$
10. $\dfrac{\sqrt{k^5}}{\sqrt{p}}$
11. $\dfrac{\sqrt{x^4y}}{\sqrt{xy^2}}$
12. $\dfrac{\sqrt{x^5y^7}}{\sqrt{xy^{10}}}$
13. $\sqrt{15a^3}\sqrt{3a}$
14. $\sqrt{18x}\sqrt{2x^5}$
15. $\dfrac{3\sqrt{25x^7}}{5\sqrt{9x}}$
16. $\dfrac{12\sqrt{3v}}{5\sqrt{12v^5}}$

For Problems 17 through 24, simplify the expression. Assume that all radicands stand for positive numbers.

17. $\sqrt{x+3}\sqrt{x-2}$
18. $\sqrt{x+5}\sqrt{x-7}$
19. $\sqrt{(x-5)^2}$
20. $\sqrt{(x+4)^2}$
21. $\sqrt{x^2+6x+9}$
22. $\sqrt{x^2-10x+25}$
23. $\sqrt{(x-7)^3}$
24. $\sqrt{(x+10)^5}$
25. Explain why the simplified form of $\sqrt{(x-3)^2}$ must have an absolute value sign, but $\sqrt{(x-3)^4}$ does not need one.
26. Let $x = \sqrt{a^2+b^2}$. Let $y = a + b$. Assume that a and b stand for positive numbers.
    a. Evaluate x and y if $a = 3$ and $b = 4$. Which is bigger, x or y? How much bigger?
    b. Evaluate x and y if $a = 15$ and $b = 8$. Which is bigger, x or y? How much bigger?
    c. Explain why y will always be bigger than x if a and b are positive numbers. If you have learned never to forget the middle term when you square a binomial, you have a good chance of being able to answer this question.
    d. Explain how what you have done in this problem proves that square root does *not* distribute over addition.

12-6 RADICAL EQUATIONS

In the last section you simplified expressions that had variables under the radical sign, such as

$$\sqrt{5x-7}.$$

There are two things you might be expected to do with such expressions.

1. Evaluate the expression if you know what x equals.
2. Find x if you know what the expression equals.

You did both of these things in Section 12-1. Substituting for x and evaluating the expression involves only arithmetic and is fairly easy. But solving a radical equation for x has some surprises, as you will see in this section.

Suppose you must find x when the expression above equals 3. Setting the expression equal to 3 gives the following *radical equation*.

$$\sqrt{5x - 7} = 3$$

DEFINITION

RADICAL EQUATION
A **radical equation** is an equation with a variable under the radical sign.

Squaring each member of this equation removes the radical sign on the left side and gives 9 on the right.

$$(\sqrt{5x - 7})^2 = 3^2 \quad \text{Square each member.}$$

$$5x - 7 = 9 \quad \text{Do the squaring.}$$

$$5x = 16 \quad \text{Add 7 to each member.}$$

$$x = 3.2 \quad \text{Divide each member by 5.}$$

Check:

$$\sqrt{5x - 7} \stackrel{?}{=} 3$$

$$\sqrt{5(3.2) - 7} \stackrel{?}{=} 3$$

$$\sqrt{16 - 7} \stackrel{?}{=} 3$$

$$\sqrt{9} \stackrel{?}{=} 3$$

$$3 = 3 \checkmark$$

$$\therefore S = \{3.2\}$$

For reasons that will soon become obvious, it is advisable to wait until *after* the check to write the solution set!

Some rather innocent-looking radical equations give perplexing results. For instance, solve

$$\sqrt{x} + 2 = x.$$

If you square each member as the equation stands now, the left member becomes

$$(\sqrt{x} + 2)^2, \quad \text{or} \quad x + 4\sqrt{x} + 4.$$

The radical is still there! In order to eliminate the radical you must isolate it on one side of the equation before squaring.

$\sqrt{x} = x - 2$	Subtract 2 from each member to isolate the radical.
$(\sqrt{x})^2 = (x - 2)^2$	Square each member.
$x = x^2 - 4x + 4$	Do the squaring.
$0 = x^2 - 5x + 4$	Make one member equal *zero* since this is a *quadratic* equation.
$0 = (x - 4)(x - 1)$	Factor the right member. (Use the Quadratic Formula, if necessary.)
$x = 4$ or $x = 1$	Set each factor equal to 0 and solve.

Before you write the solution set, you should check the answers.

$x = 4$:	$x = 1$:	
$\sqrt{x} \stackrel{?}{=} x - 2$	$\sqrt{x} \stackrel{?}{=} x - 2$	
$\sqrt{4} \stackrel{?}{=} 4 - 2$	$\sqrt{1} \stackrel{?}{=} 1 - 2$	
$2 = 2$ ✓	$1 \neq -1$	Does not check!

The first answer checks, but the second one does not! This is because there are two different original equations that you could square to get the same transformed equation.

Your equation:	Other equation:	
$\sqrt{x} = x - 2$	$-\sqrt{x} = x - 2$ ⟵	Different!
$(\sqrt{x})^2 = (x - 2)^2$	$(-\sqrt{x})^2 = (x - 2)^2$	
$x = x^2 - 4x + 4$	$x = x^2 - 4x + 4$ ⟵	Same!

The number 1 satisfies the transformed equation, but not your original equation. As you recall from Section 11-6, such a number is called an *extraneous solution*. So you would label $x = 1$ as extraneous and write only 4 in the solution set.

$$x = 4 \quad \text{or} \quad \cancel{x = 1} \rightarrow \text{Extraneous}$$

$$\therefore S = \{4\}$$

Objective

Be able to solve a radical equation involving square roots, check the answer(s), and discard any extraneous solutions.

Cover the answers as you work these examples.

EXAMPLE 1

Solve and check: $\sqrt{2x + 9} = 6$.

	Think These Reasons
$\sqrt{2x + 9} = 6$	Write the given equation.
$2x + 9 = 36$	Square each member.
$2x = 27$	Subtract 9 from each member.
$x = 13.5$	Divide each member by 2.

Check:
Check the solution.

$$\sqrt{2(13.5) + 9} \stackrel{?}{=} 6$$

$$\sqrt{36} \stackrel{?}{=} 6$$

$$6 = 6 \checkmark$$

$\therefore S = \{13.5\}$ Write the solution set.

EXAMPLE 2

Solve and check: $\sqrt{x} + 32 = 7$.

$\sqrt{x} + 32 = 7$	Write the given equation.
$\sqrt{x} = -25$	Subtract 32 to isolate the radical.
$(\sqrt{x})^2 = (-25)^2$	Square each member.
$x = 625$	Do the squaring.

Check: $\sqrt{625} + 32 \stackrel{?}{=} 7$

$$25 + 32 \stackrel{?}{=} 7$$

$$57 \neq 7$$

$\cancel{x = 625}$ → Extraneous — Discard extraneous solutions.

$\therefore S = \emptyset$ Write the solution set.

Notes:

1. The only possible solution is extraneous, so the solution set is empty.
2. You could tell at the second line,

$$\sqrt{x} = -25,$$

that the solution set is empty. Recall that $\sqrt{x}$ means the *positive* square root of x and thus cannot equal -25.

EXAMPLE 3

Solve and check: $5 - \sqrt{3x} = 2x$.

$5 - \sqrt{3x} = 2x$	Write the given equation.
$-\sqrt{3x} = 2x - 5$	Subtract 5 to isolate the radical.
$(-\sqrt{3x})^2 = (2x - 5)^2$	Square each member.
$3x = 4x^2 - 20x + 25$	Do the squaring.
$0 = 4x^2 - 23x + 25$	Make one member equal zero since the equation is quadratic.
$x = \dfrac{23 \pm \sqrt{529 - 4(4)(25)}}{2(4)}$	Use the Quadratic Formula.
$x = \dfrac{23 \pm \sqrt{129}}{8}$	Do the computations.
$x = 4.29\ldots$ or $1.455\ldots$	Finish the computations.

Check:

$x = 4.294\ldots$:	$x = 1.455\ldots$:
$5 - \sqrt{3(4.294\ldots)} \stackrel{?}{=} 2(4.294\ldots)$	$5 - \sqrt{3(1.455\ldots)} \stackrel{?}{=} 2(1.455\ldots)$
$1.410\ldots \neq 8.589\ldots$	$2.910\ldots \approx 2.910\ldots$

~~$x \approx 4.29$~~ (Extraneous) or $x \approx 1.46$	Round solutions. Discard extraneous solutions.
$\therefore S = \{1.46\}$	Write the solution set.

ORAL PRACTICE

Transform to isolate the radical.

EXAMPLE

	Answer
$5 - \sqrt{x} = 2$	$-\sqrt{x} = -3$

A. $\sqrt{x} + 3 = 8$

B. $4 + \sqrt{x} = 7$

C. $9 - \sqrt{x} = 2$

D. $6 + \sqrt{x} = x$

Give the result of squaring each member.

EXAMPLE

	Answer
$\sqrt{x+3} = 5$	$x + 3 = 25$

E. $\sqrt{x} = 9$ F. $\sqrt{x} = 3x$ G. $\sqrt{x+2} = 7$

H. $\sqrt{x-4} = 3$ I. $\sqrt{x} = x + 3$ J. $\sqrt{x} = x - 5$

K. $\sqrt{x+9} = x$ L. $\sqrt{x-1} = x + 4$

EXERCISE 12-6

Solve the equations, discarding any extraneous solutions.

1. $\sqrt{x+3} = 7$
2. $\sqrt{x+5} = 3$
3. $\sqrt{x} + 9 = 25$
4. $\sqrt{x} + 7 = 16$
5. $\sqrt{x} + 13 = 9$
6. $\sqrt{x} + 17 = 1$
7. $\sqrt{3x+4} = 5$
8. $\sqrt{5x+11} = 9$
9. $\sqrt{7x-10} = 4$
10. $\sqrt{13x-3} = 5$
11. $\sqrt{x-5} + 3 = 10$
12. $\sqrt{x-7} - 3 = 5$
13. $\sqrt{x+2} + 12 = 7$
14. $\sqrt{x+3} + 15 = 8$
15. $13 - \sqrt{x-1} = 22$
16. $11 - \sqrt{x+4} = 17$
17. $\sqrt{x} + 6 = x$
18. $\sqrt{2x} + 4 = x$
19. $2 - \sqrt{2x} = 3x$
20. $4 - \sqrt{3x} = x$

12-7 THE PYTHAGOREAN THEOREM AND APPLICATIONS

In geometry you will learn the properties of triangles. One of the most important properties concerns the lengths of sides of a **right triangle,** in which one angle is a right angle. If you square the lengths of the two shorter sides (the **legs**) and add the two numbers together, you get the square of the length of the longest side (the **hypotenuse**).

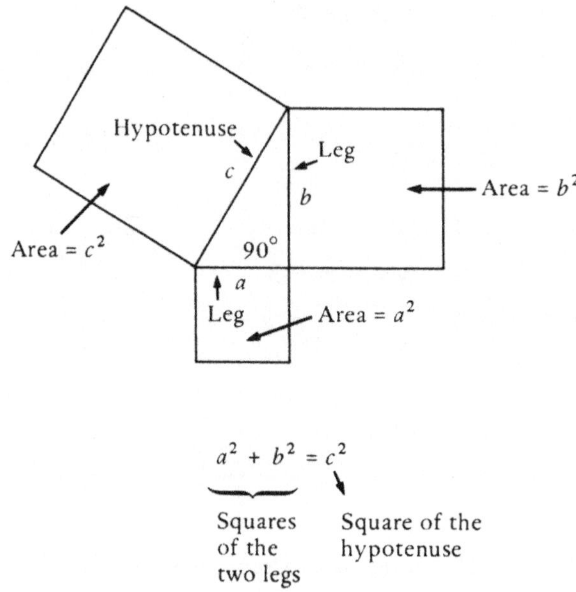

This property is called the **Pythagorean theorem** in honor of the Greek mathematician Pythagoras, who lived about 2500 years ago.

PROPERTY

PYTHAGOREAN THEOREM
In a right triangle, the square of the hypotenuse equals the sum of the squares of the two legs. That is,

$$(\text{hypotenuse})^2 = (\text{leg})^2 + (\text{other leg})^2.$$

More formally, if a and b are the lengths of the legs and c is the length of the hypotenuse, then

$$\boxed{a^2 + b^2 = c^2}$$

The word *theorem* is another name for a property that can be proved from properties, definitions, and axioms. One of the easiest ways to see why this theorem is true is to construct two squares, each with sides of length $a + b$. Then fill in the squares with *four* right triangles, as shown in the following diagrams.

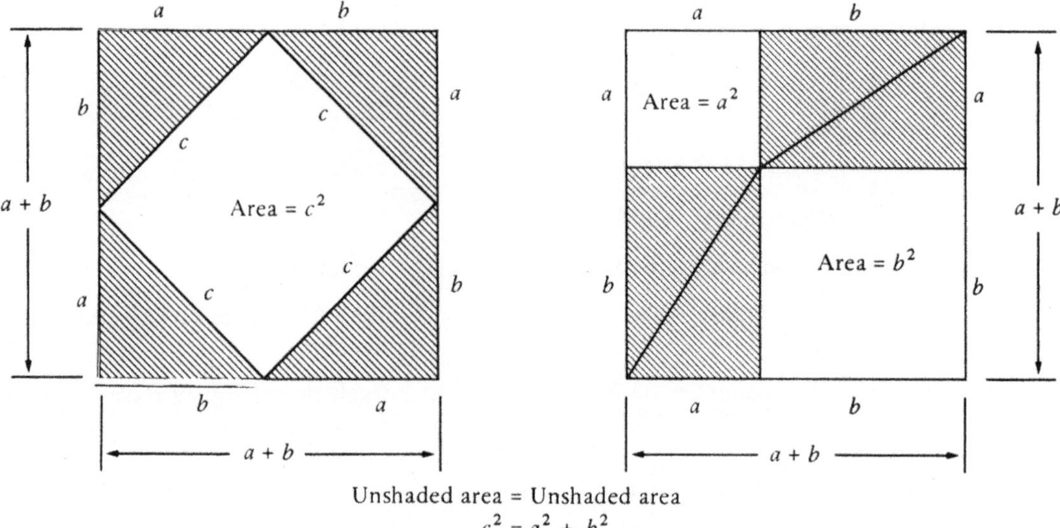

Unshaded area = Unshaded area
$c^2 = a^2 + b^2$

In the first diagram, one right triangle goes in each corner. The area of the square in the middle equals c^2, the square of the hypotenuse. In the second diagram, pairs of triangles are put together to form rectangles, and the rectangles are placed in opposite corners. Two squares remain empty, one of area a^2 and the other of area b^2. Since the same-size square is filled with the same four triangles, the unfilled areas must be equal in both figures. Therefore,

$$a^2 + b^2 = c^2.$$

In this section you will use the Pythagorean theorem to compute the length of one side of a right triangle when the lengths of the other two sides are known.

Objective

Given the lengths of two sides of a right triangle, be able to calculate the length of the third side.

Cover the answers as you work these examples.

EXAMPLE 1

Find the length of the hypotenuse.

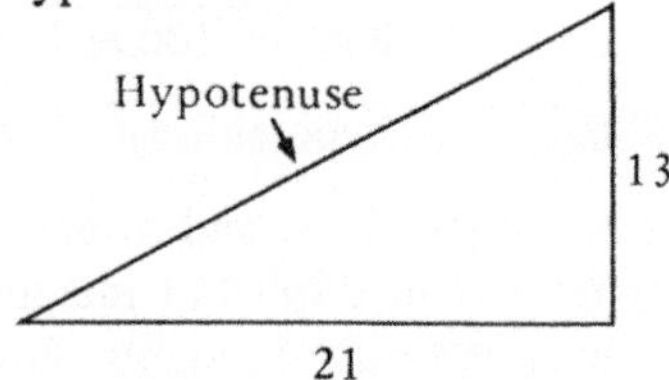

- - - - - - - - - -

Think These Reasons

$(\text{hypotenuse})^2 = 13^2 + 21^2$	Use the Pythagorean theorem.
$(\text{hypotenuse})^2 = 169 + 441$	Do the squaring.
$(\text{hypotenuse})^2 = 610$	Do the addition.
$\text{hypotenuse} = \sqrt{610}$	Take the square root of each member.
$\underline{\underline{\text{hypotenuse} \approx 24.70}}$	Evaluate the square root. Round to two decimal places.

EXAMPLE 2

Find the length of the unknown leg.

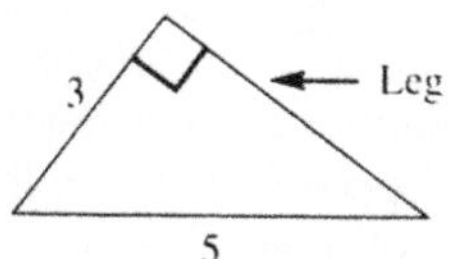

- - - - - - - - - -

$3^2 + (\text{leg})^2 = 5^2$	Use the Pythagorean theorem.
$(\text{leg})^2 = 25 - 9$	Subtract 3^2; do the squaring.
$(\text{leg})^2 = 16$	Do the arithmetic.
$\text{leg} = \sqrt{16}$	Take the square root of each member.
$\underline{\underline{\text{leg} = 4}}$	Evaluate the square root.

Notes:

1. In Example 2 it was necessary to transform the equation from the Pythagorean theorem so that $(\text{leg})^2$ was isolated on one side. Both examples can be worked more quickly if you remember the theorem in this form:

$$\text{hypotenuse} = \sqrt{(\text{leg})^2 + (\text{other leg})^2}$$

$$\text{leg} = \sqrt{(\text{hypotenuse})^2 - (\text{other leg})^2}.$$

2. In Example 2, all three sides (3, 4, and 5) are integers. There are many other such **Pythagorean triples** of integers, as you will see in the following exercise. Most right triangles, however, have at least one side whose length is an *irrational* number, as in Example 1.

EXAMPLE 3

Ship Problem A ship travels 327 kilometers due east and then turns 90° and travels 193 more kilometers due north. At that point the captain receives a message to return directly to the starting point. How far must the ship travel?

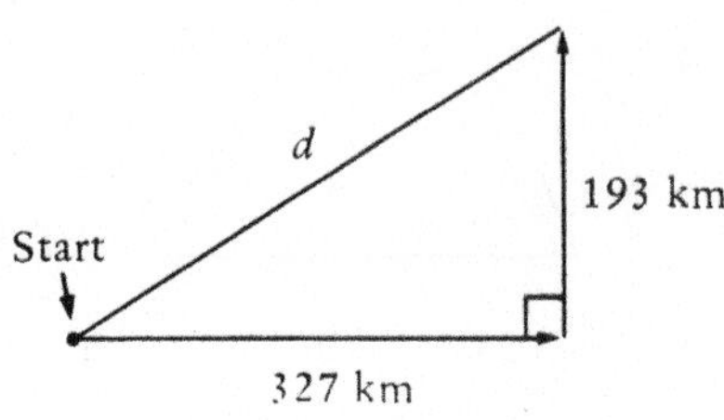

Think These Reasons

	Draw a picture, look for a right triangle, and label its sides.
$d = \sqrt{327^2 + 193^2}$	Use the Pythagorean theorem (short form).
$= \sqrt{106{,}929 + 37{,}249}$	Do the squaring.
$= \sqrt{144{,}178}$	Do the addition.
$= 379.707...$	Evaluate the square root.
$\underline{\underline{379.71 \text{ km}}}$	Answer the question. Round to two decimal places.

EXERCISE 12-7

For Problems 1 through 20, find the length of the third side of the right triangle. Round approximate answers to two decimal places.

1.

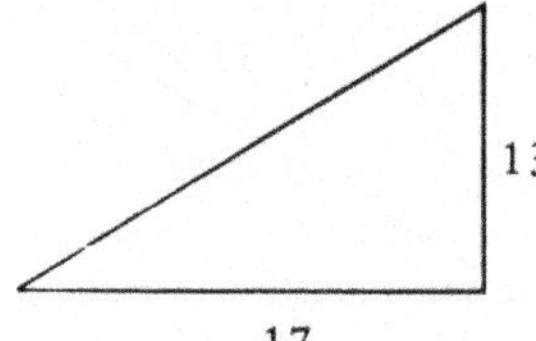

2.

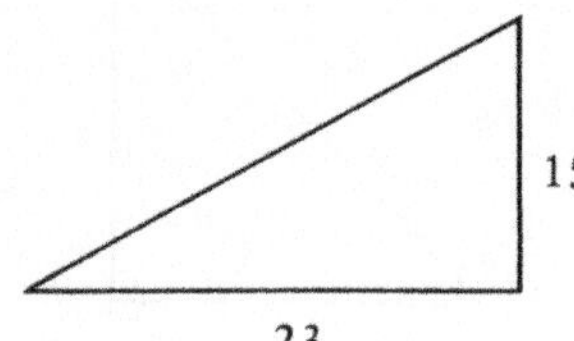

3.

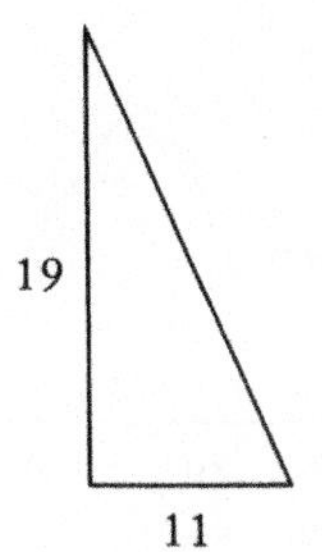

4.

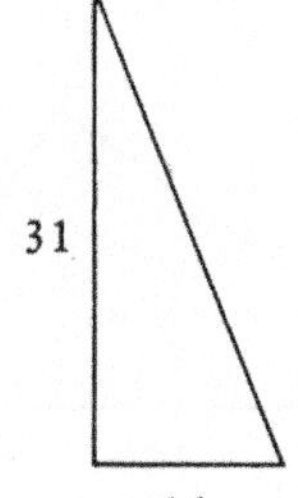

5.

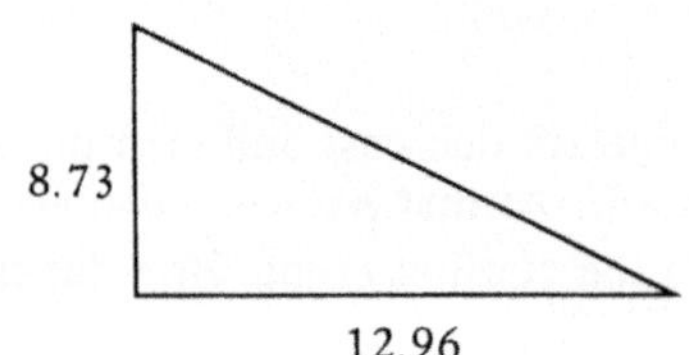

6.

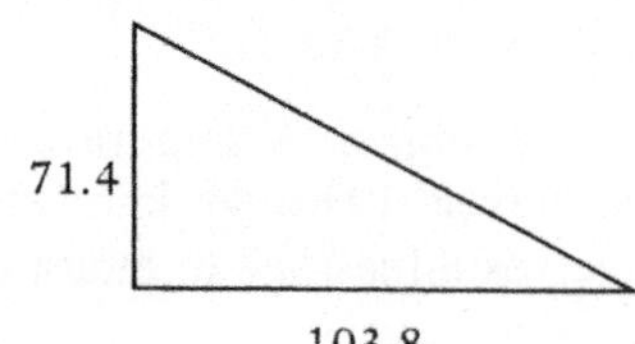

7.

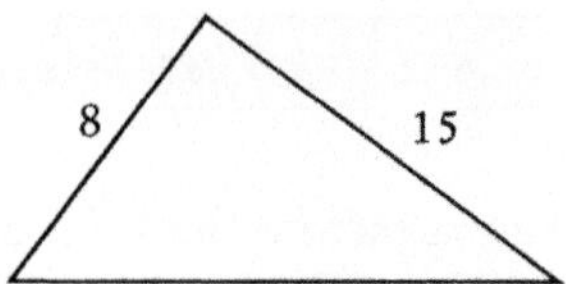

8.

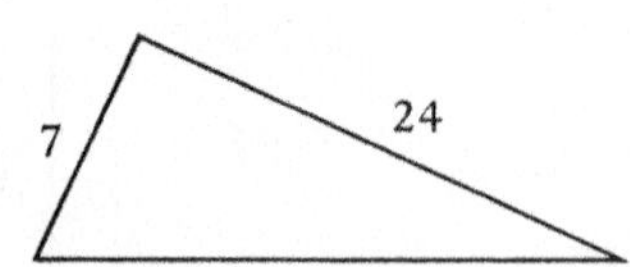

9.

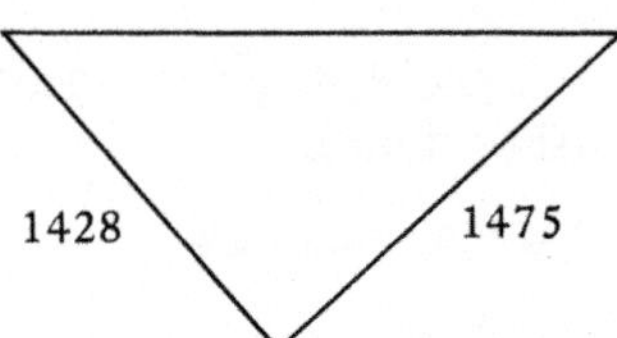

10.

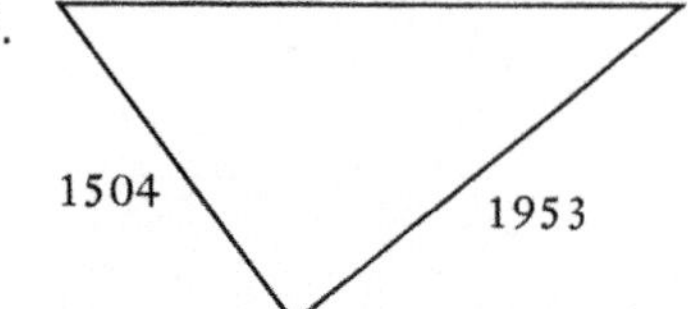

11.

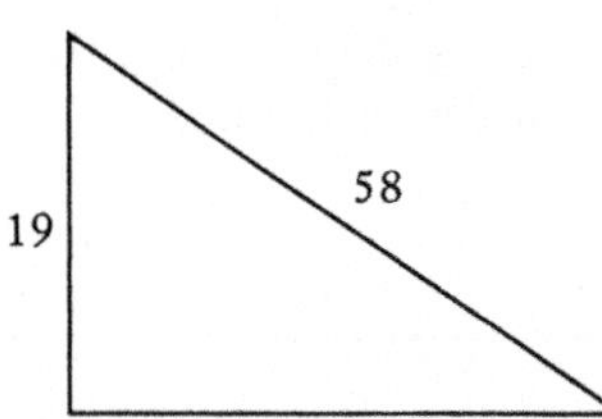

12.

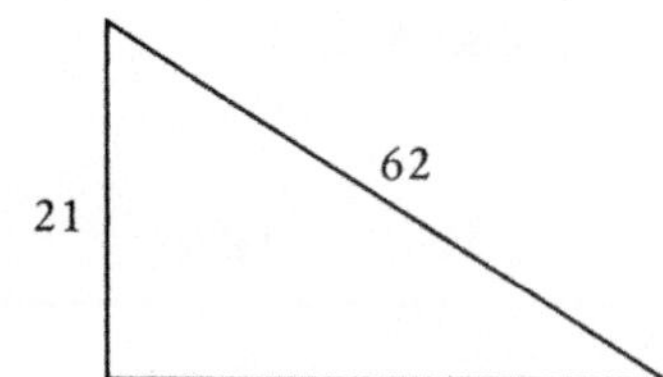

13.

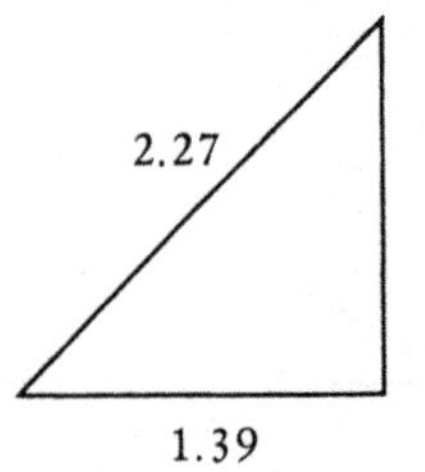

14.

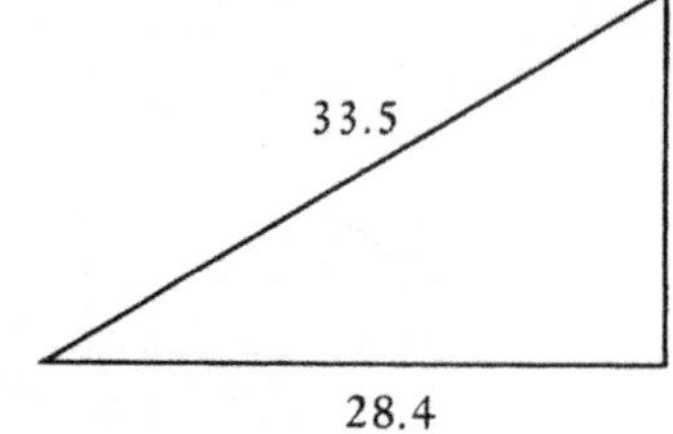

15.

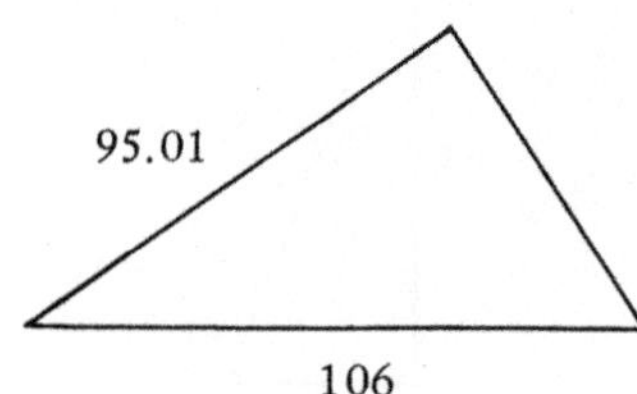

16.

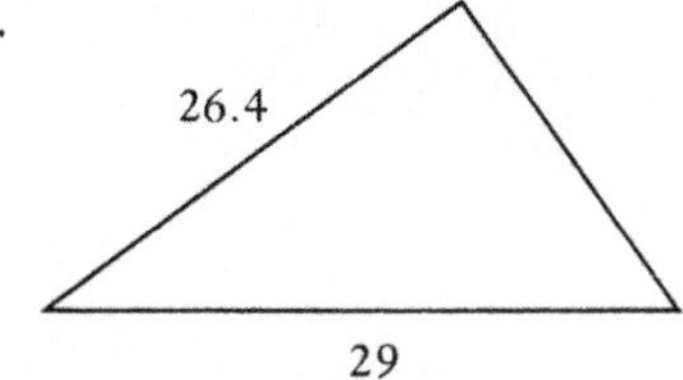

17.

18.

19.

20.

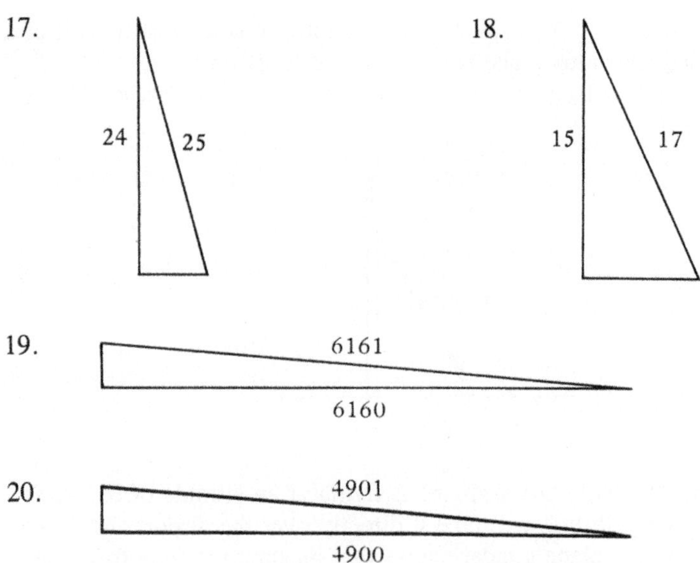

21. ***Calvin's to Phoebe's Problem*** Calvin Butterball lives on Elm Street 257 meters from its intersection with Oak. Phoebe Small lives on Oak Avenue, 113 meters from its intersection with Elm. How many meters could Calvin save by walking directly to Phoebe's instead of by walking along the roads?

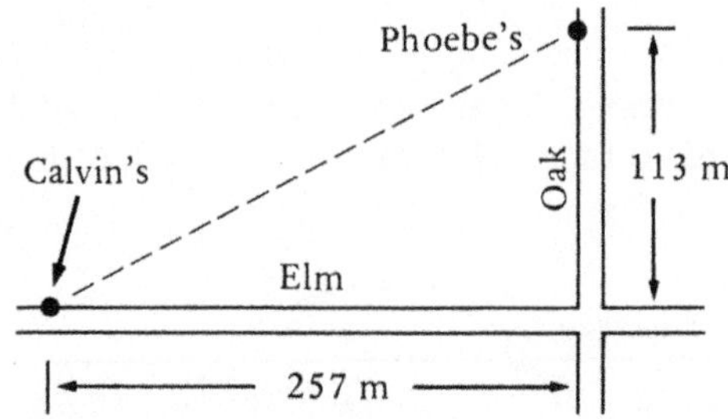

22. ***TV Transmitter Problem*** A television transmitter is atop an antenna tower 300 meters high. It is held up by guy wires from the top and from the middle, anchored in the ground 160 meters from the base of the antenna. How long is each guy wire?

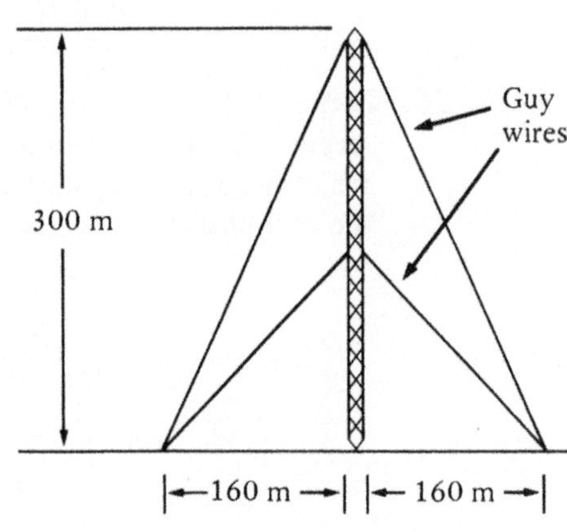

23. *Ladder Problem* A ladder 5.7 meters long rests against the sill of a second-story window. The base of the ladder is on the ground 2.3 meters from the base of the wall. How far is the window sill above the ground?

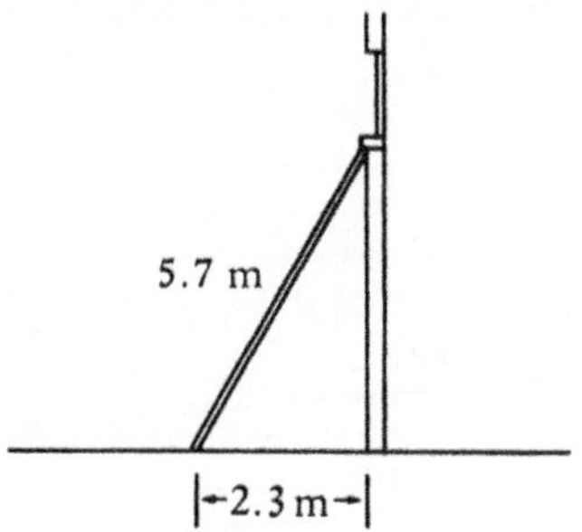

24. *Airplane Problem* An airplane is flying at an altitude of 3.7 kilometers on a path that will take it directly over the airport. At a certain instant the plane's radar shows that its slant distance from the airport is 14.2 kilometers. How far must the plane travel to be directly above the airport?

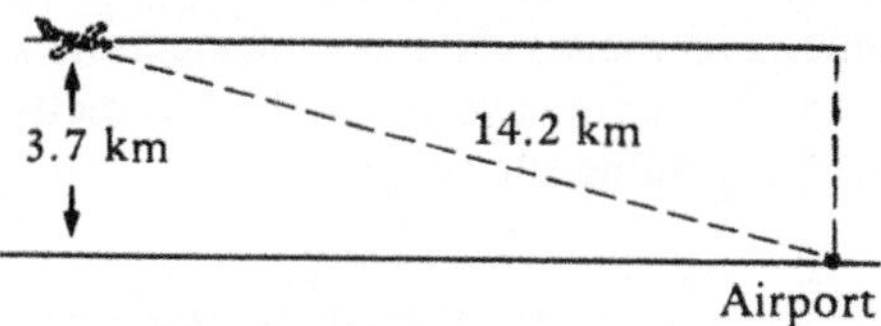

25. *CB Radio Problem* A CB radio station is located 3 km off the highway. It has a range of 7 km. What length of highway is within its range?

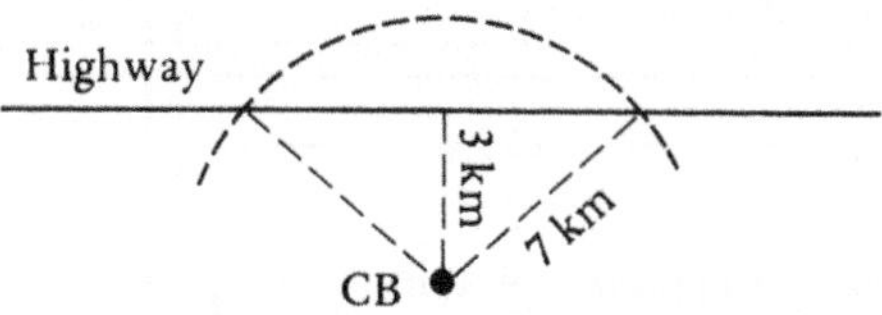

26. *Torpedo Problem* A submarine lies 2000 meters from the path of a target ship. The sub's torpedoes have a range of 5000 meters. For what distance along its path will the target ship be within range of the torpedoes?

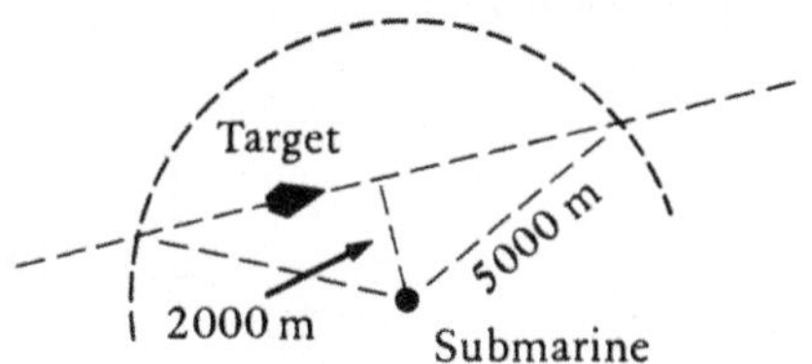

27. ***Pipeline Problem 1*** Oil well 1 is located on a side road 0.9 kilometers from the main road (see the figure). The storage tanks are on the main road, 2.5 kilometers from its intersection with the side road. A pipeline is to be built connecting the well to the tanks. It costs $3000 per kilometer if it is built along the roads or $4000 per kilometer if it is built directly to the tanks. Which way is cheaper? How much cheaper?

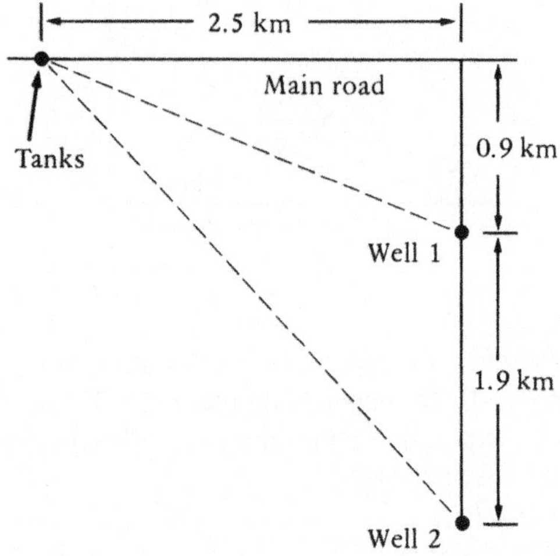

28. ***Pipeline Problem 2*** Oil well 2 is located 1.9 kilometers farther down the side road from oil well 1 (see the figure). A pipeline is to be built connecting the well to the tanks on the main road. As in Problem 27, it costs $3000 per kilometer to build pipeline along roads or $4000 per kilometer to build it directly to the tanks. Which way is cheaper? How much cheaper? Figure out an even cheaper way to connect well 2 to the tanks.

29. ***Rowing versus Walking Problem*** Keri Onward spends two weeks at a summer cottage on the beach. Each day she fishes from the end of the pier. She can either go directly by rowboat or walk 327 meters along the beach and then 204 meters along the pier. She can row 50 m/min and walk 60 m/min. Which way is quicker? How much quicker?

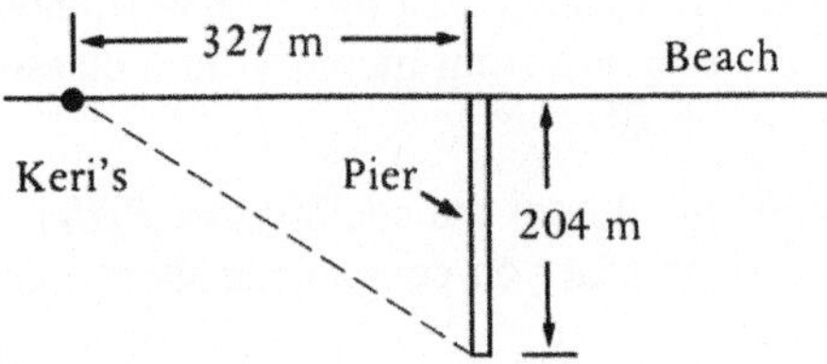

30. ***Shortcut Problem*** Perry Meter can get from Here to There either by going 52 kilometers directly along the Farm Road or by going 43 kilometers down Highway A, turning 90°, and going along Highway B. He can average 1.4 kilometers per minute (km/min) on the highways, but only 0.9 km/min on the Farm Road. Which way is quicker? How much quicker?

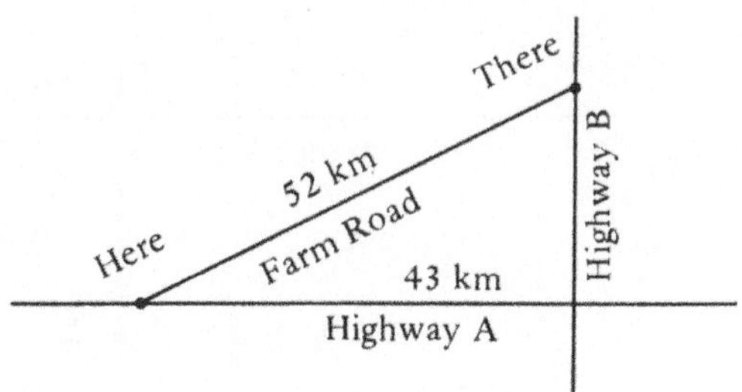

31. ***Distance Problem 1*** As a point moves along the x-axis, its distance from the point $(0, 20)$ depends on the value of x.
   a. Write an expression representing this distance in terms of x. $\sqrt{x^2 + 400}$
   b. Find the distance when:
      i. x is 37;
      ii. x is -25;
      iii. x is 0.
   c. Write an equation stating that the distance is 52. Then solve the equation to find the value(s) of x.
   d. Find the value(s) of x when the distance is 15.

32. ***Distance Problem 2*** As a point moves along the y-axis, its distance from the point $(-16, 0)$ depends on the value of y.
   a. Write an expression representing this distance in terms of y.
   b. Write an equation stating that the distance is 25. Then solve the equation to find the value(s) of y.
   c. Find the value(s) of y when the distance is 29.
   d. Find the distance when:
      i. y is -5;
      ii. y is 3.5;
      iii. y is 11.6.

33. ***Proof of the Pythagorean Theorem*** Learn the geometric justification of the Pythagorean theorem well enough so that you could draw the diagram from memory on a classroom quiz and give reasons why $a^2 + b^2 = c^2$.

34. ***Spelling Problem*** Learn the spellings of *Pythagoras* and *Pythagorean* well enough that you could write them from memory on a classroom quiz.

12-8 HIGHER-ORDER RADICALS

You have learned that a square root of x is a number that gives x for the answer when you square it. That is,

$$(\sqrt{x})^2 = x.$$

Using the same reasoning, other roots of a number can be defined. For instance, 5 is a **cube root** of 125, since

$$5^3 = 125.$$

Similarly,

3 is a **fourth root** of 81, since $3^4 = 81$,

2 is a **fifth root** of 32, since $2^5 = 32$.

The symbol for these higher order roots uses the radical sign, $\sqrt{\ }$, with a number outside to tell which root is being taken.

$\sqrt[3]{x}$ is the cube root of x.

$\sqrt[4]{x}$ is the fourth root of x.

$\sqrt[5]{x}$ is the fifth root of x.

The number 3, 4, or 5, above, is called the *root index*. The square root could be written $\sqrt[2]{x}$, but it almost never is written this way.

DEFINITION

> ***NTH* ROOT**
> An ***n*th root** of x is a number that, when raised to the nth power, gives x for the answer. That is,
>
> $\sqrt[n]{x}$ is a number such that
>
> $(\sqrt[n]{x})^n = x.$
>
> The positive integer n is called the **root index.**

An nth root of x can be evaluated using any scientific calculator. All you have to do is raise x to the power $\frac{1}{n}$. For instance, the cube root of 57 can be found as follows:

$\sqrt[3]{57}$

$= 57^{\frac{1}{3}}$ Write the cube root as a power.

≈ 3.8485011 Press 57 [y^x] 3 [$1/x$] [=], or press 57 [$\sqrt[x]{y}$] 3 [=].

You can check this answer by *cubing* it. Since the calculator rounds both in getting the answer and in checking it, you might get a number slightly different from 57, such as 56.999998.

PROPERTY

EXPONENT PROPERTY OF *N*TH ROOTS

$$\sqrt[n]{x} = x^{\frac{1}{n}}$$

Objective

Given a higher-order radical, evaluate it by calculator and use the result to work problems.

Cover the answers as you work these examples.

EXAMPLE 1

Evaluate $\sqrt[4]{32.7}$ correct to two decimal places.

	Think These Reasons
$\sqrt[4]{32.7}$	Write the given expression.
$= 32.7^{\frac{1}{4}}$	Write the radical as a power.
$= 2.3913158\ldots$	Press 32.7 [y^x] 4 [$1/x$] [=]
$\approx \underline{\underline{2.39}}$	Round the answer.

EXAMPLE 2

Evaluate $\sqrt[5]{4{,}084{,}101}$ correct to two decimal places.

$\sqrt[5]{4{,}084{,}101}$	Write the given expression.
$= 4{,}084{,}101^{\frac{1}{5}}$	Write the radical as a power.
$= \underline{\underline{21}}$	Press 4084101 [y^x] 5 [$1/x$] [=] (The answer is *exact*.)

EXAMPLE 3

The weight of a diamond is given by

$$w = 0.06\, d^3,$$

where w is the weight in carats and d is the diameter in millimeters. Find the diameter of a 7-carat diamond.

$w = 0.06\,d^3$	Write the given equation.
$7 = 0.06\,d^3$	Substitute 7 for w.
$\frac{7}{0.06} = d^3$	Divide each member by 0.06.
$\sqrt[3]{\frac{7}{0.06}} = d$	Take the cube root of each member.
$4.886324 \approx d$	Evaluate the cube root.
About 4.9 m.	Answer the question.

ORAL PRACTICE

Evaluate the radical.

A. $\sqrt[3]{8}$ B. $\sqrt[4]{16}$ C. $\sqrt[3]{27}$ D. $\sqrt[4]{81}$ E. $\sqrt[3]{64}$

F. $\sqrt[6]{64}$ G. $\sqrt[3]{1000}$ H. $\sqrt[3]{1}$ I. $\sqrt[9]{1}$ J. $\sqrt[7]{0}$

Express the radical as a power.

EXAMPLE

	Answer
$\sqrt[3]{29}$	$29^{\frac{1}{3}}$

K. $\sqrt[3]{42}$ L. $\sqrt[4]{73}$ M. $\sqrt[5]{99}$ N. $\sqrt[6]{309}$ O. $\sqrt[7]{0.95}$

EXERCISE 12-8

For Problems 1 through 20, evaluate the radical. Round approximate answers to two decimal places.

1. $\sqrt[3]{537}$
2. $\sqrt[3]{795}$
3. $\sqrt[4]{849}$
4. $\sqrt[4]{692}$
5. $\sqrt[5]{2478}$
6. $\sqrt[5]{9876}$
7. $\sqrt[6]{729}$
8. $\sqrt[6]{4096}$
9. $\sqrt[5]{1024}$

10. $\sqrt[5]{3125}$
11. $\sqrt[4]{2401}$
12. $\sqrt[4]{14{,}641}$
13. $\sqrt[3]{389{,}017}$
14. $\sqrt[3]{185{,}193}$
15. $\sqrt[3]{22.79}$
16. $\sqrt[3]{13.92}$
17. $\sqrt[4]{0.0325}$
18. $\sqrt[4]{0.0928}$
19. $\sqrt[5]{286.29151}$
20. $\sqrt[5]{24.76099}$

21. ***Cube Problem*** The volume of a cube equals the cube of the length of an edge.
    a. Find the volume of a cube of edge 3.7 cm.
    b. Find the length of the edge of a cube whose volume is 578 cubic centimeters.
    c. A person can fit into a space of about 1 cubic meter. There are approximately 4.5 billion people in the world. Thus a box of volume 4.5 billion cubic meters would hold all the people in the world. If the box were a cube, how long would the edges be?

22. ***Sphere Problem*** The volume, V, of a sphere is

$$V = \frac{4}{3}\pi r^3,$$

where r is the radius of the sphere and $\pi \approx 3.14159$.
    a. Find the volume of a basketball whose radius is 12 cm.
    b. What radius sphere would hold a liter of water (1000 cubic centimeters)?
    c. A spherical water tank is to hold 20,000 cubic feet of water. What must its radius be?

23. ***Shark Problem*** The mass of a great white shark is approximately

$$m = 9.5L^3,$$

where m is its mass in kilograms and L is its length in meters.
    a. Calculate the mass of a great white shark 2 meters long.
    b. How long would a 200-kilogram shark be?
    c. The shark in the novel *Jaws* was supposed to have been about 8 meters long. What would its mass have been? Surprising?

24. ***Height-Mass Problem*** The mass of a person of average build is approximately

$$m = 11.6h^3,$$

where m is mass in kilograms and h is height in meters.
    a. What is the mass of a person of average build who is 1.5 meters tall?
    b. What is the mass of a very tall person of average build who is 2.5 meters tall?
    c. How tall would a 50-kilogram person of average build be?
    d. What should be the mass of a person of average build who is *your* height?

25. ***Exponent Property of nth Roots Problem***
   a. Show that $\sqrt[3]{8} = 2$ by writing 8 as 2^3 and then raising 2^3 to the $\frac{1}{3}$ power, using the appropriate property of exponentiation.
   b. Show that 3 is a fifth root of 243 by writing 243 as a power and then raising it to the $\frac{1}{5}$ power, using the appropriate property of exponentiation.
   c. Write $\sqrt[n]{x}$ as $x^{\frac{1}{n}}$ and then raise it to the nth power. Explain how this computation shows that $x^{\frac{1}{n}}$ really *is* an nth root of x.

12-9 RATIONAL AND IRRATIONAL NUMBERS

In Section 5-10 you learned that *rational* numbers are numbers such as

$$\frac{2}{3},\quad 5\tfrac{1}{2},\quad -\frac{7}{2},\quad 55,$$

which can be written as ratios of two integers. You also learned that *irrational* numbers are numbers that *cannot* be written as ratios of integers. In this section you will see that repeating decimals represent *rational* numbers and that radicals such as $\sqrt{19}$ represent *irrational* numbers.

To see that rational numbers give repeating decimals, you can evaluate some numbers on a calculator.

$$\frac{2}{3} = 0.66666\ldots$$

$$\frac{3}{11} = 0.272727\ldots$$

$$\frac{2}{5} = 0.4 = 0.400000\ldots$$

You can tell *why* rational numbers give repeating decimals by looking at the long-division process. If you divide a number such as 3 by 11, there are only 11 possible remainders: 0, 1, 2, 3, 4, 5, 6, 7, 8, 9, and 10. If the remainder is ever 0, the decimal terminates. If the remainder is never 0, it is bound to be the same again after at most 10 steps in the division process. Once the remainder repeats, the decimal repeats, too.

It is possible to do the reverse problem and find the fraction equal to a given repeating decimal, such as 0.393939. . . .

Let $x = 0.393939\ldots$	Write an equation.
$\therefore 100x = 39.393939\ldots$	Multiply each member by 100 to move the decimal point over two places.

$99x = 39$	Subtract the top equation from the bottom one. The decimal parts "drop out."
$x = \frac{39}{99}$	Divide each member by 99.
$x = \frac{13}{33}$	Do any possible canceling.

This process can be done for *any* repeating decimal. At the second step, just multiply each member by a power of 10 big enough to move the decimal to where the repeating parts again line up. Then subtract the two equations to eliminate the decimal part.

CONCLUSION

> A number is rational *if* and *only* if it can be written as a repeating decimal. (Decimals that *terminate* have repeating zeros.)

With the aid of this conclusion, it is easy to construct a number that is *irrational*. Just write a decimal that clearly does *not* repeat. For instance, these numbers are irrational:

$$0.101001000100001\ldots$$

$$0.11121314151617.\ldots$$

It turns out that π, the ratio of the circumference to the diameter of a circle, is an irrational number.

$$\pi \approx 3.14159265358979323846264338327950288419716939937510\ldots$$

Computations of π to over 100,000 decimal places confirm that it does not repeat.

Roots of integers that are not whole numbers are also irrational numbers. For instance, $\sqrt{2}$ is *between* two integers, 1 and 2, and is approximately 1.414. The number 1.414 equals $\frac{1414}{1000}$ and is thus a *rational* number. But 1.414^2 is only 1.999396. So 1.414 is not exactly equal to $\sqrt{2}$.

To see why such radicals are irrational, suppose that $\sqrt{2}$ *did* equal a ratio of two integers such as

$$\frac{1414}{1000}.$$

Factoring the numerator and denominator into primes gives

$$\frac{2 \cdot 7 \cdot 101}{2^3 \cdot 5^3}.$$

Canceling common factors gives

$$\frac{7 \cdot 101}{2^2 \cdot 5^3}.$$

If this fraction is *squared,* the result is

$$\frac{7^2 \cdot 101^2}{2^4 \cdot 5^6}.$$

Squaring a fraction introduces *no* new prime factors into the numerator or denominator. Since no more canceling could be done *before* the squaring, none can be done *afterwards,* either. So $(1.414)^2$ could not possibly be the *integer* 2. The same reasoning can be used to show that *no* rational number that is *between* two integers can possibly turn out to be an integer when it is squared, cubed, or raised to a higher power.

CONCLUSION

For any integer x, if x is not a perfect n^{th} power, then $\sqrt[n]{x}$ is an *irrational* number.

That is, if x is an integer, then $\sqrt[n]{x}$ is either an *integer* or an *irrational* number.

Cover the answers as you work these examples.

EXAMPLE 1

Write $\frac{5}{7}$ as a repeating decimal.

\- - - - -　　　　- - - - -

$\frac{5}{7} = 0.714285714285714285\ldots$

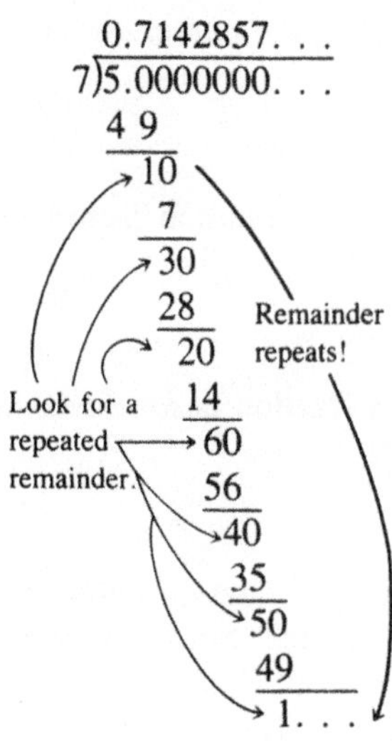

Note: When you divide a number by 7 the decimal will repeat after at most 6 digits, since there are only 6 possible nonzero remainders.

EXAMPLE 2

Write 0.405405405 . . . as a ratio of two relatively prime integers.

	Think These Reasons
$x = 0.405405405\ldots$	Write an equation.
$1000x = 405.405405405\ldots$	Multiply by 1000 to move the decimal point three places.
$999x = 405$	Subtract top equation from bottom.
$x = \frac{405}{999}$	Divide by 999.
$x = \frac{45}{111} = \frac{15}{37}$	Do the canceling to get *relatively prime* integers.

EXAMPLE 3

Is $\sqrt[4]{923521}$ a *rational* number or an *irrational* number? Justify your answer.

$\sqrt[4]{923,521}$	Write the given expression.
$= 923,521^{\frac{1}{4}}$	Write the radical as a power.
$= 31$	Press 923521 [y^x] 4 [$1/x$] [=].
$\therefore$ $\sqrt[4]{923521}$ is rational.	31 is a rational number.

EXAMPLE 4

Is $\sqrt[5]{29317}$ a *rational* number or an *irrational* number? Justify your answer.

$\sqrt[5]{29{,}317}$	Write the given expression.
$= 29{,}317^{\frac{1}{5}}$	Write the radical as a power.
≈ 7.8239111	Press 29317 [y^x] 5 [$1/x$] [=].
$\therefore$ $\sqrt[5]{29317}$ is irrational.	7.8239111 is not an integer. The only other choice is "irrational." (See the conclusion.)

EXAMPLE 5

Is 3.21221222122221 . . . a *rational* number or an *irrational* number? Justify your answer.

3.21221222122221 . . . is irrational.	It is a nonrepeating decimal.

EXERCISE 12-9

For Problems 1 through 20, write the rational number as a repeating decimal or as a terminating decimal.

1. $\frac{3}{7}$
2. $\frac{6}{7}$
3. $\frac{9}{11}$
4. $\frac{2}{11}$
5. $\frac{5}{6}$
6. $\frac{1}{6}$
7. $\frac{7}{9}$
8. $\frac{4}{9}$
9. $\frac{3}{16}$
10. $\frac{7}{16}$
11. $\frac{29}{33}$
12. $\frac{32}{33}$
13. $\frac{49}{66}$
14. $\frac{7}{66}$
15. $\frac{14}{37}$
16. $\frac{29}{37}$
17. $\frac{286}{999}$
18. $\frac{985}{999}$
19. $\frac{5}{13}$
20. $\frac{9}{13}$

For Problems 21 through 40, write the repeating decimal as a ratio of two relatively prime integers.

21. 0.333333. . .
22. 0.666666. . .
23. 0.777777. . .
24. 0.555555. . .
25. 0.565656. . .
26. 0.717171. . .

27. 0.151515. . . 28. 0.454545. . . 29. 0.909090. . .

30. 0.090909. . . 31. 0.671671. . . 32. 0.734734. . .

33. 0.303303. . . 34. 0.525525. . . 35. 0.243243. . .

36. 0.675675. . . 37. 0.037037. . . 38. 0.370370. . .

39. 0.185185. . . 40. 0.407407. . .

For Problems 41 through 60, tell whether the given number is *rational* or *irrational*. Justify your answer.

41. $\sqrt{8836}$ 42. $\sqrt{7415}$ 43. $\sqrt{3916}$

44. $\sqrt{2916}$ 45. $\sqrt[3]{7845}$ 46. $\sqrt[3]{2197}$

47. $\sqrt[4]{20{,}736}$ 48. $\sqrt[4]{75{,}802}$ 49. $\sqrt[5]{99{,}248}$

50. $\sqrt[5]{52{,}000}$ 51. 0.371371371. . . 52. 0.619619619. . .

53. 0.515115111511115. . . 54. 0.7020220222022220. . .

55. 0.005005005. . . 56. 0.010001000100010001. . .

57. 0.273 58. 0.195

59. $-\pi$ 60. π

61. ***Square Root of 5 Problem*** The square root of 5, $\sqrt{5}$, is approximately equal to 2.236.
   a. Show that 2.236 is a *rational* number by writing it as the ratio of two integers. Do any possible canceling.
   b. Factor the numerator and denominator of the simplified fraction in part (a) into primes. (*Clue:* The numerator has exactly two prime factors.)
   c. Without actually doing the multiplication, square the factored fraction in part (b). Show that the numerator and denominator of the squared fraction still have no common factors.
   d. Explain why the squared fraction in part (c) could not possibly equal 5.
   e. Square 2.236 and show that the answer is *close* to 5.

62. **0.999999. . . *Problem*** The number 0.333. . . represents $\frac{1}{3}$. Also, 2(0.333. . .), or 0.666. . . represents $\frac{2}{3}$. So 3(0.333. . .), or 0.999. . . , should represent $\frac{3}{3}$, or 1. Show that this is actually true by expressing 0.999. . . as a ratio of two integers, as in Example 2, and simplifying the result.

63. ***Cube Roots by Trial and Error*** The diagram on the next page is called a **flow chart.** Each rectangular box represents a step to be done in doing a computation. Each diamond-shaped box represents a **branch-point,** at which the flow of the computation could go either of two ways, depending on whether the answer to the question inside is Yes or No. The oval boxes mark the beginning and the end.

This particular flow chart is for a computation of cube roots. At the beginning, a number whose cube root is desired is put in. Then a variable R is started at 1, increased to 2, increased to 3, and so forth, until the *cube* of R becomes greater than N. Next, R is increased by 0.1 each step until R again becomes larger than N. The process is continued until you have a decimal approximation for the cube root of N to two decimal places.

Do the following.

a. Read through the flow chart one step at a time, doing what it says in each box as you come to it. Make a table of values for R and D, and show the output if 64 is put in for N. At the end you should find that the cube root of 64 is 4.
b. Repeat part (a) if 34 is put in for N.
c. Write a program on a graphing calculator or computer for this flow chart. Test it using 64 and 34 for N, and debug the program if necessary.

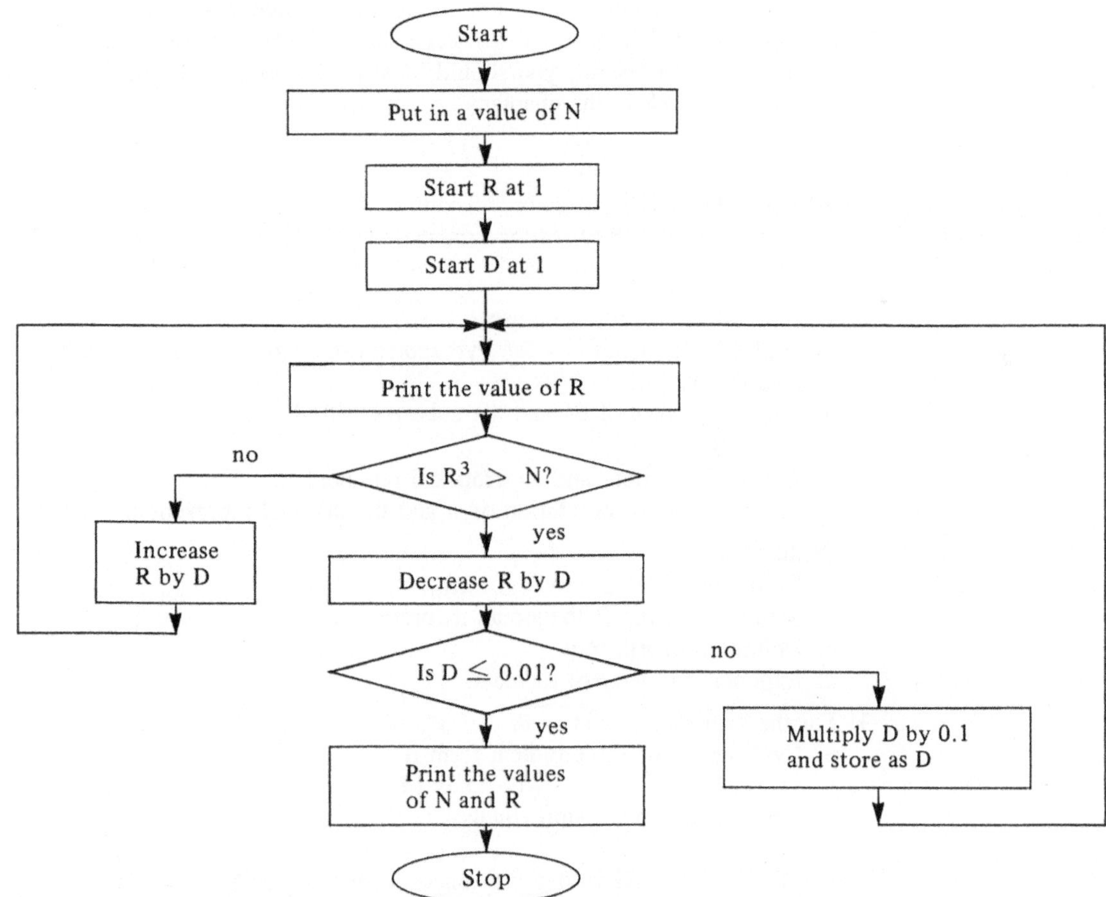

12-10 CHAPTER REVIEW AND TEST

In this chapter you have taken another look at radicals. Instead of just evaluating square roots on a calculator, you found out their properties when left in radical form. These properties allow you to simplify radicals. The process of rationalizing the denominator allows you to divide by a binomial involving square roots. When a variable occurs under a radical sign, you learned how to solve radical equations, discarding any extraneous solutions. In the real world you found radicals occurring as lengths of sides of right triangles. You learned to transform cube and higher roots to powers with fractional exponents and then evaluate them by calculator. The nth root of an integer was found to be either an integer or an irrational number.

In your review of this chapter you should realize that there are several somewhat separate topics. Unlike prior chapters, not all of these topics are tied together in the problems of the last section. So it is most important for you to look at the objective of *each* section to make sure your review leaves nothing out. The test below touches on each of these topics. If your review has been successful, you should be able to work all the problems *without* looking back in the chapter.

CHAPTER TEST

1. Tell the difference in each case.
   a. Finding a leg length by the Pythagorean theorem and finding the hypotenuse length.
   b. The square root of 64 and the cube root of 64.
   c. 8^3 and $8^{\frac{1}{3}}$.
   d. A rational number and an irrational number.
   e. The decimal representation of π and the decimal representation of $\frac{22}{7}$.
2. Write each.
   a. Definition of simple radical form.
   b. Statement of the Pythagorean theorem.
   c. Definition of nth root.
   d. Exponent property of radicals.
3. For the expression $\sqrt{3x + 8}$:
   a. Evaluate it in simple radical form if:
      i. x is 4; ii. x is 14; iii. x is 30.
   b. Find x if the expression equals:
      i. 7; ii. -4;
      iii. $x + 3$. (Give decimal answers for this part.)

4. Simplify. Write the answer in simple *radical* form.
   a. $\sqrt{252}$
   b. $\sqrt{15} \times \sqrt{21}$
   c. $\sqrt{144 + 25}$
   d. $5\sqrt{32} + 7\sqrt{8}$
   e. $9\sqrt{28} - \sqrt{28}$
   f. $\dfrac{\sqrt{10}}{\sqrt{35}}$
   g. $\dfrac{24}{\sqrt{12}}$
   h. $15\sqrt{\dfrac{3}{5}} + 15\sqrt{\dfrac{5}{3}}$
   i. $(2\sqrt{3} + 7)(5\sqrt{3} - 4)$
   j. $\dfrac{2\sqrt{7} - \sqrt{5}}{3\sqrt{5} + \sqrt{7}}$
5. Solve: $5 - \sqrt{x} = x$.
6. Find the length of the third side of these right triangles.

a.

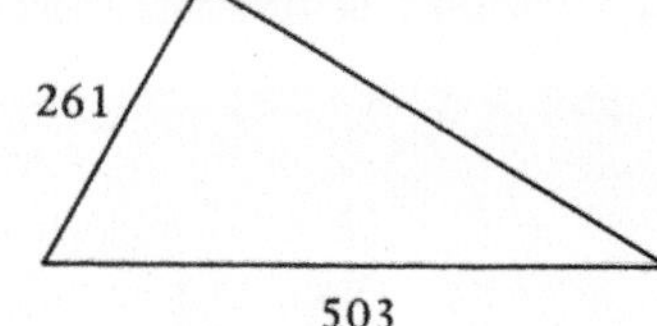

b.

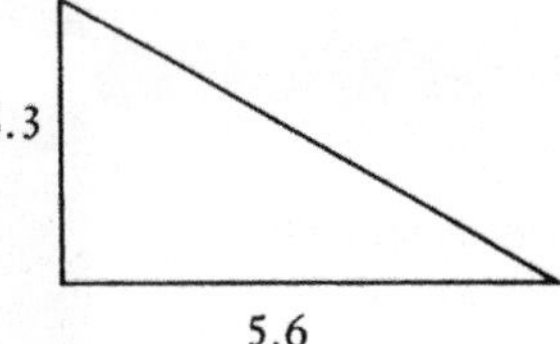

7. Evaluate the radicals. Tell which are rational numbers and which are irrational numbers.
   a. $\sqrt[3]{71}$
   b. $\sqrt[4]{28{,}561}$
   c. $\sqrt[5]{1}$
   d. $\sqrt{4{,}004{,}001}$
8. *Detour Problem* Flight 57 normally flies 275 km directly from A to B. One day it detours due to bad weather. It flies 219 km from A and then turns 90° and flies straight to B. How many extra kilometers did it fly because of the detour?

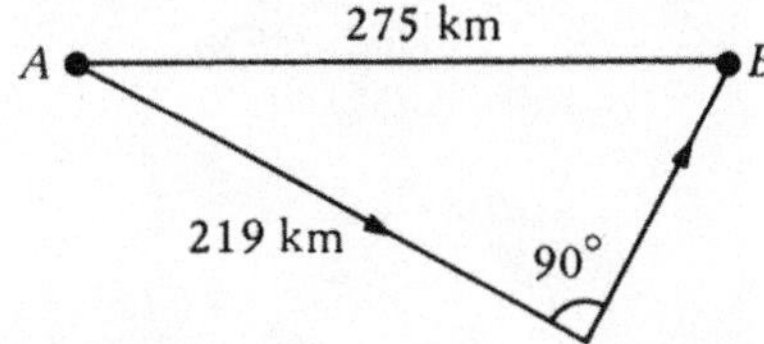

9. *Bigger Airplane Problem* The mass of a particular design of airplane is given by

$$m = 0.46L^3,$$

where m is mass in kilograms and L is the length in meters.
   a. What is the mass of a plane 20 meters long?
   b. If a plane were built big enough to have *twice* the mass you calculated in part (a), would it be *twice* as long, *more* than twice as long, or *less* than twice as long? Justify your answer.

13 Inequalities

Solving equations involves finding the value of x *when you know what number an expression equals. In this chapter you will find values of a variable when you know what number an expression is* greater *than or* less *than. The result is called an* inequality. *It could be used to say, for example, that a submarine's hull diameter is within 0.01 foot of the desired value, 33 feet.*

Variable:

x Diameter

Expression:

$|x - 33|$ Difference between x and 33 feet

Inequalities:

$|x - 33| < 0.01$

Difference is less than 0.01.

$-0.01 < x - 33 < 0.01$

$x - 3$ is between -0.01 and 0.01.

$32.99 < x < 33.01$

x is between 32.99 and 33.01.

3-1 NUMBER-LINE GRAPHS

This section introduces a new concept. However, you should be able to read part or all of it and work the problems without prior instruction from your teacher.

The number 5 is less than the number 8. To say this in a more compact way, people write

$$5 < 8.$$

The symbol $<$ means *is less than*. It is similar to an $=$ sign, but the lines have been pinched together at the smaller number and spread apart at the larger number. A similar symbol, $>$, is used in $13 > 9$, which is read "13 is greater than 9."

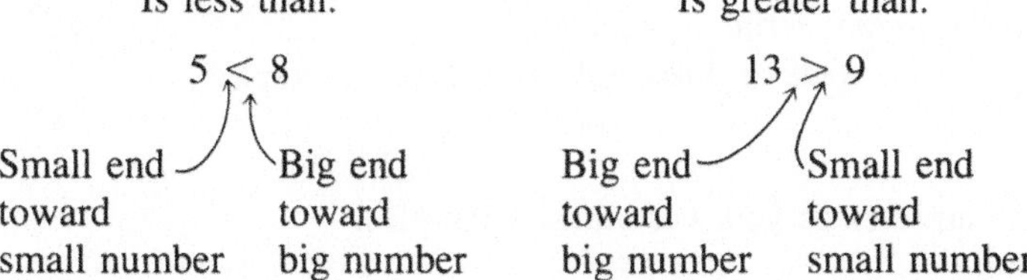

A statement such as $5 < 8$ is called an **inequality.** An inequality with a variable, such as $x < 6$, is true for *many* values of x. The inequality $x < 6$ is true for numbers such as 5, 4, 2, 3.7, 5.99, 0, and all negative numbers. This fact can be shown on a number line.

The open circle at 6 shows that x *cannot* equal 6. The shaded part of the line shows numbers that x *can* equal.

The inequality

$$x \geq 2$$

is read "x is greater than or equal to 2." A graph of the inequality looks like this.

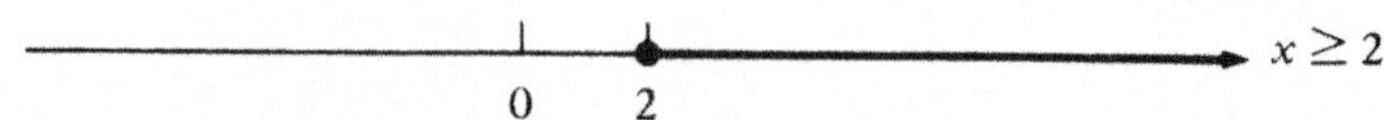

The solid dot at 2 shows that x *can* equal 2. The shaded part of the line shows the other numbers that x can equal.

These are the four inequality signs and their meanings.

DEFINITIONS

INEQUALITY SIGNS	
$<$	is less than
$>$	is greater than
$\leq$	is less than or equal to
$\geq$	is greater than or equal to

In this section you will draw number-line graphs of inequalities and write inequalities for given graphs.

Objectives

1. Given an inequality such as $x \leq 7$, draw the graph.
2. Given the graph, write an inequality.
3. Given words, write an inequality and draw its graph.

Cover the answers as you work these examples.

EXAMPLE 1

Sketch the graph of $x \leq 7$.

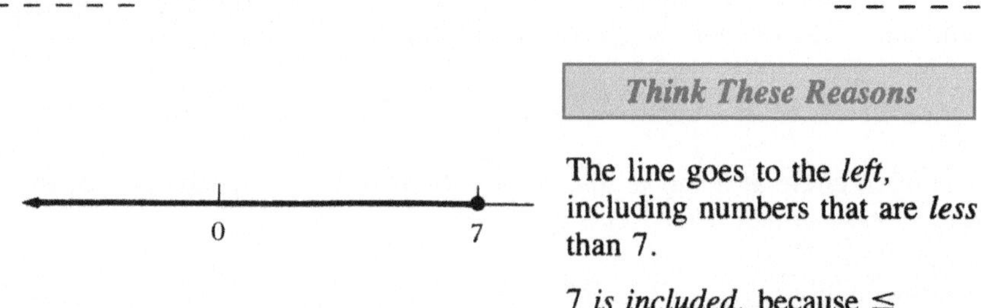

Think These Reasons

The line goes to the *left*, including numbers that are *less* than 7.

7 *is included,* because $\leq$ means less than or equal to.

Note: You should draw a neat sketch, using a ruler if you do not draw well freehand. You do not need to show numbers other than the origin, 0, and the end point, 7.

EXAMPLE 2

Sketch the graph of $x > -3$.

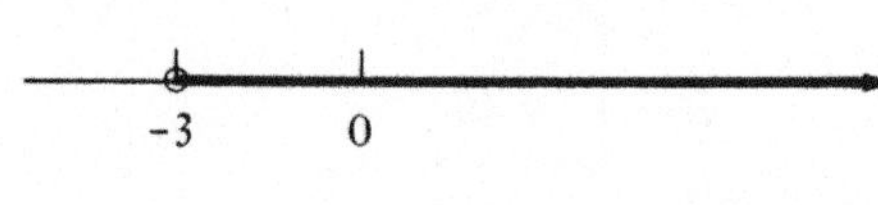

The line goes to the *right*, including numbers that are *greater* than -3.

-3 *is not* included, since the statement $-3 > -3$ is false.

EXAMPLE 3

Write an inequality for the graph.

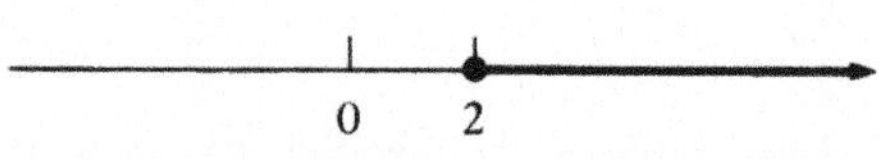

$\underline{\underline{x \geq 2}}$

The values of x can be *greater* than 2, and 2 *is* included.

EXAMPLE 4

Write an inequality for the graph.

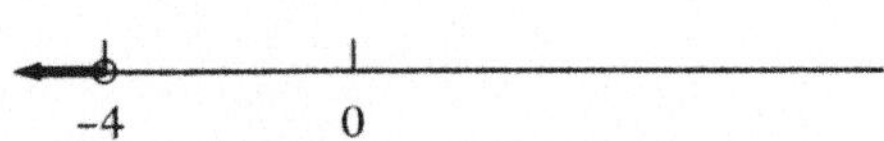

$\underline{\underline{x < -4}}$

The values of x can be *less* than -4, and -4 is *not* included.

EXAMPLE 5

Write an inequality that says x is at least 5, and draw the graph.

$\underline{\underline{x \geq 5}}$

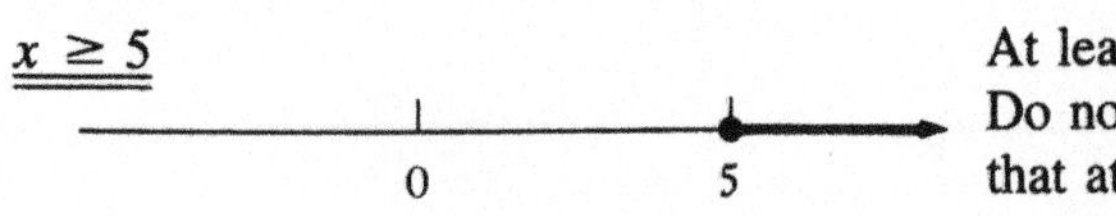

At least 5 means 5 or more. Do not be fooled into thinking that at least means less than.

EXERCISE 13-1

For Problems 1 through 20, draw a number-line graph of the inequality.

1. $x > 8$
2. $x < 10$
3. $x \leq 2$
4. $x \geq 4$
5. $x < -7$
6. $x > -5$
7. $x \geq 9$
8. $x \leq 12$
9. $x \leq -2.6$
10. $x \geq -8.3$
11. $x < 0$
12. $x \geq 0$
13. $y > 100$
14. $p < 2000$
15. $z \geq -3.146$
16. $r \leq -1.68$
17. $5 < x$
18. $3 > x$
19. $-11 \geq x$
20. $-7 \leq x$

For Problems 21 through 40, write an inequality for the given graph.

21. 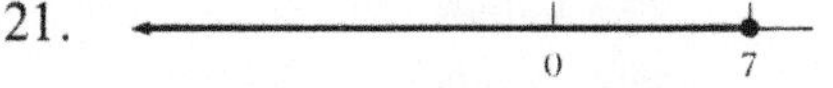

22. 
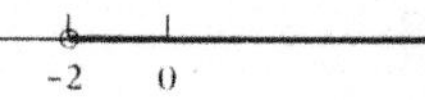

23. -4 0

24. 
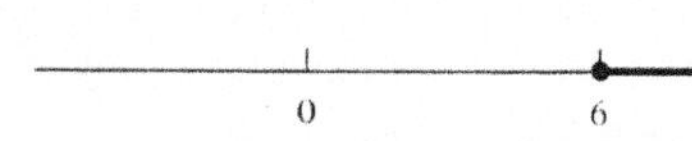

25. 0 2.5

26. 
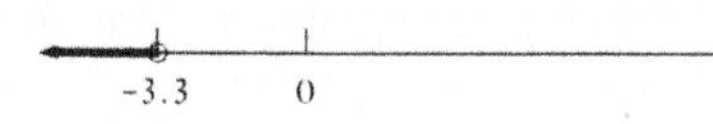

27. -8 0

28. 
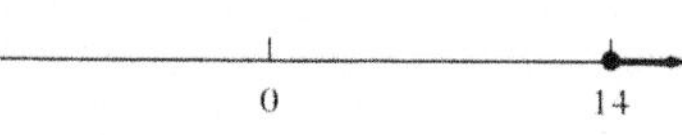

29. -50 0

30. 
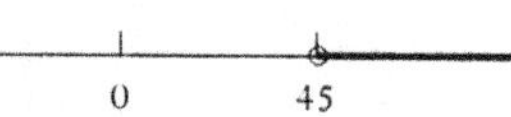

31. 0 47

32. 
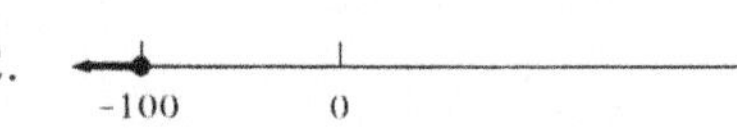

33. -0.2 0

34. 
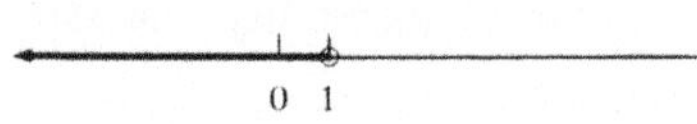

35. 0 $\sqrt{7}$

36. 
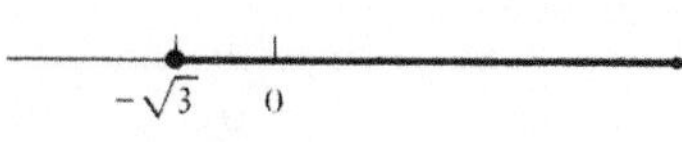

37. 

38. 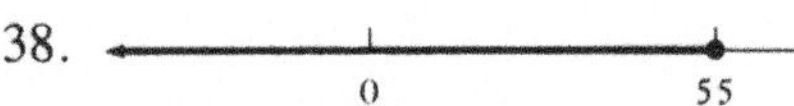

39.

40.

For Problems 41 through 50, write an inequality and draw the graph.

41. x is more than 9.
42. x is less than 18.
43. x is less than -100.
44. x is more than -5.
45. x is at least 10.
46. x is at most 13.
47. x is at most 15.
48. x is at least 1.
49. x is positive.
50. x is negative.

13-2 SOLVING INEQUALITIES

The inequality

$$3 < 7$$

tells the *order* in which 3 and 7 appear on the number line.

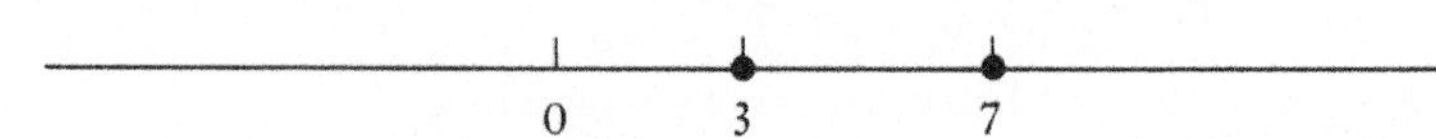

The number 3 comes first, then the number 7, as you read from left to right. Suppose that you add 2 to each member of the inequality.

$$3 + 2 < 7 + 2$$
$$5 < 9$$

The new inequality is still true. Adding 2 just moves each number an equal distance along the line. The points are still in the same order.

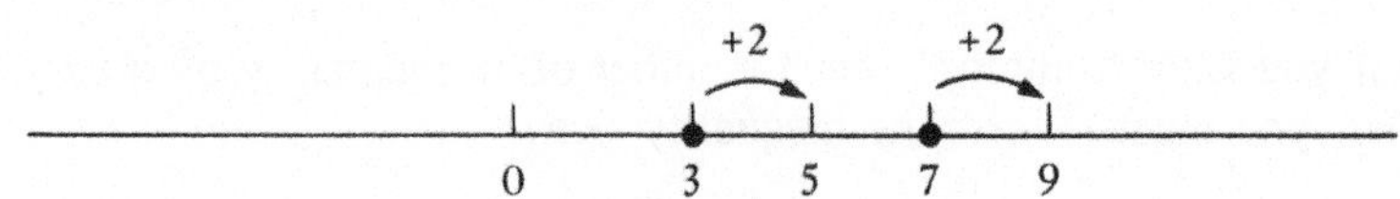

Adding the same negative number (or subtracting the same number) also leaves the points in the same order.

$$3 + (-2) < 7 + (-2)$$
$$1 < 5$$

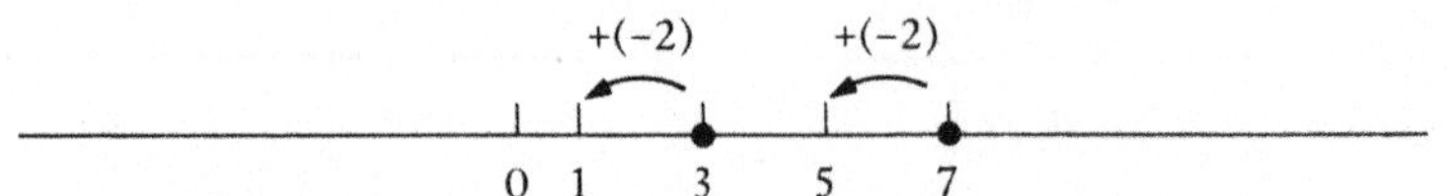

The same thing happens with $>$, $\leq$, and $\geq$. These facts are summarized in the following property.

PROPERTY

> **ADDITION PROPERTY OF ORDER**
> Given any real numbers a, b, and c.
>
> $$\text{If } a < b, \text{ then } a + c < b + c.$$
>
> $$\text{If } a > b, \text{ then } a + c > b + c.$$

The order also stays the same if you *multiply* each member by 2.

$$3 < 7$$

$$3 \cdot 2 < 7 \cdot 2$$

$$6 < 14$$

The order stays the same.

But if you multiply by a *negative* number, like -2, the order *reverses!*

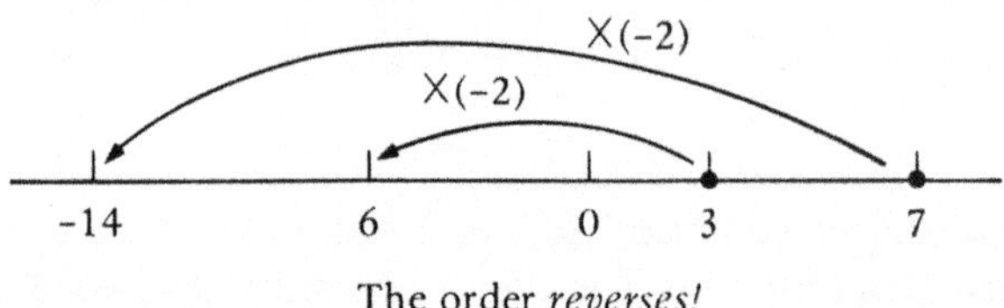

The order *reverses!*

Thus if you want to multiply each member of an inequality by a *negative* number, you must *reverse* the inequality sign.

$$3 < 7$$

$$3(-2) > 7(-2)$$

$$-6 > -14$$

These facts are summarized in the following property.

PROPERTY

MULTIPLICATION PROPERTY OF ORDER
Given any real numbers a, b, and c.

If $a < b$, then:
$ac < bc$, if c is positive;
$ac > bc$, if c is negative.

If $a > b$, then:
$ac > bc$, if c is positive;
$ac < bc$, if c is negative.

These two properties can be used to solve inequalities like

$$5x - 7 > 53.$$

You do whatever is needed to get x by itself. The process is just the same as that for solving equations. But you must remember to *reverse* the inequality signs if you multiply (or divide) by a negative number.

Objective

For an inequality such as $5x - 7 > 53$, find the values of x that make it true and draw the graph.

EXAMPLE 1

Solve and graph: $5x - 7 > 53$.

Think These Reasons

$5x - 7 > 53$	Write the given inequality.
$5x > 60$	Add 7 to each member.
$x > 12$	Divide each member by 5. The order stays the same, since you did not multiply by a negative number. (Dividing by 5 is like multiplying by $\frac{1}{5}$.)

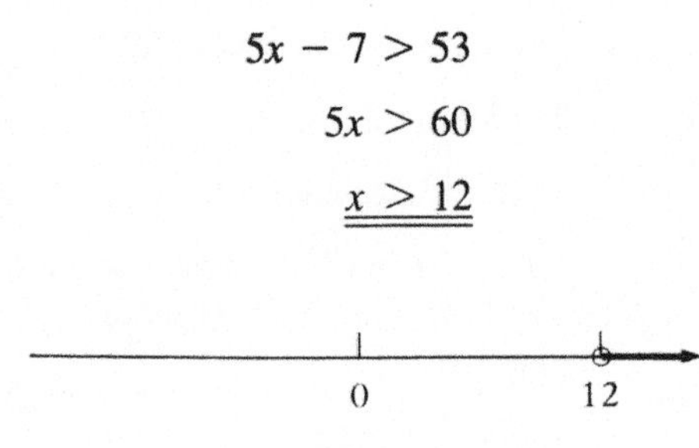

Draw the graph.

EXAMPLE 2

Solve and graph: $13 - 2x \geq 22$.

$13 - 2x \geq 22$	Write the given inequality.
$-2x \geq 9$	Add -13 to each member.
$\underline{\underline{x \leq -4.5}}$	Divide each member by -2 and reverse the inequality sign. (The order reverses when you multiply by a negative number. Dividing by -2 is like multiplying by $-\frac{1}{2}$, so you must reverse the inequality sign.)

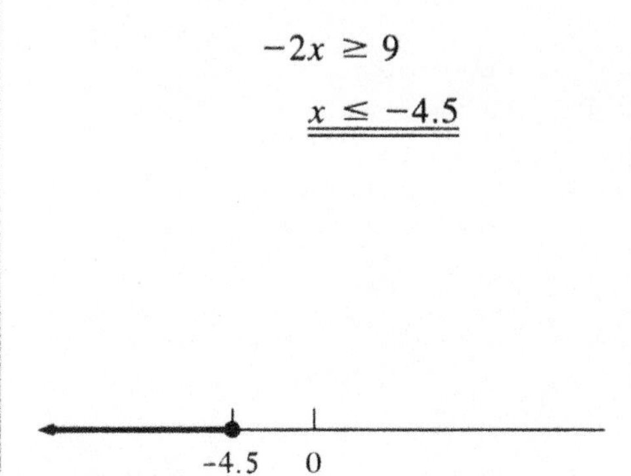

Draw the graph.

EXAMPLE 3

Solve and graph: $12 - 4(x - 5) < 8 + x$.

$12 - 4(x - 5) < 8 + x$	Write the given inequality.
$12 - 4x + 20 < 8 + x$	Distribute -4.
$-4x + 32 < 8 + x$	Combine like terms.
$-5x < -24$	Add $-x$ and -32 to each member.
$\underline{\underline{x > 4.8}}$	Divide each member by -5 and reverse the inequality sign.
0 4.8	Draw the graph.

EXAMPLE 4

Solve and graph: $3x + 11 \leq 3(x + 7)$.

$3x + 11 \leq 3(x + 7)$	Write the given inequality.
$3x + 11 \leq 3x + 21$	Distribute 3.
$11 \leq 21$	Add $-3x$ to each member.
$\underline{\underline{S = \{\text{real numbers}\}}}$	$11 \leq 21$ is *always* true! So you shade in the entire number line.
0	Draw the graph.

EXAMPLE 5

Appliance Service Problem If you work as an appliance repair person, you charge a certain amount per hour worked plus a fixed amount for the service call. Suppose that the rate is \$20 per hour, plus \$25 for the call.

a. Define a variable for the number of hours worked, and write an expression for the total number of dollars the customer would pay you.
b. What range of times could you work to earn up to and including $100?

a.	Let x = number of hours.	Define a variable.
	$\underline{\underline{20x + 25}}$ = number of dollars.	$20x$ for the $20 per hour, plus 25 for the fixed charge.
b.	$20x + 25 \le 100$	The number of dollars is up to and including 100, which means less than or equal to 100.
	$20x \le 75$	Subtract 25 from each member.
	$x \le 3.75$	Divide each member by 20.
	Up to and including 3 h 45 min.	Answer the question.

ORAL PRACTICE

Tell what you would do to transform the inequality so that x is by itself, and tell whether or not the order reverses.

EXAMPLES

	Answers:
i. $x + 3 > 7$	i. Subtract 3. Order does not reverse.
ii. $-5x > 35$	ii. Divide by -5. Order does reverse.

A. $x + 2 > 5$

B. $x + 6 < 2$

C. $x - 8 < 7$

D. $x - 4 > 1$

E. $2x > 5$

F. $6x < 2$

G. $-8x < 7$

H. $-4x > 1$

I. $3x \ge -7$

J. $-5 + x \le 3$

K. $-x \le 3$

L. $6x < -12$

M. $\frac{2}{3}x < 6$

N. $-\frac{3}{4}x > 24$

O. $x - \frac{5}{8} \ge \frac{3}{8}$

P. $x + \frac{2}{3} \le \frac{5}{3}$

EXERCISE 13-2

For each inequality:

a. solve it—that is, transform it so that x is by itself;
b. sketch the graph.

1. $5x + 4 < 39$
2. $6x + 5 > 53$
3. $3x - 7 \geq 26$
4. $2x - 13 \leq 95$
5. $13 - 4x < 25$
6. $5 - 3x > 56$
7. $\frac{1}{3}x + 5 \leq 7$
8. $\frac{1}{5}x + 3 \geq 9$
9. $-\frac{1}{6}x + 5 > 8$
10. $-\frac{1}{3}x + 6 < 10$
11. $\frac{2}{3}x - 4 < 14$
12. $\frac{3}{4}x - 5 > 7$
13. $8 - \frac{3}{5}x \leq 23$
14. $6 - \frac{5}{2}x \geq 26$
15. $5x \geq 5x + 11$
16. $22 \leq 4 + 5x$
17. $71 > 4 - x$
18. $13 < 17 - x$
19. $16x + 3 + 4x \leq 103$
20. $18x + 7 + 7x \geq 107$
21. $-5x + 17 - 8x > 56$
22. $-3x + 19 - 5x < 91$
23. $5(x + 3) - 2x \geq -21$
24. $6(x + 2) - 4x \leq 48$
25. $2(x + 3) - 5(x - 1) > 32$
26. $3(x + 4) - 5(x - 1) < 5$
27. $0 < 4(6 - x) + 7x$
28. $0 > 5(7 - x) + 12x$
29. $7x \leq -16 - 9x$
30. $11x \geq -400 - 9x$
31. $4x \leq 37 + 4x$
32. $5x + 7 \geq 4x + 7$
33. $5x + 8 > 7x + 8$
34. $5x + 7 > 5x + 8$
35. $5(9 - x) \leq 4(x + 18)$
36. $7(2 - x) \geq 3(x + 8)$
37. $2[1 - 3(x + 2)] > -x$
38. $3(1 + x) < 2[3(x + 2) - (x + 1)]$
39. $6(x + 4) - (x + 3) \geq x - 1$
40. $3(3x + 1) - (x - 1) \leq 6(x + 10)$

Two basic problems of algebra are (1) given x, find an expression's value, and (2) given an expression's value, find x. In Problems 41 and 42 you will do these two things with linear expressions.

41. For the linear expression $5x - 7$:
   a. evaluate it if:
      i. x is 6; ii. x is -2;
   b. find x if the expression is:
      i. equal to 21; ii. more than 8 (draw the graph);
      iii. at most 17 (draw the graph).

42. For the linear expression $3 - 4x$:
   a. evaluate it if:
      i. x is 7; ii. x is -2;
   b. Find x if the expression is:
      i. equal to 19; ii. less than 23 (draw the graph);
      iii. at least -21 (draw the graph).

43. ***Plumber's Fee Problem*** Suppose that you go into business doing plumbing repairs. You decide to charge $25 per hour, plus a fixed fee of $30 for the service call.
   a. Define a variable for the number of hours worked, and write an expression for the number of dollars the customer would pay.
   b. Write an inequality which says that your charge is over $100. Solve it to find the range of times for which your charge would be over $100.

44. ***Slide Problem*** The amusement park charges 75 cents to rent a mat plus 50¢ each time you ride the big slide.
   a. Define a variable for the number of times you ride. Then write an expression for the total amount you pay.
   b. Write an inequality stating that you can afford to pay no more than $6.25. Then solve it to find the range of times you could slide.

45. ***Phoebe's Loan Problem*** Phoebe Small borrows $50 from her parents to buy a dress she really likes. In return for her painting the garage, her parents agree to subtract $4 from what she owes for each hour she works. For what number of hours will her debt be below $30?

46. ***Desert Travel Problem*** Kara Vann crosses the desert on a camel. She has 200 miles to go, and she travels 30 miles per day. For what range of days will her distance remaining be more than 80 miles?

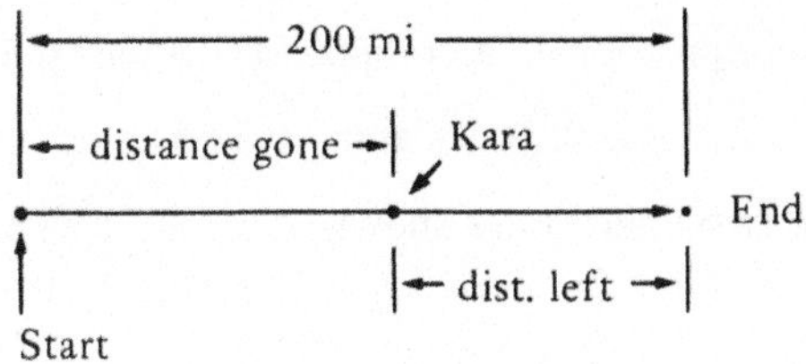

13-3 COMPOUND INEQUALITIES

You have learned how to graph inequalities like $x > 7$. Suppose that you must graph the values of x for which either

$$x > 7 \quad \text{or} \quad x \leq -2$$

is true. To see what the graph would look like, first draw each part separately.

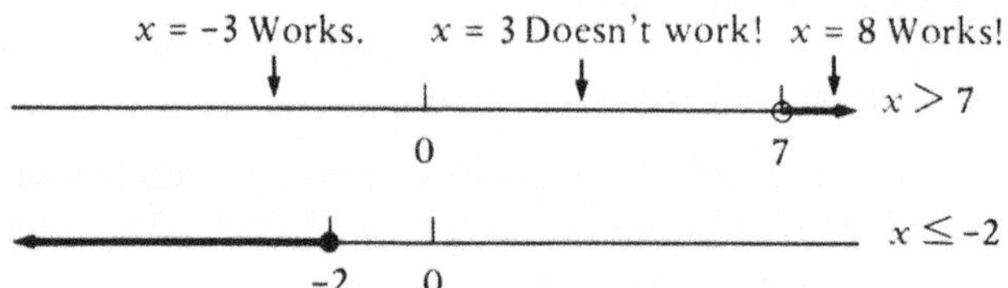

A number such as -3 or 8 *does* satisfy $x > 7$ or $x \leq -2$. Since the conjunction between the two parts is *or*, a value of x need satisfy only *one* part of the inequality. Only numbers like 3, which satisfy *neither* part, are not solutions of $x > 7$ or $x \leq -2$. The graph of this inequality would be the two parts drawn on the *same* number line.

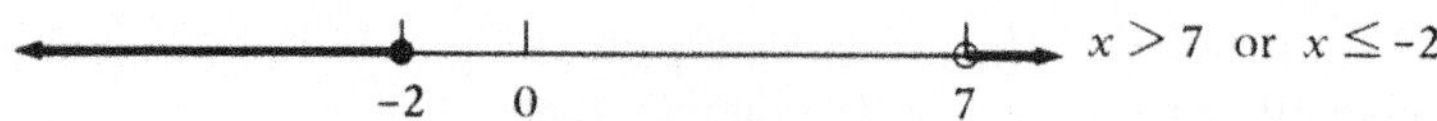

The result is called the *union* of the two graphs, since they have been put together (united). Note, however, that the two intervals are not connected.

DEFINITION

UNION
The **union** of sets A and B, abbreviated $A \cup B$, is the set of numbers that are either in set A or in set B.

The inequality $x > 7$ or $x \leq -2$ is called a *compound* inequality. Each part is called a *clause*, just like clauses of a compound sentence.

Suppose that the conjunction in a compound inequality is *and*, such as in

$$x > -1 \quad \text{and} \quad x < 5.$$

The graphs of the two clauses are shown.

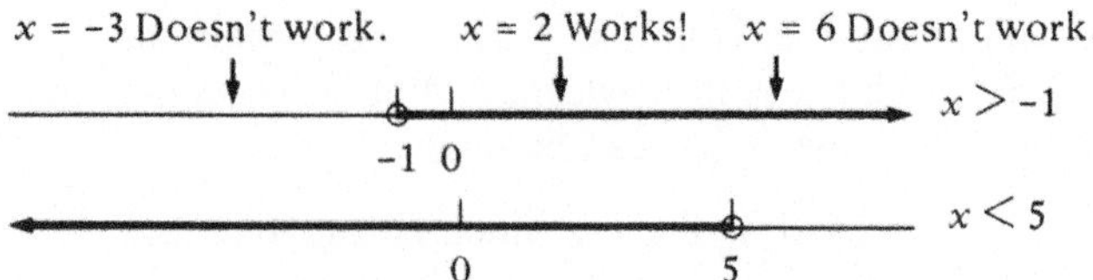

The conjunction *and* means that *both* clauses must be true. So only numbers like 2, which are *between* -1 and 5, will satisfy the inequality. Numbers like -3 and 6 do not satisfy the compound inequality, even though they do satisfy one clause of it. The graph will be the part of the number line where the two graphs overlap.

Because of this overlapping feature, the result is called the *intersection* of the two graphs.

DEFINITION

INTERSECTION
The **intersection** of sets A and B, abbreviated $A \cap B$, is the set of numbers that are in *both* sets.

For your future reference, here are the precise meanings of the words *and* and *or* as used in mathematics.

MEANING

AND* AND *OR
The statement *A and B are true* means *both* of them must be true.

The statement *A or B is true* means at least *one* of them must be true, but not necessarily both.

There is another way to write a compound inequality such as $x > -1$ and $x < 5$. Since x must be *between* -1 and 5, you simply *put* it there:

$$-1 < x < 5.$$

The lesser end point, -1, is on the left and the greater end point, 5, is on the right. The variable x is in between, and both inequality signs have the *same* direction. This inequality can be read:

-1 is less than x, which is less than 5,

or, more simply,

x is between -1 and 5.

If the end points are included, as in

$$3 \le x \le 10,$$

then the inequality is read

"x is between 3 and 10, inclusive."

Its graph would look like this.

For your future reference, here are precise definitions of *between* and *inclusive*.

DEFINITION

BETWEEN AND INCLUSIVE

x is **between** a and b means

$$a < x < b.$$

x is between a and b, **inclusive,** means

$$a \le x \le b.$$

Objectives

1. Given a compound inequality, solve it and draw the graph.
2. Given a graph or words, write a compound inequality.

Cover the answers as you work these examples.

EXAMPLE 1

Draw the graph of $x > 5$ and $x \le 8$.

Think These Reasons

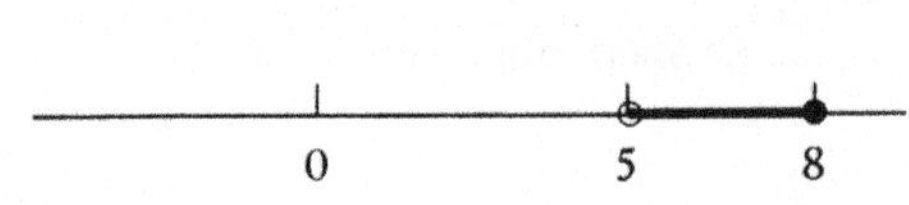

Since the conjunction is *and*, draw the intersection—that is, x is *between* the end points 5 and 8, including 8.

EXAMPLE 2

Sketch the graph of $3x + 7 < -8$ or $5 - 2x \le -9$.

- - - - -

$3x + 7 < -8$ or $5 - 2x \le -9$	Write the given inequality.
$3x < -15$ or $-2x \le -14$	Subtract 7 for the first clause. Subtract 5 for the second clause.
$x < -5$ or $x \ge 7$	Divide by 3 for the first clause. Divide by -2 and reverse the order for the second clause.
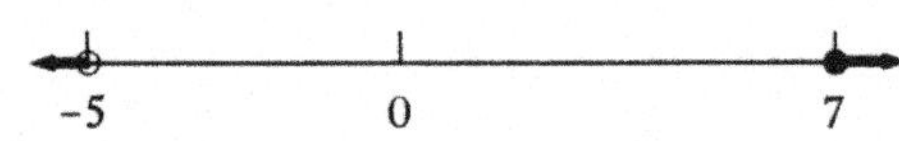	Draw the union of the two graphs.

EXAMPLE 3

Sketch the graph of $-6 < 5x - 2 < 13$.

- - - - -

$-6 < 5x - 2 < 13$	Write the given inequality.
$-4 < 5x < 15$	Add 2 to *all three* members.
$-0.8 < x < 3$	Divide all three members by 5.
	Shade *between* the end points, because x is between -0.8 and 3.

EXAMPLE 4

Write a compound inequality.

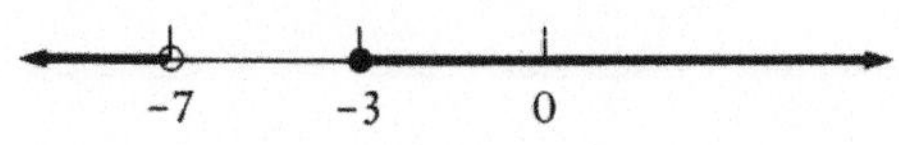

- - - - -

$\underline{\underline{x < -7 \text{ or } x \ge -3}}$	Use *or*, since x cannot be on both parts of the graph at the same time. -3 is included; -7 is not.

EXAMPLE 5

If x is between -5 and 3, inclusive, write an inequality and draw its graph.

- - - - - - - - - - -

$-5 \le x \le 3$ Put x between -5 and 3.

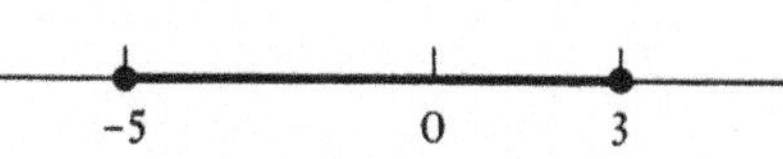

Shade between -5 and 3. Include the end points.

ORAL PRACTICE

Tell whether or not the graph is correct. If not, tell *why* not.

A. $2 < x < 5$

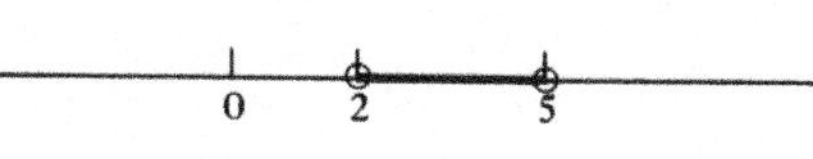

B. $3 \le x \le 7$

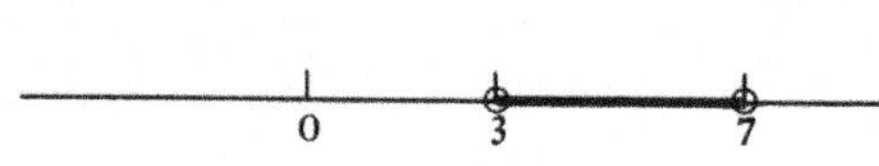

C. $-2 < x < 3$

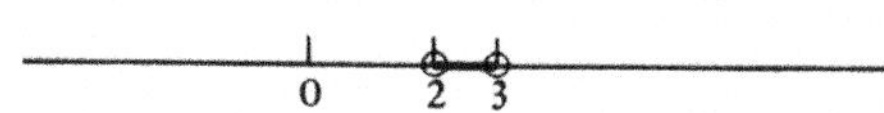

D. $x > 5$ or $x < 2$

E. $x < 5$ and $x > 2$

F. $x > 3$ or $x < -1$

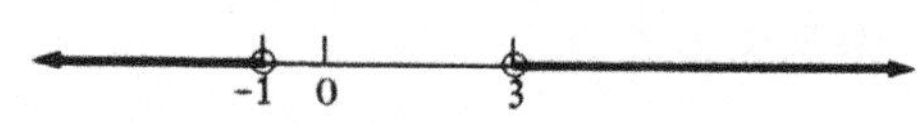

G. $4 \le x \le 6$

H. $x \le 4$ and $x \ge 6$

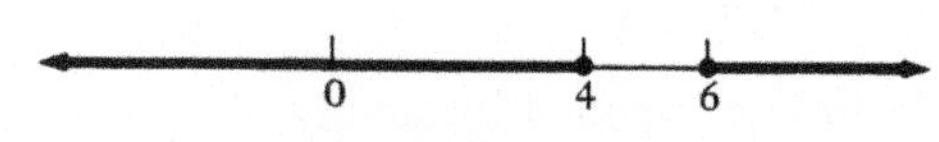

I. $x \le 4$ or $x \ge 6$

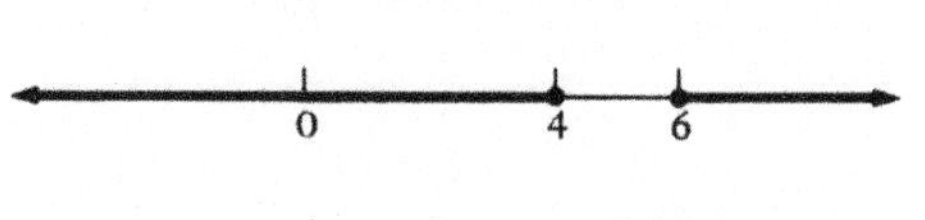

J. x is between 2 and 5.

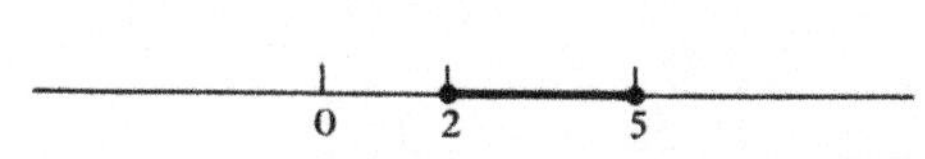

K. x is between 2 and 5, inclusive.

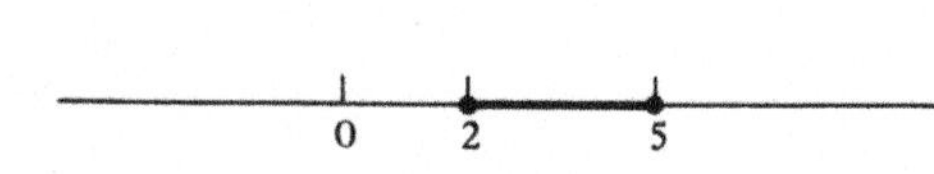

L. $9 < x < 10$ (Think!)

M. $3 > x > 5$

N. $x < 5$ or $x > 3$

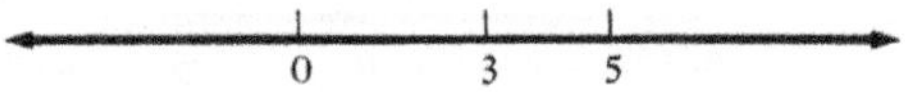

O. $x < 3$ and $x > 5$

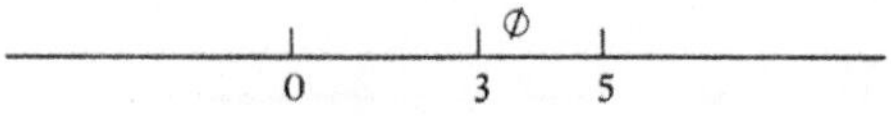

EXERCISE 13-3

For Problems 1 through 20, transform the inequality (if necessary) and sketch the graph.

1. $x \geq 5$ and $x < 9$
2. $x < -2$ and $x \geq -6$
3. $x < -2$ or $x \geq 6$
4. $x \geq 8$ or $x < 1$
5. $-7 \leq x \leq 2$
6. $-4 < x < 7$
7. $3x + 5 < 20$ or $2x - 1 > 13$
8. $3x - 4 \geq 17$ or $4x + 7 \leq 19$
9. $4 - 5x > -13$ and $3 - x \leq 10$
10. $7 - 2x > 15$ and $5 - x \leq 16$
11. $6x + 7 \leq 1$ or $6x + 7 > 28$
12. $3x + 5 < -13$ or $3x + 5 \geq 2$
13. $5 < x - 7 < 9$
14. $2 < x + 3 \leq 7$
15. $-3 \leq 2x + 11 \leq 9$
16. $-8 \leq 5x + 7 \leq 25$
17. $15 < 6 - 10x \leq 37$
18. $6 < 10 - 2x < 14$
19. $x + 5 > 19$ or $x + 5 < 24$
20. $x - 3 < 7$ and $x - 3 > 13$

For Problems 21 through 32, write a compound inequality for the graph shown.

21. 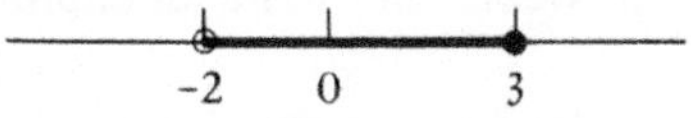

22. 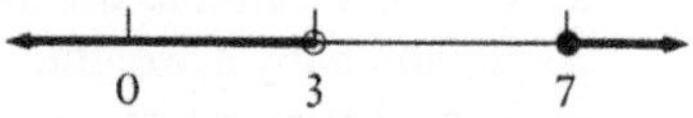

23. 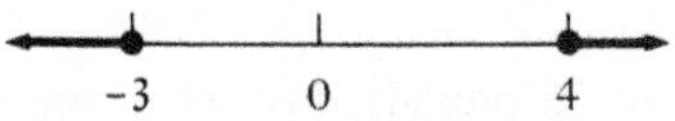

24. 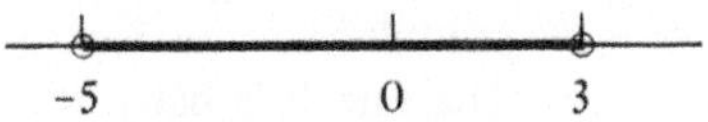

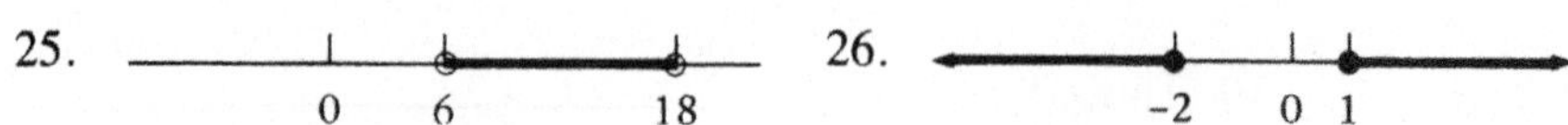

27. −10 −4 0

28. −13 −5 0

29. −5 0 5

30. −6 0 6

31. −7 0

32. 0

For Problems 33 through 40, write an inequality and draw the graph.

33. x is between 3 and 7.

34. x is between -8 and 5.

35. x is between -1 and 3, inclusive.

36. x is between 4 and 9, inclusive.

37. x is at least 3 or x is less than 1.

38. x is at least 4 or x is less than -3.

39. x is more than -2 and x is at most 7.

40. x is more than 1 and x is at most 8.

41. For the linear expression $5x - 7$:
   a. evaluate it if x is 4;
   b. find x if the expression is:
      i. equal to 8;
      ii. between -2 and 13 (draw the graph);
      iii. at least 3 or at most -12 (draw the graph).

42. For the linear expression $3 - 4x$:
   a. evaluate it if x is -9;
   b. find x if the expression is:
      i. equal to 31;
      ii. between -5 and 23, inclusive (draw the graph);
      iii. more than 3 or less than -3 (draw the graph).

43. ***Baby's Weight Problem*** Suppose that a baby weighs 7 pounds at birth, and gains 0.3 pound a week thereafter.
   a. Define a variable for the number of weeks and write an expression for the baby's weight.
   b. For what range of weeks will the baby be between 19 and 28 pounds?
   c. The family's baby scale goes up to 25 pounds. For what range of weeks will they be able to use this scale?

44. ***Savings Problem*** Penny Pincher gets a present of \$100. She puts it into a savings account. Thereafter, she adds \$4 more at the end of each week.

   a. Define a variable for the number of weeks and write an expression for the number of dollars she has put into her account.
   b. The savings account pays a certain interest rate when the amount in it is from \$200 up to, but not including, \$500. For what numbers of weeks will Penny's amount be in this range?
   c. The interest rate is much higher when the balance is over \$1000. For what range of weeks will the amount be over \$1000?

45. ***Car Wash and Fill Problem*** When you fill your gas tank, a car wash charges \$5 to wash your car. Gas costs \$1.50 per gallon. For what range of gallons will your total bill be between \$11 and \$20, inclusive?

46. ***Chartered Bus Problem*** A chartered bus travels 60 miles per hour as it makes the 500-mile trip from El Paso to Scorpion Gulch. Let t be the number of hours since the bus left El Paso. The bus driver must contact the bus station when they are between 50 and 100 mi from Scorpion Gulch. For what range of values of t will this be?

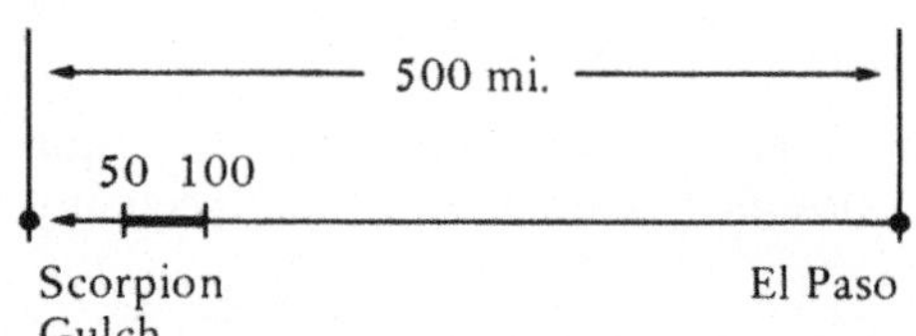

47. ***Venn Diagrams*** Intersections or unions of sets can be represented by overlapping circles. Suppose that

$$\text{Set } A = \{\text{girls in the school}\}$$

$$\text{Set } B = \{\text{athletes in the school}\}.$$

The following diagrams could be used to represent the two sets.

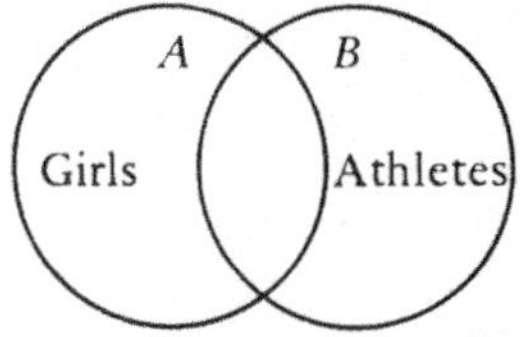

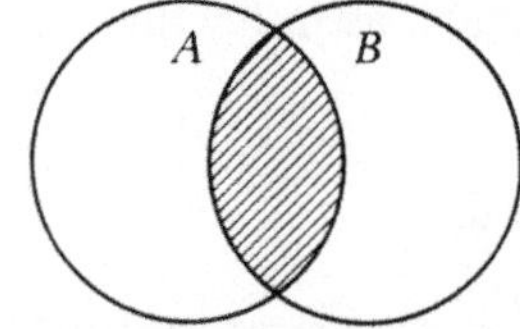

Intersection $A \cap B$. Student is a girl *and* an athlete.

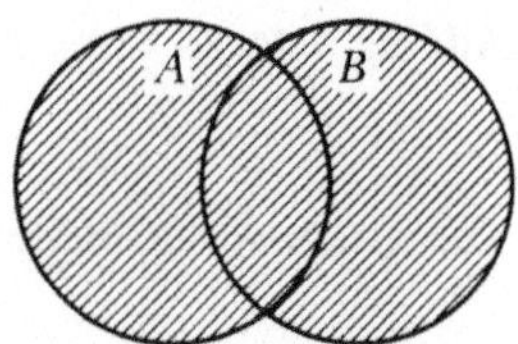

Union $A \cup B$. Student is a girl *or* an athlete.

The pictures are called **Venn diagrams.** In this problem, you will use them to represent unions and intersections of *three* sets. For each part below, copy the diagram and shade the union or intersection indicated.

a. $Q \cap R$
b. $S \cap Q$
c. $R \cup S$
d. $(R \cup S) \cup Q$
e. $(Q \cap R) \cap S$
f. $(Q \cap R) \cup S$
g. $(Q \cup R) \cap S$

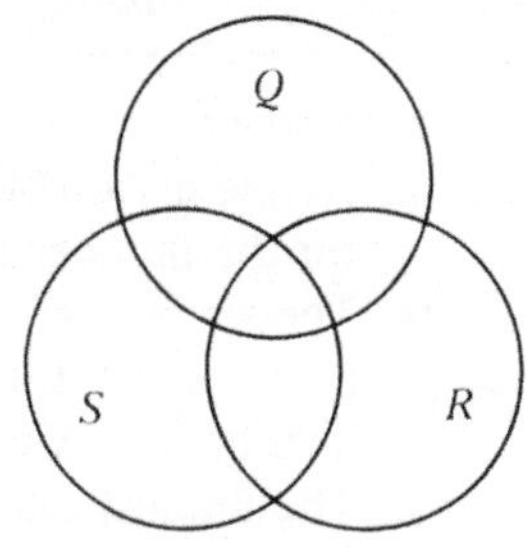

13-4 INEQUALITIES CONTAINING ABSOLUTE VALUE

In the last section you learned that an inequality such as

$$-3 < x < 3$$

can be read "x is between -3 and 3." When a variable or expression is between two numbers that are *opposites* of each other, there is another way of writing the inequality.

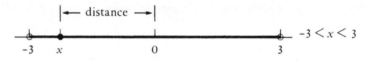

Since x is between -3 and 3, its *distance* from the origin is less than 3. This distance is the *absolute value* of x. So the inequality $-3 < x < 3$ is equivalent to

$$|x| < 3.$$

The same thought process can be used in the other direction to transform an inequality with an absolute value sign to one without. For instance,

$$|x - 7| < 5$$

really says that $x - 7$ is between -5 and 5. So you can write

$$-5 < x - 7 < 5.$$

Adding 7 to all three members, as in Section 9.3, gives

$$2 < x < 12.$$

The graph would look like this.

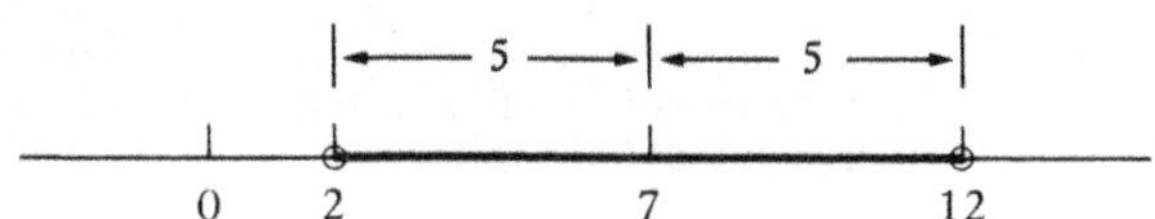

Note that the 5 and 7 in the original inequality also show up on the graph. You can think of $|x - 7| < 5$ as: x is less than 5 units away from 7.

What if the inequality sign had been > instead of <? For instance, how would you transform

$$|x + 4| > 6$$

to eliminate the absolute value sign? The inequality says that $x + 4$ is *not* between -6 and 6. So there are two possibilities,

$$x + 4 > 6 \quad \text{or} \quad x + 4 < -6.$$

This is a compound inequality like you solved in the last section. Subtracting 4 from each member of both inequalities gives

$$x > 2 \quad \text{or} \quad x < -10.$$

The graph would look like this.

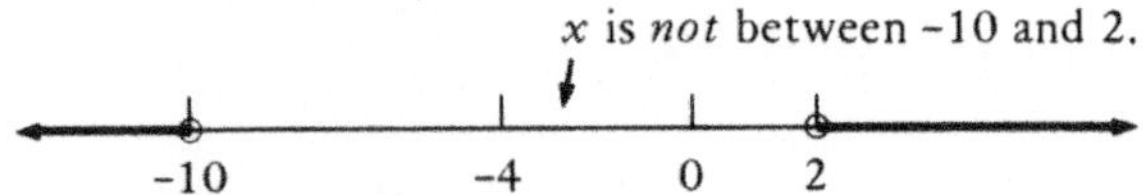

In this section you will solve and graph absolute value inequalities such as these.

Objective

Be able to solve and graph inequalities such as $|x - 7| < 5$, in which the absolute value of an expression is less than or greater than a constant.

Cover the answers as you work these examples.

EXAMPLE 1

Solve and graph: $|x + 4| < 7$.

	Think These Reasons
$\|x + 4\| < 7$	Write the given inequality.
$-7 < x + 4 < 7$	$x + 4$ is between -7 and 7.
$-11 < x < 3$	Subtract 4 from all three members.
-11 0 3	Draw the graph.

EXAMPLE 2

Solve and graph: $|4x - 17| \geq 25$.

$\|4x - 17\| \geq 25$	Write the given inequality.
$4x - 17 \geq 25$ or $4x - 17 \leq -25$	$4x - 17$ is *not* between -25 and 25. So there are *two* possibilities.
$4x \geq 42$ or $4x \leq -8$	Add 17 to each member of both clauses.
$x \geq 10.5$ or $x \leq -2$	Divide each member by 4.
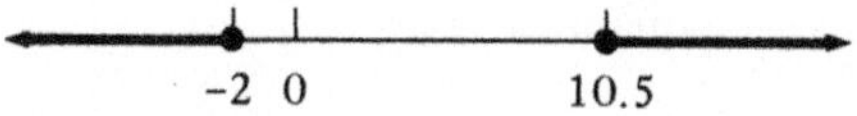	Draw the graph.

EXAMPLE 3

Solve and graph: $|x + 5| < -9$.

- - - - -

$\|x + 5\| < -9$	Write the given inequality.
No solutions.	Absolute values are never negative. So $\|x + 5\|$ cannot be *less* than -9.
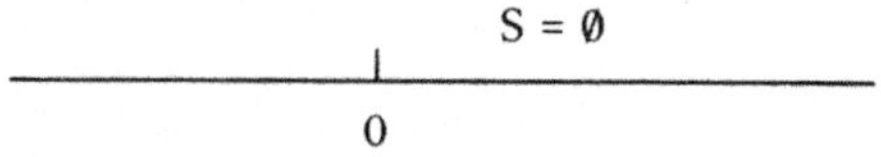	Draw an empty number line. Write the empty set symbol.

EXAMPLE 4

Solve and graph: $|x + 7| > -3$.

- - - - -

$\|x + 7\| > -3$	Write the given inequality.
S = {real numbers}.	Absolute values are never negative, so $\|x + 7\|$ is *always* greater than -3.
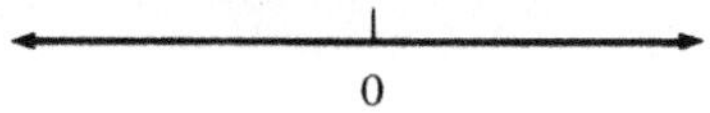	Fill in the entire number line.

EXAMPLE 5

Gas Station Problem A driver starts out across the desert, going a steady 1.2 kilometers per minute. Last Chance Gas Station is 70 km from the starting point. The driver is within 5 km of the gas station when the absolute value of the *difference* between this distance from the start and 70 km is *less* than 5 km. For what range of times will the driver be within 5 km of the gas station?

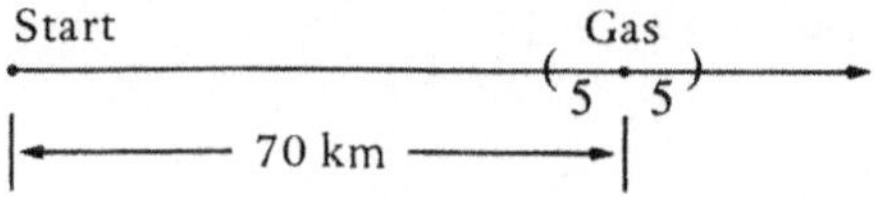

Let x = number of minutes the driver has been going.

$1.2x$ = number of kilometers from start (since $d = rt$).

$|1.2x - 70|$ = number of kilometers from gas station.

$\lvert 1.2x - 70\rvert < 5$	Write an inequality.
$-5 < 1.2x - 70 < 5$	Transform to remove the absolute value sign.
$65 < 1.2x < 75$	Add 70 to each member.
$54.2 < x < 62.5$	Divide each member by 1.2.
Between 54.2 and 62.5 min.	Answer the question.

From these examples you should be able to understand why the following conclusion is true.

CONCLUSION

TRANSFORMING ABSOLUTE VALUE INEQUALITIES
Assume that c is a positive constant.

The inequality |expression| $< c$ means:
expression is *between* $-c$ and c; that is,

$$-c < \text{expression} < c.$$

The inequality |expression| $> c$ means:
expression is *not* between $-c$ and c; that is,

$$\text{expression} > c \quad \text{or} \quad \text{expression} < -c.$$

ORAL PRACTICE

Tell in words what the inequality says.

EXAMPLES

	Answers
i. $\lvert x + 3\rvert < 5$	i. $x + 3$ is between -5 and 5.
ii. $\lvert x - 2\rvert > 7$	ii. $x - 2$ is *not* between -7 and 7.

A. $|x - 4| < 9$

B. $|x + 7| > 8$

C. $|x + 5| \leq 13$ D. $|x - 8| \geq 3$

E. $|2x - 7| \leq 6$ F. $|6x + 2| < 5$

Tell the result of transforming the inequality to remove the absolute value sign.

EXAMPLES

	Answers
i. $|x + 3| < 5$	i. $-5 < x + 3 < 5$
ii. $|x - 2| > 7$	ii. $x - 2 > 7$ or $x - 2 < -7$

G. $|x - 4| < 9$ H. $|x + 7| > 8$

I. $|x + 5| \leq 13$ J. $|x - 8| \geq 3$

K. $|2x - 7| \leq 6$ L. $|6x + 2| > 5$

The inequality shown came from transforming an absolute value inequality. Tell what that absolute value inequality was.

EXAMPLES

	Answers
i. $-2 < x + 3 < 2$	i. $|x + 3| < 2$
ii. $x + 5 \geq 9$ or $x + 5 \leq -9$	ii. $|x + 5| \geq 9$

M. $-7 < x + 8 < 7$ N. $x - 5 > 10$ or $x - 5 < -10$

O. $3x + 7 \geq 4$ or $3x + 7 \leq -4$ P. $-12 \leq 2x - 5 \leq 12$

EXERCISE 13-4

For Problems 1 through 20, transform the inequality to eliminate the absolute value signs. Then sketch the graph.

1. $|x| < 7$
2. $|x| > 10$
3. $|x| \geq 13$
4. $|x| \leq 300$
5. $|x - 3| > 8$
6. $|x - 13| < 7$
7. $|x + 7| \leq 2$
8. $|x + 4| \geq 9$
9. $|5x - 4| > 34$
10. $|2x - 7| < 19$
11. $|2x + 15| < 11$
12. $|5x + 21| > 34$
13. $|9 - 4x| \leq 15$
14. $|3 - x| \geq 15$

15. $|7x + 5| < -8$

16. $|8x + 1| > -2$

17. $|21x + 4| \geq -2$

18. $|7x - 4| \leq -5$

19. $|3x - 12| > 0$

20. $|4x + 20| > 0$

For Problems 21 through 30, first transform to the form

$$|\text{expression}| < \text{constant}.$$

(The sign could be $>$, $\leq$, or $\geq$.) Then transform and sketch the graph, as in Problems 1 through 20.

21. $|x| + 3 < 17$

22. $|x| - 4 > 9$

23. $5 + |x - 4| \geq 16$

24. $6 + |8 - x| \leq 10$

25. $3|x + 8| > 42$

26. $5|x - 2| < 45$

27. $9 - |2x + 1| \leq 3$

28. $8 - |5x + 13| \geq 1$

29. $5 \leq |x + 7| - 2$

30. $13 \geq |x - 2| - 6$

Two basic problems of algebra are (1) given x, find an expression's value, and (2) given an expression's value, find x. In Problems 31 and 32 you will do these two things with absolute value expressions.

31. For the expression $|x - 5|$:
    a. evaluate it when:
        i. x is 13;
        ii. x is -2;
    b. find x if the expression is:
        i. equal to 9;
        ii. less than 11 (draw the graph);
        iii. at least 4 (draw the graph);
        iv. less than or equal to -8 (draw the graph).

32. For the expression $|17 - 2x|$;
    a. evaluate it if:
        i. x is -3;
        ii. x is 10;
    b. find x if the expression is:
        i. equal to 13;
        ii. equal to 0;
        iii. greater than 6 (draw the graph);
        iv. no more than 21 (draw the graph).

33. ***Quiz Show Problem*** On a television quiz show, a contestant must guess the price of a new car. To be a winner, the contestant must come within a certain amount of the actual price. Suppose that the actual price is \$9826.
    a. Define a variable for the price the contestant guesses. Then write an absolute value expression for the difference between this guess and the actual price.

b. Write an inequality that says the guess must be within \$150 of the actual price, inclusive. Solve the inequality to find the range of guesses for which the contestant will win.

34. ***Estimated Tax Problem*** People who work for wages have income tax withheld from their paychecks. People who earn money from which tax is not withheld have to pay *estimated tax* during the year. Suppose that Lotta Bucks pays \$2400 in estimated tax.
   a. At the end of the year, Lotta figures out her *actual* tax bill. Define a variable for this actual tax. Then write an absolute value expression for the difference between the actual tax and the \$2400 estimate.
   b. How much is 20% of the estimated tax? Write an inequality saying that Lotta's actual tax is within 20% of the estimate, inclusive. Then solve the inequality to find the range of values her actual tax could be.

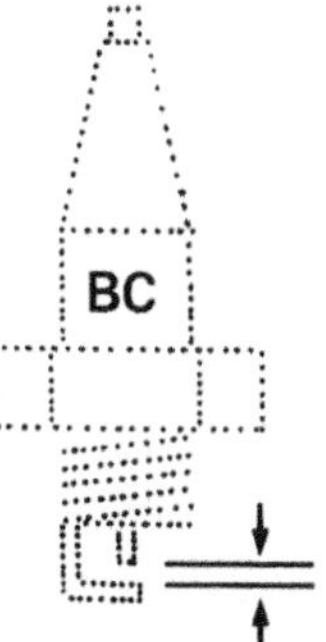

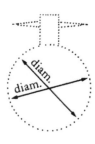

35. ***Submarine Hull Tolerance Problem*** The pressure hull of a submarine should be circular in cross section so that the water pressure will act evenly all the way around. However, the hull cannot be built exactly as a perfect circle. Suppose that the plans for a new submarine call for a diameter of 33 feet, $7\frac{1}{4}$ inches.
   a. Define a variable for the actual diameter measured at various places (see the figure). Then write an absolute value expression for the difference between the actual diameter and the 33 ft $7\frac{1}{4}$ in. called for on the plans.
   b. The plans allow for a *tolerance* of $\frac{1}{8}$ inch in the diameter. This means that the actual diameter must be within $\frac{1}{8}$ inch of 33 feet $7\frac{1}{4}$ inches, inclusive. Write an inequality stating this fact and solve it to find the range of values of the diameter.

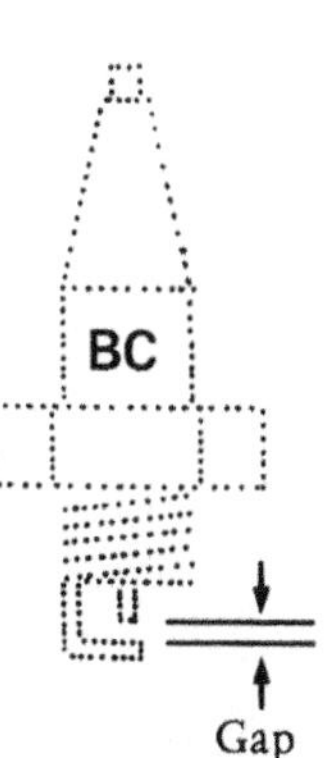

36. ***Spark Plug Tolerance Problem*** The specifications for a certain type of car state that to be within tolerance, the spark plug gap (see the figure) must be 0.03 ± 0.002 inch. The value ± 0.002 inch is called the *tolerance*.
   a. Define a variable for the actual gap width. Then write an absolute value inequality that says the gap is within tolerance.
   b. What range of gap widths is within tolerance?

37. ***Air Traffic Control Problem*** A commercial jet plane flies nonstop from San Francisco to New York at a constant speed of 900 kilometers per hour (km/h). On the way it flies directly over Chicago, 2900 km from San Francisco. Let t be the number of hours since the plane left San Francisco.

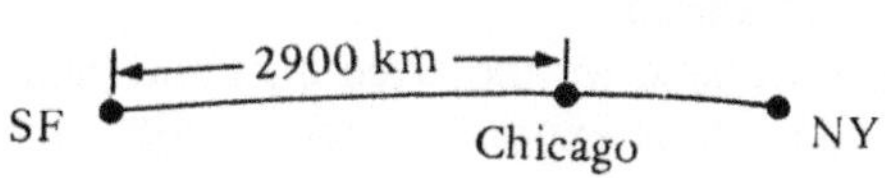

a. Write an expression in terms of t representing the plane's distance from San Francisco.
b. The plane's distance from Chicago is the *absolute value* of the *difference* between its distance from San Francisco and Chicago's distance from San Francisco (2900 km). Write an expression for the plane's distance from Chicago
c. The air traffic controllers at Chicago are responsible for the plane when it is within 500 km of Chicago. During what time interval will the Chicago controllers be responsible for it?

38. ***CB Radio Problem*** A trucker starts off from a warehouse and drives at a steady speed of 60 kilometers per hour (km/h). Fifteen minutes ($\frac{1}{4}$ hour) later his buddy starts after him from the same warehouse, going 70 km/h. Let t be the number of hours the trucker has been driving.
a. Write expressions in terms of t for (i) the number of kilometers the trucker has driven, (ii) the number of hours his buddy has been going, and (iii) the kilometers his buddy has gone.
b. The buddy eventually passes the trucker. They are within CB radio range when they are within 5 km of each other. Their distance apart is the *absolute value* of the *difference* between their distances from the warehouse. For what interval of times can they talk to each other by CB radio?
c. For what *other* time interval are they less than 5 km apart?

13-5 INEQUALITIES: GIVEN x, EVALUATE THE EXPRESSION

You have learned how to evaluate expressions such as

$$11 - 3x$$

when you know what x equals. Suppose you must find out what this expression is when x is *greater* than or *less* than some given number—for example, $x > 2$. Simply substituting 2 for x will not work. There is no good way to tell which way the inequality sign will point. One way to work this problem is to start with the inequality

$$x > 2$$

and transform it until the left member is $11 - 3x$. First, multiply each member by -3, remembering to reverse the inequality sign.

$$-3x < -6$$

Then add 11 to each member, getting

$$11 - 3x < 5.$$

So the expression $11 - 3x$ is less than 5 when x is greater than 2.

In this section you will evaluate expressions, finding out what they are greater than or less than. You will also see how this technique can be used in problems from the real world.

Objective

For linear expressions such as $11 - 3x$, find the range of values of the expression when a range of values of x is given.

Cover the answers as you work these examples.

EXAMPLE 1

Find the values of $16 - 5x$ if $x \le -3$.

- - - - - - - - - -

	Think These Reasons
$x \le -3$	Write the given values of x as an inequality.
$-5x \ge 15$	Multiply each member by -5. (The order reverses.)
$16 - 5x \ge 31$	Add 16 to each member.
Expression is greater than or equal to 31.	Answer the question.

EXAMPLE 2

Find the values of $4x - 7$ if x is between -1 and 5.

- - - - - - - - - -

$-1 < x < 5$	Write the given values of x as an inequality.
$-4 < 4x < 20$	Multiply each member by 4. (The order does *not* reverse.)
$-11 < 4x - 7 < 13$	Add -7 to each member.
Expression is between -11 and 13.	Answer the question.

Note: If the given values of x had been $-1 \le x \le 5$, you would have written "Expression is between -11 and 13, *inclusive*."

EXAMPLE 3

Hurricane Problem A hurricane is 250 miles offshore and is approaching the coast at a rate of 20 miles per hour.

a. Draw a diagram showing the coast, the starting point 250 miles offshore, and the hurricane somewhere in between.
b. Let t be the number of hours that have passed since the hurricane was 250 miles offshore. Write an expression in terms of t for the distance the hurricane is from the coast.
c. If t is at least 3 hours, where is the hurricane?
d. For what range of times will the hurricane be between 50 and 150 miles offshore?

a.

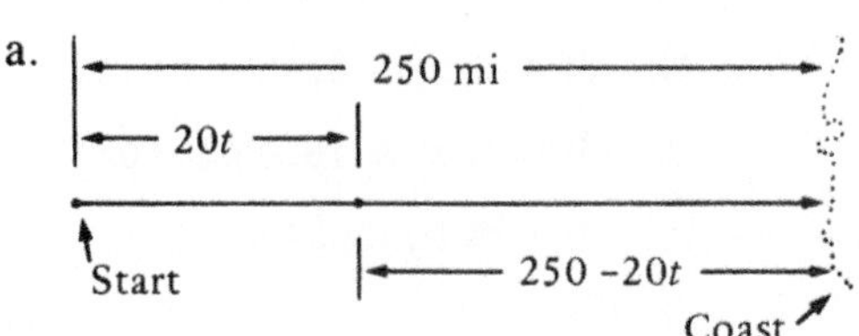

It has *gone* $20t$ miles, so it has $250 - 20t$ miles left to go.

b. t = number of hours.	Restate the definition of t.
$\underline{\underline{250 - 20t}}$ = number of miles.	Write an expression. Show it on the diagram in part (a).
c. $t \geq 3$	Write an inequality: t is at least 3.
$-20t \leq -60$	Multiply each member by -20. (The order reverses!)
$250 - 20t \leq 190$	Add 250 to each member.
Hurricane is at most 190 mi offshore.	Answer the question.
d. $50 < 250 - 20t < 150$	Write an inequality.
$-200 < -20t < -100$	Subtract 250 from each member.
$10 > t > 5$	Divide each member by -20.
Between 5 and 10 h.	Answer the question.

ORAL PRACTICE

Tell in words what the expression is for the given range of x.

EXAMPLE

	Answer
If $x > 5$, find $x + 3$.	$x + 3$ is more than 8.

A. If $x > 4$, find $x + 7$.

B. If $x < 6$, find $x + 2$.

C. If $x > 12$, find $x - 5$.

D. If $x < 1$, find $x - 4$.

E. If $x > 6$, find $3x$.

F. If $x < 30$, find $5x$.

G. If $x \geq 10$, find $\frac{1}{2}x$.

H. If $x \leq 12$, find $\frac{1}{3}x$.

I. If $x > 20$, find $-4x$.

J. If $x < 30$, find $-3x$.

K. If $x < 30$, find $-3 + x$.

L. If $x \geq 10$, find $-x$.

M. If $2 < x < 7$, find $x + 3$.

N. If $4 \leq x \leq 8$, find $x - 5$.

O. If $-6 < x < 6$, find $2x$.

P. If $0 \leq x \leq 18$, find $-6x$.

Q. If $x > 0$, find $x + 4$.

R. If $x \leq 0$, find $4x$.

EXERCISE 13-5

For Problems 1 through 20, find the range of values of the expression that corresponds to the given range of values of x. Write the answer in *words* and as an inequality.

1. If $x > 13$, find $7x + 2$.
2. If $x < 12$, find $5x + 3$.
3. If $x < 1$, find $9x - 4$.
4. If $x > 2$, find $7x - 10$.
5. If $x \leq 5$, find $9 - 2x$.
6. If $x \geq 9$, find $7 - 3x$.
7. If $x \geq -20$, find $-8x - 12$.
8. If $x \leq -6$, find $-9x - 1$.
9. If x is less than 7, find $17 + 4x$.
10. If x is more than 5, find $19 + 6x$.
11. If x is at least 2, find $-5x - 8$.
12. If x is at most 3, find $-7x - 12$.
13. If $3 \leq x \leq 5$, find $8x + 7$.
14. If $15 \leq x \leq 20$, find $2x + 37$.
15. If $-5 < x < 7$, find $13 - 6x$.
16. If $-8 < x < -3$, find $17 - 4x$.

17. If x is between 4 and 5, find $19 + 3x$.

18. If x is between 5 and 6.3, find $42 + 10x$.

19. If x is between -3 and 0, inclusive, find $-2 - 9x$.

20. If x is between 0 and 4, inclusive, find $-11 - 8x$.

21 *Vacation Financing Problem* A family goes on vacation. They start with \$1500 in traveler's checks and plan to spend \$180 per day.
   a. Define a variable for the number of days they have been on vacation. Then write an expression for the number of dollars they expect to have left.
   b. If they stay at least 5 days, what number of dollars could they expect to have left?
   c. If they want to come home with at least \$500 left, what (whole) number of days could they stay?

22. *Hamburger Help Problem* A local hamburger establishment takes in \$1700 in a day. Some of this is used to pay the employees. The wages are \$40 per employee for a day.
   a. Define a variable for the number of employees hired. Then write an expression for the number of dollars left, out of the \$1700, after the employees have been paid.
   b. The Hamburger Helper's union requires the manager to hire at least 9 employees. What range of dollars will be left?
   c. The manager wishes to make at least \$400 a day after paying the help. What (whole) number of employees could be hired? Is this compatible with union requirements? Explain.

23. *Freight Train Problem* A freight train leaves the town of Oola, La., and heads for Near, Miss., 200 miles away, at a speed of 40 miles per hour.

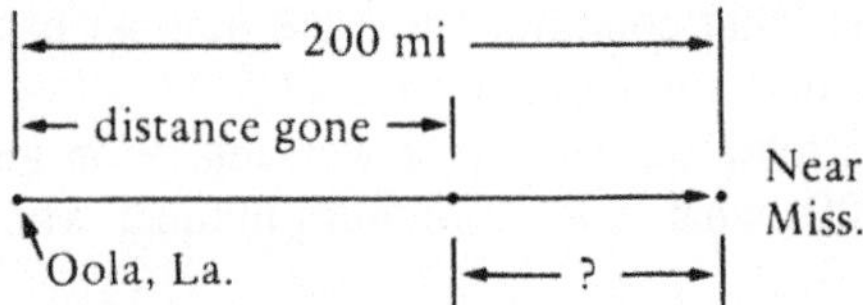

   a. Let t be the number of hours that have passed since the train left Oola, La. Write an expression for the distance the train still has to go to get to Near, Miss.
   b. If the time is greater than 3 hours, how far is the train from Near, Miss.?
   c. For what range of times will the train be between 30 and 100 miles from Near, Miss.?

24. *Raft Problem* A group of campers enters the Colorado River in the morning and travels 50 miles downstream on a raft. The raft floats with the current at 7 miles per hour.

a. Draw a diagram showing the 50-mile stretch of river with the raft somewhere on it. Show the distance the raft has left to go.
b. Let t be the number of hours the raft has been floating. Write an expression for the distance it has left to go.
c. If the raft has been going for at most 3 hours, what range of distances could it have left to go?
d. For what range of times does the raft have between 8 and 22 miles left to go?

25. ***Calvin's Height Problem*** In his early childhood, Calvin Butterball figured out that his height in inches was always 19 more than 3 times his age in years.
a. In order to sleep comfortably, one's height must be less than the length of the bed in which one sleeps. For what ages will Calvin be comfortable in:
   i. his bassinet, 31 inches long;
   ii. his youth bed, 50 inches long?
b. During his sixth year (ages 5 to 6, inclusive), what range of heights was Calvin?
c. To join the Navy, one must be between 5′6″ (66 inches) and 6′4″ (76 inches) tall, inclusive. For what ages will Calvin be eligible to join the Navy?
d. Calvin hopes to reach 7 feet tall and become a professional basketball player. How long would he have to keep growing to be over 7 feet tall? Do you think he will make it?

26. ***Workers and Guards Problem*** A primitive society on a remote tropical island has a rule that the number of people who work in the fields must be three times the number standing guard, minus 1000.
a. If fewer than 5000 people are working, how many can be on guard?
b. If more than 4000 people are on guard, how many must work?
c. Under what conditions will the number of people on guard be more than the number working?
d. If the total number either working or on guard is more than 10,000, what is the minimum number who can be working?

13-6 LINEAR INEQUALITIES WITH TWO VARIABLES

You have been solving inequalities that have *one* variable. In Chapter 7 you studied expressions that have *two* variables. In this section, expressions with two variables are set greater than or less than a specified number. You draw graphs of the resulting two-variable inequalities.

You have plotted graphs of linear equations such as

$$y = 2x - 3.$$

Substituting 2 for x gives

$$y = 2(2) - 3$$
$$y = 1.$$

The point (2, 1) is *on* the line, as shown in the graph.

Suppose that you had the *inequality*

$$y > 2x - 3.$$

Substituting 2 for x gives

$$y > 2(2) - 3$$
$$y > 1.$$

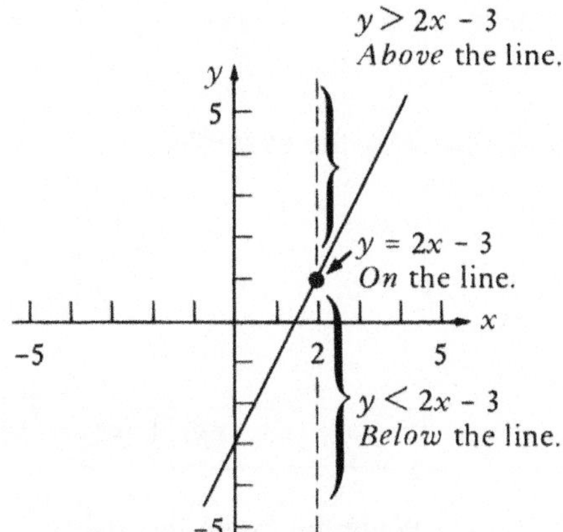

As shown in the figure, the points would be *above* the line. For the inequality

$$y < 2x - 3,$$

the points would be *below* the line. The whole graph, for all values of x, would be the entire *region* below the line, as shown in the right-hand figure below.

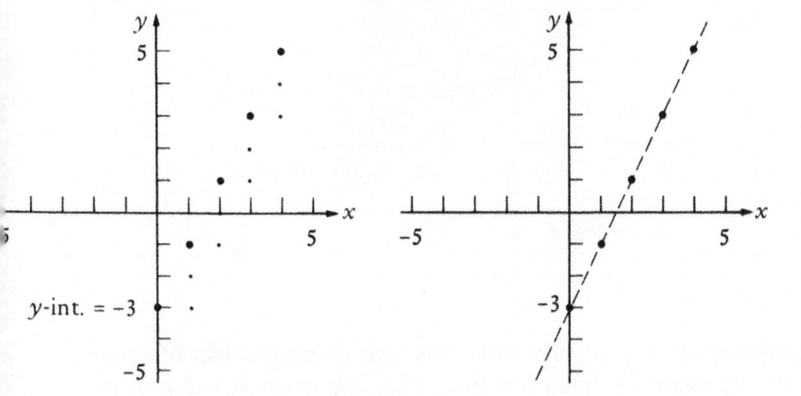

Use rise and run to plot points.

Draw the boundary line.

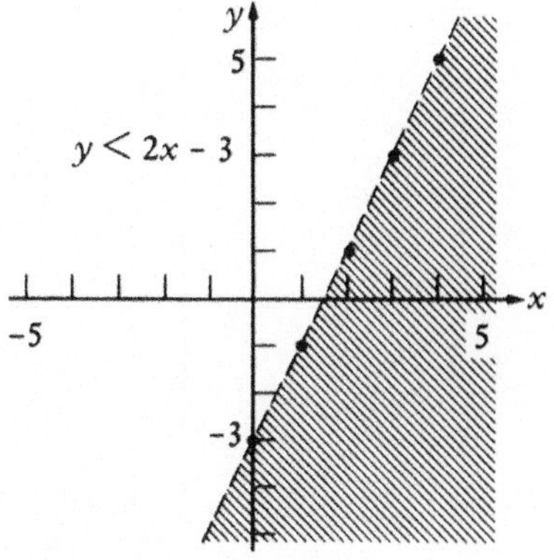

Shade the region.

Once you know what the graph looks like, you can draw it quickly. The line $y = 2x - 3$ forms the **boundary** of the region. Using the rise and run, you can plot points on this line. Then you draw the boundary line, using dashes in this case to show that the line is *not* included. (For the inequalities $\geq$ and $\leq$, you would draw a *solid* line.) Finally, you shade the proper region.

In general, for $y \geq mx + b$ or $y > mx + b$, you shade *above* the line; for $y \leq mx + b$ or $y < mx + b$, you shade *below* the line.

Objective

Given a linear inequality such as $y < 2x - 3$, draw the graph.

Cover the answers as you work the examples.

EXAMPLE 1

Draw the graph of $2x + 3y \geq 6$.

- - - - - - - - - -

	Think These Reasons
$2x + 3y \geq 6$	Write the given inequality.
$3y \geq -2x + 6$	Transform so that y is by itself on the left-hand side.
$y \geq -\frac{2}{3}x + 2$	

Plot the graph as described above.

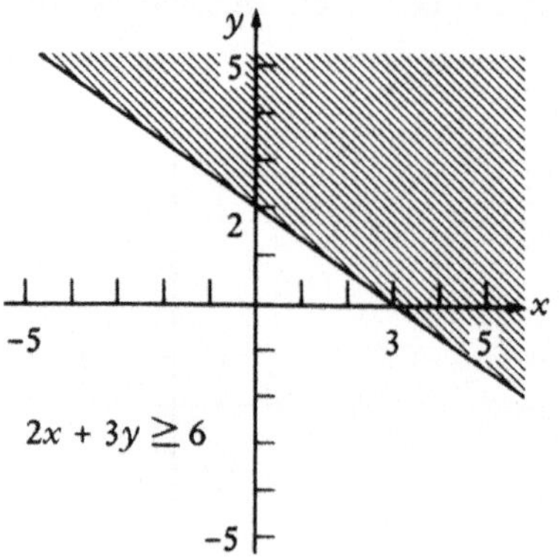

Note: The boundary line is *solid,* since the sign is greater than or *equal* to. The region is *above* the boundary line, since the inequality is *greater* than or equal to.

EXAMPLE 2

Draw the graph of the *system* of inequalities

$$x - 3y < -6 \quad \text{and} \quad y \le -\frac{5}{2}x + 1.$$

- - - - - - - - - -

$x - 3y < -6$

$-3y < -x - 6$

$y > \frac{1}{3}x + 2$

Transform the first inequality to slope-intercept form.

Note that the order *reverses*.

Plot *both* boundary lines, dotted for $>$ and solid for $\le$.

Draw small arrows to show which side of the line is shaded.

Shade the *intersection* of the two regions. This is because a solution of a system must satisfy *all* the inequalities.

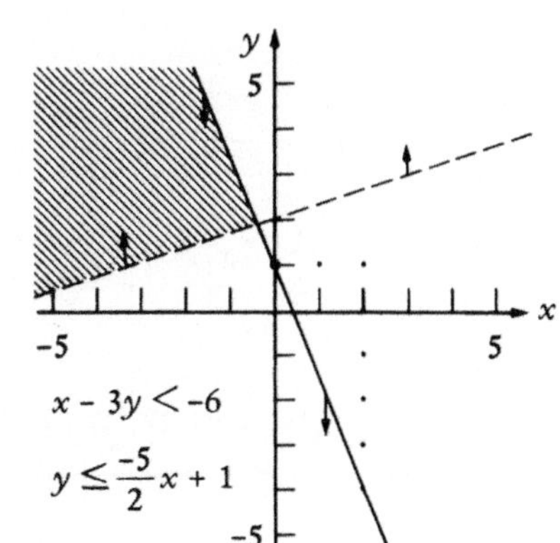

EXERCISE 13-6

For Problems 1 through 6, plot the graph of the inequality.

1. $y \ge \frac{3}{4}x - 2$
2. $y > \frac{2}{5}x - 4$
3. $3x + 5y > 20$
4. $3x + 4y \le 4$
5. $3x - y \ge -2$
6. $2x - y < -3$

For Problems 7 through 16, plot the graph of the system of inequalities.

7. $y > \frac{2}{5}x + 3$
   $y \le 2x - 1$
8. $y \le \frac{1}{3}x + 5$
   $y > \frac{7}{3}x - 2$
9. $2x + y \ge 1$
   $5x - 3y < 18$
10. $3x - 2y \ge -4$
    $x + 4y < -8$

11. $x + y < 3$
$2x - 3y < 12$

12. $x - y > -4$
$4x + y > -3$

13. $3x + y \geq 5$
$y < -x$

14. $y \geq 3x$
$3x + y \geq -6$

15. $x - 5y \leq -10$
$y < \frac{1}{5}x + 4$

16. $2x + y \leq 6$
$y > -2x + 1$

Problems 17 through 20 are systems with *three* inequalities. Plot the graph of the region that is the intersection of all three.

17. $2x + y > -2$
$x - y < -2$
$x - 3y \geq -15$

18. $y \geq -x$
$3x + 2y \leq 6$
$2x - 5y > -20$

19. $2x - 5y > -15$
$y \leq 2x$
$x + y \geq -3$

20. $x - 2y < 0$
$y > x + 1$
$x + 5y \leq 15$

13-7 SYSTEMS OF EQUATIONS AND INEQUALITIES

In Section 7-7 you graphed systems of equations and found their point of intersection. In the last section you graphed systems of inequalities. In that case, the intersection is a *region* in the Cartesian plane. Suppose that a system has one equation and one inequality, such as

$$2x + 3y > 18$$
$$x - y = -1.$$

The graph of $2x + 3y > 18$ is a region, and the graph of $x - y = -1$ is a line. The intersection is that part of the line in the shaded region.

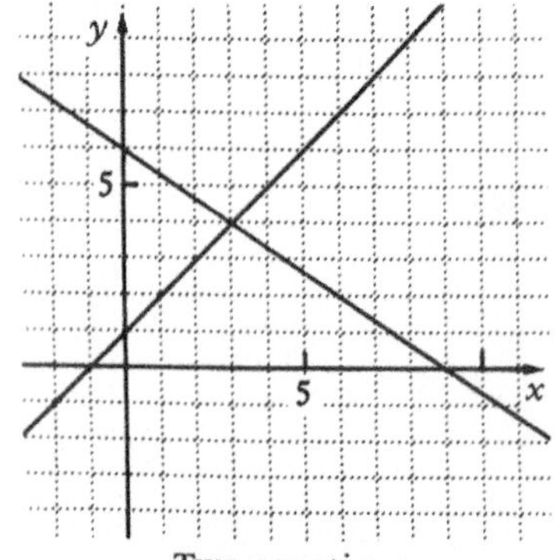

Two equations

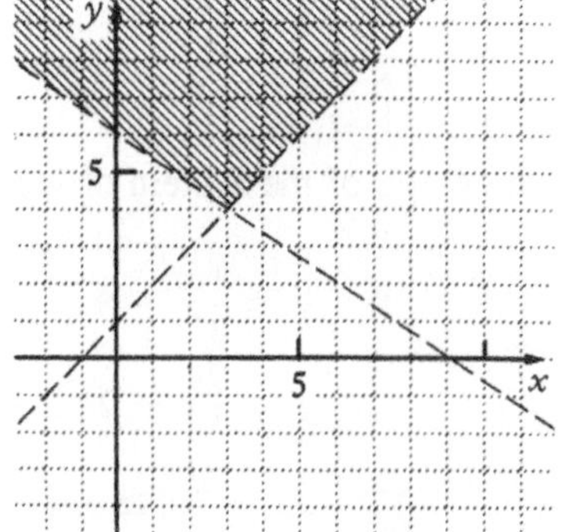

Two inequalities

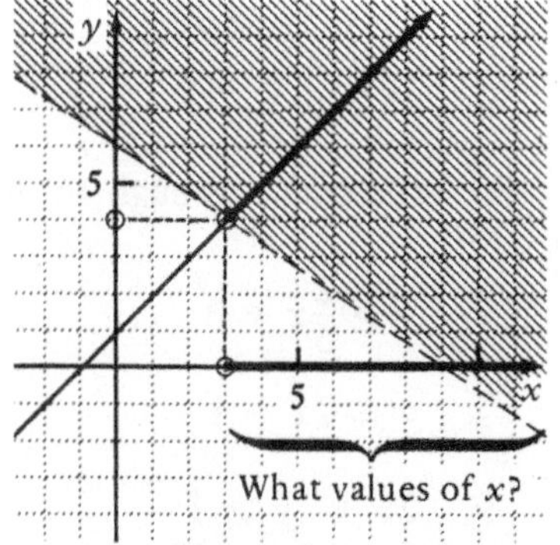

One equation, one inequality

Systems like this sometimes arise in problems from the real world. The values of x or y for the part of the line in the shaded region are easy to find using the substitution technique of Section 7.7. Here is how you would find the values of x for the system above.

	Think These Reasons
$2x + 3y > 18$ $x - y = -1$	Write the given system.
$-y = -x - 1$ $y = x + 1$	Solve the *equation* for y in terms of x.
$2x + 3(x + 1) > 18$	Substitute $x + 1$ for y in the *inequality* to eliminate y. (Now the inequality is just like the inequalities of Section 9.2.)
$2x + 3x + 3 > 18$	Distribute 3.
$5x + 3 > 18$	Combine like terms.
$5x > 15$	Subtract 3 from each member.
$x > 3$	Divide each member by 5.

As you can see from the graph, the line and the region intersect for values of x greater than 3. In this section you will solve systems like this arising in problems from the real world.

Objective

Given a problem from the real world involving two variables, write a system of one equation and one inequality and solve the system to find a range of values of a variable.

The words *equation* or *inequality* can be shortened to *open sentence*. An open sentence is simply a sentence with a variable in it. The sentence is "open" because its truth or falsity is open to question until someone gives you a value of the variable.

DEFINITION

OPEN SENTENCE

An **open sentence** is a sentence containing a variable.

(Equations and inequalities such as

$$3x + 5 = 7 \quad \text{or} \quad y < 4x - 9$$

are open sentences.)

Cover the answers as you work these examples.

EXAMPLE 1

a. Solve the system to find the range of values of y.
b. Illustrate your solution by drawing the graph.

$$x + y = 9$$
$$3x - 4y > -8$$

- - - - -

a. $x + y = 9$ / $3x - 4y > -8$ — Write the given system.

$x = 9 - y$ — Solve the *equation* for x in terms of y.

$3(9 - y) - 4y > -8$ — Substitute $9 - y$ for x in the *inequality* to eliminate x.

$27 - 3y - 4y > -8$ — Distribute 3.

$27 - 7y > -8$ — Combine like terms.

$-7y > -35$ — Subtract 27 from each member.

$\underline{\underline{y < 5}}$ — Divide each member by -7. (The order reverses.)

b.

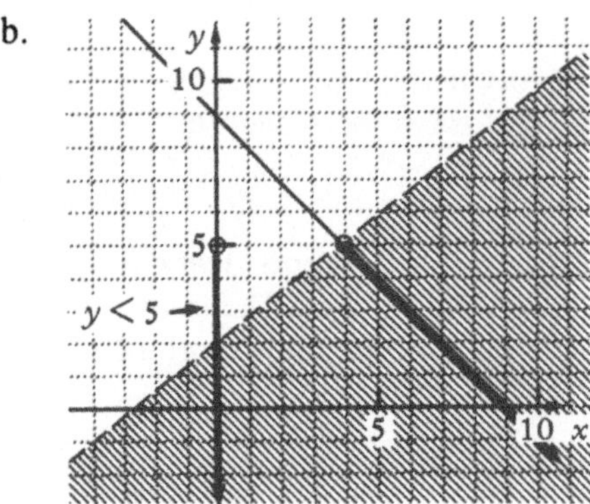

The line has intercepts $x = 9$, $y = 9$.

The inequality transforms to $y < \frac{3}{4}x + 2$.

The boundary line has $m = \frac{3}{4}$, $b = 2$.

The region is *below* the boundary line, since y is *less* than some value.

The values of y actually are less than 5.

EXAMPLE 2

School Faculty Problem A new elementary school is to have 50 faculty members. Some will be teachers and the rest will be aides. At this school, teachers will earn an average of \$20,000 a year and aides an average of \$12,000 a year.

a. Define variables for the number of teachers and for the number of aides. Then write an expression for the total amount of money paid in salaries for a year.

b. What total is paid if there are:
   i. 20 teachers and 30 aides; ii. 30 teachers and 20 aides?

c. Suppose that the total amount to be spent on salaries must be less than $896,000 a year. Write a system of open sentences, one expressing this fact and the other expressing the fact that there are 50 teachers and aides in all. Then solve the system to find the minimum number of aides that can be hired.

- - - - - - - - - -

a.	Let x = number of teachers. Let y = number of aides.	Define variables.
	$20x + 12y$ = number of thousands of dollars.	Use *thousands* of dollars to simplify the numbers.
b. i.	$20(20) + 12(30)$	Substitute 20 for x and 30 for y and evaluate the expression.
	$= 400 + 360$	
	$= 760$	
	$760,000	Answer the question.
ii.	$20(30) + 12(20)$	Substitute 30 for x and 20 for y and evaluate the expression.
	$= 600 + 240$	
	$= 840$	
	$840,000	Answer the question.

- - - - - - - - - -

c.	$20x + 12y < 896$	Write an inequality.
	$x + y = 50$	Write an equation.
	$x = 50 - y$	Solve the equation for y in terms of x, substitute into the inequality, and solve for y.
	$20(50 - y) + 12y < 896$	
	$1000 - 20y + 12y < 896$	
	$1000 - 8y < 896$	
	$-8y < -104$	
	$y > 13$	(The order reverses!)
	Minimum of 14 aides	Answer the question. Since y is an *integer* and must be greater than 13, the minimum is 14.

ORAL PRACTICE

Give the range of values of x and the range of values of y for the part of the line in the shaded region.

A.
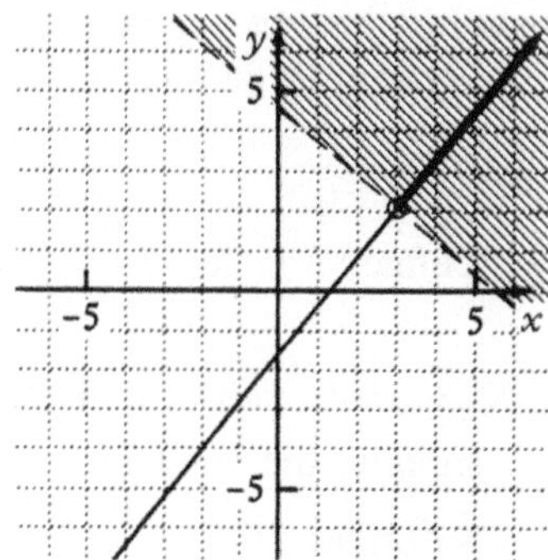

B.
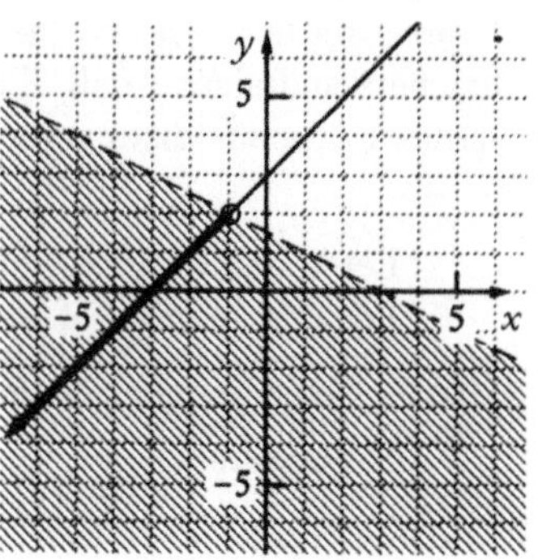

C.
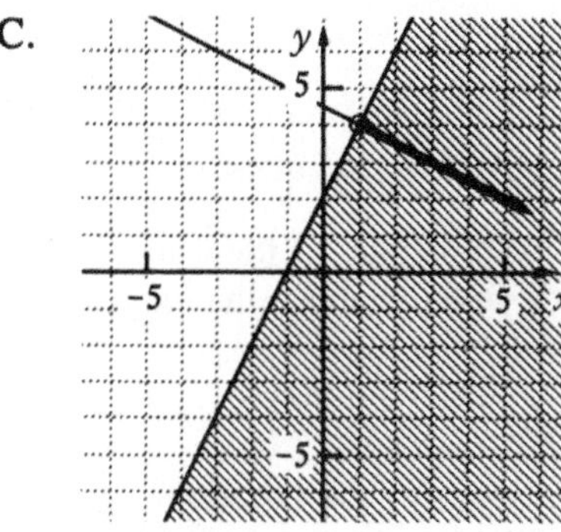

D.
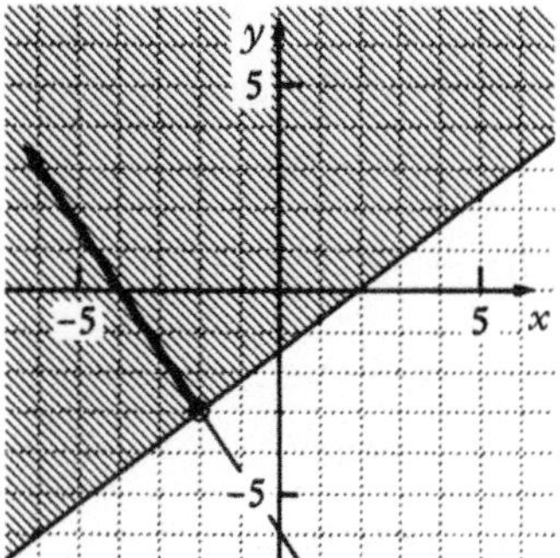

Tell which of the symbols on the right goes with the words on the left. (You may use a symbol more than once.)

E.	is less than	1.	$<$
F.	is no less than	2.	$\leq$
G.	is at least	3.	$=$
H.	is a minimum of	4.	$\geq$
I.	is down to	5.	$>$
J.	is down to . . . inclusive	6.	$< \cdots <$
K.	is up to . . . inclusive	7.	$\leq \cdots \leq$
L.	is up to		
M.	is a maximum of		

N. is at most

O. is more than

P. is no more than

Q. is greater than

R. is between

S. is between . . . inclusive

T. is unsurpassed by

U. is

EXERCISE 13-7

For Problems 1 through 4:

a. find the range of values of x and the range of values of y for which the system is satisfied;
b. draw the graph of the system.

1. $2x - 3y > -12$
   $x + y = 9$

2. $x + y = 13$
   $4x - 3y < 24$

3. $x - y = -2$
   $5x + 2y \geq 18$

4. $2x + 3y \leq 15$
   $x - y = 5$

For Problems 5 through 18, answer the questions. Problems 5 and 6 lead you step by step through the solution. For the others, you must think of what to do.

5. *TV Manufacture Problem* A manufacturer can produce 40 television sets per day, some color and the rest black-and-white. The color sets sell for \$400 each and the black-and-white sets for \$100 each.

PRODUCTION SHEET

Kind	Price	No.	\$
Color	\$400	____	____
B&W	\$100	____	____
Totals . .		40	____

   a. Define variables and write an expression for the total amount of money the manufacturer makes per day.

b. Evaluate the expression in part (a) if the manufacturer produces:
   i. 25 color and 15 black-and-white per day;
   ii. 15 color and 25 black-and-white per day.

c. The manufacturer wants to make more than $14,500 a day. Write a system of open sentences, one stating this fact and the other stating that the total number of sets is 40. Then solve the system to find the maximum number of black-and-white sets the manufacturer could produce each day.

6. *Arena Seating Problem* A new sports arena is being built to seat 10,000 people. Some seats will be reserved and the rest will be general admission. The plan is to charge $10 for a reserved seat and $6 for a general admission seat.
   a. Define variables for the numbers of tickets sold and write an expression for the total amount of money received.
   b. Evaluate the expression in part (a) for sales of:
      i. 3000 reserved and 7000 general admission tickets;
      ii. 7000 reserved and 3000 general admission tickets.
   c. Write a system of open sentences, one saying that sales are more than $68,000, total, and the other saying that all 10,000 tickets are sold. Solve the system to find the maximum number of general admission tickets that could be sold.

7. *Condominium Problem* A developer has space to build 80 condominium units near the beach. Some will be two-bedroom units selling for $100,000 each. The rest will be three-bedroom units selling for $120,000 each. The developer wishes to make more than 9 million dollars selling the condominiums. What number of two-bedroom units could be built?

8. *Silver and Gold Bracelet Problem* A jewelry manufacturer can make 20 of a particular design of bracelet each week. Some can be silver, selling for $30 each, and the rest gold, selling for $150 each. If the manufacturer wishes to make more than $1080 a week selling these bracelets, what numbers of silver bracelets could be made?

9. *Lawn Mowing Problem* A group of 30 students is going to mow grass in the community park as a public service project. Some will use power mowers and the rest will use hand mowers. Moe DeLaune figures that they must mow at least 400 square yards per minute, total, in order to finish by sunset. A person can mow 20 square yards per minute with a power mower, or 8 square yards per minute with a hand mower. What is the minimum number of power mowers they could use and still finish before sunset?

10. *Hay Bale Problem* A group of 100 people is hired to load bales of hay. An adult can load 5 bales per minute, and a teenager can load 3 bales per minute. If the group must load more than 328 bales per minute, how many teenagers could be in the group?

11. *Investment Problem* Meg A. Bucks has $10,000 to invest. She can put part of it into a certificate of deposit (CD) paying 8% per year interest and the rest into a savings account paying 5%. ("8% of . . ." means "0.08 times . . . .")
    a. How much interest will Meg get if she puts:
        i. $3000 into the CD and $7000 into savings;
        ii. $7000 into the CD and $3000 into savings?
    b. What range of amounts could Meg invest in the savings account and still get over $750 per year interest, total?

12. *Milk Mixing Problem* Cream is 30% butterfat and milk is 4% butterfat. A dairy mixes cream and milk to make 100 pounds of half-and-half.
    a. How many pounds of butterfat will there be if the dairy uses:
        i. 60 pounds of cream and 40 pounds of milk?
        ii. 40 pounds of cream and 60 pounds of milk?
    b. The Dairy Association specifies that 100 pounds of half-and-half must contain no less than 15 pounds of butterfat. What range of pounds of milk could be used?

13. *Vitamin Problem* Suppose that you must take 1000 units per day, total, of vitamins A and B. If the number of units of vitamin A must be at least $\frac{2}{3}$ of the number of units of vitamin B, what are the permissible daily doses of each?

14. *Democrats and Republicans Problem* The United States Senate has 100 members, Democrats and Republicans. The Democrats figure that to avoid political disaster the number of Democratic senators must be more than $\frac{1}{4}$ of the number of Republican senators. What range of numbers of Democratic senators will avoid disaster?

15. *Voting Problem* In order to defeat a proposed amendment to a constitution, the number of lawmakers voting against it must be more than one-half of the number voting for it. How many lawmakers voting "against" could defeat an amendment in:
    a. the United States Senate, 100 senators;
    b. the United States House of Representatives, 435 representatives;
    c. the Texas Legislature, 150 legislators;
    d. the Kansas Legislature, 125 legislators?

16. *Gold and Paper Dollars Problem* When the United States dollar was backed by gold, the law stated that the number of paper dollars could be no more than four times the number of gold dollars. Let x stand for the number of billions of gold dollars, and let y stand for the number of billions of paper dollars.
    a. Write an inequality relating x and y.
    b. If there were 40 billion gold dollars, how many paper dollars could there be?

c. If there were 200 billion paper dollars, how many gold dollars would be needed?
d. If the total number of dollars, gold and paper, were 300 billion, how many of each kind could there be?

17. *Age Problem* Roshawn Jones is 5 years younger than her sister Tonyetta. How old will each one be when:
a. the sum of their ages is at most 57 years;
b. Tonyetta is at least $\frac{11}{10}$ as old as Roshawn;
c. Roshawn's age is less than 95% of Tonyetta's age?

18. *With or Without Pepperoni Problem* The distributor of Well-Rounded Microwave Pizza found that pizzas with pepperoni sell best at small stores, but plain pizzas sell best at large stores. They deliver boxes of pizzas so that the number with pepperoni is 18 plus $\frac{2}{5}$ of the number without pepperoni.
a. If the total number of boxes delivered to the Wave 'N' Save Pizza Shoppe is at least 102, how many with pepperoni can there be? How many without pepperoni?
b. What total number of boxes will make the number without pepperoni greater than the number with pepperoni?

13-8 CHAPTER REVIEW AND TEST

In algebra you do three things with expressions.

1. Given a problem, write an expression representing a variable quantity.
2. Given x, find out the value of the expression.
3. Given the value of the expression, find x.

In this chapter you have added greater than and less than to your available symbols. You have evaluated linear expressions for a given range of x-values. You have also solved inequalities that contain linear expressions, absolute value expressions, or two-variable expressions.

You should try to work the following test within the length of time you would have for a classroom test. In order to be able to do this, you might want to look back through your class notes to make sure you are familiar with the techniques before you start the test.

CHAPTER TEST

1. What is the difference in each case?
a. The union of two sets and the intersection.
b. The graph of $x > 4$ and the graph of $x \geq 4$.

c. Multiplying each member of an inequality by a negative number and adding a negative number to each member.
d. The statements x is less than 7, and x is at least 7.
e. The statements x is between 2 and 5, and x is between 2 and 5, inclusive.

2. For the linear expression $15 - 8x$:
   a. evaluate the expression if x is 9;
   b. find x if the expression is 47;.
   c. find x if the expression is less than 71;
   d. find x if the expression is at least -577;
   e. evaluate the expression if x is at least 31.

3. For the absolute value expression $|5x - 43|$:
   a. evaluate the expression if x is 7;
   b. find x if the expression is 27;
   c. find x if the expression is at most 14;
   d. find x if the expression is less than -13.

4. Write an inequality for the graph.

a. 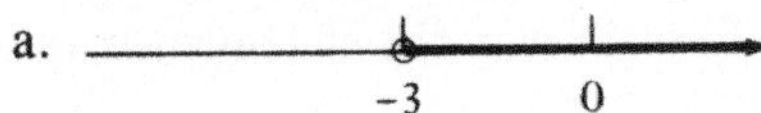

b. 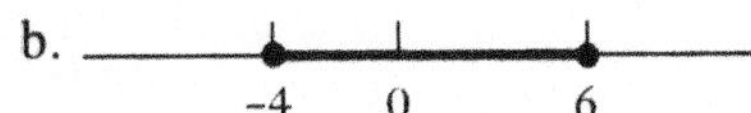

5. Graph the system of open sentences.
   a. $y \geq \frac{1}{4}x + 2$
   $5x + 2y < 10$
   b. $x + y = 2$
   $3x - 5y < 30$

6. ***Computer Service Problem*** A national computer service charges a membership fee of \$100. Thereafter, you pay \$5 per hour while your computer is connected by telephone to theirs.

COMPUTER BILL	
Fee	\$100
Service:	
___ hours @ \$5	___
Total	___

   a. Define a variable for the number of hours of "connect time," during which you use the service. Then write an expression for the total number of dollars you pay.
   b. If you pay between \$185 and \$230, for what range of times could you use the service?
   c. If your connect time is at least 30 hours, what will your bill be?

7. ***Grade Curving Problem*** Miss Calculate, the math teacher, states that students whose test scores are within 6 points, inclusive, of 73 will get a grade of C.

a. Define a variable for the test score. Then write an absolute value expression for the difference between this score and 73.
b. Write an inequality that says the student will get a C. For what range of test scores will the student get a C?

8. ***Ride and Walk Problem*** A local radio station sponsors a charity project in which students ride bikes or walk for a total of 8 hours. In return for this, people pledge to pay the students money to be given to the charity. Jim Shortz can ride at an average speed of 13 miles per hour and can walk long distances at an average of 3 miles per hour.
   a. Define variables for the numbers of hours Jim walks and rides. Then write an expression for the total distance he goes.
   b. The rules specify that each student must go more than 70 miles. Write a system of open sentences, one stating this specification and the other stating that the total time is 8 hours. Solve the system to find the range of times Jim could spend walking.

9. ***Commercial Problem*** On radio and television commercials you often hear statements like, "Save up to 30%, or more!" Let x be the percent you save. Write a compound inequality corresponding to this statement. Then draw its graph. Explain why the statement is ridiculous!

14

Functions and Advanced Topics

s equal to an expression con-
ig x, *then y is said to be a*
ion of x. *For example, the*
ure acting on a scuba diver
unction of the depth at which
she is swimming. In this
er you will be introduced to
nction concept. The things
earn will form a background
our future study of geometry,
iced algebra, trigonometry,
alculus.

ables:
Depth of diver (feet)
Water pressure (pounds per square inch)

ession:
ε Water pressure in terms of x

tion equation:
).45x

tion graph:

'ressure

Depth

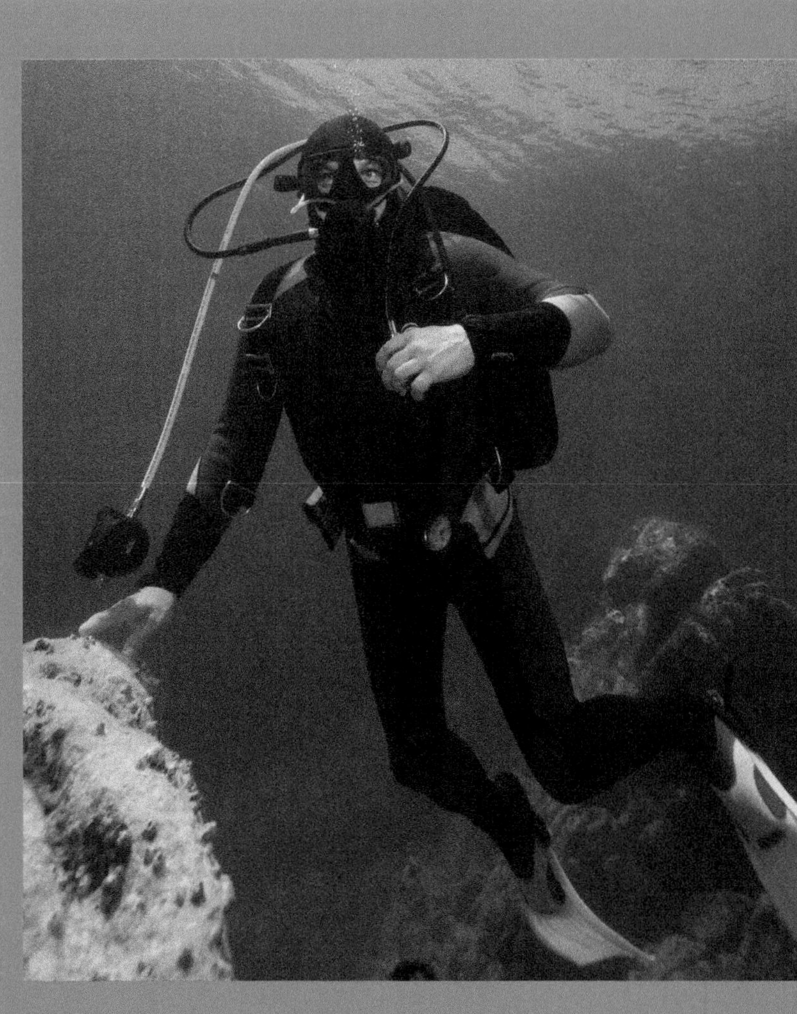

14-1 FUNCTIONS

The expression $2x - 3$ is a linear expression. If you set another variable, y, equal to this expression, you get an equation

$$y = 2x - 3.$$

As you recall, the graph of this equation is a straight line with slope 2 and y-intercept -3. For each value of x you pick, you will find that there is one and *only* one value of y. The graph shows this feature.

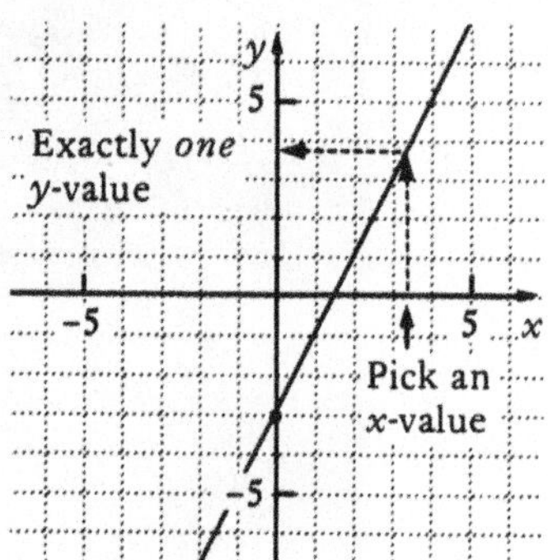

Any time there is exactly *one* y-value as the answer when you pick a value of x, y is said to be a *function* of x. Functions can have curved graphs as well as straight ones. For instance, suppose y equals a quadratic expression such as

$$y = 0.5x^2 - 2x + 1.$$

You can plot the graph by calculating points. For $x = 5$,

$$y = 0.5(5^2) - 2(5) + 1$$

$$y = 12.5 - 10 + 1$$

$$y = 3.5$$

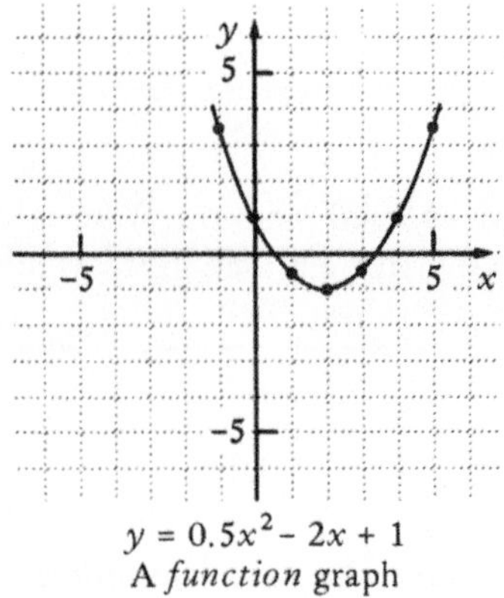

$y = 0.5x^2 - 2x + 1$
A *function* graph

Repeating this calculation for other values of x gives the following table of values.

x	y
−1	3.5
0	1
1	−0.5
2	−1
3	−0.5
4	1
5	3.5

The curved graph shown above is called a **parabola.** As you can see, there is still only *one* value of y for any single value of x you might pick, even though there may be two values of x that give the same value of y (such as $x = 0$ and $x = 4$).

There are equations for which there is more than one value of y for the same value of x. For instance, if

$$y = 2 \pm \sqrt{x},$$

then when $x = 9$,

$$y = 2 \pm \sqrt{9}$$

$$y = 2 \pm 3$$

$$y = 5 \quad \text{or} \quad y = -1$$

In this case, y is *not* a function of x.

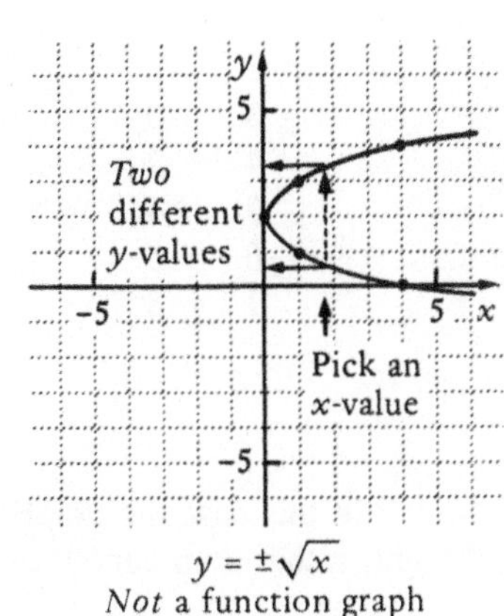

$y = \pm\sqrt{x}$
Not a function graph

DEFINITION

FUNCTION
A **function** is a set of ordered pairs (x, y) for which there is never more than one value of y for any one given value of x.

Objective

Given the equation for a function, calculate ordered pairs and use them to plot the graph.

Cover the answer as you work this example.

EXAMPLE

For the function $y = |2x - 6|$:

a. Calculate the value of y for each integer value of x, starting at $x = -1$ and ending at $x = 7$.

b. Plot the points, determine the pattern, and connect the points appropriately.

x	y
−1	8
0	6
1	4
2	2
3	0
4	2
5	4
6	6
7	8

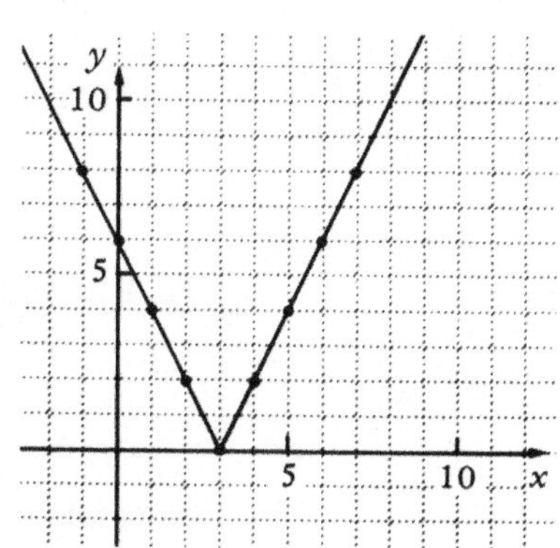

Note: In this case the graph goes down, then up. But the lines are straight, rather than curved as in the quadratic function above.

ORAL PRACTICE

Are these graphs of *functions?* Explain.

A. 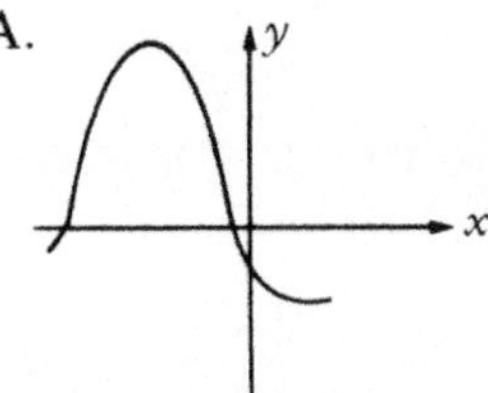

B. 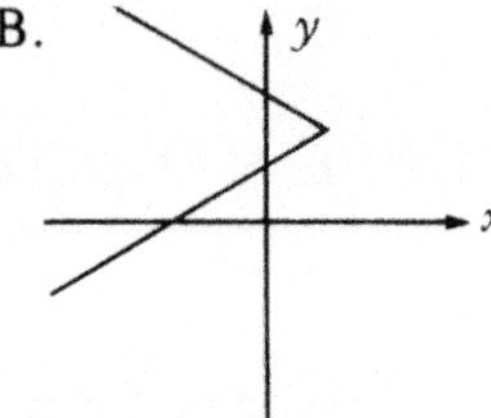

C. 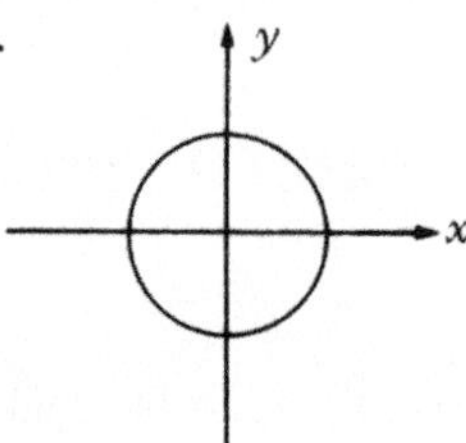

D. 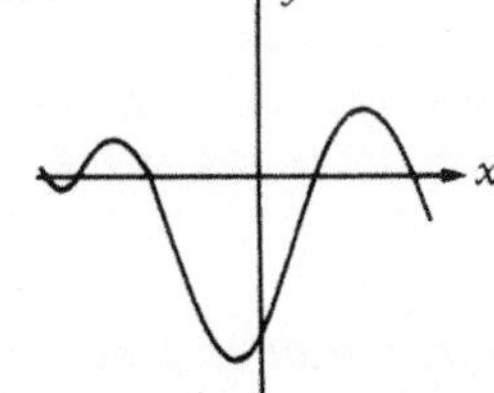

E. 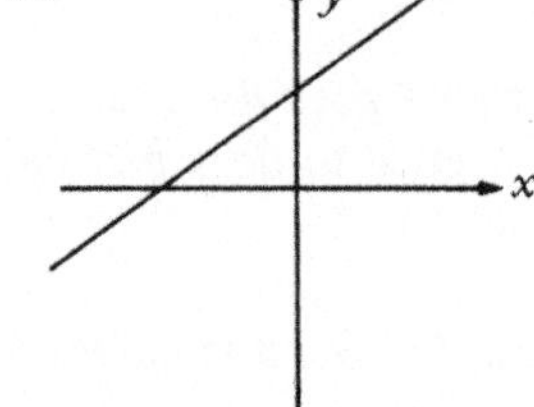

EXERCISE 14-1

For each function:

a. Calculate the value of y for each value of x indicated. Use a computer, if you like.

b. Plot the points and connect them appropriately.

1. $y = 0.3x + 4$, for all integers $-3 \le x \le 3$.
2. $y = 2.1x - 7$, for all integers $-3 \le x \le 3$.
3. $y = x^2 - 4x + 2$, for all integers $-1 \le x \le 5$.
4. $y = x^2 - 2x + 3$, for all integers $-2 \le x \le 4$.
5. $y = 0.2x^2 - 1.2x + 1$, for all integers $0 \le x \le 6$.
6. $y = 0.4x^2 - 1.6x + 3$, for all integers $-1 \le x \le 5$.
7. $y = |2x - 4|$, for all integers $-2 \le x \le 6$.

8. $y = |3x - 12|$, for all integers $0 \le x \le 8$.

9. $y = \dfrac{12}{x}$, for $x = 1, 2, 3, 4, 6, 12$.

10. $y = \dfrac{10}{x}$, for $x = 1, 2, 4, 5, 10$.

14-2 DIRECT AND INVERSE VARIATION FUNCTIONS

Sometimes in the real world two variable quantities are related in such a way that when one of them gets larger, so does the other one. For instance, as you travel in a car, the number of miles you have gone increases as the driving time increases.

In other instances, one variable goes *down* as the other goes up. For example, the length of time needed to do a particular job decreases as the number of workers increases.

The simplest function of the first kind is called a *direct variation function*. It has an equation like

$$y = 3x,$$

where the value of y is found by multiplying the value of x by a constant. In such a function, doubling x also doubles y.

$$\begin{array}{lcl} x = 10 & \xrightarrow{\text{Double } x.} & x = 20 \\ y = 3(10) & & y = 3(20) \\ y = 30 & \xrightarrow{y \text{ doubles.}} & y = 60 \end{array}$$

The simplest function of the second kind is called an *inverse variation function*. It has an equation such as

$$y = \frac{24}{x},$$

where y is found by *dividing* a constant by x. Here, doubling the value of x makes y *half* as big.

$$\begin{array}{lcl} x = 3 & \xrightarrow{\text{Double } x.} & x = 6 \\ y = \dfrac{24}{3} & & y = \dfrac{24}{6} \\ y = 8 & \xrightarrow{y \text{ is halved.}} & y = 4 \end{array}$$

For $y = (\text{constant})(x)$, y is said to *vary directly with x*, or to be *directly proportional to x*. For $y = \text{constant}/x$, y is said to *vary inversely with x*, or to be *inversely proportional to x*. In both cases, the constant is called the *proportionality constant*.

DEFINITIONS

DIRECT VARIATION FUNCTION
***y* varies directly with *x*,** or ***y* is directly proportional to *x*,** if and only if

$$y = kx.$$

where k is the **proportionality constant.**

INVERSE VARIATION FUNCTION
***y* varies inversely with *x*,** *or* ***y* is inversely proportional to *x*,** if and only if

$$y = \frac{k}{x},$$

where k is the **proportionality constant.**

An equation such as

$$y = kx \quad \text{or} \quad y = \frac{k}{x}$$

is called a **general equation.** If the value of k is known, such as

$$y = 3x \quad \text{or} \quad y = \frac{24}{x},$$

the equation is called the **particular equation.**

Objective:
Given a situation in which one quantity varies directly or inversely with another, find the proportionality constant, write the particular equation, and use the equation to predict values of variables.

Cover the answers as you work these examples.

EXAMPLE 1

Map Scale Problem The number of miles represented on a map is directly proportional to the number of centimeters you measure on that map. Suppose that the scale is 2 cm = 15mi.

a. Find the proportionality constant. Write the particular equation expressing miles in terms of centimeters.

b. It is 3.8 cm on the map from Phoenix to Scorpion Gulch. How far apart are the two places?

c. How many centimeters represent 100 mi?

- - - - -

	Think These Reasons
a. Let x = no. of centimeters. Let y = no. of miles.	Define variables.
$y = kx$ and $(x,y) = (2, 15)$	Write the general equation and the given ordered pair.
$15 = k(2)$	Substitute (2, 15).
$7.5 = k$	Solve for k.
$\therefore y = 7.5x$	Write the particular equation.
b. $y = 7.5(3.8)$	Substitute 3.8 for x.
$y = 28.5$	Do the arithmetic.
28.5 mi	Answer the question.
c. $100 = 7.5x$	Substitute 100 for y.
$13\frac{1}{3} = x$	Solve for x.
About 13.3 cm	Answer the question.

- - - - -

EXAMPLE 2

Time and Speed Problem The time it takes you to go a certain distance varies inversely with the speed at which you go. Suppose that it takes you 12 minutes to get to school riding your bike at an average speed of 15 miles per hour (mph).

a. Find the proportionality constant. Write the particular equation expressing time in terms of speed.

b. How long will it take you to get to school if you walk at 4 mph?

c. If you must get to school in 5 minutes, how fast must you go?

- - - - -

a. Let t = number of minutes.
Let s = number of miles per hour.

Define variables. You may use letters that sound like *time* and *speed*.

$t = \frac{k}{s}$, and $(s, t) = (15, 12)$ — Write the general equation and the given ordered pair.

$12 = \frac{k}{15}$ — Substitute $(15, 12)$ for (s, t).

$180 = k$ — Solve for k.

$\therefore t = \frac{180}{s}$ — Write the particular equation.

- - - - -

b. $t = \frac{180}{4}$ — Substitute 4 for s.

$t = 45$ — Do the arithmetic.

45 minutes — Answer the question.

- - - - -

c. $5 = \frac{180}{s}$ — Substitute 5 for t.

$s = \frac{180}{5}$ — Divide each member by 5. Multiply each member by s.

$s = 36$ — Do the arithmetic.

36 mph — Answer the question.

ORAL PRACTICE

Tell whether each illustrates direct or inverse variation, and why.

EXAMPLES

	Answers
i. Distance gone, and time traveled	i. Direct. Increasing time increases the distance.
ii. Time to fill the bathtub, and water flow rate	ii. Inverse. The faster the water flows, the *less* time it takes.

A. Number of left-handed people in a group, and total number of people in the group

B. Time taken to consume 100 tangerines and number of people consuming

C. Number of dollars spent on a vacation, and the number of days it lasts

D. Speed you must go, and the number of minutes you have available to get where you are going

E. A person's arm span, and his or her height

F. Electrical power used by a city, and the number of people who live in that city

G. The number of times one must stop for gas on a long trip, and the number of gallons the car's tank holds

H. The number of eggs used in a particular recipe, and the number of cups of flour used

I. The weight of a person on the earth, and his or her weight on the moon

J. The number of people sharing an apartment, and the number of dollars rent each one must pay a month

EXERCISE 14-2

1. ***Gas Consumption Problem*** The number of gallons of gas a car uses varies directly with the number of miles driven. Suppose that a car uses 3 gallons in going 120 miles.
   a. Find the proportionality constant. Write the particular equation expressing gallons in terms of miles.
   b. How many gallons would be used in driving 300 miles?
   c. How far could the car go between fill-ups if the tank holds 11 gals?

2. ***Batting Average Problem*** The number of hits a particular baseball player is expected to make is directly proportional to the number of times at bat. Suppose that Homer Fly makes 3 hits in 8 times at bat.
   a. Find the proportionality constant. Write the particular equation expressing expected hits in terms of at-bats.
   b. How many hits can Homer expect in 24 at-bats?
   c. Homer expects to make 33 hits. How many times would he have to be at bat?

3. ***Elephant Ear Problem*** The elephant ear is a semitropical plant that grows near water. The length of a leaf of the elephant ear is directly

proportional to its width. Suppose that a leaf 4 feet long has a width of 3 feet.

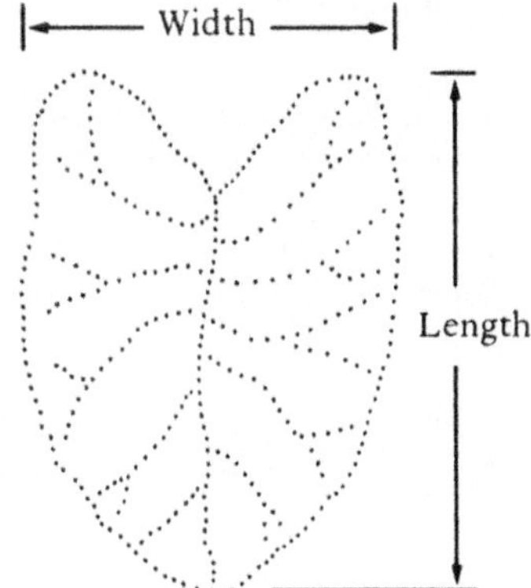

a. Find the proportionality constant. Write the particular equation expressing length in terms of width.
b. The end is torn off a leaf, so you cannot measure its length. But it is 5 feet wide. How long was it?
c. A small leaf is 1.3 feet long. How wide is it?

4. *Similar Triangles Problem* Two triangles are **similar** if their corresponding angles have equal measures. In such triangles, the altitude is directly proportional to the length of the base. Suppose that one of a set of similar triangles has base 10 cm and altitude 13 cm.

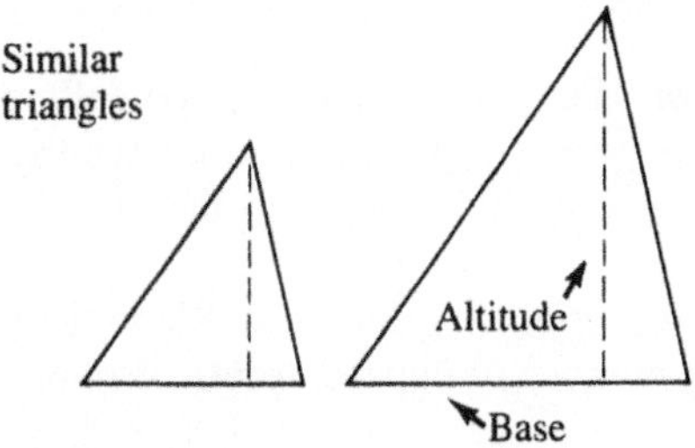

a. Find the proportionality constant. Write the particular equation expressing altitude in terms of base length.
b. What is the altitude of a triangle whose base is 52 cm?
c. How long is the base of a triangle whose altitude is 130 cm?

5. *Scuba Diving Problem* When you scuba dive, the added pressure due to the water varies directly with your depth. At 20 feet, the added pressure is about 9 pounds per square inch (psi).
   a. Find the proportionality constant. Write the particular equation expressing pressure in terms of depth.
   b. An amateur diver can safely stand an added pressure of 30 psi. How deep could he or she dive?

c. A sunken submarine lies in 120 feet of water off Lahaina in Maui, Hawaii. What added pressure would a diver experience in going to the submarine?

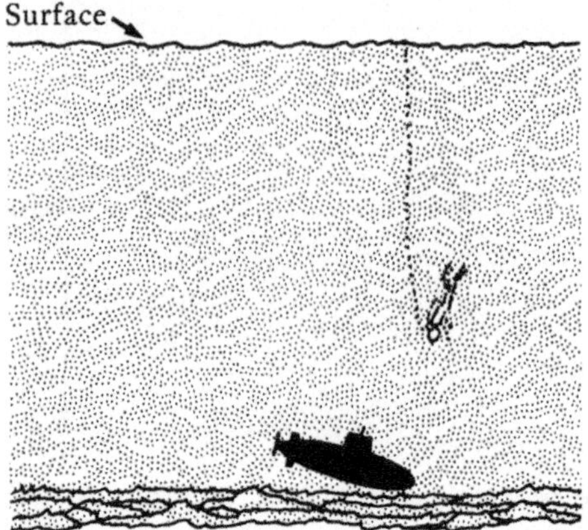

6. ***Tape Recorder Problem*** The number of feet of tape that have gone through a tape recorder varies directly with the number of minutes the recorder has been on. In 3 minutes, 40 feet of tape go through.
   a. Find the proportionality constant. Write the particular equation expressing feet in terms of minutes.
   b. A 90-minute tape plays 45 minutes in each direction. If you unwound a 90-minute tape, how long would it be?
   c. At how many feet per minute does tape go through the recorder?

7. ***Recipe Problem*** Pam Baker has a recipe calling for 3 cups of flour. The recipe serves 5 people. She knows that the number of cups to use is directly proportional to the number of people that are served.
   a. Find the proportionality constant. Write the particular equation expressing number of cups in terms of number of people.
   b. Pam wants to use the recipe in a restaurant, where 100 people will be served. How many cups of flour should be used?
   c. Pam uses the recipe for company at home. She has 7 cups of flour and hopes to serve 11 people. Does she have enough flour? Justify your answer.

8. ***Wire Length Problem*** Millie Watt is an electrical contractor. She needs to find out how many feet of wire are left on a partially used roll, without having to unroll the wire and measure it. So she cuts off a 4-foot piece, weighs it, and finds that it weighs 1.2 pounds. She knows that the length of the wire on the roll is directly proportional to the weight of the wire.

a. Find the proportionality constant. Write the particular equation expressing length in terms of weight.
b. The roll of wire remaining weighs 36 pounds. How many feet of wire are there?
c. A full roll of the same kind of wire has 200 feet of wire. Millie can lift up to 70 pounds. Can she lift a full roll? Justify your answer.

9. ***Thunder and Lightning Problem*** In a lightning storm, the number of seconds between the flash and the bang is directly proportional to the number of miles you are from the lightning. It takes 15 seconds for the thunder sound to reach you from lightning that is 3 miles away.
   a. Find the proportionality constant. Write the particular equation expressing time in terms of distance.
   b. How long does it take the sound to reach you from lightning:
      i. 5 miles away; ii. 2 miles away?
   c. How far away is the lightning if the time is only 1 second?

10. ***Diving Board Problem*** The number of centimeters a diving board bends is directly proportional to the weight of the person standing on it. An 11-year old, who weighs 90 pounds, bends the board 5 centimeters.

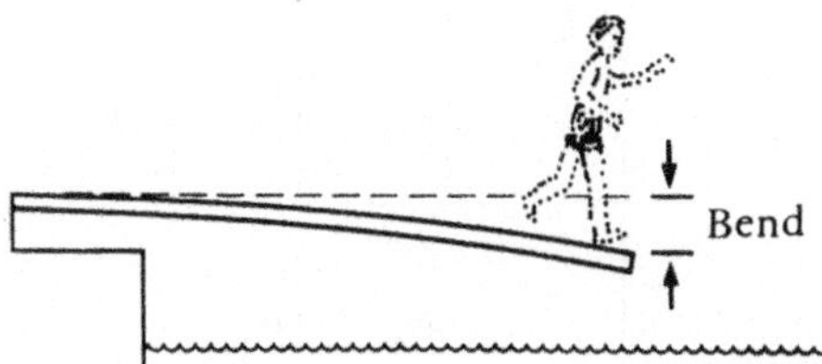

   a. Find the proportionality constant, and write the particular equation, expressing centimeters in terms of pounds.
   b. A guard on the girls' basketball team weighs 120 pounds. How far will she bend the board?
   c. A guard on the football team bends the diving board 15 centimeters. How heavy is he?

11. ***Speed versus Time Problem*** The speed you must go to cover a certain distance varies inversely with the time available for the trip. Suppose that you must travel 30 miles per hour (mph) when you have 10 minutes available.
   a. Find the proportionality constant. Write the particular equation expressing speed in terms of time.
   b. How fast must you go when there are only 5 minutes available?
   c. How fast can you go if there is half an hour available?

12. ***Book Assembly Problem*** The number of hours it takes to collate the pages for copies of a book is inversely proportional to the number of people doing the collating. Suppose that a crew of 4 people takes a total of 12 hours to do the job.
    a. Find the proportionality constant. Write the particular equation expressing time in terms of number of people.
    b. How long would it take 10 people to do the job?
    c. How long would it take one person alone to do the job? Where else have you seen this number?

13. ***Wheel Problem*** The number of times a wheel rotates in going a mile is inversely proportional to the diameter of the wheel. A 27-inch diameter bicycle wheel makes 747 revolutions in going a mile.
    a. Find the proportionality constant. Write the particular equation expressing number of revolutions in terms of diameter.
    b. How many revolutions would a locomotive wheel, 80 inches in diameter, take to go a mile?
    c. How large a diameter wheel would be needed to cover a mile with only 100 revolutions?

14. ***Heat Loss Problem*** The rate at which heat is lost through a window pane is inversely proportional to the thickness of the pane. Suppose that a normal $\frac{1}{8}$-inch-thick pane loses 400 calories per hour.

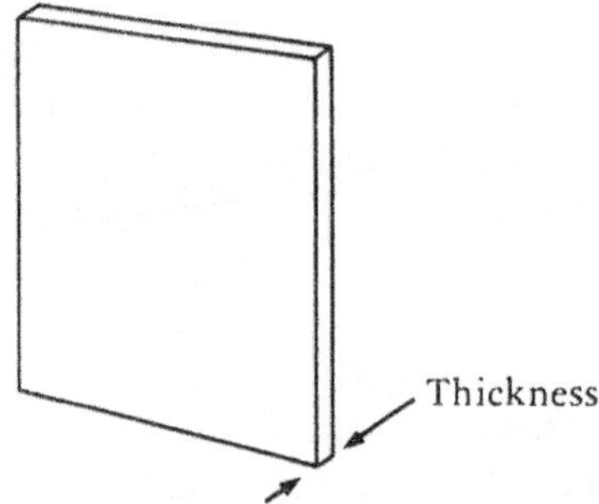

    a. Find the proportionality constant. Write the particular equation expressing calories per hour in terms of thickness.
    b. How many calories per hour would be lost through a $\frac{3}{8}$-inch-thick window pane?
    c. How thick a pane would be needed to make the loss only 50 calories per hour?

15. Demographers have a rule of thumb which says that the population of a city in a given region is inversely proportional to the *rank* of that city (largest, second largest, third largest, and so on). Suppose that the fourth-ranked city in a region has a population of 200,000.
    a. Find the proportionality constant. Write the particular equation expressing population in terms of rank.

b. What is the population of:
 i. the tenth-ranked city; ii. the largest city?
c. If a city has a population of 4000, what is its rank?

16. ***What You Can Buy Problem*** A fundamental fact of economics is that the number of things you can buy with a fixed amount of money is inversely proportional to the price of each item. Suppose that you can buy 6 records when the price is $8 each.
 a. Find the proportionality constant. Write the particular equation expressing number of records in terms of price.
 b. If the price increases to $12 each, how many records can you buy?
 c. What is the fixed amount of money you have available to spend?

17. ***Band Formation Problem*** A marching band can make various rectangular patterns with differing numbers of rows and columns. The number of columns is inversely proportional to the number of rows for a band of fixed size. Suppose that a particular band can form a rectangle with 12 rows and 9 columns.

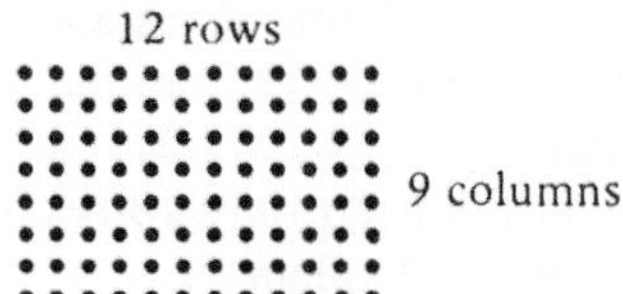

 a. Find the proportionality constant. Write the particular equation expressing number of columns in terms of number of rows.
 b. How many columns would there be if there were 6 rows?
 c. Could there be 7 rows? Explain.
 d. How many people are in this band?

18. ***Rectangle Problem*** If rectangles have equal areas, then their lengths are inversely proportional to their widths. Suppose that one of these rectangles is 40 meters long and 30 meters wide.

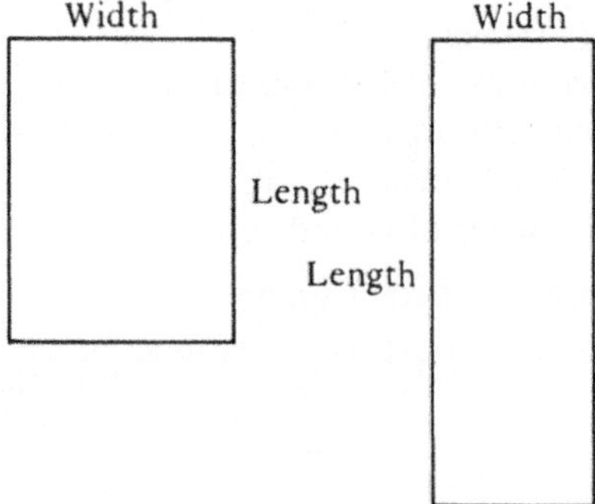

 a. Find the proportionality constant. Write the particular equation expressing length in terms of width.

b. If another of these rectangles is 20 m wide, how long must it be?

c. How long must one of these rectangles be in order for the length to equal the width?

19. ***Prying Problem*** One way to raise a heavy object is to stick a board or crowbar under it to act as a lever and pry it up. The amount of force you must exert on the lever is inversely proportional to the number of centimeters from the pivot at which you push. Suppose that 100 pounds is required at a distance of 20 cm.

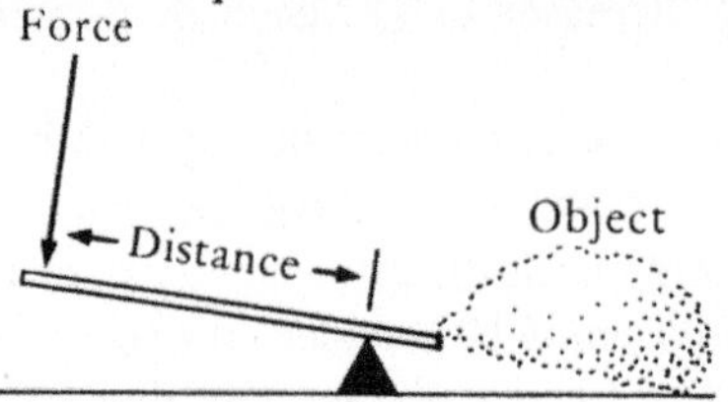

a. Find the proportionality constant. Write the particular equation expressing force in terms of distance.

b. If you move out to 60 cm from the pivot, how hard would you have to push?

c. A small child can exert only 10 pounds of force. Could the child pry up the object? Explain.

20. ***Truck Speed Problem*** If a truck starts at rest and speeds up under maximum power, its speed after a fixed length of time is inversely proportional to its total weight. Suppose that for a particular truck weighing 3000 pounds empty, the speed is 40 miles per hour (mph) after 20 seconds.

a. Find the proportionality constant and write the particular equation expressing speed in terms of weight.

b. The truck is loaded with 5000 pounds of cargo, making its total weight 8000 pounds. What will its speed be after 20 seconds under maximum power?

c. When it is partially loaded, the truck's speed is 32 mph after 20 seconds at maximum power.

   i. Find the truck's total weight.

   ii. Find the number of pounds of cargo.

21. ***Proportion Property of Direct Variation*** If (x_1, y_1) and (x_2, y_2) are two ordered pairs in a direct-variation function, $y = kx$, show that

$$\frac{y_1}{x_1} = \frac{y_2}{x_2}$$

22. ***Proportion Property of Inverse Variation*** If (x_1, y_1) and (x_2, y_2) are two ordered pairs in an inverse variation function, $y = \frac{k}{x}$, show that

$$x_1 y_1 = x_2 y_2.$$

14-3 FUNCTION TERMINOLOGY

In Chapters 7 and 8 you drew graphs of equations. For instance, the equation

$$y = \frac{2}{5}x + 1$$

has a graph with slope 2/5 and y-intercept 1. The equation

$$y = -2x + 6$$

has a graph with slope -2 and y-intercept 6. These graphs are shown in Figure 14-3a.

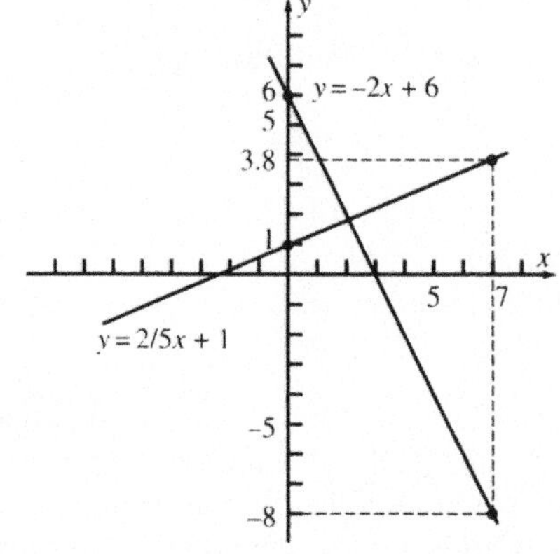

Figure 14-3a

Suppose someone tells you that x equals 7, and says, "Calculate y." You get different answers from the two equations.

$$\text{First equation: } y = \frac{2}{5}(7) + 1 = 3.8$$

$$\text{Second equation: } y = -2(7) + 6 = -8$$

In each equation, the value you get for y depends on the value you start with for x. For this reason, y is said to be a **function** of x. Since there are two different equations shown above, there are two different functions.

In order to distinguish between two different functions that use the same variables, mathematicians often call one of the functions "f" (for "function") and the other one "g" (because g comes right after f in the alphabet). The symbols used for y are $f(x)$ and $g(x)$. They are pronounced "f of x" and "g of x." (Though f and g are used most frequently, any letter may be used to name a function.)

Using these symbols, the equations we started with would be written this way:

$$f(x) = \frac{2}{5}x + 1 \qquad g(x) = -2x + 6$$

These symbols are useful for showing the number that has been substituted for x. For instance, to substitute 7 for x, as above, you would write:

$$f(7) = \frac{2}{5}(7) + 1 = 3.8$$

$$g(7) = -2(7) + 6 = -8$$

Be sure to read $f(7)$ as "f of 7." The symbol means, "The value of y in function f when x is 7." It does *not* mean f times 7.

Objective:

Become familiar with using $f(x)$ terminology for the y-value in a function.

Cover the answers as you work these examples.

EXAMPLE 1

For the function $f(x) = 0.3x - 14$:

a. Find $f(0)$, $f(52)$, and $f(-3)$.

b. Find x if $f(x) = 25$.

Think These Reasons

a. $f(0) = 0.3(0) - 14 = \underline{\underline{-14}}$ — Substitute for x and do the arithmetic.

$f(5) = 0.3(52) - 14 = \underline{\underline{1.6}}$

$f(-3) = 0.3(-3) - 14 = \underline{\underline{-14.9}}$

b. $f(x) = 0.3x - 14$ — Write the given equation.

$25 = 0.3x - 14$ — Substitute 25 for $f(x)$.

$39 = 0.3x$ — Add 14 to each member.

$\underline{\underline{130 = x}}$ — Divide each member by 0.3.

EXAMPLE 2

For the functions $f(x) = 5x + 11$ and $g(x) = x^2 - 8$:

a. Which is greater, $f(3)$ or $g(3)$?

b. Which is greater, $f(10)$ or $g(10)$?

c. Evaluate $\dfrac{f(10)}{g(10)}$.

a. $f(3) = 5(3) + 11 = 26$ — Substitute 3 for x in the f equation.

$g(3) = 3^2 - 8 = 1$ — Substitute 3 for x in the g equation.

$\therefore f(3)$ is greater than $g(3)$.

b. $f(10) = 5(10) + 11 = 61$ — Substitute 10 for x in the f equation.

$g(10) = 10^2 - 8 = 92$ — Substitute 10 for x in the g equation.

$\therefore g(10)$ is greater than $f(10)$

c. $\dfrac{f(10)}{g(10)} = \dfrac{61}{92} = \underline{\underline{0.66304...}}$ — Substitute the answers from part (b) and divide.

Note: The 10's inside the parentheses *cannot be canceled.* Remember that $f(x)$ and $g(x)$ do *not* mean multiplication.

EXAMPLE 3

For the functions $g(x) = \frac{3}{5}x - 6$ and $h(x) = -2x + 8$

a. Graph both functions on the same set of axes.
b. Find the approximate coordinates of the point where the graphs intersect.
c. Calculate the point of intersection of the two graphs.

a. Function g has slope 3/5 and y-intercept -6.
Function h has slope -2 and y-intercept 8.

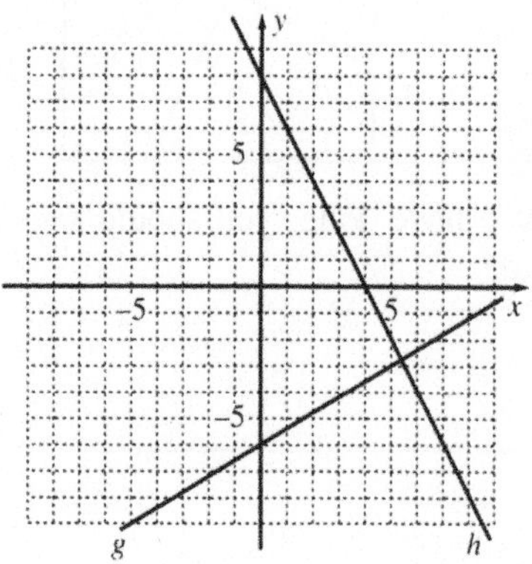

b. The graphs intersect at approximately $\underline{\underline{(5.4, -2.8)}}$.

c. $g(x) = h(x)$ — Where the graphs intersect, the two y-values are equal.

$\frac{3}{5}x - 6 = -2x + 8$ — Substitute for $g(x)$ and $h(x)$.

$\frac{3}{5}x + 2x = 14$ — Add $2x$; add 6.

$\frac{13}{5}x = 14$ — Add the like terms.

$x = \frac{70}{13} = 5\frac{5}{13}$ — Multiply by $\frac{13}{5}$.

$g\left(\frac{70}{13}\right) = \frac{3}{5} \cdot \frac{70}{13} - 6$ — Substitute $\frac{70}{13}$ for x in the g function.

$g\left(\frac{70}{13}\right) = \frac{-36}{13} = -2\frac{10}{13}$ — Do the arithmetic.

Intersection point is $\left(5\frac{5}{13}, -2\frac{10}{13}\right)$, which is about (5.38, −2.77).

Note: If you have a graphing calculator, the first part of the problem can be done by plotting both functions, then tracing to the point of intersection. The graph below shows what the display might look like.

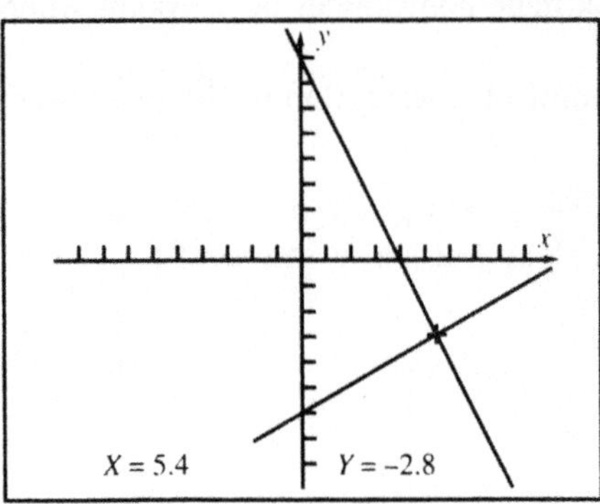

So that you can show what you have done, you should *sketch* the graph that appears on your calculator.

ORAL PRACTICE

If $f(x) = 3x$, $g(x) = x + 5$, and $h(x) = x^2$, find:

A. $f(7)$ B. $g(4)$ C. $h(5)$ D. $f(0)$
E. $h(0)$ F. $g(0)$ G. $g(-10)$ H. $f(100)$
I. $h(-11)$ J. $h(z)$ K. $g(2n)$ L. $f(p^2)$

EXERCISE 14-3

1. For the function $f(x) = 11x - 4$:
   a. Find $f(6)$, $f(-14)$, and $f(100)$.
   b. Find x if $f(x) = 62$.
2. For the function $f(x) = 13x + 9$:
   a. Find $f(5)$, $f(20)$, and $f(-10)$.
   b. Find x if $f(x) = 61$.
3. For the function $g(x) = x^2 + 7$:
   a. Find $g(9)$, $g(-5)$, and $g(20)$.
   b. Find x if $g(x) = 88$.
   c. Show that there is *no* value of x that makes $g(x) = 5$.
4. For the function $h(x) = 1000 - x^3$:
   a. Find $h(8)$, $h(-5)$, and $h(20)$.
   b. Find x if $h(x) = 0$.
   c. Find x if $h(x) = 17$.
5. For the functions $h(x) = 3x + 4$ and $g(x) = 5x - 7$:
   a. Which is greater, $h(2)$ or $g(2)$?
   b. Which is greater, $h(10)$ or $g(10)$?
   c. Evaluate $\dfrac{h(10)}{g(10)}$.
6. For the functions $c(x) = 2 + 7x$ and $p(x) = 100 - 3x$:
   a. Which is greater, $c(0)$ or $p(0)$?
   b. Which is greater, $c(8)$ or $p(8)$?
   c. Evaluate $\dfrac{p(0)}{c(0)}$
7. For the functions h and g in Problem 5, find the value of x that makes $h(x) = g(x)$. Draw a sketch showing what happens to the graphs of these two functions at this value of x.
8. For the functions c and p in Problem 6, find the value of x that makes $c(x) = p(x)$. Draw a sketch showing what happens to the graphs of these two functions at this value of x.
9. Plot accurately the graphs of $f(x) = \frac{2}{5}x + 3$ and $g(x) = 10 - \frac{4}{3}x$. From the graphs, estimate the x- and y-coordinates of the point where they intersect. Then show that your answer is close to the actual answer by calculating the point of intersection.
10. Plot accurately the graphs of $r(x) = x + 2$ and $t(x) = 9 - \frac{5}{2}x$. From the graphs, estimate the x- and y-coordinates of the point where they intersect. Then show that your answer is close to the actual answer by calculating the point of intersection.

11. ***Hourly Wage Problem*** Suppose that you get an after-school job digging ditches. The construction company pays you \$5.50 per hour, plus \$10.00 to cover transportation to the construction site, etc. Let $f(x)$ be the total number of dollars you get for working x hours.
    a. Write an equation for $f(x)$ in terms of x.
    b. Find the total numbers of dollars you would get for working 2, 3, and 4 hours
    c. How long would you have to work in one day to make at least \$50? Do you think this could be done in an after-school job?
12. ***Flea Market Problem*** To make money on weekends, you sign a contract to sell house plants at the local flea market. You get to keep \$.60 for each plant you sell, but you must pay a \$20.00 fee to rent the space at the market. Let $d(x)$ be the net number of dollars you make for selling x plants.
    a. Write an equation for $d(x)$ in terms of x.
    b. Find the net number of dollars you make for selling 15, 30, and 50 plants.
    c. How many plants must you sell in order to break even?
13. ***Handicap Race Problem*** Second-graders Randy Miles and Willie Goodspeed run a race. One of them gets a head start, but the other must start at the playground fence. At x seconds after they start, their distances from the fence are:

$$\text{Randy: } f(x) = 7x$$

$$\text{Willie: } g(x) = 5x + 25$$

    where $f(x)$ and $g(x)$ are measured in feet.
    a. How far is each one from the fence when x is 2 seconds? When x is 3 seconds?
    b. How fast is each one going, in feet per second? What part of the equation tells you this number?
    c. Who had the head start, Randy or Willie? How many feet long was the head start?
    d. At what number of seconds, x, will both be the same distance from the fence? How far from the fence will they be at that time?
    e. If the finish line is 85 feet from the fence, who crosses it first? Explain.
14. ***Delay Race Problem*** Molly Bolt and Maida Dart run a race. Both start from the same place, but one of them starts later than the other. Their distances from the starting point x seconds after the first one starts are:

$$\text{Molly: } b(x) = 11(x - 10)$$

$$\text{Maida: } d(x) = 8x$$

    where $b(x)$ and $d(x)$ are measured in feet.

a. How far is each one from the start when x is 15 seconds? When x is 16 seconds?
b. How fast is each one going, in feet per second? What part of the equation tells you this number?
c. Who started first, Molly or Maida? How many seconds was it before the other one started?
d. When the other one started, how far had the first one gone?
e. At what rate does the faster one catch up with the slower one?
f. At what number of seconds, x, will both be the same distance from the start? How far from the start will they be at that time?

15. *Graphing Calculator Problem* On a graphing calculator or computer grapher, plot the graphs of these two functions:

$$f(x) = x^3 - 3x^2 - 12x + 20$$
$$g(x) = x^2 - x - 10$$

Use a "friendly window" for x, with each space corresponding to 0.1 x-units. Then trace to find the x- and y-coordinates of each point where the two graphs intersect each other. Substitute one of these x-values into both equations, and show that the y-values actually are equal. Sketch the resulting graphs on your paper. Why do you suppose f is called a *cubic* function and g is called a *quadratic* function?

14-4 TRIGONOMETRIC FUNCTIONS

In Section 12-7 you used the Pythagorean theorem to find the length of one side of a right triangle when you knew the lengths of the other two sides. In this section you work similar problems, except you work with the measure of the *angles* in the right triangle, as well as the side lengths.

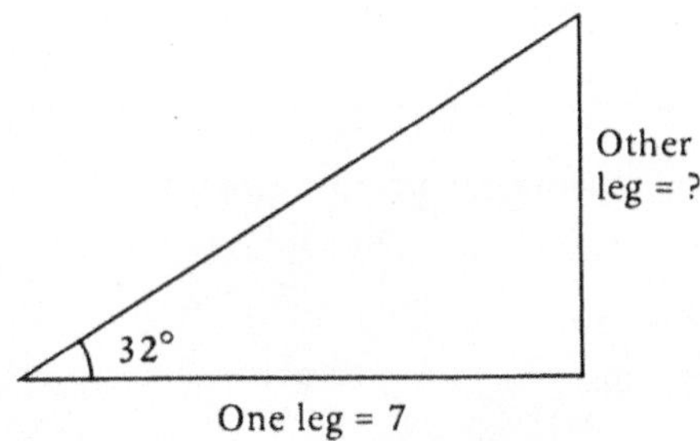

In the right triangle shown, one leg is 7 units long, and an acute angle is of measure 32°. The *ratio* of the legs in a right triangle depends only on the size of the acute angle. You learned this property when you were finding slopes of straight lines. The value of the ratio can be calculated for any angle measure. For 32° it is about 0.6249. So for this triangle,

$$\frac{\text{other leg}}{7} \approx 0.6249.$$

Multiplying each member by 7 gives

$$\text{other leg} \approx 7(0.6249) \qquad \text{other leg} \approx \underline{\underline{4.3743 \text{ units}}}$$

By knowing the ratio for any given angle, you can find lengths of legs in *any* right triangle. These values can be found on a calculator or in a table of values if you do not have a calculator.

If A is an acute angle in a right triangle, then the side opposite A is given the (obvious) name **opposite leg.** The leg next to A is called the **adjacent leg.** The word *adjacent* means *next to*. As you recall, the longest side of a right triangle is called the *hypotenuse*.

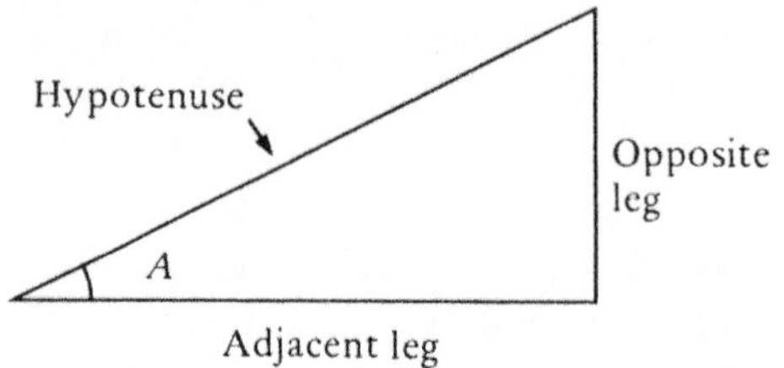

The ratio

$$\frac{\text{opposite leg}}{\text{adjacent leg}},$$

which you were using above, is called the *tangent of angle A,* abbreviated tan A. Other sides of a right triangle also have ratios that depend only on the size of the angle. Two of these are named the *sine of A*, (pronounced the same as *sign*) and the *cosine of A*. These are abbreviated sin A and cos A, respectively, and are defined below. They are called **trigonometric functions** because *trigon* is another name for *triangle,* and *metric* pertains to *measurement*.

DEFINITIONS

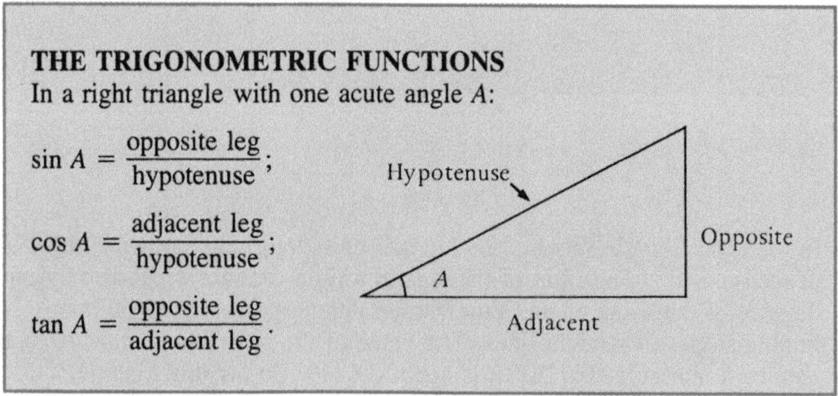

THE TRIGONOMETRIC FUNCTIONS

In a right triangle with one acute angle A:

$$\sin A = \frac{\text{opposite leg}}{\text{hypotenuse}};$$

$$\cos A = \frac{\text{adjacent leg}}{\text{hypotenuse}};$$

$$\tan A = \frac{\text{opposite leg}}{\text{adjacent leg}}.$$

Values of these functions can be found most easily on a calculator. You enter the number of degrees, then press the sin, cos, or tan key. There is also a short table of values on page 681 of this book.

Objectives:

1. Given an angle measure and a side length of a right triangle, find the lengths of the other two sides.
2. Given two side lengths of a right triangle, find the measure of an acute angle.

Cover the answers as you work these examples.

EXAMPLE 1

For the right triangle shown, find:

a. the length of the other leg;

b. the length of the hypotenuse.

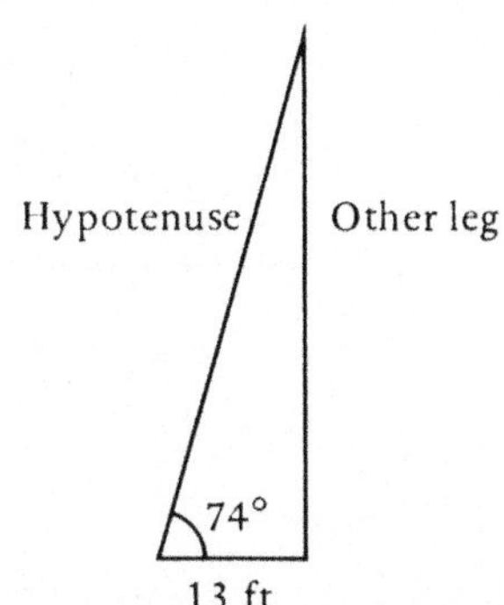

- - - - -

Think These Reasons

a. Let x = length of other leg in feet. Let y = length of hypotenuse in feet. — Define variables.

$\frac{x}{13} = \tan 74°$ — Use the definition of tangent.

$x = 13(\tan 74°)$ — Multiply each member by 13.

$x = 13(3.4874...)$ — By calculator or tables.

$x = 45.336...$ — Do the multiplication.

About 45.34 ft. — Answer the question. Round the answer.

- - - - -

b. $\frac{13}{y} = \cos 74°$ — Use the definition of cosine.

$13 = y(\cos 74°)$ — Multiply each member by y.

$\frac{13}{\cos 74°} = y$ — Divide each member by $\cos 74°$.

$\frac{13}{0.2756\ldots} = y$	By calculator or tables.
$47.163\ldots = y$	Do the division.
About 47.16 ft.	Answer the question. Round.

EXAMPLE 2

The hypotenuse of a right triangle is 50 cm and an acute angle is 19°. Find the measures of the two legs.

- - - - -

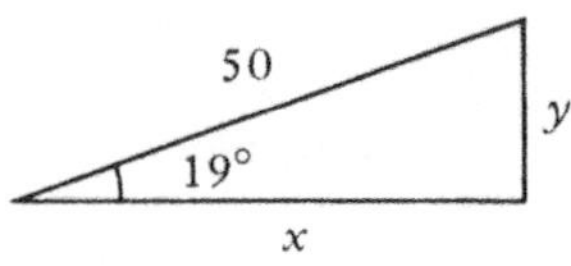

Draw a diagram. Use variables for the unknown lengths.

$\frac{y}{50} = \sin 19°$	Use the definition of sine.
$y = 50(\sin 19°)$	Multiply each member by 50.
$y = 50(0.32556\ldots)$	By calculator or tables.
$y = 16.278\ldots$	Do the multiplication.
About 16.28 cm.	Answer the question. Round.

- - - - -

$\frac{x}{50} = \cos 19°$	Use the definition of cosine.
$x = 50(\cos 19°)$	Multiply each member by 50.
$x = 50(0.9455\ldots)$	By calculator or tables.
$x = 47.2759\ldots$	Do the multiplication.
About 47.28 cm.	Answer the question. Round.

EXAMPLE 3

The hypotenuse of a right triangle is 29 inches long and one leg is 17 inches long. Find the measure of the angle opposite the 17-inch side.

- - - - -

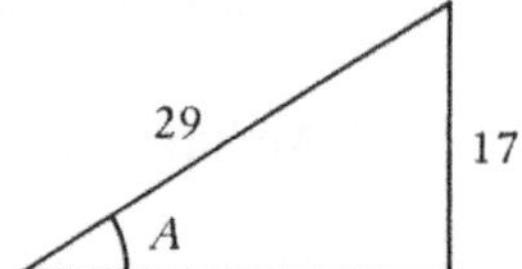

Draw a diagram. Use a variable for the angle measure.

$\sin A = \frac{17}{29}$ — Use the definition of sine.

$\sin A = 0.5862\ldots$ — Do the division.

$A = 35.888\ldots°$ — Leave 0.5862. . . in the calculator. Press [inv] [sin]. Or find the angle in the tables whose sine is closest to 0.5862.

<u>About 35.89°.</u> — Answer the question. Round.

Note: If you use the table of trigonometric functions, find the angle to the nearest degree.

EXAMPLE 4

From a point on the ground, a forester observes that the angle of elevation (see the figure) to the top of a pine tree is 37°. The forester is 123 feet from the base of the tree trunk. About how high is the tree?

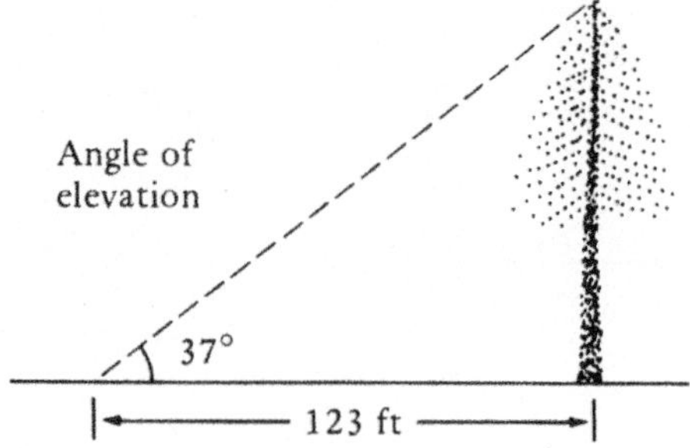

- - - - -

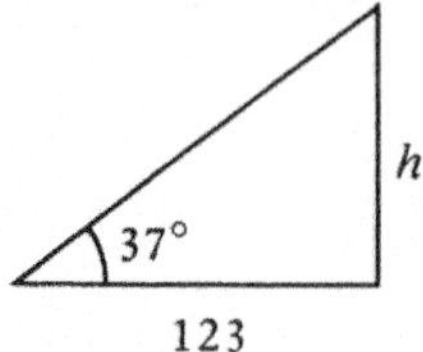

Draw a diagram. Show the known lengths, and use a variable for the height.

$\frac{h}{123} = \tan 37°$ — Use the definition of tangent.

$h = 123(\tan 37°)$ — Multiply each member by 123.

$h = 123(0.753554\ldots)$ — By calculator or tables.

$h = 92.687\ldots$ — Do the multiplication.

<u>About 93 ft high</u> — Answer the question. Round.

ORAL PRACTICE

Tell which lettered side is *opposite* the angle marked, which is *adjacent* to the angle, and which is the *hypotenuse*.

EXAMPLE

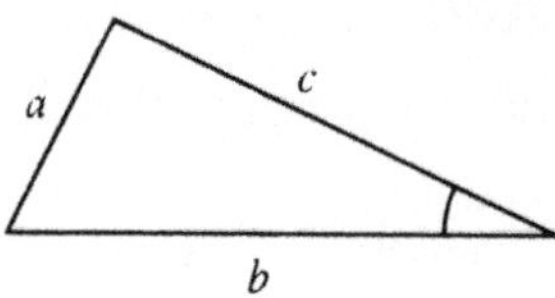

Answers
a is opposite,
c is adjacent,
b is the hypotenuse.

A.

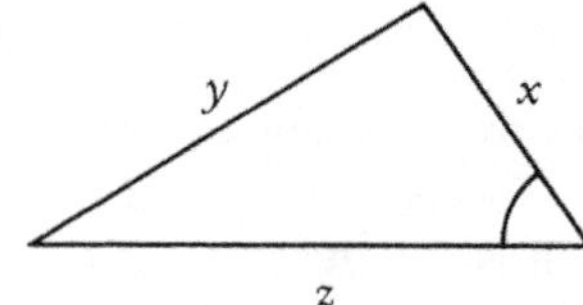

B.

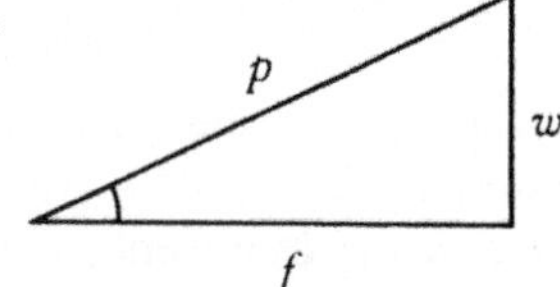

C.

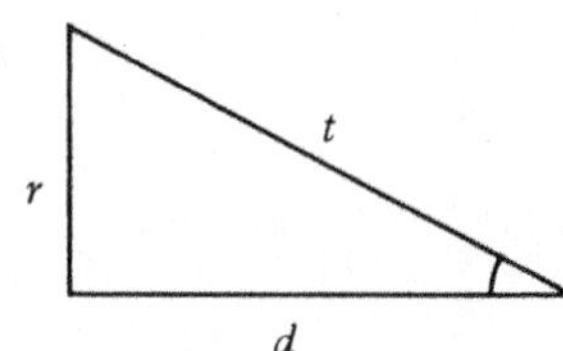

D.

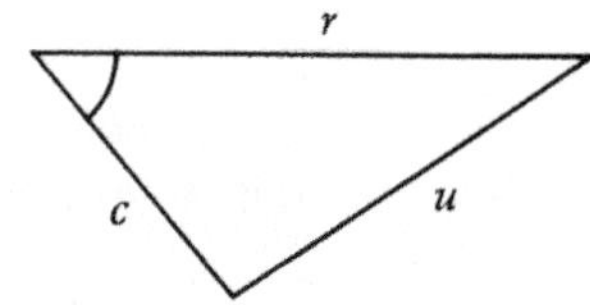

E.

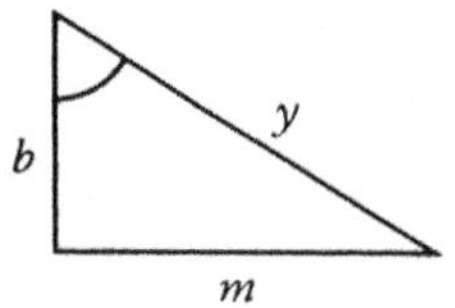

F.

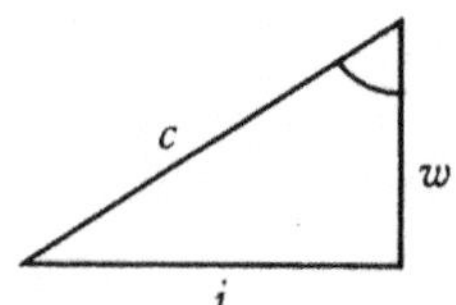

Give sin A, cos A, and tan A.

EXAMPLE

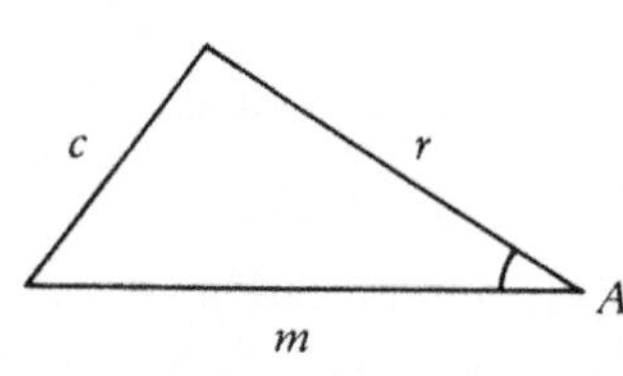

Answers

$\sin A = \frac{c}{m}$

$\cos A = \frac{r}{m}$

$\tan A = \frac{c}{r}$

G.

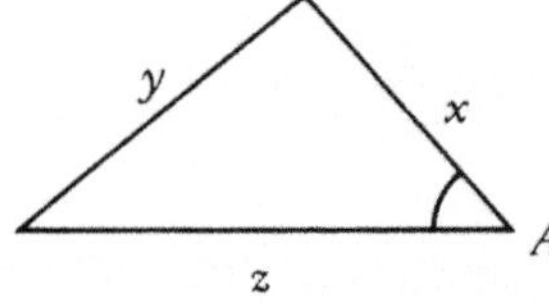

H.

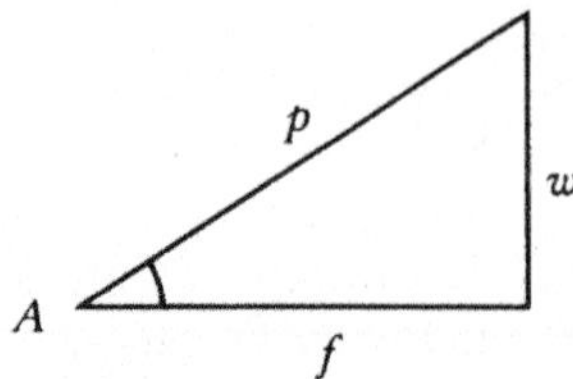

I.

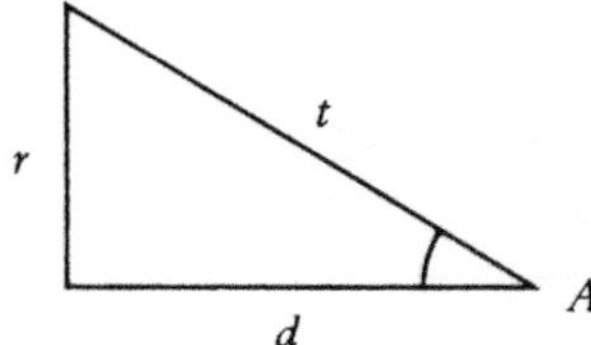

J.

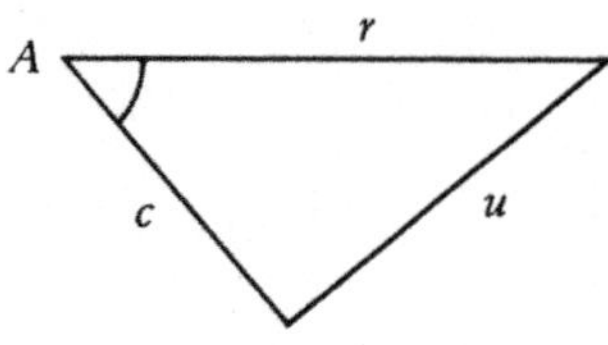

K.

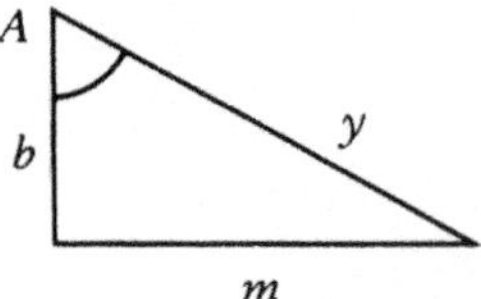

L.

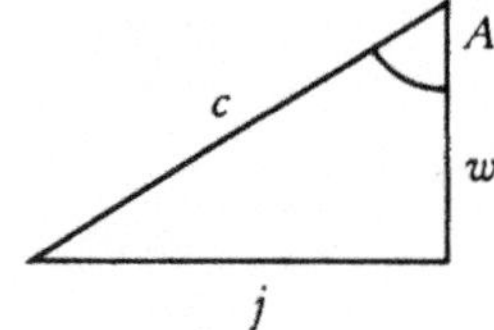

Find the following function values by calculator or from the table.

M. $\sin 14°$ N. $\cos 65°$ O. $\tan 38°$

Find the angle measure to the nearest degree. Use a calculator or the table.

P. $\sin A = 0.8356$ Q. $\cos A = 0.8954$ R. $\tan A = 1.883$

EXERCISE 14-4

For Problems 1 through 10, find the side lengths indicated in the right triangle.

1.

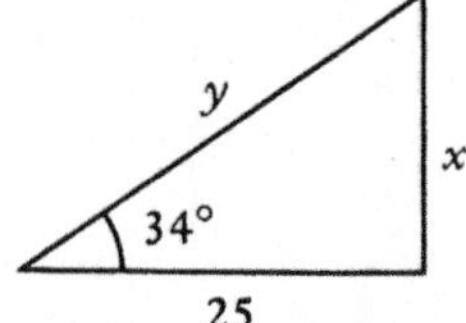

2.

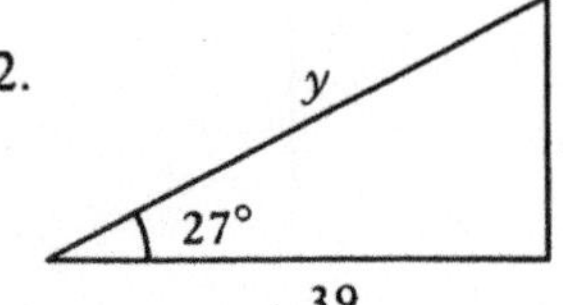

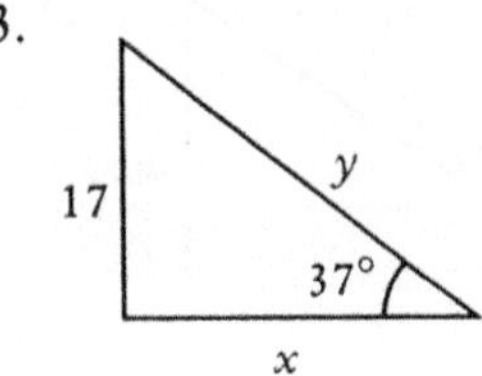

4.

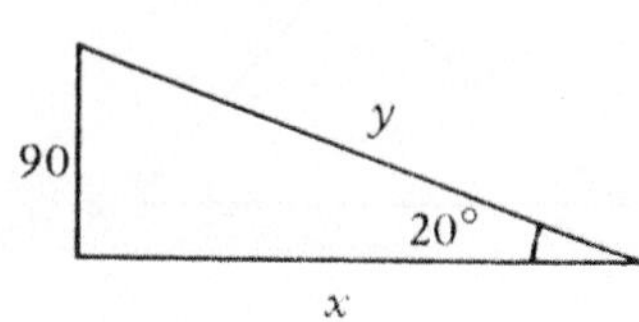

5.

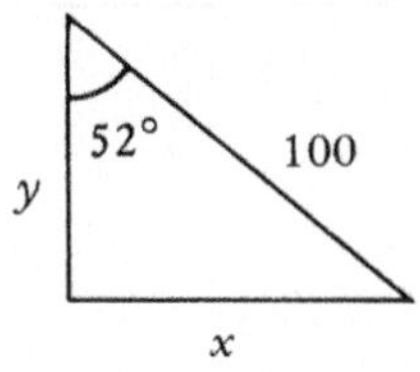

6.

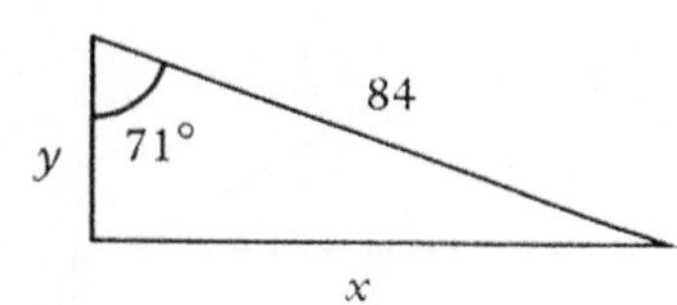

7.

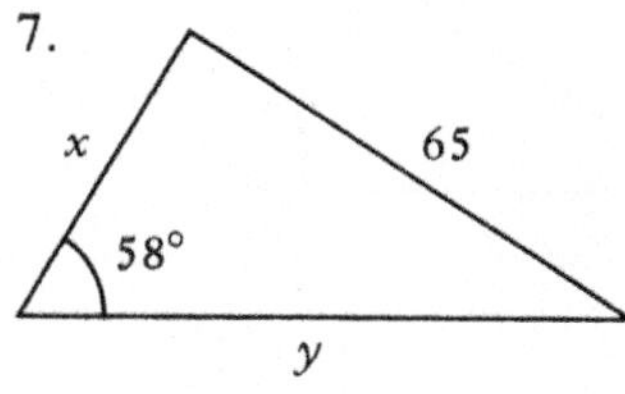

8.

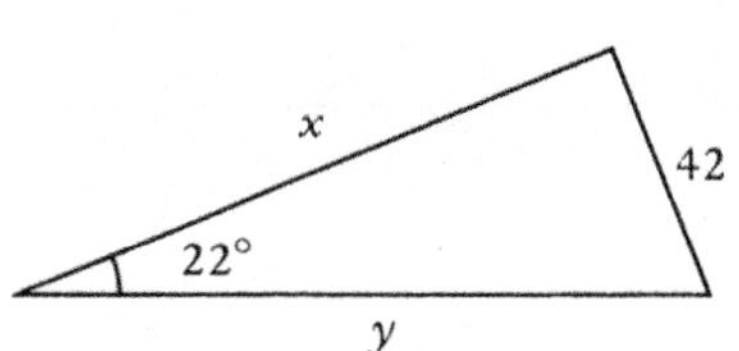

9.

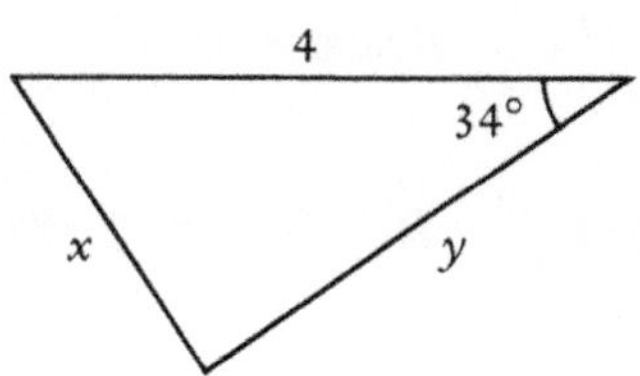

10.

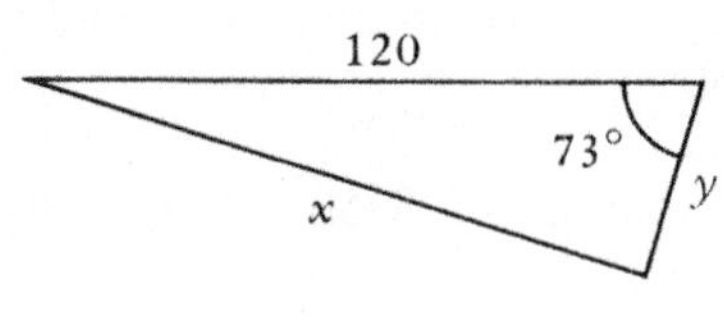

For Problems 11 through 20, find the indicated angle measure in the right triangle.

11.

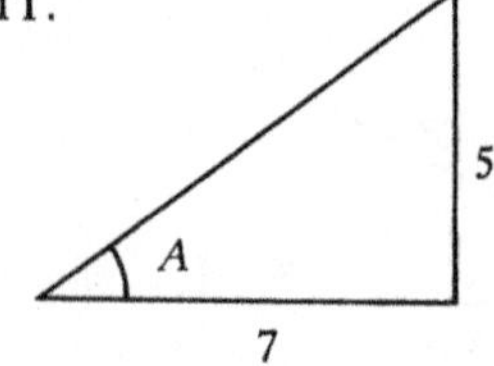

12.

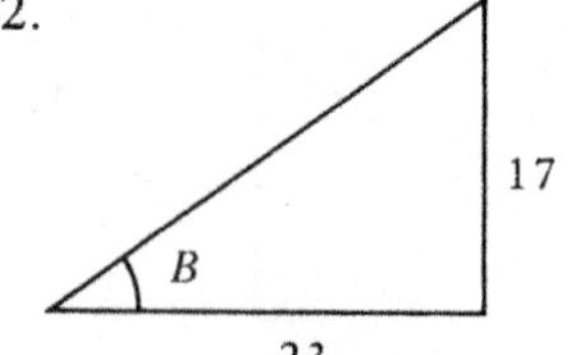

13.

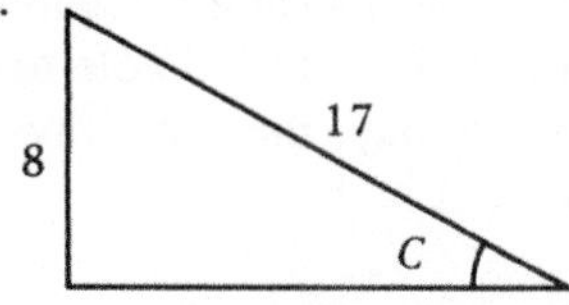

14.

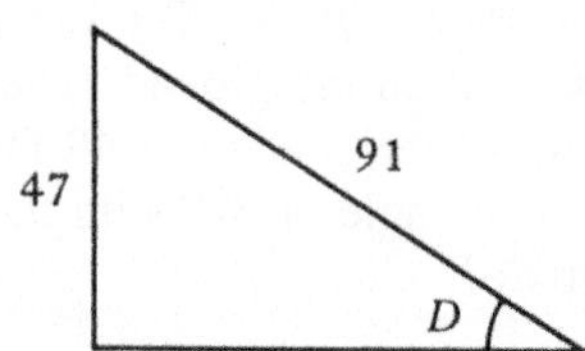

15.

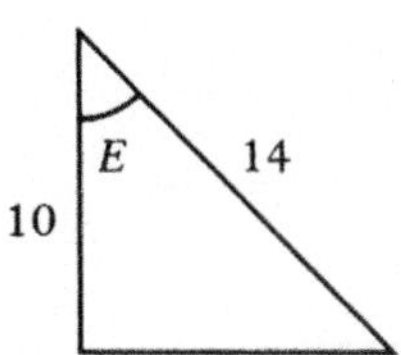

16.

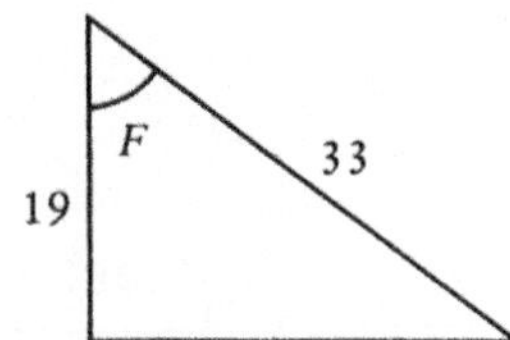

17.

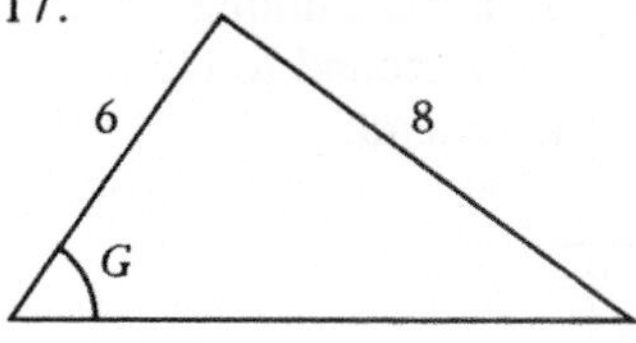

18.

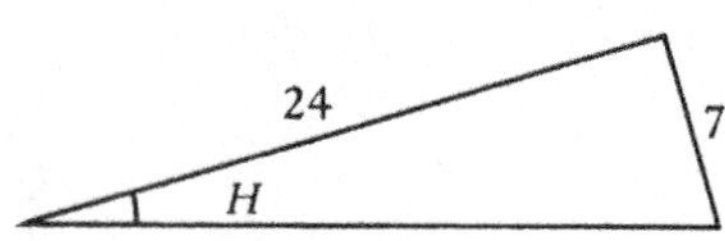

19.

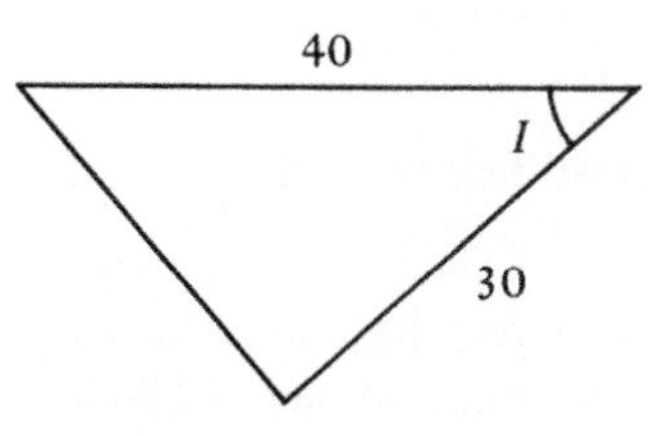

20.

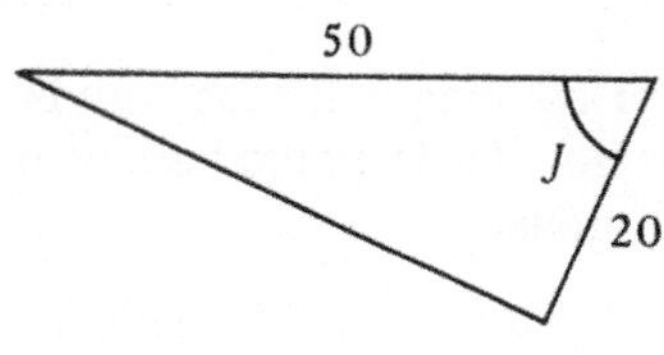

For Problems 21 through 30, answer the questions.

21. ***Building Height Problem*** From a point 78 feet from the base of a building, the angle of elevation to the top of the building is 57°. To the nearest foot, how high is the building?

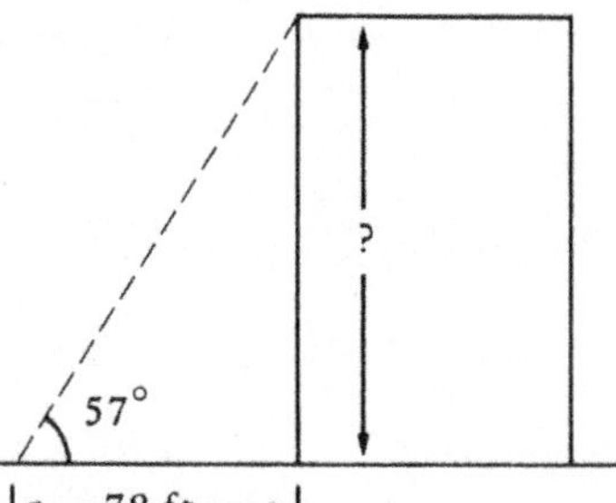

22. *Flagpole Problem* The sun shines on a flagpole, causing a shadow to be cast on the ground. The distance from the base of the pole to the tip of the shadow is 49 feet. At that time of day, the sun's rays make an angle of 38° with the ground. How tall is the flagpole?

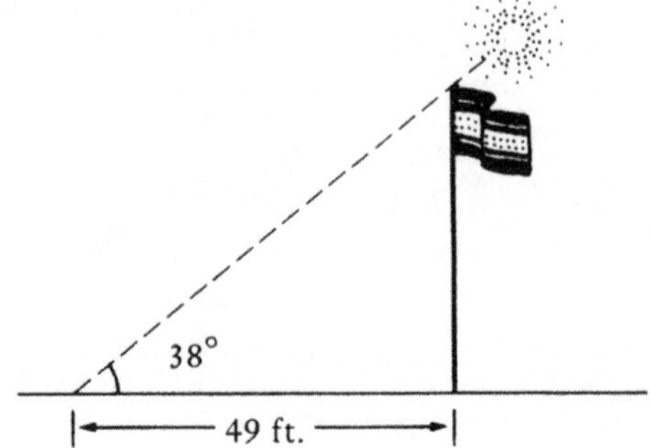

23. *Guy Wire Problem* A 2000-foot-high television transmitting tower is to be supported by guy wires running from the ground to the top. The wires must make an angle of 63° with the ground.

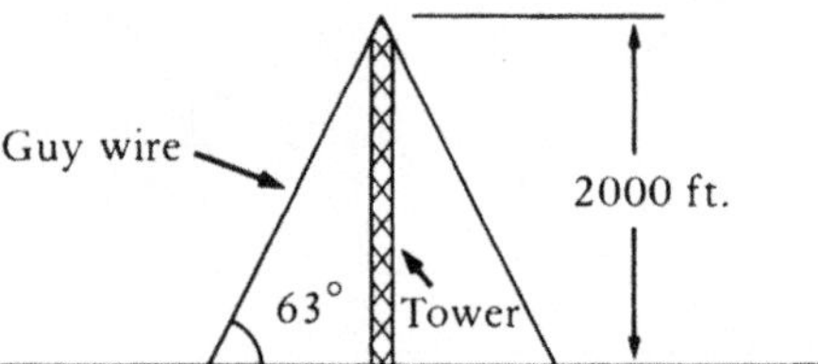

a. How long will each wire be?
b. How far from the base of the tower must they meet the ground?

24. *Ship's Path Problem* Sailors on a ship observe a lighthouse at an angle of 34° to the path of the ship. After the ship has sailed 2000 yards more, the lighthouse is at 90° to the ship's path. How far is the ship from the lighthouse:

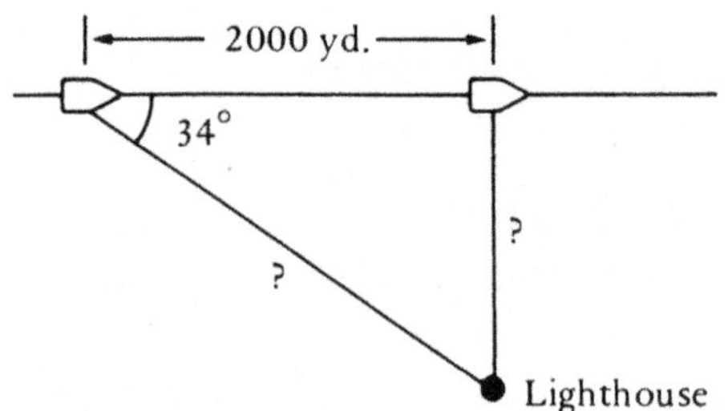

a. at the first sighting; b. at the second sighting?

25. ***Submarine Problem*** A submarine starts on the surface, and dives at an angle of 13° to the surface. It goes diagonally a distance of 890 meters before reaching the bottom.

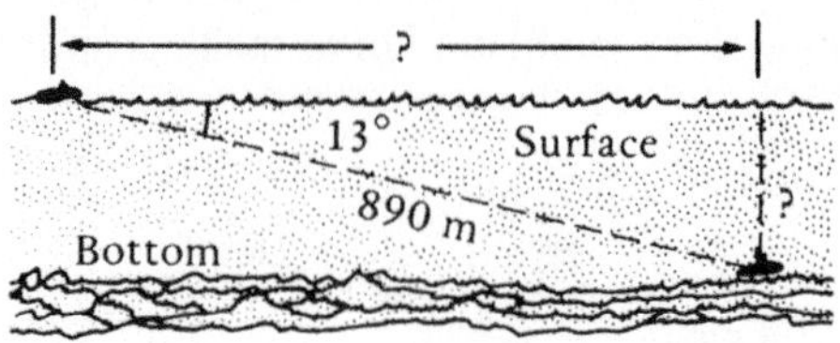

a. How deep is the water where the submarine reaches the bottom?
b. How far is it along the ocean surface from the point where the submarine started to the point directly above where it reached the bottom?

26. ***Shortcut Problem*** Calvin Butterball cuts across the field from his house to Phoebe Small's house, going 482 yards along a path that makes an angle of 28° with Alamo Street. Suppose Calvin walked along the streets instead of across the field.

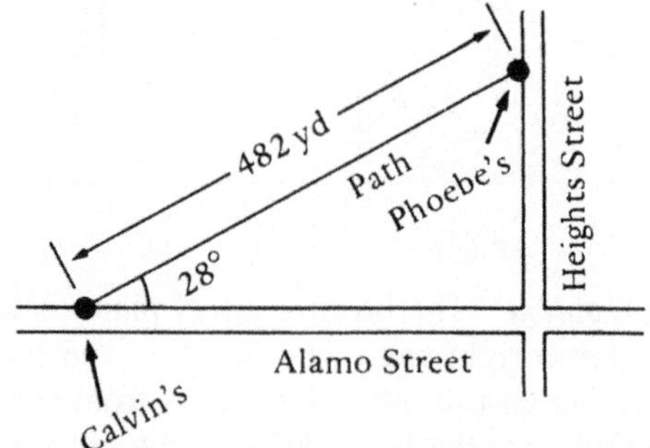

a. How far would he walk along Alamo Street?
b. How far would he walk along Heights Street?
c. How many yards does he save by using the shortcut?

27. ***Volcano Problem*** Haleakela (pronounced hallay-ah′-keh-la′) is a 10,000-foot-high dormant volcano on Maui, Hawaii. The peak is a horizontal distance of only about 30,000 feet from the ocean. At what angle would you have to look up to see the peak if you were standing at the edge of the ocean?

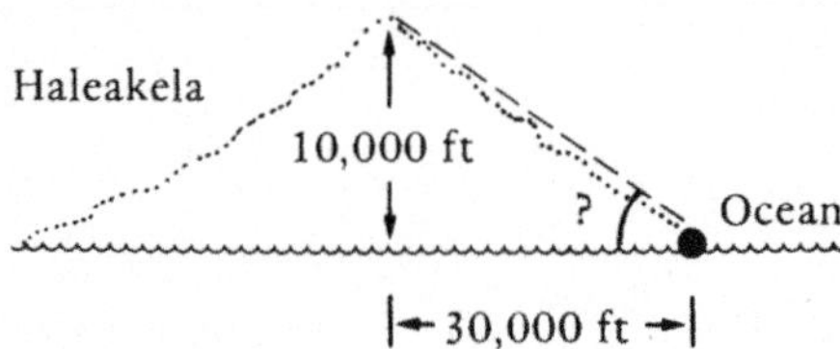

28. ***Hill Angle Problem*** One of the steepest streets in the United States is the 500 block of Highland Drive on Queen Anne Hill in Seattle. If you measure horizontally 70 centimeters from a point on the road surface, you must go down 14.2 centimeters to get back to the surface. What angle does Highland Drive make with the horizontal?

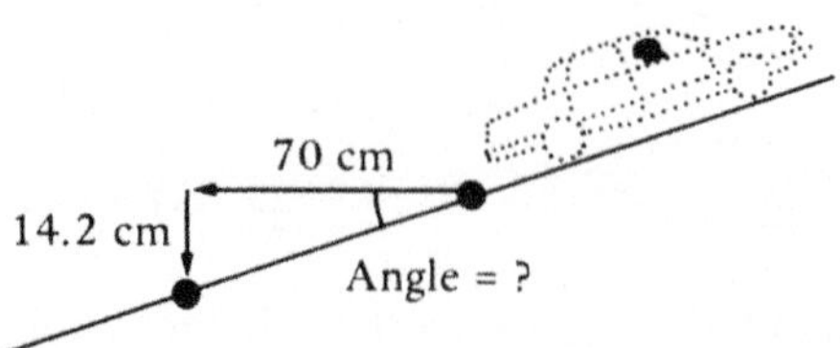

29. ***Fallen Tree Problem*** A tree is struck by lightning and snaps off 34 feet above the ground. The top part of the tree, 117 feet long, rests with the tip on the ground; the broken end rests on the stump, as shown. What angle does the top part of the tree make with the ground?

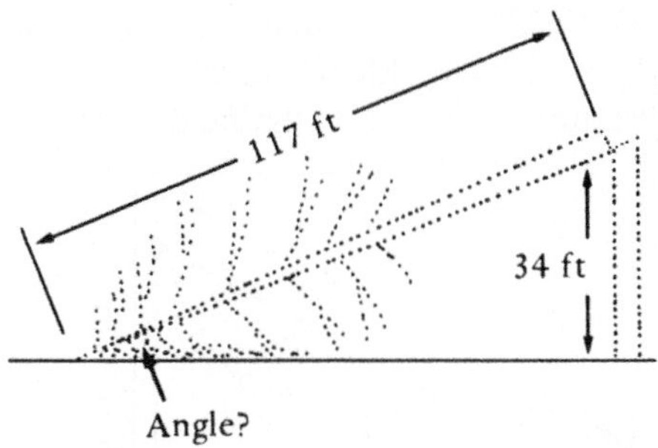

30. ***Grand Piano Problem*** The lid of a grand piano is held open by a prop, which makes a right angle with the lid. The prop is 71 centimeters long, and its base is 140 centimeters from the lid-to-piano hinge. What angle does the lid make with the piano?

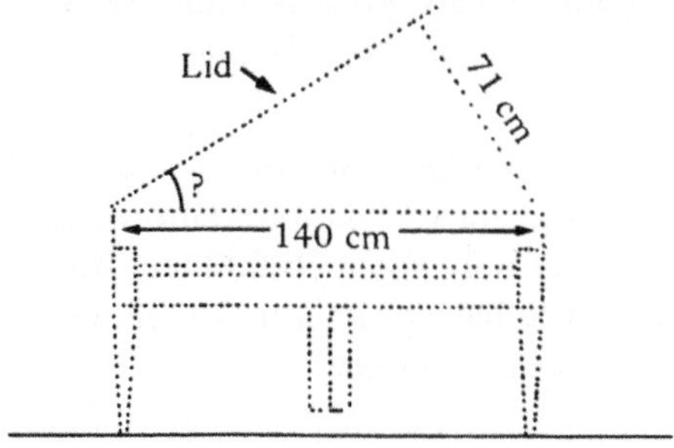

14-5 QUADRATIC FUNCTIONS

In Section 14.1 you learned that a function can have an equation such as

$$y = \text{(an expression involving } x\text{)}.$$

If that expression is quadratic, as in

$$y = x^2 - 6x + 3,$$

then the function is called a *quadratic function*.

The graph of a quadratic function can be drawn by calculating and plotting points. For the function $y = x^2 - 6x + 3$, if x is 5, then

$$y = 5^2 - 6(5) + 3$$

$$y = 25 - 30 + 3$$

$$y = -2$$

Repeating this calculation for other values of x gives the following table of values.

x	y
−1	10
0	3
1	−2
2	−5
3	−6
4	−5
5	−2
6	3
7	10

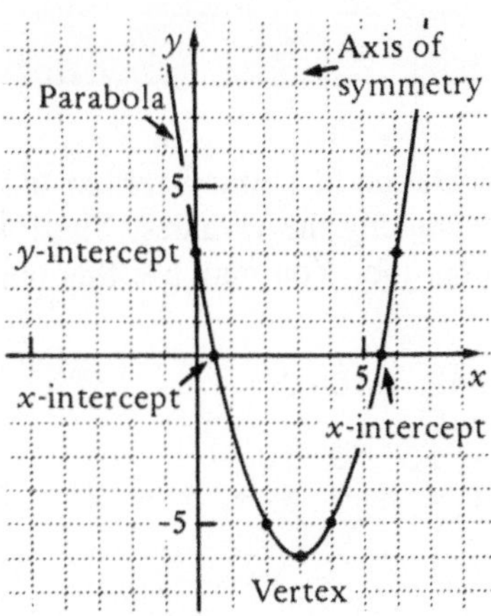

The graph is a U-shaped figure called a **parabola.** The point at which the graph turns around is called the **vertex.** If you were to fold the graph paper along a vertical line through the vertex, the two halves would fit each other. Another way of saying this is to say that the graph is **symmetric** with respect to a line through the vertex. The word comes from *sym* meaning *same,* and *metric,* meaning *measure*. The vertical line through the vertex is called the **axis of symmetry.** As you can see, there are *two* x-intercepts, as well as one y-intercept.

In this section you will plot graphs of quadratic functions by calculating points. You will also calculate the x- and y-intercepts and the vertex.

Objective:

Given the equation of a quadratic function, calculate points, plot the graph, calculate the intercepts, and find the vertex.

For your future reference, here is a formal definition of quadratic function.

DEFINITION

QUADRATIC FUNCTION

A **quadratic function** is a function with an equation of the form

$$y = \text{a quadratic expression.}$$

That is, the equation has the form

$$\boxed{y = ax^2 + bx + c}$$

for some constants a, b, and c, where $a \neq 0$.

Since the actual computation of points is rather tedious, it makes sense to use a computer for evaluating the y-values. The following is a BASIC program that will do the job. You may use this one, or write one of your own.

```
10 PRINT "TYPE A,B,C"
20 INPUT A,B,C
30 FOR X = - 10 TO 10
40 LET Y = A * X * X + B * X + C
50 PRINT X,Y
60 NEXT X
70 END
```

The following are some worked examples that show how to accomplish the objective. You may either try them on your own, or simply read them to get ideas about how to work the problems in Exercise 14-5.

EXAMPLE 1

For the quadratic function $y = x^2 - 4x - 5$:

a. calculate points;
b. plot the graph;
c. find the x- and y-intercepts;

d. find the vertex.

Think These Reasons

a.

x	y
-10	135
-9	112
-8	91
-7	72
-6	55
-5	40
-4	27
-3	16
-2	7
-1	0
0	-5
1	-8
2	-9
3	-8
4	-5
5	0
6	7
7	16
8	27
9	40
10	55

Use the computer program to calculate values.

b. Plot the graph. Note that it is not necessary to plot all the points the computer calculates. Just pick those that fit graph paper.

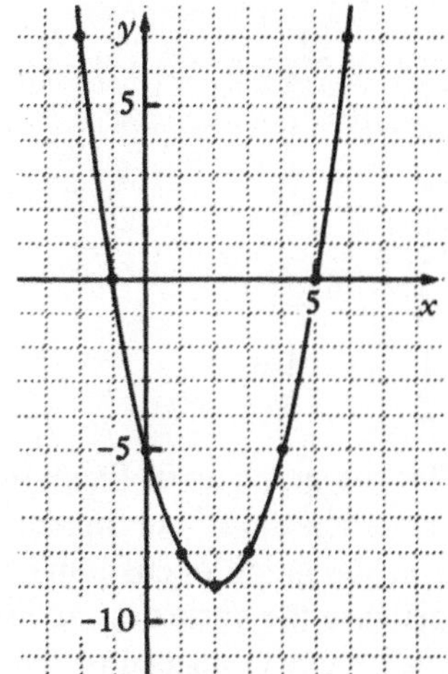

c. x-intercepts are -1 and 5.

The x-intercepts are the values of x when $y = 0$. In this case they can be found in the table.

y-intercept is -5.

The y-intercept is the value of y when $x = 0$. This, too, is in the table.

d. $x\text{-coord.} = \frac{1}{2}(-1 + 5)$
$= 2$

The axis of symmetry goes halfway between the two x-intercepts. So its x-coordinate is the *average* of the two intercepts.

$y\text{-coord.} = 2^2 - 4(2) - 5$

Substitute 2 for x and evaluate y.

$= 4 - 8 - 5$

$= -9$

Vertex: (2, −9)

Write the answer.

EXAMPLE 2

For the quadratic function $y = -x^2 - 3x + 5$:

a. calculate points;

b. plot the graph;

c. find the x- and y-intercepts;

d. find the vertex.

- - - - -

a.

x	y
-5	-5
-4	1
-3	5
-2	7
-1	7
0	5
1	1
2	-5

Use the computer program. Only part of the data is shown.

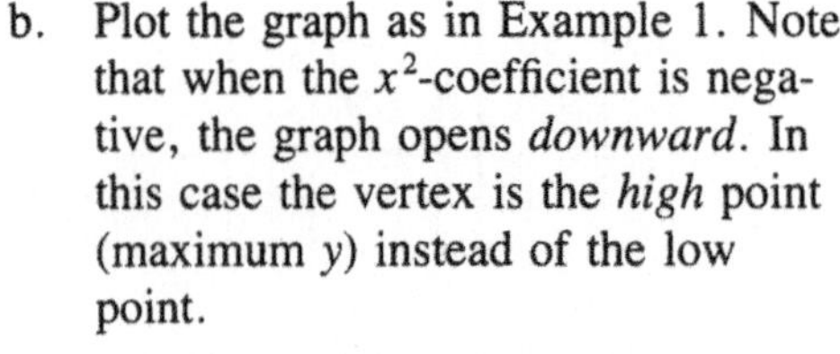

b. Plot the graph as in Example 1. Note that when the x^2-coefficient is negative, the graph opens *downward*. In this case the vertex is the *high* point (maximum y) instead of the low point.

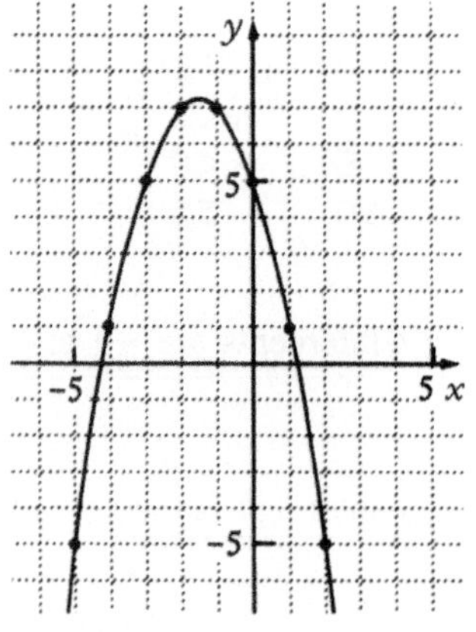

c. $0 = -x^2 - 3x + 5$ — Set $y = 0$.

$x = \dfrac{3 \pm \sqrt{9 - 4(-1)(5)}}{2(-1)}$ — Use the Quadratic Formula.

$x \approx 1.19$ or -4.19 — Do the computations.

x-intercepts are 1.19 and −4.19. — Write the answer.

$y = -0^2 - 3(0) + 5$ — Substitute 0 for x and evaluate y.

$y = 5$

y-intercept is 5. — Write the answer.

d. $x = \frac{1}{2}(-4.19 + 1.19)$ — Average the x-intercepts.

$= -1.5$ — Do the computations.

$y = -(-1.5)^2 - 3(-1.5) + 5$ — Substitute -1.5 for x and evaluate y.

$y = -2.25 + 4.5 + 5$

$y = 7.25$

Vertex: $(-1.5, 7.25)$ — Write the answer.

EXAMPLE 3

For the quadratic function $y = 6x^2 + 15x + 11$:

a. calculate points;

b. plot the graph;

c. find the x- and y-intercepts;

d. find the vertex.

-----

a. Use the computer program to calculate points.

x	y	x	y
-8	275	3	110
-7	200	4	167
-6	137	5	236
-5	86		
-4	47		
-3	20		
-2	5		
-1	2		
0	11		
1	32		
2	65		

b.

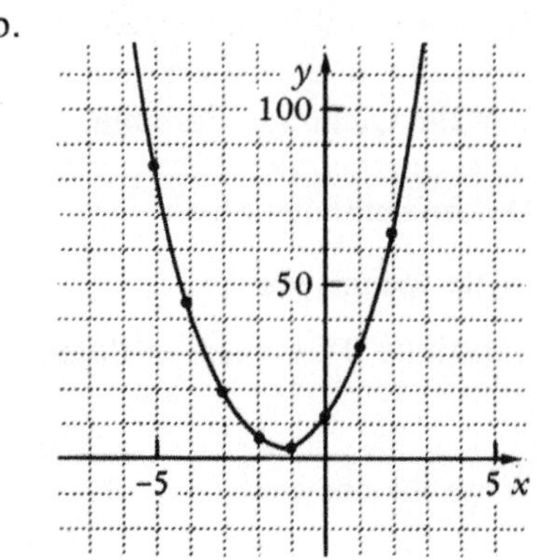

Plot the graph. Since the graph rises so steeply, you might *compress* the vertical scale as shown. Use a normal scale on the x-axis.

- - - - -

c. $0 = 6x^2 + 15x + 11$ — Set $y = 0$.

$$x = \frac{-15 \pm \sqrt{225 - 4(6)(11)}}{2(6)}$$

Use the Quadratic Formula.

$$x = \frac{-15 \pm \sqrt{-39}}{12}$$

Do the computations.

No x-intercepts.

Since $\sqrt{-39}$ is not a real number, there are *no* values of x when $y = 0$. This is obvious, because the graph does not cross the x-axis.

$$y = 6(0^2) + 15(0) + 11$$

Substitute 0 for x and evaluate y.

$$y = 11$$

y-intercept is 11. — Write the answer.

- - - - -

d. $$x = \frac{1}{2}\left(\frac{-15 + \sqrt{-39}}{12} + \frac{-15 - \sqrt{-39}}{12}\right)$$

Average the values of x from part (c).

$$= \frac{1}{2}\left(\frac{-15 + \sqrt{-39} - 15 - \sqrt{-39}}{12}\right)$$

Add the fractions.

$$= \frac{1}{2}\left(\frac{-30}{12}\right)$$

If you treat $\sqrt{-39}$ as a number, the radicals have a sum of 0. See the note at the end of the example.

$$= -1.25$$

Do the computations.

$y = 6(-1.25)^2 + 15(-1.25) + 11$ Substitute -1.25 for x and evaluate y.

$y = 1.625$

Vertex: $(-1.25, 1.625)$ Write the answer.

Note: From part (d) of Example 3, you can see that for

$$y = 6x^2 + 15x + 11,$$

the vertex is at

$$x = \frac{1}{2}\left(\frac{-30}{12}\right),$$

which reduces to

$$x = \frac{-15}{12}$$

Looking at the original equation, -15 is the *opposite* of the x-coefficient and 12 is *twice* the x^2-coefficient. This pattern is true for *all* quadratic functions.

CONCLUSION

x-COORDINATE OF THE VERTEX
For the quadratic function $y = ax^2 + bx + c$, the x-coordinate of the vertex is

$$\boxed{x = \frac{-b}{2a}}$$

You can use this fact to find the vertex *quickly*, even if there are no x-intercepts.

ORAL PRACTICE

Find the x-coordinate of the vertex using $x = \dfrac{-b}{2a}$.

EXAMPLE

$y = 3x^2 + 12x - 13$ *Ans*: $x = -2$

A. $y = 5x^2 + 30x - 7$

B. $y = 3x^2 - 6x + 4$

C. $y = 2x^2 - 12x + 5$

D. $y = x^2 + 8x + 9$

E. $y = 0.5x^2 + 7x - 3$

F. $y = 0.2x^2 - 20x - 6$

Find the y-intercept.

G. $y = 5x^2 + 30x - 7$

H. $y = 3x^2 - 6x + 4$

I. $y = 2x^2 - 12x + 5$

J. $y = x^2 + 8x + 9$

K. $y = 0.5x^2 + 7x - 3$

L. $y = 0.2x^2 - 20x - 6$

EXERCISE 14-5

For each of the following quadratic functions:

a. pick values of x and calculate values of y;

b. plot the graph;

c. find the x- and y-intercepts;

d. find the vertex.

1. $y = x^2 - 6x + 5$
2. $y = x^2 - 8x + 7$
3. $y = x^2 + 5x - 2$
4. $y = x^2 + 3x - 5$
5. $y = -0.4x^2 + 3x + 2$
6. $y = -0.7x^2 + 2.8x + 4$
7. $y = x^2 - 3x + 5$
8. $y = x^2 - 5x + 7$
9. $y = -x^2 + 6x - 10$
10. $y = -x^2 + 4x - 6$
11. $y = 8x^2 - 20x - 37$
12. $y = 5x^2 + 19x - 41$

14-6 SOLVING QUADRATIC INEQUALITIES BY COMPLETING THE SQUARE

In Chapter 9 you drew number-line graphs of linear inequalities and absolute value inequalities such as

$$3x + 2 \geq 7 \quad \text{or} \quad |x - 5| < 19.$$

In this and the next section, you will do the same thing for quadratic inequalities such as

$$x^2 - 6x + 4 < 0.$$

The main purpose of these two sections is to give you a review of most of the techniques of algebra while you learn something new.

The inequality above can be solved by completing the square. The first step is to add -4 to each member, leaving a space on the left.

$$x^2 - 6x \qquad < -4$$

To find the number that completes the square, take *half* the coefficient of x, and then *square* it. Half of -6 is -3, and $(-3)^2$ is 9. So you add 9 to each member.

$$x^2 - 6x + 9 < 5$$

The left member equals $(x - 3)^2$. The -3 is half of the x-coefficient: $\frac{1}{2}(-6)$. So you can write

$$(x - 3)^2 < 5.$$

Now you can take the square root of each member. For this, you need to know that taking the square root of each member does not reverse the order of the inequality. The following examples show you why.

$$2 < 7 \qquad\qquad 64 > 25$$

$$\sqrt{2} < \sqrt{7} \qquad\qquad \sqrt{64} > \sqrt{25}$$

$$1.41 < 2.65 \quad \text{True!} \qquad\qquad 8 > 5 \quad \text{True!}$$

The numbers *do* remain in the same order.

SQUARE ROOT PROPERTY OF ORDER
For any nonnegative numbers a and b,

$$\text{if} \quad a > b, \quad \text{then} \quad \sqrt{a} > \sqrt{b};$$

$$\text{if} \quad a < b, \quad \text{then} \quad \sqrt{a} < \sqrt{b}.$$

That is, you can take the square root of each member of an inequality without changing the order (as long as neither member is negative).

Using this property, you can take the square root of each member of the above inequality.

$$\sqrt{(x - 3)^2} < \sqrt{5}$$

Recalling that $\sqrt{(\text{number})^2}$ equals $|\text{number}|$, you can write

$$|x - 3| < \sqrt{5}.$$

From here on, it is a problem of the kind you worked in Section 9.4. Since the inequality sign is <, the quantity $x - 3$ must be *between* $-\sqrt{5}$ and $\sqrt{5}$.

$$\sqrt{5} < x - 3 < \sqrt{5}$$

Adding 3 to each member gives

$$3 - \sqrt{5} < x < 3 + \sqrt{5}.$$

By calculator, $3 - \sqrt{5} = 0.763 \ldots$. Since x must be *greater* than this number, the rounding must be *upward*. Similarly, $3 + \sqrt{5} = 5.236 \ldots$, which must be rounded *downward* since x is *less* than $3 + \sqrt{5}$.

$$0.77 < x < 5.23.$$

The graph is as follows.

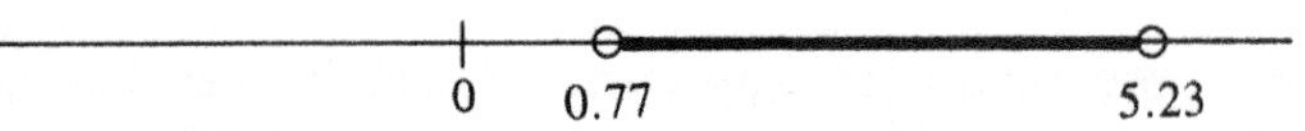

Objective:

Given a quadratic inequality such as $x^2 - 6x + 4 < 0$, solve it and graph its solution set.

Cover the answers as you work these examples.

EXAMPLE 1

Solve and graph $x^2 + 10x - 17 > 0$.

- - - - -   - - - - -

	Think These Reasons
$x^2 + 10x - 17 > 0$	Write the given inequality.
$x^2 + 10x \quad > 17$	Make space to complete the square.
$x^2 + 10x + 25 > 42$	Complete the square: $(\frac{1}{2} \cdot 10)^2 = 25$.
$(x + 5)^2 > 42$	Write the left member as a square.
$\lvert x + 5 \rvert > \sqrt{42}$	Take the square root of each member.
$x + 5 > \sqrt{42}$ or $x + 5 < -\sqrt{42}$	$x + 5$ is *not* between $\sqrt{42}$ and $-\sqrt{42}$.

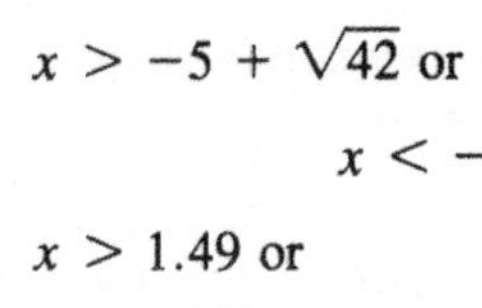

$x > -5 + \sqrt{42}$ or $x < -5 - \sqrt{42}$	Add -5 to each member.
$x > 1.49$ or $x < -11.49$	Do the arithmetic. Round in the direction of the inequality.

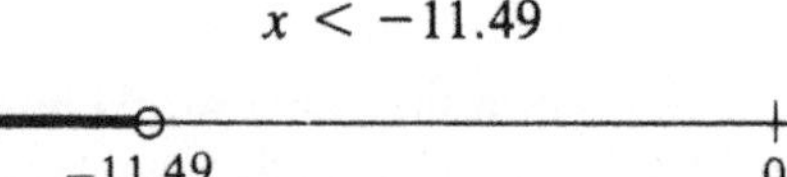

EXAMPLE 2

Solve and graph $x^2 - 13 \le 8x + 58$.

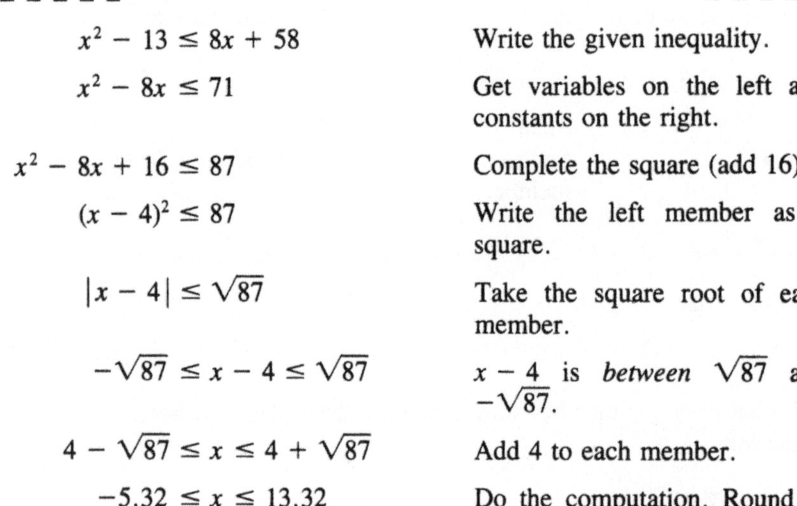

$x^2 - 13 \le 8x + 58$	Write the given inequality.
$x^2 - 8x \le 71$	Get variables on the left and constants on the right.
$x^2 - 8x + 16 \le 87$	Complete the square (add 16).
$(x - 4)^2 \le 87$	Write the left member as a square.
$\lvert x - 4 \rvert \le \sqrt{87}$	Take the square root of each member.
$-\sqrt{87} \le x - 4 \le \sqrt{87}$	$x - 4$ is *between* $\sqrt{87}$ and $-\sqrt{87}$.
$4 - \sqrt{87} \le x \le 4 + \sqrt{87}$	Add 4 to each member.
$-5.32 \le x \le 13.32$	Do the computation. Round in the direction of the inequality.

−5.32 0 13.33

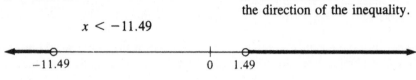

EXAMPLE 3

Solve and graph $x^2 + 14x + 60 < 0$.

$x^2 + 14x + 60 < 0$	Write the given inequality.
$x^2 + 14x \qquad < -60$	Make space to complete the square.
$x^2 + 14x + 49 < -11$	Complete the square (add 49).
$(x + 7)^2 < -11$	Write the left member as a square.

$\therefore S = \emptyset$

A square is never less than a negative number.

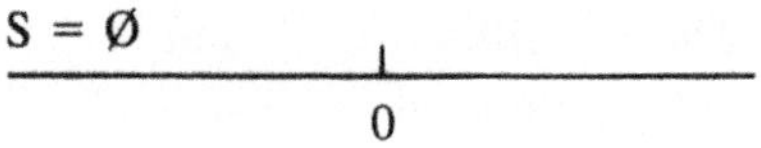

Draw the graph. It is an *empty* number line. Write $S = \emptyset$ on the number line for clarity.

Note: If the inequality were $(x + 7)^2 > -11$, then the graph would be the entire number line. Squares are *always* greater than negative numbers.

ORAL PRACTICE

Give the *two* steps that must be done in completing the square.

EXAMPLE 1

$x^2 - 12x + 7 > 0$

Answer:
Subtract 7 from each member. Add 36 to each member.

A. $x^2 - 6x + 2 > 0$

B. $x^2 + 8x - 7 \geq 0$

C. $x^2 - 10x - 3 < 0$

D. $x^2 + 4x - 3 \leq 0$

E. $x^2 - 2x - 5 < 0$

F. $x^2 + x - 7 \geq 0$

Tell what the *right* member should be after the square has been completed on the left.

EXAMPLE 2

$x^2 + 12x - 5 < 0$

Answer:
41.

G. $x^2 + 6x - 4 \leq 0$

H. $x^2 - 8x + 3 < 0$

I. $x^2 + 10x + 6 \geq 0$

J. $x^2 - 4x + 13 > 0$

K. $x^2 + 2x + 7 \geq 0$

L. $x^2 - x - 1 < 0$

EXERCISE 14-6

Transform the inequalities by completing the square, then sketch the graph.

1. $x^2 - 12x + 17 > 0$

2. $x^2 - 16x + 41 < 0$

3. $x^2 + 6x + 7 \leq 0$
4. $x^2 + 8x + 9 \geq 0$
5. $x^2 - 10x - 51 \geq 0$
6. $x^2 - 4x - 26 \leq 0$
7. $x^2 - 14x + 33 < 0$
8. $x^2 - 18x + 65 > 0$
9. $x^2 + 2x + 3 \leq 0$
10. $x^2 + 6x + 10 \geq 0$
11. $x^2 - 6x + 12 > 0$
12. $x^2 - 10x + 30 < 0$
13. $x^2 - 5x - 14 < 0$
14. $x^2 - 7x - 30 > 0$
15. $x^2 + 7x - 2 \geq 15$
16. $x^2 + 9x - 5 \leq 30$
17. $x^2 + 3x \leq 5x + 11$
18. $x^2 - 7x \geq 4 - 2x$
19. $6x + 3 < x(5 + x)$
20. $7 - 2x > x(x - 11)$

14-7 SOLVING QUADRATIC INEQUALITIES BY THE QUADRATIC FORMULA

There is a relationship between plotting graphs of quadratic *functions,* as in Section 14-5, and graphing quadratic *inequalities,* as in Section 14-6. To see what the relationship is, first look at the graph of $y = 3x^2 - 7x - 15$. The values of y may be calculated by the computer program of Section 14-5.

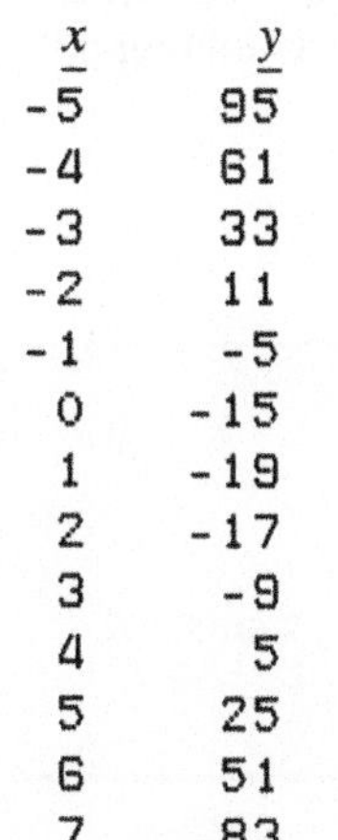

x	y
-5	95
-4	61
-3	33
-2	11
-1	-5
0	-15
1	-19
2	-17
3	-9
4	5
5	25
6	51
7	83

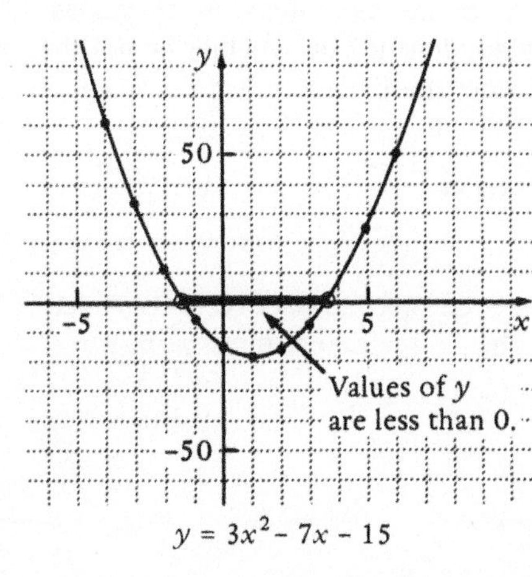

$y = 3x^2 - 7x - 15$

From the graph, you can see that when x is between the two x-intercepts, the values of y are *less* than zero. The inequality

$$y < 0$$

is equivalent to the inequality

$$3x^2 - 7x - 15 < 0,$$

because y is equal to $3x^2 - 7x - 15$. The relationship between the two kinds of problem is that the *end points* of the graph of $3x^2 - 7x - 15 < 0$ are the same as the *x-intercepts* of $y = 3x^2 - 7x - 15$.

By considering graphs of quadratic functions, you can discover that there are only four possible ways a quadratic inequality graph could look.

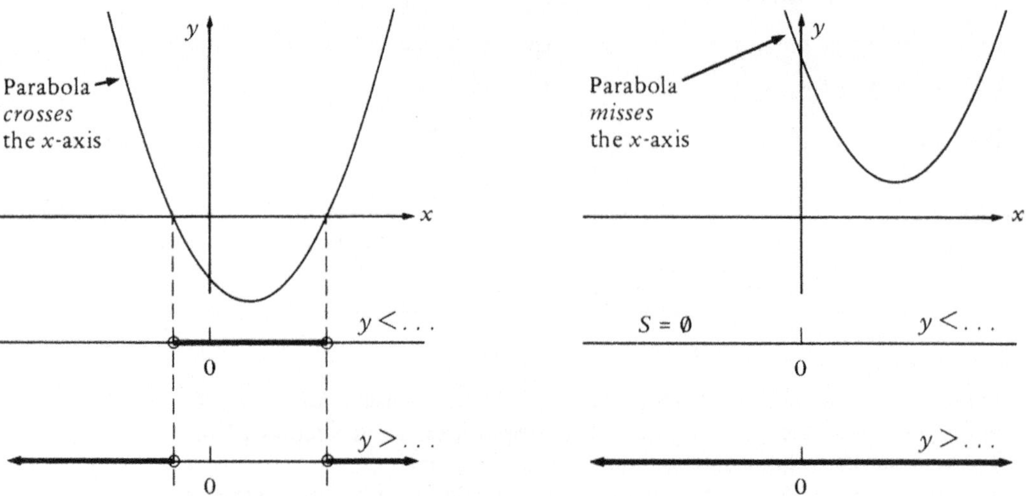

The inequality graph is one of these choices: *between* the end points, *beyond* the end points, *no* values, or *all* values. The particular graph in any given problem depends on whether or not the parabola has x-intercepts and on whether the inequality sign is $<$ or $>$.

CONCLUSION

GRAPHS OF QUADRATIC INEQUALITIES

(*Note:* The x^2-coefficient must be *positive*.)

If $ax^2 + bx + c > 0$, then the graph is *outside* the end points.

If $ax^2 + bx + c < 0$, then the graph is *between* the end points.

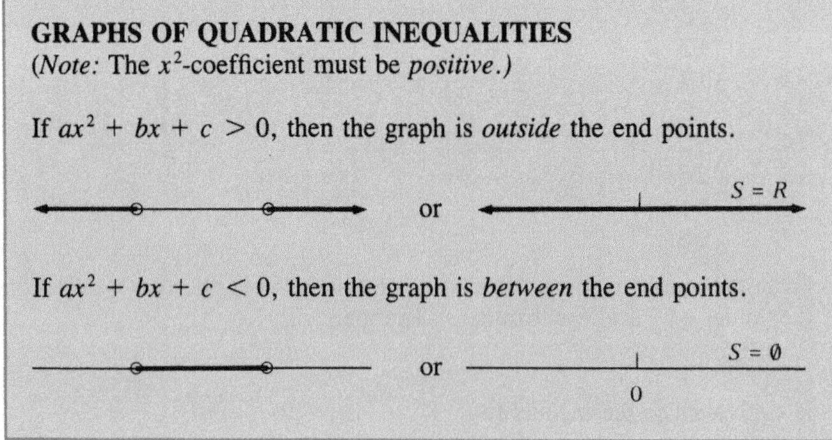

There is an easy way to draw the graph of a quadratic inequality without having to draw the parabola or to memorize the conclusion. You simply calculate the endpoints using the quadratic formula (or factoring) and then substitute a value of x to find out which of the four possible graphs it is. The following examples show you how to do this.

Objective:

Given a quadratic inequality, find the end points (if any) and draw the graph.

Study the following examples. If you like, you may try some of them on your own before uncovering the answers.

EXAMPLE 1

Find the end points and draw the graph: $3x^2 - 7x - 15 < 0$.

\- - - - -   - - - - -

	Think These Reasons
$3x^2 - 7x - 15 < 0$	Write the given inequality.
$x = \dfrac{7 \pm \sqrt{49 - 4(3)(-15)}}{2(3)}$	Use the quadratic formula to find the end points.
$x = \dfrac{7 \pm \sqrt{229}}{6}$	Do the arithmetic.
$\underline{\underline{x \approx 3.69 \quad \text{or} \quad -1.36}}$	Finish the arithmetic.
$3(0)^2 - 7(0) - 15 \overset{?}{<} 0$	Substitute a value for x. (0 is the easiest to substitute.)
$-15 \overset{?}{<} 0$ True.	
$\therefore$ 0 *is* included.	$-15 < 0$ is a *true* statement.
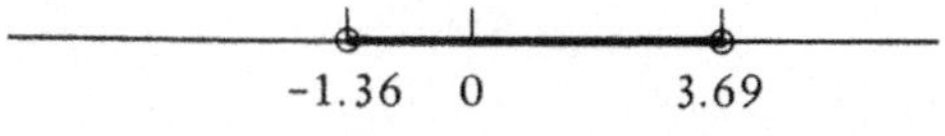	Draw the end points. Shade the portion *including* 0.

Note: This problem is the same as the one at the beginning of this section.

EXAMPLE 2

Find the end points and draw the graph: $x^2 - 6x + 13 > 0$.

\- - - - -   - - - - -

$x^2 - 6x + 13 > 0$ — Write the given inequality.

$x = \dfrac{6 \pm \sqrt{36 - 4(1)(13)}}{2(1)}$ — Use the Quadratic Formula to find the end points.

$x = \dfrac{6 \pm \sqrt{-16}}{2}$ — Do the arithmetic.

No end points. — $\sqrt{-16}$ is not a real number.

$0^2 - 6(0) + 13 \overset{?}{>} 0$ — Substitute a value for x.

$13 \overset{?}{>} 0$ True.

$\therefore$ 0 *is* included. — $13 > 0$ is a *true* statement.

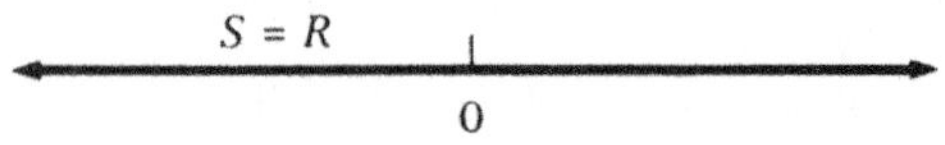

Draw the graph. Since 0 *is* included and there are *no* end points, the graph is *all* real numbers. Write $S = R$, where R means *real numbers*.

EXAMPLE 3

Find the end points and draw the graph: $x^2 - 6x + 13 < 0$.

\- - - - -

This is the same as Example 3, except the sign is <.
So there will still be no end points.
Upon substituting 0 for x, you get

$0^2 - 6(0) + 13 \overset{?}{<} 0$ — Substitute a value for x.

$13 \overset{?}{<} 0$ False.

$\therefore$ 0 is *excluded.* — $13 < 0$ is a *false* statement.

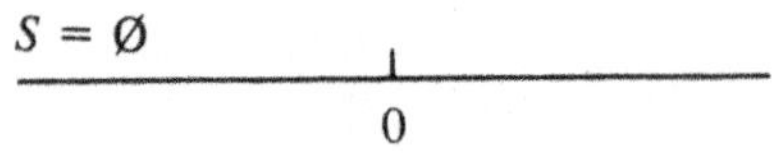

Draw the graph. Since 0 is *not* included, and there are *no* end points, the graph is the *empty* set. Write $S = \emptyset$ for clarity.

EXAMPLE 4

Find the end points and draw the graph: $2x^2 - 6x + 1 \le 7x^2 - 10$.

\- - - - -

$2x^2 - 6x + 1 \le 7x^2 - 10$ — Write the given inequality.

$-5x^2 - 6x + 11 \le 0$ — Make the right member equal 0.

$$x = \frac{6 \pm \sqrt{36 - 4(-5)(11)}}{2(-5)}$$

Use the Quadratic Formula to find the end points.

$$x = \frac{6 \pm \sqrt{36 - 4(-5)(11)}}{2(-5)}$$

Use the Quadratic Formula to find the end points.

$$x = \frac{6 \pm \sqrt{256}}{-10}$$

Do the arithmetic.

$$\underline{\underline{x = -2.2 \quad \text{or} \quad 1}}$$

Finish the arithmetic.

$$-5(0)^2 - 6(0) + 11 \overset{?}{\leq} 0$$

Substitute a value for x in the simplified inequality.

$11 \overset{?}{\leq} 0$ False.

$\therefore$ 0 is *not* included.

$11 \leq 0$ is a *false* statement.

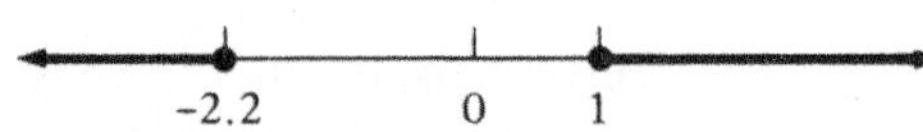

Plot the end points. Shade the portion *excluding* 0.

EXAMPLE 5

Rectangular Building Problem A rectangular building is to be built on a 30-meter by 50-meter rectangular lot in such a way that there is a path x meters wide all the way around the building. The building can occupy at most 60% of the area of the lot. What is the range of possible values of x?

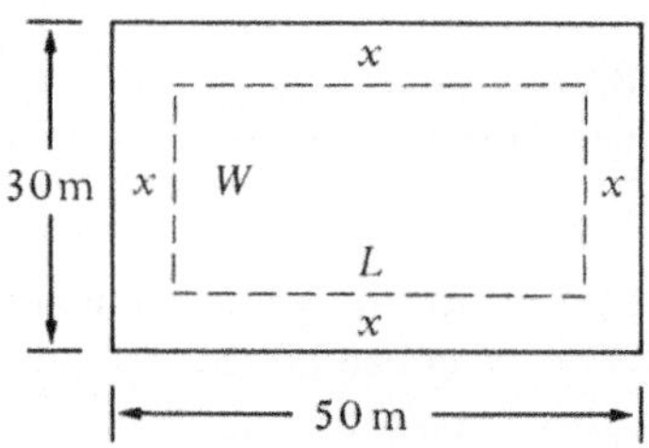

- - - - -   - - - - -

Let L = length of building in meters.
Let W = width of building in meters.

$\therefore LW \leq 0.6(30)(50)$ — Building area is at most 60% of lot area.

$LW \leq 900$ — Multiply.

$L = 50 - 2x$
$W = 30 - 2x$ — Write L and W in terms of x.

$(50 - 2x)(30 - 2x) \leq 900$ — Substitute for L and W.

$1500 - 160x + 4x^2 \leq 900$ — Multiply.

$4x^2 - 160x + 600 \leq 0$ — Make right member zero.

$x^2 - 40x + 150 \le 0$	Do any obvious simplifications.
$x = \dfrac{40 \pm \sqrt{1000}}{2}$	Use the Quadratic Formula to find the end points.
$x \approx 35.81$ or 4.19	Do the computations.
$0^2 - 40(0) + 150 \overset{?}{\le} 0$	Substitute a value for x.
$150 \overset{?}{\le} 0$ False.	
$\therefore$ 0 is *excluded.*	$150 \le 0$ is a *false* statement.
0 4.19 35.81	Plot the end points. Shade the portion *excluding* 0.
$\underline{\underline{4.19 \le x < 15}}$	Answer the question: x must be less than 15 since the walkway can be no more than half the width of the lot. Also, x cannot *equal* 15, or there would be no building!

ORAL PRACTICE

The graphs show the end points for the given inequalities. Tell in words what the graph will look like. You can do this by substituting 0 for x, as in the examples. Your answer should be one of *between, beyond, all real numbers,* or *empty set.*

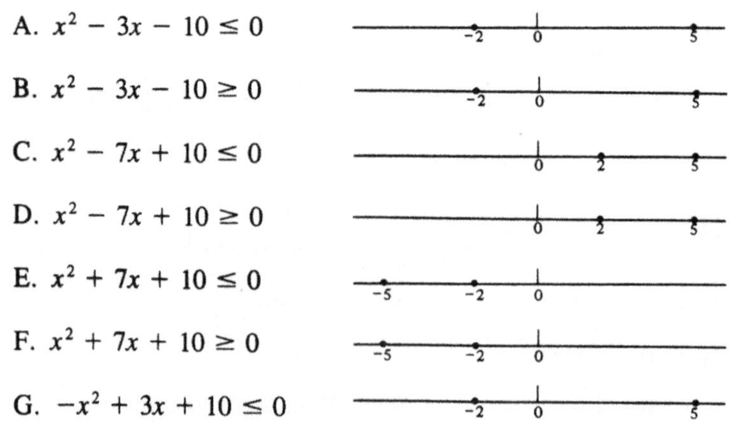

H. $-x^2 + 3x + 10 \geq 0$

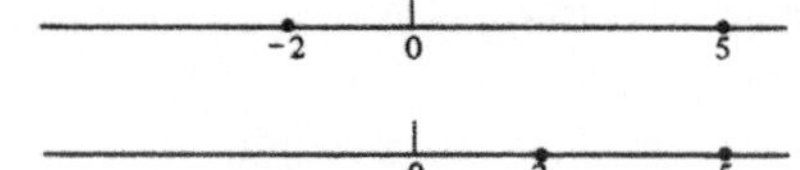

I. $-x^2 + 7x - 10 \leq 0$ 0 2 5

J. $-x^2 + 7x - 10 \geq 0$ 0 2 5

K. $x^2 + 3x + 10 \leq 0$ 0 none

L. $x^2 + 3x + 10 \geq 0$ 0 none

M. $-x^2 + 3x - 10 \leq 0$ 0 none

N. $-x^2 + 3x - 10 \geq 0$ 0 none

EXERCISE 14-7

For Problems 1 through 20, find the end points, if any, and sketch the graph.

1. $3x^2 + 5x - 19 > 0$
2. $7x^2 + 10x - 23 < 0$
3. $2x^2 - 7x - 43 \leq 0$
4. $3x^2 - 8x - 87 \geq 0$
5. $x^2 - 9x + 14 > 0$
6. $x^2 - 11x + 24 < 0$
7. $30x - 5x^2 + 47 \leq 0$
8. $79 - 7x^2 - 13x \geq 0$
9. $10x^2 + 11x + 12 \leq 0$
10. $-5x^2 - 11x + 20 \geq 0$
11. $6 + x^2 - 3x > 0$
12. $x^2 + 10 + 3x < 0$
13. $0.3x^2 - 5x - 18.9 < 0$
14. $0.9x^2 - 20x + 98.6 > 0$
15. $4x^2 - 28x + 49 > 0$
16. $25x^2 - 80x + 64 \leq 0$
17. $3x^2 - 20x \leq x^2 - 47$
18. $5x^2 + 22x > 2x^2 + 100$
19. $7x + 30 < x(x + 8)$
20. $4x + 4.8 \geq x(x + 2.3)$

For Problems 21 through 30, work the problem and answer the questions.

21. *Archery Problem* Mark Wright shoots an arrow into the air with an initial upward velocity of 70 meters per second (m/sec). Let t be the number of seconds since the arrow was shot. You recall that its distance up, d meters is

$$d = rt - 5t^2,$$

where r is the initial upward velocity. For what values of t will the arrow be:

a. more than 200 m high;
b. at most 60 m high;
c. higher than 300 m?

22. ***Diving Board Problem*** A diver leaves the 3-meter springboard with an initial upward velocity of 2 meters per second (m/sec). For what range of times will the diver be:

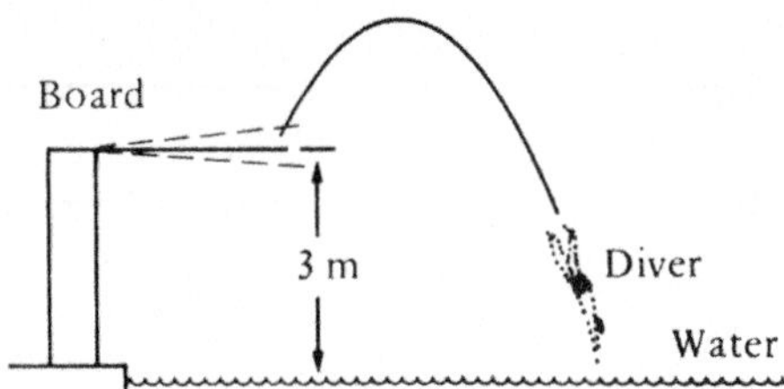

a. above the level of the board;
b. less than 5 meters above the board;
c. above the water?

23. ***Rectangle Problem*** The length of a rectangle is 5 meters plus the width. Write an inequality stating that the area of the rectangle is at least 37 square meters. Then solve the inequality to find the range of possible values of the width.

24. ***Another Rectangle Problem*** The width of a rectangle is the length minus 3 feet. Write an inequality stating that the area is at most 40 square feet. Then solve the inequality to find the range of possible values of the length.

25. ***Carpet Problem*** A room 8 meters by 6 meters is to have carpet installed in one corner, leaving a strip of floor x meters wide around the other two sides.

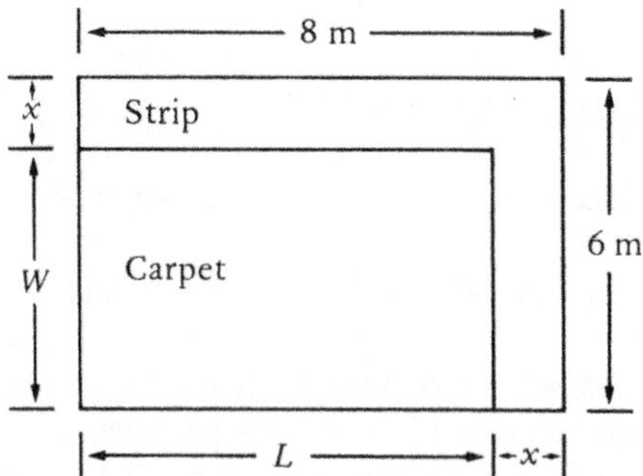

a. Write expressions for the length and for the width of the carpet in terms of x.

b. Write an expression for the area of the carpet in terms of x.
c. Write an inequality stating that the area of the carpet is at least 70% of the area of the room. Solve the inequality to find the possible values of x.
d. What values of x make the carpet no more than half of the area of the room?

26. ***Sidewalk Problem*** A sidewalk of uniform width, x, is to be built on two sides of a corner lot, as shown. The lot was originally 70 ft by 100 ft.

a. Write expressions in terms of x for the length and width of the part of the lot remaining.
b. Write an expression for the area.
c. The city agrees to leave at least 90% of the area of the original lot after the sidewalk is built. What is the range of permissible values of x?

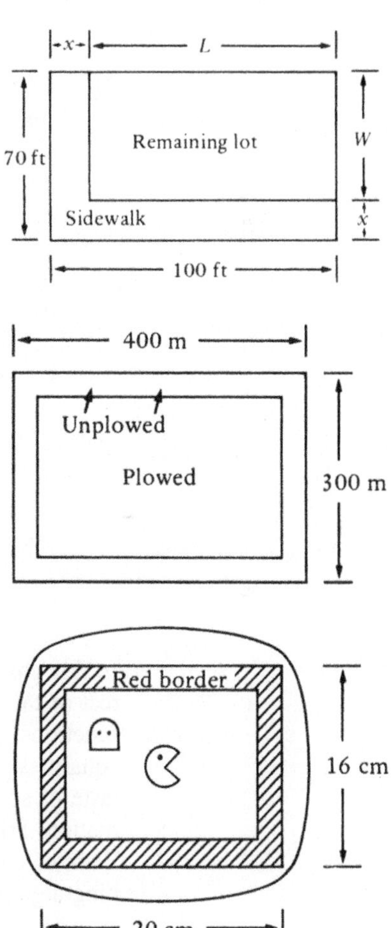

27. ***Roadway Problem*** A farmer wishes to leave unplowed a strip of land around the four sides of his field. The strip is to be of uniform width, and is to leave at least 95% of the area of the 400-m by 300-m field available for plowing. What is the range of permissible strip widths?

28. ***Video Game Problem*** A new video game is being designed. A red border of uniform width is to surround the screen, and any player running into this border will be "zapped." The author of the game wishes to have at least 90% of the area of the 20 cm by 16 cm screen left inside the red border. What is the range of possible values for the strip width?

29. ***Parabolas and Quadratic Inequalities Problem***
a. Plot the graph of $y = x^2 - 3x - 5$.
b. Solve the inequality $x^2 - 3x - 5 \geq 0$.
c. Show the solution of the inequality in part (b) on the graph of part (a).

30. ***Quadratics Computer Graphics Problem*** In this problem you will plot various quadratic functions by computer to see the effects of the coeffcients a, b, and c in the equation $y = ax^2 + bx + c$. You may use any suitable graphing program to draw the graph of this equation.
    a. Plot $y = 0.1x^2$ and $y = 0.3x^2$ on the same axes. What is the effect of the coefficient a on the shape of the graph?
    b. Plot $y = 0.1x^2$ and $y = 0.1x^2 - 5$ on the same set of axes. Does the coefficient c affect the shape of the graph, or just its position? In what way?
    c. Plot $y = 0.3x^2$ and $y = 0.3x^2 - 3x$ on the same set of axes. Does the coefficient b affect the shape of the graph, or just its position? In what way?

31. ***Absolute Value Computer Graphics Problem*** An absolute value function has the general equation $y = |ax + b| + c$, where the coeffients a, b, and c stand for constants. Use a plotting program to do the following.
    a. Plot $y = |x|$. The BASIC for |number| is ABS(number). You should find that the graph is a "V" with its point at the origin.
    b. Plot $y = |3x|$. How does the graph differ from $y = |x|$?
    c. Plot $y = |x + 4|$. How does the graph differ from $y = |x|$?
    d. Plot $y = |x| - 5$. How does the graph differ from $y = |x|$?
    e. Plot $y = |3x + 4| - 5$. By comparing the graph with the others you have plotted, tell how the coefficients a, b, and c influence the graph of $y = |ax + b| + c$.

14-8 CHAPTER REVIEW AND TEST

In this chapter you have recalled a lot of algebraic techniques from the rest of the course. You used these techniques to analyze problems about functions, direct and inverse variation, triangles, quadratics, and inequalities. In the process, you have both reviewed this course and had a taste of some mathematics yet to come. Functions are important in mathematics. Triangles are analyzed both in geometry and in trigonometry. Even calculus depends on the foundation you have acquired in this beginning algebra course.

The test below touches on materials of this chapter. There is also a problem that lets you extend your knowledge in a new direction—to *fractional* inequalities.

CHAPTER TEST

1. Tell the difference in each case:
   a. Graph of a function and a graph of a non-function.
   b. What y does as x increases in a *direct* variation function and in an *inverse* variation function.
   c. General equation and particular equation.
   d. $\sin A$ and $\cos A$.

2. Tell what is meant by each of the following.
   a. Leg *adjacent* to a given angle in a right triangle.
   b. Proportionality constant.
   c. Quadratic function.
   d. Parabola.
   e. Vertex.

3. Plot the graph of the function for the given values of x and connect the points appropriately.
   a. $y = 0.6x + 2$, for all integers $-3 \le x \le 3$.
   b. $y = |x - 2|$, for all integers $-1 \le x \le 5$.
   c. $y = \frac{6}{x}$, for $x = 1, 2, 3,$ and 6.

4. ***Food Problem*** The number of pounds of food you need to take on a camping trip varies directly with the number of days you will be gone. Suppose that a 10-day trip requires 17 pounds of food.
   a. Find the proportionality constant. Write the particular equation expressing pounds of food in terms of days.
   b. How much food should you pack for a 28-day trip?
   c. How many days can you camp if you take 51 pounds of food?

5. ***Music Practice Problem*** Clara Nett figures that the number of mistakes she will make in playing a piece of music varies inversely with the number of minutes she practices that piece. After 20 minutes of practice, she finds that she makes 4 mistakes.
   a. Find the proportionality constant. Write the particular equation expressing number of mistakes in terms of minutes of practice.
   b. Clara would like to practice long enough so that she makes only *one* mistake. How long would this be?
   c. If Clara had had only 5 minutes to practice the piece, how many mistakes might she have made?

6. a. Find the length of side x.

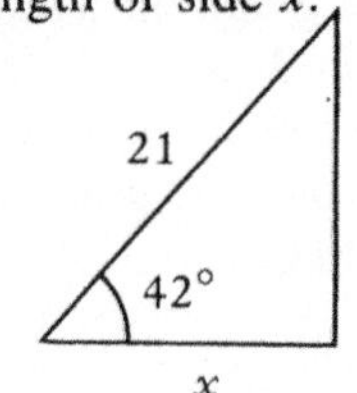

   b. Find the measure of angle A.

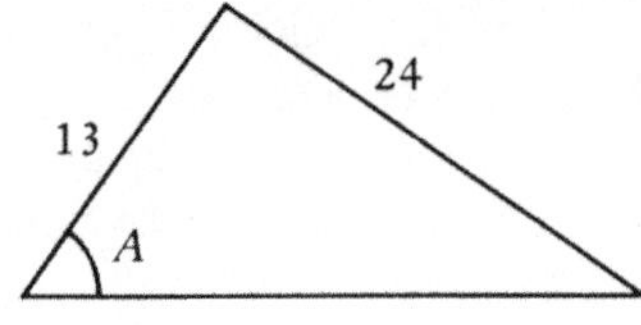

7. For the quadratic function $y = 3x^2 - 14x + 8$.
   a. Evaluate y if x is -5.
   b. Solve for x if y is more than 19. Draw the graph.
   c. Solve for x if y is at most 125. Draw the graph.
   d. Solve for x if y is at least -20. Draw the graph.

8. Sketch the graph of a parabola showing how the graph of $ax^2 + bx + c < 0$ could be:
   a. between two end points;
   b. beyond two end points;
   c. the empty set;
   d. all real numbers.

9. ***Baseball Problem*** Pop Dupp hits a baseball with an initial upward velocity of 23 meters per second. The top of the grandstands is 20 meters above where Pop hit the ball. For what time interval will the ball be at least as high as the top of the grandstands?

10. ***Rectangle Problem*** A rectangle is 7 meters by 9 meters. A new rectangle is formed that is x meters longer and x meters narrower than the original one. For what values of x will the new rectangle have less than 80% of the area of the original rectangle?

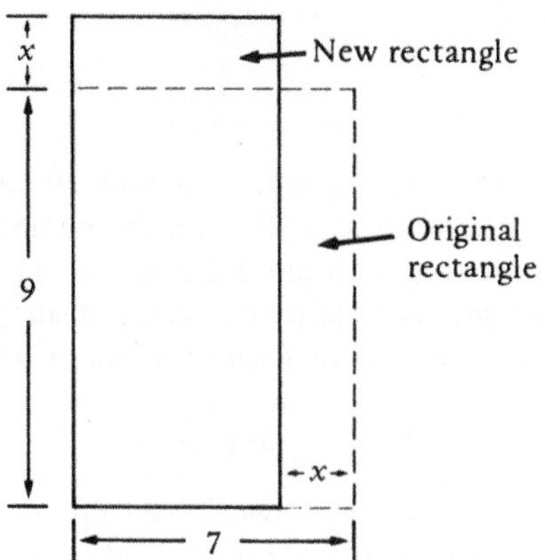

11. ***Fractional Inequality Problem*** To solve an inequality like

$$\frac{x + 5}{x - 2} < x + 4,$$

you must first multiply each member by $(x - 2)$ to get rid of the fraction. However, when $(x - 2)$ is *negative*, the order will *reverse*, and when $x - 2$ is positive, the order will *not* reverse.
   a. Let x be larger than 2, so that $(x - 2)$ is positive. Solve the above inequality, and plot the graph on that part of the number line for which x is greater than 2.
   b. Let x be less than 2, so that $(x - 2)$ is negative. Solve the above inequality again. Then plot the graph on the rest of the number line, where x is less than 2.

Final Review and Examination

REVIEW

In algebra you have learned to use *variables* to stand for numbers that can take on different values at different times. For instance, if you go on a trip, the number of kilometers you have gone varies. So does the number of minutes or hours you have been going.

The main *use* of algebra in the real world involves expressions that give the value of one variable in terms of a related variable. For instance, if you travel at 80 kilometers per hour, then your distance is given by the expression $80t$, where t is time in hours.

There are two major things you *do* with algebraic expressions. You can use them to find the value of the expression when you know what the variable equals. If distance $= 80t$ and t is 3, then the distance equals 80(3), or 240 kilometers. Or you can use them to find the value of the variable when you know what the expression equals. If the distance is 100 kilometers, you would write an *equation*, $80t = 100$, and solve it for t. The answer is 1.25 hours. If the distance is *less* than 150 kilometers, you would write the *inequality* $80t < 150$. Solving gives $t < 1.875$.

To evaluate expressions and solve equations you must often *transform* them in simpler forms. For equations and inequalities you can do the same operation to each member, such as add the same number, multiply by the same number, and so forth. To transform an expression, you can commute and associate terms or factors, distribute multiplication or division over addition or subtraction, multiply by forms of 1, add forms of 0, and so forth. Care is needed, since some tempting transformations do *not* work. For instance, subtracting, dividing, and exponentiating neither commute nor associate.

In algebra, you start with a few rather obvious *axioms*. There are *commutative, associative,* and *distributive* axioms. The facts that $x \cdot 1 = x$ and $x + 0 = x$ are called *identity* axioms, since a number remains identical after you multiply by 1 or add 0. The facts that x and $1/x$ give 1 when multiplied, and that x and $-x$ give 0 when added are called *inverse* axioms. The fact that you get a unique, real number whenever you add or multiply two real numbers is summarized in the closure axioms. Although you have not been told it before, the 11 axioms which apply to addition and multiplication are called the *field axioms*. Any set of numbers that has all 11 of these properties is called a *field*.

THE ELEVEN FIELD AXIOMS

For all of these axioms, x, y, and z stand for real numbers.

Closure Axioms

The set of real numbers is *closed* under addition and multiplication. That is,

1. $x + y$ is a *unique real* number.
2. xy is a *unique real* number.

Inverse Axioms

The set of real numbers has unique *additive* and *multiplicative inverses* for each of its elements, except that there is no multiplicative inverse for 0. That is,

3. $x + (-x) = 0$
4. $x \cdot \frac{1}{x} = 1$, provided $x \neq 0$.

Identity Axioms

The set of real numbers has an additive *identity element*, 0, and a multiplicative *identity element*, 1. That is,

5. $x + 0 = x$
6. $x \cdot 1 = x$

Associative Axioms

Addition and multiplication are *associative* operations. That is,

7. $(x + y) + z = x + (y + z)$
8. $(xy)z = x(yz)$

Commutative Axioms

Addition and multiplication are *commutative* operations. That is,

9. $x + y = y + x$
10. $xy = yx$

Distributive Axiom

Multiplication *distributes* over addition.

11. $x(y + z) = xy + xz$

The other axioms you learned apply to the equality sign. Equality is *reflexive, symmetric,* and *transitive.*

THE THREE EQUALITY AXIOMS

In all of these axioms, x, y, and z stand for real numbers.

1. **Transitive Axiom**
   If one number equals a second number, and the second number equals a third number, then the first number equals the third number. That is,
   $$\text{If } x = y \text{ and } y = z,$$
   $$\text{then } x = z.$$

2. **Symmetric Axiom**
   If one number equals a second number, then the second number equals the first. That is,
   $$\text{If } x = y,$$
   $$\text{then } y = x.$$

3. **Reflexive Axiom**
   A variable stands for the *same* number everywhere it appears in an expression. That is,
   $$x = x.$$

Various *computations* arise in algebra. If an expression such as $5x^2 - 7x + 31$ is evaluated for *many* values of x, a computer is suitable. *Single* calculations involving radicals or many-digit numbers are best done with a calculator. Easy problems like $7x = 56$ should be done in your head.

All the techniques and properties you learn come together in solving *problems* from the real world. Such problems are stated in words. The key to success is translating the words into one or more algebraic expressions. For instance, the words *the perimeter of a rectangle* would become $2L + 2W$, where L and W are the length and width of the rectangle. The two basic questions are: Find the perimeter when L and W are known, and find L and W when the perimeter is known. After you get an answer to these mathematical problems, you write the answer to whatever question was asked. For instance: The perimeter is 35 cm.

In the exam that follows you will demonstrate that you know the properties of numbers, and that you can use these properties to evaluate expressions and to solve equations and inequalities. The exam may take two or three hours. The practice you get should help you on your own final.

FINAL EXAMINATION

1. Name and state the 11 field axioms.
2. Name and state the 3 axioms of equality.
3. State the following properties or definitions.
   a. Multiplication property of 0.
   b. Multiplication property of -1.
   c. Multiplication property of fractions.
   d. Multiplication property of equality.
   e. Multiplication property of order for $<$.
   f. Distributive property of division over subtraction.
   g. Distributive property of exponentiation over multiplication.
   h. Definition of subtraction.
   i. Definition of nth root.
   j. Definition of negative exponents.
   k. Property of the power of a power.
   l. Property of the quotient of two powers with equal bases.
   m. Pythagorean theorem.
4. For the expression $3x + 5$:
   a. Tell what kind of expression it is. Linear binomial
   b. Evaluate it if $x = 7$ and if $x = -8$.
   c. Find x if the expression equals 9.
   d. Find x if the expression is greater than -10. Graph the answer.
5. For the expression $|2x - 7|$:
   a. Tell what kind of expression it is.
   b. Evaluate it if $x = 2$ and if $x = 11$.
   c. Find x if the expression equals 13.
   d. Find x if the expression is less than 5. Graph the answer.
6. For the expression $x^2 + 3x - 10$:
   a. Tell what kind of expression it is.
   b. Evaluate it if $x = 2$ and if $x = -3$.
   c. Find x if the expression equals -12.
   d. Find x if the expression equals -15.
   e. Find x if the expression is negative. Graph the answer.
7. For the expression $\dfrac{x + 3}{x - 2}$:
   a. Tell what kind of expression it is.
   b. Evaluate it if $x = 5$, if $x = -3$, and if $x = 2$.
   c. Find x if the expression equals 4.
   d. Find x if the expression equals $2x$.
8. For the expression $\sqrt{3x + 8}$:
   a. Tell what kind of expression it is.

b. Evaluate it if $x = 16$, if $x = -5$, and if $x = \frac{1}{9}$. Write the answers in simple radical form.
c. Find x if the expression equals 5.
d. Find x if the expression equals $3x$.

9. For the two-variable equation $x + 5y = 9$:
a. Find x if y is 4.
b. Find y if x is -2.
c. Transform it to the slope-intercept form.

10. For the system of equations

$$x + 5y = 9 \qquad 3x - 2y = 10$$

a. Solve the system by the *substitution* method.
b. Solve the system by the *addition-subtraction* method.
c. Plot the graph of the system of *inequalities*

$$x + 5y < 9 \qquad 3x - 2y \leq 10.$$

11. Alana wants to know how long to study to get at least a 90% on her final. Results for 6 students who took last year's exam: (x = hours studied, y = score) (3, 75), (4, 86), (1, 61), (2, 77), (5, 95), (3, 80)
a. Make a scatter plot for these data points.
b. Find values for x_{av} and y_{av}. Plot this point on your scatter plot.
c. Sketch the best line that contains this point. Write an equation.
d. About how many hours should Alana study if she wants a 90%?
e. What score would she get if she didn't study at all?
f. In what ways does this model give reasonable answers? Why might her actual score be different from the model's projection?

12. Do the following.
a. Multiply: $(3x - 5)(6x + 7)$.
b. Do the squaring: $(4x - 5)^2$.
c. Simplify: $6(3x^2)^4$.
d. Factor completely: $2x^2 - 98$.
e. Factor by grouping: $6x^2 + 4ax - 3x - 2a$.
f. Factor by splitting the middle term: $6x^2 - 13x - 8$.
g. Subtract and simplify: $\dfrac{x - 21}{x^2 - 2x - 15} - \dfrac{2}{5 - x}$.
h. Add, and write in simple radical form: $\dfrac{18}{\sqrt{3}} + 5\sqrt{12}$.
i. Write in simple radical form: $\dfrac{12}{\sqrt{7} + \sqrt{3}}$.
j. Solve by completing the square: $x^2 + 6x - 10 = 0$.
k. Simplify: $\left(\dfrac{x^3x^{-5}y^4}{y^{-6}}\right)^{-3}$.
l. Divide 2.735×10^{-5} by 3.14×10^6. Use scientific notation, and significant digits.
m. Evaluate. Round to two decimal places: $\sqrt[5]{7395}$.

13. *Lawn Mowing Problem* Arlene can mow the lawn in 30 minutes. Using the other mower, Bea can mow the same lawn in 60% of this time.
    a. How long would Bea take by herself?
    b. How long would it take if both work together?

14. *Ball Toss Problem* You recall that when an object is thrown upward into the air, its distance, d (meters) above the starting point is given by $d = rt - 5t^2$ where t is time in seconds since it was thrown and r is the initial upward speed in meters per second. Suppose that you throw a ball up with an initial speed of 30 meters per second.
    a. How high will it be after 4 seconds?
    b. To the nearest tenth of a second, what is the first time it reaches a height of 20 meters?

15. *Border Problem* A strip x cm wide is to be cut from two sides of a 30-cm by 50-cm rectangle. The remaining rectangle is to have 70% of the area of the original one. Find x.

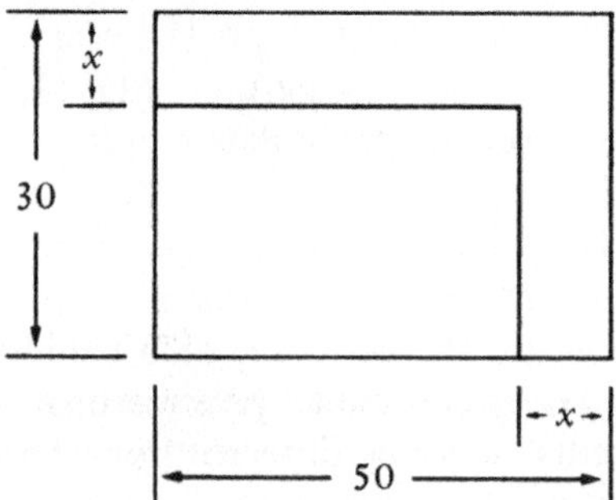

16. *Income Tax Problem* The Joneses make \$50,000 in a year. They must pay federal income tax equal to 30% of their *net* income (after subtracting state income tax). The state income tax is 10% of their *net* income after subtracting federal tax.
    a. Define variables. Then write two equations representing the above information.
    b. Solve this system of equations to find the amounts of the two taxes, correct to the nearest cent.

17. *Wheat Shipping Problem* A shipping company plans to carry wheat from an inland city to a port on the ocean. The ships will go down the river 300 km with the current and then return against the current. The current is 5 km/h.
    a. Write an expression for the total time a ship will take for the round trip in terms of the speed it moves through the water.
    b. How long will the round trip take if the ship goes 13 km/h through the water?
    c. The crew must be paid overtime wages if the trip takes more than 40 h. How fast must the ship move through the water for the round trip to take 40 hours?

18. *Cars Problem* There are about 127 million cars in the USA.
    a. A new car battery costs about $67, on the average. How much could a battery manufacturer make if they sold a battery for each car? Write the answer in scientific notation with the correct number of significant digits.
    b. Oil companies sell about 1.07×10^{11} dollars worth of gasoline per year for use in cars in the United States. How many dollars per car is this? Round to the nearest dollar.

19. *Roof Problem* A gable roof rises 4.7 meters above the housetop at its center. The house is 13.8 meters wide.
    a. What is the slant height of the roof (see sketch)?
    b. What angle does the roof make with the housetop?

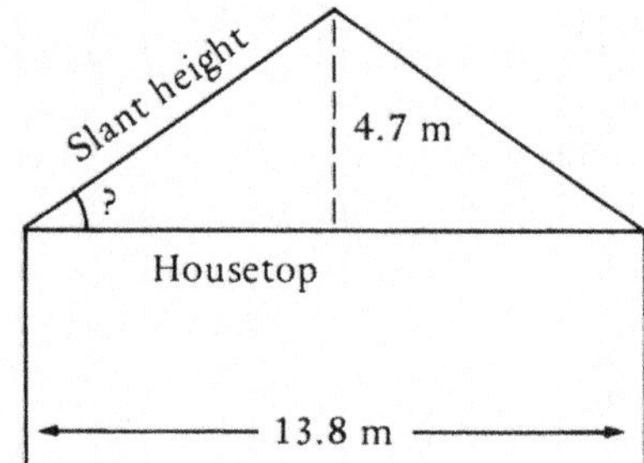

20. *Exhausted Swimmer Problem* Don Stream lost his balance and fell into Rapidan River. In his panic, he started swimming upstream, moving through the water at 72 meters per minute. When he got 120 meters upstream of the point where he fell in, Don became exhausted and stopped swimming. As he floated with the current past the place where he fell in, his friend, Hera Wynn, bent over and pulled him out. Don was in the water a total of 12 minutes. How fast does Rapidan River flow?

21. *SeeSaw Problem* The distance a person must sit from the middle of a seesaw is inversely proportional to the person's weight. Vera Young, who weighs 90 pounds, must sit 120 inches from the middle.
    a. Find the proportionality constant, and write the particular equation expressing distance in terms of weight.
    b. How far from the middle must C.A. Rider sit if he weighs 150 pounds?
    c. The Upp brothers balance the seesaw when they sit 50 inches from the middle. How heavy are they?

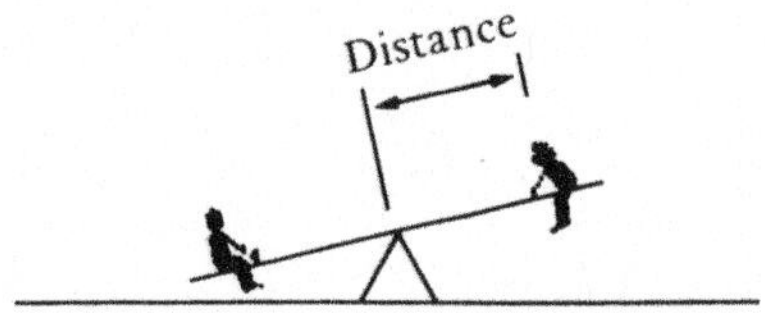

TABLE OF SQUARE ROOTS

N	N^2	$\sqrt{N}$	$\sqrt{10N}$	N	N^2	$\sqrt{N}$	$\sqrt{10N}$
1.0	1.00	1.000	3.162	5.5	30.25	2.345	7.416
1.1	1.21	1.049	3.317	5.6	31.36	2.366	7.483
1.2	1.44	1.095	3.464	5.7	32.49	2.387	7.550
1.3	1.69	1.140	3.606	5.8	33.64	2.408	7.616
1.4	1.96	1.183	3.742	5.9	34.81	2.429	7.681
1.5	2.25	1.225	3.873	6.0	36.00	2.449	7.746
1.6	2.56	1.265	4.000	6.1	37.21	2.470	7.810
1.7	2.89	1.304	4.123	6.2	38.44	2.490	7.874
1.8	3.24	1.342	4.243	6.3	39.69	2.510	7.937
1.9	3.61	1.378	4.359	6.4	40.96	2.530	8.000
2.0	4.00	1.414	4.472	6.5	42.25	2.550	8.062
2.1	4.41	1.449	4.583	6.6	43.56	2.569	8.124
2.2	4.84	1.483	4.690	6.7	44.89	2.588	8.185
2.3	5.29	1.517	4.796	6.8	46.24	2.608	8.246
2.4	5.76	1.549	4.899	6.9	47.61	2.627	8.307
2.5	6.25	1.581	5.000	7.0	49.00	2.646	8.367
2.6	6.76	1.612	5.099	7.1	50.41	2.665	8.426
2.7	7.29	1.643	5.196	7.2	51.84	2.683	8.485
2.8	7.84	1.673	5.292	7.3	53.29	2.702	8.544
2.9	8.41	1.703	5.385	7.4	54.76	2.720	8.602
3.0	9.00	1.732	5.477	7.5	56.25	2.739	8.660
3.1	9.61	1.761	5.568	7.6	57.76	2.757	8.718
3.2	10.24	1.789	5.657	7.7	59.29	2.775	8.775
3.3	10.89	1.817	5.745	7.8	60.84	2.793	8.832
3.4	11.56	1.844	5.831	7.9	62.41	2.811	8.888
3.5	12.25	1.871	5.916	8.0	64.00	2.828	8.944
3.6	12.96	1.897	6.000	8.1	65.61	2.846	9.000
3.7	13.69	1.924	6.083	8.2	67.24	2.864	9.055
3.8	14.44	1.949	6.164	8.3	68.89	2.881	9.110
3.9	15.21	1.975	6.245	8.4	70.56	2.898	9.165
4.0	16.00	2.000	6.325	8.5	72.25	2.915	9.220
4.1	16.81	2.025	6.403	8.6	73.96	2.933	9.274
4.2	17.64	2.049	6.481	8.7	75.69	2.950	9.327
4.3	18.49	2.074	6.557	8.8	77.44	2.966	9.381
4.4	19.36	2.098	6.633	8.9	79.21	2.983	9.434
4.5	20.25	2.121	6.708	9.0	81.00	3.000	9.487
4.6	21.16	2.145	6.782	9.1	82.81	3.017	9.539
4.7	22.09	2.168	6.856	9.2	84.64	3.033	9.592
4.8	23.04	2.191	6.928	9.3	86.49	3.050	9.644
4.9	24.01	2.214	7.000	9.4	88.36	3.066	9.695
5.0	25.00	2.236	7.071	9.5	90.25	3.082	9.747
5.1	26.01	2.258	7.141	9.6	92.16	3.098	9.798
5.2	27.04	2.280	7.211	9.7	94.09	3.114	9.849
5.3	28.09	2.302	7.280	9.8	96.04	3.130	9.899
5.4	29.16	2.324	7.348	9.9	98.01	3.146	9.950
5.5	30.25	2.345	7.416	10	100.00	3.162	10.000

TABLE OF TRIGONOMETRIC FUNCTIONS

Angle	sin *A*	cos *A*	tan *A*	Angle	sin *A*	cos *A*	tan *A*
1	.0175	.9998	.0175	46	.7193	.6947	1.036
2	.0349	.9994	.0349	47	.7314	.6820	1.072
3	.0523	.9986	.0524	48	.7431	.6691	1.111
4	.0698	.9976	.0699	49	.7547	.6561	1.150
5	.0872	.9962	.0875	50	.7660	.6428	1.192
6	.1045	.9945	.1051	51	.7771	.6293	1.235
7	.1219	.9925	.1228	52	.7880	.6157	1.280
8	.1392	.9903	.1405	53	.7986	.6018	1.327
9	.1564	.9877	.1584	54	.8090	.5878	1.376
10	.1736	.9848	.1763	55	.8192	.5736	1.428
11	.1908	.9816	.1944	56	.8290	.5592	1.483
12	.2079	.9781	.2126	57	.8387	.5446	1.540
13	.2250	.9744	.2309	58	.8480	.5299	1.600
14	.2419	.9703	.2493	59	.8572	.5150	1.664
15	.2588	.9659	.2679	60	.8660	.5000	1.732
16	.2756	.9613	.2867	61	.8746	.4848	1.804
17	.2924	.9563	.3057	62	.8829	.4695	1.881
18	.3090	.9511	.3249	63	.8910	.4540	1.963
19	.3256	.9455	.3443	64	.8988	.4384	2.050
20	.3420	.9397	.3640	65	.9063	.4226	2.145
21	.3584	.9336	.3839	66	.9135	.4067	2.246
22	.3746	.9272	.4040	67	.9205	.3907	2.356
23	.3907	.9205	.4245	68	.9272	.3746	2.475
24	.4067	.9135	.4452	69	.9336	.3584	2.605
25	.4226	.9063	.4663	70	.9397	.3420	2.747
26	.4384	.8988	.4877	71	.9455	.3256	2.904
27	.4540	.8910	.5095	72	.9511	.3090	3.078
28	.4695	.8829	.5317	73	.9563	.2924	3.271
29	.4848	.8746	.5543	74	.9613	.2756	3.487
30	.5000	.8660	.5774	75	.9659	.2588	3.732
31	.5150	.8572	.6009	76	.9703	.2419	4.011
32	.5299	.8480	.6249	77	.9744	.2250	4.331
33	.5446	.8387	.6494	78	.9781	.2079	4.705
34	.5592	.8290	.6745	79	.9816	.1908	5.145
35	.5736	.8192	.7002	80	.9848	.1736	5.671
36	.5878	.8090	.7265	81	.9877	.1564	6.314
37	.6018	.7986	.7536	82	.9903	.1392	7.115
38	.6157	.7880	.7813	83	.9925	.1219	8.144
39	.6293	.7771	.8098	84	.9945	.1045	9.514
40	.6428	.7660	.8391	85	.9962	.0872	11.430
41	.6561	.7547	.8693	86	.9976	.0698	14.301
42	.6691	.7431	.9004	87	.9986	.0523	19.081
43	.6820	.7314	.9325	88	.9994	.0349	28.636
44	.6947	.7193	.9657	89	.9998	.0175	57.290
45	.7071	.7071	1.0000	90	1.0000	.0000	NONE

Glossary

abscissa The first number in an ordered pair as indicated on a number-line graph; the horizontal coordinate on the graph.

absolute value The distance of a number from the origin on a number line; the number itself or the opposite of the number, whichever is positive (or zero).

addition method A method of solving equations in a system by adding.

addition property of equality For real numbers x, y, and z, if $x = y$, then $x + z = y + z$.

addition property of order Given any real numbers a, b, and c; if $a < b$, then $a + c < b + c$; if $a > b$, then $a + c > b + c$.

additive identity axiom For any real number x, $x + 0 = x$.

additive inverse axiom For any real number x, there is a number $-x$ for which $x + (-x) = 0$.

additive inverses Two numbers that add up to zero (for example -3 and 3).

adjacent leg In a right triangle, the leg next to a given angle.

associate To group two of the numbers in parentheses so that the operation between them is done first.

axiom A basic assumption about a mathematical system; a property assumed to be true without proof.

bar graph See *histogram*.

base In an expression requiring multiplication, the constant or variable that tells what number is to be multiplied. In the expression 3^2, 3 is the base.

BASIC A computer language.

binomial A polynomial with two terms.

cancel a fraction To divide the numerator and denominator by the same common factor.

Cartesian coordinate system A system of plotting the values of variables on a graph; named after the French mathematician René Descartes (1596–1650).

closure A given set of given numbers is *closed* under an operation if there is just one answer and the answer is in the given set whenever the operation is performed with the numbers in that set.

coefficient See *numerical coefficient*.

common factor A factor that is in each term of an expression. For example, in $3x + 2x$, x is the common factor.

common multiple A common multiple of a and b is a number that equals (integer) $\times\, a$ and (integer) $\times\, b$.

commute To interchange, or reverse, the positions of two numbers.

commutative operation An operation for which commuting the numbers does not change the answer.

completing the square Adding one or more terms to an expression to make it the square of a binomial.

conditional equation An equation that is true for some value(s) of the variable and not true for others.

conjugate binomials Binomials that are the same except for the sign between the terms; for example, $2x + 4$ and $2x - 4$.

constant A symbol (such as 7, 8.9, or $\frac{2}{3}$) which always stands for the same number.

converse of the multiplication property of zero If a product of real numbers equals zero, then one of its factors equals zero.

coordinates Numbers corresponding to points on a graph.

cosine A trigonometric function; in a right triangle with acute angle A, cosine $A = \dfrac{\text{adjacent leg}}{\text{hypotenuse}}$.

cross-multiplication In a proportion such as $a : b = c : d$, the product of the means equals the product of the extremes; that is, if $\frac{a}{b} = \frac{c}{d}$, then $ad = bc$.

cubic A word describing a third degree polynomial.

degree The highest power of a variable that appears in a polynomial expression. The degree of a polynomial with one variable is the exponent of the highest power of that variable.

denominator In fractions, the number under the vinculum; in $\frac{x}{y}$, y is the denominator.

dependent variable Variable dependent on independent variable.

direct variation function y varies directly with x, or y is directly proportional to x, if and only if $y = kx$, where k is the proportionality constant.

discriminant The expression $b^2 - 4ac$ which appears in the quadratic formula $x = \frac{-b \pm \sqrt{b^2 - 4ac}}{2a}$. By using the discriminant you can discriminate between quadratic equations that have solutions and those that do not.

distributive axiom For real numbers x, y, and z, $x(y + z) = xy + xz$.

division $x \div y = x \cdot \left(\frac{1}{y}\right)$

domain (of a variable) The set of numbers that can be values of the variable.

equation A sentence (such as $x + 7 = 9$) which says that one expression $(x + 7)$ is equal to another expression (9).

evaluating Finding out the value of an expression; finding the number an expression stands for.

event A successful result (or set of results) of a random experiment. (Probability.)

event space The set of all favorable outcomes of a random experiment. (Probability.)

exponent In an expression requiring multiplication, the constant or variable that tells how many bases to multiply together. For example, in the expression 3^2, 2 is the exponent.

exponentiation Raising a number to a power; for example, 3^2.

expression A collection of numbers, operation signs, and symbols of inclusion that stands for a number.

extraneous solution The solution that satisfies the transformed equation but not the original one.

extremes In a proportion, the outer terms; for example, in $\frac{a}{b} = \frac{x}{y}$, a and y are the extremes.

factor a polynomial Transform it to a product of two or more factors.

factor theorem $(x - n)$ is a factor of a polynomial if and only if the polynomial equals zero when n is substituted for x.

factoring by grouping (factoring by associating) Associating pairs of terms and factoring out their greatest common factor.

factors Numbers that are multiplied together.

fractional equation An equation that has a variable in at least one denominator.

function A set of ordered pairs (x, y) for which there is never more than one value of y for any one given value of x.

fundamental theorem of arithmetic Each positive integer has exactly one set of prime factors.

geometric probability Used in a random experiment where the probability of a successful outcome depends on a ratio of geometric quantities.

greatest common factor (GCF) The greatest common factor for two positive a and b is the greatest integer for which a/GCF = integer, and b/GCF = integer; the greatest factor that is a factor of two or more integers.

histogram (bar graph) A graph with possible outcomes plotted horizontally and the frequency of occurrence of each outcome plotted vertically.

hypotenuse In a right triangle, the side opposite the right angle.

identity An equation that is true for all values of the variable.

independent variable Variable that the dependent variable depends on.

inequality A sentence that states one expression is greater than or less than another.

integer A whole number or its opposite (for example, $-2, -1, 0, 1, 2 \ldots$), not including the fractions in between.

intersection The intersection of sets A and B is the set of numbers in both sets.

inverse variation function y varies inversely with x, or y is inversely proportional to x, if and only if, $y = \frac{k}{x}$, where k is the proportionality constant.

irrational number A real number that cannot be written as a ratio of two integers.

LCD See *least common denominator*.

LCM See *least common multiple*.

least common denominator (LCD) The smallest number that is a multiple of each denominator.

least common multiple (LCM) The least common multiple of integers a and b is the smallest positive number that is a common multiple of a and b.

like terms Two terms in an expression that have the same variable(s) raised to the same powers.

linear A word describing a first degree polynomial.

linear function A function in which the ordered pair (x, y) is related by an equation of the form $y = mx + b$, where m and b stand for constants, and $m \neq 0$.

linear regression The process of finding the best-fitting line to a set of data points.

means In a proportion, the middle terms; for example, in $\frac{a}{b} = \frac{x}{y}$, b and x are the means.

monomial A polynomial with one term.

multiple Integer multiplied by a given number.

multiplication property of equality For real numbers x, y, and z, if $x = y$, then $xz = yz$.

multiplication property of fractions To multiply two fractions, multiply their numerators and multiply their denominators.

multiplication property of −1 For any real number x, $-1 \cdot x = -x$.

multiplication property of order For any real numbers a, b, and c; if $a < b$, then $ac < bc$ if c is positive; and $ac > bc$ if c is negative. If $a > b$, then $ac > bc$ if c is positive; and $ac < bc$ if c is negative.

multiplication property of 0 For any real number x, $0 \cdot x = 0$; that is, if one factor of a product is zero, then the product equals zero.

multiplicative identity axiom Multiplying a number by 1 does not change its value $(x \cdot 1 = x)$.

multiplicative inverse axiom For any real number x, there is a number $\frac{1}{x}$ for which $x \cdot \left(\frac{1}{x}\right) = 1$ (provided $x \neq 0$).

multiplicative inverses (reciprocals) Any two numbers whose product is 1 (for example 4 and $\frac{1}{4}$).

negative exponent For any non-zero number x, and for any integer n, $x^{-n} = \frac{1}{x^n}$.

negative number A number less than zero.

n^th root An nth root of x is a number that, when raised to the nth power, gives x for the answer.

number line A way of visualizing real numbers, with zero as the origin.

numerator In fractions, the number above the vinculum; in $\frac{x}{y}$, x is the numerator.

numerical coefficient In a term, the constant that is multiplied by the variable(s). For example, in $2xy$, 2 is the coefficient of xy.

operation Something that is done to numbers, such as adding, subtracting, multiplying, or dividing.

open sentence A sentence with a variable in it.

opposite leg In a right triangle, the leg not adjacent to a given angle.

ordered pair A symbol that specifies the order in which two numbers occur.

ordinate The second number in an ordered pair; the vertical coordinate on the graph.

origin On a number line, the zero point; on a Cartesian coordinate system, the (0, 0) point.

outcomes Equally likely results of a random experiment. (Probability.)

parabola The graph of a quadratic function.

parallel Lines with equal slopes.

perimeter The sum of the lengths of a figure's sides.

perpendicular Two lines are perpendicular when the slope of one line equals the opposite of the reciprocal of the slope of the other.

point-slope form $y - y_1 = m(x - x_1)$

polynomial An expression that has no operations other than addition, subtraction, and multiplication by or of the variable(s).

positive number A number greater than zero.

power An expression containing a base and an exponent; for example, 3^2 or x^y.

prime number A positive integer that has no positive integers as factors other than 1 and itself. The number 1 is not considered to be a prime.

prime polynomial A polynomial where the only factors are 1 and the polynomial itself.

probability Number of favorable outcomes of a random experiment divided by total number of outcomes possible.

proof A set of steps starting with given information and ending with a conclusion. Each step must be justified with a reason, such as an axiom, a definition, a given piece of information, or a previously proved property.

properties Facts about mathematical processes.

proportion An equation with ratios in which the ratios are equal.

proportionality constant The constant by which two terms are directly or inversely proportional.

Pythagorean Theorem In a right triangle the square of the hypotenuse equals the sum of the squares of the two legs; named after the Greek mathematician Pythagoras.

quadrant One of the four regions in a Cartesian coordinate system.

quadratic A word describing a second degree polynomial.

quadratic equation An equation in which a variable is squared.

Quadratic Formula A formula for solving a quadratic equation. The formula is $x = \frac{-b \pm \sqrt{b^2 - 4ac}}{2a}$.

quadratic function A function with an equation of the form $y =$ (a quadratic expression).

radical An expression that has a root (square root, cube root, etc.); for example $\sqrt{25}$ is a radical.

radical equation An equation with a variable under the radical sign.

radical sign The symbol that shows a number is a radical. For example, in $\sqrt{a}$, $\sqrt{\ }$ is the radical sign.

radicand The number that appears with a radical sign. For example, in $\sqrt{9}$, 9 is the radicand.

random experiment Observing or selecting one outcome that happens by chance. Example: Rolling a die and recording the number that comes up.

range (of a variable) Set of values of the dependent variable corresponding to all values of the independent variable in the domain.

rational algebraic expressions Fractions that contain variables; a ratio of two polynomials.

rational number A number that can be written as a ratio of two integers.

real numbers All numbers on the number line, including positive numbers, negative numbers, zero, fractions, and decimals.

reciprocals See multiplicative inverses.

reflexive axiom of equality For any real number x, $x = x$; that is, a variable stands for the same number, no matter where it appears in any expression.

regression equation The equation of the best-fitting line to a set of data points.

regression line The best-fitting line to a set of data points.

relatively prime Integers with no common prime factors and whose greatest common factor is 1 are said to be relatively prime.

rise The change in y in going from one point to another in a Cartesian coordinate system; the vertical change on the graph.

run The change in x in going from one point to another in a Cartesian coordinate system; the horizontal change on the graph.

sample space The set of all possible outcomes of a random experiment. (Probability.)

scatter plot A graph of data points, usually from a real-world experiment. Used to observe relationships between the independent and dependent variables.

signed numbers Numbers presented as negative (-3) or positive (3).

simple radical form A radical is said to be in simple radical form if there are no radicals in the denominator, and the radicals in the numerator are as small as possible.

simultaneous equations Equations in a system that can be solved at the same time.

sine A trigonometric function; in a right triangle with one acute angle A, sine $A = \frac{\text{opposite leg}}{\text{hypotenuse}}$.

slope-intercept form In graphing an equation, an equation of the form $y = mx + b$, where m and b stand for constants, is in slope-intercept form.

solution (of an equation) A number that can be substituted for the variable in the equation to make the sentence (equation) true.

solution of an equation containing two variables An ordered pair that makes the equation a true statement.

solution of a system of equations An ordered pair that satisfies all the equations in the system.

solution set The set of all solutions to an equation.

solving an equation Writing the solution set to the equation.

square root n is a square root of x if $n^2 = x$.

square root of a product property The square root of a product of two nonnegative numbers equals the product of the square roots of the two numbers.

square root of a quotient property The square root of a quotient of two positive numbers equals the quotient of the square roots of the numbers.

square root property of equality If two nonnegative numbers are equal, then their positive square roots are equal.

square root property of order The square root of each member of an inequality can be taken without changing the order, as long as neither member is negative.

statistics Using data from a random experiment to make predictions about the real-world situation from which the data come.

substituting Replacing a variable (such as x) with a constant (such as 159 or 6.8).

substitution A method of solving a system of equations by solving one equation to get one of the variables and substituting the result in the other equation.

subtraction Subtracting a number means adding its opposite. That is, $x - y = x + (-y)$.

system of equations Two or more equations with the same variables.

symbols of inclusion Parentheses, brackets, and vinculums which are used in a problem to tell which operation to do first.

symmetric axiom of equality An axiom that states: for real numbers a and b, if $a = b$, then $b = a$.

tangent A trigonometric function, in a right triangle with one acute angle A, $\text{tangent } A = \frac{\text{opposite leg}}{\text{adjacent leg}}$.

terms Numbers that are added to each other or subtracted from each other.

theorem A property that can be proved.

transforming an equation Doing the same operation to each member of an equation; a step in solving a set of equations by making the variables have equal or opposite coefficients.

transforming an expression Commuting, associating, distributing, etc., in such a way that the expression still represents the same number as the original one.

transitive axiom of equality An axiom that states: if the first number equals a second number, and the second number equals a third number, then the first number equals the third number.

trigonometric functions The functions of angles in a triangle; *trigonometric* comes from Greek words meaning "measurement of a triangle." See also *sine*, *cosine*, and *tangent*.

trinomial A polynomial with three terms.

union The union of sets A and B is the set of numbers that are either in set A or in set B.

variable A letter that represents a number. It represents the same number each time it appears in an expression.

vertex The point at which the graph of a quadratic function turns around.

vertical motion formula If an object is thrown into the air with an initial upward velocity of r mls then its distance, d m, above its starting point at time t s after it was thrown is approximately $d = rt - 5t^2$.

vinculum The bar used in fractions and radicals; a symbol of inclusion.

x-intercept On a graph, the value of x when y is 0.

y-intercept On a graph, the value of y when x is 0.

zero exponent For any non-zero number x, $x^0 = 1$.

Answers to Selected Problems

Chapter 1

EXERCISE 1-1

1. 96 **3.** 61 **5.** 1 **7.** 10 **9.** 43 **11.** 54 **13.** 108 **15.** 3 **17.** 6 **19.** 14 **21.** 128 **23.** 58 **25.** 100 **27.** 10 **29.** 3 **31.** 10

EXERCISE 1-2

1. (a) 13×8 **(b)** $x \times 8$ or $8x$ **(c)** $13y$ **(d)** xy **(e)** $3 + y$ **(f)** $x + 7$ **(g)** $x - y$ **(h)** $x \div y$ or $\frac{x}{y}$ **(i)** $x + 3$ **(j)** $3x$ **(k)** $y - 5$ **(l)** $y \div 5$ or $\frac{1}{5}y$ or $\frac{y}{5}$ **3. (a)** 9 **(b)** 22 **5. (a)** 5 **(b)** 1 **7. (a)** 162 **(b)** 36 **(c)** 0 **9. (a)** 36 **(b)** 117 **11. (a)** 5 **(b)** $\frac{1}{3}$ **(c)** $\frac{2}{3}$ **13. (a)** 8 **(b)** 50 **(c)** $2\frac{1}{2}$ **15.** $5 + 2$ **17.** $x + 4$ **19.** $9 + y$ **21.** $x + y$ **23.** $15 - 8$ **25.** $7 - x$ **27.** $y - 5$ **29.** $y - x$ **31.** $6 + y + z$ **33.** $12 - 7 - y$ or $12 - (7 + y)$ **35. (a)** 61 years **(b)** $57 + y$ years **(c)** 49 years **(d)** $57 - z$ years **(e)** $x + 4$ years **(f)** $x + y$ years **(g)** $x - 8$ years **(h)** $x - z$ years

EXERCISE 1-3

1. (a) 128 **(b)** 81 **(c)** 64 **(d)** 25 **(e)** 343 **(f)** 100,000 **(g)** 64 **(h)** 0 **(i)** 13 **(j)** 1 **3. (a)** exponent **(b)** base **(c)** 216 **(d)** 1000 **(e)** "x cubed." "x to the third power." "the third power of x." "x to the third." **5.** 6^2 **7.** 4^2 **9.** y^2 **11.** 5^3 **13.** z^3 **15.** 6^4 **17.** 4^6 **19.** x^5 **21.** 2^{11} **23.** 2^y **25.** y^z **27.** $7 \cdot 7 \cdot 7 \cdot 7 \cdot 7 \cdot 7 \cdot 7$ **29.** $z \cdot z \cdot z \cdot z \cdot z$ **31.** $5 \cdot 5 \cdot 5 \cdot \ldots \cdot 5$ (x of them) **33.** $z \cdot z \cdot z \cdot \ldots \cdot z$ (x of them) **35.** 3^4 **37.** 7^3 **39.** 2^6 **41.** 10^5 **43.** 12^1 **45.** 2^{17} min

EXERCISE 1-4

1. (a) 20 **(b)** 12 **(c)** 142 **(d)** 8 **(e)** 2 **3. (a)** 16 **(b)** 31 **(c)** 19 **(d)** 49 **5. (a)** 13 **(b)** -3 **(c)** 40 **(d)** 1000 **7.** 4 **9.** 22 **11.** 328 **13.** 9 **15.** 32 **17.** 17 **19.** 92 **21.** 43 **23.** 42 **25.** 18 **27. (a)** 27 **(b)** 125 **(c)** 1 **29. (a)** 9 **(b)** 81 **(c)** 3 **31. (a)** 36 **(b)** 100 **(c)** 0 **33. (a)** 49 **(b)** 25 **(c)** 4 **35. (a)** 49 **(b)** 25 **(c)** 4 **37. (a)** 9 **(b)** 36 **(c)** 0 **39. (a)** 8 **(b)** 50 **(c)** 56

EXERCISE 1-5

1. $x - 2 + y$ **3.** $x - (2 + y)$ **5.** $\frac{x}{3} \cdot z$ or $x \div 3 \cdot z$ **7.** $x \div (3z)$ or $\frac{x}{3z}$ **9.** $3x + y$ **11.** $(x + 3) \cdot y$ **13.** $(x + y)^2$ **15.** $x^2 + y^2$ **17.** $7 - 5x$ **19.** $15 - z^3$ **21.** $3c + 5$ **23.** $5 \div p - 13$ or $\frac{5}{p} - 13$ **25.** $4(10 + x)$ **27.** $5 \div (x - 7)$ or $\frac{5}{x - 7}$ **29.** $(3x + 2) \div (1 - 3x)$ or $\frac{3x + 2}{1 - 3x}$

EXERCISE 1-6

1. (a) 10 **(b)** 13 **(c)** 23 **(d)** 103 **(e)** 2001 **3. (a)** 10 **(b)** 26 **(c)** 100 **(d)** 222 **(e)** 130

EXERCISE 1-7

1. $x = 27$ **3.** $x = 9$ **5.** $x = 18$ **7.** $x = 87$ **9.** $x = 23$ **11.** $x = 127$ **13.** $x = 16$ **15.** $x = 156$ **17.** $x = 11$ **19.** $x = 125$ **21.** $x = 476$ **23.** $x = 1000$ **25.** $x = -1$ **27.** $x = 456$ **29.** $x = 17$ **31.** $x = 153$ **33.** $x = 17$ **35.** $x = 3$ **37.** $x = 867$ **39.** $x = \frac{1}{3}$ **41.** $x = 9$ **43.** $x = 50$ **45.** $x = 8$ **47.** $x = 1$ **49.** $x = 2\frac{1}{2}$

EXERCISE 1-8

1. $4 + 8 + 7$ **3.** $x + 20$ **5.** $x + y + 14$ **7.** $x + x + x$ or $3x$ **9.** $x + y + x + y$ or $2x + 2y$ **11. (a)** $x + 28$ **(b)** $x + 28 = 47$ **(c)** $x = 19$ **13.** $x = 18$ **15.** $x = 5$

17. **(a)** $8x$ **(b)** $8x = 584$ **(c)** $x = 73$ **19.** $x = 2\frac{1}{2}$
21. **(a)** Circumference **(b)** 6.3 cm.

EXERCISE 1-9

1. **(a)** $\frac{1}{4}x$ **(b)** $\frac{1}{4}x = 312$ **(c)** 1248 students **3.** **(a)** $x - 4$ **(b)** $x - 4 = 76$ **(c)** Tip is 80.
5. **(a)** $x + 7$ **(b)** **i.** 19 cm **ii.** 44 cm **iii.** 107 cm **(c)** 36 cm wide **(d)** **i.** 84 cm **ii.** 27 cm **7.** **(a)** $x + 3$ **(b)** **i.** 8 km/h **ii.** 14 km/h **iii.** 45 km/h **(c)** 18 km/h **(d)** **i.** 6 km/h **ii.** 62 km/h **9.** **(a)** $\frac{1}{5}x$ **(b)** 235 people **(c)** **i.** 500 people **ii.** 20,000 people **(d)** **i.** 6 **ii.** 20 **iii.** 1000 **11.** **(a)** $7x$ **(b)** **i.** 56 m **ii.** 70 m **(c)** **i.** 13 m **ii.** $7\frac{1}{7}$ m
13. **(a)** $1.2x$ **(b)** **i.** \$6.00 **ii.** \$10.80 **iii.** \$168.00 **(c)** **i.** \$70.00 **ii.** \$11.00
15. **(a)** **i.** 19 **ii.** 31 **iii.** 121 **(b)** $2x + 5 = 41$ **(c)** $x = 18$

Chapter 2

EXERCISE 2-1

1. 3 **3.** 2 **5.** −3 **7.** 5 **9.** −4 **11.** −5 **13.** −17 **15.** −9 **17.** −17 **19.** −3 **21.** 2 **23.** −3 **25.** 2 **27.** −26 **29.** 24 **31.** **(a)** True **(b)** False **(c)** False **33.** **(a)** A negative number is a number less than zero. **(b)** An integer is a positive, negative, or zero "whole" number. **(c)** A real number is any number that has a place on the number line.

EXERCISE 2-2

1. 3 **3.** −5 **5.** −18 **7.** 7 **9.** −14 **11.** −13 **13.** −3 **15.** 3 **17.** −3 **19.** −38 **21.** −4.2 **23.** 1.7 **25.** −9.1 **27.** $\frac{3}{13}$ **29.** $-1\frac{3}{7}$ **31.** 7 **33.** 7 **35.** 0 **37.** −14 **39.** −7 **41.** 5 **43.** −15 **45.** −15 **47.** 5 **49.** −30 **51.** −19 **53.** 0 **55.** Real, positive, integer **57.** Real, negative **59.** Real, positive

EXERCISE 2-3

1. −165 **3.** 31 **5.** −9 **7.** −158 **9.** −199 **11.** 273 **13.** 3.6 **15.** −6.1 **17.** 6.5 **19.** −1 **21.** 15 **23.** 139 **25.** 326 **27.** 2 **29.** 4 **31.** 1558 **33.** 1 **35.** 11 **37.** −30 **39.** −9 **41.** 4 **43.** 19 **45.** 12 **47.** 13 **49.** −2

EXERCISE 2-4

1. −70 **3.** 45 **5.** −48 **7.** 6 **9.** −4 **11.** −72 **13.** 200 **15.** 0 **17.** −105 **19.** 80 **21.** −56 **23.** −30 **25.** −64 **27.** 256 **29.** −256 **31.** −1 **33.** 1 **35.** −1 **37.** −81 **39.** −72 **41.** **(a)** −125 **(b)** 25 **(c)** −5 **43.** **(a)** −125 **(b)** −25 **45.** **(a)** 16 **(b)** 1 **(c)** 0 **47.** **(a)** −5 **(b)** 3 **(c)** 1 **49.** **(a)** −5 **(b)** 3 **(c)** 1 **51.** False! $-x$ is negative only if x is *positive*. $-(-3) = 3$, a *pos.* no., if x is -3.

EXERCISE 2-5

1. −3 **3.** −3 **5.** 3 **7.** −3 **9.** 3 **11.** 3 **13.** −13 **15.** −17 **17.** 5 **19.** −100 **21.** 4 **23.** −5 **25.** −4 **27.** 4 **29.** −6 **31.** −10 **33.** 10 **35.** 0 **37.** 0 **39.** Undefined **41.** **(a)** 3 **(b)** −5 **(c)** Undefined **43.** **(a)** $-\frac{1}{6}$ **(b)** $\frac{1}{10}$ **(c)** 0 **45.** **(a)** 5 **(b)** 1.8 **(c)** 45 **47.** **(a)** 3 **(b)** 1.25 **(c)** Undefined **49.** **(a)** 3 **(b)** 0 **(c)** $1\frac{1}{3}$ **51.** There is no number such that $0 \cdot \text{number} = 1$. **53.** **(a)** $\frac{1}{7}$ **(b)** $\frac{9}{5}$ **(c)** $-\frac{3}{2}$ **(d)** −1 **(e)** 4 **(f)** None **55.** **(a)** $x \cdot \frac{1}{y}$ **(b)** $a \cdot \frac{1}{3}$ **(c)** $7 \cdot \frac{1}{p}$ **(d)** $m \cdot \frac{3}{2}$

EXERCISE 2-6

1. $x + 7$ **3.** $x + 13$ **5.** $x + 2$ **7.** $x - 4$ **9.** $24 - x$ **11.** $-x - 31$ **13.** $-x - 41$ **15.** $-x$ **17.** $7x + 12$ **19.** $-3x - 11$ **21.** $35x$ **23.** $-24x$ **25.** $4x$ **27.** $-7x$ **29.** x **31.** $6x$ **33.** $-8x$ **35.** $-100x$ **37.** $37x$ **39.** x **41.** In $2 + 3x$, the multiplication must be done *before* the addition. Calvin *added* first!

43. **(a)** **i.** $6 + x + 7$
$= (6 + x) + 7$ Associate 6 and x.
$= (x + 6) + 7$ Commute 6 and x.
$= x + (6 + 7)$ Associate 6 and 7.
$= x + 13$ Do the arithmetic.
ii. $6 + x + 7$
$= 6 + (x + 7)$ Associate x and 7.
$= 6 + (7 + x)$ Commute x and 7.
$= (6 + 7) + x$ Associate 6 and 7.
$= 13 + x$ Do the arithmetic.
(b) Commute 13 and x in $13 + x$ to get $x + 13$.
45. For example, $(2 + 3) + 4 = 5 + 4 = 9$, and $2 + (3 + 4) = 2 + 7 = 9$. But $(2 - 3) - 4 = -1 - 4 = -5$, and $2 - (3 - 4) = 2 - (-1) = 3$, not -5.
47. For example, $2 \cdot 3 = 6$, and $3 \cdot 2 = 6$, also. But $2 \div 3 = \frac{2}{3}$ and $3 \div 2 = 1.5$, not $\frac{2}{3}$.
49. For example, $2^3 = 8$, but $3^2 = 9$, not 8.

EXERCISE 2-7

1. $x = 6$ **3.** $x = 22$ **5.** $x = 7$
7. $a = 11$ **9.** $x = -18$
11. $x = -104$ **13.** $y = -3$
15. $v = 189$ **17.** $8.4 = x$
19. $x = -8$ **21.** $-67 = x$
23. $x = 18$ **25.** $x = 1.7$
27. $p = 7.75$ **29.** $x = -1$
31. Jess forgot the $-$ in front of the x in $5 - x = 11$. **33.** Noah *added* before *multiplying* in $3 + 4x = 21$.

EXERCISE 2-8

1. **(a)** $20x + 15$ **(b)** **i.** \$2.55 **ii.** \$20.15 **iii.** You must assume that the box is big enough to hold 100 donuts. **(c)** 17 donuts **3.** **(a)** $42x + 35$ **(b)** **i.** \$161 **ii.** \$224 **(c)** $2\frac{1}{2}$ hours **(d)** $\frac{1}{2}$ hour **5.** **(a)** $50 - \frac{1}{6}x$ **(b)** **i.** 48 cu ft **ii.** $33\frac{1}{3}$ cu ft **(c)** 180 scoops **7.** **(a)** **i.** 3570 cups **ii.** 3450 cups **iii.** 3600 − 30T cups **(b)** **i.** 2970 cups **ii.** 3900 cups **(c)** 40°C **(d)** −20°C
9. **(a)** $250 - 3x$ **(b)** **i.** 229 lb **ii.** 157 lb **(c)** **i.** 30 days **ii.** $33\frac{1}{3}$ days **(d)** It must keep melting at the same rate for the answers to be meaningful.
11. **(a)** (Figure) **(b)** **i.** $\frac{1}{4}x$ **ii.** $3 + \frac{1}{4}x$ **(c)** **i.** 8 mi **ii.** 18 mi **(d)** 28 min
13. **(a)** $12 + \frac{2}{3}x$ **(b)** 22 mi/hr **(c)** 9 sec **(d)** 18 sec before
15. **(a)** $24 + 10x$ **(b)** 37°C **(c)** 74°C **(d)** 3.7 km **(e)** 7.6 km

Chapter 3

EXERCISE 3-1

1. $3x + 26$ **3.** $7x + 50$
5. $6x + 56$ **7.** $72x + 30$
9. $24x + 154$

EXERCISE 3-2

1. $3x + 21$ **3.** $21x - 56$
5. $3x + xy$ **7.** $-30 + 5x$
9. $-x + y$ **11.** $x^2 + 9x$
13. $54 + 42x$ **15.** $4x - 5y$
17. $7z + 4$ **19.** $\frac{8}{3}x + \frac{1}{2}$
21. $12x + 19$ **23.** $21x - 15$
25. $13 - 16x$ **27.** $-15x - 3$
29. $-x - 1$ **31.** $6x - 23$
33. $21x + 28$ **35.** $30x - 12$
37. $8 - 5x$ **39.** $21x + 13$
41. Distribute multiplication over addition.
43. Distribute multiplication over subtraction. **45.** Distribute multiplication over subtraction. **47.** Commute
49. Associate. **51.** $S = \{9\}$
53. $S = \{55\}$ **55.** $x(y + z) = xy + xz$

EXERCISE 3-3

1. $9x - 72$ **3.** $15x - 10$
5. $4x + xz$ **7.** $cx + cy$
9. $-50 + 10y$ **11.** $-7x + 56$
13. $-r + s$ **15.** $-x - y$
17. $x^2 - 4x$ **19.** $5x + 3$
21. $20x + 7$ **23.** $6x + 7$
25. $7 - 3x$ **27.** $8 + x$ **29.** $5 - 7x$
31. $-12x + 9$ **33.** $18x + 27y + 36$
35. $-10c + 4 - 14d$
37. $-6 - 3x + 4y$ **39.** $4z - 8y - 4x$
41. $2x^2 - 4xy + 7x$ **43.** $x + 9 + 8c$
45. $6 + 13r - 20s$
47. $0.72 + 3x - 2.4y$
49. $8x - 12y + 4$ **51.** Distribute multiplication over addition and subtraction.
53. Distribute multiplication over addition.
55. Commute. **57.** Use additive inverse. **59.** Distribute multiplication over subtraction from the right.
61. 7776 7776
↑ same ↑
63. A property is a fact that is true about a mathematical system. An axiom is a property that is assumed to be true without proof.

EXERCISE 3-4

1. $14x$ **3.** $5p$ **5.** xy **7.** $5x$
9. $10x + 8$ **11.** $12y + 9$
13. $-5z - 2$ **15.** $6x - 4$

17. $13 - 13c$ **19.** $11.6 - 2.6x$
21. $3(x + y)$ **23.** $5(a - b)$
25. $7(c - 2)$ **27.** $8(2d - 1)$
29. $2(3x + 4y)$ **31.** $3a(b - c)$
33. $4x(a + 3b)$ **35.** $x(x - 9)$
37. $7x(x + 1)$ **39.** $3(x + y - 2z)$
41. $8x - 6$ **43.** $-8x - 13$
45. $5x + 1$ **47.** $x + 8$ **49.** -1
51. $42x + 56$ **53.** $10 - 8x$
55. $4x$ **57.** $x + 25$ **59.** 16
61. $7x + 37$ **63.** $-10x - 27y + 39$
65. $8x - 2x^2$ **67.** $6x - 1$
69. $0.9x - 2.9$ **71.** $S = \{19\frac{4}{5}\}$
73. $S = \{-2\frac{3}{4}\}$ **75.** $5(x + 3)$
77. $d^2 + e^2$ **79.** $15y - 3$

EXERCISE 3-5

1. Commutative axiom for addition.
3. Definition of subtraction.
5. Commutative axiom for addition.
7. Associative axiom for addition.
9. Associative axiom for multiplication.
11. Distributive axiom.
13. Commutative axiom for multiplication.
15. Multiplicative identity axiom.
17. Definition of subtraction.
19. Multiplicative inverses axiom.
21. Definition of division.
23. Multiplicative identity axiom.
25. Commutative axiom for multiplication.
27. Commutative axiom for multiplication.
29. Multiplication property of 0.
31. (a) Combine like terms. **(b)** Add.
33. (a) Sub. **(b)** Comm. for add.
35. (a) Dist. **(b)** Assoc. for add.
(c) Comm. for add. **(d)** Assoc. for add.
(e) Add. **37. (a)** Sub. **(b)** Dist.
(c) Mult. **(d)** Add. **39. (a)** Sub.
(b) Assoc. for add. **(c)** Comm. for add.
(d) Assoc. for add. **(e)** Comb. like terms. **(f)** Add. **41. (a)** Div.
(b) Assoc. for mult. **(c)** Comm. for mult. **(d)** Assoc. for mult.
(e) Mult. **43. (a)** Sub. **(b)** Assoc. for add. **(c)** Comm. for add.
(d) Assoc. for add. **(e)** Add.
(f) Add. ident. **45. (a)** Div.
(b) Assoc. for mult. **(c)** Mult. inv.
(d) Mult. ident. **47. (a)** Mult. ident.
(b) Sub. **(c)** Comb. like terms.
(d) Add. **49. (a)** Mult. ident.
(b) Sub. **(c)** Dist. **(d)** Comm. for add. **(e)** Assoc. for add. **(f)** Add.
(g) Add. **51.** $3x - 3$
53. $S = \{-1\}$ **55.** $S = \{10\}$
57. $-2x - 38.8$ **59.** $S = \{-2\frac{1}{2}\}$
61. Commutative and associative axioms for multiplication. **63.** The opposite of 0 is 0.

EXERCISE 3-6

1. Symmetric axiom of equality.
3. Distributive axiom for multiplication over addition. **5.** Commutative axiom for addition. **7.** Reflexive axiom of equality.
9. Additive inverses axiom.
11. Multiplicative inverses axiom.
13. Multiplication property of -1.
15. Multiplication property of zero.
17. Combining like terms.
19. Associative axiom of multiplication.
21. Commutative axiom for multiplication.
23. Associative axiom of addition.
25. Transitive axiom of equality.
27. Commutative axiom for multiplication.
29. Combining like terms.
31. Multiplication property of equality.
33. Multiplication property of equality.
35. Commutative axiom for addition.
37. Additive inverse axiom.
39. Definition of subtraction.
41. (a) Addition property of equality.
(b) Associative axiom of addition.
(c) Additive inverse axiom.
(d) Additive identity axiom.
(e) Arithmetic
43. (a) Multiplication property of equality and definition of division.
(b) Arithmetic. **(c)** Definition of division. **(d)** Associative axiom of multiplication. **(e)** Commutative axiom for multiplication. **(f)** Associative axiom of multiplication. **(g)** Multiplicative inverses axiom. **(h)** Multiplicative identity axiom.
45. (a) Addition property of equality.
(b) Arithmetic. **(c)** Associative axiom of addition. **(d)** Additive inverses axiom.
(e) Additive identity axiom.
(f) Multiplication property of equality.
(g) Arithmetic. **(h)** Associative axiom of multiplication. **(i)** Multiplicative inverses axiom. **(j)** Multiplicative identity axiom. **47. (a)** Addition property of equality and arithmetic.
(b) Multiplication property of equality and arithmetic. **49. (a)** Addition property of equality and arithmetic. **(b)** Addition property of equality and arithmetic.
(c) Multiplication property of equality and arithmetic. **51. (a)** Definition of subtraction. **(b)** Distributive axiom of multiplication over addition. **(c)** Associative axiom of multiplication. **(d)** Definition of

subtraction. **(e)** Transitive axiom of equality. **53. (a)** Associative axiom for addition. **(b)** Distributive axiom of multiplication over addition. **(c)** Distributive axiom of multiplication over addition.
(d) Transitive axiom of equality.
55. (a) Multiplicative identity axiom.
(b) Distributive axiom of multiplication over addition. **(c)** Multiplicative identity axiom. **(d)** Definition of subtraction.
(e) Transitive axiom of equality.
57. The multiplication property of equality is true for real numbers, not for $\frac{1}{0}$.
59. (a) If $x = y$, then $y = x$.
(b) $x = x$. **(c)** If $x = y$ and $y = z$, then $x = z$. **(d)** $xy = yx$
(e) $x + (-x) = 0$ **(f)** $x \cdot 1 = x$
61. $S = \{-5\frac{2}{5}\}$ **63.** $13 + 3x$
65. $15x - 2$ **67.** $S = \{\frac{2}{5}\}$
69. $30x$

Chapter 4

EXERCISE 4-1

1. $x = 7$ **3.** $x = 5$ **5.** $x = 2$
7. $x = -4$ **9.** $x = -3$ **11.** $x = 6$
13. $x = 1$ **15.** $x = 10$ **17.** $x = 9$
19. $x = 3$ **21.** $8x - 4$ **23.** 19.9
25. 9 **27.** $x - 12$ **29.** Associative axiom of multiplication.

EXERCISE 4-2

1. $x = 4$ **3.** $x = -15$ **5.** $x = 5$
7. $r = 11$ **9.** $c = -3$
11. $-26 = x$ **13.** $t = 17$
15. $x = -7$ **17.** $x = -10.8$
19. $x = 9$ **21.** $x = -12$
23. $x = 4$ **25.** $x = 2$
27. $x = -1$ **29.** $x = 9$ **31.** $x = 7$
33. $x = -7$ **35.** $6 = x$
37. $-8 = x$ **39.** $a = 5$
41. $x = -7$ **43.** Any real no.
45. Multiplication property of -1.
47. $55 - 18x$ **49.** $14x - 10$

EXERCISE 4-3

1. $x = -9$ **3.** $x = -14$
5. $x = -13$ **7.** $5 = x$ **9.** $x = 8$
11. $c = 17$ **13.** $y = -28$
15. $a = 10$ **17.** $x = 34$
19. $z = -1$ **21.** No solution
23. $x = 0$ **25.** $x = -9$ **27.** All real nos.; identity **29.** $x = 13$
31. $6 = x$ **33.** $-3 = x$ **35.** $20 = s$
37. No solution **39.** Identity
41. $x = -2$ **43.** $x = -5\frac{1}{2}$
45. $12x - 6.9y + 2z$ **47.** 12.2
49. $4x - 25.3$

EXERCISE 4-4

1. $x \approx 5.29 \uparrow$ **3.** $x \approx 2.88 \downarrow$
5. $x \approx -2.62 \uparrow$ **7.** $c \approx -6.79 \uparrow$
9. $x \approx 5.09 \downarrow$ **11.** $x = 1.5$ (exact)
13. $x \approx -1.98 \downarrow$ **15.** $s = 4.25$ (exact)
17. $x \approx 9.76 \downarrow$ **19.** $z \approx 30.67 \uparrow$
21. $12(2x + 3y)$ **23.** 180
25. $3x + (4 + y)$ **27.** $\frac{1}{3}$ **29.** 4^3

EXERCISE 4-5

1. $x = \dfrac{17 - t}{5}$ **3.** $x = \dfrac{4 - g}{2}$
5. $x = \dfrac{c - a}{6}$ **7.** $x = \dfrac{k + b}{a}$
9. $x = 2a + b$ **11.** $x = 6v$
13. $x = \dfrac{2}{c}$ **15.** $x = \dfrac{12b}{a}$
17. $x = 7w$ **19.** $x = \dfrac{6a}{5}$
21. $W = 28$ **23.** $C = 125.6$
25. $V = 33.49$ **27.** $r = 25$
29. $A = 33$ **31. (a)** 15 Newtons
(b) $A = \dfrac{F}{M}$ **(c)** 6.67 m/s^2

EXERCISE 4-6

1. (a) $16x$ **(b)** $x - 3$, $10(x - 3)$
(c) 5 days **(d)** 20 tons
3. (a) x = no. of days. $100 - 3x$ = Phil's no. of dollars $20 + 5x$ = Ernest's no. of dollars **(b) i.** Phil has \$24 more.
ii. Ernest has \$32 more. **(c)** After 10 days. **(d)** $100 - 3x = 100 - 3(10) = 70$ ←same→ $20 + 5x = 20 + 5(10) = 70$
5. (a) x = no. of hours $38 - 1.7x$ = no. of deg. in S. G. $25 + 2.1x$ = no. of degrees in C.J. **(b)** After about 3.42 hours
(c) About 32.18 degrees **7. a.** Let x = no. of hours worked. $3 + 26x$ = Kay's no. of eqns. $8 + 20x$ = Dan's no. of eqns.
(b) Kay $11\frac{2}{3}$, Dan $14\frac{2}{3}$ **(c)** $\frac{5}{6}$ hour (50 minutes) 24.6 **(d)** Kay finishes first. After $24\frac{2}{3}$ equations they are tied, and Kay works faster than Dan. **9. (a)** x = Nick's no. of hours $x - 4$ = Ivan's no. of hours
(b) $30x$ = Nick's no. of dollars $20(x - 4)$ = Ivan's no. of dollars **(c)** 11 hours
(d) Nick \$330, Ivan \$140 **11. (a)** t = no. of hr for patrol car. $100t$ = no. of km for patrol car. $10 + 70t$ = no. of km for truck.
(b) i. Truck is 5 km further. **ii.** Patrol car is 5 km further. **(c)** $\frac{1}{3}$ hour or 20 minutes. **(d)** $100t = 100(\frac{1}{3}) = 33\frac{1}{3}$ ←same→ $10 + 70t = 10 + 70(\frac{1}{3}) = 33\frac{1}{3}$.

13. (a) t = Robin's no. of minutes. $1.7t$ = Robin's no. of km **(b)** $t - 5$ = Willie's no. of minutes $2.9(t - 5)$ = Willie's no. of km **(c)** About 12.08 min after R. starts **(d)** About 20.54 km from bank
15. (a) (diagram) **(b)** x = Lois' no. of hours $50x$ = Lois' no. of km
(c) $x - 3$ = Superman's no. of hours
$300(x - 3)$ = Superman's no. of km
(d) $50x = 300(x - 3)$ **(e)** After 3.6 hours. **17. (a)** (diagram)
(b) x = no. of hours $80x$ = car's no. of km $13 + 80x$ = bus's no. of km
(c) 9.75 minutes **(d)** 1 hour 27.75 minutes **(e)** $80x = 13 + 80x$ $0 = 13$
No solution! This is reasonable. Since each is going the same speed, the car never catches up. **19. (a)** x = no. of $ for subscr. sold
$0.6x - 100$ = publisher's no. of $
$0.4x + 100$ = school's no. of $
(b) $166.67 **(c)** $166.67 **(d)** $1000
21. (a) 2800 − 300t
(b) i. 1000 km **ii.** 4000 km
(c) $431(t - 7)$
(d) $2800 - 300t = 431(t - 7)$;
$t \approx 7.96$ min; about
413 km from station

Chapter 5

EXERCISE 5-1

1. (a) $5x^2 + 3x + 4$ **(b)** $4 + 3x + 5x^2$
3. (a) $x^5 + x^3 + x^2 + 9$
(b) $9 + x^2 + x^3 + x^5$
5. (a) $2x^5 + 5x^4 - 9x^3 + x^2 + 8x$
(b) $8x + x^2 - 9x^3 + 5x^4 + 2x^5$
7. $8x - 7$ **9.** $-x + 41$ **11.** 71

EXERCISE 5-2

1. $x^3 + 4x$ Polynomial. No ops. besides +, −, ×. **3.** $x^3 + \frac{4}{x}$ Not poly. Div. by a variable. **5.** y^5 Poly. No ops. besides +, −, ×. **7.** x Poly. No ops. besides +, −, ×. (no ops. *at all*!)
9. 3 Poly. No ops. besides +, −, ×.
11. $|x + 4|$ Not poly. Abs. val. of variable. **13.** 3, 2, −4, 7
15. 1, −5, 2 **17.** 4, 1
19. 1, −1, 5 **21.** Quadratic trinomial
23. Cubic monomial **25.** Quadratic binomial **27.** Linear monomial
29. 5th degree monomial
31. 4th degree binomial **33.** Cubic, 4 terms **35.** Linear binomial
37. $x + 1$, eg. **39.** $x^2 + x + 1$, eg.
41. $x^3 + x^2 + 1$, eg. **43.** x^2, eg.
45. $x^6 + 1$, eg. **47.** $7x^2 + 5x + 2$
49. $-x^7 + x^5 + x^3 + 11$
51. $x^4 + 2x^3 - x - 3$
53. $x^5 + 3x^4 - 9x^3 + x^2 + 7x$
55. $-x^5 + 4^5$ **57.** $x = 5$; division by zero undefined **59.** 24 **61. (a)** $10x$, $12(x - 7)$ **(b) i.** 13 min **ii.** 42 min.

EXERCISE 5-3

1. $x^2 + 7x + 12$ **3.** $x^2 + 3x - 40$
5. $x^2 - 5x - 14$ **7.** $r^2 + 3r - 28$
9. $s^2 - 5s - 6$ **11.** $x^2 - 12x + 32$
13. $x^2 - 3x + 2$ **15.** $2x^2 + 11x + 12$
17. $3x^2 - 5x - 2$ **19.** $2x^2 - 11x + 5$
21. $3x^2 + 17x + 20$ **23.** $8x^2 - 6x - 9$
25. $10x^2 - 27x - 28$
27. $16x^2 + 24x + 9$ **29.** $16x^2 - 9$
31. $4x^2 - 28x + 49$ **33.** $4x^2 - 49$
35. $x^2 + 12x + 36$ **37.** $x^2 - 18x + 81$
39. $9x^2 + 30x + 25$
41. $x^3 + 5x^2 + 11x + 10$
43. $x^3 + x^2 - 10x - 6$
45. $x^3 + 3x^2 - 7x + 15$
47. $x^3 - 10x^2 + 19x + 30$
49. $6x^3 + x^2 - 2x + 15$
51. $x^3 + 9x^2 + 26x + 24$
53. $x^3 - 2x^2 - 13x - 10$
55. $x^3 - 2x^2 - 33x + 90$
57. $x^3 - 6x^2 - 9x + 14$
59. $x^3 - 12x^2 + 44x - 48$
61. $-8x^5 - 3x^2 + 7x + 4$ **63.** eg. x
65. (a) Polynomial **(b)** Polynomial
(c) Not polynomial. Division by a variable.
(d) Polynomial. **67.** $19x - 32$
69. −25 **71.** $6x^2 + 2x - 20$
73. 40 = 40 Same!

EXERCISE 5-4

1. $(x + 1)(x + 6)$ **3.** $(x + 1)(x + 5)$
5. $(x - 1)(x - 25)$ **7.** $(r - 2)(r - 6)$
9. $(z + 2)(z + 3)$ **11.** $(x + 3)(x + 3)$
13. $(x + 1)(x + 9)$ **15.** $(x - 3)(x - 7)$
17. $(a - 5)(a - 8)$
19. $(x + 4)(x + 12)$ **21.** $(x + 6)(x + 8)$
23. $(x - 3)(x - 16)$ **25.** Prime
27. $(x - 2)(x - 24)$
29. $(m + 2)(m + 9)$
31. $(x - 2)(x - 50)$
33. Prime **35.** $(b + 10)(b + 15)$
37. $(y - 12)(y - 25)$

39. $(x - 13)(x - 77)$
41. $3x^2 + 17x + 20$
43. $10x^2 - 27x - 28$
45. $4x^2 - 28x + 49$ 47. $4x^2 - 49$
49. $x^2 - 18x + 81$ 51. $x = 8$
53. $13x - 7$
55. $-2x^3 + x^2 - 5x + 11$

EXERCISE 5-5

1. $(x - 2)(x + 5)$ 3. $(x - 2)(x + 4)$
5. $(x - 1)(x + 9)$ 7. $(r + 2)(r - 6)$
9. $(a + 5)(a - 6)$ 11. $(x - 4)(x + 5)$
13. $(x + 5)(x - 10)$
15. $(x + 2)(x - 25)$ 17. Prime
19. $(u + 1)(u - 72)$ 21. Prime
23. $(u + 4)(u - 18)$
25. $(u - 8)(u + 9)$ 27. $(x - 6)(x - 7)$
29. $(x - 1)(x + 6)$ 31. $(x - 2)(x - 3)$
33. $(x + 6)(x + 20)$
35. $(x - 4)(x + 30)$
37. $(x - 7)(x - 14)$
39. $(x - 3)(x + 17)$ 41. $x^2 - 5x - 14$
43. $4x^2 - 5x - 6$
45. $21x^2 + 68x + 32$ 47. María
49. (a)

Factors	*Sum*	*Trinomials*
$-1 + 6$	$+5$	$x^2 + 5x - 6$
$-2 + 3$	$+1$	$x^2 + x - 6$
$-3 + 2$	-1	$x^2 - x - 6$
$-6 + 1$	-5	$x^2 - 5x - 6$

(b)

Factors	*Sum*	*Trinomials*
$-1 + 8$	7	$x^2 + 7x - 8$
$-2 + 4$	2	$x^2 + 2x - 8$
$-4 + 2$	-2	$x^2 - 2x - 8$
$-8 + 1$	-7	$x^2 - 7x - 8$

(c)

Factors	*Sum*	*Trinomials*
$1 + 10$	11	$x^2 + 11x + 10$
$2 + 5$	7	$x^2 + 7x + 10$
$-2 + (-5)$	-7	$x^2 - 7x + 10$
$-1 + (-10)$	-11	$x^2 - 11x + 10$

(d)

Factors	*Sum*	*Trinomials*
$1 + 18$	19	$x^2 + 19x + 18$
$2 + 9$	11	$x^2 + 11x + 18$
$3 + 6$	9	$x^2 + 9x + 18$
$-3 + (-6)$	-9	$x^2 - 9x + 18$
$-2 + (-9)$	-11	$x^2 - 11x + 18$
$-1 + (-18)$	-19	$x^2 - 19x + 18$

(e)

Factors	*Sum*	*Trinomials*
$1 + 25$	26	$x^2 + 26x + 25$
$5 + 5$	10	$x^2 + 10x + 25$
$-5 + (-5)$	-10	$x^2 - 10x + 25$
$-1 + (-25)$	-26	$x^2 - 26x + 25$

EXERCISE 5-6

1. $(x + 1)(5x + 3)$ 3. $(x + 2)(2x + 1)$
5. $(y + 3)(2y + 1)$ 7. $(x + 4)(2x + 1)$
9. $(x - 5)(3x - 1)$ 11. $(x - 1)(3x - 2)$
13. $(p - 2)(3p - 2)$
15. $(x - 3)(3x + 1)$
17. $(v + 1)(3v - 2)$
19. $(x - 2)(5x + 2)$
21. $(2x + 3)(2x + 1)$
23. $(x + 1)(4x + 3)$
25. $(2u + 5)(2u - 1)$
27. $(4x + 5)(x - 1)$
29. $(2x + 3)(3x + 4)$
31. $x^2 + 3x - 28$ 33. $3x^2 + 19x - 40$
35. $14x^2 - 15x + 4$ 37. Both.
39. (a) $(3 + x)(2 + x)$
(b) $(1 + 3x)(1 + 2x)$
(c) $(x + 5)(x + 5)$ (d) $(x + 5)(x - 5)$
(e) $(5x + 1)(5x + 1)$
(f) $(2x - 3)(2x - 3)$
(g) $(2x + 3)(2x - 3)$
(h) $(a + b + 1)(a + b + 6)$
(i) $(r - s + 1)(r - s + 2)$
(j) (number + 2)(number − 5)

EXERCISE 5-7

1. $(x + 4)(x - 4)$ 3. $(x + 8)(x - 8)$
5. $(a + 2)(a - 2)$ 7. $(c + 3)(c - 3)$
9. $(x + 1)(x - 1)$
11. $(2x + 5)(2x - 5)$
13. $(3x + 7)(3x - 7)$
15. $(5a + 6)(5a - 6)$
17. $(9r + 2)(9r - 2)$
19. $(3x + 10)(3x - 10)$
21. $(2 + 5x)(2 - 5x)$
23. $(10 + 3x)(10 - 3x)$
25. Prime 27. $(1 + p)(1 - p)$
29. Prime 31. $(2x + 3y)(2x - 3y)$
33. $(5x + 9y)(5x - 9y)$
35. $(x + 7y)(x - 7y)$
37. $(6a + b)(6a - b)$
39. $(c + d)(c - d)$
41. $(a + b + 2)(a + b - 2)$
43. $(3x + c + d)(3x - c - d)$
45. $(9 + 8xy)(9 - 8xy)$
47. $-4(x + 4)$ 49. (5 number +1)(5 number −1) 51. $12x^2 - 22x - 14$
53. $(x - 2)(x + 15)$
55. $(x + 3)(x + 10)$ 57. $13 = x$
59. $41 - 5x$ 61. -10

EXERCISE 5-8

1. $x^2 + 18x + 81$ 3. $x^2 - 20x + 100$
5. $25x^2 + 60x + 36$
7. $16x^2 - 56x + 49$ 9. $36 - 12x + x^2$
11. $x^2 + 16x + 64$ 13. $x^2 + 6x + 9$
15. $h^2 - 12h + 36$
17. $x^2 + 24x + 144$
19. $k^2 - 14k + 49$
21. $16x^2 + 24x + 9$

23. $25x^2 - 20x + 4$
25. $49x^2 - 14x + 1$
27. $36x^2 + 84x + 49$
29. $9c^2 - 42c + 49$
31. $25 + 10x + x^2$
33. $81 - 72x + 16x^2$
35. $t^2 + 2t + 1$ **37.** $x^2 - 4x + 4$
39. $81a^2 - 126a + 49$
41. $x^2 + 8xy + 16y^2$
43. $25a^2 - 10ab + b^2$
45. $4y^2 + 20yz + 25z^2$
47. $a^2 + 2ab + b^2$ **49.** $a^2 - 2ab + b^2$
51. $(x + 3)(x + 5)$
53. $(5w - 3)(w + 1)$
55. $(d + 7)(d - 7)$
57. $(10x + 3)(10x - 3)$
59. $4x^2 + 5x - 21$ **61.** The middle term is missing. **63. (a)** $x^2 - 6x + 9$ **(b)** $9 - 6x + x^2$ **(c)** Equivalent
65. (a) $(x + y)^3 = (x + y)(x + y)(x + y)$
(b) $= (x + y)(x^2 + 2xy + y^2)$
(c) $= x^3 + 2x^2y + xy^2 + x^2y + 2xy^2 + y^3$
$= x^3 + 3x^2y + 3xy^2 + y^3$
(d) The powers of x start at x^3 and *drop* 1 each term. The powers of y *increase* 1 each term. The coefficients are 1, 3, 3, 1.
(e) i. $a^3 + 3a^2b + 3ab^2 + b^3$
ii. $r^3 - 3r^2s + 3rs^2 - s^3$
iii. $x^3 + 6x^2 + 12x + 8$
iv. $x^3 - 15x^2 + 75x - 125$

EXERCISE 5-9

1. $(x + 3)^2$ **3.** $(x - 5)^2$
5. $(x + 8)^2$ **7.** $(x - 2)^2$
9. $(x - 1)^2$ **11.** 20 is *not* a perf. sq.
13. $(x - 4)^2$ **15.** $\sqrt{-16}$ is *not* a real no. **17.** $20 \neq 2\sqrt{81}$ **19.** $(a + 10)^2$
21. $(x - 15)^2$ **23.** $(x + 31)^2$
25. $(x - 47)^2$ **27.** $(x + 89)^2$
29. $(x - 74)^2$ **31.** Middle term $\neq 2 \times 68$ **33.** $(x - 111)^2$
35. $20 \neq 2\sqrt{400}$ **37.** $(x - 100)^2$
39. 1000 is *not* a perf. sq.
41. $3x^2 + 10x - 8$
43. $16x^2 + 24x + 9$
45. $(3x - 1)(x - 7)$ **47.** $x = 12.5$
49. 15 **51. (a)** 7^2 **(b)** 2^2 **(c)** 6^2 **(d)** 8^2 **53. (a)** $7^2 = 49$ and $(-7)^2 = 49$. So 7 and -7 are both square roots of 49. **(b)** $\sqrt{49} = 7$ because the symbol $\sqrt{\ }$ means the *positive* square root. **(c)** $\sqrt{49} = -7$, but $\sqrt{-49}$ is *not* a real number because no real number gives a *negative* answer when it is squared.

EXERCISE 5-10

1. Closed e.g. $3 \times 4 = 12 \leftarrow$ real
3. Closed e.g. $-3 + (-4) = -7 \leftarrow$ neg.
5. Not closed e.g. $2 \div 3 = \frac{2}{3} \leftarrow$ not an int. **7.** Closed e.g. $2 \div 3 = \frac{2}{3} \leftarrow$ pos.
9. Not closed e.g. $-3 \times (-2) = 6 \leftarrow$ not neg. **11.** Closed e.g. $2 - 7 = -5 \leftarrow$ real
13. Closed e.g. $2 + 5 = 7 \leftarrow$ pos. int.
15. Closed e.g. $\frac{3}{5} \times \frac{1}{4} = \frac{3}{20} \leftarrow$ rational
17. Closed e.g. $3 + (-7) = -4 \leftarrow$ integer
19. Not closed e.g. $0 - 1 = -1 \leftarrow$ not in set **21.** Closed e.g. $(0)(1) = 0 \leftarrow$ in set **23.** Not closed e.g. $|-3| = 3 \leftarrow$ not neg. **25.** Closed e.g. $2^3 = 8 \leftarrow$ pos. int. **27.** Not closed e.g. $\sqrt{-9}$ is not a real no. **29.** Closed e.g. $\sqrt{1} = 1$ **31.** rational **33.** irrational
35. rational **37.** rational
39. irrational **41.** neither
43. rational **45.** $8x^2 + 22x + 15$
47. $(2x + 3)(x - 4)$ **49.** $(c - 9)^2$
51. $x = 5$ **53.** $3x - 15$

Chapter 6

EXERCISE 6-2

1. 7.94 **3.** 4 **5.** 5.65 **7.** 10
9. 21 **11.** 0.88 **13.** No value
15. 29.93 **17.** 8.31 **19.** 3.83
21. 5 **23.** -1.81 **25.** -2.76
27. -5.29 **29.** -1.68 **31.** 0.31
33. (a) $6 = 6$
↑ same ↑
(b) $4.5825756 = 4.5825756$
↑ same ↑
(c) $30 = 30$
↑ same ↑
(d) $4.6010868 = 4.6010868$
↑ same ↑
35. (a) $7.8102496 \neq 11$
↑ Not the same! ↑
(b) $7.1414284 \neq 3$
↑ Not the same! ↑
37. $\sqrt{289329955237}$ is *irrational*. Perfect squares end in only 0, 1, 4, 5, 6, or 9. Since the radicand ends in 7, it is *not* a perfect square, and its square root is thus *irrational*. However, the next *lower* integer, 289329955236, *is* a perfect square, 537894^2.

EXERCISE 6-3

1. $S = \{15, -15\}$ **3.** $S = \{132, -132\}$
5. $S = \{9, -5\}$ **7.** $S = \{16, -22\}$
9. $S = \emptyset$ **11.** $S = \{-26, 36\}$
13. $S = \{17, -12\}$ **15.** $S = \{9.5, -13\}$

17. $S = \{11, 2.2\}$ **19.** $S = \{-3.1, 4.5\}$
21. $S = \emptyset$ **23.** $S = \{8\}$
25. $S = \{30, -30\}$ **27.** $S = \{24, -24\}$
29. $S = \{9.5, -12.5\}$ **31.** $S = \{10, -8\}$
33. $S = \{3, 6\}$ **35.** $S = \{x: x \geq 0\}$
37. $x = (-3 \pm 5)/7$

EXERCISE 6-4

1. $S = \{12, -2\}$ **3.** $S = \{7, -13\}$
5. $S = \{6.60, -10.60\}$
7. $S = \{14.24, 1.76\}$
9. $S = \{16.28, -2.28\}$ **11.** $S = \{2, -7\}$
13. $S = \{5.12, 2.21\}$
15. $S = \{-2.31, -3.29\}$
17. $S = \{\frac{2}{3}\}$ **19.** $S = \{9.74, 2.26\}$
21. $S = \{-1.40, -6.80\}$
23. $S = \{1.85, -0.85\}$
25. $S = \{20.68, -57.18\}$
27. $S = \{16, 0\}$
29. $S = \emptyset$ **31.** $S = \{21, -29\}$
33. $S = \{13, -1\}$ **35.** $S = \{8, -13\}$
37. $S = \{-11, 13.5\}$ **39.** $S = \emptyset$
41. $\sqrt{(x-3)^2}$ means the *positive* square root. Since $x - 3$ can be a *negative* number, the answer must be $|x - 3|$.

EXERCISE 6-5

1. $S = \{1, -7\}$ **3.** $S = \{7, -3\}$
5. $S = \{5.48, -7.48\}$
7. $S = \{53.73, -35.73\}$
9. $S = \{5.93, -13.93\}$
11. $S = \{11.39, 0.61\}$
13. $S = \{12.93, 7.07\}$ **15.** $S = \emptyset$
17. $S = \{0, -14\}$ **19.** $S = \{-5\}$
21. $S = \{4.5, -9.5\}$
23. $S = \{6.5, 0.5\}$
25. $S = \{13.04, -4.04\}$
27. $S = \{1.09, -3.69\}$
29. $S = \{1.29, 0.11\}$
31. $S = \{41, -31\}$
33. $S = \{1700, -2300\}$
35. $S = \{3, -2.6\}$ **37.** $S = \{3, -17\}$
39. $S = \{1, -0.4\}$ **41.** $S = \{\frac{1}{3}, -1\}$
43. $S = \{\frac{12}{5}, -\frac{6}{5}\}$ **45.** $S = \{-2, -\frac{1}{3}\}$
47. $S = \{2, -\frac{3}{4}\}$
49. (a) $x^2 + 10x + 13 = 47$ Constant term would have to be $[\frac{1}{2}(10)]^2 = 5^2 = 25$. **(b)** So *add 12* to each member. $x^2 + 10x + 13 + 12 = 47 + 12$
(c) $x^2 + 10x + 25 = 59$ $(x + 5)^2 = 59$
$x = -5 \pm \sqrt{59}$ $S = \{2.68, -12.68\}$

EXERCISE 6-6

1. $x^2 + 12x + 36$ **3.** $x^2 - 10x + 25$
5. $x^2 + 18x + 81$ **7.** $x^2 - 4x + 4$
9. $x^2 + 2x + 1$ **11.** 25 **13.** 9
15. 144 **17.** 625 **19.** 1
21. 6.25 **23.** 42.25 **25.** 3.61
27. 6.5025 **29.** 0.0225
31. $S = \{0.39, -10.39\}$

EXERCISE 6-7

1. $S = \{-0.76, -5.24\}$
3. $S = \{7.61, 0.39\}$
5. $S = \{17, -1\}$
7. $S = \{2.59, -16.59\}$
9. $S = \{7, 3\}$ **11.** $S = \{0.95, -20.95\}$
13. $S = \{6.87, -4.87\}$ **15.** $S = \emptyset$
17. $S = \{6\}$ **19.** $S = \{0, -18\}$
21. $S = \{-0.70, -4.30\}$
23. $S = \{7.53, -0.53\}$
25. $S = \{6.22, -3.22\}$
27. $S = \{6, 5\}$ **29.** $S = \{1.28, -4.68\}$
31. $S = \{8, -2\}$ **33.** $S = \{-1, -7\}$
35. $S = \{1.3, 0.5\}$ **37.** $S = \{0.2, -10\}$
39. $S = \{1.19, -4.19\}$
41. $S = \{3.37, 1.63\}$
43. $S = \{-0.76, -1.84\}$
45. $S = \{5.72, -26.22\}$
47. $S = \{6.5, -1.5\}$ **49.** $S = \emptyset$
51. $S = \{69, -59\}$ **53.** $S = \{-4, -10\}$
55. $S = \{16, -4\}$ **57.** $S = \{4.3, -13.7\}$
59. $S = \{32\}$

EXERCISE 6-8

1. $S = \{-1\frac{2}{3}, -3\}$ **3.** $S = \{2.30, 0.56\}$
5. $S = \{0.71, -1.26\}$
7. $S = \{-6.16, 2.56\}$
9. $S = \emptyset$ **11.** $S = \{3, -\frac{1}{6}\}$
13. $S = \{-0.32, -21.68\}$
15. $S = \{7, -3\}$ **17.** $S = \{1.52, -8.52\}$
19. $S = \{-1.62, 0.62\}$
21. $S = \{1.34, -1.34\}$ **23.** $S = \emptyset$
25. $S = \{0, -1\frac{2}{3}\}$ **27.** $S = \{1, 0\}$
29. $S = \{2.5\}$ **31.** $S = \{-\frac{2}{3}, -1\}$
33. $S = \{0.29, -0.69\}$
35. $S = \{4.54, -1.54\}$
37. $S = \{5, -6\}$ **39.** $S = \{-1, -7\}$
41. $S = \{2.41, -5.41\}$
43. $S = \{2, -\frac{23}{6}\} = \{2, -3.83\}$
45. $S = \emptyset$ **47.** $S = \{-0.32, 0.62\}$
49. $S = \{-6\}$ **51.** $S = \{0.3, -4.3\}$
53. $S = \{15.4, -4.2\}$
55. $S = \{-3, -11\}$ **57.** $S = \{3, -5\}$
59. $S = \{3.24, 2.16\}$ **61. (a)** -56 No solutions **(b)** 61 Has solutions **(c)** 401 Has solutions **(d)** -47 No solutions

EXERCISE 6-9

1. (a) i. 30 m **ii.** 30 m **(b)** At 1 sec, and at 4 sec **(c)** (Diagram)

(d) After 5 sec **3. (a)** 40 m
(b) After 1 sec and after 5 sec
(c) After 6 sec **(d) i.** 3 sec
ii. 45 m **(e)** (Diagram)
5. (a) 4 sec **(b)** 20 sec
(c) 24 sec **(d)** 30 sec
7. (a) 2.4 m **(b)** After 0.4 sec and after 1 sec **(c)** After 1.4 sec
(d) After 2.82 sec **9. (a)** 5.95 m
(b) After 1.2 sec **(c)** It was neither going up nor down. It had reached its high point since there was only *one* value of t.
(d) 2.4 sec **(e)** 32 m deep
11. (a) 1.35 m **(b)** 4.35 m
(c) 1.2 sec **(d)** 0.6 sec; 4.8 m
13. (a) 54 m **(b)** 5.56 sec or 1.04 sec
(c) Ball is *never* 60 m high!
(d) (Diagram) **15. (a)** 0.8 sec
(b) 0.4 sec, 3.8 m **(c)** 1.27 sec
(d) i. 5 sec **ii.** 8 m **iii.** 5.66 sec
17. (a) i. 2.80 sec **ii.** 11.59 m
(b) i. 18.10 m/sec **ii.** 18.74 m
(c) She'll *never* be 9 m above ground. No times at which distance is 9.

EXERCISE 6-10

1. D = 76 Irrational
3. D = −76 none
5. D = 176 Irrational
7. D = 529 = 23^2 Rational
9. D = 0 = 0^2 Rational
11. D = 29 Irrational
13. D = −23 None
15. D = 25 = 5^2 Rational
17. D = −3 None
19. D = 5 Irrational
21. D = 109 Irrational
23. D = 49 = 7^2 Rational
25. D = 289 = 17^2 Rational
27. D = −31 None
29. D = 8.97 Irrational
31. D = 2.39^2 Rational
33. D = 0 Rational
35. D = −2000 Never reaches!
37. D = 2.01 Can dunk!
39. D = −0.36 Can't make it!

Chapter 7

EXERCISE 7-1

1. (a) 31 **(b)** 41 **(c)** 13.25
(d) −10 **3. (a)** 16 **(b)** −1
(c) 4.6 **(d)** −13.2 **5. (a)** −62
(b) 7 **(c)** 85 **7. (a)** 79
(b) 649 **(c)** 12,400 **(d)** 70

EXERCISE 7-2

1. A (2, 5) **B** (−3, 2) **C** (−3, −2)
D (1, −5) **E** (5, 0) **F** (0, 3)
G (−3, 5) **H** (−5, 1) **I** (−5, −4)
J (−2, 0) **3.** (Graph)
5. A (1.8, 1.6) **B** (−1.7, 1.5)
C (−0.3, −1.9) **D** (1.6, −0.8)
7. (Graph) **(a)** (4, 4) **(b)** (5, 6)
(c) (3, 2) **(d)** (2, 0) **9.** (Graph)
(1.7, 2.8) **11.** (Graph) The lines are *parallel*. **13. (a)** (2, 1) (examples only!)
(b) (−1, 2) **(c)** (−1, −5)
(d) (3, −1) **(e)** (−1, 0)
15. (Graph)

EXERCISE 7-3

1. (Graph) **3.** (Graph) **5.** (Graph)
7. (Graph) **9.** (Graph)
(a) $y = -3x + 12$
(b) x: −1, 0, 1, 2, 3, 4 y: 15, 12, 9, 6, 3, 0
11. (Graph) **(a)** $y = 2x - 6$
(b) x: 0, 1, 2, 3, 4 y: −6, −4, −2, 0, 2
13. (Graph) **(a)** $y = -\frac{4}{5}x + 8$
(b) x: 0, 5, 10, −5 y: 8, 4, 0, 12
15. (Graph) **(a)** $y = \frac{3}{2}x + 9$
(b) x: −6, −4, −2, 0 y: 0, 3, 6, 9
17. (Graph) **(a)** $y = -x + 7$
(b) x: 7, 6, 5, 4, 3, 2, 1, 0
y: 0, 1, 2, 3, 4, 5, 6, 7 **19.** (Graph)
(a) $y = \frac{1}{3}x$ **(b)** x: −3, 0, 3, 6
y: −1, 0, 1, 2

EXERCISE 7-4

1. (Graph) x: 6 y: 8 **3.** (Graph)
x: −10 y: −4 **5.** (Graph) x: 12 y: −9
7. (Graph) x: −8 y: 5 **9.** (Graph)
x: 5 y: 10 **11.** (Graph) x: −2 y: 12
13. (Graph) x: 6 y: 2 **15.** (Graph)
x: 4 y: 4 **17.** (Graph) x: −3 y: 3
19. (Graph) x: 7.5 y: 5 **21.** (Graph)
x: 7.6 y: 6.5 **23.** (Graph) x: 5.2
y: −2.9 **25. (a)** $3x + 2y$
(b) i. \$44 **ii.** \$46
(c) $3x + 2y = 30$ **(d)** x: 10 y: 15
(Graph) **(e)** (0, 15), (2, 12), (4, 9), (6, 6), (8, 3), (10, 0) **27. (a)** $100x + 300y$
(b) i. 1600 yd **ii.** 2400 yd
(c) $100x + 300y = 6000$ **(d)** x: 60
y: 20 (Graph) **(e)** 16 min

EXERCISE 7-5

1. (a) $\frac{4}{9}$ **(b)** $-\frac{4}{3}$ **(c)** 2 **(d)** −2
(e) 0 **(f)** No slope **3.** (Graph)
$m = -\frac{5}{7}$ **5.** (Graph) $m = -\frac{4}{3}$
7. (Graph) $m = \frac{8}{3}$ **9.** (Graph) $m = -\frac{4}{7}$

11. (Graph) **13.** (Graph) **15.** (Graph) **17.** (Graph) **19.** (Graph) **21.** (Graph) **23.** (Graph) $y = -\frac{7}{2}x + 5$; $m = -\frac{7}{2}$, y-int = 5 **25.** (Graph) $y = \frac{1}{4}x - 3$; $m = \frac{1}{4}$, y-int = −3 **27.** (Graph) $y = \frac{2}{3}x - 1$; $m = \frac{2}{3}$, y-int = −1 **29.** (Graph) $y = -\frac{1}{4}x - 4$; $m = -\frac{1}{4}$, y-int = −4 **31.** $y = 3x + 5$ **33.** $y = \frac{2}{3}x - 1$

EXERCISE 7-6

1. **(a)** $m = \frac{2}{5}$, (1, 4)
3. **(a)** $m = 4$, (3, −2)
5. **(a)** $m = \frac{1}{3}$, (−4, 5)
7. **(a)** $m = \frac{3}{2}$, (−5, −1)
9. $y = 2x + 5$ **11.** $y = -5x + \frac{2}{3}$
13. $y - 9 = -3(x - 4)$
15. $y - 5 = \frac{4}{9}(x - 2)$
17. $y - 2 = -13(x + 7)$
19. $y + 4 = \frac{1}{8}(x + 2)$
21. $y - 5 = \frac{7}{2}(x - 4)$
23. $y - 2 = -(x + 1)$
25. $y + 1 = -\frac{1}{3}(x + 8)$ **27.** $x = 3$
29. $y = -7$ **31.** $y = -\frac{3}{5}x + 4$
33. $y - 5 = \frac{4}{3}(x - 2)$
35. $y - 6 = -2(x + 5)$ **37.** $y = -7$
39. $y + 1 = \frac{2}{7}(x - 6)$ **41.** $y = 7x + 4$
43. $y = -\frac{3}{7}x + 5$ **45.** $y = -\frac{7}{5}x + 4$
47. $y - 9 = -\frac{1}{7}(x - 4)$
49. $y + 10 = -\frac{5}{4}(x + 3)$
51. $y = 4(x - 5)$ **53.** no such line
55. $y = kx$ for any real $k \neq 0$.

EXERCISE 7-7

1. (Graph) $2x + 3y = 18$: $x = 9$, $y = 6$ $x - y = 5$: $x = 5$, $y = -5$ (6.6, 1.6) **3.** (Graph) $2x + y = 8$: $x = 4$, $y = 8$ $5x - 3y = 15$: $x = 3$, $y = -5$ (3.6, 0.9) **5.** (Graph) $8x - 5y = -40$: $x = -5$, $y = 8$ $2x + y = -6$: $x = -3$, $y = -6$ (−3.9, 1.8) **7.** (Graph) $3x + 2y = -12$: $x = -4$, $y = -6$, $x - y = -2$: $x = -2$, $y = 2$ (−3.2, −1.2) **9.** (Graph) $2x + 3y = -12$: $x = -6$, $y = -4$ $8x - 5y = 40$: $x = 5$, $y = -8$ (1.8, −5.2) **11.** (Graph) $3x + 5y = 15$; $x = 5$, $y = 3$ $3x + 5y = 30$: $x = 10$, $y = 6$ No intersection!

EXERCISE 7-8

1. (2, 4) **3.** (−1, −3) **5.** (3, 7) **7.** (−1.4, 3.6) **9.** (1, 9) **11.** (−4, 3) **13.** (5, −1) **15.** (0, 5) **17.** (12.41, 10.59) **19.** (2.5, −3.5) **21.** (2, −4) **23.** (1, 3) **25.** (3, 5) **27.** (245.45, 109.09) **29.** (729.73, 189.19) **31.** (Graph) (2, 7) **33.** (Graph) (−3, 5)

EXERCISE 7-9

1. (4, 7) **3.** (−3, 5) **5.** (1.6, 8.2) **7.** (11, −3) **9.** (6, −1) **11.** (5.1, 2.7) **13.** (−3, 0) **15.** (1, −17) **17.** (3, 2) **19.** (4.31, 2.02) **21.** (4, 1) **23.** (−1, 3) **25.** (2, 0) **27.** (0.4, 1.3) **29.** (1, 2) **31.** (1.2, 0.7) **33.** (−4, 3.4) **35.** (10, 2) **37.** (4, −1) **39.** (0, 2.7) **41.** $y = 2x - 2$ **43.** $y = \frac{1}{4}x + 3$

EXERCISE 7-10

1. (a) $2x + 3y$, $4x + 5y$ **(b) i.** \$2.50 for reg., \$4.40 for spec. **ii.** \$2.40 for reg., \$4.30 for spec. **(c)** 37¢ for taco, 55¢ for enchilada **3. (a)** 70¢ for an egg, 83¢ for a sausage **(b)** \$9.31 **5.** 48¢/liter for reg., 52¢/liter for unleaded **7. (a)** 41¢/scoop for ice cream, 5¢ for cone **(b)** \$1.69 **9.** 47.9¢/liter for regular, 52.9¢/liter for unleaded **11. (a)** $3x + 5y$ **(b) i.** 146 **ii.** 163 **iii.** 163 **(c)** $x + y = 49$, $3x + 5y = 181$; 32 cars, 17 trucks **13.** 431 reserved, 1356 gen. adm. **15.** 103 cars, 57 trucks **17. (a)** $0.43x + 0.27y$ **(b)** 1670 **(c)** 33.4% **(d)** 500 mg CO, 1100 mg CO_2 **19.** 140.74 kg coins, 59.26 kg silver solder **21. (a)** 79.5% **(b)** 60 advanced, 30 regular **23. (a)** $20(x + y)$ = no. of ft out, $30(x - y)$ = no. of ft back **(b) i.** 10000 ft out, 9000 ft back **ii.** 2600 ft out, 900 ft back **(c)** Shark swims 87.5 ft/min, current is 17.5 ft/min **25.** 35 km/h through air, 25 km/h wind **27.** Ann runs 5 ft/sec, escalator moves 1 ft/sec

29. They pedal 33 m/min, current is 7 m/min. **31.** Aquaman swims about 140.5 m/min, water flows about 73.8 m/min **33. (a)** \$80 from mother, \$120 from father **(b)** \$110.64 from mother, \$153.19 from father **(c)** \$63.83 **35. (a)** $s = 0.1(50{,}000 - f)$ $f = 0.2(50{,}000 - s)$ **(b)** \$4081.63 state tax, \$9183.67 federal tax **(c)** \$1734.70 **37. (a)** 5.6 min uphill, 7.4 min downhill **(b)** 432 m uphill, 1752 m downhill **39.** 30 5-member, 10 3-member

Chapter 8

EXERCISE 8-1

1. (a) −25 **(b)** 6

3. Positive slope, negative y-intercept

5. (Graph)

7. (a) Let T = total cost in dollars.
Let f = square feet of floor space.
$\underline{T = 40{,}000 + 60f}$
(b) $T = 40{,}000 + 60(2500)$
$= \underline{\$190{,}000}$
(c) $220{,}000 = 40{,}000 + 60f$
$f = \underline{3{,}000 \text{ ft}^2}$
(d) (Graph)

9. (a) Let P = total daily pay in dollars.
Let t = tip money received during day.
$\underline{P = 40 + 0.7t}$
(b) $100 = 40 + 0.7t$
$t = \underline{\$85.71}$
(c) $P = 40 + 0.7(57)$
$= \underline{\$79.90}$
(d) Domain and range would depend on the reasonable limit on tips for this restaurant.

11. (a) Let T = total time in hours.
Let m = miles of center strip painted.
45 min. = 0.75 h
$\underline{T = 0.75 + 2.3\,m}$
(b) $T = 0.75 + 2.3(2)$
$T = \underline{5.35 \text{ h or } 5 \text{ h } 21 \text{ min}}$
(c) $8 = 0.75 + 2.3m$
$m \approx \underline{3.15 \text{ mi}}$
(d) (Graph)

13. (a) Let w = number of ounces in box.
Let d = cost in dollars for a box.
(24, 1.95), (18, 1.49)
(b) $m = \dfrac{1.95 - 1.49}{24 - 18}$
$\approx \underline{0.0767}$
(c) $d - 1.95 = 0.0767(w - 24)$
or
$d - 1.49 = 0.0767(w - 18)$
(d) Transform the equation to slope-intercept form. The y-intercept is the fixed cost.

$$d = 1.95 + 0.0767w - 1.84$$
$$d = 0.0767w + 0.11$$

The fixed cost is about $\underline{\$0.11}$.

EXERCISE 8-2

For **1–13,** all answers also have graphs. Equations are for regression lines. Estimated answers will vary somewhat.
1. $x$av = 8.1, $y$av = 5.0; $y = .24x + 3.09$ **3.** $x$av = 5.2, $y$av = 4.8; $y = -1.34x + 11.75$ **5.** $x$av = 11.2, $y$av = 7.3; $y = .32x + 3.70$ **7.** $x$av = 5.1, $y$av = 5.5; $y = 0.64x + 2.2$ **9.** $x$av = 5.0, $y$av = 3.8; $y = -0.2375x + 4.99$ **11.** $x$av = 2.55, $y$av = −2.25; $y = 1.27x - 5.49$ **13. (c)** 0.6 **(d)** $y = 0.6x - 4.84$ **(e)** approx 57 inches **15.** If you assume sports records are linear, showing a downward trend, then there will be a year when the time for the event—for instance, the mile run—is *zero* (and then becomes negative)!

EXERCISE 8-3

1. (a) 1/11 **(b)** 2/11 **(c)** 6/11 **(d)** 4/11 **(e)** 9/11 **(f)** 10/11 **(g)** 10/11 **(h)** 0/11 = 0 **3. (a)** 12/24 = 1/2 **(b)** 1/2 **(c)** 2/3, 3/4 **(d)** 1/2 **(e)** it is the same as those two probabilities **(f)** 19.5/24 = 0.8125 **5. (a)** 1/25 **(b)** 4% **(c)** 28% **(d)** Ann hits bull's eye 10/72 ≈ 14% of the time, more than the 4% from part **(a)** This is because her arrows are not striking the target randomly, as we assumed in part **(a)** **7. (a)** $x \in \{0, 1, 2, \ldots, 10\}$ **(b)** $0 \le x \le 10, x \in \mathrm{R}$ **(c)** $0 \le w \le 6, 0 \le h \le 4$

(d) $x \in \{1, 2, 3, 4, 5, 6\}$, $y \in \{1, 2, 3, 4\}$ **(e)** all points on the target **(f)** all points on the screen **(g)** $x \in \{0, 3, 6, 9\}$ **(h)** $4 \le x \le 10$ **(i)** $w \le 4$ and $h \le 3$ **(j)** the ordered pairs (1, 1), (1, 2) (1, 3), (1, 4), (2, 1), (2, 2), (2, 3), (3, 1), (3, 2), (4, 1), (5, 1), (6, 1) **(k)** all points in the 3rd ring **(l)** all points on the screen at least 1/2 mm away from all wires **9. (a)** smallest is 10000, largest is 99999; 90000 possibilities **(b)** 9 **(c)** 81 **(d)** 8; 648 **(e)** 27216 **(f)** 0.3024 = 30.24% **11. (a)** 24 **(b)** 5040 **(c)** 362880 **(d)** 3628800 **(e)** 8.321×10^{81} **(f)** 19958400 **(g)** 144 **(h)** F **(i)** F **(j)** F **(k)** F

EXERCISE 8-4

1. (a) 50% **(b)–(e)** Answers will vary **(f)** Answers will vary, but results should confirm the law.
3. (a) Histogram will have 5 boxes for 1, 2, 3, 4, 5, and 6. **(b)** Answers will vary **5. (a)–(f)** Answers will vary

Chapter 9

EXERCISE 9-1

1. $2^3 \cdot 5$ **3.** $3^2 \cdot 5^2$ **5.** $2^2 \cdot 3^2 \cdot 7$ **7.** $2^4 \cdot 7^2$ **9.** $3^4 \cdot 11$ **11.** $11^2 \cdot 17$ **13.** $2^2 \cdot 3^3 \cdot 5^2$ **15.** $5^3 \cdot 7^2$ **17.** $7 \cdot 13^3$ **19.** $2 \cdot 3 \cdot 5 \cdot 7 \cdot 11 \cdot 13$ **21. (a)** $2 \cdot 2 \cdot 3$ **(b)** If 1 were a prime then these would *also* be prime factorizations of 12: $1 \cdot 2 \cdot 2 \cdot 3$; $1 \cdot 1 \cdot 2 \cdot 2 \cdot 3$; $1 \cdot 1 \cdot 1 \cdot 2 \cdot 2 \cdot 3$; $1 \cdot 1 \cdot 1 \cdot 1 \cdot 2 \cdot 2 \cdot 3$, etc. **(c)** The set of prime factors of 1 is $\emptyset$, the *empty* set!

EXERCISE 9-2

1. (a) 8 **(b)** 125 **(c)** −27 **3. (a)** 64 **(b)** 4096 **(c)** 1 **5. (a)** 48 **(b)** 3888 **(c)** 30,000 **7. (a)** 2000 **(b)** 8 **(c)** −72 **9. (a)** 59,049 **(b)** 1024 **(c)** 1,048,576 **11.** x^7 **13.** x^9 **15.** x^{13} **17.** x^8 **19.** x^{15} **21.** x^3y^3 **23.** a^6b^6 **25.** $81x^4$ **27.** $25x^2$ **29.** x^8y^4 **31.** $5^3 = 5 \cdot 5 \cdot 5$. There are three 5's, not 3 "times" signs.

EXERCISE 9-3

1. (a) 64 **(b)** 64 **3. (a)** 8000 **(b)** 8000 **5. (a)** 59 049 **(b)** 59 049 **7.** x^{18} **9.** y^{80} **11.** z^8 **13.** a^{87} **15.** $15x^{13}$ **17.** $63r^{52}$ **19.** $-48s^{59}$ **21.** $200x^{88}$ **23.** $30x^{27}$ **25.** $-1001b^{31}$ **27.** x^{54} **29.** p^{60} **31.** y^{14} **33.** $125r^{18}$ **35.** $-32x^{50}$ **37.** $81x^{28}$ **39.** x^{140} **41.** x^9y^9 **43.** $a^{17}b^{17}$ **45.** $243r^5s^5$ **47.** $0.001x^9y^{15}$ **49.** $36c^{10}d^{12}$ **51.** $-8x^{18}y^{21}$ **53.** $10\,000x^4y^{40}$ **55.** $3^{xz}5^{yz}$ **57.** $11x^6$ **59.** $-8y^7$ **61.** $9x^{14}$ **63.** $45x^6$ **65.** $14x^3$ **67.** Can't be simp. **69.** x^{12} **71.** Can't be simp. **73.** $2x^5$ **75.** 0 **77.** $2x^5$ **79.** x^{10} **81.** $-8x^3$ **83.** $16x^4$ **85.** $-16x^4$ **87.** x^8 **89.** x^4y^4 **91.** $16x^8y^{12}$ **93.** $x^{32}y^{24}$ **95.** $4x^3$ **97.** Can't be simp. **99.** $3x^7 - 3x^5y^3$

EXERCISE 9-4

1. x^4 **3.** s^{14} **5.** $3x^4$ **7.** $3c^5$ **9.** x **11.** y^4 **13.** 1 **15.** 3 **17.** $-2x^6$ **19.** $-4x^9$ **21.** x^3y^2 **23.** a^8b^4 **25.** $4x^5y$ **27.** $3x^8y^{10}$ **29.** $7y^6$ **31.** $4x^3y$ **33.** x^2y^3 **35.** r^2t **37.** $2x^2$ **39.** 135 **41.** $\frac{x^{10}}{y^8}$ **43.** $\frac{a^{12}}{b^6}$ **45.** x^2y^5 **47.** x^7y^6 **49.** 16 **51.** x^4y **53.** x^3y^6 **55.** x^9y^7 **57.** $3x^{18}$ **59.** $125b^9$

EXERCISE 9-5

1. $\frac{1}{9}$ **3.** $\frac{1}{64}$ **5.** $\frac{1}{25}$ **7.** 1 **9.** $-\frac{1}{8}$ **11. (a)** x^{-5} **(b)** $\frac{1}{x^5}$ **13. (a)** y^{-4} **(b)** $\frac{1}{y^4}$ **15. (a)** a^{-4} **(b)** $\frac{1}{a^4}$ **17. (a)** c^{-1} **(b)** $\frac{1}{c}$ **19. (a)** x^5 **(b)** x^5 **21. (a)** 1 **(b)** 1 **23. (a)** x^2 **(b)** x^2 **25. (a)** x^{-6} **(b)** $\frac{1}{x^6}$ **27. (a)** x^{-13} **(b)** $\frac{1}{x^{13}}$ **29. (a)** x^7y^{-3} **(b)** $\frac{x^7}{y^3}$ **31. (a)** x^5 **(b)** x^5 **33. (a)** x^{-7} **(b)** $\frac{1}{x^7}$ **35. (a)** $r^{-4}s^{-6}$ **(b)** $\frac{1}{r^4s^6}$

37. **(a)** a^{-2} **(b)** $\frac{1}{a^2}$ **39.** **(a)** c^3d^{-7} **(b)** $\frac{c^3}{d^7}$ **41.** $t^{15}v^{-3}$ **43.** x^6y^{-4} **45.** x^2y^{-4} **47.** $x^{10}y^{-15}$ **49.** $16x^{-12}$ **51.** x^6y^{-8} **53.** $\frac{1}{9}x^8$ **55.** x^{-10} **57.** a^{13} **59.** h^2 **61.** p^5 **63.** y^7 **65.** x^2y^{-16} **67.** $r^{-12}y^{-2}$ **69.** c^{-8} **71.** $5x^2$ **73.** $\frac{4}{5}a^3$ **75.** $\frac{1}{2}r^{13}$ **77.** $3m^2p^{10}$ **79.** $\frac{1}{5}t^{-1}v^1$ **81.** x^2y^{-1} **83.** $m^{16}x$ **85.** b^{-2} **87.** r^4s^{-12} **89.** x^{-3} **91.** $x^{10}y^{-8}$ **93.** $x^{-6}y^{-15}$ **95.** x^2y^{-2} **97.** $a^{-2}b^{-9}$ **99.** $x^{-2}y^{-9}$ **101.** $r^{-21}s^{14}$ **103.** $3x^{30}$ **105.** $\frac{1}{2}t^{-5}p^2$ **107.** $625s^{-14}$ **109.** $3r^{12}$

EXERCISE 9-6

1. **(a)** 57.3 **(b)** 291 **(c)** 3040 **(d)** 0.68 **(e)** 0.0907 **3.** **(a)** 6.39 **(b)** 0.791 **(c)** 8.2 **(d)** 0.048 **(e)** 0.000014 **5.** 7100 **7.** 465,000 **9.** 0.00038 **11.** 86 **13.** 0.98 **15.** 4.38×10^4 **17.** 2.917×10^2 **19.** 3.45×10^7 **21.** 7.39×10^{-3} **23.** 1.14×10^{-6} **25.** 2.75×10^7 **27.** 2×10^5 **29.** 6.24×10^4 **31.** 5.48×10^{-5} **33.** 7×10^6 **35.** 9.71×10^{-3} **37.** 6×10^{15} **39.** 8×10^6 **41.** 3.5×10^{16} **43.** 4.2×10^{-4} **45.** 5.4×10^1 **47.** 5.6×10^{-23} **49.** 4×10^{11} **51.** 2×10^{-7} **53.** 5×10^{-6} **55.** 3.5×10^8 **57.** 5×10^8 **59.** 8×10^{-17} **61.** 6.40×10^{13} **63.** 6.6×10^{12} **65.** 1.99×10^{-14} **67.** 1.7×10^{-12} **69.** 1.28×10^3 **71.** 6.1×10^{-14} **73.** 7.7×10^{12} **75.** 1.308×10^4 **77.** 1.70×10^{-5} **79.** 6.17×10^6 **81.** 5.48×10^{10} **83.** 1.66×10^{-9} **85.** 7.22×10^{14}

EXERCISE 9-7

1. \$4280 per person **3.** About 253 million years **5.** About 3.2 billion dollars! **7.** 29.239% **9.** **(a)** 50688 days **(b)** 139 years **11.** **(a)** 750,000 **(b)** 375 **13.** About 9.5 trillion km **15.** **(a)** About 32 million **(b)** 415 gal **17.** **(a)** 1.2 kw **(b)** 2920 h **(c)** 3504 kwh **(d)** \$273.31 **(e)** **(i)** \$109.32 **(ii)** \$68.33 **19.** **(a)** 3×10^6 **(b)** 8×10^{13} sq ft **(c)** 1.7×10^{16} cu ft **(d)** 1.3×10^{25} grains

Chapter 10

EXERCISE 10-1

1. $x^2 + 14x + 33$ **3.** $2x^2 - 3x - 20$ **5.** $6x^2 - 37x + 56$ **7.** $x^2 - 25$ **9.** $9x^2 + 24x + 16$ **11.** $(x + 5)(x + 9)$ **13.** $(x + 3)(x - 7)$ **15.** $(x - 2)(x - 10)$ **17.** $(2x + 7)(2x - 7)$ **19.** $(2x - 1)(x + 5)$ **21.** **(a)** **i.** -12 **ii.** 9 **(b)** $(x + 3)(x - 5)$ is easier to evaluate.

EXERCISE 10-2

1. The greatest common factor of two positive integers a and b is the greatest integer for which a/GCF = integer and b/GCF = integer **3.** 6 **5.** 4 **7.** 11 **9.** 1 Relatively prime. **11.** 18 **13.** 150 **15.** 45 **17.** 1 Relatively prime. **19.** 500 **21.** x^3 **23.** a^7 **25.** b^6 **27.** x^2y^2 **29.** r^9s^{11} **31.** $5x^4$ **33.** $4m^2$ **35.** $3ab^6$ **37.** $8c^3$ **39.** $6x^2y^3z^3$ **41.** $3x^2$ **43.** $4a^2$ **45.** $3c^5$ **47.** $5x^2y$ **49.** x^8 **51.** 6 **53.** 5 **55.** 1 Relatively prime. **57.** 10 **59.** 36

EXERCISE 10-3

1. $2(x + 3)(x + 5)$ **3.** $3(x + 4)(x + 6)$ **5.** $4(x - 2)(x + 3)$ **7.** $5(r + 5)(r - 7)$ **9.** $2(x + 3y)(x + 4y)$ **11.** $6(x - 1)(x - 3)$ **13.** $10(s - 1)(s + 12)$ **15.** $8(a + 3b)(a - 5b)$ **17.** $x^2(x - 2)(x - 6)$ **19.** $2c^3(c - 1)(c + 4)$ **21.** $4(x + 5)(x - 5)$ **23.** $5(x + 6)(x - 6)$ **25.** $7x(x + 1)(x - 1)$ **27.** $10(x + 3y)(x - 3y)$ **29.** $xy(x + y)(x - y)$ **31.** $6(x - 4)^2$ **33.** $2(m + 5p)^2$ **35.** $3a(x + 2)(x + 10)$ **37.** $6x^2(c + 10d)(c - 10d)$ **39.** $2x^2y^3(x + 3y)(x - 12y)$ **41.** $3(2x + 5)(x + 1)$ **43.** $5(3x - 1)(x + 3)$ **45.** $4(5e - 2)(e - 1)$ **47.** $6(3x + 2y)(x - 2y)$ **49.** $2y^4(2y - 1)(y - 4)$

EXERCISE 10-4

1. $(x + 2)(x + 10)$ **3.** $(x - 5)(x - 8)$ **5.** $(x + 4)(x - 7)$ **7.** $(x - 21)(3x + 4)$

9. $3(2r - 9)(2r - 1)$
11. $(4a + b)(7a - 6)$
13. $(3x - 1)(12 + x)$
15. $(x + 3)(6x + 1)$
17. $(8m - 5)(m - 1)$
19. $(3x - 7)(1 + 2x)$
21. $(x - j)(p - k)$
23. $(x + 4)(x + 3)(x - 3)$
25. $(r - 5)(a + b)(a - b)$
27. $(a + 2)(a - 2)(x + y)(x - y)$
29. $(4 + r)(4 - r)(x + 1)(x - 1)$
31. $(x + 3)(2x - 5)$
33. $2(2x - 7)(x + 3)$
35. $(3a + 4)(5x - 3)$
37. $(x + 7)(x + 2)(x + 3)$
39. $(2x - 1)(x + 1)(x - 4)$
41. $(5y - z)(x - 2)(x - 10)$
43. $(x + 1)(x + 5)(x + 2)$ **45.** $(x - 3)^3$
47. $x(x + 3)(x + 5)(x - 5)$
49. $x(x + 2)(x + 1)$
51. $(x + 1)$ **53.** $(x - 2)$ **55.** 1
57. $(x - 3)$ **59.** $(x + 1)(x + 3)$

EXERCISE 10-5

1. $(a + 3)(a + b)$
3. $(2x + 3y)(4x + 5z)$
5. $(b + 3c)(x - 2r)$
7. $(3a - 7)(2x + 5)$
9. $(m - 6v)(c - 5)$
11. $(x + 5y)(x + 1)$
13. $(5r + 2s)(z - 1)$
15. $2(5b + 6)(3a + 7)$
17. $(2x - 3)(x^2 - 2)$
19. $(4x + 15)(3x^2 + 8)$
21. $3(4x - 3)(2x^2 + 5)$
23. $(2x + 1)(x + 3)(x - 3)$
25. $5(x - 2)(x + 4)(x - 4)$
27. $(2x + 3)(6x + 5)$
29. $(2x - 3)(x + 7)$
31. $(5x - 2)(3x + 1)$
33. $(8x - 3)(x - 1)$
35. $(x + 3 + y)(x + 3 - y)$
37. $(x - 5 + 3a)(x - 5 - 3a)$
39. $(x + y + 4)(x - y - 4)$
41. $(5x + a - 2)(5x - a + 2)$
43. $(x - 5 + 7c)(x - 5 - 7c)$
45. $(x + 3)(x + 2 - a)$
47. $(x + 3)(x - 1 + r)$
49. $(x + 5)(3s + x - 2)$
51. $(x - 2)(x^3 + x + 5)$
53. $(x + 5)(c(x + 3) + d(x - 7))$

EXERCISE 10-6

1. $(3x + 4)(x + 4)$
3. $(3x + 4)(2x + 5)$
5. $(2x - 9)(x + 10)$
7. $(4x + 1)(5x - 12)$
9. $(3x - 5)(3x - 8)$ **11.** *Prime*
13. $(8x + y)(3x + 2y)$
15. $(r - s)(4r - 5s)$
17. $8(3x + 2)(2x - 3)$
19. $-3(x - 1)(4x + 15)$
21. $(2x + 1)(x + 3)$
23. $(3x + 4)(x + 2)$
25. $(5x - 1)(x - 4)$
27. $(3x + 5)(2x - 1)$
29. $(6x + 5)(x - 1)$
31. $(3r + 2s)(2r + 3s)$
33. $(5a + 2b)(3a + 2b)$
35. $(m - 4)(6m - 1)$
37. $(2m - 5)(m + 10)$
39. $4(x + 1)(x + 8)$
41. $(7x + y)(x - y)$
43. $x^3(4x + 3)(2x - 1)$
45. $ax(a - 5x)(2a - 3x)$
47. $3r(3u + 2)^2$
49. $2(x + 3)(3x - 2)(2x + 1)$

EXERCISE 10-7

3. $S = \{3, 7\}$ **5.** $S = \{\frac{5}{3}, -4\}$
7. $S = \{-\frac{8}{7}, \frac{11}{2}\}$ **9.** $S = \{-\frac{13}{5}, -\frac{21}{4}\}$
11. $S = \{3, -4, 5\}$ **13.** $S = \{\frac{5}{6}, -7, \frac{9}{2}\}$
15. $S = \{1, -2, -3, 4\}$
17. $S = \{-2, -5\}$ **19.** $S = \{-3, 4\}$
21. $S = \{1, -5\}$ **23.** $S = \{2, 3\}$
25. $S = \{-0.81, -6.19\}$
27. $S = \{-\frac{3}{2}, -1\}$ **29.** $S = \{\frac{4}{3}, -2\}$
31. $S = \{-\frac{3}{5}, 2\}$ **33.** $S = \{\frac{5}{6}, 1\}$
35. $S = \{3.18, -0.38\}$ **37.** $S = \{-\frac{2}{3}, \frac{3}{2}\}$
39. $S = \{\frac{3}{8}, \frac{5}{2}\}$ **41.** $S = \{3, -2, 2\}$
43. $S = \{-4, -5, 5\}$
45. $S = \{-\frac{4}{3}, -1, 1\}$
47. $S = \{-6, -\sqrt{5}, \sqrt{5}\}$
49. $S = \{\frac{1}{2}, \sqrt{\frac{4}{3}}, -\sqrt{\frac{4}{3}}\}$

EXERCISE 10-8

1. *A* is 9, *B* is 5 **3.** *E* is 12, *F* is 6 **5.** *J* is 10, *K* is 7 **7.** *N* is 14, *M* is 20 **9.** *O* is 11, *N* is 14, *J* is 17. **11.** *M* is 22, *L* is 17 **13.** 8, 9 or −8, −9 **15.** 58, 59 or −59, −58 **17.** 41, 42 **19.** −63, −64, −65 **21.** 83, 85 or −85, −83 **23.** 47, 49, 51 or −47, −49, −51 **25.** No such integers. **27.** −84, −82 **29.** −44, −42, −40 **31.** 86, 88 **33.** 8, 10, or −10, −8 **35.** 52 **37.** 27 **39.** 47 **41.** 63 **43.** 71 **45.** 7 dimes, 5 quarters **47.** 13

pennies, 5 nickels **49.** 120 \$50 bills, 200 \$20 bills **51.** 7 tuna sandwiches, 3 cheese sandwiches **53.** 10 and 10 **55.** 45 minutes **57.** 30 minutes **59.** *J*: 30 km/h, *K*: 20 km/h **61.** $L = 9$, $W = 7$ **63.** $L = 12$ km, $W = 8$ km **65.** 6.33 m by 8.33 m **67.** 12 by 5 **69.** 2 km **71.** Rectangle is 12 ft by 6 ft **73.** 1.5 units **75.** 1.5 cm wide **77.** 30.36 m by 36.36 m

Chapter 11

EXERCISE 11-1

1. (a) $\frac{-3}{10}$ **(b)** 14 **(c)** 0
3. (a) $\frac{23}{3}$ **(b)** $-\frac{1}{8}$ **(c)** No value
5. (a) $\frac{4}{5}$ **(b)** 0 **(c)** $\frac{3}{5}$
7. (a) $x = -10.5$ **(b)** $x = -1.4$
9. (a) $x = 7.125$ **(b)** No value

EXERCISE 11-2

1. $\frac{2}{3x^2}$ **3.** $\frac{5y^3}{2x}$ **5.** $\frac{x+3}{x+5}$
7. $\frac{x+2}{x+4}$ **9.** $\frac{2x+5}{2x-5}$ **11.** $\frac{x+3}{x+2}$
13. $\frac{x-1}{x+4}$ **15.** $\frac{x+7}{x+6}$ **17.** $\frac{x^2}{2}$
19. $\frac{5(x-2)}{x+3}$ **21.** $\frac{x-3}{x-2}$
23. $\frac{4x+3}{3x+4}$ **25.** $\frac{5x-2}{5x-3}$ **27.** $\frac{x+4}{x-1}$
29. $\frac{6x-9}{2x-4}$ **31.** -10 **33. (a)** 3 **(b)** -5

EXERCISE 11-3

1. (a) $\frac{56}{45x^2}$ **(b)** $\frac{72}{35}$ **3. (a)** $\frac{55}{216x^2}$ **(b)** $\frac{15}{22}$ **5. (a)** $\frac{x^2+3x}{48}$ **(b)** $\frac{x}{3x+9}$
7. (a) $\frac{x^2-11x+30}{x^2-4x-21}$
(b) $\frac{x^2-13x+42}{x^2-2x-15}$
9. (a) $\frac{8x^2+22x+15}{3x^2+5x-2}$
(b) $\frac{2x^2+7x+6}{12x^2+11x-5}$
11. $\frac{3}{2}$ **13.** $\frac{3}{5}$ **15.** $\frac{12p^2}{7s^2}$
17. $\frac{8m^2}{t^2}$ **19.** $\frac{2a}{5}$ **21.** $\frac{1}{2p^2c^2}$
23. $\frac{r^2}{2s^2}$ **25.** $\frac{5}{2}$ **27.** $\frac{3c^3-3c^2d}{2c+2d}$
29. $\frac{2u+1}{u-4}$ **31.** $\frac{x^2+xy-6y^2}{x+6y}$
33. 1 **35.** $\frac{x-5}{3x^2}$
37. $\frac{2y-6}{y^2-12y+36}$ **39.** $\frac{1}{3}$
41. $\frac{a-2b}{a}$ **43.** $\frac{x-3}{2x-4}$ **45.** $\frac{x}{3}$
47. 1 **49.** $\frac{4x+6}{4x+5}$ **51.** $\frac{13}{4}$
53. (a) 7 **(b)** -2

EXERCISE 11-4

1. a^2b^2c **3.** $12x^5$ **5.** $294a^3b^2c$
7. $4x(a-x)$ **9.** $6(a-x)(a+x)$
11. $21(a+x)$ **13.** $c^2m^2(c-m)$
15. $xyz(x-y)$ **17.** $4(a-b)$
19. $j(j+3)(j-3)$
21. $(x-y)^2(x+y)$
23. $(x-3)(x+2)(x-7)$
25. $(x-2)^5(x+3)^3(x+2)^4$
27. $(x+2)(x+4)(x+3)$
29. $(2x+3)(x-1)(x+5)$
31. $36(x+2)(x+1)(x-1)$
33. $(x-2)(x+1)(x-1)$
35. $4(x-2)(x+2)$
37. $(x+3)(x+2)(x-2)(x-4)$
39. $x^5(x+1)^2(x-1)$ **41.** a^4x^3
43. $60v^4c^3$ **45.** $36x^3y^4z^4$
47. 2: 2 4 [6] 8 10 (12) 14 16 (18) 20
3: 3 [6] 9 (12) 15 (18)
49. LCM = 72
GCF = 12
(LCM)(GCF) = (72)(12) = 864 = (24)(36)
51. $\frac{4}{5}$ **53.** $-\frac{1}{4}$ **55.** $\frac{7}{6}$ **57.** $\frac{11}{35}$
59. $\frac{19}{12}$ **61.** $\frac{1}{24}$

EXERCISE 11-5

1. (a) $\frac{107}{45x}$ **(b)** $\frac{37}{45x}$ **3. (a)** $\frac{37}{36x}$
(b) $-\frac{7}{36x}$ **5. (a)** $\frac{4x+9}{12}$
(b) $\frac{-2x-9}{12}$ **7. (a)** $\frac{2x^2-15x+27}{x^2-4x-21}$
(b) $\frac{-11x+57}{x^2-4x-21}$

9. **(a)** $\frac{14x^2 + 18x + 1}{3x^2 + 5x - 2}$

(b) $\frac{-10x^2 - 4x + 11}{3x^2 + 5x - 2}$ **11.** $\frac{8}{x}$

13. $-\frac{x}{y}$ **15.** $\frac{x}{2}$ **17.** $\frac{3a + 2b}{ab}$

19. $\frac{3s - 4r}{rs}$ **21.** $\frac{7}{4a}$ **23.** $\frac{1}{10p}$

25. $\frac{22}{15a}$ **27.** $\frac{7}{12x}$ **29.** $\frac{7}{12x}$

31. $\frac{3y + 2x}{axy}$ **33.** $\frac{3x - 1}{6}$

35. $\frac{4c - 13}{12}$ **37.** $\frac{8a - 13b}{20}$

39. $\frac{9m - 7}{18}$ **41.** $-\frac{a}{21}$ **43.** $\frac{1}{12x}$

45. $\frac{1}{2}$ **47.** $\frac{1}{3}$ **49.** $\frac{1}{12r - 12s}$

51. $\frac{3}{4a - 4b}$ **53.** $\frac{2x}{x^2 - 1}$

55. $\frac{x^2 - 2xy - y^2}{x^2 - y^2}$ **57.** $\frac{x^2 + 2x - 6}{x^2 + 7x + 12}$

59. $\frac{2x^2 + x + 8}{x^2 + 2x - 8}$ **61.** $\frac{9x + 23}{x^2 + 2x - 3}$

63. $\frac{7x - 30}{x^2 - 12x + 20}$ **65.** $\frac{x^2 - x + 2}{x - 2}$

67. $\frac{-5x + 4}{x + 2}$ **69.** $\frac{x - 3}{x - 1}$

EXERCISE 11-6

1. $\frac{x + 7}{x - 7}$ **3.** -1 **5.** $-\frac{a - 3}{a + 3}$

7. $-\frac{2 + x}{x - 2}$ **9.** $\frac{x - 4}{2 - x}$ **11.** $\frac{1}{x}$

13. 1 **15.** 3 **17.** $c + d$

19. $-6 - x$ **21.** $\frac{2a^2 - 3a + 4}{a^3}$

23. $-\frac{20}{x^9}$ **25.** $\frac{18u}{11}$ **27.** 13

29. $-\frac{5 + p}{2}$ **31.** $\frac{6x}{x^2 - 16}$

33. $\frac{20}{x^2 - 25}$ **35.** $\frac{3}{x - 3}$ **37.** $\frac{1}{a + 2}$

39. $\frac{2}{r^2 + 5r}$ **41.** 0

43. $\frac{x^2 + 2x - 24}{-x^2 - 2x + 15}$ **45.** $-\frac{x + 7}{x - 7}$

47. $\frac{5}{x - 3}$ **49.** $\frac{5}{x - 5}$ **51.** $\frac{2}{x + 1}$

53. $\frac{1}{x + 4}$ **55.** $-\frac{3}{x + 5}$

57. **(a)** Answers may vary. 4.85
(b) Answers may vary. 7.831, 7.833, 7.835, 7.837, 7.839 **(c)** 379.5, between
(d) $n = \frac{x + y}{2}$ **(e)** $\frac{29}{56}$ or $0.517 \cdots$, between **(f)** ratio of integers
(g) Any number which can be written in the form $\frac{m}{n}$, where m and n are integers, and $n \neq 0$, is called a rational number. The average of two rational numbers,
$\frac{\frac{a}{b} + \frac{c}{d}}{2}$ or $\frac{ad + bc}{2bd}$, lies between them as shown above and is a rational number, since the sums or products of integers are integers.
(h) yes; no; no integer between adjacent integers

EXERCISE 11-7

1. $x + 2 - \frac{17}{x + 3}$ **3.** $3x - 2 + \frac{3}{2x - 1}$

5. $4x + 7$ **7.** $x^2 - 4x + 5 + \frac{2}{x + 2}$

9. $x^2 - 3x + 2$

11. $4x^2 - x - 5 - \frac{5}{2x + 3}$

13. $x^2 + 2x - 10 + \frac{1}{x + 5}$

15. $4x^2 + 28x - 4$ **17.** $x^2 + 9x + 81$

19. $x - 2 - \frac{11}{x^2 - 2x - 5}$ **21.** $2x - 8$

23. $x^3 + x^2 - x - 2 - \frac{2}{x + 6}$

25. **(a)** 8 **(b)** 8 **(c)** 8 **(d)** 0

EXERCISE 11-8

1. $S = \{5\}$ **3.** $S = \{4\}$
5. $S = \{5\frac{1}{12}\}$ **7.** $S = \{17.5\}$
9. $S = \{6\frac{2}{3}\}$ **11.** $S = \{1\frac{1}{2}\}$
13. $S = \{-3\}$ **15.** $S = \{\emptyset\}$
17. $S = \{-0.5\}$ **19.** $S = \{-2, 18\}$
21. $S = \{2.63, -4.30\}$
23. $S = \{-2.38, -12.62\}$

25. $\frac{23}{10x}$ **27.** $\frac{5x + 11}{x^2 + 5x + 4}$

29. $\frac{8x}{x^2 - 9}$ **31.** $x + 5$ **33.** $\frac{9}{x - 2}$

EXERCISE 11-9

1. 117 **3.** 576 and 448 **5. (a)** 3:2 **(b)** 4320 acres and 2880 acres **7. (a)** 13:2 6.5:1 **(b)** $21,840,000 **9.** 4800 women **11.** 112 cartons generic, 48 cartons national **13.** 10,000 ℓ. regular. 14,000 ℓ. unleaded 4,000 ℓ. super unleaded **15.** 28 m, 40 m, 44 m **17.** Length = 21.9 cm, width = 14.6 cm **19.** 750 fish **21.** 33 years from now **23. (a)** 5 : 7 **(b)** 55 cm^2

EXERCISE 11-10

1. (a) i. 150 km/h **ii.** 100 km/h **iii.** $120 - x$ **iv.** $120 + y$ **(b) i.** $\frac{1}{2}$hr **ii.** 0.6 hr **iii.** 0.4 hr **iv.** $\frac{60}{120 + y}$ **3. (a)** $\frac{60}{120 - x} + \frac{60}{120 + y}$ **(b)** 1.21 h **(c)** About 57.65 km/h **5. (a)** $\frac{60}{120 - x} + \frac{60}{120 + x}$ **(b)** 0.07 h longer or 4 minutes **7. (a)** 476.19 sec **(b)** 7.22 m/sec **(c)** −667 sec **9.** 2.78 m/sec **11.** 20 m/min **13. (a)** 0.75 h **(b)** $13\frac{1}{3}$ km/h **(c)** less **15.** $\frac{2xy}{x + y}$ **17.** 1.06 ft/sec **19.** $1\frac{5}{7}$ hours **21.** 75 min **23.** 17.5 hours **25.** $2\frac{2}{11}$ min **27.** 17 and 53 **29.** 21 and 37 **31. (a)** $P(\text{girl}) = \frac{173}{312}$ or 0.554 . . . ; $P(\text{boy}) = \frac{139}{312}$ or 0.445 . . . **(b)** 6 or 7 girls (6.653 . . .) **33. (a)** $P(1) = \frac{1}{6}, P(5) = \frac{1}{6}$ **(b)** 5 times **(c)** Answers may vary.

Chapter 12

EXERCISE 12-1

1. (a) 4.58 **(b)** 9 **3. (a)** 3 **(b)** 0 **(c)** No value **5. (a)** 1 **(b)** 5 **(c)** 10 **(d)** No value **7. (a)** $x = 50$ **(b)** $x = 4.5$ **9. (a)** $x = 139$ **(b)** $x = -1$ **(c)** $x = -5$

EXERCISE 12-2

1. (a) 14 = 14 **(b)** 4.5825756 = 4.582575 **(c)** $5 \neq 7$ **(d)** $5 \neq 1$ **3.** $2\sqrt{3}$ **5.** $2\sqrt{10}$ **7.** $3\sqrt{3}$ **9.** $3\sqrt{5}$ **11.** $4\sqrt{2}$ **13.** $6\sqrt{3}$ **15.** $10\sqrt{2}$ **17.** $7\sqrt{3}$ **19.** $9\sqrt{5}$ **21.** $3\sqrt{5}$ **23.** $7\sqrt{3}$ **25.** 4 **27.** 6 **29.** $15\sqrt{2}$ **31.** $42\sqrt{15}$ **33.** $80\sqrt{6}$ **35.** $60\sqrt{11}$ **37.** $180\sqrt{7}$ **39.** 1050 **41.** $9\sqrt{5}$ **43.** $5\sqrt{7}$ **45.** $12\sqrt{6}$ **47.** $7\sqrt{3}$ **49.** $10\sqrt{5}$ **51.** $8\sqrt{2}$ **53.** $7\sqrt{3}$ **55.** $-2\sqrt{7}$ **57.** $\sqrt{5}$ **59.** $2\sqrt{2} - 4\sqrt{3}$ **61. (a)** $x^2\sqrt{x}$ **(b)** $y^4\sqrt{y}$ **(c)** x^3 **(d)** $x^4y\sqrt{y}$ **(e)** xy^5

EXERCISE 12-3

1. $\frac{\sqrt{33}}{11}$ **3.** $\frac{2\sqrt{15}}{5}$ **5.** $\sqrt{5}$ **7.** $\frac{\sqrt{39}}{13}$ **9.** $\frac{5\sqrt{42}}{12}$ **11.** $2\sqrt{10}$ **13.** $\frac{\sqrt{15}}{9}$ **15.** $7\sqrt{3}$ **17.** $5\sqrt{3}$ **19.** 1 **21.** $\frac{3\sqrt{2}}{4}$ **23.** $\frac{6\sqrt{5}}{5}$ **25.** $\frac{4\sqrt{14}}{7}$ **27.** $\frac{9\sqrt{2}}{10}$ **29.** $3\sqrt{3}$ **31.** $\sqrt{5}$ **33.** $5\sqrt{6}$ **35.** 0 **37.** $7\sqrt{7}$ **39.** $2\sqrt{2}$ **41.** $\frac{3}{\sqrt{21}}$ **43.** $\frac{1}{2\sqrt{6}}$ **45. (a)** $x\sqrt{x}$ **(b)** $\frac{\sqrt{z}}{z^2}$ **(c)** $\frac{y^2\sqrt{x}}{x}$ **(d)** $\frac{1}{x^2y^5}$ **(e)** $\frac{1}{n^2}$

EXERCISE 12-4

1. $5\sqrt{2} + 7\sqrt{5}$ **3.** $6\sqrt{7} + 14$ **5.** $5\sqrt{3} - 3\sqrt{5}$ **7.** −9 **9.** $40\sqrt{2} + 14\sqrt{15}$ **11.** $13 + 7\sqrt{3}$ **13.** $-22 - 3\sqrt{6}$ **15.** $-17 + 5\sqrt{7}$ **17.** $17 - 8\sqrt{5}$ **19.** $11 + 4\sqrt{10}$ **21.** $12 - 15\sqrt{2}$ **23.** $240 - 150\sqrt{3}$ **25.** $52 - 14\sqrt{3}$ **27.** $9 + 6\sqrt{2}$ **29.** $113 - 30\sqrt{14}$ **31.** −4 **33.** 11 **35.** 74 **37.** −57 **39.** −1000 **41.** $10\sqrt{6} - 20$ **43.** $4\sqrt{15} + 12$ **45.** $8 + 2\sqrt{3}$ **47.** $-9\sqrt{2} + 9\sqrt{7}$ **49.** $8\sqrt{11} + 8\sqrt{5}$ **51.** $\frac{2\sqrt{13} + 7}{3}$ **53.** $\frac{27 - \sqrt{3}}{22}$ **55.** $6 + \sqrt{35}$

57. $4 - \sqrt{15}$ **59.** $\dfrac{1421 + 4\sqrt{118326}}{355}$

EXERCISE 12-5

1. x^3 **3.** $3a^4$ **5.** $a^3\sqrt{a}$
7. $2r^4\sqrt{3r}$ **9.** $\dfrac{x\sqrt{xy}}{y}$ **11.** $\dfrac{x\sqrt{xy}}{y}$
13. $3a^2\sqrt{5}$ **15.** x^3
17. $\sqrt{x^2 + x - 6}$ **19.** $|x - 5|$
21. $|x + 3|$ **23.** $(x - 7)\sqrt{x - 7}$
25. Both $(x - 3)^4$ and $(x - 3)^2$ must be nonnegative, but $x - 3$ may be negative.

EXERCISE 12-6

1. $S = \{46\}$ **3.** $S = \{256\}$
5. $S = \emptyset$ **7.** $S = \{7\}$
9. $S = \{3.71\}$ **11.** $S = \{54\}$
13. $S = \emptyset$ **15.** $S = \emptyset$ **17.** $S = \{9\}$
19. $S = \{0.38\}$

EXERCISE 12-7

1. 21.40 **3.** 21.95 **5.** 15.63
7. 17 **9.** 2053 **11.** 54.80
13. 1.79 **15.** 47.00 **17.** 7
19. 111 **21.** 89.25 m **23.** 5.22 m
25. 12.65 km **27.** Road cost is $428.26 cheaper. **29.** Rowing is 1.14 min. quicker. **31. (a)** $d = \sqrt{x^2 + 400}$
(b) i. 42.06 **ii.** 32.02 **iii.** 20
(c) 48 or −48 **(d)** No values

EXERCISE 12-8

1. 8.13 **3.** 5.40 **5.** 4.77 **7.** 3
9. 4 **11.** 7 **13.** 73 **15.** 2.84
17. 0.42 **19.** 3.1
21. (a) 50.65 cm³ **(b)** 8.33 cm
(c) 1650 m **23. (a)** 76 kg
(b) 2.76 m **(c)** 4864 kg
25. (a) $\sqrt[3]{8} = \sqrt[3]{2^3} = (2^3)^{1/3} = 2^1 = 2$
(b) $\sqrt[5]{243} = \sqrt[5]{3^5} = (3^5)^{1/5} = 3^1 = 3$
(c) $x^{\frac{1}{n}} = \sqrt[n]{x} : (x^{\frac{1}{n}})^n = x^1 = x \therefore x^{\frac{1}{n}} = \sqrt[n]{x}$

EXERCISE 12-9

1. $0.\overline{428571}$ **3.** $0.\overline{81}$ **5.** $0.8\overline{3}$
7. $0.\overline{7}$ **9.** 0.1875 **11.** $0.\overline{87}$
13. $0.\overline{742}$ **15.** $0.\overline{378}$ **17.** $0.\overline{286}$
19. $0.\overline{384615}$ **21.** $\dfrac{1}{3}$ **23.** $\dfrac{7}{9}$
25. $\dfrac{56}{99}$ **27.** $\dfrac{5}{33}$ **29.** $\dfrac{10}{11}$
31. $\dfrac{671}{999}$ **33.** $\dfrac{101}{333}$ **35.** $\dfrac{9}{37}$
37. $\dfrac{1}{27}$ **39.** $\dfrac{5}{27}$
41. Rational **43.** Irrational
45. Irrational **47.** Rational
49. Irrational **51.** Rational
53. Irrational **55.** Rational
57. Rational **59.** Irrational
61. (a) $\dfrac{559}{250}$ **(b)** $\dfrac{13 \times 43}{2 \times 5^3}$
(c) $\dfrac{13^2 \times 43^2}{2^2 \times 5^6}$ **(d)** It cannot equal 5.
(e) 4.999696

63. (a)

N	64
R	~~1~~ ~~2~~ ~~3~~ ~~4~~ ~~5~~ ~~4~~ ~~4.1~~ ~~4~~ ~~4.01~~ 4
D	~~1~~ ~~0.1~~ 0.01

```
Output: 1
        2
        3
        4
        5
        4
        4.1
        4
        4.01
Cube root of 64 is 4
```

(b)

N	34
R	~~1~~ ~~2~~ ~~3~~ ~~4~~ ~~3~~ ~~3.1~~ ~~3.2~~ ~~3.3~~ ~~3.2~~
	~~3.21~~ ~~3.22~~ ~~3.23~~ ~~3.24~~ 3.23
D	~~1~~ ~~0.1~~ 0.01

```
Output: 1
        2
        3
        4
        3
        3.1
        3.2
        3.3
        3.2
        3.21
        3.22
        3.23
        3.24
Cube root of 34 is 3.23
```

(c) A BASIC program is shown.

```
10  INPUT N
20  LET R = 1
30  LET D = 1
40  PRINT R
50  IF R ^ 3 > N THEN 80
60  LET R = R + D
70  GOTO 40
80  LET R = R - D
90  IF D < = 0.01 THEN 120
100 LET D = D * 0.1
110 GOTO 40
```

```
120 PRINT
130 PRINT "CUBE ROOT OF ";N;"
    IS ";R
140 END

]RUN
?64
1
2
3
4
5
4
4.1
4
4.01

CUBE ROOT OF 64 IS 4

RUN
?34
1
2
3
4
3
3.1
3.2
3.3
3.2
3.21
3.22
3.23
3.24

CUBE ROOT OF 34 IS 3.23
```

Chapter 13

EXERCISE 13-1

1. (Graph) $x > 8$ **3.** (Graph) $x \le 2$ **5.** (Graph) $x < -7$ **7.** (Graph) $x \ge 9$ **9.** (Graph) $x \le -2.6$ **11.** (Graph) $x < 0$ **13.** (Graph) $y > 100$ **15.** (Graph) $z \ge -3.146$ **17.** (Graph) $5 < x$ **19.** (Graph) $-11 \ge x$ **21.** $x \le 7$ **23.** $x < -4$ **25.** $x \ge 2.5$ **27.** $x > -8$ **29.** $x \le -50$ **31.** $x > 47$ **33.** $x \ge -0.2$ **35.** $x < \sqrt{7}$ **37.** $x \ge -13$ **39.** $x \le 0$ **41.** (Graph) $x > 9$ **43.** (Graph) $x < -100$ **45.** (Graph) $x \ge 10$ **47.** (Graph) $x \le 15$ **49.** (Graph) $x > 0$

EXERCISE 13-2

1. (Graph) $x < 7$ **3.** (Graph) $x \ge 11$ **5.** (Graph) $x > -3$ **7.** (Graph) $x \le 6$ **9.** (Graph) $x < -18$ **11.** (Graph) $x < 27$ **13.** (Graph) $x \ge -25$ **15.** (Graph) $S = \emptyset$ **17.** (Graph) $x > -67$ **19.** (Graph) $x \le 5$ **21.** (Graph) $x < -3$ **23.** (Graph) $x \ge -12$ **25.** (Graph) $x < -7$ **27.** (Graph) $x > -8$ **29.** (Graph) $x \le -1$ **31.** (Graph) S = {Real nos.} **33.** (Graph) $x < 0$ **35.** (Graph) $x \ge -3$ **37.** (Graph) $x < -2$ **39.** (Graph) $x \ge -5.5$ **41.** (Graph) **(a) i.** 23 **ii.** -17 **(b) i.** $x = 5.6$ **ii.** $x > 3$ **iii.** $x \le 4.8$ **43. (a)** $25x + 30$ **(b)** Over 2.8 hr **45.** Over 5 hr

EXERCISE 13-3

1. (Graph) $x \ge 5$ and $x < 9$ **3.** (Graph) $x < -2$ or $x \ge 6$ **5.** (Graph) $-7 \le x \le 2$ **7.** (Graph) $x < 5$ or $x > 7$ **9.** (Graph) $x < 3.4$ and $x \ge -7$ **11.** (Graph) $x \le -1$ or $x > 3.5$ **13.** (Graph) $12 < x < 16$ **15.** (Graph) $-7 \le x \le -1$ **17.** (Graph) $-0.9 > x \ge -3.1$ **19.** (Graph) $x > 14$ or $x < 19$ S = {real nos.} **21.** $-2 < x \le 3$ **23.** $x \le -3$ or $x \ge 4$ **25.** $6 < x < 18$ **27.** $x \le -10$ or $x > -4$ **29.** $-5 \le x \le 5$ **31.** $x < -7$ or $x > 0$ **33.** (Graph) $3 < x < 7$ **35.** (Graph) $-1 \le x \le 3$ **37.** (Graph) $x \ge 3$ or $x < 1$ **39.** (Graph) $x > -2$ and $x \le 7$ **41. (a)** 13 **(b) i.** $x = 3$ **ii.** $1 < x < 4$ (Graph) **iii.** $x \ge 2$ or $x \le -1$ (Graph) **43. (a)** $7 + 0.3x$ **(b)** Between 40 and 70 weeks **(c)** Up to 60 weeks **45.** From 4 to 10 gal, inclusive

EXERCISE 13-4

1. (Graph) $-7 < x < 7$ **3.** (Graph) $x \ge 13$ or $x \le -13$ **5.** (Graph) $x > 11$ or $x < -5$ **7.** (Graph) $-9 \le x \le -5$ **9.** (Graph) $x > 7.6$ or $x < -6$ **11.** (Graph) $-13 < x < -2$ **13.** (Graph) $6 \ge x \ge -1.5$ **15.** (Graph) $S = \emptyset$ **17.** (Graph) S = {real nos.} **19.** (Graph) $x > 4$ or $x < 4$ **21.** (Graph) $-14 < x < 14$ **23.** (Graph) $x \ge 15$ or $x \le -7$

25. (Graph) $x > 6$ or $x < -22$
27. (Graph) $x \geq 2.5$ or $x \leq -3.5$
29. (Graph) $x \geq 0$ or $x \leq -14$
31. **(a) i.** 8 **ii.** 7 **(b) i.** $x = 14$ or $x = -4$ **ii.** (Graph) $-6 < x < 16$ **iii.** (Graph) $x \geq 9$ or $x \leq 1$ **iv.** (Graph) $S = \emptyset$ **33.** **(a)** $|x - 9826|$
(b) Between \$9676 and \$9976
35. **(a)** $|x - 33'7\frac{1}{4}''|$ **(b)** Between $33'7\frac{1}{8}''$ and $33'7\frac{3}{8}''$, inclusive
37. **(a)** $900\,t$ = no. of km from SFO.
(b) $|2900 - 900t|$ = no. of km from Chicago
(c) Between 2.67 and 3.78 hours

EXERCISE 13-5

1. $7x + 2 > 93$ Expr. is more than 93.
3. $9x - 4 < 5$ Expr. is less than 5.
5. $9 - 2x \geq -1$ Expr. is at least -1.
7. $-8x - 12 \leq 148$ Expr. is at most 148.
9. $17 + 4x < 45$ Expr. is less than 45.
11. $-5x - 8 \leq -18$. Expr. is at most -18.
13. $31 \leq 8x + 7 \leq 47$ Expr. is between 31 and 47, inclusive. **15.** $43 > 13 - 6x > -29$ Expr. is between -29 and 43.
17. $31 < 19 + 3x < 34$ Expr. is between 31 and 34. **19.** $25 \geq -2 - 9x \geq -2$ Expr. is between -2 and 25, inclusive.
21. **(a)** $1500 - 180x$ **(b)** At most \$600 **(c)** At most 5 days
23. **(a)** $200 - 40t$ **(b)** Less than 80 miles **(c)** Between 2.5 and 4.25 hours
25. **(a) i.** Till he's 4 **ii.** Till he's $10\frac{1}{3}$
(b) Between 34 and 37 in., inclusive
(c) Between $15\frac{2}{3}$ and 19, inclusive
(d) Till he's over $21\frac{2}{3}$

EXERCISE 13-6

1. (Graph) $y \geq \frac{3}{4}x - 2$ **3.** (Graph) $y > -\frac{3}{5}x + 4$ **5.** (Graph) $y \leq 3x + 2$
7. (Graph) $y > \frac{2}{5}x + 3$ $y \leq 2x - 1$
9. (Graph) $y \geq -2x + 1$ $y > \frac{5}{3}x - 6$
11. (Graph) $y < -x + 3$ $y > \frac{2}{3}x - 4$
13. (Graph) $y \geq -3x + 5$ $y < -x$
15. (Graph) $y \geq \frac{1}{5}x + 2$ $y < \frac{1}{5}x + 4$
17. (Graph) $y > -2x - 2$ $y > x + 2$ $y \leq \frac{1}{3}x + 5$ **19.** (Graph) $y < \frac{2}{5}x + 3$ $y \leq 2x$ $y \geq -x - 3$

EXERCISE 13-7

1. **(a)** $x > 3$ $y < 6$ **(b)** (Graph)
3. **(a)** $x \geq 2$ $y \geq 4$ **(b)** (Graph)
5. **a.** $400x + 100y$ **b. i.** 11500 **ii.** 8500 **c.** Maximum no. is 4
7. From 0 through 29 2-bedroom
9. Minimum no. is 14 power mowers

11. **(a) i.** \$590 **ii.** \$710 **(b)** From \$0 through \$1666.66 **13.** At least 400 units of A At most 600 units of B
15. **(a)** Min. no. is 34. **(b)** Min. no. is 146 **(c)** Min. is 51 **(d)** Min. is 42 **17.** **(a)** Roshawn is at most 26. Tonyetta at most 31. **(b)** Roshawn is at most 50. Tonyetta is at most 55.
(c) Roshawn is less than 95. Tonyetta is less than 100.

Chapter 14

EXERCISE 14-1

1. (Graph)

X	Y
-3	3.1
-2	3.4
-1	3.7
0	4
1	4.3
2	4.6
3	4.9

3. (Graph)

X	Y
-1	7
0	2
1	-1
2	-2
3	-1
4	2
5	7

5. (Graph)

X	Y
0	1
1	0
2	-.6
3	-.8
4	-.6
5	0
6	1

7. (Graph)

X	Y
-2	8
-1	6
0	4
1	2
2	0
3	2
4	4
5	6
6	8

9. (Graph)

X	Y
1	12
2	6
3	4
4	3
6	2
12	1

EXERCISE 14-2

1. **(a)** $y = 0.025x$ **(b)** 7.5 gal **(c)** 440 mi **3.** **(a)** $L = \frac{4}{3}w$ **(b)** $6\frac{2}{3}$ feet **(c)** About 0.975 ft
5. **(a)** $y = 0.45x$ **(b)** About 66 feet **(c)** 54 psi **7.** **(a)** $c = 0.6p$ **(b)** 60 cups **(c)** Yes. 7 is enough. Yes. She can serve more than 11 people.
9. **(a)** $y = 5x$ **(b) i.** 25 sec **ii.** 10 sec **(c)** 0.2 mi **11.** **(a)** $y = \dfrac{300}{x}$
(b) 60 mph **(c)** 10 mph

13. (a) $n = \frac{20169}{d}$ **(b)** About 252 rev **(c)** About 202 in. **15. (a)** $p = \frac{800,000}{r}$ **(b) i.** 80,000 people **ii.** 800,000 people **(c)** Rank is 200*th* **17. (a)** $c = \frac{108}{r}$ **(b)** 18 columns **(c)** Yes, with 15 columns and 3 people left over **(d)** 108 people **19. (a)** $F = \frac{2000}{d}$ **(b)** $33\frac{1}{3}$ lb **(c)** Yes, if the lever is at least 200 cm long **21.** $y = kx$

$$\therefore y_1 = kx_1, \text{ and } y_2 = kx_2$$

$$\frac{y_1}{x_1} = k \text{ and } \frac{y_2}{x_2} = k$$

$$\therefore \frac{y_1}{x_1} = \frac{y_2}{x_2}, \text{ which was to be proved}$$

EXERCISE 14-3

1. (a) 62, −158, 1096 **(b)** 6 **3. (a)** 88, 32, 407 **(b)** ±9 **(c)** If $5 = x^2 + 7$, $-2 = x^2$; x^2 can't be negative **5. (a)** $h(2) = 10 > g(2) = 3$ **(b)** $g(10) = 43 > h(10) = 34$ **(c)** $34/43 \approx 0.7907$ **7.** 5.5; the graphs intersect at (5.5, 20.5) **9.** Point of intersection is $\left(4\frac{1}{26}, 4\frac{8}{13}\right) \approx (4.04, 4.615)$ **11. (a)** $f(x) = \$5.50x + \$10.00$ **(b)** 2 hrs = \$21, 3 hrs = \$26.50, 4 hrs = \$32 **(c)** $7\frac{3}{11}$ hrs ≈ 7.27 hrs ≈ 7 hrs 16 minutes; this would be very difficult (and may even violate child labor laws!) **13. (a)** at 2 sec: Randy: 14 feet, Willie 35 feet; at 3 sec: Randy 21 feet, Willie 40 feet **(b)** Randy: 7 ft/sec, Willie 5 ft/sec, the coefficient of x tells you this **(c)** Willie had a 25 ft head start **(d)** At 12.5 sec they will both be 87.5 ft from the fence **(e)** Willie will win **15.** Points of intersection: (−3, 2), (2, −8), (5, 10) Quadratic function: highest-order term x^2; cubic, highest-order term x^3

EXERCISE 14-4

1. $x \approx 16.86$ $y \approx 30.16$
3. $x \approx 22.56$ $y \approx 28.25$
5. $x \approx 78.80$ $y \approx 61.57$
7. $x \approx 40.62$ $y = 76.65$ **9.** $x \approx 2.24$ $y \approx 3.32$ **11.** 35.54° **13.** 28.07° **15.** 44.42° **17.** 53.13° **19.** 41.41° **21.** Approx. 120 ft **23. (a)** About 2244 ft **(b)** About 1019 ft **25. (a)** About 200 m (b) About 867 m **27.** 18.43° **29.** 16.89°

EXERCISE 14-5

1. (a)

x	y
-7	96
-6	77
-5	60
-4	45
-3	32
-2	21
-1	12
0	5
1	0
2	-3
3	-4
4	-3
5	0
6	5
7	12
8	21
9	32
10	45

(b) (Graph)
(c) $x = 1, 5$
$y = 5$
(d) (3, −4)

3. (a)

x	y
-10	48
-9	34
-8	22
-7	12
-6	4
-5	-2
-4	-6
-3	-8
-2	-8
-1	-6
0	-2
1	4
2	12
3	22
4	34
5	48

(b) (Graph)
(c) $x \approx 0.37, -5.37$
$y = -2$
(d) (−2.5, −8.25)

5. **(a)**

x	y
-3	-10.6
-2	-5.6
-1	-1.4
0	2
1	4.6
2	6.4
3	7.4
4	7.6
5	7
6	5.6
7	3.4
8	.4
9	-3.4
10	-8

(b) (Graph)

(c) $x \approx -0.62, 8.12$
$y = 2$

(d) (3.75, 7.63)

7. **(a)**

x	y
-3	23
-2	15
-1	9
0	5
1	3
2	3
3	5
4	9
5	15
6	23

(b) (Graph)

(c) x: none
$y = 5$

(d) (1.5, 2.75)

9. **(a)**

x	y
-2	-26
-1	-17
0	-10
1	-5
2	-2
3	-1
4	-2
5	-5
6	-10
7	-17
8	-26

(b) (Graph)

(c) x: none
$y = -10$

(d) $(3, -1)$

11. **(a)**

x	y
-3	95
-2	35
-1	-9
0	-37
1	-49
2	-45
3	-25
4	11
5	63
6	131

(b) (Graph)

(c) $x \approx 3.74, -1.24$
$y = -37$

(d) $(1.25, -49.5)$

EXERCISE 14-6

1. (Graph) $x > 10.36$ or $x < 1.64$
3. (Graph) $-4.41 \le x \le -1.59$
5. (Graph) $x \ge 13.72$ or $x \le -3.72$
7. (Graph) $3 < x < 11$ **9.** (Graph) $S = \emptyset$ **11.** (Graph) $S = \{\text{real nos.}\}$
13. (Graph) $-2 < x < 7$
15. (Graph) $x \ge 1.91$ or $x \le -8.91$
17. (Graph) $-2.46 \le x \le 4.46$
19. (Graph) $x > 2.31$ or $x < -1.31$

EXERCISE 14-7

1. (Graph) $x \approx 1.82$ or -3.48
3. (Graph) $x \approx 6.70$ or -3.20
5. (Graph) $x = 7$ or 2 **7.** (Graph) $x \approx 7.29$ or -1.29 **9.** (Graph) No endpoints **11.** (Graph) No endpoints
13. (Graph) $x \approx 19.84$ or -3.17
15. (Graph) $x = 3.5$ (only)
17. (Graph) $x \approx 6.22$ or 3.78
19. (Graph) $x = 5$ or -6
21. **(a)** Between 4 and 10 sec
(b) Before 0.92 sec or after 13.08 sec
(c) Never above 300 m **23.** (Graph) At least 4.08 m **25.** **(a)** Length $= 8 - x$ Width $= 6 - x$ **(b)** $48 - 14x + x^2$
(c) (Graph) $0 \le x \le 1.11$ m
(d) (Graph) $2 \le x \le 6$ m
27. (Graph) At most 4.33 m
29. **(a)** (Graph) **(b)** (Graph) $x \approx 4.20$ or -1.20 **(c)** (Graph, part (a))

Problem Title Index

General Index

Skills Handbook

Problem Solving Strategies

You may find one or more of these strategies helpful in solving a word problem.

STRATEGY	WHEN TO USE IT
Draw a Diagram	The problem describes a picture or diagram.
Try, Check, Revise	Solving the problem directly is too complicated.
Look for a Pattern	The problem describes a relationship.
Make a Table	The problem has data that need to be organized.
Solve a Simpler Problem	The problem is very complex.
Use Logical Reasoning	You need to reach a conclusion using given information.
Work Backward	You need to find the number that led to the result.

Problem Solving: Draw a Diagram

Two cars started from the same point. One traveled east at 45 mi/h and the other west at 50 mi/h. How far apart were the cars after 5 hours?

Draw a diagram.

West ← 50 mi/h • 5 — Start — 45 mi/h • 5 → East

The first car traveled $45 \cdot 5$ or 225 mi. The second car traveled $50 \cdot 5$ or 250 mi.

The diagram shows that the two distances should be added: $225 + 250 = 475$ mi.

After 5 hours, the cars were 475 mi apart.

EXERCISES

1. Jason, Lee, Melda, Aaron, and Bonnie want to play one another in tennis. How many games will be played?

2. A playground, a zoo, a picnic area, and a flower garden will be in four corners of a new park. Straight paths will connect each of these areas to all the other areas. How many pathways will be built?

3. Pedro wants to tack 4 posters on a bulletin board. He will tack the four corners of each poster, overlapping the sides of each poster a little bit. What is the least number of tacks that Pedro can use?

Problem Solving: Try, Check, Revise

When you are not sure how to start, guess and test an answer. In the process, you may see a way of revising your guess to get closer to the answer or to get the exact answer.

Maria bought books and CDs as gifts. Altogether she bought 12 gifts and spent \$84. The books cost \$6 each and the CDs cost \$9 each. How many of each gift did she buy?

Trial 6 books, 6 CDs — **Test**

$$\begin{array}{rr} 6 \cdot \$6 = & \$36 \\ 6 \cdot \$9 = & +\ \$54 \\ \hline & \$90 \end{array}$$

Revise your guess. You need fewer CDs to bring the total cost down.

Trial 7 books, 5 CDs — **Test**

$$\begin{array}{rr} 7 \cdot \$6 = & \$42 \\ 5 \cdot \$9 = & +\ \$45 \\ \hline & \$87 \end{array}$$

The cost is still too high.

Trial 8 books, 4 CDs — **Test**

$$\begin{array}{rr} 8 \cdot \$6 = & \$48 \\ 4 \cdot \$9 = & +\ \$36 \\ \hline & \$84 \end{array}$$

Maria bought 8 books and 4 CDs.

EXERCISES

1. Find two consecutive odd integers whose product is 323.
2. Find three consecutive integers whose sum is 81.
3. Find four consecutive integers whose sum is 138.
4. Mika bought 9 rolls of film to take 180 pictures on a field trip. Some rolls had 36 exposures and the rest had 12 exposures. How many of each type did Mika buy?
5. Tanya is 18 years old. Her brother Shawn is 16 years younger. How old will Tanya be when she is 3 times as old as Shawn?
6. Steven has 100 ft of fencing and wants to build a fence in the shape of a rectangle to enclose the largest possible area. What should be the dimensions of the rectangle?
7. The combined ages of a mother, her son, and her daughter are 61 years. The mother is 22 years older than her son and 31 years older than her daughter. How old is each person?

Problem Solving: Look for a Pattern and Make a Table

Some problems describe relationships that involve regular sequences of numbers. To solve you need to be able to recognize and describe the pattern that gives the relationship. One way to organize the information is to make a table.

A tree farm is planted as shown at the right. The dots represent trees. The lot will be enlarged by adding larger squares. How many trees will be in the fifth square?

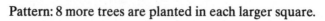

Make a table to help find a pattern.

Square position	1st	2nd	3rd	4th	5th
Number of trees	4	12	20	■	■

Pattern: 8 more trees are planted in each larger square.

The fourth square will have 28 trees. The fifth square will have 36 trees.

EXERCISES

1. Kareem made a display of books at a book fair. One book was in the first row, and each of the other rows had two more books than the row before it. How many books does Kareem have if he has nine rows?
2. Chris is using green and white tiles to cover her floor. If she uses tiles in the pattern G, W, G, G, W, G, G, W, G, G, what will be the color of the twentieth tile?
3. Jay read one story the first week of summer vacation, 3 stories the second week, 6 stories the third week, and 10 stories the fourth week. He kept to this pattern for eight weeks. How many stories did he read the eighth week?
4. Jan has 6 coins, none of which is a half dollar. The coins have a value of $.85. What coins does she have?
5. Sam is covering a wall with rows of red, white, and blue siding. The red siding is cut in 1.8-m strips, the white in 2.4-m strips, and the blue in 1.2-m strips. What is the shortest length that Sam can cover with uncut strips to form equal rows of each color?
6. A train leaves a station at 8:00 a.m. and averages 40 mi/h. Another train leaves the same station one hour later and averages 50 mi/h traveling in the same direction on a parallel track. At what time will the second train catch up with the first train? How many miles would each train have traveled by that time?

Problem Solving: Solve a Simpler Problem

By solving one or more simpler problems you can often find a pattern that will help solve a more complicated problem.

How many different rectangles are in a strip with 10 squares?

Begin with one square, and then add one square at a time. Determine whether there is a pattern.

Squares in the strip:	1	2	3	4	5
Number of rectangles:	1	3	6	10	15
Pattern:		$1 + 2 = 3$	$3 + 3 = 6$	$6 + 4 = 10$	$10 + 5 = 15$

Now continue the pattern.

Squares in the strip:	6	7	8	9	10
Number of rectangles:	21	28	36	45	55
Pattern:	$15 + 6 = 21$	$21 + 7 = 28$	$28 + 8 = 36$	$36 + 9 = 45$	$45 + 10 = 55$

There are 55 rectangles in a strip with 10 squares.

EXERCISES

1. Lockers in the east wing of Hastings High School are numbered 1–120. How many contain the digit 8?
2. What is the sum of all the numbers from 1 to 100? (*Hint:* What is $1 + 100$? What is $2 + 99$?)
3. Suppose your heart beats 70 times per minute. At this rate, how many times had it beaten by the time you were 10?
4. For a community project you have to create the numbers 1 through 148 using large cardboard digits covered with glitter, which you make by hand. How many cardboard digits will you make?
5. There are 64 teams competing in the state soccer championship. If a team loses a game it is eliminated. How many games have to be played in order to get a single champion team?
6. You work in a supermarket. Your boss asks you to arrange oranges in a pyramid for a display. The pyramid's base should be a square with 25 oranges. How many layers of oranges will be in your pyramid? How many oranges will you need?

Problem Solving: Use Logical Reasoning

Some problems can be solved without the use of numbers. They can be solved by the use of logical reasoning, given some information.

Joe, Mel, Liz and Greg play different sports. Their sports are running, basketball, baseball, and tennis. Liz's sport does not use a ball. Joe hit a home run in his sport. Mel is the sister of the tennis player. Which sport does each play?

Make a table to organize what you know.

	Running	Basketball	Baseball	Tennis
Joe	✗	✗	✓	✗
Mel				✗
Liz	✓	✗	✗	✗
Greg				

Home run means Joe plays baseball.

Mel is not the tennis player.

Liz must run, since running does not involve a ball.

Use logical reasoning to complete the table.

	Running	Basketball	Baseball	Tennis
Joe	✗	✗	✓	✗
Mel	✗	✓	✗	✗
Liz	✓	✗	✗	✗
Greg	✗	✗	✗	✓

Tennis only option for Greg.

Greg plays tennis, Mel plays basketball, Liz runs, and Joe plays baseball.

EXERCISES

1. Juan has a dog, a horse, a bird, and a cat. Their names are Bo, Cricket, K.C., and Tuffy. Tuffy and K.C. cannot fly or be ridden. The bird talks to Bo. Tuffy runs from the dog. What is each pet's name?
2. A math class has 25 students. There are 13 students who are only in the band, 4 students who are only on the swimming team, and 5 students who are in both groups. How many students are not in either group?
3. Annette is taller than Heather but shorter than Garo. Tanya's height is between Garo's and Annette's. Karin would be the shortest if it weren't for Alexa. List the names in order from shortest to tallest.
4. The girls' basketball league uses a telephone tree when it needs to cancel its games. The leader takes 1 min to call 2 players. These 2 players take 1 min to call 2 more players, and so on. How many players will be called in 6 min?

Problem Solving: Work Backward

To solve some problems, you need to start with the end result and work backward to the beginning.

On Monday, Rita withdrew \$150 from her savings account. On Wednesday, she deposited \$400 into her account. She now has \$1000. How much was in her account on Monday before she withdrew the money?

money in account now	\$1000
Undo the deposit.	−\$400
	\$600
Undo the withdrawal.	+\$150
	\$750

Rita had \$750 in her account on Monday before withdrawing money.

EXERCISES

1. Ned gave Connie the following puzzle: I am thinking of a number. I doubled it, then tripled the result. The final result was 36. What is my number?

2. Fernando gave Maria the following puzzle: I am thinking of a number. I divide it by 3. Then I divide the result by 5. The final result is 8. What is my number?

3. A teacher lends pencils to students. She gave out 7 pencils in the morning, collected 5 before lunch, and gave out 3 after lunch. At the end of the day she had 16 pencils. How many pencils did the teacher have at the start of the day?

4. This week Sandy withdrew \$350 from her savings account. She made a deposit of \$125, wrote a check for \$ 275, and made a deposit of \$150. She now has \$225 in her account. How much did she have in her account at the beginning of the week?

5. Jeff paid \$12.50, including a \$1.60 tip, for a taxi ride from his home to the airport. City Cab charges \$1.90 for the first mile plus \$.15 for each additional $\frac{1}{6}$ mile. How many miles is Jeff's home from the airport?

6. Ben sold $\frac{1}{4}$ as many tickets to the fund-raiser as Charles. Charles sold 3 times as many as Susan. Susan sold 4 fewer than Tom. Tom sold 12 tickets. How many did Ben sell?

7. Two cars start traveling towards each other. One car averages 30 mi/h and the other 40 mi/h. After 4 h the cars are 10 mi apart. How far apart were the cars when they started?

Divisibility

An integer is divisible by another integer if the remainder is zero. You can use the following tests to determine whether a number is divisible by the numbers below.

Number	Divisibility Test
2	The ones' digit is 0, 2, 4, 6, or 8.
3	The sum of the digits is divisible by 3.
4	The number formed by the last two digits is divisible by 4.
5	The ones' digit is 0 or 5.
6	The number is divisible by 2 and by 3.
8	The number formed by the last three digits is divisible by 8.
9	The sum of the digits is divisible by 9.

EXAMPLE

Use the divisibility tests to determine the numbers by which 2116 is divisible.

2: Yes; the ones' digit is 6.

3: No; the sum of the digits is $2 + 1 + 1 + 6 = 10$, which is not divisible by 3.

4: Yes; the number formed by the last two digits is 16, which is divisible by 4.

5: No; the ones' digit is 6, *not* 0 or 5.

6: No; 2116 is not divisible by 3.

8: No; the number formed by the last three digits is 116, which is *not* divisible by 8.

9: No; the sum of the digits is $2 + 1 + 1 + 6 = 10$, which is not divisible by 9.

2116 is divisible by 2 and 4.

EXERCISES

Determine whether each number is divisible by 2, 3, 4, 5, 6, 8, or 9.

1. 236 **2.** 72 **3.** 105 **4.** 108 **5.** 225 **6.** 364

7. 1234 **8.** 4321 **9.** 7848 **10.** 3366 **11.** 1421 **12.** 1071

13. 78,765 **14.** 30,303 **15.** 4104 **16.** 700 **17.** 868 **18.** 1155

19. Reasoning Since 435 is divisible by both 3 and 5, it is also divisible by what number?

Simplifying Fractions

Different names for the same fraction are called equivalent fractions. You can find an equivalent fraction for any given fraction by multiplying the numerator and denominator of the given fraction by the same number.

Write five equivalent fractions for $\frac{3}{5}$.

$\frac{3}{5} = \frac{3 \cdot 2}{5 \cdot 2} = \frac{6}{10}$ $\frac{3}{5} = \frac{3 \cdot 3}{5 \cdot 3} = \frac{9}{15}$ $\frac{3}{5} = \frac{3 \cdot 4}{5 \cdot 4} = \frac{12}{20}$ $\frac{3}{5} = \frac{3 \cdot 5}{5 \cdot 5} = \frac{15}{25}$ $\frac{3}{5} = \frac{3 \cdot 6}{5 \cdot 6} = \frac{18}{30}$

The fraction $\frac{3}{5}$ is in simplest form because the only common factor of the numerator and denominator is the number 1. To write a fraction in simplest form, divide its numerator and denominator by their greatest common factor (GCF).

Write $\frac{6}{24}$ in simplest form.

Step 1 Find the GCF of 6 and 24.

$6 = 2 \cdot 3$ **Multiply the common prime factors.**

$24 = 2 \cdot 2 \cdot 2 \cdot 3$ **GCF = 2 · 3 = 6.**

Step 2 Divide the numerator and denominator of $\frac{6}{24}$ by the GCF, 6.

$\frac{6}{24} = \frac{6 \div 6}{24 \div 6} = \frac{1}{4}$ **simplest form**

EXERCISES

Write five equivalent fractions for each fraction.

1. $\frac{4}{7}$ **2.** $\frac{9}{16}$ **3.** $\frac{3}{8}$ **4.** $\frac{8}{17}$ **5.** $\frac{5}{6}$ **6.** $\frac{7}{10}$

Complete each statement.

7. $\frac{3}{7} = \frac{■}{21}$ **8.** $\frac{5}{8} = \frac{20}{■}$ **9.** $\frac{11}{12} = \frac{44}{■}$ **10.** $\frac{12}{16} = \frac{■}{4}$ **11.** $\frac{50}{100} = \frac{1}{■}$

12. $\frac{5}{9} = \frac{■}{27}$ **13.** $\frac{3}{8} = \frac{■}{24}$ **14.** $\frac{5}{6} = \frac{20}{■}$ **15.** $\frac{12}{20} = \frac{■}{5}$ **16.** $\frac{75}{150} = \frac{1}{■}$

Which fractions are in simplest form?

17. $\frac{4}{12}$ **18.** $\frac{3}{16}$ **19.** $\frac{5}{30}$ **20.** $\frac{9}{72}$ **21.** $\frac{11}{22}$ **22.** $\frac{24}{25}$

Write in simplest form.

23. $\frac{8}{16}$ **24.** $\frac{7}{14}$ **25.** $\frac{6}{9}$ **26.** $\frac{20}{30}$ **27.** $\frac{8}{20}$ **28.** $\frac{12}{40}$

29. $\frac{15}{45}$ **30.** $\frac{14}{56}$ **31.** $\frac{10}{25}$ **32.** $\frac{9}{27}$ **33.** $\frac{45}{60}$ **34.** $\frac{20}{35}$

Fractions and Decimals

You can write a fraction as a decimal and a decimal as a fraction.

1 EXAMPLE

Write $\frac{3}{5}$ as a decimal.

$$\begin{array}{r} 0.6 \\ 5\overline{)3.0} \\ \underline{-30} \end{array}$$

Divide the numerator by the denominator.

The decimal for $\frac{3}{5}$ is 0.6.

2 EXAMPLE

Write 0.38 as a fraction.

$0.38 = 38 \text{ hundredths} = \frac{38}{100} = \frac{19}{50}$

Some fractions have decimal forms that do not end, but do repeat.

3 EXAMPLE

Write $\frac{3}{11}$ as a decimal.

Divide 3 by 11. The remainders 8 and 3 keep repeating. Therefore 2 and 7 will keep repeating in the quotient.

$\frac{3}{11} = 0.2727\ldots = 0.\overline{27}$

$$\frac{3}{11} = \begin{array}{r} 0.2727 \\ 11\overline{)3.0000\ldots} \\ \underline{22} \\ 80 \\ \underline{77} \\ 30 \\ \underline{22} \\ 80 \\ \underline{77} \\ 3 \end{array}$$

You can write a repeating decimal as a fraction.

4 EXAMPLE

Write 0.363636 ... as a fraction.

Let	$x = 0.363636\ldots$	
Then	$100x = 36.36363636\ldots$	**When 2 digits repeat, multiply by 100.**
	$99x = 36$	**Subtract the first equation from the second.**
	$x = \frac{36}{99}$ or $\frac{4}{11}$	**Divide each side by 99.**

EXERCISES

Write as a decimal.

1. $\frac{3}{10}$	**2.** $\frac{13}{12}$	**3.** $\frac{4}{20}$	**4.** $\frac{25}{75}$	**5.** $\frac{5}{7}$	**6.** $4\frac{3}{25}$
7. $\frac{5}{9}$	**8.** $5\frac{7}{8}$	**9.** $\frac{2}{7}$	**10.** $\frac{3}{15}$	**11.** $\frac{16}{100}$	**12.** $2\frac{2}{5}$

Write as a fraction in simplest form.

13. 0.07	**14.** 0.25	**15.** 0.875	**16.** 0.4545...	**17.** 6.333...	**18.** 7.2626...
19. 0.77...	**20.** 3.1313...	**21.** 0.375	**22.** 0.8333...	**23.** 6.48	**24.** 0.8

Adding and Subtracting Fractions

Fractions with unlike denominators are called unlike fractions. To add or subtract fractions with unlike denominators, find the least common denominator (LCD) and write equivalent fractions with the same denominator. Then add or subtract the like fractions.

EXAMPLE

Add $\frac{3}{4} + \frac{5}{6}$.

$\frac{3}{4} + \frac{5}{6} = \frac{9}{12} + \frac{10}{12}$ **Find the LCD. The LCD is the same as the least common multiple (LCM). The LCD of 4 and 6 is 12.**

$\approx \frac{9+10}{12} = \frac{19}{12}$ or $1\frac{7}{12}$ **Write equivalent fractions with the same denominator.**

To add or subtract mixed numbers, add or subtract the fractions. Then add or subtract the whole numbers. Sometimes when subtracting mixed numbers you may have to regroup.

EXAMPLE

Subtract $5\frac{1}{4} - 3\frac{2}{3}$.

$5\frac{1}{4} - 3\frac{2}{3} = 5\frac{3}{12} - 3\frac{8}{12}$ **Write equivalent fractions with the same denominator.**

$= 4\frac{15}{12} - 3\frac{8}{12}$ **Write $5\frac{3}{12}$ as $4\frac{15}{12}$ so you can subtract the fractions.**

$= 1\frac{7}{12}$ **Subtract the fractions. Then subtract the whole numbers.**

EXERCISES

Add. Write each answer in simplest form.

1. $\frac{2}{7} + \frac{3}{7}$ **2.** $\frac{3}{8} + \frac{7}{8}$ **3.** $\frac{6}{5} + \frac{9}{5}$ **4.** $\frac{4}{9} + \frac{8}{9}$ **5.** $6\frac{2}{3} + 3\frac{4}{5}$

6. $1\frac{4}{7} + 2\frac{3}{14}$ **7.** $4\frac{5}{6} + 1\frac{7}{18}$ **8.** $2\frac{4}{5} + 3\frac{6}{7}$ **9.** $4\frac{2}{3} + 1\frac{6}{11}$ **10.** $3\frac{7}{9} + 5\frac{4}{11}$

11. $8 + 1\frac{2}{3}$ **12.** $8\frac{1}{5} + 3\frac{3}{4}$ **13.** $11\frac{3}{8} + 2\frac{1}{16}$ **14.** $9\frac{1}{12} + 8\frac{3}{4}$ **15.** $33\frac{1}{3} + 23\frac{2}{5}$

Subtract. Write each answer in simplest form.

16. $\frac{7}{8} - \frac{3}{8}$ **17.** $\frac{9}{10} - \frac{3}{10}$ **18.** $\frac{17}{5} - \frac{2}{5}$ **19.** $\frac{11}{7} - \frac{2}{7}$ **20.** $\frac{5}{11} - \frac{4}{11}$

21. $8\frac{5}{8} - 6\frac{1}{4}$ **22.** $3\frac{2}{3} - 1\frac{8}{9}$ **23.** $8\frac{5}{6} - 5\frac{1}{2}$ **24.** $12\frac{3}{4} - 4\frac{5}{6}$ **25.** $17\frac{2}{7} - 8\frac{2}{9}$

26. $7\frac{3}{4} - 3\frac{3}{8}$ **27.** $4\frac{1}{12} - 1\frac{11}{12}$ **28.** $5\frac{5}{8} - 2\frac{7}{16}$ **29.** $11\frac{2}{3} - 3\frac{5}{6}$ **30.** $25\frac{5}{8} - 17\frac{15}{16}$

Multiplying and Dividing Fractions

To multiply two or more fractions, multiply the numerators, multiply the denominators, and simplify the product, if necessary.

1 EXAMPLE

Multiply $\frac{3}{7} \cdot \frac{5}{6}$.

$$\frac{3}{7} \cdot \frac{5}{6} = \frac{3 \cdot 5}{7 \cdot 6} = \frac{15}{42} = \frac{15 \div 3}{42 \div 3} = \frac{5}{14}$$

To multiply mixed numbers, change the mixed numbers to improper fractions and multiply the fractions. Write the product as a mixed number.

2 EXAMPLE

Multiply $2\frac{4}{5} \cdot 1\frac{2}{3}$.

$$2\frac{4}{5} \cdot 1\frac{2}{3} = \frac{14}{\cancel{5}} = \frac{\cancel{5}}{3} = \frac{14}{3} = 4\frac{2}{3}$$

To divide fractions, change the division problem to a multiplication problem. Remember that $8 \div \frac{1}{4}$ is the same as $8 \cdot 4$.

3 EXAMPLE

Divide $4\frac{2}{3} \div 7\frac{3}{5}$.

$$4\frac{2}{3} \div 7\frac{3}{5} = \frac{14}{3} \div \frac{38}{5}$$

$$= \frac{\cancel{14}}{3} \cdot \frac{5}{\cancel{38}}$$ ← **Multiply by the reciprocal of the divisor.**

$$= \frac{35}{57}$$ ← **Simplify the answer.**

EXERCISES

Multiply. Write your answers in simplest form.

1. $\frac{2}{5} \cdot \frac{3}{4}$ **2.** $\frac{3}{7} \cdot \frac{4}{3}$ **3.** $1\frac{1}{2} \cdot 5\frac{3}{4}$ **4.** $3\frac{4}{5} \cdot 10$ **5.** $5\frac{1}{4} \cdot \frac{2}{3}$

6. $4\frac{1}{2} \cdot 7\frac{1}{2}$ **7.** $3\frac{2}{3} \cdot 6\frac{9}{10}$ **8.** $6\frac{1}{2} \cdot 7\frac{2}{3}$ **9.** $2\frac{2}{5} \cdot 1\frac{1}{6}$ **10.** $4\frac{1}{9} \cdot 3\frac{3}{8}$

11. $3\frac{1}{5} \cdot 1\frac{7}{8}$ **12.** $7\frac{5}{6} \cdot 4\frac{1}{2}$ **13.** $1\frac{2}{3} \cdot 5\frac{9}{10}$ **14.** $3\frac{3}{4} \cdot 5\frac{1}{3}$ **15.** $1\frac{2}{3} \cdot 3\frac{9}{16}$

Divide. Write your answers in simplest form.

16. $\frac{3}{5} \div \frac{1}{2}$ **17.** $\frac{4}{5} \div \frac{9}{10}$ **18.** $2\frac{1}{2} \div 3\frac{1}{2}$ **19.** $1\frac{4}{5} \div 2\frac{1}{2}$ **20.** $3\frac{1}{6} \div 1\frac{3}{4}$

21. $5 \div \frac{3}{8}$ **22.** $\frac{4}{9} \div \frac{3}{5}$ **23.** $\frac{5}{8} \div \frac{3}{4}$ **24.** $2\frac{1}{5} \div 2\frac{1}{2}$ **25.** $6\frac{1}{2} \div \frac{1}{4}$

26. $1\frac{3}{4} \div 4\frac{3}{8}$ **27.** $\frac{8}{9} \div \frac{2}{3}$ **28.** $\frac{1}{5} \div \frac{1}{3}$ **29.** $2\frac{2}{5} \div 7\frac{1}{5}$ **30.** $7\frac{2}{3} \div \frac{2}{9}$

Fractions, Decimals, and Percents

Percent means per hundred. 50% means 50 per hundred. $50\% = \frac{50}{100} = 0.50$

You can write fractions as percents by writing the fractions as decimals first. Then move the decimal point two places to the right and write a percent sign.

1 EXAMPLE

Write each number as a percent.

a. $\frac{3}{5}$ $\quad \frac{3}{5} = 0.6 = 60\%$

b. $\frac{7}{20}$ $\quad \frac{7}{20} = 0.35 = 35\%$

c. $\frac{2}{3}$ $\quad \frac{2}{3} = 0.66\overline{6} = 66.\overline{6}\% \approx 66.7\%$

Follow these examples to write percents as fractions or decimals.

2 EXAMPLE

Write each number as a decimal and as a fraction or mixed number.

a. 25%

$25\% = 0.25$

$25\% = \frac{25}{100} = \frac{1}{4}$

b. $\frac{1}{2}\%$

$\frac{1}{2}\% = 0.5\% = 0.005$

$\frac{1}{2}\% = \frac{\frac{1}{2}}{100} = \frac{1}{2} \div 100$

$= \frac{1}{2} \cdot \frac{1}{100} = \frac{1}{200}$

c. 360%

$360\% = 3.6$

$360\% = \frac{360}{100} = \frac{18}{5} = 3\frac{3}{5}$

EXERCISES

Write each number as a percent. If necessary, round to the nearest tenth.

1. 0.56 **2.** 0.09 **3.** 6.02 **4.** 5.245

5. 8.2 **6.** 0.14 **7.** $\frac{1}{7}$ **8.** $\frac{9}{20}$

9. $\frac{1}{9}$ **10.** $\frac{5}{6}$ **11.** $\frac{3}{4}$ **12.** $\frac{7}{8}$

Write each number as a decimal.

13. 7% **14.** 8.5% **15.** 0.9% **16.** 250% **17.** 83% **18.** 110%

19. 15% **20.** 72% **21.** 0.03% **22.** 36.2% **23.** 365% **24.** 101%

Write each number as a fraction or mixed number in simplest form.

25. 19% **26.** $\frac{3}{4}\%$ **27.** 450% **28.** $\frac{4}{5}\%$ **29.** 64% **30.** $\frac{2}{3}\%$

31. 24% **32.** 845% **33.** $\frac{3}{8}\%$ **34.** 480% **35.** 60% **36.** 350%

37. 2% **38.** 16% **39.** 66% **40.** $\frac{4}{7}\%$ **41.** 125% **42.** 84%

Line Graphs

Line graphs are used to display the change in a set of data over a period of time.

Graph the data in the table below.

Households with VCR and Cable TV (millions)

Year	1985	1990	1995	1996	1997	1998
VCR	18	63	77	79	82	83
Cable TV	36	52	60	63	64	66

SOURCE: Television Bureau of Advertising, Inc., *Trends in Television*

Since the data show changes over time for two sets of data, use a double line graph.

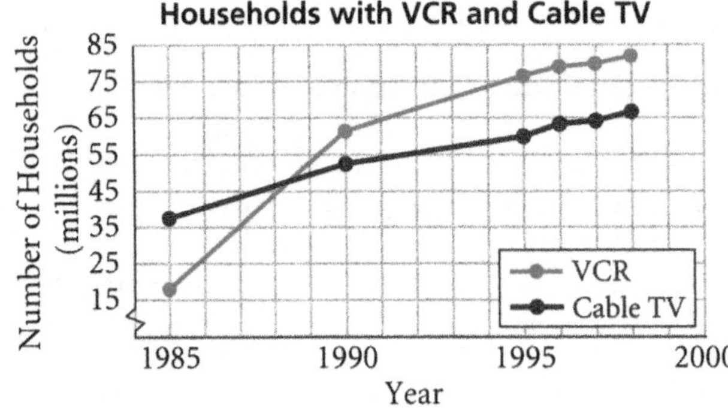

The zigzag line on the vertical axis indicates a break from 0 to 15 since there is no data to graph.

EXERCISES

Graph the following data.

1. **Market Shares (percent)**

Year	1994	1995	1996	1997	1998	1999	2000
Rap/Hip Hop	7.9	6.7	8.9	10.1	9.7	10.8	12.9
Pop	10.3	10.1	9.3	9.4	10.0	10.3	11.0

SOURCE: The Recording Industry of America

2. **Percents of Schools with Internet Access**

Year	1995	1996	1997	1998	1999
Elementary	46	61	75	88	94
Secondary	65	77	89	94	98

SOURCE: U.S. National Center for Education Statistics

Circle Graphs

A circle graph is a way to present certain types of data. The graphs show data as percents or fractions of a whole. The total must be 100% or 1.

EXAMPLE

The table at the right shows the number of people in the United States who have at least one grandchild under the age of 18. Draw a circle graph for the data.

Ages of U.S. Grandparents

Age	People (millions)
44 and under	3.6
45–54	10.3
55–64	15.0
65 and over	18.2

Step 1 Add to find the total number:
$3.6 + 10.3 + 15.0 + 18.2 = 47.1$ (million).

Step 2 For each central angle, set up a proportion to find the measure. Use a calculator to solve each proportion.

$\frac{3.6}{47.1} = \frac{a}{360°}$ $\quad$ $\frac{10.3}{47.1} = \frac{b}{360°}$ $\quad$ $\frac{15.0}{47.1} = \frac{c}{360°}$ $\quad$ $\frac{18.2}{47.1} = \frac{d}{360°}$

$a \approx 27.5°$ $\quad$ $b \approx 78.7°$ $\quad$ $c \approx 114.6°$ $\quad$ $d \approx 139.1°$

Step 3 Use a compass to draw a circle. Draw the approximate central angles with a protractor.

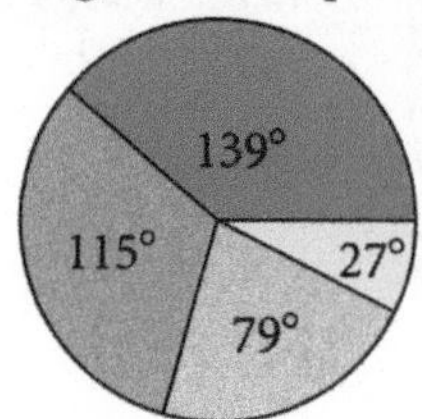

Step 4 Label each sector. Add any necessary information.

Ages of U.S. Grandparents

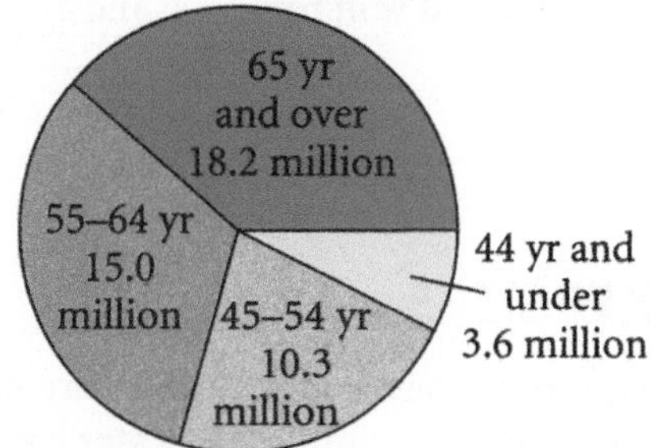

EXERCISES

1. Use the data in the table to draw a circle graph.

Transportation Mode	Walk	Bicycle	Bus	Car
Number of Students	252	135	432	81

2. **Data Collection** Survey your class to find out how they get to school. Use the data to draw a circle graph.

Spreadsheets

You can use a spreadsheet to evaluate formulas. Spreadsheets use the symbols + for addition and − for subtraction, but different symbols for other operations.

Multiplication: * Division: / Exponent: ^

EXAMPLE

Evaluate the formula $P = 2\ell + 2w$ for $\ell = 3$ and forwhole-number values of w from 8 to 11.

Enter the values of ℓ and w into the first two columns. Cell A2 has the value of ℓ. Cell B2 has the first value of w. In cell C2, enter the expression = 2*A2 + 2*B2 to find the perimeter of a figure with length 3 and width 8.

	A	B	C
1	L	W	2L + 2W
2	3	8	= 2*A2 + 2* B2
3	3	9	
4	3	10	
5	3	11	

The spreadsheet evaluates the expression automatically.

Copy the expression in cell C2 into cells C3, C4, and C5. The spreadsheet automatically updates for the values of ℓ and w in rows 3, 4, and 5.

= 2*A2 + 2* B2

	A	B	C
1	L	W	2L + 2W
2	3	8	22
3	3	9	24
4	3	10	26
5	3	11	28

EXERCISES

Suppose the values of *a*, *b*, and *c* are in cells A2, B2, and C2 of a spreadsheet. Write the expression you would use to enter each formula in the spreadsheet.

1. $P = a + b + c$ **2.** $T = \frac{3a + 5b}{8}$ **3.** $R = \frac{1}{2}bc$ **4.** $A = c^2$

5. You deposit \$200 in an account that earns 6% compounded annually for three years. The spreadsheet below shows the balance at the end of each year. In which cell of the spreadsheet would you find the formula = B3 * C3? = B4 + D4?

	A	B	C	D	E
1	Year	Start of Year	Rate	Interest	End of Year
2	1st	\$200.00	0.06	\$12.00	\$212.00
3	2nd	\$212.00	0.06	\$12.72	\$224.72
4	3rd	\$224.72	0.06	\$13.48	\$238.20